Rendezvous
with Destiny

Rendezvous
with Destiny

HOW FRANKLIN D. ROOSEVELT

AND FIVE EXTRAORDINARY MEN

TOOK AMERICA INTO THE WAR

AND INTO THE WORLD

MICHAEL FULLILOVE

THE PENGUIN PRESS
New York
2013

THE PENGUIN PRESS
Published by the Penguin Group
Penguin Group (USA) Inc., 375 Hudson Street,
New York, New York 10014, USA

USA • Canada • UK • Ireland • Australia
New Zealand • India • South Africa • China

Penguin Books Ltd, Registered Offices: 80 Strand, London WC2R 0RL, England
For more information about the Penguin Group visit penguin.com

LIBRARY OF CONGRESS CATALOGING-IN-PUBLICATION DATA
Fullilove, Michael, 1972-
Rendezvous with destiny : how Franklin D. Roosevelt and five extraordinary men
took America into the war and into the world / Michael Fullilove.
pages cm—
Includes bibliographical references and index.
ISBN 978-1-59420-435-7
1. Roosevelt, Franklin D. (Franklin Delano), 1882–1945.   2. Roosevelt, Franklin D.
(Franklin Delano), 1882–1945—Friends and associates.   3. Welles, Sumner, 1892–1961.
4. Donovan, William J. (William Joseph), 1883–1959.   5. Hopkins, Harry L. (Harry Lloyd),
1890–1946.   6. Willkie, Wendell L. (Wendell Lewis), 1892–1944.   7. Harriman, W. Averell
(William Averell), 1891–1986   8. United States—Foreign relations—1933–1945.   9. World War,
1939–1945—Diplomatic history.   10. World War, 1939–1945—United States.   I. Title.
E806.F85 2013
973.917092—dc23   2012047003

Printed in the United States of America
1   3   5   7   9   10   8   6   4   2

Book design by Meighan Cavanaugh

For Gillian

And our three little special envoys

There is a mysterious cycle in human events. To some generations much is given. Of other generations much is expected. This generation of Americans has a rendezvous with destiny.

—Franklin D. Roosevelt,
Philadelphia, June 1936

I have always taken the view that the fortunes of mankind in its tremendous journey are principally decided for good or ill—but mainly for good, for the path is upward—by its greatest men and its greatest episodes.

—Winston S. Churchill,
London, January 1941

Contents

Rendezvous with Destiny

Prologue

At 2:50 a.m. on Friday, September 1, 1939, a telephone rang in a darkened bedroom on the second floor of the White House. Franklin Delano Roosevelt, fifty-seven years old, the twice-elected president of the United States, stirred in his narrow iron cot and pushed himself up with his powerful arms and shoulders. His useless, withered legs trailed behind. He switched on a light, illuminating the clutter with which he liked to surround himself: an old rocking chair; a bureau and a heavyset wardrobe; a mess of family pictures and naval prints covering the walls; a litter of small china pigs and a herd of carved donkeys occupying the marble mantelpiece; a horse's tail hanging over the door to remind him of his privileged childhood in New York's Hudson River Valley. He picked up one of the telephones that competed for space on his bedside table with books, aspirin, a pack of cigarettes, an ashtray, a prayer book, odd bits of paper, and pencil stubs. On the line was Roosevelt's ambassador in Paris, William C. Bullitt, relaying a message from his counterpart in Warsaw. Germany's legions had breached Poland's frontiers. The Luftwaffe was bombarding Poland's cities.

The greatest, bloodiest war in history had begun. "Well, Bill, it's come at last," said FDR. "God help us all."[1]

As the news spread, it reached the ears of five other men scattered across North America. Sumner Welles, the highborn under secretary of state and principal diplomatic adviser to the president, was the first to hear. Welles was brilliant, fastidious, and imperturbable; one minister from Central America compared him to "a tall glass of distilled ice water." Welles subscribed fully to Talleyrand's famous advice to a young diplomat: "above everything, do not allow yourself to become excited about your work." When Roosevelt put down the telephone to Bullitt, he called Welles at Oxon Hill, his lordly 250-acre estate on the Potomac River. A few hours later, the under secretary arrived at the State Department for an emergency meeting with his boss, Secretary of State Cordell Hull, and other senior officials. Soon he was conferring with the president at his bedside: Welles, "stiff and correct as always," sat in a chair by the bed; FDR leaned up against his pillows wearing a blue cape over his pajamas.[2]

Over the next two days, as British prime minister Neville Chamberlain dithered, then rallied, and eventually declared war on Germany on September 3, followed quickly by France, Welles was never far from Roosevelt's counsels. From his State Department office, a beautifully decorated, book-lined space with dark blue leather chairs, a gleaming mahogany table, and a marble bust of a statesman on a corner pedestal, Welles helped to coordinate Washington's response to European events, starting with an emergency meeting of Latin American foreign ministers.[3]

If Sumner Welles was at the heart of things, Bill Donovan was literally in the wilderness: camped beside Teepee Lake in Canada's Yukon Territory, 250 miles from the nearest town. "Wild Bill" was an Irish American war hero, New York lawyer, and muscular Republican in the mold of Franklin Roosevelt's distant cousin Theodore. TR certainly would have approved of Donovan's monthlong hunting expedition in the Yukon with three other wealthy Republicans, including retired general Robert E. Wood, the chairman of Sears, Roebuck & Co. The men had a special permit from the Canadian authorities to collect taxidermy specimens for a natural history museum in Boston, and they were enthusiastic about their work. Riding on horseback through the spectacular Saint Elias Mountains and Kluane Lake country, accompanied by Native guides and a pack train, they hunted mountain sheep, moose, caribou, and bear, and caught grayling and arctic trout. Without a radio, they were oblivious to the worsening situation in Europe. Donovan nearly perished when he was thrown from his horse and almost tumbled over a cliff. He recovered to bring down a ram with an extraordinary long-range shot and bag a nine-foot-tall grizzly, "the great-grandfather of them all," according to one of his companions. Meals were prepared by the Jacquot brothers, well-known local outfitters and guides who had trained in France as chefs. A typical camp dinner consisted of soup, roast lamb or duck with all the trimmings, a hot fluffy biscuit, lemon cream pie, tea, scotch, and cigars.[4]

Around midnight on September 2, after just such a dinner, the gentlemen were enjoying a few rubbers of bridge when there was movement at the tent flaps. A stranger entered. "Me, Indian runner," he said. "Message." The man had ridden for thirty hours over difficult country to get the latest news through to General Wood, who despite his isolationist tendencies had recently been appointed to a new five-member government advisory body, the War Resources Board. Wood opened the envelope with which he was presented, scanned the radiogram it contained, and uttered a single word: "War!"[5]

Also a long way from the national capital was Harry Hopkins, Roosevelt's commerce secretary and confidant. Whatever Hopkins had in common with Welles and Donovan was not apparent at first glance. When the president's cousin Daisy Suckley was first introduced to the social worker turned politician, she thought him "one of the most unattractive people I've ever met . . . A strange, weak-looking face, thin, slouching, untidy." Yet she warmed to him, as most people did. Hopkins combined a fierce idealism with a wisecracking sense of humor and "ten-carat charm." He also possessed a rare ability to reduce the most formidable and abstruse problem to its essence, a gift that would later lead Winston Churchill to confer on him the mock title "Lord Root of the Matter."[6]

In that first week of September, Hopkins faced his own formidable problem: a mysterious nutritional disease that his doctors at the Mayo Clinic in Rochester, Minnesota, feared threatened his very life. Hopkins was skeletal and bedridden, his eyesight was failing, and he had serious edema in his feet. His family was told he had only weeks to live. Yet he cheerfully underwent a series of unpleasant experimental treatments in the hope of recovering, staying in touch with FDR by phone and following events in Europe over the wireless. Having listened to the world news "at all hours of the day and night," he told a friend, "I now look upon myself as a full blown authority." Hopkins knew that he could not return to "the active list" until he had licked his ailment. But he admitted he was restless, writing that "with all the excitement going on it is tough quarterbacking from the bench."[7]

In New York City, news of Germany's invasion of Poland was flashed up on the moving electric bulletin board that wrapped around Times Tower, the *New York Times*' old building in Times Square. As darkness descended on Manhattan, New Yorkers congregated silently on the curbs and in the gutters of Broadway and Seventh Avenue to watch the board, buy a late edition, or cluster around a radio-equipped taxicab. The crowds stretched from 39th Street right up to 47th, where the statue of Father Francis Duffy, chaplain of New York's "Fighting 69th" Regiment in the First World War and comrade and admirer of Bill Donovan, appeared to be blessing the congregation. Periodically the traffic in Times Square came to a jarring stop when pedestrians, motorists, or streetcar motormen paused to look up and take in the dreadful facts.[8]

Most New Yorkers were not standing vigil in Times Square that night, however. As they settled into the three-day Labor Day weekend, they were thinking of rest, not war. Many were headed for the shore or the mountains, even as tens of thousands poured into the city to visit the World's Fair at

Flushing Meadows. "The country as a whole does not yet have any deep sense of world crisis," admitted FDR privately. The vast majority of Americans detested Adolf Hitler and wanted the Allies to win, but helping them to win was another matter. Only one in six believed the country should enter the war at some stage, and only one in forty supported an immediate declaration of war. Twenty percent were in favor of helping the Allies in other ways, but more than half believed the United States should maintain an impartial neutrality. The war seemed very distant, and not especially threatening.[9]

Wendell Willkie was a corporate lawyer and the president of the giant Commonwealth & Southern public utility holding company, headquartered downtown at 20 Pine Street. A product of small-town Indiana, he and his wife, Edith, now lived at 1010 Fifth Avenue, a grand apartment building opposite the Metropolitan Museum of Art. Willkie was a big, bearlike, rumpled man with a magnetic personality: a reporter observed that people who met him "often came away talking as if he were 14 feet tall and shot lightning bolts from his eyes."[10] Even though he was a lifelong Democrat, he was positioning himself to run against Franklin Roosevelt in 1940. His presidential candidacy had crystallized a fortnight earlier when he visited the editor of *Fortune* magazine, Russell Davenport, at his summer home on Saugatuck Harbor in Westport, Connecticut. His hosts had planned for tennis, golf, and poker. However, Willkie spent most of the weekend on the porch, "sprawled in a wicker armchair with one leg thrown over the arm of the chair," his jacket off and cigarette ash tumbling down his shirt front, "talking hard" with Davenport about his political beliefs and prospects. Davenport soon signed up to be his campaign manager.[11]

When the Wehrmacht rolled into Poland, Willkie was enjoying praise for a review of Lord David Cecil's book *The Young Melbourne* that he had just had published in the *New York Herald Tribune*. The article revealed something of its author's own approach to life. Willkie admired the "earthy exuberance" of the Whigs, the aristocratic statesmen who dominated eighteenth- and early-nineteenth-century English public life and were the subjects of Cecil's book. "Rowdy, reckless and robust," Willkie wrote, "they could eat their twelve-course dinners, dance until dawn and gamble, drink and make love until breakfast—and still put in a hard day's work on their estates or in Parliament." Book reviewing was new to Willkie, and he told a friend, "I am almost childishly happy about writing a review that somebody would accept."[12] In fact, he had an advantage on that front: the *Herald Tribune*'s influential literary editor, Irita Van Doren, was Willkie's mistress. Indeed, he may have been with her at her farmhouse in West Cornwall, New York, on the weekend of the invasion.[13]

The fifth man, Averell Harriman, was a different kind of New York businessman. He was chairman of the board of his family railroad, the Union Pacific, and a senior partner at Brown Brothers Harriman & Co., a private banking firm located at 59 Wall Street, three hundred yards from the offices of Commonwealth & Southern. Tanned, athletic, and well-heeled, he spent much of each summer at his house on the North Shore of Long Island, where he played competitive croquet with friends on the lawns of Sands Point, Manhasset, and Great Neck.[14] Harriman's days as a world-class polo player were behind him, but that summer he and his wife had attended several big polo matches at the prestigious Meadow Brook Club in Westbury.[15]

Harriman was not a typical Long Island socialite, however. He had a nose for power and a taste for hard work. Even more unusually, he was a Democrat, and had spent much of the past decade trying to inveigle his way into a big job in the Roosevelt administration. To this end, he assiduously tended his friendship with Harry Hopkins. In June 1939, he tried to persuade Hopkins to vacation at his private cottage at the resort he had established in Sun Valley, Idaho. Over the summer, he kept tabs on the ailing commerce secretary's health, checking in with his personal secretary in Washington and pestering him in Rochester. "I am happy to hear through Miss Van Meter today that you are making satisfactory progress," he cabled Hopkins on September 1. "When you feel like seeing me please let me know as I would gladly come down any time," he offered on another occasion.[16] Like Donovan, Willkie, and Hopkins himself, Harriman in September 1939 was at the margins of world events. They all wanted to get to the center.

The period between the outbreak of the European war in September 1939 and America's entry into the war in December 1941 was the turning point of the twentieth century.[17] Over those two years, the disposition of forces in the world changed utterly. In 1939, the wind was at Adolf Hitler's back; in 1940, he conquered much of western Europe; but by the end of 1941, he faced the deadly combination of the United States, the Soviet Union, and the British Empire. In 1939, America was nervous and parochial; in 1940, she rearmed and remobilized; by the end of 1941, she was at war, and her course was set toward global leadership.

The position of the United States in these momentous years was precarious.[18] America was the most powerful neutral nation in a world of belligerents, a supporter of the democracies but not their ally. The U.S. president was by instinct an internationalist, inclined to apply a broad definition of American interests. Yet the limits on Franklin Roosevelt's freedom of movement were severe, including historical precedent, public anxiety and congressional opposition at home, and unreliable partners abroad. FDR's extraordinary achievement over the years 1939–1941 was to navigate these constraints and move a divided and hesitant America toward ever greater involvement in the European war.

Roosevelt never threw over his natural caution. Democratic governments cannot "swing so far or so quickly" as individuals, he told an interventionist newspaper publisher in June 1940. "They can only move with the thought and will of the great majority of the people."[19] Accordingly, he avoided sudden moves and abrupt shifts in policy; indeed, he received almost as much criticism for moving too slowly as for moving too swiftly. Under his leadership, America's involvement in the war deepened in stages, and always in response to events. Yet if the process was gradual, it was also relentless. With each reversal abroad and each advance at home, U.S. policy toward the dictators hardened.

Roosevelt had five unusual helpers in this process, and he sent them to Europe on special missions that proved crucial to the course of the Second World War. Sumner Welles toured European capitals in the spring of 1940, during the so-called Phony War, when FDR was still feeling his way toward an effective policy. Four months later, after France's disastrous collapse, Bill Donovan visited a lonely United Kingdom at the president's behest. His eyewitness report, as well as the exploits of the Royal Air Force in the skies over Britain, convinced FDR that this was a country worth backing.

After his reelection in November 1940, Roosevelt threw a lifeline to Britain in the form of Lend-Lease, and dispatched three envoys to secure it. In January 1941, he sent Harry Hopkins on a monthlong mission to London, and also co-opted Wendell Willkie, who had been the 1940 GOP presidential nominee, to deliver a symbolic message to the new prime minister, Winston Churchill. A week after Willkie's return, he asked Averell Harriman to serve as his personal representative in London, with responsibility for expediting Lend-Lease aid to Britain.

Finally, in the aftermath of Hitler's invasion of the Soviet Union in June 1941, FDR sent Hopkins on two further assignments—back to London to see Churchill again, and to Moscow to meet with Soviet leader Joseph Stalin for the first time. Through these last two missions, Hopkins helped to establish the triangular relationship between the "Big Three"—Roosevelt, Churchill, and Stalin—who would go on to direct the Allied war effort after the Japanese attack at Pearl Harbor in December.

Winston Churchill said there were four "climacterics"—intense, pressurized turning points—in the period 1939–1941. These were the fall of France, the Battle of Britain, Lend-Lease, and Germany's invasion of the Soviet Union.[20] Each climacteric produced a sharpening of Roosevelt's position toward the war. Remarkably, FDR's five special envoys were vital at each juncture—urging a course of action on the president, giving him comfort that he had laid a wise bet, helping him to implement a decision, explaining it to British or Soviet leaders, or selling it to the American people.

It is significant that the president sent his personal emissaries across the Atlantic rather than the Pacific. A Europeanist by experience and instinct, FDR believed that the most potent threat to U.S. interests and global security came from Germany, not Japan. Consequently, his mind was concentrated on developments in Europe; he left the implementation of his Asia policy, which sought to contain the Japanese without causing a war, to Hull and the State Department. Perhaps, as events unfolded, this disparity betrayed a dangerous Rooseveltian blind spot. On the other hand, few could dispute that the greater evil resided in Berlin rather than Tokyo.[21]

Over this critical period, then, Roosevelt entrusted five very different men, only one of whom was a professional diplomat, with seven important assignments in Europe. This represents an extraordinary passage of politics and diplomacy. Several of the missions were dangerous. Most were undertaken alone. All trespassed on the sacred turf of the State Department. They took the president's men into the middle of the war and exposed them to the century's leading figures. Taken together, the missions plot the arc of America's transformation from a reluctant middle power into the global leader.

We often think of Harry S. Truman, George Marshall, Dean Acheson, and George F. Kennan as the authors of America's global primacy in the second half of the twentieth century: men who built the institutions of global order, rescued Europe from financial ruin, and set the conditions for victory in the Cold War. But all their achievements were enabled by the earlier work of Roosevelt and his envoys, who took the United States into the Second World War and, by defeating domestic isolationists and foreign enemies, into the world. In these two years, America turned. FDR and his envoys were responsible for the turn.

FEW PRESIDENTS HAVE ELICITED more hatred from their enemies than Franklin D. Roosevelt. Many scholars, too, disoriented by what speechwriter

Robert Sherwood called his "heavily forested interior," have dismissed him as facile and lacking fixedness of purpose.[22] Some have mistaken his love of improvisation, and the flexibility of means he employed, for an absence of sure and certain ends.

In fact, Roosevelt was the most important statesman of the twentieth century. He saved American democracy from the Depression, led the Allies to victory over fascism, won an unprecedented four consecutive presidential elections—and did all this with a broken body.

FDR was a seductive figure and an effervescent one: to encounter him, said Churchill, was like opening your first bottle of champagne.[23] He was, perhaps, the most patrician of all presidents, having grown up as the cosseted son of leisured grandees from Dutchess County in upstate New York. Yet he spurned the conventional career choices of his class and instead entered politics, serving as state senator, assistant secretary of the navy, vice presidential candidate, and governor of New York before his election to the White House. Roosevelt was no snob. He took a generous view of humanity, preferring the company of rogues to preachers, and attracting to his person a colorful menagerie of cronies. He was charming, but also tricky and sometimes heartless. He wore his friendships lightly; at times, he discarded them easily.

Roosevelt was also elusive. When flying over Egypt in 1943, it is said, he looked down and said in recognition, "Ah, my friend the Sphinx." He wrote afterward to his personal secretary, "I've seen the Pyramids and made close friends with the Sphinx. Congress should know her."[24] Congress, and the rest of Washington, knew very well that FDR was sphinxlike. He dissembled, advising his friends to "never let your left hand know what your right is doing." He disdained formal record keeping, and, in the opinion of brains truster Rexford G. Tugwell, "put every possible obstacle in the way" of future scholars who sought to scrutinize him. He drew a heavy veil over his own thinking.[25] Divining his intentions is, therefore, a task of classical proportions. Historians must piece together a mosaic of the man from thousands of tiny tesserae.

The picture that emerges, for the most part, is one of coherence and purpose, not ambivalence and reaction. If the doctors at the Bethesda Naval Hospital had been able to sequence Roosevelt's political genome, they undoubtedly would have found the gene for pragmatism. He "listened to every rustle in the leaves," wrote one canny observer, "and built up his own position with unending care and subtlety."[26] He was cautious in his movements, and highly sensitive to public opinion. He had periods of inertia that seemed to outsiders like paralysis. His tactical shifts were ceaseless, yet behind them all a clear and inexorable direction can be discerned. To adapt his own metaphor, FDR steered his government like one of his beloved sailboats, tacking this way and that for advantage, sometimes drifting, but finally bringing her into his chosen port.[27]

That is not to say that Roosevelt's governing method was tidy or graceful. He "practised a highly personal form of government," wrote philosopher and wartime diplomat Isaiah Berlin, that "maddened sober and responsible officials used to the slower tempo and more normal patterns of administration." He uncoupled the chains of command. He set aside protocols and created intersecting administrative empires. Often he allocated a single task to multiple people. To his courtiers, FDR was a faithless prince, giving none of them a monopoly on his attention and regard. As a result, his administration never coursed with esprit de corps. But there was method to this administrative madness. By seeking intelligence everywhere, he avoided capture by any one source. By setting his advisers against each other, he tested the strength of their arguments. By diffusing authority, he maintained control.[28]

FDR's professional and domestic lives were analogous. Arthur M. Schlesinger Jr. observed that "co-existence with disorder was almost the pattern of his life." From the day he married his distant cousin Eleanor—to the displeasure of his formidable mother, Sara, who preferred not to share him—Roosevelt "had lived in a household of unresolved jurisdictions, and it had never occurred to him to try to settle lines finally as between mother and wife."[29]

Settled lines were not Roosevelt's style. On foreign policy, this proclivity was strengthened by his distrust of the State Department. The career men in the diplomatic service were mainly Republicans, he believed, and out of step with his policies, being disinclined toward interference in the European conflict. His confidants agreed. Interior Secretary Harold L. Ickes felt the department was "undemocratic in its outlook" and "shot through with fascism." Harry Hopkins hooted that foreign service officers were "cookie pushers, pansies—and usually isolationists to boot." Not long after the bombing of Pearl Harbor, FDR is supposed to have joked that his State Department was neutral in this war and he hoped it would at least remain that way.[30]

Aside from ideological misgivings, FDR found State to be a poor instrument for his purposes. "You should go through the experience of trying to get any changes in the thinking, policy and action of the career diplomats and then you'd know what a real problem was," he told one visitor. On the day he died, he reviewed a letter prepared for his signature and observed with a laugh, "A typical State Department letter—it says nothing at all." He felt the department was littered with "dead wood."[31] He had little faith in the security of its cables, leading him to conduct many of his communications with foreign leaders via naval channels.[32] On top of all that, FDR shared the public conception of diplomats as effete dandies—the "boys in the striped pants." Other White House terms of abuse for foreign service officers included "old maids" and "stuffed shirts."[33]

FDR never sought seriously to reform the State Department: instead, he sidelined it. He asked his key ambassadors to stay in touch with him via personal letters.[34] Wherever possible, he cultivated personal relationships with crowned heads and other foreign leaders. In June 1939, for instance, he delighted in hosting King George VI and Queen Elizabeth for a weekend at his family estate in Hyde Park during their tour of North America. His idea was to increase Americans' sympathies toward the British—and to stiffen British spines. "Roosevelt set the stage for their reception with the care and gusto of a Broadway director," observed historian James MacGregor Burns. He deliberately treated the royal couple like old family friends, driving them in his Ford (which had been outfitted with custom-made hand controls) to a picnic lunch consisting of hot dogs, baked beans, and strawberry shortcake. Much to his mother's displeasure, he even served Their Majesties cocktails before dinner. When FDR saw off his visitors at Hyde Park railway station, the crowd sang "Auld Lang Syne." "Good luck to you!" called the president. "All the luck in the world!"[35]

FRANKLIN ROOSEVELT WAS, THEN, a leader who disliked faceless bureaucracies, distrusted his foreign ministry, craved information, and enjoyed personal diplomacy. If these factors were insufficient to predispose him to the use of personal envoys, there was another: the polio attack in 1921 that paralyzed him from the waist down and forced him to rely, for the sake of political success and his very survival, on family, friends, and aides. For nearly a decade after that calamity, as FDR sought unsuccessfully to regain his ability to walk, he relied on his wife Eleanor and close adviser Louis Howe to keep his name in the public eye.[36]

When he returned to public life, he continued to encourage his wife in this role of emissary and investigator. As governor of New York, Franklin toured the state each summer with Eleanor, visiting hospitals, prisons, and insane asylums. It was on those early trips, she recalled later, that "she received some of her best training as a reporter." While the head of an institution sat in the car talking to the governor, Eleanor would inspect the place on her husband's behalf. If she reported that there was no overcrowding, "he would laugh heartily at her amateurishness." "Idiot, didn't you look to see if there were beds put away in closets or behind doors?" On one occasion, he asked her what the patients had to eat, and she relayed what she had seen on their menus. "Look into the pots on the stove," FDR admonished her.[37]

Eleanor never stopped looking into the pots. During their years in the White House, Roosevelt asked her to investigate poverty in Appalachia and labor conditions in Puerto Rico; during the war, she visited Britain, the South Pacific, and the Caribbean.[38] Eleanor was able to represent her husband to people who would never see him in person. From her reports, and those of other intimates, FDR could pick up intelligence and gauge the public mood. Her visibility as a spokesperson for liberal causes also served a political function, enabling Franklin to hold on to his left-wing constituency even as he moved to the center. If conservatives complained, he simply pointed out that she was her own person. "Well, you know my Missus . . . ," he would tell the press with an affectionate grin.[39]

If personal envoys were an integral element of FDR's domestic political apparatus, they played an even more prominent part in his diplomacy. Roosevelt savored personal diplomacy, but the perils of international travel and the questionable security and poor transmission quality of international telephone calls circumscribed its reach, causing him to look for alternative conduits.[40] He was also intrigued by the practice of President Woodrow Wilson (whom he served as assistant secretary of the navy and whose portrait he hung in the Cabinet Room when he was president) of using Colonel Edward M. House as a roving diplomatic envoy. FDR corresponded with House until his death in 1938 and on several occasions expressed a wish that the colonel could undertake special missions on his behalf. In the spring of 1934, Roosevelt wrote, "I so wish you could go over [to Europe] and get a true picture for me!" He repeated the sentiment a year later: "I do wish I had someone to fulfil for me the splendid missions which you carried out in Europe before we got into the war—but there is only one *you* and I know of no other."[41]

The unavailability of the aged House, however, did not put Roosevelt off the idea of personal envoys. From the first years of the Republic, presidents have assigned individuals to execute diplomatic missions outside of the conventional channels. But there has been no more enthusiastic practitioner of envoy diplomacy than FDR, whose stable of emissaries included friends, allies, cronies, and the occasional political opponent, very few of them with much experience. He dispatched them practically everywhere—to western Europe, Russia, the Middle East, China, India, Latin America. Secretary of State Cordell Hull referred to such amateur diplomats as "raw materials" and believed they tended to "create havoc."[42] But the president was very taken with the approach, so much so that he tried to extend it from the diplomatic to the divine, appointing a personal representative to the Vatican[43] and exploring the accreditation of emissaries to the Greek Orthodox Church and "the Mohammedan world."[44]

FRANKLIN ROOSEVELT NEVER CALLED on envoys to greater effect than during 1939–1941, as the European war developed into a world war. As FDR edged the United States closer to the conflict, five uncommon individuals— a well-bred diplomat, a Republican lawyer, a political fixer, a former presidential candidate, and a tycoon—were the inspirations and instruments of his policy.

1.

"A One-Man American Mission of Curiosity"

SUMNER WELLES IN ROME, BERLIN, PARIS,

AND LONDON, FEBRUARY—MARCH 1940

B efore war pounced on the United States," historian Waldo Heinrichs has written, "it crept up, stage by stage, over many years." The stealthiness of its approach was enabled by the historical predisposition of Americans, flanked by vast oceans and unthreatening neighbors, to isolate themselves from conflict and strife abroad. High tariff walls symbolized their desire for separation. This tendency was reinforced in the 1930s by the devastating effects of the Great Depression and a persistent belief that the country had been tricked into entering the First World War.

In the mid-1930s, accordingly, Congress limited expenditure on the military and passed a series of Neutrality Acts that were intended to "fence off the United States from future conflict." This legislation banned most commercial dealings with warring nations, including financial aid and arms sales, although the 1937 Neutrality Act gave the president the power to authorize trade in nonlethal items on a "cash-and-carry" basis; that is, where the items were paid for and transported by the belligerents.[1]

While America looked inward, the world slid ever closer to the brink, with the rapid accumulation of arms, conflicts within Spain and between China and Japan, and the steady progress of the dictators. In retrospect, the decade's bleak milestones have all the tragic inevitability of the Stations of the Cross. Adolf Hitler consolidated his personal grip on Germany, began his vicious persecution of the Jews, remilitarized the Rhineland, and looked abroad for Lebensraum. Benito Mussolini invaded Abyssinia, exposing the weakness of the League of Nations, and tied Italy's fortunes tightly to those of Germany. The government in Tokyo, which increasingly resembled a military dictatorship, extended its brutal rule in northeastern China and eyed the resource-rich European colonial territories to its south.

On the periphery, Franklin Roosevelt began to shift his focus from the New Deal and domestic politics to foreign policy. He searched fitfully for ways that war could be averted—calling for the quarantining of aggressors in October 1937, then sketching a possible American peace initiative a few months later—but political opposition as well as his innate caution stayed his hand, even when Germany annexed Austria in March 1938. "It's a terrible thing," FDR told his speechwriter Judge Samuel Rosenman, "to look over your shoulder when you are trying to lead—and to find no one there."[2] Winston Churchill is supposed to have observed that "kites fly highest against the wind," but Roosevelt preferred his kites to fly with the wind.

FDR's equivocation began to abate after the Munich agreement of September 1938, by which Britain and France capitulated to German demands for the dismemberment of Czechoslovakia so that the Sudetenland could be incorporated into the Reich. Munich showed that it was futile to negotiate with Hitler: a lasting peace in Europe was unachievable while the Nazis remained in power. Roosevelt signaled his determination to rearm and to revise the neutrality legislation, but again he met domestic resistance.[3]

On November 9–10, 1938, a night that would become known as *Kristallnacht*, the Nazis orchestrated a nationwide pogrom against the Jews. Synagogues were burned and shops looted; twenty thousand Jews were sent to the concentration camps; the rights of those who remained at liberty were curtailed severely. "I myself could scarcely believe that such things could occur in a twentieth-century civilization," FDR revealed to the White House press corps. Then, less than six months after agreeing to terms at Munich, Hitler violated them and invaded what remained of Czechoslovakia. After years of sipping from what Churchill, the leader of Britain's anti-Hitlerite forces, called the "bitter cup" of appeasement, the British and French steeled themselves and guaranteed the territorial integrity of Poland. In Washington, Roosevelt renewed his efforts on neutrality reform and accelerated his efforts to shape American public opinion on European affairs.

Events in Europe were also speeding up. In late August, Berlin and Moscow signed a nonaggression pact, and on September 1, despite final pleas from Roosevelt, Hitler invaded Poland, prompting William Bullitt's late-night call to the White House.[4]

DESPITE A BRAVE DEFENSE, Poland fell quickly before the combined forces of the Nazis and their Soviet accessories, who intervened in mid-September 1939. Hitler and Stalin then proceeded to divide Poland's carcass between them. For the moment, Mussolini declined to join in, his desire for easy gains trumped by Italy's military unpreparedness. Roosevelt pledged to keep the United States out of the conflict, but he did not conceal where his sympathies lay. At the start of the First World War, Woodrow Wilson had promised that Americans would be neutral in thought and deed. FDR could not go so far as that. "This nation will remain a neutral nation," he declared in a fireside chat, "but I cannot ask that every American remain neutral in thought as well. Even a neutral has a right to take account of facts. Even a neutral cannot be asked to close his mind or his conscience."

Taking his own account of the facts, Roosevelt moved quickly to achieve a sharper version of the neutrality reform that had previously eluded him. He wanted a kind of neutrality that favored the democracies, and increasingly the country agreed with him. At the president's urging, Congress repealed the arms embargo and applied the cash-and-carry principle to all trade with belligerent nations. The main effect was to make America's industrial output available to Britain and France, both wealthy trading powers that were able to pay for and transport their purchases safely across the Atlantic Ocean, which traditionally had been policed by the Royal Navy.[5]

Roosevelt also reached out to Winston Churchill, who had been brought into the British cabinet by Prime Minister Neville Chamberlain and given charge of the Royal Navy as first lord of the admiralty. "I shall at all times welcome it if you will keep me in touch personally with anything you want me to know about," wrote the president on September 11, 1939. This was the first of nearly two thousand letters, cables, and memoranda that would pass between the two men over the course of the war.[6] As usual with FDR, the political was personal.

In September and October, Moscow moved to establish its hegemony over the Baltic states: Latvia, Lithuania, and Estonia. At the end of November, the Soviets initiated their "Winter War" against the Finns, who put up an impressive resistance. Apart from these peripheral engagements, however, the European armies remained still. Between the great powers, there was some fighting at sea but none on land. The Germans and the French dug in along their frontier but did not push across it. Awful crimes against civilians were committed within the occupied countries, but on the surface, things seemed so benign that two elderly British ladies asked the American Express office in Paris to organize for them a guided tour of the front. No wonder that isolationist senator William Borah of Idaho said, "There is something phony about this war." The French also thought it a *drôle de guerre* (strange war); Germans dubbed it the *Sitzkrieg* (sitting war). Most observers knew, however, that the Wehrmacht would not stay seated forever. A spring offensive loomed.[7]

AT THIS UNCERTAIN MOMENT, Roosevelt decided to send a personal envoy to Europe to confer with a key neutral power, Italy, and the three principal belligerents, Germany, France, and Great Britain. The man he selected, Benjamin Sumner Welles, was described by *Time* as "a casting director's dream of a diplomat." Very tall, with a high forehead, noble nose, and neat mustache, Welles literally looked down on his interlocutors. He spoke three foreign languages and, according to one ambassador, had "a mind like a Swiss watch." Welles's voice was deep, his accent cultured, and his grooming impeccable. He carried himself with papal dignity: when he testified before Congress, he appeared to feel he was slumming it. One observer compared Welles's self-control to that of a surgeon.[8] But appearances were deceiving. Behind the haughty demeanor he was a pleasure-seeker whose reckless pursuit of his unconventional tastes would ultimately lead to his ruin.

Welles was born on October 14, 1892, in New York City, into an old patrician, Episcopalian family. There had been Welleses in America since 1636, and their ranks included statesmen, clergymen, and scholars. Astors and Schermerhorns nestled in Sumner's family tree like turtledoves. Edith Wharton was his great-aunt, and he could have passed for a character from one of her novels. He inherited his middle name, which he preferred, from his great-uncle, the famous abolitionist senator from Massachusetts, Charles Sumner.[9]

Benjamin and Frances Swan Welles brought up their children, Sumner and Emily, in the moneyed, high-caste world of the Social Register. Summers were spent at Welles House, an estate on the South Shore of Long Island that had its own stables and greenhouses. Playmates were drawn from other established families, although it is surely apocryphal that Sumner never went out to mingle with them without wearing white gloves. It is said that for his commute to Miss Kearny's Day School for Boys on 42nd Street, ten-year-old Sumner eschewed the roller skates that were fashionable at the time in favor of a slow walk. The following year, his parents signed him up for the Knickerbocker Greys, a cadet corps based at the Seventh Regiment Armory on Park Avenue and 67th Street, which drew its members from the higher reaches of New York society. "Whatever else the Greys taught him," Welles's son and biographer recalled later, "he held himself like a guardsman throughout his life."[10]

Shortly before his twelfth birthday, Welles started at Groton School, a prep school recently established in a bucolic setting outside Boston by the Reverend Endicott Peabody, and Franklin Roosevelt's own alma mater. An apostle of "muscular Christianity," Peabody had a profound influence on the education of the mid-twentieth-century American elite. His prescription for young men—cold showers, calisthenics, and church—must have come as a shock to the pampered, nonathletic Welles, who was interested in opera and Japanese art. In 1910 he received his Groton diploma and entered Harvard, only thirty miles to the southeast. During his freshman year, his beloved mother, Frances, died. For the rest of his days, Welles wore neckties of mourning black.[11]

Welles did not fit in terribly well at Harvard, but he found more congenial company in the grand brownstones of the Back Bay, to which cousins and family friends gave him entrée. It was in this elevated society that he met his first wife, heiress Esther Slater. He was also well known in other, less refined Boston establishments, including an infamous brothel in the South End. Cramming his studies into three years, Welles spent his final year in Paris with an old Groton chum, ostensibly studying architecture but in fact sampling all the pleasures of the Belle Époque capital. Several older Parisiennes were attracted by this dignified young American with his black cravat, gray spats, and golden-topped cane. Welles returned to the United States just as Europe sank into war.[12]

In 1915 Welles joined the clubby world of the State Department, having topped the diplomatic examinations. His application was sponsored by various eminent relatives and connections, including the assistant secretary of the navy, Franklin Roosevelt, who wrote that Welles "should give a very good account of himself in the service." The two Groton-Harvard men were bound together by family ties; as a boy, Sumner had served as a page at Franklin and Eleanor's wedding, at which the bride was given away by her uncle, President Theodore Roosevelt. True to FDR's prediction, Welles proved a model foreign service officer in his early postings in Tokyo and

Buenos Aires. Latin America would prove to be his abiding professional interest; the sensual aspects of its culture appealed to that side of his own character, which was otherwise masked by his solemnity. To his wife Esther's sadness, Welles took lovers in Argentina, men as well as women.[13]

In 1920, not yet thirty years old, Welles returned to Washington to run the State Department's Latin American affairs division. The department, adjacent to the White House, was housed in a hulking granite building designed in the French Second Empire style, with mansards, pillars, and porticos. Two antique bronze cannon guarded its Pennsylvania Avenue entrance. Inside, the floors were a checkerboard of black slate and white marble; the offices were high-ceilinged and commodious. Welles pleased his superiors with his work. He came to believe that Washington needed to edge away from its hegemonic, interventionary position in Latin America toward something more likely to encourage hemispheric solidarity. In 1925, however, he resigned from the foreign service at the behest of President Calvin Coolidge. It would not be the last time that Welles's unorthodox private life threatened his career.[14]

A few years earlier, Welles had met the love of his life, Mathilde Townsend Gerry, a famous Washington beauty. John Singer Sargent had painted a well-known portrait of Mathilde as a debutante, but with her oval face and large, heavy-lidded eyes she resembled more closely a Modigliani. Eight years older than Welles, she was the only child of a wealthy railroad family, and a noted equestrienne. Her residence on Massachusetts Avenue was a magnificent French Renaissance mansion fashioned after Versailles's Petit Trianon. Known as "the house with a hundred rooms," it would later accommodate the Cosmos Club. In all these respects, Mathilde was perfect for Welles. The only problem was that she was married to Senator Peter Goelet Gerry of Rhode Island. After a long affair, Sumner and Mathilde each obtained a divorce and were married in June 1925. Publicity attended the newlyweds, and it must have reached the dour, puritanical Coolidge. The president viewed divorce very darkly, and this, along with the enmity of those who had felt the sting of Welles's pen, was enough to cut short his government service.[15]

THE NEXT FEW YEARS were spent in exile, but at least it was a gilded exile. The Welleses built a magnificent manor house at Oxon Hill, Maryland, overlooking the Potomac. Guests to the estate were impressed by the Louis XV chandeliers, the fresh flowers from the gardens and hothouses, and the life-size portrait of Sumner hanging over the marble fireplace in the drawing room. The master of the house rose early in the mornings to ride his thoroughbreds along the estate's bridle paths; in the evenings, he retreated to his book-lined study to read or listen to classical records with his eyes closed.[16]

During these years, Welles grew closer to his old mentor Franklin Roosevelt, now governor of New York and increasingly a national Democratic leader. As Roosevelt closed on the Democratic presidential nomination, Welles helped draft the foreign policy section of the party platform and even paraded, in his shirtsleeves and waving an FDR placard, with the Maryland delegation at the raucous 1932 Democratic convention in Chicago. It was quite a turnaround for the austere Brahmin from the old Republican family.[17]

In April 1933, President Roosevelt appointed forty-year-old Welles his assistant secretary of state for Latin America. Welles performed well in the job, contributing to the development of FDR's Good Neighbor policy, according to which Washington renounced its right to intervene in the affairs of its sister republics and generally played a more respectful role in the Western Hemisphere. In 1936, he emerged the victor of a nasty bureaucratic contest for the position of under secretary, then the penultimate post in the department. This promotion brought him directly into the path of Cordell Hull, Roosevelt's secretary of state. Hull looked the part of America's chief diplomat: six feet tall with courtly southern manners, silver hair, and a manly jaw. A former Democratic senator from Tennessee, he had enormous cachet with Congress and the country for his service and his public rectitude.[18]

But Hull's defects were also numerous, albeit invisible to the public. He was prickly and sensitive to slights, with a foul mouth when provoked. As an administrator, he was cautious and unimaginative. Furthermore, his international interests were narrow, being principally concerned with trade treaties (or as FDR rendered the phrase behind Hull's back, making fun of his lisp, "twade tweaties"). Years later, Welles wrote that Hull's conversations with foreign diplomats were like "a train with twenty cars from which emerged a single passenger"—and always the same passenger, the reciprocal trade agreement. In a complex and dangerous world, this was simply not enough.[19]

As under secretary, Welles expanded his influence throughout the department. He reorganized its divisions according to his own preferences and the urgent demands of the time. He worked punishing hours, plowing through stacks of incoming cables and turning out elegant memoranda of conversations. He made decisions quickly, and few details evaded his demanding eye. Reports appeared in the press that ambassadors preferred Welles's "acute and precise comments" to discussions with "his vaguer and somewhat rambling superior." So did the president. Welles was the one career diplomat Roosevelt really respected. More and more often, reporters spotted Welles crossing West Executive Avenue from the State Department to the White House, his ivory-handled walking stick in hand. FDR would sometimes motor across to Oxon Hill at the end of a summer's day to discuss events over a mint julep.[20]

Naturally, all this disturbed the equilibrium of the State Department. Even as Welles won the president's trust, he incurred the enmity of the secretary of state, who felt overlooked and underappreciated.[21] Hull was stung by FDR's neglect and embittered by his subordinate's behavior. But the trend away from him was irresistible. Hull was afflicted by several chronic illnesses, including tuberculosis and diabetes, which increasingly kept him from his duties and left Welles as acting secretary. As the pace of international developments quickened, Welles's strengths were all the more obvious. He was a "field marshal" in the "war of brains" against the Axis, concluded one magazine. "Sumner Welles is naturally fitted to his work, tailored to it as accurately as his clothes are tailored to him."[22]

The quality of Welles's tailoring was a cause of much comment, indeed wonder, among Washington's scruffy press corps. Whatever the occasion, he was elegantly done out in the appropriate attire. Observers noted that on humid days his valet reported to the State Department at lunchtime with a fresh change of clothes for his master. Welles's grooming—sober, punctilious, and superior—served as reportorial shorthand for his character. He was invariably described in wintry terms. The *Washington Post* declared that "his chill, frosty, icy demeanor" was "guaranteed to congeal a finagling foreign diplomat at ten paces." *Time* compared the receipt of a diplomatic rebuff from the "enigmatic, icy, shiny-domed Sumner Welles" to "being stabbed to the heart with an icicle."[23]

Welles's colleagues did not demur from these assessments. Harold Ickes, Roosevelt's earthy secretary of the interior, observed that Welles was "glacially toplofty even when he is engaged in a fight." "If he ever smiles," Ickes recorded on another occasion, "it has not been in my presence. He conducts himself with portentous gravity and as if he were charged with all the responsibilities of Atlas." Even the British Conservative politician Anthony Eden, an Eton-educated son of a baronet, thought Welles was "rather a stiff dog."[24]

JUST BEFORE 11 A.M. on February 9, 1940, Franklin Roosevelt held one of his regular press conferences in the Oval Office. Nearly 150 newspaper reporters crowded around his desk, almost filling the bright, spacious room. After a bit of jovial banter, the president produced a typewritten sheet and read aloud from it:

At the request of the President, the Under Secretary of State Mr. Sumner Welles will proceed shortly to Europe to visit Italy, France, Germany and Great Britain. This visit is solely for the purpose of advising the President and the Secretary of State as to present conditions in Europe. Mr. Welles will, of course, be authorized to make no proposals or commitments in the name of the Government of the United States. Furthermore, statements made to him by officials of Governments will be kept in the strictest confidence and will be communicated by him solely to the President and the Secretary of State.[25]

The announcement brought forth from the newsmen a barrage of questions, most of which the president waved away. He was particularly concerned with dampening speculation that his envoy's remit went beyond fact-finding. When a reporter asked whether Welles would be discussing the administration's views on a possible peace, FDR sounded exasperated. "There you go," he said. "Now, do not get didactic. You have to stand on this statement: 'for the purpose of advising the President and the Secretary of State as to present conditions in Europe.' . . . That is the whole thing. It is all in one sentence and probably anything you add . . . to enlarge on this, will be wrong."[26]

Of course, no one writing about such a dramatic intervention, which seemed to presage a deepening of America's involvement in European affairs, could be expected to confine their speculations to Roosevelt's single sentence. Many theories were propounded, but FDR refused to lift the curtain on his reasoning. He told an adviser that he himself was "the only person who knew why Welles had been sent abroad."[27] He gave his instructions to Welles orally, and told his cabinet that any information collected by the emissary would not be shared with them. Even one of Welles's companions on his travels confessed to being "quite in the dark as to what it is all about."[28]

As usual with Roosevelt, there were wheels within wheels. Drawing on his private conversations at the time,[29] it is possible to discern five motives for his decision to send Welles to Europe.[30] The first was to delay the feared spring offensive by the Germans and buy time for the British and French to prepare for the onslaught. FDR told an intimate that he "wanted them to have as much time as they could have before the German attack commenced in all its ferocity."[31] Second, he hoped to weaken the Axis by keeping Italy neutral. An Italian declaration of war would not only complicate matters for France and endanger Britain's freedom of movement in the Mediterranean; it would demonstrate that the tide of events was moving against the democracies. The Welles mission was one of several attempts FDR made in 1939–1940 to lever Mussolini away from Hitler, or as he put it, "to drive a wedge between the two madmen."[32]

The third purpose was in fact the mission's official raison d'être: to obtain firsthand impressions of Europe's circumstances and glean political intelligence on her leaders. *Time* ventured that the mission was ordered "on the theory of let's-take-one-last-look-around-before-the-explosion."[33] Arthur Schlesinger once observed of Roosevelt, "Detail stuck in his mind like sand in honey."[34] Here was an opportunity for him to get some detail on Europe—and to take the measure of the dictators in Rome and Berlin. For some time, the Fascists and the Nazis had frozen out American diplomats, thereby depriving Roosevelt of the intelligence to which he was partial.[35]

Fourth, the Welles mission promised to serve Roosevelt's domestic political ends. In recent months, he had made a series of dramatic gestures to focus Americans' minds on the European war in general and German culpability in particular—"to put the bee on Germany," as he phrased it.[36] This new maneuver was in the same tradition, he told the British ambassador Lord Lothian, helping to satisfy public opinion that "every possibility of ending the war had been exhausted."[37] Many believed there was a more naked political motive. Electoral politics were never far from FDR's mind, especially in an election year. Many believed the Welles mission was his play for the peace vote should he run for reelection in November.[38] After all, 96 percent of Americans still opposed entering the war against Germany. Congress was preparing to cut the U.S. armed forces budget by 10 percent. Isolationists and pacifists were urging Roosevelt to "explore every road of mediation for peace."[39] By sending Welles abroad, the president hoped both to nudge Americans toward greater engagement with international affairs and prove his bona fides as a peace-loving leader.[40]

Finally, Roosevelt wanted to assure himself that there were in fact no lingering possibilities of making peace.[41] He had made earlier peace moves, and he occasionally mused to visitors about being "a kind of umpire" or "moderator" in world affairs.[42] Early drafts of his Oval Office statement indicate that he initially intended for his envoy to ask the belligerent governments to state "the basis upon which they would be prepared to make peace," but he diluted the text when the British reacted adversely.[43] Sumner Welles certainly conducted himself on his mission as if he were interested in striking a peace deal between the European powers.[44]

This does not mean that in the spring of 1940, FDR was willing to countenance the appeasement of Hitler. Roosevelt had been convinced, probably by the time of Munich but certainly from the outbreak of the European war, that a lasting peace could not be made with the Nazis. On September 11, 1939, for example, he instructed Hull to warn his ambassador in London, Joseph P. Kennedy, whom he privately labeled an "appeaser," that the "people of the United States would not support any move for peace initiated by this government that would consolidate or make possible a survival of a regime of force and of aggression."[45]

Furthermore, the organization of the trip indicates that Roosevelt never contemplated serious peace negotiations. Before announcing the mission, he consulted London but not Berlin.[46] He provided Welles with personal letters of introduction, written in longhand and brimming with goodwill, to Mussolini, Chamberlain, and Édouard Daladier, prime minister of France—but not to Hitler.[47] The order in which Welles visited the different European capitals favored the Allies, and the itinerary did not include Moscow—a strange omission if Roosevelt was really seeking to make a European peace.[48] Elements of the State Department favored a compromise peace, including Welles himself, but Roosevelt's views should never be conflated with those of his advisers, for he had advisers of every stripe.[49] When a window on peace negotiations opened during the mission, FDR himself slammed it shut.

What was the explanation for this apparent disjunction in Roosevelt's thinking? If he was against peace negotiations with the Nazis, why would he allow Welles to explore them? The answer is that FDR was always comfortable holding contradictory views, until the contradiction resolved itself. Republican Henry L. Stimson, whom the president would soon appoint to his cabinet, observed that his "mind does not follow easily a consecutive chain of thought . . . it is very much like chasing a vagrant beam of sunshine around a vacant room."[50] Like Walt Whitman, Roosevelt was large; he contained multitudes.

In the spring of 1940, FDR's policy was as tentative as the Phony War itself. He was looking for ways to help the democracies without involving the United States in the war. He estimated the odds of a peace settlement at "one in a thousand," a scenario that probably involved a complete capitulation by Berlin, or as Welles put it, "the German army laying down on Hitler" and compelling a change of regime.[51] If there were any chance of averting a disaster, why not let one of his officials test it, even if he got out in front of FDR's own position? The Welles mission was serving other purposes; why not this one, too? This was experimentation, not deliberate, clearheaded statecraft; but Roosevelt was capable of both these things.

Despite FDR's Oval Office injunction not to "get didactic," most of the American press presented the mission as a peace move. The *New York Times* saw it as the start of the "the President's long-awaited 'offensive for peace.'" Isolationist publications such as the *Chicago Daily Tribune* reacted shrilly to this creeping involvement in European affairs, likening the mission to Colonel House's secret diplomacy prior to American entry into the First World War. Other newspapers charged FDR with playing politics.[52]

The reaction next door to the White House, at the State Department, was overwhelmingly negative. Cordell Hull told a confidant he was "rather shocked" by the development, which he believed would "create confusion," raise "false hopes," and cause "five hundred different rumors."[53] Judge R. Walton Moore, who had been Hull's candidate for under secretary of state, compared the mission to "shooting at the moon."[54] A rare supporter was

Joseph Davies, a former ambassador to Moscow. "Sumner is just the man to get an objective perspective and procure it simultaneously from the principals involved," he wrote the president. "No single Ambassador assigned to a European post could do that."[55]

The U.S. diplomats posted along Welles's route all had concerns about the mission. The ambassador in Rome was William Phillips, another highborn, well-tailored New Englander. Phillips was an admirer of Welles, but he wondered privately what the envoy could achieve "surrounded by a bevy of American correspondents" and worried that the whole exercise would play into the Germans' hands.[56] In Berlin, U.S. interests were represented by the chargé d'affaires, Alexander Kirk, FDR having recalled his ambassador to Germany after *Kristallnacht*. Kirk was chagrined by the lack of information forthcoming from Washington on the Welles mission.[57]

The ambassadors to Paris and London, William Bullitt and Joseph Kennedy, were both in the United States at the time of the announcement and were furious about it. Bullitt was the brilliant and headstrong scion of a prominent Philadelphia family, who had previously served as the first U.S. ambassador to the Soviet Union. He was black with rage at the news of Welles's appointment because he regarded himself as FDR's principal adviser on European affairs. Bullitt vented to various cabinet members and journalists, who duly reported on dissension in the State Department. To signal his displeasure, he refused to return to France until Welles had left, preferring to vacation on Hobe Sound in Florida.[58]

Joe Kennedy was the Irish American businessman and patriarch—and outspoken isolationist—whom Roosevelt had unaccountably made ambassador to the Court of St. James's. Kennedy was a friend of Welles's rather than a rival, but he too was riled by the news of his European assignment. "Now just where does that put me?" he roared when he heard of the mission. "You would think I had just been pouring tea over there instead of working my head off. If they think they need a special ambassador over there to get all the British secrets I failed to get, they can count me out."[59]

The reaction from the countries to which all these gentlemen were accredited was also mixed. The status-conscious Italians affected skepticism but were secretly delighted that Welles would visit Rome before Berlin.[60] The British, French, and Germans, on the other hand, each interpreted Roosevelt's decision through the prism of their own private fears.

London and Paris worried that Roosevelt was going wobbly. Sir Robert Vansittart, a fierce old Foreign Office lion and sworn enemy of appeasement, thought His Majesty's Government should "warn President Roosevelt off any undesirable grass, before we have to receive the grass-snake, Mr Welles." His acerbic colleague Sir Alec Cadogan, the most senior civil servant at the Foreign Office, was horrified at the "awful, half-baked idea of sending Sumner Welles (!) over here with a flourish of trumpets to collect data on which Roosevelt is to proclaim [the] basis of peace!"[61] Taking advantage of his extra week's notice, Prime Minister Neville Chamberlain wrote to FDR admitting to "a good deal of anxiety" lest the mission embarrass the democracies and advantage Germany. FDR moved to reassure the British, promising to make clear that it was not a peace mission. London was partly mollified, and when the final announcement came across the wires, even Cadogan conceded it was "not too bad."[62]

The French government, lacking the advantage of prior notice, was flustered by the news of Welles's appointment. The foreign ministry, the Quai d'Orsay, expressed to the U.S. embassy in Paris its "reserve as to the purposes of the visit." Privately some Frenchmen muttered about American appeasement. Both the British and French press took their lead from their governments, protesting loudly against suggestions that the mission was a peace move and declaring their countries' resolve to defeat the Nazis.[63]

Far from viewing the Welles mission as an indication of the strength of its position, however, the German government feared it would expose its weakness. Worried that it might encourage popular hopes for peace, Adolf Hitler's propaganda chief, Joseph Goebbels, quickly imposed a press blackout on the subject. Hitler believed the mission's purpose was "to prevent an offensive." Elements of the regime fretted that it could strengthen Washington's ties to London—or, more damagingly, to Rome. The Führer moved to consolidate the Axis, writing to Mussolini that "the only purpose of this intervention is to gain time for the Allies; that is, to paralyze any German intentions for an offensive." Germany's official response to Washington was cold. Berlin signaled it was willing to receive Welles, but that was all.[64]

Sumner Welles sailed from New York City for Naples on February 17, 1940, aboard the liner SS *Rex*. The *Rex* was a svelte, twin-funneled 51,000-ton vessel of the Italian Line, dubbed "the Riviera afloat." She was fast, having in 1933 captured the westbound Blue Riband as the fastest passenger liner to cross the Atlantic.[65]

Welles's traveling party had a hint of grandness about it. It included Mathilde Welles, looking handsome in glossy furs, her niece Miss Thora Ronalds, and their respective maids, all of whom were to stay in Rome while the mission unfolded across Europe; dark-haired Jay Pierrepont Moffat, yet another Groton-Harvard man, who was chief of the European Affairs Division at the State Department; and Welles's English valet, Reeks. Rounding out the entourage was the under secretary's West Highland terrier, Toby, who habitually accompanied him to diplomatic conferences and was rumored once to have "barked most intemperately" at Cordell Hull. A reporter covering the departure admitted she hoped the "spunky little Scot" would return from Europe "with shreds of brown shirts in his teeth." (Sadly, Toby would not get his chance, as he stayed in Italy with Mrs. Welles.)[66]

Pier 92 at the foot of West 52nd Street, in the middle of "Luxury Liner Row," was crawling with reporters there to see off Roosevelt's enigmatic envoy. Media interest ran high. One radio correspondent observed that Welles had been described as "a listening post, a fact-finder, a sprinting Sphinx, a one-man American mission of curiosity, and a 1940 edition of Colonel House."[67]

———

"One sea voyage is much like another," wrote Jay Pierrepont Moffat in his diary. "It is time-out in the march of life, and hence to be treasured." Other passengers on board the *Rex* included minor Belgian royals, a Swedish magnate, the prominent columnist Walter Lippmann and his wife, and a group of reporters detailed to follow Sumner Welles. There was "no sense of strain," wrote Moffat, "no feeling that war was being fought on the waters of the Atlantic, perhaps just beyond the horizon."[68]

However, at Gibraltar, the British stronghold at the entrance to the Mediterranean, the war came into view. The British maintained a naval blockade of Europe in an effort to prevent Germany from obtaining succor from abroad. The *Rex* was invited to heave to near other detained ships, and Welles was spotted leaning on the rail, watching impassively as a British tender came alongside. While Welles joined the senior British officers at tea on the veranda deck, their colleagues seized 334 bags of U.S. mail addressed to Germany and Poland and covered the *Rex*'s cargo with navicerts—navigational certificates specifying the cargo was not contraband. The censoring of the mails was an ongoing irritant in the relationship between Washington and London. After a speedy turnaround of three and a half hours, which was attributed to Welles's presence on board, the *Rex* was allowed to proceed.[69]

The *Rex* sailed in to the calm, cobalt-blue Bay of Naples shortly after lunch on Sunday, February 25, a beautiful springlike day. "All the trappings of an official visit" were on display in Naples, Moffat noted, including civilian and military officials, flashing photographers' bulbs, and whirring motion-picture cameras. At the train station on Piazza Garibaldi, attendants had "brushed and rebrushed yards of red plush carpet" laid for the occasion. Welles's party made the three-hour run to Rome in a private railway coach, rolling through beautiful countryside, past fortified towns and castles, across the Pontine Marshes, and finally onto the flower-decked royal platform at the capital's central train station, Stazione Termini. The welcoming ceremony there was splashed with color, including the red and blue of the Carabinieris' plumed hats and the black shirts of the Fascist paramilitaries. Unimpressed, Toby lifted his leg on a stately urn. Reeks, who was holding the terrier's leash, was mortified; the dark-suited Welles "looked stonily the other way."[70]

Pink blossoms covered the city's almond trees; Romans hummed jaunty songs and flocked to American movies. Yet something was amiss: Welles felt that "the hand of Fascism lay heavy over Italy." The newspapers were uniformly mute about his mission. Walking the streets, he could sense the restrictions that were strangling the country's natural exuberance. Italians ate silently in cafés under signs forbidding the discussion of politics. Coffee shortages hit home particularly hard. "Italy sees dark days ahead," diarized Moffat. "People are afraid of the currency, and are indulging in a buying orgy; gambling is rife."[71]

Welles made a brief call on King Victor Emmanuel III the next morning, then spent two hours with Italy's foreign minister, Count Galeazzo Ciano, at his opulent official residence, the Palazzo Chigi. Ciano was a vain, slick-haired, excitable aristocrat in his late thirties, Mussolini's son-in-law and his creature. Yet he was contemptuous of the Nazis and opposed to Italy's participation in the war, believing the West would defeat Germany in the end. Welles emphasized Roosevelt's desire for closer Italo-American ties, and stressed the benefits to Italy of a policy of neutrality. Both men came away from the meeting impressed. Ciano wrote in his diary that Welles was "a gentleman," unlike the German officials with whom he dealt—"that pack of presumptuous vulgarians." Welles thought Ciano was intelligent, frank, and caustic. It was only after the meeting, when moving-picture footage of the two was recorded, that Ciano adopted a Fascist-style "chest out, chin up" pose.[72]

That afternoon Ciano escorted Welles and Ambassador Phillips to meet the originator of that pose. The Duce's office in the Palazzo Venezia, a former papal palace, was known as the Sala del Mappamondo (the Hall of Two Hemispheres). The room was monumental, sixty feet long and forty feet wide, and as high as it was wide. A balcony overlooked the Piazza Venezia; it was from here that Mussolini delivered his diatribes to the crowds below. At the end of the room, an ugly pyramidal painting of an ax blade emerging from a bundle of sticks—the fasces—sat over a massive fireplace. The immense room was empty of furniture save for a desk in the corner and a few visitors' chairs; it was gloomy and sepulchral, the whole vast space illuminated by a single reading lamp on the desk.[73]

In a nod to his visitor's mission, Mussolini had eschewed his uniform for civilian clothes. From his pictures and descriptions, Welles had expected the Duce to be active and animated. But the man before him, with white close-cropped hair and "rolls of flesh," seemed much older than his fifty-six years. "He was ponderous and static," Welles remembered in his report to FDR. "He moved with elephantine motion. Every step appeared an effort." He bragged that he rode every morning and had beaten his tennis professional 6–2 that very day. To Welles, however, he appeared to be "a man laboring under some tremendous strain"—partly explained, Welles thought, by the fact that he had recently taken a new mistress. Unfortunately, some of Welles's observations on his host's appearance later made their way back to an indignant Duce via an intercepted British telegram.[74]

Mussolini was visibly pleased to receive FDR's letter of introduction and said he agreed on the importance of close relations between Rome and Washington. Welles was heartened when Mussolini agreed that a "real and lasting peace" between the Allies and Germany was possible. Berlin's terms would include, the Duce thought, the retention of Austria in the Reich; an independent Slovakia; German control of parts of Poland and the Czech rump; German hegemony in central Europe; and restoration of Germany's colonies. He declared Italy's right to free access to the Mediterranean and the oceans.[75] The American was taken with Mussolini's shrewdness, and told the British ambassador in Rome that he was surprised to have been received in "a friendly and cordial way."[76]

In fact, Welles had misread his man. Mussolini had played the role of mediator at Munich, and enjoyed it. But since the outbreak of war he had lost interest in a compromise peace. He believed that his country's status as a great power, as well as its "national virility," required war. Jealous of Hitler's victories, and hungry for an empire of his own, he was moving quickly toward committing Italy to fight beside Germany. Mussolini had no interest in a "real and lasting peace."[77]

Late the following evening, Welles and his party left Italy by train, riding in Ciano's private car. They left behind a satisfied U.S. ambassador in Rome. William Phillips felt that the visit had been "exceedingly helpful," introducing "a new spirit" of cooperation into the bilateral relationship.[78] At the border town of Chiasso, the party switched to a Swiss wagon-salon for the glorious Alpine run over the St. Gotthard Pass to Zurich. Their twenty-four-hour stopover in the Swiss city loosed a "flood of rumors and speculation." The press wondered about mysterious meetings, German peace plans, and a drive to mediate the Russo-Finnish War. In fact, all Welles wanted was a decent sleep and a chance to recover from a cold he had brought with him from Washington.[79]

There was, however, a certain cloak-and-dagger quality to the layover in Zurich. Welles was followed by unknown persons. An American diplomat dined with him under the alias "Mr. Smith," a disguise that was penetrated by the press in a few hours. A female reporter from a New York tabloid poured herself into a revealing black dress in an unsuccessful attempt to prise free some of Welles's secrets. A mysterious Austro-Hungarian princess claiming to carry a message from Goebbels asked to be received. "We politely declined to make contact with the Princess," observed Moffat, "who, it is said, burst into tears at her failure. I wonder whose agent she really was."[80]

THE FOLLOWING DAY, Welles and his party departed for Berlin, and at the frontier they transferred to a special train Hitler had sent to collect them. The train's blinds were drawn at the insistence of the authorities, but they were too flimsy a barrier to prevent the travelers from sensing the atmosphere in Germany. In Stuttgart, Welles stepped out onto the station platform in the "inky" blackness that lay over the countryside, and his "feeling of oppression was almost physical." This feeling was heightened when he read the ugly and fantastical lies that filled the German newspapers provided for him in his coach. In conformity with Goebbels's orders, however, none of the periodicals reported on his own visit.[81]

Welles's train pulled into Anhalter Station on the morning of Friday, March 1. There were no flags or military escorts to welcome the envoy. Driving up Unter den Linden to the Hotel Adlon, Welles noticed a contingent of Polish prisoners shoveling snow under armed guard. The Adlon was the grandest hotel in Berlin, located near the Brandenburg Gate and the U.S. embassy, which accounted for the American diplomats and reporters who could always be found at its bar. But it also abutted Wilhelmstrasse, the home of many Reich ministries, including the Foreign Office, the propaganda and air ministries, and Hitler's new Chancellery. Welles would sleep at the heart of the gangster capital.[82]

As Welles's car pulled up outside the Adlon, deafening sirens split the air, signifying an air raid drill. He noticed that the hotel was flying not the American flag, but the pennant of the Slovak Republic, a Nazi client state. At that very moment, a Slovakian delegation headed by a young paramilitary commander drew up outside the hotel. *Time* recorded that Welles remained poker-faced as the air raid siren screamed and "the Adlon's lobby filled with gesticulating, heel-clicking, heiling Slovakians, obscuring his own arrival."[83]

Berlin had recently enjoyed hints of the spring to come, but with Welles's arrival winter returned. The war was evident in the troop trains passing through the capital each day heading west, and in the shortages of meat, fresh vegetables, and chocolate. Theaters and opera houses remained open, however, and restaurants were full. In the main, Germany at war was not so different from Germany at peace. "In a state created expressly for the purpose of waging war," wrote American correspondent Howard K. Smith, "the line dividing the two conditions was bound to be a fine, almost invisible one." The mobilization of several million soldiers to fight in Poland had "had no more effect on the German home front than the wash of a motor-boat on a giant liner at sea."[84]

For a visitor like Welles, who had not been to Berlin in many years, the dark trappings of the Nazi regime were shocking. Banners of red and white, with the black hooked cross at their center, hung everywhere. Senior Nazis were driven around at extreme speed in powerful saloon cars. SS uniforms mingled with those of the military. Propaganda posters featuring Chamberlain or Churchill as warmonger, gas poisoner, or starver of children were plastered on walls. Signs on doorways declared, "Jews unwanted."[85]

In his three days in Berlin, Welles spoke with the most important Nazi leaders. But as Hitler's interpreter recalled later, the conversations played out like a series of identical gramophone records.[86] The Führer had already moved to ensure that German officials spoke with one voice, instructing his officials to stress both Germany's innocence and her will to victory. No discussion of peace was to be entered into, he directed. "I request rather that Mr Sumner Welles not be given the slightest reason to doubt that Germany is determined to end this war victoriously and that the German people—united today as never before in their thousand year history—and their leadership are unshakeable in their confidence in victory."[87]

At noon on the day of his arrival, Welles, now in morning dress and a silk top hat, was escorted to the Foreign Office for his meeting with Foreign Minister Joachim von Ribbentrop.[88] All the German diplomats, including the minister, were uniformed; sentries were stationed at the top of the stairs, their faces "subnormal in their startling brutality." After a three-minute wait in an anteroom (Welles always measured such intervals precisely), Welles and the U.S. chargé, Alexander Kirk, were received by Ribbentrop at the door to his office, "glacially, and without the semblance of a smile or a word of greeting." The minister was fluent in English—as Welles noted sniffily in his report, he had worked as a wine salesman in North America as well as serving as Germany's ambassador in London—but he insisted on conversing via an interpreter.[89]

Welles began by explaining, as he had done in Rome, that his mission was "to ascertain whether there existed any possibility of the establishment of a sound and permanent peace in Europe." In reply, Ribbentrop subjected him to a two-hour diatribe on the Nazi version of European history since Hitler had come to power. While he delivered these familiar catechisms, he sat "rigid in his chair with eyes closed, as if he were a man having a vision."[90] Afterward, Welles's judgment was scathing. "Ribbentrop has a completely closed mind," he reported to Roosevelt. "It struck me as also a very stupid mind . . . he was guilty of a hundred inaccuracies in his presentation of German policy during recent years. I have rarely seen a man I disliked more." Welles told the Washington columnist Drew Pearson that Ribbentrop was "one of the weirdest individuals in history."[91]

At eleven o'clock the next day, Welles and Kirk were taken to the Reich Chancellery to meet Adolf Hitler. The Chancellery, completed only a year before, consisted of a string of rooms laid out along a rectangular site. Much of the interior was constructed out of highly polished marble the color of blood. This made for slippery floors and stairs, but Hitler's view was that "diplomats should have practice in moving on a slippery surface." A state guest calling on the Führer was required to walk nearly the entire length of the building before being received. "On the long walk from the entrance to the reception hall they'll get a taste of the power and grandeur of the German Reich!" exulted Hitler when he first saw the design.[92] The Chancellery was in fact designed specifically to impress someone like Sumner Welles.

Welles was first driven through great bronze gates into the court of honor, a rectangular courtyard with high blank walls and plain round columns. An honor guard of black-garbed SS troops was drawn up, their rifles glinting in the sunshine. Welles mounted a few steps and entered the Chancellery, passing between twin monumental bronze nudes symbolizing "The Party" and "The Army," and beneath a bas-relief stone eagle sitting atop a swastika. At the same instant, the SS stiffened into a Nazi salute.[93] All the glamour of evil was on display.

In the entrance hall, Welles noticed "a group of flunkeys" dressed in "light blue satin liveries, with powdered hair." A factotum led Welles and his entourage through high double doors and a succession of dramatic rooms until he was brought to an immense gallery that was 480 feet long—twice the length of the Hall of Mirrors at Versailles. Hitler's architect Albert Speer had modeled this gallery on the ballroom of the Château de Fontainebleau outside Paris; to Welles's eye, it resembled more closely the main salon of a German ocean liner. After a short wait, the party was brought to Hitler's reception hall, overlooking the gardens of Bismarck's old residence, in which Hitler now lived.[94]

The chancellor met Welles at the door and quickly made a good impression on his visitor. He was taller than Welles had expected, relaxed and in good health. "He was dignified both in speech and movement, and there was not the slightest impression of the comic effect from moustache and hair which one sees in his caricatures," reported Welles. Only occasionally did Hitler lose his composure, at which point his eyes lost their pleasant look and his voice acquired "the raucous stridency which is heard in his speeches."[95]

Welles began by observing that in Rome he had "happily gained the impression . . . that the Duce believed the foundations of a just and lasting peace might still be laid." He "hoped the Chancellor would find it possible to confirm that impression." But Welles was to be disappointed. Hitler's survey of the wrongs Germany had suffered and his own government's policies, although milder in form than Ribbentrop's, was similar in substance. "The German people had every right to demand that their historical position of a thousand years should be restored to them," including economic hegemony in central and southeastern Europe. The colonies stolen from Germany at Versailles must be returned to her. All the blame for the war lay at the feet of London and Paris. "I can see no hope for the establishment of any lasting peace," he intoned, "until the will of England and France to destroy Germany is itself destroyed." Clutching at straws, Welles declared that he would not forget Hitler's closing statement that "Germany's aim, whether it must come through war or otherwise, is a just peace."[96] But the outlook was not promising.

A driving storm struck Berlin on Sunday, bringing rain, sleet, and snow and, in the view of the *New York Times*, "a note of gloom to the conclusion of this extraordinary visit." In the morning, Welles met with the deputy Nazi Party leader, Rudolf Hess, at the party headquarters, which were as stark and bare of decoration as a prison. Welles thought that Hess bore "the unmistakable appearance of being devoid of all but a very low order of intelligence. His forehead is low and narrow, and his deep-set eyes are very close together. He is noted for his dog-like devotion to Hitler." Also joining the meeting was a rowdy group of young Nazis who "appeared to have previously rehearsed with Hess every word of what he was to say."[97]

Hess produced a set of typewritten cards, from which he read throughout the meeting. His spiel was identical to Ribbentrop's statement of the position. He emphasized that the German people and National Socialism were inseparable: the people "stood as one man behind their Fuehrer." The only route to a lasting peace was through "a total and crushing German military victory." The chorus of young Nazis behind him nodded their approval, their eyes burning with "an almost insane fanaticism."[98]

The day now got even stranger. Welles's final substantive appointment in Germany was with Field Marshal Hermann Göring at his hunting lodge, Carinhall. Göring was not just the head of the Luftwaffe but an extremely powerful figure in the regime, and Hitler's nominated successor. Göring's succession was an outcome greatly desired by some in the West, who believed that his aims were more moderate than the Führer's. Carinhall was located in the Schorfheide forest north of Berlin, in a national game reserve. On each side of the long entrance drive were enclosures where Göring kept exotic animals, including a herd of large cattle that were the product of his attempt to reintroduce the ancient aurochs—extinct giant cattle—to Europe through cross-breeding. Carinhall was Göring's folly: a modest hunting lodge, named for his deceased first wife, that had been rebuilt into a Norse-style baronial estate as large and ostentatious as its lord. Welles, who was not unfamiliar with grand residences, noted that Carinhall was the size of Washington's new National Gallery.[99]

Welles and the lupine Göring spoke for almost three hours in front of an open fire, next to huge picture windows framing the falling snow. Welles's pen portrait of his host was lethal. "His thighs and arms are tremendous," Welles wrote, "and his girth is tremendous." Göring's face "gave the impression of being heavily rouged"; he wore a white tunic covered with various colorful insignia. An Iron Cross hung from his neck, along with a monocle on a black cord. "His hands are shaped like the digging-paws of a badger," observed Welles. "On his right hand he wore an enormous ring set with six huge diamonds; on his left hand he wore an emerald at least an inch square."[100]

Welles recalled that Göring "spoke with far greater frankness and clarity" than other German officials, but the message was no different. He doubted that Hitler could ever believe "there was any way of destroying the British will to destroy Germany, except through military victory." He cautioned Welles that this time, unlike in the last war, Germany had "all the trumps in her hands." He wished Welles success in his mission to avert war, but there was not a cigarette paper between his position and Hitler's. Later, Göring gave Welles a tour of his house, which served as a treasure chest for the loot he had extorted over the years. The walls were hung with hundreds of paintings of mixed quality; glass cases displayed golden cups and other gifts from foreign governments and German organizations eager to stay in the field marshal's good graces. Welles was offended by Göring's vulgarity and disheartened by his remarks. On the long twilight drive back to the capital, Welles motored past long lines of Berliners waiting to buy food, or tickets to a movie theater. He did not see a single smiling face.[101]

That evening, Welles proceeded through the blackout to Anhalter Station. His Berlin conversations had been an anticlimax. They contained no hints of a possible peace deal. Each of his official interlocutors had rehearsed an increasingly familiar historical survey and pinned all the blame on Britain and France. Furthermore, his talks with foreign diplomats in Berlin revealed that internal opposition to Hitler was weak. The hope in Washington that the army would push Hitler aside was naïve; in reality, all authority sprang from the head of the Führer. For his part, Welles gave no sign in his meetings that he was actively feeling for the outlines of a negotiated peace. The German interpreter who sat in on all the key conversations recalled that Welles's "frigid, reserved attitude" would scarcely have encouraged Hitler to start peace talks even if he had been so inclined. (He did not know that Welles was frigid and reserved on a good day.)[102]

In a brief conversation at the blackened railway station with a German diplomat, Welles gave an indication that he was thinking about his mission's other aims, including forestalling the spring offensive and complicating Italian-German ties. He expected his trip to be successful, he told the German, if Europe remained quiet "in the next four to five weeks." But even in the short term, the Welles mission was not a stick in Hitler's spokes. Welles's presence in Berlin did not stop the Führer from ratcheting up preparations for his next campaigns, against Denmark and Norway. A week later, Hitler would send Ribbentrop to Rome to stiffen Mussolini's spine. For the first time, the Duce indicated privately that at the appropriate moment he would take Italy into the war on Germany's side.[103]

None of this was known to Welles as his train rolled out of Berlin shortly after nine o'clock. But he could divine Hitler's intentions from the stories in the German press. As he departed, the Wilhelmstrasse briefed reporters in depressing detail about the recent talks. Hitler had told Welles, they indicated, that there was no chance of a negotiated peace and the war must be fought to the bitter end.[104] If Welles had arrived in Berlin with questions, he now had his answers.

WELLES'S TRAIN RACED SOUTHWARD during the night toward Switzerland, where he intended to rest before proceeding to Paris. Close to Heidelberg, German fortifications started appearing as the train came within range of French heavy artillery. For the last fifty miles before the Swiss border, it rolled down the east bank of the silvery Rhine, between the Maginot Line and its German twin, the Siegfried Line. Immediately below them, the party saw German trenches and artillery positions; just across the river, sometimes as little as a hundred yards away, they observed French fortifications. Franklin Roosevelt's envoy was literally between the two belligerents, and the position afforded him an excellent view of the Phony War. French and German soldiers went about their business as he passed. Their laundry flapped in the wind. Couriers dashed to and fro on motorcycles. Civilians worked in the fields and tied up vines in the vineyards. "Not a gun was fired, not a disturbing sound broke the stillness," recorded Jay Pierrepont Moffat. "Never have I had so strange a feeling of the unreality of this war."[105]

Walter Trohan of the *Chicago Daily Tribune*, who was on Welles's train, wrote an evocative dispatch describing the view from its windows:

> Soldiers piled off the Welles train at various points along the line to report for front line duty. All along the line soldiers engaged in building railroads, concrete forts, pillboxes, trenches, and other defenses, halted to watch the passing train after the manner of railroad workers in the United States. Soldiers who were stripped down to their undershirts in the bright sun which lifted the early morning haze over the Rhine went about their work after the fashion of Works Progress Administration workers at home. They showed no concern for the war or their enemy . . . Children were everywhere. Three boys, all less than eight years old, dangled their legs from a stone bridge while they watched mixers pour concrete into a fort in the fashion of Tom Sawyer and Huckleberry Finn watching steamers on the Mississippi.[106]

Six miles before the frontier, the train passed right under the Siegfried Line. Fluttering Swiss flags soon signaled it had passed into neutral territory. Moffat immediately felt the mood of the train shift. "The sense of strain lifted. People were smiling and even laughing. Food was no longer rationed. News was no longer controlled. Thought was free."[107]

At Basel, Welles and company boarded an express train to the pretty resort town of Lausanne on the northern shore of Lake Geneva, facing the French Alps. Here he spent two restful days at the Hotel Beau-Rivage Palace, guarded by Swiss police, trying to recover from his persistent cold. Late in the evening of Wednesday, March 6, he boarded a special railway car that had been dispatched by the French government to Lausanne, to be attached to the Simplon-Orient-Express. The coach was not, however, up to scratch. "Whereas the Italian and German cars were clean and comfortable and luxurious," complained Moffat, "this one was dirty, down at heel, and worse yet, the sheets were so damp we couldn't sleep in them." Bismarck famously heard the approach of history in distant hoofbeats; Welles and his party saw it in sloppy housekeeping.[108]

BACK IN WASHINGTON, a different phony war was being fought—over whether Franklin Roosevelt would run for a third consecutive term as president and, if so, whether he would win. The two-term limit was an ancient American tradition, and the only reason a departure from precedent was conceivable was the gravity of the foreign danger. Reporters probed relentlessly for some hint of the president's thinking. The *Washington Post* ran a cartoon portraying the Sphinx drawn with FDR's face. One of its paws rested on a bundle of papers labeled "Welles Report?," the other on papers reading "Third Term?"

Roosevelt treated political matters such as this with "the utmost care and finesse," observed his speechwriter Robert Sherwood, and he studied this issue "from every conceivable angle." For many months, he was undecided what to do. He had already achieved a great deal as president; by running again, in the face of convention, he risked a humiliating defeat. Part of him was ready to return to his estate on the Hudson, where he was presiding over the construction of a presidential library for his papers and a private hilltop hideaway, Top Cottage. His speech at the laying of the library's cornerstone was full of nostalgic stories from his Dutchess County boyhood, when he sailed toy boats, picked the sickle pears from the trees, dug into woodchuck holes in the fields, and lay between the strawberry rows eating "sun-warmed strawberries—the best in the world."

When Daniel Tobin of the Teamsters Union visited the White House around this time and urged him to run again, the response was unequivocal. "No, Dan," replied FDR, "I just can't do it. I tell you, I have been here a long time. I am tired. I really am. You don't know what it's like . . . No, I can't be President again . . . I want to go home to Hyde Park. I want to take care of my trees. I have a big planting there, Dan. I want to make the farm pay. I want to finish my little house on the hill. I want to write history. No, I just can't do it, Dan."

And yet—who could Roosevelt trust with the keys to the White House? Who else could preserve the gains of the New Deal and prepare America to face the threats from abroad? At different times, FDR toyed with various Democratic successors, including Cordell Hull and Harry Hopkins. But he never got around to putting in place a succession plan; perhaps he never intended to. Instead, he waited for events to play themselves out. "I do not want to run," he told Treasury Secretary Henry Morgenthau, "unless between now and the [July 1940 Democratic] convention things get very, very much worse in Europe."[109]

THE ORIENT-EXPRESS PULLED IN to the art nouveau Gare de Lyon at 10 a.m. on March 7, four years to the day since Germany had remilitarized the Rhineland. The French authorities put on a good show at the station, including a detachment of special constables from the Garde Mobile as well as plainclothes policemen. Welles was whisked off to his accommodations at the Ritz Hotel, the storied establishment overlooking the octagonal Place Vendôme, in an armored Renault with motorcycle outriders.[110]

Welles wrote later that he found "a Paris wholly changed" and characterized by "sullen apathy." Springtime weather now created as much anxiety as joy, as it presaged the fighting season. There was an awful sense of anticipation in the air. Millions of Frenchmen had been mobilized, and they could be seen everywhere in their uniforms. Important structures, such as the Arc de Triomphe, and the Marly Horses and Obelisk of Luxor in the Place de la

Concorde, were all sandbagged. Another visitor to the city at the time, Canadian diplomat Vincent Massey, observed that Paris was "not all herself—rather like a lovely woman a bit distressed in mind."[111]

Yet for other observers, the similarities to the peacetime condition were more striking than the differences. Sunshine had "brought tables back to café terraces and cheerful strolling crowds back to the Champs-Élysées." English newspapers were available at the kiosks and restaurants were well patronized. "The French ideas of rationing made us smile," noted Moffat. "On meatless days, one can none the less eat duck, turkey, goose, birds, et cetera; on spiritless days, one cannot have a cocktail, but one can (and does) have a glass of champagne as an apéritif."[112] At night, Paris was as seductive as ever. Theaters and music halls were open; a revival of *Cyrano de Bergerac* was staged at the Comédie-Française and *La Traviata* played at the Opéra-Comique; Maurice Chevalier and Josephine Baker performed at the Casino de Paris. The blackout was nowhere near as effective as that in London or Berlin; in fact, it was actually "a subdued blue."[113]

Reports of Welles's hauteur spread quickly in the French capital. Within two hours of his arrival, a reporter noted, "all Paris was chuckling over the story that a new cocktail had been created in honor of Welles" at the bar of the Hotel Crillon, much frequented by Americans, and "its sole ingredient was ice water."[114]

Welles called on the president of the Republic, Albert Lebrun, at the Élysée Palace on rue du Faubourg Saint-Honoré. The guard of honor did not look nearly so fearsome as the SS at Hitler's Chancellery. Lebrun was an elder statesman, gentle, cautious, and high-minded, but lacking toughness and vision—and, unfortunately, the power of recall. His memory was failing, and as he described France's previous wars with Germany he had difficulty remembering names and dates. When he took Welles on a tour of the main rooms of the palace, he struggled to identify the subjects of the official portraits. President Lebrun personified the frailty of the Third Republic.[115]

The French secret service drove Welles and his party "at lightning speed" from the Élysée across the Seine to his meeting with Édouard Daladier, who was not only prime minister but also minister of national defense and war. Daladier spent most of his days at the defense ministry's headquarters in the splendid eighteenth-century town house Hôtel de Brienne, on the narrow rue Saint-Dominique. Daladier's office, decorated in the Empire style, looked out on to a small garden. Its most striking feature was a large tapestry depicting King Louis XIV signing the Treaty of Dover, which had established a brief alliance between France and its old enemy, England.[116]

Welles liked Daladier, a burly machine politician whose apparent fortitude concealed a certain indecisiveness. The prime minister had signed the Munich Pact but had no illusions about Hitler, whose ambition was not, he said, "the unity of the German peoples of Central Europe," but rather "ultimate domination of Europe and of the Near East." Whatever he might state in public, however, Daladier revealed to Welles that he "would not refuse to deal with the present German regime" so long as France's security was guaranteed.[117] That evening, the PM hosted a dinner for Welles's party in the banquet hall of the Quai d'Orsay, the French foreign ministry's home on the banks of the Seine. A number of French ministers and diplomats were present. Notwithstanding the peril in which the Republic found herself, the traditional formalities were observed and the guests were served by footmen in knee breeches.[118]

Welles got a sense of the virulence of European anti-Semitism when he met with Léon Blum, the former socialist prime minister and leader of the Popular Front coalition government in 1936–1937. Blum, a well-known admirer of Franklin Roosevelt, was living in a small apartment on the Quai de Bourbon on Île Saint-Louis, overlooking the Seine. Welles and Blum spoke for a long time in his charming little study, overflowing with the remnants of a public life. Welles perceived in Blum's remarks an undercurrent of "profound sadness and an almost corroding discouragement," a feeling that, for the Republic, "the hours were numbered, and time was passing very swiftly." Blum's sadness was not misplaced. In the next few days, the U.S. embassy received several thousand letters from Frenchmen, many of them abusive, protesting that a representative of the president of the United States had called on a Jew.[119]

The following month, after Ambassador Bullitt's belated return to France, he reported to Roosevelt that Welles had made a bleak impression in Paris. French politicians had told him, he wrote, "that Welles 'eulogized' Mussolini to everyone" and gave "the impression that Germany could not be beaten." A clearly piqued Bullitt concluded, with his usual pigheadedness, "I have been highly restrained in this report since certain of the remarks which have been made to me have been violent in the extreme. Now let's forget the matter for good."[120]

Welles certainly went out of his way to assuage French animosity toward Mussolini and his regime, as a means of snarling up the Axis. This was, after all, one of his commissions. But a more nuanced account of his visit was provided by the British ambassador in Paris, Sir Ronald Campbell, who reported to London that Welles had made "an excellent personal impression." Although Welles had been "somewhat too easily impressed by Signor Mussolini," he had clearly been displeased by what he had seen in Germany, and his "sympathies were definitely on the side of the Allies."[121]

As for the press, editorialists argued that someone so intelligent could hardly fail to be impressed with the freely expressed opinions he heard in France, compared with the strictly enforced line in Germany. *Paris-Soir* addressed FDR's envoy directly: "In Germany you were the guest of an oligarchy. In Paris the whole people welcomes you . . . on one side the tyranny of a party; on the other a people that is free." It also restated the official view that "there could be no peace so long as the Nazi regime remained in power; bitter experience had revealed that Nazi pledges did not count." The only paths to peace, the Daladier government declared publicly, were victory over Germany or regime change within it. In private, the position expressed to Welles had not been so clear.[122]

ON SUNDAY MORNING, Welles and his colleagues flew to England in a passenger aircraft, accompanied by three French fighters and a British reconnaissance plane. Within a few minutes of taking off from Le Bourget

Airport, all they could see of Paris was the tip of the Eiffel Tower poking through the clouds. Ninety minutes later they were flying over England, so low that Welles could see workers in the countryside preparing for the spring planting. He stepped from the plane, wearing his black bowler hat, at Heston Aerodrome to the west of the capital. This was the same field to which Neville Chamberlain had returned from Munich in September 1938, waving a piece of paper that seemed to signify peace, when it fact it only signified submission.[123]

Joe Kennedy met Welles at the plane and drove the party back to their hotel, the modern and luxurious Dorchester. Its lobby was full of reporters, interested onlookers, and one frock-coated gentleman with bulging hip pockets who was taken for a detective. The original intention had been to put Welles in another Mayfair hotel, Claridge's, but the embassy had heard that its Italian manager had Fascist leanings and worried that Welles's suite might be wired. The British Security Service, MI5, was called in. It could not locate any listening devices but it could not guarantee they had not been inserted into the walls, so Welles was shifted. "Perhaps the British wanted to move the mission to a hotel where they instead of the Italians had the microphone privileges," Moffat suggested archly.[124]

That afternoon, Kennedy took the party to Kew Gardens, which were full of Londoners enjoying the warm Sunday afternoon. While they walked, Kennedy gave the visitors his take on things. Chamberlain's government was determined not to deal with the "gang" in Berlin, he said, but it knew that a long war would bankrupt Britain, and the upper classes were "bitterly worried." Washington's reluctance to enter the war was stirring up anti-American feelings, which were not helped by Kennedy's own cloth-eared interventions. "For Christ's sake, stop trying to make this a holy war, because no-one will believe you," was his challenge to British officials, he told Welles. "You're fighting for your life as an Empire, and that's good enough."[125]

The war certainly seemed closer at hand in London than it had in Paris. Silver barrage balloons dotted the sky above the capital and the streets were full of sandbags and barbed wire. The Guard at Buckingham Palace wore khaki and the police wore metal helmets. One correspondent wrote that "the gas mask in England seems now to be a badge of national unity, equivalent to the swastika in Germany."[126] The blackout, the Americans would discover, was more uncompromising than in France, and Londoners were more fastidious about darkening their windows than Parisians. Welles saw no evidence in Britain that "German propaganda, which had so fatally undermined French morale, had made any headway." He sensed an underlying determination to "fight to the last ditch" rather than capitulate before Hitler as they had done in the autumn of 1938.[127]

On the surface, His Majesty's Government seemed sanguine about the Welles mission. Prime Minister Chamberlain told Kennedy that he had been "very much concerned at first," but "it had been made so clear by Washington that the trip was not for the purpose of 'putting over a peace plan' that he was now completely happy." In reality, Whitehall was still unsure of what Cadogan called "the ultimate underlying purpose of Mr Welles' visit."[128] Moreover, it came at a nervous time for the Allies, coinciding with Russia's defeat of Finland, which was seen as a major reverse for both Britain and France. (Within ten days, Daladier would resign as prime minister.) Consequently, most of Welles's interlocutors in London testified to the impossibility of dealing with Hitler, and Britain's determination to win a complete victory over Germany. The king was given a crib sheet to use in his audience with Welles that, according to one historian, "read more like a Ministry of Information propaganda briefing."[129]

Accompanied around town by a detective from Scotland Yard, Welles met with most of the country's leaders, including members of the Chamberlain government; the leader of the opposition, Labour leader Clement Attlee; former prime minister Lloyd George; ambassadors and high commissioners; and diplomats from the Foreign Office.[130] Naturally, Welles was perfectly attired for each occasion and every kind of company. Sometimes this required fancy footwork. On one particular day, for instance, he had to change from his business suit to striped trousers, frock coat, and topper, and then in the evening to white tie, tails, and silk hat. No wonder the *Chicago Daily Tribune* jeered that he had been "put aboard the British social merry-go-round." London's fashion critics, on the other hand, were impressed by his taste, and even named him the second-best-dressed man in public life, after the king.[131]

Welles picked up a good deal of intelligence in his London meetings, although in contrast to later missions by other envoys, his status as a presidential emissary did not translate into privileged access to secret British information. The Foreign Office view was that "we should expose to him fully our policy and aims," but not provide him with "full military information." The war cabinet concluded that, given Britain was at war, such information should not be shared with the neutral United States.[132]

Late one afternoon, Welles called in to Admiralty House to see FDR's correspondent Winston Churchill. The sixty-five-year-old first lord of the admiralty had served in the same post in the First World War, before resigning over the part he had played in devising the disastrous Allied landings at Gallipoli. Now, he said, a quarter of a century later, he sat in the same dark-paneled room, at the same octagonal table, under the same portrait of Lord Nelson, confronting the same situation and the same enemy. "The objectives of the German people had not changed, and would not change," he told Welles. "These were world supremacy and military conquest; objectives which endangered the security of the United States as much as they imperilled the safety of the British Empire. He had foreseen the present crisis; time and again he had pointed out to previous British Governments the dangers they were incurring, but he had not been listened to, and now the crisis once more was upon them."[133]

Welles was a little catty when he described this encounter to the president. Churchill was "smoking a 24-inch cigar and drinking a whiskey and soda" when Welles entered his room, and the American thought "it was quite obvious that he had consumed a good many whiskeys before I arrived." Churchill gave him the benefit of a two-hour address, during which Welles had no opportunity to speak. "It constituted a cascade of oratory, brilliant and always effective, interlarded with considerable wit," Welles recalled. "It would have impressed me more had I not already read his book 'Step by

Step' (of which incidentally, he gave me an autographed copy before I left) and of which his address to me constituted a rehash." In fact, though, Churchill's charm did pierce Welles's reserve. The envoy told an acquaintance he had entered the first lord's room exhausted and left it feeling "mentally refreshed," having found Churchill "one of the most fascinating personalities he had ever met."[134]

The most noteworthy of the London meetings were those with Prime Minister Neville Chamberlain and his foreign secretary, Lord Halifax. Welles and Kennedy arrived at 10 Downing Street early in the evening of Monday, March 11, for the first such conference. The grand old house had first been home to a British prime minister more than two centuries earlier. They found Chamberlain in the long, high-windowed Cabinet Room, sitting at his place at the baize-covered cabinet table, in front of a white marble chimneypiece. Welles thought that he looked younger and stronger than he did in his photographs, with none of the infamous "puzzled hen" effect. "His hair is dark, except for a strand of completely white hair across his forehead . . . The dominating features are a pair of large, very dark and piercing eyes, and a low and incisive voice." Soon they were joined by Halifax, who by contrast was "exactly like his photographs: exceedingly tall, gangling, and with a rather inchoate face."[135]

Welles indicated to the two men that his stay in Berlin had convinced him that regime change in Germany was not imminent, so any peace deal would involve coming to terms with Hitler. He outlined a series of ideas which he thought might address all the parties' security concerns: a German withdrawal from Poland and the Czech region of Bohemia, the disarming of the belligerents, and the creation of an international air force to prevent Germany from falling on small nations in the future. For Welles, disarmament was the key to the whole problem. Chamberlain protested that he had made "every possible concession to Germany during the past two years" and all he had received in return was deceit and lies. Germany was "the author of all the world's present troubles," he stated. Speaking with "a white-hot anger," the prime minister said flatly that "so long as the present Government of

Germany continued there could be no hope of any real peace." Disarmament could not be achieved without the reestablishment of confidence, he declared, which required the German people to change their rulers.[136]

Welles replied that the issue reminded him of "the old conundrum as to which came first, the hen or the egg." Whereas Chamberlain spoke of disarmament being impossible until confidence in Europe was recreated, Welles felt that no nation could have any confidence until disarmament had taken place, in particular the abolition of bomber aircraft and other offensive weapons. Welles stressed that he "had no proposal" to offer, but it seemed to Chamberlain and Halifax that the American was searching for a peace proposal that he could put to Roosevelt, which might prove embarrassing to London.[137] Sir Robert Vansittart, already hostile to Welles, was outraged when he heard of this exchange. Of course confidence must precede disarmament, Vansittart spluttered, and Welles was "hopelessly wrong in putting it the other way round and then seeking refuge in some rubbish about the hen and the egg."[138] It must indeed have seemed strange to hear an American ruminating about poultry while Hitler plotted conquest and murder in Berlin.

The second and final interview took place at Downing Street two nights later, on Welles's final evening in London. This time, Chamberlain's resolution wavered. Welles asked the prime minister directly if he would still refuse to negotiate with the Nazis even if they vacated Poland and the Czech regions of Bohemia and Moravia and a disarmament scheme was instituted, to which Halifax added a few other conditions including self-determination for Austria. Welles reported that the Duce had thought "a solution along these lines was not impossible." At this point Joe Kennedy, who was trailing around town after his fellow American, made a particularly discreditable intervention. If Britain refused to enter discussions when a lasting peace was at hand, he exploded, its position would be untenable. "If you took that position," he said, "why I myself would like to lead the opposition to the Chamberlain government." The PM's response was that if such a miraculous reversal of policy on Hitler's part occurred, he could not refuse to parley.[139]

Later that night, Chamberlain gave a dinner for the Americans and a few British colleagues. The dining room upstairs at Downing Street was bedecked with heavy paneling and portraits of Wellington, Nelson, Pitt, and Fox. Chamberlain spoke affectionately of his old friend "Cotty," the Reverend Endicott Peabody, schoolmaster of Welles, Moffat, and Roosevelt. Churchill gave the party his view of the British people's mentality. "Take the workman," he suggested. "His back is up. He will stand for no pulling of punches against Germany." For once, even Joe Kennedy found a gracious line. "If you can show me one Englishman that's tougher than you are, Winston, I'll eat my hat."[140]

Welles departed London the next morning, having created a mixed impression. Chamberlain described him in Parliament as "a man of outstanding ability and of quick and powerful understanding." Halifax was surprised to find he liked Welles, but he thought him "a bit remote from the facts still, and inclined to feel that the problem can be solved by paper ingenuity."[141] Robert Vansittart took a less charitable view, claiming in a series of blistering minutes that Welles was naïve, "glib and facile," and "an international danger."[142]

Sumner Welles had shifted gears in London. For the first time, he voiced opinions rather than soliciting them; he was groping for the outlines of a peace plan. Many of his interlocutors believed that in doing so, he was freelancing. The Foreign Office felt the emissary had got ahead of the president, and the two men's minds were "working on different lines." "Mr Welles has his own ideas," mused one British diplomat, "but it remains to be seen if he can 'sell' them to Mr Roosevelt."[143] This test would transpire sooner than anyone thought.

THE WELLES ENTOURAGE FLEW OUT of Hendon Aerodrome on the morning of March 14, in the prime minister's own plane, into a terrible blizzard. It was a blind flight, and the passengers were "buffeted unmercifully," but they finally spotted Le Bourget Airport through a hole in the clouds and came down "at such a pace that we were all deaf for a few hours." The party spent only a few hours in Paris before boarding a train for Rome. A fortnight earlier, Welles had agreed to a request from Count Ciano that he meet with the Italians again on his way back to America. He wanted to have one more go at undermining the Axis before the armies started marching; perhaps he could even stop them marching altogether.[144]

In Rome, there was more febrile press speculation. Reporters watched Welles closely during his second visit to Rome, feeling that "something very big is in the air." The smallest coincidence involving Welles—a German diplomatic courier arriving in the capital on the same night; the appearance of the German ambassador at the Palazzo Chigi at the same time—was written up as a sensation.[145]

In his second round of meetings with Ciano and Mussolini, Welles again ladled out the flattery, emphasizing Italy's centrality to events in Europe. He played down French and British intransigence and reported his sense that a peace could possibly be made on the basis of independence for Poland and a reconstituted Czech state, a plebiscite for Austria, and general disarmament. He gave Ciano the impression that if the Allies "had certain guarantees of security they would be ready to give in more or less and to recognise the *fait accompli*"—which went well beyond what Chamberlain and Halifax had conceded. Welles was straining to bridge the gap between the parties.[146]

In his shadowy office at the Palazzo Venezia, a more vigorous-looking Duce warned Welles that the German offensive was very close: "The minute hand is pointing to one minute before midnight." In two days' time, he was to confer with Hitler at the Brenner Pass, high in the Alps between Italy and Austria. If he were to have any hope of postponing the offensive, Mussolini said, he needed to offer the Führer hope that the Allies would not be intransigent when it came to Germany's Lebensraum. Mussolini asked whether Welles would authorize him to pass on to Hitler Welles's views as to the possibility of a negotiated European peace. The envoy replied that he would need to seek instructions from Washington, and that evening he made his only telephone call to Roosevelt for the whole trip. The president rejected the suggestion immediately.[147]

The content of this call will never be known for sure. Welles's version was that he recommended that Roosevelt refuse Mussolini's offer, lest the president be seen to help Hitler determine the basis of a negotiated peace.[148] This seems at odds with the direction of Welles's diplomacy over the previous few days. Ciano believed, on the basis of a phone tap by the Italian intelligence services, that Welles had sought "permission to undertake a certain vague attempt for peace, but the answer is in the negative."[149] Perhaps the transatlantic telephone line was particularly scratchy that evening. Regardless of what the call reveals about Welles, however, Roosevelt's position was clear: given the opportunity, he was not interested in peace talks with Berlin.

On the very same day that he turned down Mussolini's offer, FDR made a thinly veiled public attack on Germany that effectively ruled out treating with the Nazis. "Today we seek a moral basis for peace," he said from the White House in a radio broadcast honoring Christian missionaries. "It cannot be a real peace if it fails to recognize brotherhood. It cannot be a lasting peace if the fruit of it is oppression, or starvation, or cruelty, or human life dominated by armed camps. It cannot be a sound peace if small nations must live in fear of powerful neighbors. It cannot be a moral peace if freedom from invasion is sold for tribute. It cannot be an intelligent peace if it denies free passage to that knowledge of those ideals which permit men to find common ground. It cannot be a righteous peace if worship of God is denied." The speech was carefully noted in Europe. British sources told the *New York Times* they were "in agreement with every passage of the address."[150]

The Welles mission to Europe was over. On March 18, Hitler and Mussolini and their respective toadies met at the Brenner Pass; the Duce confirmed privately that Italy's entry into the war beside Germany was "inevitable."[151] Back in Rome, Welles was presented to the pope at the Vatican.[152] That evening, he witnessed a different kind of performance. Upon learning Welles was an opera buff, the governor of Rome arranged for a special performance of Verdi's *Un Ballo in Maschera (A Masked Ball)* to be put on at Rome's Opera House, which was "filled to overflowing with men in white ties and women *en grande toilette*." The leading man, the famous

Italian tenor Beniamino Gigli, who had appeared often at New York's Metropolitan Opera, was in excellent voice.[153] In *Un Ballo in Maschera*, a powerful New Englander's forbidden love leads to his destruction. Within a few short years, Welles's own life would mirror the opera's plot.

WELLES TOOK HIS LEAVE of Europe, accompanied once more by his wife, her niece, their maids, and Toby the terrier, who had all remained in Italy during his mission. The party sailed from Genoa on March 20 on the *Conte de Savoia*, a smaller and even more elegant liner than the *Rex*, and her running mate on the Atlantic route. Eight days later, she berthed at her midtown pier on the Hudson River; that afternoon, reporters observed Welles and Cordell Hull entering the White House together. They "stepped along the rubber mat of the White House entrance; the gleaming glass-and-bronze doors swung wide under the hands of the blue-uniformed Negro doorman," reported *Time*. "Hats and coats taken, Hull and Welles stepped into the whirring little elevator, creaked up to the oval second-floor study where sat Franklin Roosevelt at the huge desk carved from timbers of the *Resolute*. There ended Welles's trip."

He had covered fourteen thousand miles, conferring with two kings, two prime ministers, a Führer, a Duce, and a pope, and numberless foreign ministers, statesmen, and officials. "If looking and listening could do it," said *Time*, "in those 41 days Sumner Welles had become the best-informed man in the world on the world's biggest problem—World War II." Little wonder that newspapers offered Welles as much as $50,000, a massive sum at the time, for his account of the mission.[154]

Welles's official report, which he had completed on board the *Conte di Savoia*, consisted of a separate memorandum for each of his conversations in Europe, with all of the rich descriptive detail that Roosevelt savored. Even Hull allowed that it was "superb." The concluding section dealt with the role of Italy and the prospects of peace. He predicted that Italy would "move as Mussolini alone determines. Mussolini is a man of genius, but it must never be forgotten that Mussolini remains at heart and in instinct an Italian peasant . . . He admires force and power." The United States should seek to improve relations with Rome, Welles recommended, by deepening commercial relations and speaking more mildly about the Fascists.[155]

On the broader question, Welles thought there was "a slight chance for the negotiation of a lasting peace if the attack for peace is made upon the issue of security." "The German people," he wrote, "are living a life which seems the existence of people on another planet. To them lies have become truth; evil, good; and aggression, self-defense. But yet, back of all that, their real demand is security, the chance to live reasonably happy lives, and peace." The "one slight hope of peace," so long as the Nazis remained in power, was to rig up "some practicable plan of security and of disarmament." Fashioning such a scheme would require "statesmanship of the highest character, marked by vision, courage and daring." Welles had found no signs of such leadership in Europe: only the United States, supported by other neutral states, could pull it off.[156]

But Roosevelt had no interest in action along these lines. While he was conferring with Welles and Hull upstairs in the residence, his press secretary, Steve Early, called in White House reporters and warned them not to "write yourselves out on the end of a limb" by quoting "allegedly authorized or unimpeachable or reliable sources." The under secretary's report would be seen only by the president and Hull, and Early stressed that neither would be revealing its contents.[157]

The next day, the president announced that the Welles mission had concluded. "The information which he has received," FDR stated, "will be of the greatest value to this Government in the general conduct of its foreign relations . . . To Mr. Welles go my thanks and full appreciation for carrying out this difficult mission with extraordinary tact and understanding, and in accordance with the best American diplomatic traditions."[158]

The mission then faded from public view. The administration remained tight-lipped about the report, and Hull rebuffed a request from the Senate Foreign Relations Committee that Welles appear before it.[159] Within a fortnight, the mission had been lost in the quickening pace of events in Europe.

ARTHUR SCHLESINGER'S VERDICT, delivered half a century later, was that "Sumner Welles did not cover himself in glory in Europe."[160] He neither delayed the German offensive nor weakened the Axis. Although the visits to Rome occasioned a temporary improvement in Italo-American relations, this did not translate into lasting gains. Rather, the mission encouraged Hitler to bolster his ties with Mussolini. The Welles mission probably caused as much consternation among the Allies as within the Axis.

It certainly caused discord within the State Department, with devastating effects. The mission heightened Cordell Hull's jealousy of his deputy, and won Welles a vicious enemy in the person of William Bullitt.[161] In time, the ill-feeling created by Welles's appointment would contribute to his downfall.

Roosevelt never seriously envisaged the Welles mission as a vehicle for peacemaking. However, FDR's failure to define the limits of the exercise, and Welles's willingness to exceed them, led to mission creep. When Welles reached London, his mission veered into the territory of high-stakes shuttle diplomacy as he sought, albeit tentatively and briefly, to define the contents of a negotiated peace. "Reality only came crashing back in," argues one historian, "when Welles and Roosevelt talked by phone and the president crushed any possibility of U.S. participation in peace talks."[162] Welles was partly to blame for this—but the ultimate responsibility was Roosevelt's. In February–March 1940, the president's sympathies were clear but his policy was not. The Welles mission reflected this uncertainty.

The effect of the mission as a domestic political maneuver is more difficult to measure. The mission seems to have stirred Americans' interest in European events, and it coincided with a sharp jump in the number of Americans who believed the United States would enter the war.[163] Very quickly, however, it was swamped by developing news from Europe. It probably had little lasting impact on the country's attitude to the conflict or FDR's reelection.

In retrospect, however, the mission played its part in the evolution of Roosevelt's policy. Unlike other American diplomats, Welles gained access to the persons of Hitler and Mussolini, and helped FDR to size them up.[164] The president was keen to have the observations of "one mind" on the whole European situation, rather than a plethora of separate and unrelated reports. Welles's colorful report brought the European situation to life for FDR. It confirmed his belief that an unappeasable Hitler would soon launch "totalitarian war" and dispelled illusions of forthcoming regime change in Berlin.[165] And it showed that as long as America remained uninvolved, her influence would be limited.

In the end, the defects of the Welles mission were a reflection of the policy of which it was an expression. Over the next few months, as Europe exploded, Franklin Roosevelt's position clarified and hardened. So did the uses to which he put his special envoys. For all its limitations, the Welles mission foreshadowed the most important diplomatic campaign of the century.

2.

"A Sensible Colonel House"

The world changed considerably in the four months between Sumner Welles's return to Washington and Colonel William J. Donovan's departure for London. In the late spring of 1940, what Franklin Roosevelt called a "hurricane of events," which had been forming for years, finally made landfall in Europe.[1] Hitler had already conquered Czechoslovakia and Poland; in April he invaded Denmark and Norway. One of his many victims was Neville Chamberlain, replaced as British prime minister on May 10 by Franklin Roosevelt's correspondent Winston Churchill. A new coalition government was constituted, including Conservative, Labour, and Liberal members. In his first speech to the House of Commons as prime minister, Churchill set a new course for Great Britain:

> You ask, what is our policy? I will say: It is to wage war, by sea, land and air, with all our might and with all the strength that God can give us: to wage war against a monstrous tyranny, never surpassed in the dark, lamentable catalogue of human crime. That is our policy. You ask, what is our

aim? I can answer in one word: Victory—victory at all costs, victory in spite of all terror, victory, however long and hard the road may be; for without victory, there is no survival.[2]

As if to prove the truth of Churchill's words, the Führer unleashed Blitzkrieg. His forces quickly overwhelmed Belgium, the Netherlands, and France, which succumbed in terrifyingly short order for a great power. The feebleness of the Third Republic, so apparent on Sumner Welles's visit to Paris, was now revealed to the world. On June 16, Marshal Philippe Pétain became premier of France and immediately asked Germany for an armistice. A number of Welles's interlocutors, including Édouard Daladier and Léon Blum, were soon arrested by the Vichy authorities. Few were drinking champagne now in Paris, except its German occupiers and their French accomplices.

Only Britain and her empire remained standing—and who knew for how long? Washington's view of the world was suddenly transformed. "Almost overnight," wrote the historian Waldo Heinrichs, "the 'free security' enjoyed by the United States since the Napoleonic Wars disappeared. The Atlantic was no longer a friendly ocean: Hitler controlled the far shore ... A very real possibility existed that the Americas would find themselves an island in a world dominated by the Axis." The ripples from Hitler's victories reached the Pacific, too. A new administration came to power in Tokyo, which resolved to strengthen Japan's bonds with Germany and Italy and establish a new order in Asia, to the detriment of the European powers.[3]

Roosevelt's foreign policy was also transformed. His response to these shocking events, articulated in a stirring commencement speech at the University of Virginia, was not to withdraw into the Western Hemisphere as urged by many outside and inside his administration, but to hasten American rearmament and expedite the flow of aid to "the opponents of force," especially France and Britain. FDR's Charlottesville remarks were delivered on the day that Mussolini took Italy into the war against those two countries, a decision that angered Roosevelt deeply because of the effort he and

Welles had put into keeping her out of it. "The hand that held the dagger," he declared indignantly, "has struck it into the back of its neighbor."[4]

Roosevelt's dual policy comprised rearmament and aid. Rearmament was an urgent necessity. After a decade of miserly congressional appropriations, the country's armed forces were puny. With the surrender of the Belgian army in late May, observers calculated, the U.S. Army was promoted to the rank of eighteenth largest in the world, slightly ahead of Bulgaria's. GIs were drilling with drainpipes instead of trench mortars, and broomsticks instead of machine guns. Now, after the reversals in Europe, senators and congressmen fell over themselves to atone for their earlier sins. They appropriated the full amounts that Roosevelt requested, and more—and gave him a rollicking ovation when he asked them for fifty thousand warplanes a year. Not everyone was so pleased, however. In a national address over the Columbia Broadcasting System, the famous aviator Colonel Charles Lindbergh was sharply critical of FDR's emergency defense program and denounced the "hysterical chatter of calamity and invasion that has been running rife." The United States was not in danger of foreign invasion, he said, unless Americans "bring it on" by meddling in other nations' affairs. "If we desire peace, we need only stop asking for war." An irritated FDR told an associate that "it could not have been better put if it had been written by Goebbels himself."[5]

Historians J. Garry Clifford and Samuel R. Spencer Jr. have noted that in the president's message to Congress calling for a much larger military, he "failed to mention one significant fact—namely, that a vast force of trained men was needed to drive the tanks, pilot the planes, and shoulder the rifles." Such a force would almost inevitably require a system of compulsory military training and service. Yet FDR was reluctant to call for the first peacetime draft in the history of the United States, at least until he knew it would pass in Congress. Instead, a group of New York bankers and lawyers, officers from the First World War, stepped in to prepare the ground for a "selective service" system that would register and draft millions of young American men.[6]

In May and June 1940, Roosevelt was more focused on the second, even more contentious arm of his policy: sending aid to the Allies. He was field-ing increasingly desperate requests from Paris and London for equipment that could be used to fight off the advancing Germans. Using various sub-terfuges to get around legislative restrictions, he ordered the release of large quantities of U.S. matériel, including a quarter of a million rifles (which later armed the British Home Guard), 130 million rounds of ammunition (a quarter of the U.S. Army's stocks), 80,000 machine guns, 900 artillery pieces, and 140 bombers. Such transfers were unpopular with many in Con-gress, who supported building up America's defenses, not breaking them up. They were also controversial within the War Department, which was under-standably anxious about parting with its own meager resources. FDR's deci-sion showed considerable political nerve. Some White House allies believed it "represented suicide for Roosevelt and quite possibly for the nation."[7]

By the time of France's collapse, public opinion was swinging behind the president's policy of aiding Britain, but two-thirds of Americans still doubted that the British would prevail. Many Americans suspected they would soon lapse back into appeasement and sue for peace. FDR could not dismiss these concerns, especially when they were held by people close to him and con-firmed by reports from the field. In particular, the cables sent back from London by Joe Kennedy were, according to one State Department official, "tinged with deep-dyed pessimism . . . [Kennedy] gives the impression that Britain's race is nearly run and says that if we should ever get into the war we would be left holding the entire bag."[8]

At this time of unusual danger, William J. "Wild Bill" Donovan stepped onto the stage. Donovan was an Irish American war hero who had once aspired to public office in New York but now occupied himself with a busy law practice and the occasional bout of freelance diplomacy. He would go on to become America's wartime spymaster, but in 1940 he remained on the margins of national politics. Arthur Schlesinger, who worked for Dono-van during the Second World War, described him as "a remarkable man, a winning combination of charm, audacity, imagination, optimism and energy . . . a disorderly administrator and an impetuous policymaker, racing from here to there, coming up with ideas and initiatives and then cheerfully moving on to something else."[9] He shared many traits, in other words, with Franklin Roosevelt. But in other respects, Donovan was the president's opposite: a Catholic Republican born into Buffalo's working class rather than an Episcopalian Democrat born into the Hudson River Valley aristocracy.

William Donovan was the grandson of Irish immigrants who came to America from County Cork during the potato famine of the 1840s. They ended up in the booming city of Buffalo in western New York, a magnet for newcomers because of the plentiful jobs that were available in the mills, grain elevators, and warehouses on its busy waterfront. Donovan's grandfather Timothy, a devout Catholic and rumored sympathizer of the Fenians, found work as a scooper in the grain holds of ships. He inculcated in his family a distrust of liquor and a personal code based on self-discipline. His son, also called Timothy, began as a greaser on the locomotives and ended up as yardmaster at the main terminal. Regretting his lack of education, he acquired a library stocked with Shakespeare, Dante, and Dickens, and bucked his class to become a Republican. He took as his wife Anna Letitia Lennon, an Irish girl who, like him, loved to read.[10]

Like most of the Buffalo Irish, the Donovans lived in the city's First Ward, a tough, tribal neighborhood buffeted by the chilly winds that blew across Lake Erie from Canada. William Donovan was born there on New Year's Day 1883; later, when he was confirmed into the Roman Catholic Church, he took the middle name of Joseph. He was one of nine children, of whom only five survived, and his family lived on the second floor of his grandparents' house until they had saved enough money to move out of the First Ward. Young William grew up scrapping with his brothers in a makeshift boxing ring in the yard; on Saturday nights his father would take them to one of Buffalo's thousand saloons to listen to the men arguing and singing, although being Donovans they themselves touched nothing stronger than ginger ale.[11]

At church schools and later at Niagara University, a small Catholic college just outside Buffalo, Donovan proved to be a middling student but a prodigious reader and confident public speaker. He was dissuaded from joining the Dominicans by a perceptive priest who saw that his talents lay elsewhere. Instead, he transferred to Columbia College in New York City, where he managed his fraternity house in return for room and board. Donovan was no great scholar at Columbia, but he rowed in the varsity crew and sometimes played quarterback for the Columbia Lions. Later, he was a classmate of Franklin Roosevelt at Columbia Law School, although they were not close friends. After graduation, Donovan returned to Buffalo to practice law, this time moving in loftier circles than he had as a boy. With his fancy education and native charm, he was accepted into the clubs and societies of the old Buffalo families, institutions whose doors had rarely been darkened by a Catholic. He and some other society men established a cavalry troop in 1912, officially designated Troop I, 1st Cavalry Regiment, New York National Guard, but known around town, in light of its members' pedigrees, as the "Silk Stocking Boys." Donovan was elected the troop's captain.[12]

The handsome Bill Donovan was popular with the ladies of Buffalo, and he was known to spread his affections widely and generously. In 1914, however, he was captivated by Ruth Rumsey, a blonde Episcopalian whose late father had been the richest man in Buffalo. Ruth was slim, blue-eyed, well traveled, and quick-witted. At first her mother was not impressed that her daughter was going around with an Irish Catholic with a roving eye, but she was soon won over. Presently, Bill and Ruth were married. Buffalo society noted that the First Warder had certainly married up.[13]

Donovan was called to the colors in July 1916, when Troop I was ordered to the Mexican border to assist in the hunt for the revolutionary bandit Pancho Villa. U.S. forces tracked their elusive quarry all along the Rio Grande, but Donovan and his men saw no action, and were mustered out of service in March of the following year. By this time, America's participation in the world war seemed inevitable, and Donovan was recruited as a battalion major in the famous Irish 69th Infantry Regiment of New York. The regiment had a storied history dating back to the Civil War, during which the

Confederate commander Robert E. Lee is said to have christened it "the Fighting 69th." Newly redesignated the 165th U.S. Infantry Regiment, it was selected to go to Europe in the first ranks of the American Expeditionary Forces, as part of the 42nd or so-called Rainbow Division, which was drawn from National Guard units across the country.[14]

The regiment trained at Camp Mills on the Hempstead Plains of Long Island. Donovan told his commanding officer he intended to "turn out the best battalion in the entire army," and he proceeded literally to whip his men into shape: one of his sergeants cracked a bullwhip over their heads during training. Donovan may have been dubbed "Wild Bill" in this period by troops who were exhausted by his relentless drills and cross-country runs. He even ordered boxing gloves and presided over boxing lessons for the battalion. When former president Theodore Roosevelt heard of this innovation, he invited Donovan and his officers to his home at Sagamore Hill in nearby Oyster Bay and declared them to be "good fighting stuff." To Donovan, who had always admired TR's virile approach to life, this was high praise. In August, Bill and Ruth's second child, a girl named Patricia, was baptized at Camp Mills with water from the canteen of the regimental chaplain, Father Francis Duffy. Pat was named the Daughter of the Regiment, and the canteen became a prized Donovan family heirloom.[15]

In late October 1917, the old 69th shipped out for France, where Bill Donovan would make his name. Combat did not unnerve him; indeed, he told his wife it made him feel like "a youngster at Halloween." He was often among the leading elements, urging his men on with a shout. "Come on," he would cry, "we'll have them on the run before long." Once he turned his back to the enemy and called out with a smile, "Come on now, men, they can't hit me and they won't hit you!" One of his sergeants, Richard O'Neill, who was New York's most decorated hero of the war, marveled at Donovan's calm under fire: "You'd think he was standing at the corner of Broadway and Forty-second Street, not in the middle of a barrage." Sometimes Donovan was rough with malingerers, but he could be sympathetic, too, putting an arm around the shoulders of a scared lad and bucking him up.[16]

When a German shell exploded on the roof of an American dugout in the Rouge Bouquet wood in northern France, burying a platoon in tons of rocks and clay, Donovan led the rescue party personally despite the danger to himself. For this and other gallantries the French awarded him the Croix de Guerre, which Donovan refused to accept until it was also given to a deserving Jewish sergeant who was initially passed over for the honor. The journalist and poet Joyce Kilmer, who served as Donovan's adjutant in France, memorialized those who died in the cave-in in his poem "Rouge Bouquet," which included the lines:

> *Now over the grave abrupt and clear*
> *Three volleys ring:*
> *And perhaps their brave young spirits hear*
> *The bugle sing:*
> *"Go to sleep!*
> *Go to sleep!*
> *Slumber well where the shell screamed and fell.*
> *Let your rifles rest on the muddy floor,*
> *You will not need them anymore.*
> *Danger's past;*
> *Now at last,*
> *Go to sleep!"*[17]

In July 1918, Donovan led his battalion's advance across the Ourcq River, for which he received the Distinguished Service Cross. The 69th lost most of its fighting strength in that battle; Major Donovan lost all his company commanders and his adjutant, Kilmer.[18] Donovan was promoted to lieutenant colonel and regimental chief of staff. His finest moment came during the Meuse-Argonne offensive in October. He went into battle looking immaculate—neatly shaven, in a spotless uniform that displayed all his ribbons, medals, and insignia of rank, with his boots and Sam Browne belt polished to a high sheen. When a bullet smashed into his shinbone near

Landres-et-Saint-Georges, he refused to give up command, continuing to direct the attack and calling in artillery and mortars. More than four years later, after much army politics, he was awarded America's highest military decoration, the Medal of Honor, for this episode of conspicuous gallantry under fire. In a grand gesture, he gave the medal to the 69th and deposited it at the regimental armory on Lexington Avenue.[19]

Father Duffy said of Donovan, "His men would have cheerfully gone to hell with him, and as a priest, I mean what I say." His exploits made him a hero in the AEF, and due to the efforts of Ruth, who typed out his letters home and sent them to the newspapers for publication, in the country at large. Teddy Roosevelt wrote to him praising him as "the finest example of the American fighting gentleman." In March 1919, Donovan was given his colonelcy and command of the regiment, and the following month he took it home to New York City. Its victory parade was a famous one. The weather that day had "a hint of Flanders" about it, some veterans thought. The 165th U.S. Infantry—the old 69th—assembled in Washington Square Park and marched in close formation under the Victory Arch and up Fifth Avenue to 110th Street. Every soldier wore his helmet and carried his rifle; seven hundred invalided men rode in open cars at the end of the parade. A million New Yorkers lined Fifth Avenue to watch the Fighting Irish pass north in time to "Garryowen," "Killarney," "The Wearing of the Green," and other marches and songs. The crowds threw flowers upon the ranks, the regimental colors, and the gold-starred service flag; ticker tape fluttered down from office windows. At the regiment's head, marching with his men rather than riding before them as was his right, was Colonel William J. Donovan.[20]

DONOVAN PROSPERED BETWEEN THE WARS, but his star never rose as high as the manner of his homecoming seemed to promise. He returned to his law practice, and was appointed part-time U.S. attorney for Buffalo and western New York. As vigorous as ever, he dashed about prosecuting rum-runners, racketeers, bootleggers, and opium kings. He closed down saloons that breached the Prohibition laws, but crossed a class line when he raided the exclusive Saturn Club, of which he was a member. This was too much for the city's leading citizens, and Donovan found himself ostracized from polite society. He lost friends, his law partner, and any prospect of a successful political career in Buffalo. It probably came as a relief, then, when in 1924 he was appointed assistant attorney general of the United States: Calvin Coolidge's succession to the presidency, which proved so damaging for Sumner Welles's career, was highly advantageous for Bill Donovan's. He was a hit in Washington: energetic, colorful, and effective in his advocacy before the Supreme Court and Congress.[21]

He also became tight with the Republican Party's nominee to succeed Coolidge in 1928, Herbert Hoover, helping him with campaign speeches and hosting private meetings in the imposing house he and Ruth bought at the corner of 30th and R Streets in Georgetown. Once elected, however, Hoover reneged on his promise to make Donovan attorney general, offering him the governorship of the Philippines as a consolation prize. Donovan refused it, resigned from the Justice Department, and departed the capital. A sketch at the annual Gridiron Dinner, held shortly after Hoover's inauguration, had the new commander in chief awarding Donovan one of the few decorations he did not already possess: "The Order of the Boot."[22]

The Donovans moved to New York City, establishing themselves in a grand duplex at 1 Beekman Place, with a fine view of the East River. Bill conjured up a successful private practice despite the onset of the Depression, representing public utilities, corporations, and Hollywood stars. He grew stout and lived large, dining at Manhattan's toniest clubs and patronizing its most exclusive tailors, shirtmakers, and cobblers. Lawyering was not enough for Donovan, however, and in 1932 he accepted the Republican nomination for governor of New York with the aim of succeeding Governor Franklin D. Roosevelt, who was running for president. But it was a bad year to be on the Republican ticket, and to make matters worse, Donovan turned out to be a lackluster campaigner. He also ran into the contradictions of his own political identity, being too exotic for some GOP voters and too moneyed for some blue-collar Irish. Finally, there were whispers about the Donovans' marriage, whispers that could not be rejected out of hand by anyone who had seen Bill turn on the charm for a beautiful woman. Election day found FDR in Hyde Park, concluding a triumphant campaign that propelled him into the White House; in Buffalo, 350 miles to the west, Donovan discovered he had lost not only the gubernatorial race but a majority of votes in his own hometown.[23]

For the rest of the decade, Donovan's law work was punctuated with increasing frequency by trips abroad to various trouble spots. Even as a young man, he was known for talking his way onto official delegations and scouting out overseas business opportunities for clients. In the 1930s, as his political prospects dimmed, the pace of his travel abroad accelerated. He could often be found poking around a foreign capital or combat zone, usually at his own invitation. In 1935, Donovan called on Benito Mussolini in his cavernous room in the Palazzo Venezia and secured his permission to inspect the Italian headquarters in Libya and Abyssinia. In the spring of 1939, he visited the front lines of the Spanish Civil War. Over the summer, just before his trip to the Yukon, he traveled all through the febrile countries of western Europe.[24]

In the months after the outbreak of war, rumors circulated that the president was looking to bring Republicans into his cabinet in order to promote national unity. In December, Roosevelt sounded out Colonel Frank Knox, the publisher of the *Chicago Daily News* and former GOP vice presidential nominee, who had once served with Teddy Roosevelt's Rough Riders, about becoming secretary of the navy. Knox was interested and suggested his old friend Bill Donovan for the War Department. FDR and Donovan had had their run-ins during the 1932 campaign, but now the president seemed well-disposed to his fellow New Yorker, who was making helpful comments on the need to ratchet up the country's military preparations. "Bill Donovan is also an old friend of mine—we were in the law school together," he wrote Knox. "I should like to have him in the Cabinet, not only for his own ability, but also to repair in a sense the very great injustice done him by President Hoover in the winter of 1929." Nothing came of this exchange, however, and the closest Donovan got to the action in the early months of 1940 was when he helped to publicize *The Fighting 69th*, a new Warner Bros. film about the regiment's exploits in the last world war.[25]

Now aged fifty-seven, Donovan cut an attractive figure on the publicity trail. Years of prosperity had rounded him out and ruddied his complexion, yet his blue eyes were as clear and striking as ever. Not especially tall, he nevertheless gave the impression of being a big man. Charming, humorous, and shrewd, he had a remarkable memory for names and faces. He was much milder than his nickname indicated: the *New York Times* decreed that he was "about as wild as a good baby's nurse." He did not smoke and, like all Donovans, drank very little. He did not brag about his soldiering or his chestful of medals; indeed, he declined to wear in his lapel the blue silk rosette given to a recipient of the Medal of Honor. Yet his restless energy and thrusting ambition were immediately apparent. Donovan rose early and ate a big breakfast: as one associate remarked, "he needed some ammunition on which to work." He devoured two or three books a week, typically about history and war, which he read standing up at a special lectern in his office. "His imagination was unlimited," recalled another friend. "Ideas were his plaything. Excitement made him snort like a race horse."[26]

In April 1940, Donovan suffered a terrible blow when his adored twenty-two-year-old daughter Patricia was killed in an automobile accident in Virginia. He nearly collapsed from grief, and his hair turned white almost overnight. Franklin Roosevelt cabled from the White House, "My heart goes out to you in the sorrow which has come to you with such sudden and tragic force. Please accept for yourself and for all who mourn with you an assurance of sincere sympathy and of my warm personal regard." Donovan was grateful for the president's message, but it hardly dulled the pain. On a rainy day the following month, the "Daughter of the 69th" was buried at Arlington National Cemetery, a privilege accorded to her as the child of a recipient of the Medal of Honor.[27]

As Bill Donovan struggled with his loss, Washington was in a frenzy of activity in response to the frightening news from Europe. On June 20, Roosevelt gave his dual policy of rearmament and aid some bipartisan ballast by appointing two high-profile interventionist Republicans, Henry Stimson (who had served as Herbert Hoover's secretary of state) and Frank Knox, to the cabinet as secretaries of war and the navy. Once more Donovan was left on the sidelines, but he did what he could to smooth his friend Knox's path to office, urging fellow Republicans to accept the two appointments without rancor. When Knox arrived at Washington airport at the beginning of July he found Donovan waiting for him. Donovan insisted that Knox stay at his Georgetown mansion while he prepared for his confirmation hearings. Donovan's handsome eight-bedroom residence, with its wide lawns and circular drive, offered Knox the perfect base. It was well-appointed, private, and cool in the evenings. Ruth was away at the Donovans' holiday home in Maine, but there were three servants on duty to look after the two men.[28]

Donovan had his own commitments in Washington that week, including testifying before Congress in favor of the draft. The New York group of former officers, of which he was a member, had drafted a selective-service bill requiring the registration of all American men between the ages of twenty-one and thirty-five. It was presented to Congress in the names of Senator Edward R. Burke of Nebraska, an anti–New Deal Democrat, and Republican congressman James W. Wadsworth of New York. The bill was introduced into the Senate on the same day that Roosevelt brought Stimson and Knox, both supporters of the draft, into his cabinet. Donovan testified before the Senate Committee on Military Affairs on July 3, the first day of formal hearings, along with liberal Republican lawyer Grenville Clark, Harvard president James B. Conant, and others. Donovan told the committee that in France he had seen the bloody consequences of sending an ill-trained army into battle. Many of the soldiers in the 69th had arrived at the front "never having had on a gas mask . . . never having opened the bolts of their

rifles," which "were still filled with grease." The draft was "the most democratic method" to raise a well-prepared army, he said. It would also serve
to "bring home to the youngsters of this country, and the older fellows, too,
that there is still the simple virtue of duty. We are not going to get anywhere
unless some degree of sacrifice is made, and if the underlying purpose of
that bill is sacrifice, I think it is a great thing for our country."[29]

Knox and Donovan probably cooked up the idea of a mission to Britain
during that week they spent together in Georgetown.[30] Knox may have
hoped the trip would help his friend get over Patricia's death.[31] On or around
July 9, Donovan was summoned to a White House meeting at which Knox,
Stimson, Hull, and probably Roosevelt himself were present. The participants discussed the urgent need for information from Britain, and Knox put
forward Donovan's name for a fact-finding mission. Donovan left the White
House as a special envoy.[32]

Whose special envoy was he, though? This was a question that would vex
diplomatic minds on both sides of the Atlantic. The administration declined
to issue a statement about Donovan's appointment. Officially he was a representative of the new secretary of the navy, who penned letters of introduction for him on July 11, his first day in office. However, Donovan was clearly
the president's agent, too. Knox told a British minister that Donovan was on
"an official mission for me, with the full approval of the President," and the
secretary of state confirmed the president's approval of the trip when he
alerted the embassies in Lisbon and London.[33]

The purposes of the mission were also left opaque. After the war, Donovan stated he had two objectives in visiting Britain: "(1) to find out about the
fifth column there, (2) to learn whether the British were 'falling on their
faces' as everybody said."[34] FDR had been concerned by the work of Nazi
saboteurs and spies in western Europe and Scandinavia and feared the spec-
ter of a fifth column operating in the United States, so it made sense to commission a firsthand study on British counterespionage.[35] While the fifth
column was an important factor, though, Donovan told several associates
that his "real assignment" was to consider the second, broader issue. He

confided to the crusading journalist Edgar Mowrer that his job was "finding out for President Roosevelt the thing he needed most to know: would and could the British hold out against the Germans?" The question, at its simplest, was whether London was "a worthwhile ally."[36]

Mowrer, a European correspondent for the *Chicago Daily News* who was hated in Germany for his anti-Nazi reporting and admired in Britain for the same, would act as Donovan's associate during the mission. In March 1940, he had vented at members of the Welles mission in Paris about the wickedness of the Nazis and declared that any attempt to make peace with them was "treachery to God and man." Mowrer fled France after the Germans invaded, a wise move given that Hitler became enraged at the mention of his name and Goebbels said on radio that he would give a division to lay hands on him. Mowrer was in Lisbon en route to America when Frank Knox, in his capacity as publisher of the *Daily News*, ordered him to fly to London instead and place himself at the disposal of Colonel Donovan. Over the course of Donovan's stay, Mowrer acted as a semi-independent collector of information, meeting up with Donovan from time to time to compare notes.[37]

Two insights emerge from all this about Roosevelt's thinking and modus operandi. The president's approval of Donovan as an envoy demonstrates that he was predisposed to ramping up support to Britain. Like his mentor, Frank Knox, and his assistant, Edgar Mowrer, Donovan was a well-known supporter of an interventionist foreign policy and all-out aid to London.[38] In tapping Donovan, FDR did not commission an objective, unbiased diagnosis of British conditions. Rather, Roosevelt was inclined to help, but he wanted his instinct that Britain could survive confirmed by a firsthand report. Furthermore, the strong suggestion that the fifth-column task was a cover story for the broader mission indicates that Roosevelt was prepared not only to bypass his official representatives, but to deceive them.[39]

THE IDEA OF THE DONOVAN MISSION outraged Joe Kennedy, who had just dealt with the Welles mission and was increasingly galled by the direct communications between Roosevelt and Churchill.[40] On July 10 and 11, Cordell Hull informed the ambassador that Donovan would soon arrive in London on a mission for Knox, and asked that "arrangements and preparations" be made in advance.[41] Kennedy's reply took the form of three cables in little more than twelve hours. At 5 p.m. on July 12, he cabled, "I will render any service I can to Colonel Donovan whom I know and like. It is impossible to make any arrangements or preparations in advance because I do not know the nature of his mission . . . to send a new man in here at this time, with all due respect to Colonel Knox, is to me the height of nonsense and a definite blow to good organization." Four hours later, having spoken to Mowrer, Kennedy fumed that "this is utter nonsense . . . If Colonel Knox does not stop sending Mowrers and Colonel Donovans over here this organization is not going to function efficiently." The next morning, he fired off his third complaint, stating that the situation was personally embarrassing and concluding that "this whole picture is full of dynamite."[42]

The ambassador was so angry that he placed a transatlantic call to Sumner Welles in Washington, asking him to show his correspondence to the president. "He feels very strongly," Welles minuted Roosevelt, "that Colonel Donovan cannot possibly get any information except through our existing military and naval attachés and that his mission will simply result in creating confusion and misunderstanding on the part of the British. I told him that I would lay his message before you but that I understood your decision had already been made." The president's note to Knox in response was gleeful: "Please take this up with Secretary Hull and try to straighten it out. Somebody's nose seems to be out of joint!"[43]

Hull's cable to Kennedy of the same day was the administration's final reply to the barrage of communications from London. It addressed Kennedy's concern that the emissaries were in fact newspaper correspondents rather than government representatives, but the smooth words would not have mollified the infuriated ambassador. "The Secretary of the Navy advises me that he is taking these steps in his official capacity," Hull reported. "Colonel Knox appreciates fully the excellent reporting of the Embassy and the Military and Naval Attachés, and does not desire that this step will interfere in any way with the functions of the Embassy or the Attachés."[44]

The question of the precise status of Donovan and his sidekick, Mowrer, also caused consternation in Whitehall. Between July 10 and 13, the British ambassador, Lord Lothian, sent four cables informing London of the appointment of the two men to "make investigations in England" with respect to fifth-column activities and requesting that appropriate assistance be provided to them. He pointed out that Donovan "may exercise considerable influence here on his return owing to his close association with Mr Knox."[45] The resulting Foreign Office minutes reveal confusion and a sense of violated bureaucratic propriety. One diplomat wrote, "We should definitely not treat Mr Mowrer as a high official of the US Government . . . We are telegraphing to Lord Lothian to discover how to treat Colonel Donovan."[46] On July 16, Lothian confirmed that Donovan was "on a very important mission which has the full approval of both the President and the Secretary of State," and urged that the emissary be afforded the opportunity to meet with the prime minister and "other leading personalities at home." Two days later, Lothian advised that, in addition to investigating the fifth-column issue, Donovan had some "special commissions" to carry out.[47]

Having resolved Donovan's status, the British set about preparing to impress him, but Mowrer's position remained unsettled. An official in the Security Service worried that he would be like "a fifth wheel in the coach."[48] The ambiguity of Mowrer's accreditation had amusing results. The U.S. embassy and the British Ministry of Information agreed "to regard Mr Mowrer as being possessed of two wholly separate positions"; each time he asked for assistance, it would need to be clarified whether he did so as a representative of Secretary Knox or the *Daily News*.[49]

On Saturday, July 13, Donovan spent his final afternoon in Washington cruising the Potomac with Knox and other friends aboard the navy secretary's yacht, USS *Sequoia*. A 104-foot luxury vessel with polished oak decks and mahogany paneling, the *Sequoia* was the nicest perk of Knox's new job. Donovan and Knox then changed into dinner clothes and adjourned to the

British embassy on Massachusetts Avenue for dinner with Lord Lothian and Richard Casey, the Australian minister in Washington. Casey was troubled by U.S. ambivalence toward the war, but he found Wild Bill "very refreshing" on this count. Donovan attributed the "softness" abroad in the nation to "lack of leadership." His approach, by contrast, was, "Be hanged to safety first." He left for New York City at midnight.[50]

Donovan flew out of LaGuardia Field the following day, having called Ruth to inform her that he was going abroad on "a secret mission."[51] Donovan told reporters at the airport he was traveling on "private business," but the customs men let slip that he carried a special passport. Knox refused to comment on Donovan's departure when asked, but reporters ascertained that the administration had exempted the envoy from the Neutrality Act's restriction on Americans entering the war zone.[52]

The elegant art deco Marine Air Terminal at LaGuardia Field, on the shoreline of Bowery Bay, had been completed only a few months earlier to accommodate Pan American's giant silver Boeing 314 flying boats, or "Clippers," which were revolutionizing transatlantic travel. The all-metal, double-decked, four-engined Clippers were the largest aircraft in the world— 106 feet long with a 152-foot wingspan. Clipper crews dressed in a nautical style and the onboard luxuries also rivaled those of an ocean liner: passengers could move around, eat their steak lunches and lamb-chop dinners from fine china, take cocktails in the lounge, and sleep in comfortable bunks in their staterooms. Every Clipper passenger was a first-class passenger. "Fifty years from now," wrote Clare Booth Luce, "people will look back upon a Pan American Clipper flight of today as the most romantic voyage of history."[53]

The *Atlantic Clipper* took off shortly after 4 p.m. on July 14 and made its way across the Atlantic to Bermuda, the Azores, and finally Lisbon. The capital of neutral Portugal was a nest of spies, so it appealed to Donovan. Only the most important of these agents, as well as couriers, diplomats, wealthy refugees, and royals, stayed at Donovan's digs, the baronial Hotel Aviz. Here he caught up with another internationalist-minded Republican, John G. "Gil" Winant, a former governor of New Hampshire who was serving as the director of the International Labour Office (ILO). Winant was heading in the opposite direction from Donovan, on Pan American's *Dixie Clipper*. He was moving the ILO's operations from Geneva to Montreal to protect it from the dictators. Winant provided Donovan with a list of people to call on in London and a letter of introduction to go with the others Donovan had received.[54]

WHILE DONOVAN WAS FLYING OVER the Atlantic, Franklin Roosevelt was nominated by the Democratic Party for a third term as president. FDR's intimates believed that the dire international situation had impelled him to run again. Roosevelt did not attend the Democratic National Convention in Chicago in mid-July, sending Harry Hopkins to stage-manage affairs on his behalf from a suite at the Blackstone Hotel. (A direct line to the White House was set up in Hopkins's bathroom to enable the two men to speak privately.) A message from the president was read out to the convention stating his supposed reluctance to continue in office. At that moment, a disembodied voice boomed out a repeated demand from loudspeakers around the Chicago Stadium: "We want Roosevelt!" The speaker was later identified as Chicago's superintendent of sewers, a stalwart of the city's Democratic machine who was known thereafter as "the voice from the sewers." The undoubted pro-Roosevelt feelings of delegates were further stoked by the Chicago police band's rendition of "Happy Days Are Here Again" and the fire department band's version of the popular Broadway tune "Franklin D. Roosevelt Jones." The president was renominated overwhelmingly on the first ballot, a vote that was soon made unanimous. He accepted the nomination in the early hours of Friday, July 19, in a speech broadcast to Chicago from the White House.[55]

———

DONOVAN ARRIVED IN BRITAIN that same evening. America's neutrality legislation prevented Pan American's Clippers from entering belligerent ports, so he traveled the last leg on a British commercial aircraft. An embassy officer took him to his Mayfair hotel, Claridge's, which would serve as his London headquarters for the next fortnight. (The Italian manager who had so troubled the U.S. embassy in March had since been dismissed.) Inside, past the sandbags and blackout curtains, Donovan found a brilliantly lit, mirrored, black-and-white-tiled art deco foyer in which much of London society, including the exiled European royals who used Claridge's as their boarding-house, regularly assembled.[56]

The fall of France had knocked the stuffing out of the British establishment on which Sumner Welles had called a few months earlier. The replacement of Chamberlain by Churchill had proved a tonic, but it could not disguise the seriousness of the situation. Dominating all else in the British public's mind was the threat of invasion. While Donovan was en route, Hitler had secretly ordered his high command to begin preparing for the landing operation, code-named "Sea Lion"; on the day Donovan flew in, the Führer publicly promised "annihilation" for Britain unless she submitted to terms, an offer Churchill was pleased to refuse. The British countryside was being transformed by pillboxes, camouflaged gun pits, and hundreds of miles of barbed wire. The *Illustrated London News* ran features with titles such as "How to build trenches efficiently." Desperate measures were imposed: the minister of food, Lord Woolton, even asked Britons to observe a tea ration of no more than two ounces, or about twenty-five cups, per week. "Drink less tea and win the war," was the minister's slogan.[57]

Donovan's visit coincided with the prelude to the Battle of Britain, Germany's attempt to establish air supremacy over the country prior to the planned invasion. The full symphony would not begin until mid-August, but there was more than enough happening in July to stimulate the senses.

In addition to attacking shipping in the English Channel, the Luftwaffe was steadily escalating its assault on Royal Air Force (RAF) airfields as well as other ground targets such as factories producing aircraft equipment and explosives. Aerial dogfights between British and German fighters were occurring daily; on July 20, reporters counted more than one hundred warplanes wheeling and diving above the Channel waters as the British sought to repel a mass attack on a convoy. Britain returned the favors it received, sending its bombers on raids against German factories, docks, refineries, and industrial areas.[58]

In this dangerous phase of the war, the British government had to make two difficult, and potentially contradictory, arguments to the Roosevelt administration: that Britain was fighting bravely and was worth backing; and that the consequences to U.S. security of not backing her would be dire. It is not surprising that Whitehall latched on to the visit of an American who, like Welles before him, was thought to have the president's confidence, but who, unlike the under secretary, was regarded as a "great friend of Britain."[59] Every possible effort was made to draft him as an ally.

Several people had a hand in pulling together a program.[60] Donovan drew on the wide network of acquaintances he had built over the course of many years and many foreign adventures. The U.S. naval attaché, Captain Alan G. Kirk, made arrangements with the Admiralty. Old friends such as Ronald Tree, an Anglo-American member of parliament (MP) and heir to Chicago's Marshall Field fortune, gave him the inside track.[61] Help also came from Stewart Menzies, the chief of Britain's Secret Intelligence Service (SIS), otherwise known as MI6. Like all SIS chiefs, Menzies wrote in green ink and signed himself "C," after an illustrious predecessor. The connection between the two men made sense: Donovan had an interest in espionage and a job to do in London on fifth columns; Menzies had an interest in Anglo-American intelligence cooperation, as well as the broader relationship. Having been forewarned of Donovan's arrival by his New York representative, William Stephenson, Menzies set about opening doors for the visitor. He received

Donovan at Broadway Buildings, the SIS headquarters opposite St. James's Park Underground station, early in his mission and briefed him on what to expect.[62]

Donovan was able to meet officials such as Menzies discreetly during his time in Britain. He was not troubled by the press. His trip was the antithesis of Sumner Welles's, which was, said the *Washington Post* columnist Dorothy Thompson, "about as secret as a Hollywood divorce."[63] Donovan's mission really was secret.

In his first full week in Britain, Donovan received detailed briefings at the Admiralty, where he saw Churchill's successor as first lord, the Labour politician A. V. Alexander. He met the director of naval intelligence, Rear Admiral John Godfrey, who would become an important associate, later helping Donovan to become America's spy chief. At the Air Ministry he saw the secretary of state, the Liberal Sir Archibald Sinclair, and discussed an idea he had been promoting for American volunteers to join the RAF.[64] He also breakfasted with the military attaché at the U.S. embassy, Brigadier General Raymond E. Lee, who had butted heads with Kennedy over the ambassador's negative assessments and who liked Donovan instantly. "I welcome anyone who gets the intelligence and sends it home," Lee diarized. Donovan told Lee that in addition to his other jobs in London, he wanted to gain firsthand knowledge of Britain's conscription laws, given the discussions in Washington over the proposal for a peacetime draft. America's attitude toward conscription, he told Lee, "will be a test of our soul."[65]

In the late afternoon of Thursday, July 25, Donovan called on Winston Churchill at 10 Downing Street.[66] The meeting had been urged on the prime minister by various parties, including Lothian and Sir Robert Vansittart at the Foreign Office, who took a considerably kinder view of this presidential representative than he did of the previous one. Vansittart suggested that Churchill meet with Donovan in order to press home Britain's urgent need for destroyers. "It would be very easy to introduce the subject in the course of a ten minute conversation with him," wrote Vansittart. "If you could spare the time I think that in any event you should see him for a short while. He is an important person, and will be still more important to us in the future. And it would probably pay you to give him the pleasure."[67]

No account survives of their meeting, although it was said that Donovan was struck by the gossipy, aristocratic, "eighteenth century atmosphere" of Churchill's entourage, which convened at endless lunches and dinner parties, and "in which unofficial persons (women, for instance) sometimes have as much importance as officials."[68] Later Rooseveltian envoys would be drawn right into this entourage.

That evening Donovan dined with Rear Admiral John Godfrey at the fashionable Royal Thames Yacht Club. The stern naval spymaster was one of the models for the character "M" in the James Bond novels written by Godfrey's aide, Commander Ian Fleming.[69] Some Americans found Godfrey crafty and devious, but Donovan took to him immediately. He told Godfrey that he had been warned he would find the British "difficult, secretive and patronising." His "actual experience . . . has been exactly the opposite." Godfrey observed that Donovan had "very little use" for Kennedy, who was "preaching a gospel of 'all is lost.'" The envoy had sensed a "general air of defeatism at the Embassy."[70]

Over the weekend, Donovan spent time "gadding around with British Army friends." He visited army posts and observed maneuvers on the Salisbury Plain and at other locations in the south of England.[71] On Sunday evening, Donovan motored out to Windsor to have dinner with Joe Kennedy at his country house, St. Leonard's. The seventy-room estate had been lent to the ambassador by an American automobile heir in case London was bombed. Kennedy had already sent his family home to the United States, and his practice of retreating to St. Leonard's on weekends and some evenings attracted accusations of cowardice from his enemies. Also at the dinner was Kirk, the U.S. naval attaché, who hoped the meal would clear the air between the two men. It did not. Donovan later boasted of chiding Kennedy that "the American policy was to help in every way we can and it doesn't help these people any to keep telling them that they haven't got a chance."[72]

Donovan could hardly be blamed for feeling a little grumpy that night.

In order to see Kennedy he had forgone an evening in Churchill's company, at a party at the Dorchester hosted by the society beauty Lady Diana Cooper, wife of the notorious philanderer and information minister, Duff Cooper. Donovan sent Lady Diana flowers to apologize, for which she thanked him in a kittenish note:

Dear wild Colonel,

Thank you so much for the yellow roses. They comforted me a little for your absence. I was so disappointed that the interest of our two countries came between us.

I am happy to tell you that Winston was in his most amusing and invigorating form and I am sure you would have enjoyed it enormously. I had too, for your delight, the beautiful Eve Curie [daughter of Pierre and Marie Curie, attached to the Free French in London] and my prettiest niece. I hope you had a hideous evening with Joe and I hope too that you will lunch or dine another day.

Yours, Diana Cooper[73]

The historical record is silent on whether Wild Bill dined another day with Lady Diana.

On the morning of Monday, July 29, Kirk drove the visitor south to the coast, where they inspected naval shore establishments for the training of officers and seamen. Kirk was "at pains to caution Donovan that the British are showing him the best side of the picture" and felt sure that Donovan was canny enough to understand that.[74] The following morning, Donovan was shown around the RAF's Coastal Command headquarters, before returning to London for a small lunch party at the home of Conservative MP Lady Nancy Astor in St. James's Square, which seems to have been attended by the king and queen. In the afternoon, he visited a fighter squadron in Essex and was flown by the RAF to a Bomber Command station. He spent the night at the station and was able to talk to bomber crews returning from raids over Germany.[75]

Donovan was a highly sought-after man during his time in Britain, bombarded with invitations from ministers, service chiefs and officers, and various aristocrats. He conferred with Brendan Bracken, the redheaded Irish-born businessman and MP who served as Churchill's parliamentary private secretary, and Sir Alan Brooke, the new commander in chief of Home Forces.[76] He called on Ernest Bevin, the shrewd, forceful former union leader who now served as minister of labor—a large man with "small and glittery eyes." Bevin impressed Donovan with his account of the resolute support that organized labor and the working class had shown for the war effort.[77] Another Labour man, Herbert Morrison, the minister of supply, took Donovan to munitions and ordnance factories and introduced him to the workers.[78]

Donovan received reports from MI5 on the government's detention of foreigners who were suspected of being subversives. He also saw Hugh Dalton, the minister of economic warfare, who had been tasked by Winston Churchill a week earlier with overseeing a new clandestine organization responsible for waging guerrilla war, the Special Operations Executive. Churchill's order to Dalton had been to "set Europe ablaze." Dalton gave Donovan papers to take back to the United States on economic warfare and briefed him on the British naval blockade of Europe.[79]

On Friday, August 2, Donovan's last full day in the country, he had a long breakfast meeting at Claridge's with Brigadier General Lee and some of his colleagues from the embassy. The military attaché was relieved to find that after "talking to an extraordinary list of well-posted people, from [the] King and Churchill down," Donovan "agrees with our conclusions and is not at all defeatist. He gives odds of 60–40 that the British will beat off the German attack." Donovan also requested that a series of reports be provided to him so he could put them before decision makers in Washington.[80]

That night, Admiral Godfrey hosted Donovan for dinner at his large home outside London. The two men stayed up until 2 a.m. talking, and Donovan laid out his conclusions, all of them gratifying to his host, who promptly passed them up the line to his superiors. To the questions of whether the British were "earnest about the war" and were "worth supporting," Donovan's answer was "definitely Yes." Britain would succumb neither to air raids nor invasion. He had seen "the spiritual qualities of the British race—the imponderables that make for victory which have evaded Joe Kennedy." He did not base this view solely on paranormal indicators, but also on the quality of the British services, especially the RAF; the dispersal of British airfields, which would make it difficult for the Luftwaffe to achieve superiority in the air; and the condition of Britain's coastal defenses.[81]

Britain deserved support, Donovan believed, and the United States should provide it. "There is still time," he told Godfrey, "for American aid, both material and economic, to exercise a decisive effect on the war." Furthermore, he believed that "as long as we are determined to help we ought to do it now." He was going home with "definite proposals" of specific assistance that should be provided, including U.S. destroyers; flying boats and bombers; rifles; artillery pieces; access to America's Sperry bombsight technology, which enabled accurate high-altitude bombing; the use of American airfields for the training of British Empire pilots; and collaboration on intelligence matters.[82] Godfrey was delighted by Donovan's "stout hearted point of view."[83]

Finally, Donovan revealed that he had a proposal to enhance bilateral diplomatic relations. In addition to the nomination of a "sensible Ambassador," he intended to urge FDR to appoint "a sensible Colonel House." This person should "travel backwards and forwards . . . and keep the feelings of each country 'fresh' in the minds of the other country's rulers." He should identify "all the various ways by which the two countries can concede to each other, and co-operate," while also explaining "the prickly matters where national sovereignty and prestige are involved, and where perhaps the ignorant and too insistent demand for concession should be avoided."[84] Colonel

Donovan no doubt imagined himself playing the role of the "sensible Colonel House."

On Saturday, August 3, the front pages of America's newspapers reported that President Roosevelt had made a dramatic intervention in the selective-service debate. To date, he had hung back from issuing an unambiguous public endorsement of a peacetime draft. Now, with floor debates looming and the mail running ten to one against conscription, he came out for it. In an Oval Office press conference, he declared that he was "distinctly in favor of a selective service bill" and considered it "essential to adequate national defense." Adequate training was "a case of saving lives," he said, and it had to be initiated in advance of a crisis, not on the day that war came. Privately, FDR feared the issue might cause his defeat in the fall. But as he explained to a wavering senator, "I would be derelict in my duty if I did not tell the American people of the real danger which confronts them at the present time." It took a year to get an army ready, Roosevelt said, and he could not "guarantee such a period free from attack in the days to come." "Do please reconsider this whole vital matter," concluded the president, "and give me your aid for the protection of your nation and mine."[85]

That same day, Bill Donovan departed Britain on board a British Overseas Airways Corporation (BOAC) flying boat, the *Clare*, on which the Air Ministry had found him a berth. His suits and laundry followed later in the U.S. diplomatic pouch. As this was the first transatlantic passenger flight from the British Isles to America in a year and there were fears of interception, the aircraft was camouflaged in olive-and-blue paint. Even her propellers were painted black to avoid sun glare that might betray her position to the Luftwaffe. The *Clare* was seen off at Poole by Sir Archibald Sinclair, secretary of state for air, and she was escorted westward across the Irish Sea by British fighters. Despite expectations, the flight was uneventful—"as boring as the Clipper," complained Donovan. Fortunately, he had been provided with some onboard entertainment: a collection of books from Brendan Bracken, including a volume of Edmund Burke, and a bottle of champagne from the chief of the air staff.[86]

The *Clare* set down on the Shannon Estuary in Foynes in County Limerick, Ireland, where Donovan chatted with a young lieutenant in charge of a detachment of Irish troops. "Are you ready to meet the invader?" asked the former commander of the Fighting 69th. "The first that comes," replied the young Irishman. From Foynes the boat flew across the Atlantic to Botwood, Newfoundland, and on to Boucherville, Quebec. Early Sunday evening, the *Clare* circled LaGuardia Field twice before landing on the waters of Bowery Bay and taxiing to the Marine Terminal. Her dark paint made her look drab beside the gleaming silver Clippers, but she proudly flew a British flag. Donovan was the only passenger on board the *Clare*, the other two having disembarked in Canada. In the waiting crowd were two FBI agents, who met Donovan at the pier, and a gaggle of reporters. Donovan refused to answer the reporters' questions about his trip beyond saying that he had undertaken a mission for Frank Knox. "I went abroad for the Secretary of the Navy," Donovan remarked, "and you'll have to ask him."[87]

Just as Donovan arrived back in the United States, another famous colonel, Charles Lindbergh, addressed a crowd of forty thousand people at Soldier Field in Chicago rallying against participation in the European war. The popular Lindbergh called for cooperation with the German Reich should it win the war. "In the past," he said, "we have dealt with a Europe dominated by England and France. In the future we may have to deal with a Europe dominated by Germany." Over dinner with intimates the following night at Hyde Park, Franklin Roosevelt agreed that Lindbergh's speech was a worrying development. "It was serious," he said.[88]

DONOVAN HEADED STRAIGHT FOR WASHINGTON to report his conclusions to political leaders. He conferred with Frank Knox for an hour on the morning of Monday, August 5; that evening, the navy secretary hosted a dinner on board the *Sequoia* at which administration officials could hear from both Donovan and Edgar Mowrer, who had also returned. "Both were extraordinarily interesting," recorded Knox, "and we had a long evening of talk—very informative. Both men brought home a great fund of useful information . . . Both Bill and Edgar are inclined to think the British can defeat an attempted invasion. They agree British morale is high but say British equipment is deficient." Donovan had "a heated discussion" with Admiral Harold R. "Betty" Stark, the chief of naval operations, who worried that providing military supplies to Britain would denude America, but he reported to Kirk that the admiral "came 'round handsomely."[89]

By now the first mentions of Donovan's trip were appearing in the press, albeit with scant detail. The *New York Times* complained that his mission was "one of the present day mysteries of the navy." The mystery man joined Secretary of War Henry Stimson for dinner that evening at Woodley, his gracious colonial residence overlooking Rock Creek Park. "Donovan told us at length of his recent trip to England to find out the real situation there," diarized Stimson. "Donovan had come into contact with all the Chiefs of the British Army; had been taken all over their country and had gone up and down the islands, so that he knew everything that an outsider could learn. He described the morale as very high now and his final summary was that if an attack was made now, the British would probably win." Stimson concluded his diary entry, "He was determined to get into the war some way or another and was the same old Bill Donovan that we have all known and been so fond of."[90]

On August 7, Lord Lothian reported to his foreign secretary, Lord Halifax, that Donovan had been "deeply impressed and grateful for the frankness and courtesy of everybody he saw. He is pressing everybody here vigorously to supply us with destroyers and other equipment asked for, immediately." The Secret Intelligence Service's representative in the United States confirmed the same to "C." Donovan was telling his countrymen that Britons were "determined" and "resolute," with "an unconquerable quality," and "there would not be a defeat of England by the winter months." Americans should not regard Britain as "a beggar at the gate," Donovan argued; rather, she was "our shield" against danger and "our laboratory." That Donovan was an Irish Catholic, Republican war hero only increased the salience of his message.[91]

TWO DAYS LATER, Donovan briefed the president. Roosevelt was escaping the Washington heat at Springwood, his family estate on the Hudson River, and preparing to embark on a tour of naval defenses in New Hampshire, Massachusetts, Connecticut, and Rhode Island. Traveling by presidential train, yacht, and limousine, he and Frank Knox would spend three days inspecting navy yards, fortifications, and submarine docks as well as an arsenal, a torpedo factory, a training station, and other establishments. The intention was to dramatize for the American public the unprecedented quickening of defense preparations initiated by the administration since Germany had launched its spring offensive.

The itinerary included no campaign rallies and the trip was supposedly nonpolitical, but cynics noted that it would take the president across large stretches of the Democrats' northeastern stronghold and involve a drive through Boston along a publicly announced route. (The motorcade would also cross a corner of Maine, one of only two states that voted the Republican ticket in 1936.) This being a Roosevelt expedition, it also mixed some pleasure in with the business: a little fishing off the Massachusetts coast and a visit with family.[92]

At 11 a.m. on Friday, August 9, FDR received the press corps in his study at Springwood, in which he had done his schoolwork as a boy. The room was so small and full of books and knickknacks that reporters spilled out the door onto the porch. "I will tell you who is coming up with [Secretary Knox] and going to be on the train and going down on the *Potomac*," said Roosevelt. "Bill Donovan, so he can tell me what he found on the other side when he went over." A reporter asked whether the president could give "any indication of the nature of Donovan's mission abroad," to which he replied cheerfully, "I cannot and he won't tell you."[93]

Knox and Donovan arrived at Hyde Park shortly before 6 p.m. and were taken across to Val-Kill, Eleanor Roosevelt's retreat, two miles east of the Big House. FDR had designed the little fieldstone cottage in the Dutch Colonial style for his wife. Eleanor served her guests a picnic supper of hot dogs and hamburgers and peppered Donovan with questions about Britain. The colonel, who struck his interlocutors as "mild-mannered" and "silken-voiced," declared he was sure that Britain would hold out. He delighted the First Lady by praising the Labour Party figures who had joined Churchill's cabinet, even predicting that Ernest Bevin would be the next prime minister.[94]

Late that evening, FDR's train left Hyde Park railroad station. The President's Special typically consisted of eight cars to transport the White House staff, reporters, and Secret Service. The last car was a private Pullman car for Roosevelt himself.[95] As the train rolled through the dark countryside, Donovan shared his impressions of Europe. He reported later that he had "a long talk" with the president in which he spoke "very frankly." FDR "had at first tended to make the interview a monologue," but Donovan pressed upon him Britain's "excellent prospects of pulling through." Donovan advocated the provision of American destroyers and bombers, "prepared" the president's mind on the question of training British pilots, and suggested that he make the Sperry bombsight technology available to the RAF. The discussion continued even after Roosevelt had retired to his stateroom, with Donovan and Harry Hopkins, who was also on board, speaking until dawn. In retrospect, this conversation represented the passing of the baton from one presidential envoy to the next.[96]

The president's train arrived in Portsmouth, New Hampshire, on the morning of Saturday, August 10. The Secret Service assisted FDR, attired in a lightweight gray suit and panama hat, into his limousine—a twenty-one-foot-long black, armor-plated Cadillac convertible that evoked an ocean liner and accordingly was known as the "Queen Mary." Riding with Knox and the New Hampshire governor, the president drove through the streets of Portsmouth, once the home port of John Paul Jones's famous sloop-of-war USS *Ranger*, now lined with fifteen thousand well-wishers. At the Portsmouth Navy Yard, he spent twenty minutes inspecting new submarines on the ways and in the fitting-out docks. Then he was piped aboard his yacht, USS *Potomac*, where Hopkins, Donovan, and the rest of his party awaited him. The yacht set sail southward on a gorgeous New England day, shadowed by a destroyer. It stopped in at the little cove at Nahant, Massachusetts, so that FDR could view his youngest grandchild, two-month-old Haven Roosevelt, for the first time. Donovan had more time with Roosevelt as they cruised down the Massachusetts coast. Shortly after 3 p.m., the *Potomac* passed the ancient, wooden-hulled USS *Constitution* and drew up to the dock at the Boston Navy Yard in Charlestown. The band of the spanking-new aircraft carrier USS *Wasp* played the national anthem and a salute of twenty-one guns echoed across Boston Harbor.[97]

Bill Donovan disembarked at Boston. Roosevelt continued with his inspection tour, driving past new destroyers lying at anchor and viewing millions of dollars' worth of new buildings and machine works at the Boston Navy Yard, including a dry dock for the repair of capital ships. Under the rearmament program, the yard now employed nine thousand men working three shifts a day. Next, FDR motored along the Charles River to the Watertown Arsenal, one of the U.S. Army's gun factories. He was driven through the arsenal's machine shops and assembly lines, inspected a new antiaircraft gun, and watched the construction of railway carriages and emplacements for the big guns. The defense effort was "going along really well," he told reporters in an impromptu press conference conducted from his car. "I am very well pleased with everything that I saw today . . . It shows we are really getting into our stride." He predicted the yards and arsenals would be operating at full capacity by the late fall.[98]

The newspapermen thought that since Knox was sitting beside FDR in the "Queen Mary," they would raise the subject of Wild Bill, whose London adventures were now creeping into the press in greater detail.

REPORTER: Have you and Mr. Knox anything to say about Mr. Donovan's mission to Europe?

KNOX: May I answer that question?

FDR: Yes.

KNOX: He went over as my eyes and ears to see what he could find.

REPORTER: Anything to say, sir?

FDR: Well, you see it is his mouth.

REPORTER: Your eyes and ears and Colonel Donovan's mouth? *(Laughter)*[99]

The presidential tour of defense establishments continued for another couple of days, taking in a torpedo base, a training station, and the U.S. Naval War College in Newport, Rhode Island; a new naval air station at Quonset Point, Rhode Island; a submarine base in New London, Connecticut; and a submarine plant in nearby Groton, Connecticut. In between stops, there was time to throw the line over the side of the *Potomac* in Buzzards Bay, where bass, tautog, flounder, and scup were known to run, and later in Narragansett Bay. When asked by reporters whether he had fished, FDR replied, "Not officially." By mistake, the navy secretary and others had caught "some litty-bitty mackerel," he claimed jovially. "It was purely an accident."[100]

BACK IN WASHINGTON, Donovan continued to spread the good word. On Sunday, August 11, he visited with General Robert E. Wood, his hunting companion in the Yukon. The general had just agreed to head up the new isolationist movement America First, and Donovan tried his best to soften his opposition to aid to Britain. On Monday, he lobbied Treasury Secretary Henry Morgenthau on the need to press FDR strongly to send military supplies across the Atlantic.[101]

That evening, he was the guest of honor at a dinner at the Army and Navy Club on Farragut Square, given by Nebraska senator Edward R. Burke,

the sponsor of the selective-service bill in the Senate. The conscription debate was proving bitter, a product of both the intensity of the issue and the
unusually humid Washington weather. Isolationist Senator Hiram Johnson
of California called the bill "the most sinister law" he had encountered in
public life. The so-called Mothers of the USA, their faces veiled, held a
"death watch" against the bill and hanged a proconscription senator in ef-
figy from a tree on Capitol Hill. At the Army and Navy Club, Donovan told
his audience that England faced a "terrible test" but that she would survive.
He said he favored conscription for the United States as both "democratic
and necessary."[102]

Later that month, Donovan and Mowrer published a series of articles
about the techniques used by German-sponsored fifth columnists in Europe, which were picked up by newspapers across America. The articles
were designed, said Knox in an introduction, to familiarize Americans with
the dictator states' methods in case they were employed against the United
States. "I regard defense against possible enemy propaganda as second only
to defense against enemy armaments," he wrote. The *Chicago Daily Tribune*
questioned whether Donovan could be considered an "expert" after spending only a fortnight in Europe, but this quibble did not limit the articles'
impact. Donovan boasted to Bracken that they had "served to arouse the
people to the danger that exists."[103]

Donovan was quickly becoming a British favorite. One Air Ministry official commented that he was "worth his weight in either platinum or alu-
minium (whichever is scarcer)." Lord Beaverbrook, the Anglo-Canadian
newspaper baron, Churchill crony, and minister of air production, reached
for a biblical comparison. "You are like . . . rivers of water in a dry place," he
cabled Donovan in September.[104]

The lesson the British learned from the Donovan episode was that being
open with a Roosevelt envoy paid dividends. They did not share all their secrets with Wild Bill, but they shared many of them.[105] In the months after his
mission, British officials made available to him more data on issues in which
Washington had an interest, including counterespionage techniques,[106] the

structure of the British army and the ministries of information and supply,[107] the European food situation,[108] and merchant shipping.[109] Seven British officials were assigned to the preparation of one report for FDR on economic controls in Britain.[110]

The contrast with the Welles mission is striking: Britain had realized that all its hopes lay with America, and set about satiating the American hunger for information. Donovan's continuing support convinced the British that the new policy of openness was a success. The head of the British Purchasing Commission in the United States, Arthur Purvis, told Churchill that Donovan had been "most impressed with the welcome accorded to him," particularly "the extent to which we had disclosed secret information to him." As a result he was "working with great energy in our interest" and Britain now had "a firm friend in the Republican camp."[111] All of Joe Kennedy's predictions about Donovan's mission, in other words, had been dead wrong. Whitehall would soon extend this policy of transparency to new envoys from President Roosevelt.

MEANWHILE, THE TRENCH WARFARE over the selective-service bill continued on Capitol Hill. There were fisticuffs on the floor of the House of Representatives. So feverish was the atmosphere (and the climate) in Washington that after one key vote the Speaker, William B. Bankhead of Alabama, suffered a stroke and died. Donovan played his part in the air war, recording a national radio address in Chicago, the headquarters of midwestern isolationism. Conscription would be "an inspiration to our own people," he argued, and "a warning to those who would attack us." The bill finally passed on September 14, accompanied by a few last bursts of violent rhetoric. Senator Burton K. Wheeler warned that the bill would "slit the throat of the last democracy still living." "You will have a country of Al Capones," said the senator. "You will have a country where robbery and murder will run riot."[112]

Two days later, Franklin Roosevelt signed the Selective Training and Service Act in the Cabinet Room at the White House, in the presence of

Stimson; General George C. Marshall, chief of staff of the U.S. Army; and congressional supporters. "Time and distance have been shortened," he stated. "A few weeks have seen great nations fall. We cannot remain indifferent to the philosophy of force now rampant in the world . . . We must and will marshal our great potential strength to fend off war from our shores. We must and will prevent our land from becoming a victim of aggression." Bill Donovan was delighted. "Conscription has come," he wrote to Robert Vansittart, "and I look to it as the real means of revealing us to ourselves."[113]

For the first time in its peacetime history, the United States would draft its citizens into the armed forces. Scholars Garry Clifford and Samuel Spencer record that forty-five million men would eventually be registered under selective service, and ten million drafted. Between 1940 and 1945, the system permitted the army to increase in size from fewer than three hundred thousand men to more than eight million. In the Cabinet Room that afternoon, then, Roosevelt signed the birth certificate of the military that would help win the Second World War.[114]

Another great shift was taking place in the United States at the same time. It was during the summer and fall of 1940, historian Wayne S. Cole recounts, that "isolationism lost its majority position in American public opinion." In May and June, nearly two-thirds of Americans regarded it as more important that they stay out of the war than that they aid Britain at the risk of war. When FDR signed the Selective Training and Service Act, Americans were evenly divided on the issue. But by November, the pendulum had swung right over, and a strong majority believed it was more important to help Britain, even at risk of war, than it was to keep out of the war. No one was more responsible for this epochal development than Franklin Roosevelt.[115]

BILL DONOVAN was also near the center of all these debates that steamy summer. FDR and Knox had commissioned him to obtain an eyewitness report on conditions in Britain. They got what they asked for, and his reports served to boost the view in Washington that the British could withstand the

German onslaught, and that aiding them made good strategic sense. Donovan was not shy about claiming credit in this regard. He told his British friends that on his return to the United States he had found "a feeling of helplessness," for which he held Kennedy partly responsible.[116] Fortunately, he wrote, his own "report on conditions has restored morale to many of our people in authority."[117]

To be fair, others also gave him credit. Secretary Knox received Edgar Mowrer at the Navy Department and told him that FDR had been "encouraged by Donovan's report." The columnist Walter Lippmann wrote that Donovan "almost single-handed overcame the unmitigated defeatism which was paralyzing Washington." Donovan's efforts were reinforced by events in Europe: on the same day that Roosevelt finished his defense inspection tour, Germany sent nearly fifteen hundred aircraft over the British Isles in an attempt to knock out its airfields and aircraft factories. The Luftwaffe's "Eagle Day" marked the formal commencement of the Battle of Britain, in which the airmen of Fighter Command did so much to convince the world of their country's resilience. Later, in the Blitz, the citizens of London would perform a similar role.[118]

DONOVAN'S REPORT was also a factor in President Roosevelt's critical decision in August to transfer fifty overage U.S. destroyers to Britain.[119] The British had sought American destroyers since May, less for their intrinsic value than as a sign of support. FDR had been reluctant to make the transfer until early August, when his thinking began to shift. There were several reasons for this change. The appointment of Stimson and Knox had given his administration a newly hawkish character. An interventionist lobby, the "Century Group," massaged public opinion and the Republican leadership, and procured an opinion from a group of lawyers (including a young Dean Acheson) that a deal could be done via executive fiat rather than legislation. Ever guileful, Roosevelt insisted on sweetening the deal with some "molasses," namely leases to British territory in Western Hemisphere locations such as Newfoundland, Bermuda, and the Caribbean, and a guarantee that the Royal Navy would never be surrendered into enemy hands. But the other crucial factor, argues historian David Reynolds, was the president's growing optimism about Britain's prospects, to which Donovan's "upbeat report" contributed.[120]

The man himself was certain of his central role in persuading FDR, as he told British officials with whom he met in December. "Without any self-conceit," recorded one official generously, "he took credit to himself for having been instrumental in giving impetus to the Destroyer-Bases Agreement" on the trip through New England. Donovan also appears to have briefed journalists that he helped to make the deal.[121]

It does seem that the mission and the transfer of the destroyers were linked. FDR decided to proceed with the deal on August 13, the day he returned to Washington from the trip he took with Donovan. Lord Lothian, who was at the center of the negotiations, believed that Donovan "helped a lot."[122] The British Secret Intelligence Service believed that without Donovan "it could not possibly have happened at this time."[123] Donovan's bullish firsthand report probably nudged FDR over the line; even if the president's mind was made up by other developments, it reassured him that the destroyers would be put to good use.

As it happened, negotiations on the details dragged on, and even by the end of 1940 fewer than one-fifth of the destroyers were ready for service with the British fleet. When the ships were transferred, they performed yeoman service fighting U-boats, escorting convoys, and patrolling Britain's coasts.[124] However, the primary significance of the deal was not military but symbolic, signaling a new Anglo-American intimacy to the Axis and the world. That was certainly the British spin. Winston Churchill ended a speech to the House of Commons in late August with this peroration:

> These two great organizations of the English-speaking democracies, the British Empire and the United States, will have to be somewhat mixed up together in some of their affairs for mutual and general advantage. For my

own part, looking out upon the future, I do not view the process with any misgivings. I could not stop it if I wished; no one can stop it. Like the Mississippi, it just keeps rolling along. Let it roll. Let it roll on full flood, inexorable, irresistible, benignant, to broader lands and better days.[125]

DONOVAN'S LEDGER WAS NOT all positive, however. As with Sumner Welles's travels, the Donovan mission raised diplomatic hackles, although this time Joe Kennedy was the malcontent. One insider characterized the Donovan-Kennedy imbroglio as "melancholy monkey-business."[126] The week after Donovan left England, Kennedy complained bitterly to Cordell Hull about a newspaper story revealing that a "secret Roosevelt envoy" had met the king and the prime minister and was reporting back to the White House. "The least . . . that can be done for the American Ambassador in London," Kennedy wrote, "is to let him, subject to the State Department's policy, run his own job . . . Now there is probably a good reason why it is necessary to go around the Ambassador in London . . . However, I do not like it and I either want to run this job or get out." Kennedy took his complaint up with FDR directly in late October at the White House; however, the president "promptly denied everything," blaming Knox and the State Department. This was vintage Roosevelt behavior. Because personal envoys were informal, they were deniable, and FDR used this fact to keep Kennedy in his tent until the 1940 presidential election.[127]

Shortly after the election, Kennedy resigned from his post. So well regarded was Bill Donovan in Whitehall that Sir Alec Cadogan suggested that Lothian "drop a hint in the appropriate quarter" that Donovan would be welcome as the next ambassador. In the end, the idea was not pursued, as the Foreign Office decided that "Colonel Donovan can do us more good by expounding our cause in the US—as he has been doing since his visit."[128]

The benefits of Bill Donovan's investigative diplomacy plainly outweighed any damage done to Joe Kennedy's dignity. Franklin Roosevelt was a glutton for information, particularly when it had been collected in person and confirmed his own prejudices. In this case, Donovan displayed what his companion Edgar Mowrer called "a lawyer's ability . . . to sift the grain from the chaff" and provided the president with vivid, timely, discreet intelligence.[129] His visit to London coincided with the first two of Churchill's climacterics, and helped produce a stiffening of U.S. policy. FDR was certainly pleased with Donovan's work; soon he would entrust him with an even more sensitive mission.

3.

"History's Foremost Marriage Broker"

HARRY HOPKINS IN LONDON,

JANUARY—FEBRUARY 1941

I n the early months of 1941, Washington witnessed a remarkable burst of diplomatic activity. Within the space of seven weeks, the president appointed a new ambassador to the United Kingdom and dispatched three personal envoys to London, of whom the first and most important was Harry L. Hopkins.

All these appointments can be traced back to the sobering events in Europe over the previous six months: the fall of France in June; the Battle of Britain, which began in August and gave way in September to the Luftwaffe's terrifying bombing campaign against London and other British cities; and the establishment in the same month of the Tripartite Pact between Germany, Italy, and Japan. This pact was intended to discourage Washington from responding more forcefully to Germany's assault on Britain and Japan's attempts to establish suzerainty over East Asia. It threatened to link the hitherto largely separate conflicts in the Atlantic and the Pacific. As Americans' attitudes hardened in tandem with these events, the president authorized the Destroyers-Bases Deal and Congress enacted the first peacetime draft in American history. The export of scrap metal to Japan was embargoed. After these initiatives, however, U.S. policy stalled.[1]

Roosevelt's natural circumspection was reinforced by the deadening effect of the 1940 presidential election campaign. Notwithstanding the pro-British stance of his Republican opponent, Wendell Willkie, FDR was branded a warmonger. Worried that frankness might cost him the election, he dissembled instead. On October 29, he stood on the stage of the neoclassical Departmental Auditorium on Washington's Constitution Avenue and watched a blindfolded Henry Stimson draw the first number in the historic peacetime draft lottery. In his remarks, however, the president took care to describe selective service as a "muster" that had been put on for "one purpose only: the defense of our freedom." As historians have noted, his choice of words evoked Lexington and Concord rather than London and Dunkirk. The next day, in an infamous speech at the Boston Garden, Roosevelt made Americans an explicit promise: "Your boys are not going to be sent into any foreign wars."[2]

With the president's convincing victory on November 5, however, the anesthesia started to wear off. No one was happier with the electoral result than the British—"my heart leapt like a young salmon when I heard that Roosevelt had won," recorded one member of parliament—and now they took their chance.[3] While FDR was on a post-election holiday cruise in the Caribbean in December, a navy seaplane delivered to him a long letter from Winston Churchill that the British premier would later describe as "one of the most important I ever wrote."[4] The letter set out the increasingly grave difficulties London was having in paying for its vast American purchases and maintaining its supply routes in the face of German raids on its convoys. Cash-and-carry was not much use if you were out of cash and could not carry. Over the next few days, Roosevelt considered Churchill's plea. By the time the cruiser USS *Tuscaloosa* returned to American waters, he had identified a way around Britain's dollar shortage: Lend-Lease.

Back in Washington, a tanned and refreshed President Roosevelt reiterated his policy of providing Britain with the maximum assistance short of war. The "best defense of Great Britain is the best defense of the United States," Roosevelt told journalists, so it is "important from a selfish point of view . . . that we should do everything to help the British Empire to defend itself."[5] In his famous fireside chat on national security, FDR warned a huge radio audience, "If Great Britain goes down, the Axis powers will control the continents of Europe, Asia, Africa, Australasia, and the high seas . . . It is no exaggeration to say that all of us, in all the Americas, would be living at the point of a gun."[6]

Roosevelt proposed that the United States should lend Britain the supplies it needed to continue the fight, accepting in-kind repayment "when the show was over." Telling newsmen at the White House that he intended to "get rid of the silly, foolish old dollar sign," he compared this extraordinary transfer of arms between two nations to a man lending his neighbor a length of garden hose in order to douse a fire.[7] "We must be the great arsenal of democracy," urged the president over the wireless.[8] To that end, he prepared to lay before the Congress the Lend-Lease bill, the stated purpose of which was "to promote the defense of the United States." As a patriotic note, the statute was designated "H.R. 1776."[9]

FDR was not yet ready to enter the war, but he was prepared to risk war by betting on Britain. He was offering London what would later be called a "common-law alliance"—an informal but intimate military partnership.[10] To make this proposal in person, Roosevelt called on the most important of all his envoys, who also happened to be the unlikeliest.

HARRY LLOYD HOPKINS was born in Sioux City, Iowa, on August 17, 1890, the fourth of five surviving children to David "Al" Hopkins and Anna Pickett. His parents were an unusual match. After periods as a prospector and traveling salesman, Al settled down as a harnessmaker-cum-storekeeper who sold newspapers, magazines, and candy above the counter and cigarettes under it. Large in both body and personality, he was easygoing, gregarious, and irreligious. He was far less interested in bookkeeping than in bowling, his great obsession. Anna was a stern, straitlaced, and devout Methodist who hailed originally from a speck of a town in Ontario, Canada, called Lowville. A schoolteacher as a young woman, she endured the financial vicissitudes of life with Al and tried to raise hardworking, God-fearing children. In his teens, the *New Yorker* recorded, young Harry "beat carpets, scrubbed floors, milked cows; summers he earned money by working on nearby farms. He also spent a good deal of time swapping funny stories with his father, a man who believed in letting carpets alone."[11]

If he got his father's gift of gab, Harry also acquired his taste for gambling and his "champagne appetites." He inherited Anna's features, her sense of social responsibility, and her fearsome determination, which was behind the family's move to Grinnell, Iowa, in 1901. With a fine Congregational school, Grinnell College, and no saloons, Grinnell was Anna's kind of town. Harry was a popular student at Grinnell College and, despite his scrawny build, a champion basketball player. He was also voted senior class president, the highest elected office he would ever hold. After graduating in 1912, he maneuvered his way into a social-work career in New York City. In later life, he would sometimes cite his small-town roots, but as a young man, his son recalled, "he wanted to get to the big city."[12]

"I've liked New York since the first day I saw it," said Hopkins. "I like everything about that town." He enjoyed the way that all the elements of city life—bankers from Millionaires' Row and immigrants from Avenue B; good-government activists and gangsters; opera houses and speakeasies— bumped up against each other.[13] He married twice in this period, first to a fellow social worker, Ethel Gross, a Hungarian Jewish immigrant, with whom he had three sons and a daughter who died in infancy; and after their divorce, to Barbara Duncan, ten years younger than he, with whom he had a daughter. In his work, he displayed sympathy, ambition, and phenomenal energy. Over two decades, he rose through a succession of charities that served New York's poor, whose numbers grew as the Depression threatened to overwhelm the country. In 1931, Governor Franklin D. Roosevelt tapped him to serve as his point man for unemployment relief, providing assistance to one-tenth of the state's population. When Roosevelt was elected president, Hopkins joined him in Washington as the boss of the new Federal Emergency Relief Administration (FERA). The president wanted action immediately, and in his first two hours on the job, Hopkins disbursed $5 million.[14] Roosevelt did not yet know Hopkins well, but he always appreciated a man who enjoyed his work.

In short order, Hopkins became the whirling dervish at the center of Roosevelt's program for getting the country moving again. Heading up a series of federal relief and works agencies that employed millions and spent billions—FERA, the Civil Works Administration (CWA), and the Works Progress Administration (WPA)—he quickly "came to be regarded as the Chief Apostle of the New Deal and the most cordially hated by its enemies." Many friends of the New Deal also disliked Hopkins, including Interior Secretary Harold Ickes, who oversaw the rival Public Works Administration (PWA). But Hopkins's star continued to rise, especially after Louis Howe died in 1936 and other Roosevelt cronies fell from favor.[15]

From the president's point of view, Hopkins had unimpeachable qualifications for membership of the inner circle. First, he had an uncanny ability to get to the crux of an issue. FDR marveled at how Hopkins would sit in a meeting watching everyone else haggle and talk at cross purposes and then, with a single sentence, "put his finger on the point of the argument, and clarify the whole thing."[16] Second, Hopkins was a stranger to bureaucratic orthodoxies. He "never hesitated to act." FDR would say, "Now Harry, get that God damn thing done," and two hours later it was done. Finally, he was utterly, unshakably loyal. He was once asked in a confirmation hearing what he would do if he disagreed with a presidential decision. "Once the policy is set," he replied, "I'm in there fighting for it fifteen minutes later."[17]

Apart from all this, Roosevelt just liked Hopkins. He was shrewd, candid, and laconic. He was delightfully informal—even with junior officials, remembered one, "it was banter and jokes and wisecracks." He had a writer's eye for detail and a good ear for listening. He played practical jokes and a mean game of poker. He told the bawdy stories that FDR relished. He could be impertinent, but he never called the president by his first name.[18] Amid all the pomp and toadyism of the capital, Hopkins's easy manner was like a gust of air-conditioning on a humid Washington day.

It emerged, too, that Hopkins had a particular gift for Washington's most important parlor game: "understanding, sensing, divining, often guessing—and usually guessing right—what is in Franklin Roosevelt's mind." According to one observer, Hopkins had "almost an extrasensory perception of Roosevelt's moods; he knew how to give advice in the form of flattery and flattery in the form of advice; he sensed when to press his boss and when to desist, when to talk and when to listen, when to submit and when to argue."[19]

If Hopkins was good company for Roosevelt, he was also good copy for reporters. He did not look like a sleek Washington heavyweight; indeed he struck one foreign visitor as a "gangling yokel." With an elongated, curved face and irregular features, Hopkins was not a handsome man. His suits looked "as though they had been slept in or had spent the night in a heap on the floor," and they "always reflected the angles of bony knees and elbows." He gave off the suggestion, wrote one correspondent, of "quick cigarettes, thinning hair, dandruff, brief sarcasm, fraying suits of clothes, and a wholly understandable preoccupation." Yet there was also a machine-gun intensity about him. Reporters noticed that he "talks without commas, like an old-fashioned telegram." He was pretty handy with telegrams, as it happened, and he also spent hours each day fixing and straightening things on the telephone. Hopkins had the passion of the idealist and the sharp elbows of the pragmatist.[20]

He was certainly no earnest liberal. "He is no more like the accepted pattern of the social worker," reported the *Boston Sunday Globe*, "than a race horse is like a farmer's old gray mare." The metaphor was well chosen, because Hopkins loved the racetrack, which he often visited in the company of society types and business tycoons. His political sympathies were with the underdogs, but Hopkins enjoyed running with the thoroughbreds. He "didn't give a damn about being rich," allowed one of his rivals. "The President's people never played for such small stakes as money." Sometimes

Hopkins needed an advance to pay his rent, even when he was disbursing billions. This did not stop him enjoying the finer things in life—cocktails and fancy meals, chauffeur-driven cars and first-class travel—and the company of those who could afford them.[21]

In 1937, Hopkins's life changed gears. In the fall, his second wife, Barbara, died of cancer. Two months later, Hopkins was admitted to the Mayo Clinic in Rochester, Minnesota, where doctors removed a large tumor from his stomach, in the process cutting away much of the organ itself. A cover story was circulated that Hopkins had suffered a perforating gastric ulcer, because at that point Roosevelt was positioning Hopkins to replace him in the White House in 1940 should he not run again. To bolster his credentials, Roosevelt appointed him to the cabinet as his commerce secretary. Any chance he had of succeeding in this unlikely position, however—let alone as a presidential candidate—was ruined by his worsening health. From the spring of 1939, Hopkins's medical sorrows came not as single spies but in battalions: weakness, pain, weight loss, swollen feet, poor vision, vomiting, and diarrhea. By the time Hitler's armies marched into Poland, he was back at the Mayo Clinic.[22]

Hopkins's cancer had not returned. He was suffering from malnutrition, unable to absorb nutrients from his food, which, in a reporter's words, "slid through his stomach as it would through glass tubing." The cause was never fully established, nor was it ever cured, but it was probably either celiac disease or a mechanical problem stemming from his cancer surgery. Urged on by FDR, he endured a diversity of treatments, including blood transfusions, intravenous feeding, and injections of iron and vitamins into his arms, ankles, and hands. "They gave me stuff they'd never given before," he told a reporter proudly. He returned to Washington a frail man and spent most of the winter at home in bed, listening to the news of the Phony War in Europe on the radio. He seemed to be sidelined; the common view around town, Harold Ickes recorded with satisfaction, was that "Harry has practically completely faded from the political picture." On May 10, 1940, however, the day that Hitler invaded the Low Countries and Churchill became prime minister, an "emaciated, sad-eyed" Hopkins dined with Roosevelt at the White House. The president invited him to stay for the weekend. He lived there for most of the next three and a half years.[23]

A new stage in Hopkins's career now began. Robert Sherwood wrote that the president "converted his friend to war purposes just as surely and as completely as, in the general upheaval of that same year, a Chicago industrialist . . . converted his wallpaper factory into a plant for the production of incendiary bombs." With complete access to Roosevelt's person and his thinking, Hopkins became the ultimate counselor, sounding board, and gatekeeper—"the right arm," FDR's son called him.[24] If the president's military and foreign policy advisers were chary of Hopkins in the early days, they were soon won over by his abilities. Henry Stimson, for instance, thought it was "phenomenal how quickly he came to understand the basic principles of grand strategy and to shape his whole thinking and his course of action accordingly." The British were also pleased, finding him "very much for our side."[25] Hopkins's residence in the executive mansion attracted criticism; Arthur Krock of the *New York Times* observed that he was "as much a marked man as a courted man." Roosevelt's reply was simple: "There is a tremendous job to be done. I need what Harry has to give and I need him here in this house."[26]

Hopkins was quartered on the second floor of the White House, a drafty collection of rooms occupied by the Roosevelts and their guests, furnished haphazardly and decorated with family photographs and nautical prints. He lived in a large bedroom in the southeast corner of the building that had once been Abraham Lincoln's study. A bronze plaque over the fireplace marked the signing of the Emancipation Proclamation. Tall windows looked out across the South Lawn toward the Washington Monument and the Jefferson Memorial. In the corner stood Hopkins's leather cabinet chair, given to him when he resigned as commerce secretary in September 1940. If he wasn't ambling down the hall to confer with the president, or accidentally crashing one of Eleanor's press conferences in his bright silk dressing gown, Hopkins could be found in this room, working off a small card table or surrounded by official papers on the enormous green-canopied four-poster bed, with a telephone to his ear and a Lucky Strike between his lips. He would sit with distinguished visitors on the edge of his bed, talking of high policy while they looked at his shaving brush and toothbrush. He thrived, stronger than he had been in several years. A reporter wrote that he was "rising as a trout to the fly, to this biggest of all crises."[27]

IF HARRY HOPKINS was now in the president's innermost circle, Sumner Welles remained FDR's man at the State Department. Early in the fall of 1940, however, an incident took place that would set off a vicious campaign against Welles and eventually drive him from public office forever.[28]

The evening of September 17, 1940, found Roosevelt on board the presidential train, returning to Washington from the funeral of House Speaker William Bankhead in Jasper, Alabama. Thousands of mourners, including nearly a hundred members of Congress, had turned out in Jasper's stifling heat to mourn the Speaker and see the president. Accompanying FDR back to the capital were half a dozen members of his cabinet and, in the place of an ailing Cordell Hull, Sumner Welles. The under secretary of state sometimes unwound from his ferocious work schedule by turning to alcohol. That evening, he joined Vice President Henry A. Wallace and others in the dining car and drank "one whiskey after another." By the early hours of the following morning, he was heavily intoxicated and muttering about his mission to Europe in the spring. At 4 a.m., Welles summoned a series of African American Pullman porters to his sleeping compartment and made homosexual advances toward them. They refused the advances, and alerted railway officials and the head of the president's security detail. When Welles saw the Secret Service man in his car, he closed the door of his compartment and made no further trouble. That afternoon he alighted at Union Station.

Within twenty-four hours, reporters started to hear rumors of the incident, although they were loath to print such a story. Soon isolationists in the

Senate had the information and sought to disseminate it in order to damage the administration. By November, the news had reached the ears of Welles's most implacable enemy, William Bullitt, the former U.S. ambassador to France who had felt sidelined by the Welles mission. For Sumner Welles, this was the beginning of the end.

THE IDEA FOR HARRY HOPKINS to visit London was conceived on board USS *Tuscaloosa* in December 1940, after delivery of Churchill's long letter. "A lot of this could be settled if Churchill and I could just sit down together for a while," remarked Roosevelt. He didn't see how it could be arranged, however, because the recent resignation of Joseph Kennedy and sudden death of Lord Lothian, the British ambassador in Washington, meant that both countries were without ambassadors in each other's capitals. "How about me going over, Mr. President?" asked Hopkins. FDR turned him down flat, saying he needed him in Washington. When the party returned home, Hopkins recruited two of FDR's intimates, personal secretary Missy Le-Hand and Supreme Court justice Felix Frankfurter, to put in their "plugs" for the idea, but the president seemed reluctant—he was being "slow Dutch," as Frankfurter put it. For the next few weeks, Roosevelt teased Hopkins about the suggestion: "You weren't thinking of taking a long airplane trip, were you? I hear that life in those air-raid shelters is pretty congested, Harry."[29] Still, he gave no hint that anything was afoot.

Then, without warning, at a press conference on January 3, 1941, the president announced that Hopkins would go "as my personal representative for a very short trip to the other side, just to maintain—I suppose that is the word for it—personal contact between me and the British Government." When press secretary Steve Early told the president's new envoy about his assignment, Hopkins was incredulous. "Think of it!" he said to Early, as he stood in the Lincoln Study in his frayed bathrobe. "My father was a harness maker and my mother was a schoolteacher. And I'm going over to talk to

Winston Churchill and the men who run the British government. If that isn't democracy, I don't know what is."[30]

Roosevelt was typically evasive about the nature of the Hopkins mission in his press conference:

REPORTER: Does Mr. Hopkins have any special mission, Mr. President?

FDR: No, no, no!

REPORTER: Any title?

FDR: No, no! . . .

REPORTER: Mr. President, with regard to Mr. Hopkins, you said he was going over as personal representative; will he have a status of ambassador?

FDR: No, he has no status at all; he is going over as my representative. The question of title doesn't enter into it . . .

REPORTER: Mr. President, is it safe to say Mr. Hopkins will not be the next Ambassador?

FDR: You know Harry isn't strong enough for that job . . .

REPORTER: Will anyone accompany Mr. Hopkins?

FDR: No. And he will have no powers.

REPORTER: Will he have any mission to perform?

FDR: No; you can't get anything exciting. *(Laughter)* He's just going over to say "How do you do?" to a lot of my friends! *(Laughter)*[31]

Maintaining personal contact with Roosevelt's friends was certainly one of Hopkins's tasks. In January 1941, FDR needed to communicate to His Majesty's Government his program for all-out aid to Britain short of war. "I have just got to see Churchill myself in order to explain things to him," FDR told an intimate. In the meantime, he was dispatching an emissary who was completely conversant with his views. Roosevelt told a jealous Ickes that he was sending Hopkins over "so that he can talk to Churchill like an Iowa farmer." "Harry is the perfect ambassador for my purposes," said

FDR. "He doesn't even know the meaning of the word 'protocol.' When he sees a piece of red tape he just pulls out those old garden shears of his and snips it."[32]

One of Hopkins's jobs, then, was to establish a closer rapport between Roosevelt and Churchill. The other was to survey the local political terrain on behalf of his boss. FDR told another secretary, Grace Tully, that Hopkins was to be "a glorified reporter . . . There are more things I want to know than I seem to be finding out through the so-called channels . . . So instead of sending another career man I'm sending somebody who looks like a farmer and acts like a farmer and probably will find out more than all the others combined."[33]

The president was still fielding divergent assessments of Britain's situation, and now he was deprived of ambassadorial reports. Furthermore, the stream of military secrets and intelligence from Whitehall to Washington that Donovan had brought forth had dried up somewhat.[34] Roosevelt needed a trusted adviser to bring him "the clearest picture" of Britain's ability to withstand the German onslaught, confirm that he had backed a winner, and identify the country's most urgent needs.[35]

Perhaps most importantly, FDR wanted intelligence on Churchill. The prime minister was "still an unknown quantity." Was he "an odd-ball" and "a lot of hot air," as many felt? There were widespread rumors about his alcohol consumption, which Sumner Welles's report from Europe had tended to confirm. Roosevelt told the cabinet in May 1940 that "he supposed that Churchill was the best man England had, even if he was drunk half of his time." Then there was the matter of criticisms Churchill had made of the New Deal, admittedly quite ancient but recently excavated by Wendell Willkie during the presidential campaign.[36] Was this a man with whom FDR could do business?

Hopkins was, therefore, to be Roosevelt's proxy in London, bringing him into closer touch with the British government and gathering information essential to his political calculus. He would be just the kind of "sensible Colonel House" envisaged by Bill Donovan five months earlier.

———

MEANWHILE, THE FOREIGN OFFICE was wondering what to make of all this. The day after Roosevelt's press conference, Hopkins called on the British chargé d'affaires in Washington, Nevile Butler, and told him FDR wanted someone with an "intimate knowledge of his own mind and of the Administration to talk to those who were governing England and bring back the over-all picture," including precise details of the ships, airplanes, and munitions required. On his return, Hopkins and the president could use this information to "override any Departmental attempts to whittle down [British] orders." Hopkins made it clear to Butler that he planned to operate independently from the State Department. He also emphasized Roosevelt's unneutral intent, commenting that "one issue that mattered a heap was that the United States in their own interest should enable Great Britain to defeat Hitler. This was the spirit in which he was undertaking his mission."

Butler concluded that Hopkins was "a thorough-going supporter" of aid to Britain and "a person to be cultivated, and I hope therefore that everything will be done to welcome him and assist him in London." Whitehall was initially unimpressed, however. "I do not think that any very subtle significance must be read into Mr Hopkins's visit," sniffed the Foreign Office's resident U.S. expert, T. North Whitehead. "The President is notorious for his tendency to send special representatives off in all directions at the least provocation and he often has two or more balls in the air simultaneously."[37]

Luckily, unofficial channels worked better than official ones. Two individuals, sitting on either side of the Atlantic like mismatched bookends, now came into the picture. The first was Felix Frankfurter, the Jewish, Austrian-born Harvard Law School professor whom Roosevelt had appointed to the Supreme Court. Small and dapper, with a quick mind and an inability to suffer fools, he had admirers and detractors in equal numbers. Many from both camps would have agreed with reporter Marquis Childs that Frankfurter was "the greatest busybody in the world."[38] He was also a passionate

Anglophile and regarded by some in the State Department as "the power behind the throne" of the administration's interventionist faction.[39]

Frankfurter had urged the Hopkins mission on Roosevelt, feeling that it "might accomplish vast good," but also aware that "if these chemicals failed to fuse it might mean vast mischief." Now Frankfurter was worried lest Hopkins depart with "a chip on his shoulder." He arranged a three-way conversation with Hopkins and Jean Monnet, the influential Frenchman who was posted in Washington with the British Purchasing Commission. The two men's minds were, as Frankfurter observed, entirely different—the one "darting, intuitive, penetrating," the other "orderly, precise, logical, French"— but at Frankfurter's house, they met. Monnet warned Hopkins against looking for authority in London except in the person of the prime minister: "Churchill *is* the War Cabinet." Hopkins seemed "tired of hearing about the Churchill legend," remarking that he supposed that Churchill thought "he's the greatest man in the world." But Frankfurter told him not to go to the United Kingdom "with the attitude of a chauvinistic Middle Westerner," and he was delighted when Hopkins "got the idea that his whole mission depended upon interpreting Roosevelt correctly to Churchill and then vice versa—'to act as history's foremost marriage broker.'"[40]

For his part, Frankfurter was determined to be the marriage broker's marriage broker. Having briefed Hopkins on Churchill, he now set out to brief Churchill on Hopkins, using the good offices of Richard Casey and Stanley Bruce, Australian diplomats in Washington and London. Casey and Bruce were both upper-class, Cambridge-educated Tories—Bruce was famous in Australia for wearing spats—as well as sensitive and adroit operators. After visiting Frankfurter in his chambers at the Supreme Court, Casey sent Bruce a cable suggesting that he urge Churchill to "go out of his way at an early stage to express to Hopkins his great and cordial admiration for the president . . . There is no surer way of reaching Hopkins' heart and there is no one who can do this more convincingly than Churchill." Two days later, Bruce replied, "Have seen the Prime Minister tonight and conveyed your point. He was most grateful and will certainly act on it."[41]

On the day of Hopkins's arrival in the United Kingdom, accordingly, Churchill delivered a speech lavishing praise on Roosevelt. Casey forwarded reports of it to Frankfurter, observing that it was "probably not unconnected" with his correspondence with Bruce. In the aftermath of the trip, Frankfurter would make the bolder claim that "the success of Harry Hopkins' London mission was fundamentally due" to the Frankfurter-Casey-Bruce correspondence.[42]

The other bookend was Brendan Bracken, Churchill's aide. Bracken was as close to Churchill as Hopkins was to Roosevelt; indeed, some believed wrongly that he was not only the prime minister's confidant but his illegitimate son. Shortly after Hopkins took up residence in the White House, Bracken moved into 10 Downing Street, where he was available for the midnight conversations Churchill enjoyed. Three years earlier, Bracken had met Hopkins at Keewaydin, the Long Island mansion of the celebrated newspaper editor Herbert Bayard Swope. Keewaydin was a gracious white clapboard house perched on Sands Point, squarely in Gatsby country. It was a place of legendary hospitality, with a tennis court, a saltwater swimming pool, and a famous croquet court. At the end of "a most pleasant day" of games and conversation, Hopkins had given Bracken a ride back to Manhattan, and Bracken was pleased to "listen without interruption to a first-rate talker." When Churchill was apprised of Hopkins's assignment in January 1941, his initial reaction was that "he can't be an important man or the president would have told me he was coming."[43] But Bracken, who had followed Hopkins's career and maintained a correspondence with him, set him straight. Hopkins was "the most important American visitor to this country we had ever had," he informed the Churchill circle. "He could influence the President more than any living man." When the prime minister heard this, Sherwood reports, "he ordered the unrolling of any red carpets that might have survived the blitz."[44]

Americans were just as confused by the appointment as the British. State Department hands saw it as an expression of Roosevelt's fondness for

Hopkins, not an important diplomatic initiative. They were dismissive of Hopkins's qualifications and concerned that he would disrupt the work of the properly accredited representatives. "One might say that Roosevelt was being very kind to an incompetent," remarked the Republican foreign policy figure William R. Castle sharply. "But kindness is no reason for sending the man to London as 'personal representative of the president.' " Harold Ickes, ever attentive to palace politics, feared that Roosevelt's purpose was "to give Harry some kind of a buildup in the eyes of the country." Many well-informed observers, such as the columnist Raymond Clapper, assumed mistakenly that Hopkins's job was to investigate social and economic changes in Britain since the outbreak of war—that he was the emissary of the "New Deal Roosevelt" rather than the "win-the-war Roosevelt." The isolationist *Chicago Daily Tribune* got much closer to the truth, warning against "one of the biggest moves to date to link peaceful America with warring Britain."[45]

On his way to London, Hopkins stopped in New York City to run an errand. Roosevelt had been buoyed by a flood of supportive letters and telegrams after his "garden hose" press conference and his Arsenal of Democracy speech, and his aides were hard at work on drafting the Lend-Lease bill. But the president was concerned about the effect that Joe Kennedy's rumored opposition to Lend-Lease might have on passage of the bill. Accordingly, Hopkins called on the former ambassador at the Waldorf Hotel and played down the administration's commitment to the British cause, giving Kennedy the impression that neither he nor FDR were "sold on the British."[46] With this task behind him, and spurred on by good-luck cables from Eleanor Roosevelt and Felix Frankfurter, Harry Hopkins prepared to depart.[47]

Shortly after eight in the morning of January 6, Hopkins arrived at La-Guardia Field, accompanied by several family members and Juan Trippe, the president of Pan American, but without any aides. For an hour he sat waiting inside the terminal, sipping black coffee and fending off newsmen hungry for a story. "I don't know how long I'll be in London," he told them. "I'll be back when I've finished and it won't be too long. I can't answer your other questions." He frowned when one reporter compared him to Colonel House, but refused to comment. Above this scene, running right around the marble rotunda of the Marine Air Terminal's interior, stretched James Brooks's immense mural depicting the history of flight, which had been sponsored by the WPA's Federal Arts Project. ("Hell! They've got to eat just like other people!" was Hopkins's response to criticisms of New Deal support for artists when he was WPA administrator.)[48]

Finally, it was time for Hopkins to head out along the walkway to where the *Yankee Clipper* sat on the water. With a few jokes and kisses for his children, he gathered up his battered gray felt hat, his newspaper, and a couple of paperbacks and climbed aboard the flying boat. A few minutes later, it taxied across the waters of Bowery Bay and lifted off into the air.[49]

Hopkins carried one other item with him—an extraordinary personal letter from the president of the United States:

My dear Mr. Hopkins:

Reposing special faith and confidence in you, I am asking you to proceed at your earliest convenience to Great Britain, there to act as my personal representative. I am also asking you to convey a communication in this sense to His Majesty King George VI.

You will, of course, communicate to this Government any matters which may come to your attention in the performance of your mission which you may feel will serve the best interests of the United States.

> *With all best wishes for the success of your mission, I am,*
>
> *Very sincerely yours,*
> *Franklin D. Roosevelt*[50]

———

WHILE HOPKINS WAS EN ROUTE, Roosevelt delivered his annual message to Congress on the State of the Union. The mood was more somber than was usually the case on such occasions. Massive steel braces, erected to compensate for structural weaknesses in the roof of the House chamber, gave the scene a somewhat martial appearance. Observers noted that the diplomatic gallery contained no representatives from the Axis countries. FDR arrived under heavy guard, wearing a grave expression. The new Speaker, Sam Rayburn of Texas, was so tense that he banged his elaborate mesquite-wood gavel too hard and broke it, sending pieces flying off in several directions.

"I address you, the Members of the Seventy-seventh Congress," the president began, "at a moment unprecedented in the history of the Union. I use the word 'unprecedented,' because at no previous time has American security been as seriously threatened from without as it is today." Roosevelt denounced "the new order of tyranny that seeks to spread over every continent today," declaring that the "American people have unalterably set their faces against that tyranny." He warned against "those who with sounding brass and a tinkling cymbal preach the 'ism' of appeasement," and called for "a swift and driving increase in our armament production." His message to "the democracies" was this: "We shall send you, in ever-increasing numbers, ships, planes, tanks, guns. This is our purpose and our pledge." "In fulfillment of this purpose," he added, "we will not be intimidated by the threat of dictators."

The most famous section of the address came at its close:

In the future days, which we seek to make secure, we look forward to a world founded upon four essential human freedoms.

The first is freedom of speech and expression—everywhere in the world.

The second is freedom of every person to worship God in his own way—everywhere in the world.

The third is freedom from want—which, translated into world terms, means economic understandings which will secure to every nation a healthy peacetime life for its inhabitants—everywhere in the world.

The fourth is freedom from fear—which, translated into world terms, means a world-wide reduction of armaments to such a point and in such a thorough fashion that no nation will be in a position to commit an act of physical aggression against any neighbor—anywhere in the world.

FDR had written these words himself. A few days earlier, during a drafting session in his White House study with Harry Hopkins, Robert Sherwood, and Sam Rosenman, he had suddenly announced that he had "an idea for a peroration." "We waited as he leaned far back in his swivel chair with his gaze on the ceiling," Rosenman recalled. "It was a long pause—so long that it began to become uncomfortable." Then he leaned forward in his chair and dictated the passage in one go. He had alluded to these freedoms only once before, at a press conference some months previously, but "the words seemed now to roll off his tongue as though he had rehearsed them many times to himself." Hopkins registered a protest at the phrase "everywhere in the world." "That covers an awful lot of territory, Mr. President. I don't know how interested Americans are going to be in the people of Java." "I'm afraid they'll have to be some day, Harry," replied FDR. "The world is getting so small that even the people in Java are getting to be our neighbors now."

The members of Congress received Roosevelt's address solemnly and without the usual raucous applause; journalists noted that Republican members were largely silent. The reported responses of senators and congressmen ranged over the entire scale. Democratic senator Morris Sheppard of Texas thought it was "one of the greatest deliverances of all time, not merely of American history." On the other hand, Representative Robert F. Rich of Pennsylvania thought the speech meant "war and dictatorship in this country"; his fellow Republican, Representative George H. Tinkham of Massachusetts, claimed that Roosevelt had "declared war on the world."

But columnist Arthur Krock thought that the sobriety of the representatives during the address "was more eloquent than the published comment." They had already read in the newspapers about the president's plans for Lend-Lease. Now, having been officially informed of the administration's intentions in his speech, "the members, while not shrinking from the consequences, were thinking of them hard. And they must have thought especially hard when Mr Roosevelt said: 'When the dictators—if the dictators—are ready to make war upon us, they will not wait for an act of war on our part.'"[51]

IN THE LATE AFTERNOON of January 9, Hopkins landed in Poole, on England's south coast, aboard a BOAC plane. Unfavorable flying conditions had delayed him by a day in Lisbon, where he met with conservative Portuguese prime minister António de Oliveira Salazar and British ambassador Sir Ronald Campbell. Sir Ronald, who was ambassador in Paris during the Welles mission, unwittingly offended Hopkins's liberal instincts by pronouncing haughtily on the wonderful morale of Britain's "lower classes."[52]

After four days of travel, Hopkins was a wreck. Brendan Bracken, dispatched by Churchill to meet the distinguished American visitor, found him slumped in his seat after the other passengers had disembarked the aircraft, looking "sick and shrunken and too tired even to unfasten his safety belt." Another observer thought he seemed "so ill and frail that a puff of wind would blow him away." But Hopkins had remarkable powers of recovery, which were soon supplemented by the large scotch he was served by white-gloved waiters on the special train Churchill had rustled up to bring him to the capital. "Are you going to let Hitler take these fields away from you?" he asked Bracken as the train sped through the countryside. He could hardly have been surprised by the one-word answer he received.[53]

Hitler's labors were soon obvious to Hopkins. His train pulled into a heavily guarded Waterloo Station in the middle of an air raid, with incendiaries falling on the tracks behind it. Stepping off the blacked-out train into the darkened terminus, Hopkins had to raise his voice in order to be heard above the roar of the antiaircraft guns. "I had a good trip and I feel fine," he told the waiting newsmen with a smile. The barrage had resumed a few minutes later when an embassy car delivered him to Claridge's, and a reporter caught him turning for a moment to look at the London skies before he passed through its fortified entranceway. Too exhausted to accept an invitation to dine at Downing Street, he adjourned instead to his room for a quiet supper with Herschel Johnson, the U.S. chargé in London. The encounter had a lasting effect on the unpretentious foreign service officer. For months, while Berlin had sent its bombers to London, Washington had sent only instructions to maintain the strictest neutrality, leaving Johnson feeling like a man in a burning building who is told "to take no sides as between the Fire Department and the flames." Now, with the arrival of an envoy who was determined to help Britain prevail, "the first real assurance of hope had at last come through."[54]

Johnson had welcome news for Hopkins, too—a briefing on Churchill's remarks about Roosevelt, delivered that day to a luncheon of the Anglo-American society the Pilgrims at the Savoy Hotel:

I have always taken the view that the fortunes of mankind in its tremendous journey are principally decided for good or ill—but mainly for good, for the path is upward—by its greatest men and its greatest episodes.

I therefore hail it as a most fortunate occurrence that at this awe-striking climax in world affairs there should stand at the head of the American Republic a famous statesman, long versed and experienced in the work of government and administration, in whose heart there burns the fire of resistance to aggression and oppression, and whose sympathies and nature make him the sincere and undoubted champion of justice and of freedom, and of the victims of wrongdoing wherever they may dwell.

And not less—for I may say it now that the party struggle in the United States is over—do I rejoice that this pre-eminent figure should newly have received the unprecedented honour of being called for the third time to lead the American democracies in days of stress and storm.[55]

Hopkins awoke the next morning to a breakfast of toast, fruit, and American-style coffee, and some banter with the hotel valet. The poor man, accustomed to serving a different sort of guest, was horrified to find that Hopkins had arrived with only a few shirts—none of them with the detachable collars that were favored by the London quality—and no winter underwear. This was the beginning of a sympathetic relationship between Hopkins and the hotel staff, who found him generous with little gifts such as eggs he received from his well-placed friends, and generally more lovable than the usual Claridge's clientele. The valets tried to be present when Hopkins left his room each morning in order to straighten up his outfit, with Hopkins muttering, "Oh yes—I've got to remember I'm in London now—I've got to look dignified." They would steam and block his dilapidated old hat when he wasn't looking, and take his wrinkled suit off for ironing, only to find that he had left his passport, wallet, or even secret documents in the pockets. Hopkins's dishevelment presented quite a contrast to the dashing figure cut by Sumner Welles in London the previous year.[56]

At 10:30 a.m., after a briefing from the U.S. military and naval attachés, Hopkins was driven to the Foreign Office, a grand, ornate classical building located between Whitehall and St. James's Park, for meetings with the new foreign secretary, Anthony Eden, and his predecessor, Lord Halifax, who was heading to Washington as ambassador. The building's richly decorated interiors spoke of imperial power, but wartime visitors also noticed the unlit corridors and the broken windows covered with black cloth. Hopkins was unimpressed with Eden, finding him "suave, impeccable, unimportant." "I gained the impression," he reported to FDR, "that Mr. Anthony Eden had little more to do with the prosecution of the war than the Supreme Court"— a conclusion that was a little unfair to the Court, given Justice Frankfurter's recent efforts. On the other hand, he found Halifax "a different and somewhat tougher breed . . . A tall stoop shouldered aristocrat with one hand in a gray glove" to hide an arm that was withered from birth. Hopkins briefed Halifax on the people he should meet in Washington but admitted that "when I got beyond the President and Hull I was in deep water and quit." Hopkins presumed Halifax was "a hopeless Tory—but that isn't important now if we can but get on with the business of licking Hitler." In fact, Halifax was not just a hopeless Tory: he was a hopeless appeaser, who was still open to treating with Hitler rather than licking him.[57]

After midday, Hopkins made his way to 10 Downing Street for lunch with Churchill. Brendan Bracken met him at the famous black door, with its lion's head knocker and brass letterbox. To Hopkins, the place seemed "a bit down at the heels," and no wonder. As the prime minister's residence was highly vulnerable to the Luftwaffe's bombs, many of the functions of government had been moved out of it and most of its rooms stripped of valuable paintings, furniture, and carpets. Most of the windows were out and workmen were everywhere repairing bomb damage. Churchill and his wife had also been shifted to safer accommodation in the Number 10 Annexe at Storey's Gate, located a few hundred yards away, above the underground Cabinet War Room. But the PM was allergic to the Annexe and preferred to continue using Number 10 during the day for working and dining.

Downstairs, the Garden Rooms had been buttressed with sturdy beams and pillars, and the windows were protected by steel shutters, producing an atmosphere likened to a ship's wardroom. Bracken led Hopkins to a small dining room on this level, gave him a glass of sherry, and left him to wait for Churchill.[58]

Hopkins's report of what happened next included just the kind of observations Roosevelt had relied on for years in order to form long-distance character judgments:

A rotund—smiling—red faced gentleman appeared—extended a fat but none the less convincing hand and wished me welcome to England. A short black coat—striped trousers—a clear eye and a mushy voice was the impression of England's leader as he showed me with obvious pride the photographs of his beautiful daughter-in-law and grandchild.[59]

Hopkins plainly liked the cut of Churchill's jib—and who can blame him? Churchill was at the very height of his prestige, lifted up by the half dozen magnificent speeches he had given over the summer, living in the precise moment toward which his whole life had thrust, sitting in the cockpit of the British Empire at its time of greatest peril. Churchill, too, was immediately attracted to Hopkins. "I soon comprehended his personal dynamism and the outstanding importance of his mission," he wrote later. "It was evident to me that here was an envoy from the President of supreme importance to our life." Churchill was known for making snap judgments of people (not all of them correct) based on a single "searching gaze." In this case, he had stronger evidence, namely the powerful message Hopkins had brought with him from Washington. "The President is determined that we shall win the war together," said the American. "Make no mistake about it. He has sent me here to tell you that at all costs and by all means he will carry you through, no matter what happens to him—there is nothing that he will not do so far as he has human power."[60]

Lunch was a simple affair of soup, cold beef, green salad, cheese, coffee, port, and wine, served by "a very plain woman who seemed to be an old family servant," with the host leaning over to put more jelly on his guest's plate. (The meal was not so simple that Churchill neglected to take snuff, from a small silver box.) Discussion centered on possible dates and locations for a summit meeting between Roosevelt and Churchill. The prime minister was just as keen as the president for a rendezvous, and "the sooner the better." Hopkins was able to put over the president's plans for Lend-Lease, and elicited a promise from Churchill to "make every detail of information and opinion available" to him to convince him of "the urgent necessity of the exact material assistance Britain requires to win this war." Hopkins also raised the perception in some quarters of Washington that Churchill was anti-American or hostile to Roosevelt. Churchill "denied it vigorously," launched "a bitter though fairly restrained attack on Ambassador Kennedy whom he believes is responsible for this impression," and sent a secretary to fetch a telegram he had sent FDR expressing "his warm delight at the

President's re-election." (To the PM's disquiet, Roosevelt had never acknowledged this telegram.)[61]

Churchill gave Hopkins the first of what would turn out to be many *tours d'horizon*, setting out his views on the likelihood of invasion (if it comes, he said, "we shall drive them out") and developments in the Mediterranean. The lecture concluded upstairs in the Cabinet Room in front of a healthy fire, with Churchill pointing out on his maps the routes taken by Britain's transatlantic convoys and Germany's bombers. The two men "were so impressed with each other," recorded one of the PM's private secretaries, John Colville, "that their tête-à-tête did not break up till nearly 4.00."[62]

"I have never had such an enjoyable time as I had with Mr. Churchill," Hopkins told the U.S. military attaché Brigadier General Lee shortly afterward, "but God, what a force that man has!" For his part, the prime minister felt he had at last established "a definite heart-to-heart contact with the President."[63]

The length of this contact caused Hopkins to be two hours late for press conferences he had scheduled with British and American reporters. He received the newsmen in the ambassador's office at the embassy, sitting behind Joe Kennedy's old desk, "tapping the arms of his chair and looking as though he might burst with secrets." He revealed nothing, however, beyond the fact that he was there "to discuss matters of mutual interest to our two countries." (One editor recalled that Hopkins "rewarded the zeal of one particularly determined questioner by agreeing, 'Yes, I think you can say urgent matters.'") The *New York Times* correspondent noted that Hopkins "managed to convey the impression that it would be a little unpatriotic for any one to pry too deeply." Reporters compared him to an "oyster" and a "clam." And yet they liked Hopkins; they were charmed even when he turned away their questions with a twisted little smile or a joke. The *Daily Herald* correspondent, noticing the way Hopkins's feet danced while he talked but surely also thinking of his deft media moves, imagined that he was Fred Astaire, starring in a movie called *President's Pal*.[64]

Hopkins was more forthcoming over dinner that evening with the broadcaster Edward R. Murrow. Hopkins had listened to Murrow's radio reports from London at the outbreak of war, as he lay in the Mayo Clinic fighting for his life. Now he summoned the correspondent to his room at Claridge's and spent hours interrogating him about British political figures. "I have come here to try to find a way to be a catalytic between two prima donnas," confided Hopkins. "I want to get a real understanding of Churchill and of the men whom he sees after midnight."[65]

THE PRESIDENT'S REPRESENTATIVE spent the weekend as Churchill's guest at Ditchley, a fine stately home in Oxfordshire that was regarded by the chiefs of staff as offering a safer haven from the attentions of the Luftwaffe than Chequers, the prime minister's official country residence. A few months earlier, Churchill had called Ditchley's owner, Ronald Tree, MP, to his rooms in the House of Commons. "Would it be possible for you to offer me accommodation at Ditchley for certain weekends when the moon is high?" he asked. Special telephones and equipment were soon installed, and on a dozen or so weekends in 1940–1942, when visibility was forecast to be clear, the prime minister and his entourage decamped to Ditchley. On a Friday afternoon, two detectives would arrive to search the premises, followed by a valet and a maid with the luggage, and a detachment of soldiers from the Oxfordshire and Buckinghamshire Light Infantry for guard duty. Then promptly at five o'clock, Tree recalled, the Churchills' caravan would arrive, "complete with secretaries, red dispatch-boxes, motor-cars and an antiquated armoured car which the Prime Minister much disliked, would not enter, and which, consequently, spent its weekend out of sight in the garage."[66]

Hopkins made it to Ditchley for lunch on Saturday, motoring along the double avenue of beech trees up to the main gates, passing through a wood and then along another avenue of elms, until the house itself appeared— Palladian in style and proportions, with a façade of golden stone topped by two lead figures, Loyalty and Fame. The trip had taken longer than expected, as the chauffeur had got lost in the countryside, which had been shorn of signposts at the first hint of invasion. The company at lunch was small, but Colville recorded that Hopkins's "quiet charm and dignity held the table." He assured Churchill that the Lend-Lease bill would pass despite opposition, and spoke warmly of the king and queen's North American tour in 1939. In the afternoon, Bracken took Hopkins for a visit to nearby Blenheim Palace, the ancestral home of the Churchills, where Winston was born and in the grounds of which, in a small lake house modeled on a Greek temple, he proposed marriage to Clementine. During the drive, Hopkins told him that Roosevelt "was resolved that [Britain] should have the means of survival and victory"—even if those means had to be taken from the U.S. armed forces.[67]

Dinner was served by candlelight, on a table dressed with a simple gilt setting. More guests had arrived, interested to meet this "mystery man" Harry Hopkins, including Churchill's scientific adviser Frederick "the Prof" Lindemann, who had driven up from Oxford in his old Rolls-Royce, and the president of the Board of Trade, businessman and MP Oliver Lyttelton. Two of England's most charming women, socialites Venetia Montagu and Freda Dudley Ward, mistress of Edward VIII, had also been invited for the weekend by Bracken, who knew that their liveliness would bring out the best in Churchill. Over dinner, the prime minister launched into one of his favorite themes, the need for greater intimacy between the United States and Britain. After the ladies withdrew, Hopkins complimented Churchill on his speeches of the previous year, revealing that FDR had brought a wireless set into the Cabinet Room in the White House so that everyone could listen to him. Churchill replied, a little too modestly, that he hardly knew what he said last summer, he only knew "it would be better for us to be destroyed than to see the triumph of such an imposter."[68]

Like an actor called back to the stage by an ovation, Churchill then delivered a "majestic monologue" on the origins and course of the war to date. When he turned to the future, he described Britain's postwar goals in a way that seemed calculated to appeal to his liberal visitor, one that rhymed with Roosevelt's Four Freedoms speech. "We seek no treasure," Churchill promised, "we seek no territorial gains, we seek only the right of man to be free; we seek his right to worship his God, to lead his life in his own way, secure from persecution. As the humble labourer returns from his work when the day is done, and sees the smoke curling upwards from his cottage home in the serene evening sky, we wish him to know that no rat-a-tat-tat"— and here Churchill rapped on the table—"of the secret police upon his door will disturb his leisure or interrupt his rest. We seek government with the consent of the people, man's freedom to say what he will, and when he thinks himself injured, to find himself equal in the eyes of the law. But war aims other than these we have none. What will the President say to all this?"[69]

Hopkins was silent for almost a minute, and when his reply finally came, one guest thought that its halting delivery formed "a remarkable contrast to the ceaseless flow of eloquence to which we had listened." Another guest described Hopkins's response:

> Exaggerating his American drawl, he said, "Well, Mr Prime Minister, I don't think the President will give a dam' for all that." Heavens alive, it's gone wrong, thought I. There was another pause, and then Harry said, "You see, we're only interested in seeing that that Goddam sonofabitch, Hitler, gets licked." There was loud laughter, and at that moment a friendship was cemented which no convulsion ever undermined.[70]

On Sunday, Hopkins got his first proper look at Churchill's weekend routine. While at Ditchley, Churchill would breakfast at nine o'clock or so, on bacon and eggs, toast and marmalade, and some leftovers from the previous night—a partridge, perhaps. The morning was spent in bed with his newspapers and dispatch boxes, an unlit cigar in his mouth and a secretary taking dictation. He would emerge in time for lunch, and linger over brandy in the dining room. In the afternoon, he might disappear with his private secretary into the Chinese Room, named for its chinoiserie wall decorations, or take a guest between the pair of large Venetian stone lions guarding the back door for a quick turn around the gardens. At five in the afternoon, Churchill would don an ankle-length nightgown and retire to his bed, with a hot-water bottle, for a nap. His guests would usually entertain themselves in Ditchley's magnificent hall, one of the grandest in all of England and furnished by the Trees with comfortable chairs. It may have been on this Sunday afternoon that militant teetotaler Lady Nancy Astor called to berate her niece, Ronald Tree's wife, Nancy, for exposing Hopkins to Churchill's bad habits. "How can you have that nice Sunday School teacher . . . together with that drinking Prime Minister in your house?" she demanded. "He'll go home with all the wrong impressions." It so happened that at that very moment, Hopkins was playing poker, with a large whiskey in his hand.[71]

Churchill was often grumpy at dinner, especially if the war news was poor—and that evening he learned that the light cruiser HMS *Southampton* had been destroyed by German dive bombers in the Mediterranean. As the night wore on and the brandy had its effect, however, Churchill "thawed out." At midnight that evening, the party was seated in a collection of scarlet leather armchairs grouped around one of the two fireplaces in Ditchley's library, an elegant room nearly fifty feet long, with bookshelves that went right up to the cornices. Smoking a "phenomenally large cigar," Churchill walked up and down in front of the fire and "sketched the whole history of the war," while Hopkins made the occasional comment and the other guests "sat and goggled." This was *tour d'horizon* as tour de force. Churchill's manner on these occasions, a contemporary recalled, was to "steep himself (and you) in gloom on some grim aspect of the war . . . only to proceed to 'fight his way out' until he is pacing the floor with the light of battle in his eyes." This particular evening, the battle finished at 2 a.m. and the party crept to bed. Before Lyttelton could fall asleep, however, Hopkins "slunk into his room and ensconced himself in a chair in front of the fire, muttering at intervals, 'Jesus Christ! What a man!'"[72]

ON TUESDAY, CHURCHILL AND HOPKINS left together for Scotland, in order to see off Lord Halifax, who was traveling to his post in the United

States on board the Royal Navy's new battleship HMS *King George V.* Both men were in contact with Roosevelt before they departed. Churchill telegraphed, "I am most grateful to you for sending so remarkable an envoy, who enjoys so high a measure of your intimacy and confidence."[73] Hopkins's message was longer but no less effusive. This was his first substantive report to FDR, written in longhand on Claridge's notepaper, for delivery to the president by U.S. military attaché Brigadier General Lee, who was traveling home with Halifax:

> The people here are amazing from Churchill down, and if courage alone can win—the result will be inevitable. But they need our help desperately, and I am sure you will permit nothing to stand in the way ... *Churchill* is the government in every sense of the word—he controls the grand strategy and often the details—labour trusts him—the army, navy, air force are behind him to a man. The politicians and upper crust pretend to like him. I cannot emphasize too strongly that he is the one and only person over here with whom you need to have a full meeting of minds ... I am convinced this meeting between you and Churchill is essential—and soon—for the battering continues and Hitler does not wait for Congress ... This island needs our help now, Mr. President, with everything we can give them.[74]

He concluded in more familiar terms: "the bombs aren't nice and seem to be quite impersonal ... a tin hat and gas mask have been delivered—the best I can say for the hat is that it looks worse than my own and doesn't fit—the gas mask I can't get on—so I am all right. There is much to tell but it will have to wait—for I must be off to Charing Cross."[75]

As it happened, the train for Scotland was leaving from King's Cross, not Charing Cross. An unkempt Hopkins arrived at the last possible minute, trailing ripe opinions about confusing British place names. Waiting for him were the prime minister and his wife, Clementine; the Halifaxes; Churchill's military assistant Major-General Sir Hastings "Pug" Ismay; his aide-de-camp Commander Charles "Tommy" Thompson; his private secretary John Martin;

and his personal physician, Sir Charles Wilson. Wilson had learned of the trip less than an hour earlier, and had tried to dissuade Churchill from taking it on the grounds of his bad cold. "What damned nonsense! Of course I am going," responded Churchill, throwing off his bedclothes. Furthermore, he declared, Wilson was coming, too. So it was that a miserable Wilson found himself heading to the frigid north without even a toothbrush, although the PM lent him a greatcoat with an astrakhan collar.[76]

When the party awoke the next morning, their train was stuck in Caithness in northern Scotland, "in the middle of a deserted heath, the ground white with snow and a blizzard howling at the windows." When they eventually made it to Thurso at Scotland's northern tip, they boarded an Australian destroyer, HMAS *Napier*, for the voyage to Scapa Flow, the vast natural harbor in the middle of the Orkney Islands that served as the principal anchorage of the Home Fleet. Visitors to the Orkneys at this time of year usually found "cold, stormy weather with a few hours of bleak daylight sandwiched between great slabs of darkness." But as the destroyer turned into the Flow on this occasion, Ismay recalled, "the sun broke through the clouds, and the first sight of the Home Fleet riding at anchor was inspiring." He wanted Hopkins to see this vision, but found him "disconsolate and shivering with cold in the wardroom," and not even the gift of an extra sweater and fur-lined flying boots could persuade him to take a brisk walk around the ship. Instead, Hopkins found a sheltered spot on the deck and sat down to rest his bones, only to be told by a chief petty officer that he was perched on a depth charge.[77]

After bidding farewell to Lord and Lady Halifax on *King George V*, the prime minister spent two days inspecting the fleet and the shore establishments while Hopkins remained bundled up in the captain's cabin of the flagship HMS *Nelson*. An embarrassing incident occurred when Churchill asked for a demonstration of a UP gun, an experimental rocket-propelled antiaircraft weapon that had been mounted on one of the *Nelson*'s turrets. One of the rocket projectiles got caught in the rigging, and a shell the size of a jam jar flew toward the bridge and landed with "a great bang" about five feet from where Hopkins was standing. He thought the incident was funny; the prime minister did not. With his cigar clenched tightly between his teeth, Churchill stared up at the mast and observed, "I think there is something not quite right about the way you are using this new weapon." On the day of departure, tempestuous seas made it difficult to effect a transfer from the admiral's barge to the destroyer that would take them back to Thurso. As Hopkins climbed aboard the destroyer, a rung of the ladder gave way beneath him; he would have fallen into the sea had he not been caught by the collar by two burly sailors. "I shouldn't stay there too long, Harry," Churchill commented helpfully, leaning over the rail and puffing on a large cigar as Hopkins hung on for his life. "When two ships are close together in a rough sea, you are liable to get hurt."[78]

The party stopped in Glasgow on January 17 on the way back to London and inspected the ranks of the city's civil defense workers, including Air Raid Precautions wardens, fire brigades, police, and members of the Red Cross and Women's Voluntary Service. Churchill made a point of introducing Hopkins to everyone as the president's personal representative, in order to impress the citizenry with the American's presence and impress the visitor with the British spirit. Stirring it may have been, but it was also tiring, and Hopkins soon fell behind and tried to hide in the crowd. As Ismay observed, though, no such escape was possible: "'Harry, Harry, where are you?' came the call; and poor Harry had to reappear."[79]

That evening, Harry Hopkins gave one of the few speeches of his mission. Those who heard it never forgot it. The Scottish Labour MP and civil defense commissioner Tom Johnston hosted a private dinner in the prime minister's honor at the North British Station Hotel, a stately railway hotel located on George Square. There, in room 21 overlooking the square, the visitors supped with the lord provost of Glasgow and one or two other local notables.[80]

After toasts to the king and the president, Johnston prevailed upon an exhausted Hopkins, whose face was white and drawn, to say a few words to the table. "Mr Chairman, I am not making speeches over here," said Hopkins. "I am reporting what I see to Mr Franklin Delano Roosevelt, my President, a great man, a very great man. But now that I am here and on my feet perhaps I might say in the language of the old book"—and here he paused, and looked straight down the table at Churchill—"Whither thou goest, I will go; and where thou lodgest, I will lodge: thy people shall be my people, and thy God my God." And then he lowered his voice and said, very quietly, "Even unto the end."[81]

Hopkins sat down in silence. Everyone in the room was moved. Churchill was in tears, just as he would weep afterward when retelling the story. "He knew what it meant," recalled the prime minister's doctor, Charles Wilson. "Even to us the words seemed like a rope thrown to a drowning man."[82]

THE CHURCHILL-HOPKINS roadshow concluded at Chequers that weekend. A handsome Tudor manor house of mellowed red brick, located in the Chiltern Hills about forty miles from London, Chequers was bequeathed to the nation in the early twentieth century to provide respite for prime ministers. Unless the moon was high, Churchill spent most of his weekends during the war at Chequers. He entertained there in style, once joking that the official Chequers entertainment allowance just about covered food and drink for the chauffeurs who brought his guests down for the weekend.[83]

If the hospitality at Chequers was warm, however, the house was not. Hopkins suffered greatly from the cold during the three weekends he spent there during this winter mission. The Great Hall, in which the guests spent much of their time, was poorly insulated and warmed only by a log fire and a couple of radiators. The central heating system was rudimentary. Hopkins usually refused to remove his overcoat in the house, and often repaired in it to the downstairs bathroom, which he found more temperate than the rest of the building, to read his official papers. Clementine Churchill, who had quickly grown fond of Hopkins, took great pains to warm his bedroom and supply him with hot soup. "She tried to temper the wind to the shorn lamb," recalled her daughter Mary. In return, Hopkins vowed that after the war the

U.S. government would install proper central heating at Chequers as a victory present.[84]

His service this particular weekend, however, was to facilitate a telephone call between the two leaders. After conversing with Roosevelt, Hopkins passed the receiver to a delighted Churchill, who began by saying, "Mr President—it's me—Winston speaking!" Very soon, it was reported, the two men were calling each other by their first names, and a few days later Hopkins told journalists that "in future Roosevelt and Churchill would probably be in regular telephone contact."[85] Apparently it was not only telephonic relations that were improved. Churchill later wrote of his Scotland trip with Hopkins, "I got to know this man—and to know about his Chief. Hopkins was about ten days with me, and in this time he put me into harmonious mental relations with the newly re-chosen Master of the great Republic."[86]

As Hopkins was weekending at Chequers, an intriguing piece of correspondence was winging its way to him by Clipper. On January 15, Roosevelt wrote to his envoy requesting that he inquire into a "tale that is told" of Joseph Kennedy making a large profit by selling Czech securities short just before the invasion of Czechoslovakia. "I hate to think of even the possibility of Joe having made a short sale of this kind while he was Ambassador and, therefore, in possession of confidential information," said FDR. "However, it must be looked into, and I suggest that you . . . try to run it down, and if necessary get the help of the British Government to discover the broker or brokers, if there were any. That should not be an impossible thing. I know of no other way in which this can be done, and I ask you to do it only because you happen to be in London."[87]

This is a remarkable piece of correspondence: a presidential direction to an unofficial emissary to ask a foreign government for assistance in investigating allegations of malfeasance by the man who until very recently had been accredited to it as ambassador. Kennedy had a reputation for questionable moneymaking activities. The Czech rumor came to FDR via Harold Ickes, who speculated in his diary that "if this can be nailed to Kennedy, we need have no fears of what he may do along the appeasement line" because the story "would utterly ruin him in public estimation."[88] This was information Roosevelt would undoubtedly have liked for the White House files in case Kennedy, who had flirted with the idea of opposing the president's re-election the previous year, now proved difficult on Lend-Lease. The speed with which he launched the Hopkins inquiry indicates he was anxious for an answer.[89]

Having asked for vinegar, Roosevelt also doled out honey, meeting with Kennedy the day after he wrote to Hopkins and showing a "very friendly" attitude. The president reported to the cabinet afterward that he thought "Kennedy would not go too far overboard," and he was right. Kennedy's two principal interventions in the Lend-Lease debate, a radio broadcast and testimony before the House Committee on Foreign Affairs, were less hostile to the idea of aid to Britain than had been anticipated, and he expressed confidence in President Roosevelt's management of U.S. foreign policy. Unfortunately, there is no trace of Hopkins's investigation into the matter of the Czech securities.[90]

HOPKINS RETURNED TO LONDON on Monday and continued his tasks of fact-finding and temperature-gauging. Over the next three weeks, he met with all the key British decision makers, talking to each of them in his direct, informal way, getting a sense of the country's prospects and its needs. He spoke with most of Churchill's ministers; all the relevant officials in the realms of production, shipping, and finance; the heads of the British military establishment; newspaper proprietors, industry leaders, intellectuals such as Harold Laski and John Maynard Keynes, foreign diplomats, crowned heads, and other leaders in exile. He got the broadest possible view of the situation. In fact, Hopkins felt his schedule was too crowded, complaining that the appointments secretary assigned to him by the embassy "let in all sorts of crackpots who had no business coming to see me." The press noticed the frenetic pace of this "pocket blitz of a man," christening him "Mr Harry (Hop, Skip and a Jump) Hopkins" and "Mr Harry-in-a-Hurry."[91]

All this activity took place against a dramatic setting. London wore the effects of war and Blitz much more plainly now. At Charing Cross, the statue of King Charles now rode his horse within "a corrugated iron container." Signs for air raid shelters were common. Printed notices in Westminster Abbey advised that in the event of an alert, "the Choir will leave the Abbey with all reverent speed and proceed to their posts of duty" as Air Raid Precautions officials. Rubble and craters left by air raids could be seen everywhere. The society photographer Cecil Beaton described a small dwelling with its front cut away like a doll's house, with a half-eaten meal on the table, pictures knocked off-kilter by the blast, and a staircase leading up to a floor that no longer existed.[92]

And yet there was a strange glamour to the city, too. "One felt oneself to be at the centre of big events," recalled one Londoner, as well as "a sense of pride in having provided the first check to the German menace." Big cars dashed about with mysterious letters on their license plates indicating their importance. Clothes rationing had not yet begun, so people looked stylish, and good food and drink was still available in restaurants. In the evening blackout, you could make out only dim forms in the street, but then a chink opened in a door and you entered a room full of light and gaiety. The presence of death enhanced the joie de vivre. When Hopkins was in London, a revival of J. M. Barrie's comedy Dear Brutus was showing in the West End. In one performance, the leading lady cocked her head and murmured, "I think I hear someone," only to have the wail of an air raid siren shatter the silence of the theater. The audience responded with cheers and laughter.[93]

Some of the same bonhomie was in the air when Lord Beaverbrook gave an off-the-record dinner for Hopkins at Claridge's, attended by London's most prominent media figures. The editor of the Daily Herald, Welshman Percy Cudlipp, recalled that the journalists present were beaten down by the Blitz but intensely curious about the guest of honor, who had made few public comments since arriving in Britain. After the meal, looking "lean, shy and untidy, grasping the back of his chair," Hopkins addressed the group.[94] His tour with the prime minister had shown him, he told his listeners (including a Foreign Office informant), "the fine spirit of the country . . . and the extraordinary hold which Mr Churchill exercised over all classes—a point which he said President Roosevelt did not thoroughly realise." Hopkins assured the audience that FDR was "determined 'to whip Hitler' and to this end would use to the utmost the vast powers he was acquiring by current legislation."[95] The FBI also had agents at Claridge's that evening, and its director, J. Edgar Hoover, reported to Roosevelt that the audience had found Hopkins's manner "very charming . . . very vigorous and dynamic." A *Sunday Times* columnist described Hopkins as "an American Hamlet . . . When he makes a speech he soliloquises—and to excellent effect."[96] Cudlipp drew a different Shakespearean analogy:

> His speech left us with the feeling that although America was not yet in the war, she was marching beside us, and that should we stumble she would see we did not fall. Above all, he convinced us that the President and the men about him blazed with faith in the future of Democracy . . . We went away content . . . we were happy men all; our confidence and our courage had been stimulated by a contact for which Shakespeare, in *Henry V*, had a phrase: "A little touch of Harry in the night."[97]

HOPKINS WAS BACK in the prime minister's hands on Friday, January 24, for a tour of the gun batteries at Dover that glared across the Channel. During the afternoon he heard one worker say to another, as Churchill passed by, "There goes the bloody British Empire." In the oak-paneled dining room at Chequers that night, Hopkins reported this exchange to its subject. Colville recalled, "Winston's face wreathed itself in smiles and, turning to me, he lisped, '*Very* nice.' I don't think anything has given him such pleasure for a long time." Churchill was in an expansive mood, declaring that Hitler's window for invading the United Kingdom had closed and that he now woke up in the mornings "as if he had a bottle of champagne inside him and glad that another day had come." Neither did he worry about being bombed, citing French statesman Raymond Poincaré: "I take refuge beneath the impenetrable arch of probability."[98]

Hopkins awoke on Saturday to "a cold, dreary morning" and a breakfast in bed of kidney and bacon, followed by prunes. He lay there for a while reading an "amazing document" Churchill had given him—a war cabinet document, printed on light green paper, containing the telegrams Churchill had sent his Middle East commander, Sir Archibald Wavell, during the initial phase of the Western Desert campaign in late 1940. Hopkins thrilled at the "boldness" and "daring" of the telegrams, in which Churchill encouraged and resupplied Wavell's forces even as Egypt was threatened by the Italians and Britain was bombarded by the Germans, and then urged them forward in their December counterattack in which they pushed the Italians back and pursued them into Libya. This was grand stuff. "Ask, and it shall be given to you; seek, and ye shall find; knock, and it shall be opened unto you," read part of a recent message.[99] At dinner that evening, Hopkins heard some Churchillian prose of a different order. If the Nazis ever invaded Britain, Churchill said, his speech would conclude simply, "The hour has come; kill the Hun."[100]

Sunday evening found the party in the Great Hall. The ladies had retired and brandy had been consumed. Sitting in a circle around the fireplace, with its great alabaster chimneypiece decorated with heraldic devices, were Hopkins; Colville; Lindemann; Churchill's brother, Jack; and Air Chief Marshal Sir Charles Portal. Meanwhile, the prime minister orated from the mantelpiece, "a cigar between his teeth, his hands in the armpits of his waistcoat," glaring at one or other of his guests as he made his points about the sins of his predecessors, the "Carthaginian peace" of Versailles, and the principles that should govern the postwar settlement. Finally, he "sat down heavily on the sofa, said he had talked too much, and asked Hopkins for his views." In reply, the American gave Churchill a lesson on the domestic constraints on the president. He sketched the different strains of U.S. public opinion but emphasized "the President's determination to send the maximum assistance at whatever risk."[101]

"The important element in the situation," a guest recalled Hopkins saying, "was the boldness of the President, who would lead opinion and not follow it, who was convinced that if England lost, America, too, would be encircled and beaten. He would use his powers if necessary; he would not scruple to interpret existing laws for the furtherance of his aim; he would make people gape with surprise, as the . . . Foreign Office must have gaped when it saw the terms of the Lease and Lend Bill. The boldness of the President was a striking factor in the situation. He did not want war, indeed he looked upon America as an arsenal which should provide the weapons for the conflict and not count the cost; but he would not shrink from war." Such a candid account of the position could only have been delivered in private, and by a presidential intimate. It did much to alleviate Churchill's lingering anxieties about FDR's steadfastness.[102]

Hopkins spent most of the following week passing intelligence between Washington and London. He updated the British on Roosevelt's thoughts about how the Lend-Lease bill was being received in the United States, and sent a stream of reports back to Washington.[103] He told FDR, for example, that his decision to sail out to sea on his yacht the *Potomac* to welcome Lord Halifax off HMS *King George V*, a radical departure from diplomatic convention, had been "received very warmly here," with "full accounts carried on the front page of all newspapers and repeatedly described in broadcasts."[104]

Hopkins was a perfect medium for communication between the two heads of government. He was less a catalytic than an adhesive, drawing them together, aligning their expectations, and coordinating their activities. On Wednesday, January 29, he saw the Canadian high commissioner, Vincent Massey, at the U.S. embassy. More important than his "advertised mission to report on the progress of the war," he told Massey, "was the task of helping Roosevelt and Churchill to understand each other's mind." Hopkins felt that "they didn't *really* understand each other and that there were inherent dangers in this. He was impressed with the similarity between the two leaders in temperament—their sense of history, their imaginative outlook, their feeling for the technique of things—in all of which there are virtues and dangers as well."[105]

Reporter Emrys Jones had an imaginative way of describing Hopkins's role. Churchill and Roosevelt had staged no spectacular meetings such as Hitler and Mussolini had at the Brenner Pass, he wrote in the *Daily Mail*. "Yet between the British Prime Minister and the President of the United States there is a Brenner, not a pass in the Alps, but a man—Harry Hopkins."[106]

In a series of dispatches, Hopkins laid out his central conclusions from his trip. "Your 'Naval Person,'" he telegraphed Roosevelt, using the code name Churchill employed in his correspondence with the president, "is not only the Prime Minister, but . . . the directing force behind the strategy and the conduct of the war in all of its essentials. He has an amazing hold on the people of Britain of all groups and classes." Even if an invasion occurred, Hopkins said, the "spirit and determination of these people is beyond praise and no matter how fierce the attack may be you can be sure it will be resisted, and resisted effectively." (In fact, Hitler had already made the crucial strategic decision to shelve the invasion of Britain and begin planning his invasion of the Soviet Union.)[107]

Along with the judgment that Britain could survive, Hopkins listed the "urgent ways in which we can help England immediately," including the provision of further obsolete destroyers; more merchant ships; B-17 bombers, PBY Catalinas, and other aircraft and assistance in ferrying them to Britain; flying training schools; and rifles and ammunition. "I hesitate to urge upon you matters about which I know you are already convinced, or to assume to advise one who has seen the needs here far clearer than anyone in America," Hopkins concluded. "I would not do it now but for the compelling conviction which the military men of England have impressed upon me. Decisive action now may mean the difference between victory and defeat. I feel sure that at no time in your administration have the actions which you have taken and the words that you have spoken meant so much to freedom as have the things that you have done and will do to defeat the dictators."[108]

On Thursday, January 30, Hopkins joined King George and Queen Elizabeth for lunch at Buckingham Palace. He had met them on their North American tour, at a tea party held on a sunny White House lawn, when he briefed them on the workings of the U.S. relief system. In private, the king was more talkative and well informed than his subjects might have guessed from his pained public performances. The small, dignified queen had charmed Hopkins in 1939 by allowing his young daughter Diana to see her in her state costume of white crinoline, jewelry, and tiara. "Oh, Daddy," Diana said to her father at the time, "I have seen the Fairy Queen." Now Hopkins got to see behind the famous façade of a building that had been bombed several times during the Blitz and was maintained in a spartan style befitting the wartime conditions. Many of the palace's rooms were closed; the central heating was turned down; windows were covered over by wooden boards if their panes had been shattered by bombs; a five-inch "Plimsoll line" was painted around the insides of palace bathtubs to indicate the maximum height to which they should be filled.[109]

Hopkins was led by a courtier and an equerry down "long, cold, narrow, windowless passages" into the royal presence. The king questioned Hopkins on his ministers and gave his own verdicts on them. The queen betrayed a little of the British dependence on the United States when she remarked "quite casually" to Hopkins that "she had written to Mrs Roosevelt three times and had no answers to any of her letters, but that she was going to be persistent and send a fourth." (Her husband ventured that "he was never quite able to understand" why Eleanor was always busy at press conferences and lectures, Hopkins recalled, but "added smilingly that he did not presume to criticize the ways of my country.") The queen told Hopkins an anecdote about attending a service at the little graystone St. James Episcopal Church in Hyde Park with the Roosevelt family, including FDR's mother, Sara, a lady with her own regal sense of self-importance. "It appears that the old lady dropped her Prayer Book over and over again and the Queen had to pick it up," noted Hopkins drily. "This was no sooner done than she would drop her handkerchief. Eventually the Prayer Book went over the bench and there was nothing further that could be done."[110]

As the threesome sat down to lunch the air raid alarm sounded, and as they had their coffee and port a bell in the palace rang, indicating that a roof spotter had sighted planes overhead. "That means we have got to go to the air raid shelter," said the king, and so with the guns "firing fairly briskly," the group "walked down two or three flights of stairs, through a dark hallway led by a guard," and "finally landed in a small lighted room with a table and chairs." The royal shelter, located in a deep cellar, contained a radio and telephone, boxes of snacks, an electric stove for brewing beverages, and some knitting to occupy the queen. They talked in the shelter for a further hour on Anglo-American relations, and Hopkins recorded that when he "emphasized the President's great determination to defeat Hitler, his deep conviction that Britain and America had a mutuality of interest in this respect, and that they could depend upon aid from America, they were both very deeply moved."[111]

ON THAT DAY IN WASHINGTON, the president celebrated his fifty-ninth birthday. In line with tradition, a series of "birthday balls" were held in Roosevelt's name at fancy hotels around the capital to raise funds for children crippled by polio. The theme of the balls, which were attended by more than fifteen thousand people, was "dance so that others may walk." Ordinary Washingtonians mingled with political notables and show business stars who had flown in for the occasion, including Lana Turner, Deanna Durbin, Maureen O'Hara, George Raft, and Benny Goodman. Eleanor stopped in at all the balls, pausing at the Wardman Park Hotel in Woodley Park to cut a six-layered birthday cake that was decorated with an American flag made of spun sugar and a picture of her husband.

As was his custom on his birthday, FDR dined at the White House with members of the so-called Cuff Links Gang. The original gang, consisting of a dozen or so old chums from Roosevelt's unsuccessful campaign for vice president in 1920, had grown to include other friends such as Henry Morgenthau, Sam Rosenman, Robert Sherwood, Steve Early, Missy LeHand, and Grace Tully, as well as Eleanor and a couple of her female friends. The president had given each member a pair of gold cuff links engraved with his own initials and those of the recipient. The annual meeting of the club comprised a dinner and, for the gentlemen, a friendly game of poker. On this particular occasion the host received a cable from another member in good standing—Harry Hopkins. "I wish I might be with you tonight," he wrote, but "as you are sitting down to dinner with the old friends I too will raise my glass and wish you long life and good health. Harry."

After dinner, the president delivered a nationally broadcast radio address from the oval-shaped Diplomatic Reception Room, in the presence of the Cuff Links Gang and the Hollywood stars. He did not mention his own two-decades-old paralysis, a struggle that had remade his life. He stated merely that he was pleased that "definite progress has been made in these past twenty years on a national scale in the fight against infantile paralysis." He gave thanks "for the rarest birthday present of all—the gift of your charity, the gift of your kindliness to each other and to the Nation." Even on this occasion, though, FDR could not ignore events in Europe: "I cannot say, as you can well understand, that this is for me a completely happy birthday. These are not completely happy days for any of us in the world." But at least American birthdays are happier than they might otherwise be, he commented, "because all of us are still living under a free people's philosophy." "We believe in and insist on," he affirmed, "the right of the helpless, the right of the weak, and the right of the crippled everywhere to play their part in life—and survive."[112]

HARRY HOPKINS'S MISSION to the United Kingdom was wrapping up. The day after his lunch at the palace, he took his final excursion outside London with the Churchills, this time to the south coast of England. Pausing on the steps of the Southampton Civic Centre, the prime minister cried, "Are we down-hearted?" A terrific reply of "No!" came back from the crowd. At the Portsmouth dockyard, the party was greeted by spontaneous cheering and Churchill was at his lovable best. He was introduced to some young survivors of HMS *Jervis Bay*, an old liner turned convoy escort that had recently been sunk in the North Atlantic in a famous action that won her captain a posthumous Victoria Cross. He stood talking to a dockworker with his arm around the man's shoulder; upon being asked for a souvenir, he gave him the cigar he was smoking. A gent in the crowd gave him the "thumbs-up" gesture and Churchill responded in kind; soon two hundred thumbs were in the air. He asked for three cheers for "the President of the United States" and received a deafening response. To the Portsmouth city council, meeting at a local hotel since its Guildhall was destroyed in a bombing raid, he pointed out "Mr Hopkins, the envoy and friend of President Roosevelt, that great statesman and friend of freedom and democracy."[113]

After dinner that night at Chequers, Hopkins produced a big box of American gramophone records. Churchill walked around the Great Hall, commenting on "what a remarkable thing that the two nations should be drawing so much together at this critical time" and "dancing *a passeul*, in time with the music." One guest recalled that they "all got a bit sentimental and Anglo-American, under the influence of the good dinner and the music."[114]

The following week, Hopkins's last in London, he sent through further reports to the White House; spoke by telephone with FDR and General George Marshall; was taken to lunch at Claridge's by the exiled Queen Wilhelmina of the Netherlands; and met several times with Anthony Eden, to whom he had warmed since their first encounter. Hopkins passed on to Roosevelt Eden's concern that the Japanese were preparing to move against British possessions in Asia and his hope that America could "find a way to accent [its] determination to prevent Japan from making further encroachments." Eden believed that a positive line from Washington "might make them pause." But Roosevelt was unwilling to risk a forceful response, for fear that it would rebound on the domestic Lend-Lease debate or divert U.S. naval resources from the conflict in the Atlantic.[115]

On Saturday, February 8, Hopkins said farewell to Churchill at Chequers. The two men spent some hours discussing a speech the prime minister was writing for broadcast the following evening, addressed principally to Americans. Hopkins was by now an intimate counselor to two serving heads of government. When he departed, Churchill gave him a gift of his autobiography, *My Early Life*, inscribed for Diana Hopkins, as well as a bottle of pink pills that he said he took regularly for their great recuperative properties. (A chemical analysis performed later in Washington indicated they could do neither much harm nor much good).[116]

Hopkins scrawled his feelings down on a piece of Chequers notepaper:

My dear Mr. Prime Minister:

I shall never forget these days with you—your supreme confidence and will to victory—Britain I have ever liked—I like it the more.

As I leave for America tonight I wish you great and good luck—confusion to your enemies—victory for Britain.

Ever so cordially,
Harry Hopkins.[117]

At 11 p.m., Hopkins boarded a special train at Princes Risborough station on the first leg of his journey home. His aircraft took off on Monday morning from Poole, the port at which he'd arrived a month earlier. "Nobody even knew Mr. Hopkins had gone until after he had climbed in a plane with no ceremony whatsoever," reported the *New York Times*. From Lisbon he caught the *Yankee Clipper* home, although he flew one leg of the trip in a U.S. Navy PBY flying boat when the Clipper was grounded by bad weather.[118]

This was certainly a more prosaic journey than it might have been. Churchill and the first lord of the admiralty had earlier discussed the possibility of sending Hopkins home in one of His Majesty's battleships, but Hopkins's insistence that no special arrangements be made for him scuttled the idea. Even so, the British were determined to ensure Hopkins's safe passage. When he decided to return to the United States via Clipper, the Admiralty assured Churchill that in the event of an emergency, a cruiser could be sent to Lisbon to pick him up within twenty-four hours.[119]

Other precautions were taken, too. The British authorities detailed a dashing Irish Guards officer to travel home with Hopkins and carry his secret papers in a sealed bag, as well as "to hold Mr Hopkins's hand and look after him" by taking care of hotels, tips, and the like.[120] Hopkins also asked Hull to ensure there were no German or Italian passengers on the Clipper. Given Hopkins's experiences in the United Kingdom and the documents he carried on his person, one London newspaper predicted he would be able to tell Roosevelt "more about Britain's war secrets than any other man outside the British Cabinet."[121]

The *Yankee Clipper* touched down on the choppy waters of Bowery Bay just after 8 a.m. on the morning of Sunday, February 16. (The Clipper was "not a bit rough," Hopkins said—it was "just like riding in a baby carriage.") Waiting for Hopkins at the Marine Air Terminal were Hopkins's son David, his friend Averell Harriman, a crowd of sightseers, and New York mayor Fiorello LaGuardia. Just before Hopkins stepped out onto the landing float, a giant B-24 bomber, bearing the insignia of the Royal Air Force and camouflaged in mottled gray-green, appeared over the field. This was the first of twenty-six such bombers being manufactured in San Diego for service in the RAF.[122]

Inside the terminal building, Hopkins gave a statement for the newsreels. "I have just got back from a mission for the President," he said. "In my four weeks in England I have seen their defenses, their fleet, their soldiers and their air force, and there is one thing I can say: I am convinced the British people are going to win this war. They need our help; they need it desperately; they need it now; and I am sure they are going to get it. They deserve to win." LaGuardia and Harriman then took him in the mayor's car to the Roosevelt Hotel in midtown Manhattan, for a meeting with Roosevelt's newly appointed ambassador to the United Kingdom, the former ILO director Gil Winant. After briefing Winant on what he had seen in Britain, Hopkins caught the 3:30 p.m. train for Washington. Newsmen at Union Station later that evening reported that a "pouch-eyed, gaunt, battered" Hopkins climbed out of a parlor car with a "bulging black briefcase" and into a government limousine for the final leg of his journey. Back at the White House, he stayed up talking with FDR until 2 a.m. Hopkins no doubt gave his chief the same message he gave to his colleagues at the Roosevelt Hotel: Britain's prospects were good and her spirit was tremendous—but so were her needs and her expectations.[123]

The conference resumed first thing the next morning, and in the afternoon the secretaries of war, navy, treasury, and agriculture and the budget director were called to the White House to hear from Hopkins. "They are taking time by the forelock," press secretary Steve Early told reporters. "When the Lend-Lease Bill passes, many of the administrative requirements will be set and ready." On the same day, Henry Luce published his famous essay "The American Century" in *Life* magazine, calling on Americans to intervene in the war and assume global leadership responsibilities.[124]

In the weeks that followed, Hopkins communicated his sense of urgency about aid to the British throughout Washington. Lord Halifax, now ensconced in the British embassy in Washington, recorded that Hopkins's mission had been "very constructive."[125] The envoy visited the War Department to provide a rousing briefing to senior officers on Britain's immediate military needs and her defense preparations. Henry Stimson was initially concerned that Hopkins, who had been "living very close" to British leaders, had imbibed their "undue optimism," but a week later he concluded, "It is a Godsend that he should be at the White House and that the President should have sent him to Great Britain where he has gotten on such intimate terms with the people there."[126]

GODSEND OR NOT, the Hopkins mission was a success. In a very brief period, the president's envoy earned the trust and affection, indeed admiration, of the prime minister. "My father wanted to like him, wanted to get on with him, it was vital to the progress of the war," admitted Churchill's daughter Mary. "But at the same time it was perfectly obvious that the chemistry was right between them."[127] This chemistry transformed the nature of the relationship between the two heads of government, persuading each of the other's reliability.[128] Very soon, notes Waldo Heinrichs, "the two were exchanging messages briskly, Churchill usually seeking and Roosevelt occasionally providing."[129]

The principals themselves testified to this success. On January 28, the prime minister cabled the president, "It has been a great pleasure to me to make friends with Hopkins, who has been a great comfort and encouragement to everyone he has met. One can easily see why he is so close to you."[130] As for Roosevelt, we have Ickes's account of a cabinet meeting on February 7:

> The President started off by handing himself large bouquets for having sent Harry Hopkins to London . . . He wanted us to know that he had worked it out in his mind that his friend from Iowa was just the right kind of human being who would make the greatest impression on Winston Churchill, son of a duke, English gentleman, etc. And, according to the President, the deeply laid plot had worked out even better than he had anticipated. Apparently the first thing that Churchill asks for when he gets awake in the morning is Harry Hopkins, and Harry is the last one whom he sees at night.[131]

Ickes could not resist adding his own acidic caveat, however: "I suspect that if, as his personal representative, the President should send to London a man with the bubonic plague, Churchill would, nevertheless, see a good deal of him."[132]

If Hopkins was able to channel his master's voice during his mission, he was also the president's eyes and ears, traveling the length and breadth of the British Isles to collect information and providing timely and persuasive reports of all he had seen to Roosevelt. These reports confirmed that FDR's gamble on the British had been a prudent one—and that he would need to double down in the future. Although Hopkins went out of his way to shun publicity, the British public was well aware of his presence, not least because of Churchill's habit of introducing him to crowds. The effect was to bolster the British spirit without implicating Roosevelt directly and opening him to domestic criticism. This allowed FDR to play different tunes to different audiences—just as Eleanor's role at home enabled him to keep his liberal constituency on board even when the administration was moving too slowly for liberal tastes. Roosevelt was undoubtedly delighted for the British to play up the visit's significance while he played it down.

Hopkins certainly had a great effect on the Britons he met. In Herschel Johnson's evocative phrase, the envoy "acted on the British like a galvanic needle."[133]

Some back in Washington believed that Hopkins became a yes-man for the British. "We can't take seriously requests that come late in the evening over a bottle of port," said one military officer. Clearly the British were alive to the fact that Hopkins's visit might, as one official noted, "prove of greatest value to ourselves."[134] Churchill deliberately courted Hopkins,[135] and other officials sought to bring him into the British camp through the payment of special courtesies.[136] Yet Hopkins was shrewd enough to identify flattery and blandishments.[137] His behavior throughout the mission was consistent with his devotion to Franklin Roosevelt. He kept his head down in public and in no way embarrassed his boss. He made no commitments on Roosevelt's behalf or forced his hand on any issue. The reports that Hopkins sent home were pro-British but accurate and insightful. No doubt he was affected emotionally by the situation in Britain, the exhilaration of being an envoy, and the force of Churchill's character.[138] But hero worship was not Hopkins's style; indeed, close observers testify that part of his appeal to Churchill lay in his willingness to speak the truth, no matter how unpleasant.[139]

Hopkins performed his task as personal representative in precisely the manner the president wanted. Roosevelt had decided to provide massive support to the United Kingdom and he sent Hopkins over there in that spirit.

He was kept fully informed of Hopkins's activities in Britain and the company he was keeping by the press coverage and Hopkins's cables, and he was delighted by the intimacy that developed between Churchill and Hopkins.[140]

Harry Hopkins's first foreign mission for the president had been a great success. Other, more dangerous missions would soon follow.

4.

"Sail On, Oh Ship of State!"

WENDELL WILLKIE IN LONDON AND DUBLIN,

JANUARY—FEBRUARY 1941

W hile Harry Hopkins was swanning around Britain, Franklin Roosevelt was fighting his latest set-piece battle against isolationist forces. Weakened by their defeat on selective service and discombobulated by the shift in national sentiment toward aiding Britain, they were nevertheless determined to resist Lend-Lease. If anything, their recent setbacks made them more shrill, determined, and dangerous.

"None of the leading isolationists approved dictatorship by Hitler in Germany or by Mussolini in Italy," cautions historian Wayne Cole. But by the time of the Lend-Lease fight, "many of them believed that Roosevelt was more of a danger to democracy within the United States than either Hitler or Mussolini was." With Lend-Lease, Roosevelt fed their darkest fears. He proposed sending mind-boggling quantities of American arms to a country they did not trust and that could not pay, while making the counterintuitive claim that this was the best way to avoid war. The *Chicago Daily Tribune* called Lend-Lease "the war dictatorship bill." The new isolationist pressure group America First, led by Bill Donovan's hunting partner General Wood, promised to oppose the bill "with all the vigor it can exert." FDR joked privately to an intimate that it might make sense to intern America First's leaders on "Nantucket . . . for the duration."[1]

Most Republican leaders were livid about the bill. "Lending war equipment is a good deal like lending chewing gum," said one senator, not unreasonably. "You don't want it back." Other Republicans referred to Lend-Lease as a "Fascist" initiative, and claimed it "would bring an end to free government in the United States." Opposition was not wholly partisan, of course: many progressives from America's western states were just as isolationist as the extreme conservatives. It was a Democratic senator, Burton Wheeler of Montana, who infamously labeled Lend-Lease "the New Deal's triple A foreign policy; it will plow under every fourth American boy." Roosevelt told reporters this was "the most untruthful . . . the most dastardly, unpatriotic thing that has ever been said."[2]

Still, the strongest opposition came from the Grand Old Party. And when it came to winning over (or at least neutralizing) Republicans, Roosevelt had an unlikely ally—his opponent in the 1940 presidential election, Wendell Lewis Willkie. Willkie was one of the most appealing figures of twentieth-century American public life. One of his supporters said he had the "personality to charm a bird from a tree—if he wanted to." Another described him as a "great hulk of a man, with attractively shaggy hair, a booming voice, and a genial homespun manner."[3] Broad-shouldered and broad-minded, Willkie made a remarkable journey from registered Democrat to the Republican Party's presidential nominee in less than a year. A few months later, he followed it up with another remarkable journey.

WENDELL WILLKIE was born on February 18, 1892, in Elwood, Indiana. The recent discovery of natural gas in the area had made Elwood a boomtown with all the usual accoutrements, including a sevenfold increase in its citizens and forty poolrooms and forty brothels for their pleasure. Herman and Henrietta Willkie and their six children, however, were ornaments to the town, expressions of the ideals of self-improvement and community service. All four of Willkie's grandparents had left autocratic Germany for America in search of freedom. Herman was a person of great integrity and kindness, a schoolmaster and superintendent of schools who became Elwood's leading trial lawyer. A liberal and a Democrat, who mainly represented workers and labor unions, he read aloud to his children for an hour each night from the family library of six thousand books. Years later, when Wendell was famous, a childhood friend would remind him, "Don't get too cocky. Your father was twice as big a man as you are." And Wendell would reply, "I know it."

Henrietta was a more remote figure to her children, but she was no less impressive than her husband. The first woman admitted to the Indiana bar and reputedly the first woman in Elwood to smoke cigarettes, she painted china, learned foreign languages, and practiced law; until her death in 1940 she read widely and wore French heels. To Wendell, she passed on her perpetual energy and ambition. The epitaph chosen by the Willkie sons for their father was, "He dedicated his life to his children"; that for their mother, "A woman driven by indomitable will."[4]

Willkie and his siblings led an idyllic existence as children, flying kites and visiting swimming holes, building wigwams and huts, hiking around the countryside, and boating on local rivers. After an undistinguished first year at high school, however, his parents packed him off to Culver Military Academy summer camp to straighten out his character and his posture. But it was probably less Culver's military discipline than the arrival of an inspirational teacher at Elwood High that turned Willkie around, and soon he was captain of the debate team. At the same time, his questing personality began to emerge. His summer jobs included working in the local tin plate factory, where the intense heat could scorch and curl shoe leather; running a tent hotel in South Dakota; cutting hay on a Montana ranch; and driving a tourist stagecoach in Yellowstone National Park (he flipped the stage on his first outing and was promptly fired).

At Indiana University, he acquired a reputation as a turtleneck-wearing radical who campaigned against inheritances and fraternities, although he later joined one at the insistence of a girlfriend who thought he needed some polish. After graduation, he spent a period as a popular schoolteacher in Coffeyville, Kansas, and a chemist in Puerto Rico, before returning to Bloomington to complete his law degree. The young Democrat finished at the top of his class and delivered a sensational oration at his graduation ceremony, criticizing the law school's teaching methods and calling for tougher regulations on Indiana's businesses. Wendell Willkie always made an impression.[5]

Willkie enlisted in the U.S. Army on the same day that President Woodrow Wilson asked Congress for a declaration of war against Germany. At the artillery school in Fort Sill, Oklahoma, he displayed his fearlessness by jumping out of a hot-air balloon with a parachute (but without any training) in order to win a fifty-dollar wager. In September 1918, Lieutenant Willkie sailed for Europe, leaving behind his new wife, Edith, a small, shy librarian. Unlike Bill Donovan, however, Willkie had no chance to be a hero. Shortly after his regiment arrived in France, the war ended, leaving him to cool his heels defending enlisted men who were being court-martialed for violations of the military code, especially for going AWOL. Back in the United States after being discharged, he flirted with politics but instead returned to the law, working at the Firestone Tire and Rubber Company in Akron, Ohio, and then in private practice.

Willkie's big career move came in 1929, just weeks before the stock market crash, when he moved his young family to New York City to take up a position as counsel to the giant Commonwealth & Southern utilities holding company. Through its operating companies, C&S provided electric power to six million Americans, principally in the Midwest and Southeast. Like Harry Hopkins, Willkie thought that New York was "the most exciting, stimulating, satisfying spot in the world . . . I wouldn't live anywhere else."

He prospered in New York and at C&S, and he was appointed president of the corporation in 1933, only five weeks before Franklin Roosevelt was inaugurated president of the United States. Most of Willkie's energies over the rest of the decade went into fighting high-profile battles with Roosevelt's administration over the activities of New Deal regulators and the operation of the Tennessee Valley Authority (TVA) public power project, which threatened C&S's position in the south. The battle concluded in 1939, when the TVA purchased most of C&S's Tennessee Valley properties.[6]

Willkie's rising prominence led to suggestions that he was presidential timber. In February 1939, Arthur Krock mentioned him as a possible candidate in the 1940 election, albeit "the darkest horse in the stable." The C&S president stepped up his public appearances and began hinting that he might run, and plotting how he would do so with *Fortune* managing editor Russell Davenport and others. In late 1939, expecting that Roosevelt would stand for reelection under the Democratic banner, Willkie quietly changed his registration to Republican.

The GOP had reasons to be hopeful about the 1940 election, given the ten million unemployed, the $36 billion of national debt, and the general unease about the prospect of FDR defying convention to run for a third term. The three leading candidates to take him on were Thomas E. Dewey, New York's racket-busting, mustachioed young district attorney; Senator Arthur H. Vandenberg of Michigan, a perennial favorite with a verbose manner and a magnificent comb-over; and Ohio senator Robert A. Taft, the son of a president and the most conservative candidate in the mix. Next to these men, Willkie's vulnerabilities were obvious. He had no money, no program, and no organization. His aides were not professional politicians but novices who had thrown in their jobs to work for him. As a supporter of much of the New Deal, he was outside the Republican mainstream. Perhaps most damaging of all, he was known to have voted for the hated FDR in 1932, and even contributed $150 to his campaign. This was a lot for the Grand Old Party to swallow.[7]

On the other hand, Willkie had three significant advantages. The first was his personality. In the words of investment banker Thomas W. Lamont, "Mr. Willkie is *sui generis.*" At six foot one and 220 pounds, he stood out in any gathering like "a buffalo bill in a herd of cattle," said the *New York Herald Tribune.* A "four-puff chainsmoker," he averaged three packs of Camels a day but could go through six "in a tough speech-writing session." He neither drove an automobile nor wore a watch, which added to the cloud of chaos that hung about him. He loved a yarn, and would drape his arm over another man's shoulder while he talked to him. The editor of the *Jackson Citizen Patriot* in Michigan wrote that Willkie was "as approachable as a Pullman porter, as democratic as a candidate for sheriff." He lacked Roosevelt's subtlety, but he had none of his deviousness either. In spirit, he was bold, energetic, and generous.[8]

This personal dynamism created Willkie's second advantage: the enthusiasm of his supporters, especially the young people who collected petitions and formed Willkie Clubs all around the country, and the publishers who championed his cause in their newspapers and magazines.[9]

But Willkie's biggest advantage was the course of events. Vandenberg and Taft were isolationists in principle; at this point in his career, Dewey was one in practice. Only Willkie had clearly identified Hitler as a threat to American security and urged the dispatch of military aid to the Allies. When Willkie formally declared his candidacy in June 1940, Hitler's armies were on the march in Europe. Ten days later the French surrendered, and the Willkie boomlet became a boom. At the Republican convention in steamy Philadelphia at the end of the month, the galleries were full of fans chanting, "We want Willkie!" and delegates were inundated with hundreds of thousands of telegrams demanding his nomination—which he won, against all odds, well after midnight, on the sixth ballot. The result was astounding, not least for U.S. foreign policy. "Isolationists, riding high, wide and handsome, were set to make an issue of the Administration's policy abroad," wrote the columnist Raymond Clapper. In Willkie's acceptance speech, however, "he rewrote the Republican platform into a frank support of the Administration course."[10]

The general election failed to live up to the hype, however. The candidate whistled around the country in his twelve-car "Willkie Special," enthusing his supporters but never arriving at a unifying theme. The disorder of his campaign, which was riven by jealousies and rivalries, raised questions about his managerial capacities. (The train was soon dubbed by its passengers the "Organized Chaos.") Meanwhile, Roosevelt did his best to ignore him, refusing to mention him by name and disdaining campaign tours in favor of "inspection tours" of defense facilities, like the one he took to New England in August with Bill Donovan. For the most part, Willkie stuck to his internationalist principles, supporting aid to Britain and the draft. However, as his prospects dimmed, he warned that a Democratic victory would carry the United States into the war—a deviation that he later regretted and vowed never to repeat. On November 5, Willkie received more popular votes than any previous Republican candidate for president, but five million fewer than Roosevelt. The New Deal coalition—the South, the big cities, blue-collar workers, and the poor—had held. In alarming times, with bombs falling on British cities, Americans had stuck with what they knew. "The same factors that had compelled his nomination worked against his election," concluded Willkie's biographer Steve Neal. "FDR was the political beneficiary of the worsening international situation."[11]

IN MID-NOVEMBER, Wendell and Edith Willkie decamped to a winter cottage on Jupiter Island in Hobe Sound, Florida, for a six-week vacation. Willkie had countless career options before him, including lawyer, college president, company director, and columnist. But when he returned to New York in the first week of January 1941, he decided instead to plunge right back into politics in support of aid to Britain, specifically Roosevelt's new Lend-Lease concept. Most leading Republicans, including Willkie's closest rivals for the 1940 nomination and the two previous GOP nominees, opposed the Lend-Lease bill. However, on January 12, two days after its introduction to Congress, Willkie summoned reporters to his political headquarters at the Commodore Hotel on 42nd Street and Lexington Avenue and announced he would support its passage with only a few modifications.[12]

"Appeasers, isolationists or lip-service friends of Britain will seek to sabotage the program for aid to Britain behind the screen of opposition to this bill," he said. Willkie's message to Americans was very different. "Much as we would like to withdraw within ourselves," he warned, "we cannot. We cannot be indifferent to what happens in Europe. We cannot forget the fighting men of Britain. They are defending our liberty as well as theirs. If they are permitted to fail I say to you quite deliberately that I do not believe liberty can survive here . . . America will not stay out of the war merely by persons asserting bravely in speeches that she will not go into the war. We will however stay out of the war, in my judgment, if the men of Britain are supported to the utmost and immediately."[13]

At his Commodore Hotel press conference, Willkie declared that he would visit the United Kingdom to witness the conditions firsthand and get a perspective on the Lend-Lease issue and other problems that would confront the United States "while democracy is under attack." Willkie said the notion had come to him while he was writing a magazine article on U.S. foreign policy. "I put down a statement about Great Britain. Then I thought, how do I know that? The idea popped into my head, why not go to the source? Why not go to England and find out?" Mrs. Willkie had been "a good sport about it," he reported.[14]

Willkie's mistress and confidante, the *New York Herald Tribune*'s book editor Irita Van Doren, was also a good sport about the trip; indeed, she may have been involved in its genesis. Van Doren, a gracious and intelligent divorcée with a soft southern accent, captivated Willkie when they met in 1937. As their affair deepened, she lent him intellectual breadth, guiding his reading, polishing his articles and speeches, and introducing him to important figures on the New York literary scene. Rumors about their relationship threatened to spike Willkie's chances in 1940, and FDR speculated privately to an aide, "Awful nice gal, writes for the magazine and so forth and so on, a book reviewer. But nevertheless, there is the *fact*."[15] In the end, however, the story never broke.

On New Year's Day 1941, the ubiquitous Felix Frankfurter, who had a passing acquaintance with Willkie, had entered the picture. Frankfurter and the liberal publishing figure Harold Guinzburg suggested to Van Doren that Willkie could "profitably make a trip to England as a means of putting himself in a position to reply, on the basis of first-hand knowledge, to the Republican isolationists who are ganging up on him." Apparently she passed this idea to Willkie, or perhaps he had already thought of it himself, or perhaps it had occurred to him when he heard of Harry Hopkins's London mission. Regardless of its origins, however, the trip's purpose was to arm Willkie against isolationist criticism and enable him to prosecute the cause of aid to Britain. Willkie's view on the European conflict was already set, which is why he resisted suggestions that he should visit France, Germany, and Italy as well as England.[16] He was going to London on a "selling job," he told an acquaintance, "not to educate himself."[17]

The reactions to Willkie's announcement showed that Republicans needed a lot of selling. Senator Robert Taft stated that Willkie no longer spoke for Republicans; the *Chicago Daily Tribune* tried to read him out of the party. "If Mr. Willkie had revealed his position before the Republican convention he would never have been nominated," said the 1936 presidential candidate, former Kansas governor Alf Landon. "Out of the 190-odd Republican members of the House and Senate," another GOP leader estimated, "Willkie couldn't dig up ten friends if his life depended upon it."[18] One of Willkie's most influential backers, the diminutive press baron Roy Howard of the Scripps-Howard newspaper chain, told him he had missed "the biggest chance of his life." Howard said he now saw that "all the time and effort I have spent on helping you has been wasted," and warned him that his papers were going to "tear your reputation to shreds." "If Howard wasn't such a little pipsqueak," Willkie told a dinner party at Van Doren's Upper West Side apartment later, "I'd have felt like knocking him down."[19]

Administration officials were much more supportive. Henry Stimson thought his fellow Republican was "rather a prima donna," but he was pleased by Willkie's choice of a Stimson intimate, retired New York investment banker Landon K. Thorne, as one of his traveling companions. After meeting with them the night before Willkie's announcement, the secretary of war concluded that the trip "offered a good opportunity to help keep him informed and straight on the situation," and arranged for briefing documents to be provided to the party.[20]

Cordell Hull also played an important role. Realizing after the election that Willkie was in a position "to either help or hamper our very difficult and delicate efforts," Hull had sought to keep him in the interventionist tent, even suggesting that the defeated candidate be shown incoming diplomatic cables about the European conflict "so he could judge for himself."[21] When Willkie telephoned Hull in January seeking permission to visit Britain (travel to belligerent countries being strictly limited), Hull secured FDR's approval and set about facilitating the trip, instructing passport authorities to assist Willkie and asking U.S. embassy officials in Lisbon and London to meet his plane and arrange his appointments.[22]

Hull passed on the details of the trip to Roosevelt, who invited Willkie to visit the White House en route to London.[23] Just prior to the meeting, Willkie's resolution wavered, and Thorne told Stimson that "Willkie is a little reluctant to meet the president for fear that it will give his trip abroad too much of an official appearance and deprive him of some standing as an independent observer."[24] However, Stimson's arguments prevailed, and a meeting was set for January 19, the day before FDR's third inauguration.

That morning, Willkie flew to the capital, but severe winds diverted his plane to the unfinished Washington National Airport at Gravelly Point. The new field lacked even basic ground transport facilities, so Willkie hitched a ride into town with a photographer who had driven out to take his picture. First he called on the secretary of state at his Washington residence, a seventh-floor suite at the swanky Carlton Hotel. When they made to leave after nearly two hours of discussions, they found the hotel lobby jammed by several hundred people, many of whom had heard that Willkie was in the building. The cheering crowd was so thick that hotel attendants had to clear a path for the two men; one woman shoved her way through and grabbed at Willkie's coat, shouting, "Bless his heart! Bless his heart!" Finally they made it outside, and Hull gave Willkie a ride two blocks south to the White House.[25]

Roosevelt and Willkie had known each other for some years, although they had not seen each other since 1937. The president liked Willkie, but the feeling was not mutual. Magnanimity is easier in victory, after all, than in defeat. When Willkie first met FDR early in his presidency, he cabled his wife, "Charm greatly exaggerated." After the election campaign, he told associates that Roosevelt was shallow, untrustworthy, and lacking a "moral sense."[26] No such animus was evident on this chilly January afternoon, however.

When Willkie arrived at the White House, Roosevelt was working on his inaugural address in the Cabinet Room with two speechwriters, Robert Sherwood and Sam Rosenman. The printers were waiting on the final text. FDR shifted into his wheelchair and started moving through his secretary's office into the Oval Office, where he would meet the man whom he had recently fought for possession of it. However, when he came to the door and looked into the handsome office with the presidential seal set into the ceiling and Hudson River prints on the walls, he paused. Turning his wheelchair around, he asked his aides to pass him some literature from the cabinet table. "Which particular papers do you want, Mr. President?" one asked. "Oh, it doesn't matter," replied FDR. "Just give me a handful to strew around on my desk so that I will look very busy when Willkie comes in." Shortly the Republican was ushered in, saying, "I won't be long—I know what it is to be interrupted while laboring on a speech." Roosevelt extended his hand and, playing his usual trick of addressing a visitor by his first name, said he was glad to see "Wendell."[27]

The two former rivals talked for half an hour about the European crisis and U.S. production schedules. Willkie reiterated that he supported Lend-Lease but favored three modifications: that the president's powers be returned at a certain date; that Congress retain more financial control; and that a study be undertaken to ensure all the new powers were strictly necessary. The discussion turned to Harry Hopkins's mission, and Willkie asked FDR why he kept Hopkins so close, given his unpopularity. "I can understand that you wonder why I need that half-man around me," replied Roosevelt. "But—some day you may well be sitting here where I am now as President of the United States. And when you are, you'll be looking at that door over there and knowing that practically everybody who walks through it wants something out of you. You'll learn what a lonely job this is, and you'll discover the need for somebody like Harry Hopkins, who asks for nothing except to serve you."[28]

In the course of the meeting, Roosevelt took a sheet of White House stationery and wrote a letter to Winston Churchill for delivery by his recent rival. It was addressed to "A Certain Naval Person" and the envelope was marked "Kindness of Honorable Wendell Willkie."[29] The letter, containing lines from Henry Wadsworth Longfellow's poem "The Building of the Ship," read as follows:

Dear Churchill

   Wendell Willkie will give you this—He is truly helping to keep politics out over here.
   I think this verse applies to your people as it does to us:

> *"Sail on, Oh Ship of State!*
> *Sail on, Oh Union strong and great.*
> *Humanity with all its fears,*
> *With all the hopes of future years,*
> *Is hanging breathless on thy fate."*

As ever yours
Franklin D. Roosevelt[30]

The meeting broke up with banter and laughter. FDR said he wished "Wendell" were going to be out on the frigid inaugural stand the following day instead of himself. Willkie replied that when he was in the middle of all the excitement in London, the president would once again want to change places with him. Someone observed later that given Willkie's fame, he needed a letter of introduction as much as Charles Lindbergh needed a letter of introduction when he made the first nonstop flight from New York to Paris in 1927. Nevertheless, Willkie was pleased and declared that the conference had been "delightful." Later that night he returned by train to New York, where he was due to have shots for typhoid and smallpox. This appointment also spared him the ordeal of attending Roosevelt's inauguration.[31]

"Roosevelt never made a more graceful or effective gesture" than writing the Longfellow letter, observed Robert Sherwood, and "none of us who were with him in the White House at the time had any idea how he happened to think of it."[32] It was the kind of diplomatic flourish, like his decision to sail out in person to greet Lord Halifax, for which Roosevelt had a particular gift. Willkie went to Europe for his own reasons. He was not sent there by FDR in the manner of Sumner Welles or Harry Hopkins. Nevertheless, by entrusting Willkie with a foreign mission—the delivery of a personal message of support to the British prime minister—Roosevelt turned his former opponent into an instrument of his diplomacy. Roosevelt was able to capitalize on Willkie's news value, which was substantially higher than Hopkins's, and send a symbolic message to the British people.

Roosevelt's gesture also promised to build bipartisan support within the United States for aid to Britain and, in the long term, a more expansive role for America in the world.[33] Roosevelt had already tried to bring Republicans on board by appointing Frank Knox and Henry Stimson to the cabinet and sending Bill Donovan to London. After he won the 1940 election, he resolved to reach out to Willkie, telling Labor Secretary Frances Perkins, "He is a very good fellow. He has lots of talent. I want to use him somehow. I want to offer him an important post in the government . . . I think it would be a good thing for the country, it would help us to a feeling of unity."[34]

The "important post" that Roosevelt hit on was that of de facto presidential envoy. Another guileful politician, Harold Ickes, saw the cleverness of the move. Entrusting Willkie with the Longfellow letter "created a good impression," he commented, and was "sound political strategy."[35] Ickes no doubt perceived Roosevelt's other motive: to further his own personal political agenda as well as the larger national interest. Bipartisan support for the administration's policies would likely translate into a strong electoral position. And what better way for FDR to demonstrate his mastery over the political scene than by getting his defeated opponent to run an errand for him?[36]

Naturally, Willkie bridled at suggestions he was Roosevelt's emissary and insisted he was his own man. He was "going to England as a private citizen," he stressed.[37] For reasons of personal pride and political viability, it was important that he be seen as an independent force, not a messenger boy for the man who had bested him. But the perception lingered.

IN BRITAIN, early news of the Willkie mission led to speculation in London about its purpose: "I think we ought to know more about this. Why is Mr Willkie coming here?" asked one Foreign Office mandarin.[38] The official presumption, though, was that in light of Willkie's stance on aid to Britain, and the dramatic White House meeting with FDR, "he should be accorded any facility and given a good welcome."[39] Herschel Johnson told the Foreign Office that after his visit to England, Willkie should prove to be a "tower of strength" to Roosevelt's policy of aiding Britain. The Nazi press drew the opposite conclusion, claiming that the Willkie mission showed that Americans didn't believe the British and wanted to "see everything with their own eyes."[40]

Winston Churchill was kept apprised of developments with Willkie's program, and sent a friendly telegram to the defeated presidential candidate at his Commodore Hotel headquarters.[41] Even Clementine Churchill weighed in on scheduling issues, suggesting that when Willkie and his companions came to Chequers for the weekend, it be left "a wholly man's party," without female distractions.[42] The prime minister approved the selection of a "sort of *aide de camp*" to Willkie, who could "fix up his appointments etc."[43] As usual, the suggestion had an ulterior motive. The man selected for the job, Thomas Brand, an aristocratic merchant banker who was now in government harness as part of the war effort, was also asked "to keep a close watch on Mr Willkie's reactions during his visit."[44]

As Willkie prepared to depart American shores, he was preceded by an avalanche of letters of introduction to the great and the good in London. "I think everybody in the United States gave me a letter to somebody," Willkie said with a chuckle to a reporter later. President Roosevelt's note to Churchill was one of four the prime minister received on Willkie's behalf.[45] Ministers, officials, and the governor of the Bank of England, Sir Montagu Norman, all received letters.[46] Introductions were not confined to official circles, either. Sympathizers suggested Willkie meet with educators such as the vice chancellor of Oxford and the master of Balliol College, John Maynard Keynes at Cambridge, and professors at the London School of Economics; cables were sent to churchmen, merchant bankers, diplomats, newspaper proprietors, and assorted personal friends among the British aristocracy.[47]

The authors of all these missives were no less distinguished than their recipients, including the actor Douglas Fairbanks Jr., publishers Helen Rogers Reid and Condé Nast, and banker Thomas Lamont of J.P. Morgan, who sent more than a dozen letters of introduction.[48] The tidal wave of correspondence demonstrates the reach of the well-educated, well-traveled northeasterners who had been laboring away for the cause of interventionism for some years, and now saw an opportunity to influence U.S. policy through Willkie's travels. It also reveals the strength of the web binding transatlantic elites together—a web that caught many of FDR's men when they landed in the United Kingdom.

———

AT 8:30 A.M. ON JANUARY 22, Wendell Willkie departed from LaGuardia on the flying boat *Yankee Clipper*, seen off by a crowd of three hundred.[49] It was an extraordinary moment. American political leaders of this era did not practice shuttle diplomacy. The last president to cross the Atlantic while in office was Woodrow Wilson; FDR himself had not even been in an aircraft since 1932. Now Wendell Willkie, only recently defeated for the presidency, was catching a plane, during wartime, to visit one of the belligerents.[50] For companions on this epic trip he had the banker Landon Thorne and the publisher of the *Minneapolis Star Journal*, John Cowles Jr. Willkie had invited them on a whim, and told reporters he had since been forced to turn down requests from "enough people to load down a ship." When a third escort, campaign aide Russell Davenport, canceled, Willkie had the spare outbound seat transferred to a ukulele-playing reporter from the Associated Press, Eddy Gilmore.[51]

Willkie was in fine fettle aboard the *Yankee Clipper*, chatting to the other passengers about the war and commenting that a "presidential campaign plus England in the space of twelve months is a lot in a man's life. I feel mine is as rich as any man alive." When he was not conversing, he read from a so-called knapsack book of verse like those carried by British soldiers, printed on India paper and containing everything from Matthew Arnold's "Dover Beach" to William Blake's "Proverbs of Hell." "If I felt any better," he told Gilmore as the flying boat landed in Bermuda, "I would be dangerous."[52] A reporter observed that Willkie's "eyes widened" at the RAF's flying-boat station on Darrell's Island in Bermuda's Great Sound when he spotted two thirteen-ton bombers refueling on their way to Britain. Standing beside them was a group of famous American flyers "lazily tossing pennies"—Bernt Balchen, the first man to fly over the South Pole; aerial showman Clyde "Upside-Down" Pangborn; and First World War ace, test pilot, and star of advertisements for Camel cigarettes Homer Berry. "Ferrying bombers is getting dull," said Berry, who was wearing the uniform of the Royal Canadian

Air Force. "I am joining a fighting unit soon." "Who says the world has no more adventures?" marveled Willkie to reporters.[53]

En route to Lisbon, a severe gale diverted the Clipper to the city of Horta in the Azores. Eddy Gilmore reported that "Willkie 'carried' this island of 20,000," many of whom were under the misapprehension that they were entertaining the president of the United States. "Not since the last big earthquake in the twenties has excitement run so high on this pinpoint in the Atlantic west of Portugal," he wrote. A delegation of locals told Willkie that the last American visitor had been Mark Twain, who thought Horta was "a good place to wear out old clothes." "Not to me," replied Willkie, who enthusiastically inspected local farms like a political candidate, even getting down into the mud to examine the livestock. "'I'm delighted to find Indian corn and Berkshire hogs like in Indiana.' The delegation was a bit hazy as to Indiana, but smiled its approval."[54]

Willkie had a smooth crossing to Lisbon, where he was met by the U.S. minister and a crowd of newspapermen, photographers, and curious onlookers, and taken to the Hotel Palácio in Estoril, a seaside resort a few miles down the coast. The Palácio was a gilded cage for all sorts of exotic birds, including refugees, exiled European royals, businessmen from Vichy France, and spies. British politician and diarist Henry "Chips" Channon stayed at the hotel at the same time and saw various "impoverished grandees . . . including Rothschilds down to their last two millions." As the number of Clipper berths was limited, the hotel was full of people who were marooned while waiting for their passages. When the Pan American representative entered the dining room at lunch or dinner, "he would be surrounded by a score of people anxiously enquiring what were their chances on the next flight."[55]

And everywhere, there were Germans. In January 1941, with Hitler's forces in the ascendant, neutral Portugal was listing away from its ancient alliance with Britain. The Anglo-American MP Ronald Tree also stopped in Portugal at this time and observed that "Lisbon was filled with Germans . . . wherever you went you saw groups of extremely affable young Germans making themselves agreeable to the Portuguese." Newsstands were plastered with German propaganda. "Everywhere there were pictures of healthy young Germans encased in the newest form of helmet, sitting on the latest form of tank, armoured car, or aeroplane, smilingly acknowledging the plaudits of the countries they had just overrun. We, on the other hand, had little or nothing to show: pictures of pre-war cricket matches and village greens were relied on to convey the British way of life, which looked to the Portuguese as if it were to disappear for ever."[56]

Willkie took in some of the sights of Lisbon, which included the baroque Queluz Palace, the Fronteira Palace with its magnificent magnolias, and the fine botanical gardens at Montserrat. He visited the National Assembly Palace to call on the dour Dr. Salazar, and met with newsmen at the U.S. legation, reiterating, "My position is for aid to Britain as against any form of appeasement."[57]

The following day, he was off again, headed for London on a BOAC plane. Willkie was in an "exuberant" mood during the seven-hour flight, pacing up and down the aircraft, even volunteering his assistance to the pilots in charting their course. He was so eager to see England that when the plane descended toward Filton airfield near Bristol, he stood up and fell in the aisle. Unhurt and unfazed, he picked himself up and brushed off his suit—the same one he had been wearing when he climbed aboard the *Yankee Clipper* in New York the previous week.[58]

WILLKIE STEPPED ONTO ENGLISH SOIL in the midafternoon of January 26. His appearance fulfilled expectations, thought the *Times*: "His necktie was awry, his famous unruly lock of black hair was straggling over his forehead, and as he shook hands he radiated a spirit of friendliness." The tie was a campaign special—"a blue four-in-hand with white stripes woven in such fashion that they spelled his name." He was met by the usual retinue of U.S. and British officials but was more interested in a bunch of American flyers he noticed on the tarmac. "Glad to meet you boys," he declared with a disarming grin. Over the roar of the aircraft, he told the newsreel reporters, "I feel fine. As a matter of fact I never felt better in my life. I am very glad to be in England, for whose cause I have the utmost sympathy." After twenty minutes on the ground, he flew to an airfield near London on Churchill's own de Havilland Flamingo, with its prominent RAF roundel on the side of the fuselage. In contrast to Hopkins's dramatic arrival, Willkie drove into the wartime capital in the gathering dusk during an "all quiet."[59]

Willkie's headquarters in London was the Dorchester Hotel. Constructed from steel and heavily reinforced concrete, it was thought to offer the safest lodgings in the city during the Blitz. Cecil Beaton laughed at the "mixed brew" who gathered at the Dorchester while the battery of antiaircraft guns across the road in Hyde Park roared away: "Cabinet ministers and their self-consciously respectable wives; hatchet-jawed, iron grey brigadiers; calf-like airmen off duty; tarts on duty; actresses (also); déclassé society people, cheap musicians and motor-car agents." It was, thought Chips Channon, "the modern wartime Babylon." Any of these types might be encountered, as well as royals and foreign diplomats, in a diverse array of dressing gowns and formal dress, in the luxurious shelter in the Dorchester's basement during an air raid. Beaton compared the scene during one such raid to "a transatlantic crossing in a luxury liner, with all the horrors of enforced jocularity and expensive squalor."[60] Willkie took a suite of three rooms on the first floor, which was protected from German bombs by the seven floors above it. He arrived to find an enormous quantity of fan mail and telegrams. Soon he would engage three secretaries and take an additional hotel room to cope with the correspondence and callers. The British were treating Willkie as if he were America's leader of the opposition.[61]

Willkie started his fact-finding the next morning, Monday, January 27, asking the chambermaid who served him tea in his room how the war was going. "Of course we're going to win," she replied, "but I think we'd like a little more help from America." Out on the sidewalk he talked to a traffic policeman and buttonholed a British private walking past with his arm in a sling. American newspapermen detected "typical British understatement" when the bemused soldier told Willkie the war was going "not so bad, sir." A few minutes later Willkie arrived at the Ministry of Information for a press conference, walking into a terrific reception. "Huge crowds jammed the courtyard," reported the *Chicago Daily Tribune*'s correspondent. "Girl typists gazed down on him from windows and balconies. Thirty photographers stalked his every movement." The three hundred British and foreign newspapermen received him with "four rounds of cheers and two hear-hears." Attendants cleared a path to the front of the proceedings, where Willkie told the reporters to "shoot" their questions, and "shoot them fast." The reporters responded like stockbrokers in a bourse. He told them he was in the country to find out about local conditions and what they would be "following your victory." Of the English people he had met so far, he declared, "I like their nerve."[62]

Over at the Foreign Office, he spent an hour with Anthony Eden. At first Eden was not a fan, writing that Willkie "has none of the charm of Hopkins." Whereas Hopkins was "quiet, subtle, with a sense of humour" and "speaks with all the added appeal of a man who appears not to want to," Eden noted that Willkie talked "with the healthy pleasure of a man who likes to hear his own voice." After Willkie had plied him with questions, however, Eden started to modify his opinion. On the other hand, Willkie remained unimpressed with the foreign secretary. "Your people must think up somebody better than that to succeed Churchill," he later told Lord Halifax. "We have an expression in the United States: 'You open the front door and find yourself in the alley.' "[63] As Eden showed Willkie out, they came upon a workman patching windows that had been broken in an air raid. Willkie strode up and started interrogating the man, who plainly had no idea who his questioner was. Eden recorded the exchange:

"How do you feel about this war?" "How d'yer mean?" Willkie persisted: "Want to go through with it?" The man looked at him quickly: "Hitler ain't dead yet, is he?" and turned back to his work. I could not have staged it as well.[64]

Next came a brief tour of the financial district around St. Paul's Cathedral, the City of London, which had been leveled by a heavy German raid in December. Eight churches designed by Sir Christopher Wren were destroyed in the firestorm that night. "We have known Ypres in the heart of London," wrote Cecil Beaton the morning after. Now police officers allowed Willkie through the barricades so he could pick his way over the debris and inspect the eviscerated Guildhall. Willkie was most affected by the ruins of Paternoster Row, a medieval street where monks once chanted the Lord's Prayer as they processed toward St. Paul's, and which had been a center of London's book trade. "I thought that the burning of Paternoster Row, the street where the books are published, was rather symbolic," he told reporters. "They have destroyed the place where the truth is told." By this stage Willkie was getting worked up. "Take me to your toughest shelters," he said. "I want to see the very worst ones you have got. I will talk to everyone who will talk to me—the people in the street, in the shelters, in the hotel, in the trains—everywhere."[65]

"Everywhere" began at 10 Downing Street, where he joined Winston and Clementine Churchill for lunch. Willkie was careful to explain that under the U.S. system, he held no position of responsibility and could state only his personal views. When Churchill lamented the fact that defeated presidential candidates were lost to politics, Willkie replied with equal geniality "as a loyal American in defense of our system, that perhaps ours had the advantage because the English had with them political figures always, while we had a convenient method of retiring them."[66] For the better part of two hours, over a meal of fish and eggs ("I hope we did not break any of the rationing rules," said Willkie later), they discussed the war and Anglo-American relations. "I knew he was a great man," Willkie told reporters afterward. "I know it now even more."[67]

In the course of the meeting, Willkie handed over Roosevelt's letter to the prime minister. Churchill was "deeply affected," remarked an aide, and "took this as an earnest" of the president's good intentions.[68] Churchill's telegram to Washington the following day reveals that FDR's message of support had found its mark. "I received Willkie yesterday," he wrote, "and was deeply moved by the verse of Longfellow's which you had quoted. I shall have it framed as a souvenir of these tremendous days, and as a mark of our friendly relations, which have been built up telegraphically but also telepathically under all the stresses."[69] In fact, Churchill was to do much more with Longfellow's verse than have it framed.

FOUR THOUSAND MILES AWAY from Downing Street, in Washington, D.C., secret staff conversations between senior U.S. and British military officers were commencing on the same day, on the same topics. In order not to excite controversy, the members of the visiting delegation wore civilian clothes and styled themselves as "technical advisers to the British Purchasing Commission." These discussions affirmed that if the United States were forced to enter the war, both she and Britain would pursue a "Germany first" strategy. They would concentrate their energies on controlling the Atlantic and defeating Germany, which represented the greatest threat to their security, while waging a war of attrition against Japan. These plans were contingent in nature, but they foreshadowed the grand strategy that would animate the Allies after Pearl Harbor.[70]

ON HIS SECOND DAY in London, Willkie returned to the City and visited Wren's greatest building, St. Paul's. The cathedral's high altar, its crypt, and much of its glass had been damaged in the December raid, but the rest of it remained whole. Willkie "climbed over great blocks of masonry littering the choir floor" and accepted, as a souvenir from the dean, a piece of an incendiary bomb that had landed on the great dome and burned itself out. As he stepped out of St. Paul's, the first air raid warning of the day sounded. Willkie "cocked an ear, smiled and said, 'Fine, that's just fine!'"[71]

Willkie also attended a debate in the Neo-Gothic House of Commons, during which a Labour member of parliament denounced the government for suppressing the communist newspaper the *Daily Worker*. No sooner had he taken his seat in the Distinguished Strangers' Gallery than the sirens shrieked a daylight alert; soon there was the "menacing hum of German planes overhead, anti-aircraft guns yapping and occasional bombs crumping down." Willkie thought this was "the most dramatic example of democracy at work any one could wish to see . . . here Britain is fighting a war for her life. Yet a free house meets and people can get up and denounce the administration, and while they are talking their country is being attacked from the air." He only narrowly managed to see this example of democracy at work, as he lacked the gas mask usually required for entry to the Palace of Westminster, and he had left his own First World War–vintage helmet back at the hotel. He was admitted on the ground that he was "a temporary resident of London." When Churchill heard of this, he immediately sent Willkie's party a package containing gas masks and steel helmets.[72]

The two men saw each other that evening, when Lord Beaverbrook hosted a dinner for Willkie at Claridge's that was very similar in tone and attendance to the one he had put on for Hopkins. Although both men could only be Americans, a columnist in the *Sunday Times* observed that "surely two men were never less alike." Willkie struck the writer, who wrote under the pseudonym Atticus, as "big, human, generous, and reassuring . . . Temperamentally and physically he is the kind of man you would like to have as a mountain guide or as a companion in the rough quarters of a seaside port. One feels that he could punch with the force of a heavyweight or be strangely gentle with a child. If that reads like an excursion into sentimentality I cannot help it. Mr Willkie is a romantic figure."[73]

On Wednesday, Willkie communed with the British left. In the morning, he had breakfast with the pacifist Vera Brittain and a chat with the socialist Harold Laski, who later told FDR he found Willkie "shrewd, very agreeable, and warm-hearted; but incredibly inexperienced in political argument."[74] Willkie then attended a meeting of the general council of the Trades Union Congress, the peak labor union organization, at its headquarters on Smith Square. He told its members about his own log-cabin origins—"I grew up in a tin-mill town in Indiana, and my father was the lawyer there for the local trade union"—and heard from them about the unity of the British war effort. "To know there is no dissentient voice among the five million workers represented by the TUC . . . that they are solidly behind the war effort . . . boy, I tell you, it was grand. I enjoyed one of the grandest meetings of my life." Like many other Americans, Willkie was discomfited by his exposure to the British class system, and he liked that these unionists—"a grand bunch of fellows"—were more interested in improving workers' standard of living than the kind of "theoretical socialism" he had heard from Laski.[75]

Willkie saw another side of the British left at lunchtime. He was dining with a businessman at the Savoy Hotel when he unwittingly got caught up in a Communist Party–inspired food demonstration. Food scarcity was a major issue in Britain, one that FDR would shortly move to address. On this occasion more than sixty well-dressed women, many of them in furs, some believed to be employed by the *Daily Worker*, entered the hotel lobby in twos and threes. In the dining room, they sat down at tables reserved for others and refused to move. At a signal, they unfurled banners featuring slogans such as "Omelettes for the rich, one egg a week for us" and "Ration the rich." A few of the women had to be dragged out by the good-tempered bobbies who were called to the scene.[76]

That evening, Willkie got his chance to visit London's air raid shelters. Hopkins also dropped in on public shelters on his mission, but his visits were unheralded; the first news of it came through on the ticker after he had left. Willkie's tour, by contrast, was announced in advance and described in detail afterward to scores of reporters. Over the course of three emotional hours, as German planes flew overhead, Willkie visited with Londoners in their underground refuges. It was as if he were campaigning again. In one shelter people got up from their beds to cheer him as he entered, and to sing along with a harmonica player who had struck up "The Star-Spangled Banner." At another, people shouted, "We are not down!" and "Send us all you've got!" A woman dashed up to show off her newborn baby. An elderly man told him he had been living in shelters for five months and would stay there forever if it helped to win the war: "We'll die before the Germans take this island." "When you get an old chap and the old fight like that," admitted Willkie, "I tell you, it gets to you." Another gent offered him coffee from his cup—which Willkie accepted, "smacking his lips, saying it was better than the coffee in his hotel." Nowhere did he hear a complaint. "I'm a pretty hardboiled egg, I think, but this moves me deeply," he said. "I am almost spilling over." As he stood in the midst of a calm, smiling crowd in one particularly deep shelter, he nearly wept. "I had to turn my head a couple of times."[77]

Willkie's British campaign continued the next day. In the morning he popped into the Old Chesterfield Arms, a pub near Shepherd Market in Mayfair, for a drink with the locals. He played a game of darts with a demolition squad worker for a pint of draft beer, and when he lost he also bought a round for a group of soldiers from the Royal Irish Rifles who were lounging about in their khaki uniforms. He flirted with the girl behind the bar, who cautioned that her husband was in the armed forces. "Fancy pulling that husband stuff on me!" Willkie retorted. Someone up the back shouted out, "If only the missus knew!" and quick as a flash Willkie replied, "What? Does your missus know when you go out?" As word of Willkie's presence spread, the pub filled up, and before long the American was behind the bar pulling, and drinking, beers. As he made to leave, the proprietor produced a bottle of champagne. "I was keeping this for Armistice Day, but your visit is as good as Armistice Day to us. Shall we split this now?" The two men pledged each other with the champagne, and the room cheered.[78]

After lunch, the lord chancellor gave Willkie a briefing on the operation of the British judicial system during wartime, and took him for a walk around the bomb-damaged Temple area of London, where the Inns of Court are located. Willkie visited the Middle Temple Hall and saw the remains of its elaborately carved wooden screen, before which Queen Elizabeth danced and Twelfth Night was first performed. It had been stoved in by a German bomb. In the ruins of the Inner Temple Hall, Willkie raised a glass of brandy from the cellars and proposed a toast "to the restoration of the Temple." Much of the afternoon was spent receiving briefings on naval matters at the Admiralty.[79]

Not everyone was an instant fan of Willkie. That evening, he hosted a cocktail party at the Dorchester that was attended by the Canadian high commissioner, Vincent Massey. When Massey had met with Hopkins, he found him "a quiet, unassuming, shrewd, and sensitive man." He was much less impressed with Willkie's glad-handing style. "His visit here seems like an extension of his election campaign and his sitting room at the Dorchester was like a campaign committee room—henchmen and secretaries running about while the Great Man shook hands with everyone," Massey diarized. "I tried to make conversation with my host but he shook me by the hand while he was . . . looking at others and I gave it up. Soon he retreated into his bedroom and left his guests for good."[80]

On Friday, Willkie traveled to Dover to inspect Britain's coastal defenses, only twenty miles from German-occupied France. Wearing his "white steel helmet at a jaunty angle," he inspected the big guns that had taken part in cross-Channel duels, and twice witnessed British antiaircraft batteries fire on a Dornier "flying pencil" bomber that had taken advantage of the miserable weather and low clouds to cross the coast. Back in London, he didn't even bother to change out of his muddy boots and clothes before speaking with journalists. "I think the Germans have got a tough job on if they try invasion around where I have been," he said. "I certainly would not like to be a German coming over."[81] That evening, Willkie received a cable from Washington inviting him to testify before the Senate Foreign Relations Committee on the Lend-Lease bill. The mission would have to be cut short.[82]

THE CONGRESSIONAL DEBATE on the bill was grinding along.[83] Two weeks of hearings had taken place before the House Foreign Affairs Committee, and the Senate Foreign Relations Committee had begun taking testimony. The administration's witnesses, including Cordell Hull, Frank Knox, Henry Stimson, and Henry Morgenthau, argued that an aggressive Germany threatened the United States and that British naval power was critical to the country's defense, especially in light of German penetration of the Western Hemisphere. The testimony of military leaders, including General Marshall and Admiral Stark, was particularly effective.

The opposition charged that Lend-Lease would turn the president into a dictator and entangle the United States in the European conflict. Colonel Lindbergh announced that he preferred "to see neither side win" and opposed all aid to Britain. For the second time that century, critics declared, the cunning British were looking to take America for a ride. Willkie's recent opponent Senator Robert Taft claimed the bill would "make Uncle Sam the best and biggest Santa Claus the world has ever seen." One Irish American congressman proposed a new, Anglophobic battle hymn to be sung to the tune of "God Bless America":

God save America from British rule:
Stand beside her and guide her
From the schemers who would make of her a fool.
From Lexington to Yorktown,
From blood-stained Valley Forge,
God save America
From a king named George.

From the outset, the administration was confident it had the votes to pass Lend-Lease: the Democratic majorities in the House and Senate made it a virtual certainty. But as Warren F. Kimball, the historian of Lend-Lease, argues, FDR had a broader ambition: to use the congressional debate as a means of achieving a public consensus in favor of his program of massive aid to the British. As he had foreseen, the discussions in the capital were replicated all over the country—in homes and churches, in Rotary Clubs and American Legion posts, on the radio and the letters pages of newspapers. As they listened to the arguments from both sides, growing numbers of Americans were persuaded by the merits of Lend-Lease.

Before Wendell Willkie could play any role in lifting those numbers further, he had hands to shake in Britain. He dropped in on the American Eagle Club in Charing Cross Road, a place where Americans serving in the British armed forces could get a hamburger or read a newspaper from home. Wishing them "all kinds of luck," he even posed for a photograph at the piano, purporting to play the popular song "Thanks Mister Roosevelt."[84] On the morning of Saturday, February 1, he hopped on a double-decker bus, earning the wrath of the female conductor when he didn't know how to pay his fare. "Now then, sir, either get on or get off," she snapped before recognizing her famous passenger. Willkie grinned, then moved from seat to seat, chatting to the Londoners on board. He made his way to Lambeth Walk, a working-class street in south London that had inspired the song of the same name, and which had suffered badly in the Blitz. Mobbed by locals, he autographed everything from tea packets to family photographs. When police attempted to intervene to protect him, he waved them away, telling them "everything's dandy." He went for a ride on someone's bicycle and enjoyed a cup of tea with a woman whose house had been reduced to a pile of rubble. Privately, the poverty of the district "struck him forcibly." His British aide Thomas Brand reported to his superiors that Willkie felt "the people in slum areas had no stake in the country," but he was "impressed by the obvious determination of those areas to fight it out."[85]

That night Willkie experienced a noticeable change of scenery as an overnight guest at Chequers. Outside, a company of Coldstream Guards stood watch; detectives were known to beat the undergrowth for spies. Inside, Willkie received eight hours of the Churchill treatment, probably delivered in the "siren suit" the prime minister was wont to wear at Chequers, a "dull blue overall with a zip fastener up the front." Churchill is "the most brilliant conversationalist and exchanger of ideas," Willkie recalled later. "He can thrust. He can take, appreciate and acknowledge your thrusts."[86] Willkie noticed at one point, as the two men were discussing the U.S. Civil War, that Churchill was looking off into the distance. Suddenly he came to and asked for his guest's honest opinion as to whether Britain could pull through. When Willkie said he believed it could, "Churchill immediately jumped up, went to the piano and played a few notes, and danced a jig."[87]

On Sunday morning, Willkie's party departed on a tour of the battered cities of England's industrial heartlands in the Midlands and the north. He wanted, he told reporters, "to speak to the men of the lathes and the women at the counters," in the provinces as well as the capital.[88] He began by visiting the ancient city of Coventry, once filled with monuments and ringed by factories, which had been desolated in a bombing raid that the Germans christened Operation Moonlight Sonata. On the night of November 14, 1940, the Luftwaffe dropped five hundred tons of high explosive on Coventry, delivered by between twelve hundred and sixteen hundred bombs. The next morning, the center of town was a landscape of ruins, craters, smoldering incendiary devices, and human torsos. Five hundred and sixty-eight people were killed and nearly a thousand were seriously injured. A legend arose of "gallant little Coventry," a town that woke up the next morning and opened for business on time. Instead of playing down the success of the raid, the Ministry of Information played up its barbarity in the British and American press.[89]

As Willkie's car sped into the city, people "ran through side lanes and main streets to catch a sight of him." American flags waved from windows and doorways. In the Coventry Council Chamber, he told a large gathering, "All over the world the news of the devastation of your city aroused the greatest sympathy, proving that in the face of totalitarian attack free men feel a common brotherhood." He gazed on the ruins of St. Michael's Cathedral, once the jewel of Coventry, still starkly beautiful against the open sky. Showers of incendiaries had struck the cathedral's roof on the evening of November 14, far too many to be doused by the fire trucks. The cathedral's defenders had watched it burn, along with the famous organ on which Handel had once played. "All night long the city burned and the Cathedral burned with her," recalled its provost, Dick Howard, "emblem of the eternal truth that, when men suffer, God suffers with them." Willkie was deeply moved by Coventry's condition and her spirit, telling a newspaperman "it was a little overwhelming." But he also appreciated the moral advantage it gave to the British, believing it was worth £5 million in propaganda. Indeed, it was characteristic of the whole Blitz: "The Germans had spent a lot of powder, destroyed a large number of slums and some fine old buildings, and united a nation."[90]

That afternoon, he saw similar destruction in Birmingham. He was greeted on the outskirts of the town by the lord mayor, who was wearing the chains of office once worn by his predecessor Neville Chamberlain, and a wildly cheering crowd that swarmed around the two men. Shouts of "Send us all the help you can, Mr. Willkie!" and "Tell them we can take it, Mr. Willkie!" rang out.[91] High spirits were also evident the next day at the Liverpool docks; a convoy of fifteen merchant ships had just come through the German blockade without loss. When Willkie strode into the middle of a group of grimy dockers with a cheery "Hullo, boys," they returned fire with a "Good old Willkie" and jostled to shake his hand.[92]

The trip was rounded out in Manchester, where a large and enthusiastic crowd waited for him outside the Midland Hotel. When he was told that German radio had broadcast calls for Mancunians to demonstrate against Willkie's presence, he walked out on his balcony to test the feeling. "The crowd yelled, cheered, and sang 'Marching Through Georgia' as he stood there, smiling and waving," recorded a reporter. "Back in the room, Mr. Willkie said, 'That seems to settle that. I guess these German guys haven't been reading the papers!'" In mock protest at the enthusiasm of his reception, he said to a newsman, "I am here on a serious job. You people make me feel that I am being entertained. I am told that it is Northern hospitality and I love it—but do you know there's a war on?"

Everywhere Willkie went, he was fêted. Air Raid Precautions workers and soldiers clapped him on the back. An elderly woman gave him a bottle of beer and a kiss on both cheeks. A young woman offered him a hold of her baby, but he begged off with a grin, confessing, "I'm so darned awkward, I might drop him." Summing up his provincial tour, Willkie said, "I have been staggered at the warmth of my reception . . . It has been the experience, the thrill of a life-time. But the calm, precise, magnificently efficient turning of your wheels of industry is, perhaps, an even greater thrill." In fact, it was the bonhomie of the people amid all the destruction that would stay with him. "Willkie was almost frightened by the extent of the crowds which welcomed him," his British aide Brand reported up the line, "and at times wondered whether this was not a sign of a feeling of desperation."[93]

Due to the shortened itinerary, Tuesday, February 4, was Willkie's last full day in-country—and it was busy even by his manic standards, involving calls on chiefs of state in both Ireland and Great Britain. In the morning, he took a charter flight to Dublin to meet the Irish *taoiseach*, or prime minister, Éamon de Valera. Willkie's motivations for this surprise visit related to both high policy and electoral politics. He hoped to persuade de Valera to modify the Irish policy of strict neutrality and make available to Britain key ports on the west coast of Ireland that she had relinquished in 1938. He was also determined that Irish Americans not be "able to say that he had not heard both sides of the case."[94]

Willkie had been criticized by Irish American organizations as being too pro-British, and his trusted campaign manager Russell Davenport cabled him on February 2 that enemies at home were interpreting his scheduled early return to Washington as a further sellout to the administration. An

"Irish trip would help," said Davenport, urging him to spend a "few hours" with de Valera.[95] Churchill counseled against the trip, believing the cause was hopeless and de Valera was a "wicked man," and it fell off the itinerary when the trip was shortened. But at the last minute, when he discovered that Dublin was little more than an hour by air from Manchester, Willkie decided to go.[96]

"I am very happy to be in Ireland," said Willkie at Dublin airport late in the morning, "the land to which so many millions of Americans look as the land of their forefathers." On the ten-minute drive to the Edwardian-era Government Buildings, he was struck by Dublin's handsome wide streets, which looked peaceful and cheerful next to bombed and harried London. De Valera met Willkie for forty minutes in his office, which had portraits of Irish revolutionaries on the walls and a telephone box on his desk into which he was wont to speak in Gaelic. Afterward they joined ministers and officials for lunch in the *taoiseach*'s private room near the Dáil Éireann, the lower house of the Irish parliament.[97]

Foreign visitors who encountered de Valera rarely found him to be the "fanatic" described by King George and others. British member of parliament Harold Nicolson was surprised to see "benevolent cold eyes behind steel-framed glasses," "a firm gentle voice with a soft Irish accent," and a "deep spiritual certainty underneath it all, giving to his features a mark of repose."[98] Australian prime minister and Anglophile Robert Menzies visited de Valera in Dublin shortly after Willkie. He reported his observations of de Valera to a nonplussed war cabinet in London:

He is educated, I think sincere, and with a mind in which acute intelligence is found to contain many blind spots occasioned by prejudice, bitter personal experience, and marked slavery to past history. It was clear to me that . . . he has a large and fanatical following in Dublin. He is the "chief." The very clerks in the offices stand promptly to attention as he strides past. His ministers speak with freedom in his absence, but are restrained and obedient in his presence . . . On the whole, with all my prejudices, I liked him and occasionally succeeded in evoking from him a sort of wintry humour, which was not without charm.[99]

It does not seem that Willkie noticed de Valera's finer qualities, however, nor indeed the statue of Abraham Lincoln and the facsimile of the Declaration of Independence in his outer office.[100] By his own account, he was "brutally frank" and "pretty rude" with the *taoiseach*. He had an American's impatience with the Old World's quarrels. He told him straight out that he ought to allow Britain use of the harbor facilities and airfields, but found him immovable. When de Valera tried to give him a lecture on Anglo-Irish history—"they had to be suspicious of Britain as history had made them suspicious," was the Irishman's argument—Willkie "retorted that he knew all that, that he had once studied the matter and had been about to write a book on the subject, and that all that could be taken for granted." The war against the fascists was "a war for liberty," said Willkie; having won his own war for liberty, de Valera was neglecting a new one that was being fought around him. When de Valera admitted he was worried that unneutral acts would lead to the bombing of Dublin, Willkie, straight off the plane from Coventry and Birmingham, was "disgusted." "If Ireland did not help England," he warned, "it would lose the sympathy of the American people."[101]

Given Dublin's sensitivity to American views, this was a most unwelcome message. The U.S. minister was pleased that Willkie had communicated the "solidarity of American opinion" to the Irish government. Willkie took his leave and returned to the airport, taking care to keep his public comments bland. With his aircraft's engines ticking over, he had a quick word with the officials seeing him off, "waved a cheery farewell to everyone around," and climbed aboard. He was back in the air three hours after he had arrived.[102]

LATE THAT AFTERNOON, Willkie took tea with the king and queen at Buckingham Palace. In fact, although he had been invited to tea and it was advertised as such, he asked for a scotch and soda, and the king joined him in having one. Willkie engaged in a little risqué repartee with the queen, replying to her comment that he must be very tired: "Well, Your Majesty, never *too* tired." Alluding to Joe Kennedy's imperviousness to British charm, he told her, "You are doing a better job on me than you did on another person." "Well, Mr. Willkie," Her Majesty replied, "it wasn't because I didn't try on him." This social call demonstrated the reach of the visitor's celebrity. While Willkie was inside with the royals, he recalled later, "one of the gorgeously caparisoned footmen timidly tugged" at John Cowles's sleeve and asked if he could get him Willkie's autograph.[103]

That evening, Willkie relaxed at a dinner party in his Dorchester suite organized by banker Henry Andrews and his wife, Cicely, a writer friend of Irita Van Doren's who used the pen name Rebecca West. Other guests included Kingsley Martin of the *New Statesman*, playwright and broadcaster J. B. Priestley, and Harold Nicolson, MP.[104] Willkie had asked for an opportunity to meet "a small number of men of lively intellect, for a private talk, where you could shoot straight." Most of the attendees were thrilled by the encounter: West wrote Van Doren that she felt "the better for having warmed my hands at that fire." However, one guest, a diplomat at the Foreign Office, complained that the occasion was a "virtual monologue . . . He treated the party more like a press conference." Nicolson thought he was bored: "He turns his charm on but drums with his fingers." Willkie confirmed to the party that "he was here, quite frankly, on a selling job"—selling the war to Americans, and selling the idea of a united America to the British and the Germans. "He had carried this function . . . throughout the whole of his trip, down to letting himself be kissed by the most unlikely people in Manchester, because it would make a good story."

Willkie's key observations were that Britain was unified behind the government's policy of fighting on, and that Churchill was "a grand leader . . . for a country to have in these times." He was not sure, however, that the prime minister would be the right leader for the postwar period of reconstruction—

he might, in fact, be "lousy." The assembled diners applauded this final comment, but the Foreign Office mandarins who received a report of the dinner were less impressed. The ornery Sir Robert Vansittart, who was already miffed that Willkie never called on him, was horrified:

> What an awful party . . . I wonder . . . that we didn't keep him from these no-goods. It is, in fact, a dreadful lack of stage-management to let a man like this fall into hands like these. I suggest that if we have any more distinguished visitors we should take care to fill up their leisure, lest others should fill up their heads. This point is really rather important . . . When one wishes to get the right stuff into the naifs, one should be very careful to keep them occupied with the right people and not a moment to spare for the wrong and third rate. This is a first principle of propaganda. The Germans understand it. We don't.[105]

At 11:30 p.m., Willkie left the Dorchester for America, still wearing his dinner jacket. The guests were amazed at his stamina, one remarking "what an astonishing animal he is." With a parting shout of "Keep smiling, boys!" to some U.S. servicemen at the station, he boarded a train to Bristol, on the southwest coast of England. Arriving before dawn, he toured the bombed sections of that city with its mayor and recorded a message for the German people, which was broadcast by BBC radio into Germany and printed on leaflets and dropped over Germany by the RAF. "I am proud of my German blood," said Willkie, "but I hate aggression and tyranny . . . We German-Americans reject and hate the aggression and lust for power of the present German government." This broadcast took some courage, given that there were whispers about Willkie's German ancestry during the presidential campaign. Nazi propagandist Joseph Goebbels responded to the broadcast by claiming that Willkie's ancestors were actually Jewish. "Any American could be proud of having Mr. Goebbels as an enemy," was Willkie's riposte.[106]

Churchill had asked the Admiralty to look into the possibility of placing a cruiser at Willkie's disposal for the journey home, but his date with the Foreign Relations Committee ruled out such a leisurely passage. Instead, on the morning of February 5, he took a flight from Bristol to Lisbon, with an RAF fighter escort. At Lisbon, his party joined Pan American officials and government aeronautical inspectors on the *Dixie Clipper* for the first proving flight over an experimental winter transatlantic route. This new southern route was nearly twice as long as the usual course, passing through Portuguese Guinea, Trinidad, and Puerto Rico rather than the Azores and Bermuda; however, it enabled the Clipper to fly with the trade winds at her back rather than fifty-mile-an-hour westerlies in her face.[107]

The twenty-four-hour layover on the island of Bolama, off the west coast of Africa, was the most colorful part of the pioneer flight. Willkie accepted an invitation from the Portuguese colonial governor to go lion hunting in the jungle, but he bagged nothing more than a few wild ducks. He also jawboned with a native chieftain who had twenty-seven wives. When Willkie asked how he could afford it, the chief explained that "every time he married a new wife he got a new field hand." This encounter nearly ended in tears when Willkie mentioned that he had seen one of the chief's daughters bathing in the river. Early the next morning, as the crew was readying the Clipper for departure, a canoe approached carrying the daughter and her mother. Tribal custom dictated that by mentioning the daughter, Willkie had incurred the obligation to take her as his wife, for the price of twelve silver dollars. Swift negotiations ensued, leaving the girl with her freedom, the mother with the purchase price, and Willkie without a second wife.[108]

Just after 8 a.m. on February 9, a reporter watched as the *Dixie Clipper*, "glittering in the bright morning sun, loomed over the Whitestone Bridge and came down for a perfect landing in the choppy water off New York's LaGuardia Airport." Willkie strode up the walkway, slapped his son Philip on the back, and kissed his wife, Edith. He said a few words for the newsreels and waved a native sword from Bolama at the press photographers. That afternoon, he received reporters at the Commodore Hotel. The previous day, the House of Representatives had passed the Lend-Lease bill by 260 votes to 165, mainly on party lines. Looking ahead to his Senate testimony, Willkie was determined to refute the isolationist argument that aid to Britain would draw America into the European war. "In my judgment," he told reporters, "if we do give aid to Britain we are likely to stay out of war, while if we do not give aid to Britain we shall probably become involved in war." Was the trip worthwhile? he was asked. The answer, from a man who had recently run a remarkable campaign to become president of the United States, was surprising but emphatic: "It was the most stimulating experience I ever had in my life."[109]

On the same day that Willkie arrived in New York, Americans heard a stirring radio address from Winston Churchill—the same address on which Hopkins had counseled Churchill at Chequers. The speech reviewed British victories in the Middle East and in the skies over Britain before declaring that "a mighty tide of sympathy, of goodwill and of effective aid, has begun to flow across the Atlantic in support of the world cause which is at stake." The prime minister referred to the visits by the "distinguished Americans" Hopkins and Willkie, and rejected attacks on Lend-Lease as a war measure by claiming that Britain would not need "the gallant Armies which are forming throughout the American Union." Rather, he asserted, Britain needed "an immense and continuous supply of war materials and technical apparatus of all kinds." Churchill recounted the fact that "President Roosevelt gave his opponent in the late Presidential Election a letter of introduction to me, and in it he wrote out a verse, in his own handwriting, from Longfellow." Churchill repeated the verse, and then concluded his address as follows:

What is the answer that I shall give, in your name, to this great man, the thrice-chosen head of a nation of 130 millions? Here is the answer which I will give to President Roosevelt: Put your confidence in us. Give us your faith and your blessing, and, under Providence, all will be well.

We shall not fail or falter; we shall not weaken or tire. Neither the sudden shock of battle, nor the long-drawn trials of vigilance and exertion will wear us down. Give us the tools, and we will finish the job.[110]

The speech was the perfect Churchillian intervention in the American debate, demonstrating British resolve to fight on, emphasizing the links between the English-speaking peoples, calming public concerns about the need for U.S. troops, drawing attention to Hopkins's and Willkie's support for the cause, and advocating brilliantly the passage of Lend-Lease. It is remarkable that two of Roosevelt's envoys were involved, in different ways, in its composition.

Two days later, on February 11, Willkie provided further support to Lend-Lease in dramatic testimony before the Foreign Relations Committee. He was the final witness, appearing after advocates from the administration as well as Harvard president James Conant, theologian Reinhold Niebuhr, and Mayor Fiorello LaGuardia, and opponents such as Charles Lindbergh and Alf Landon. The crowd began gathering in the ornate, marble-pillared Senate Caucus Room before sunrise, and by the time Willkie appeared in the midafternoon, well over a thousand people, including senators' wives in mink coats and jewels, were crowded into a room that seated less than half that number. The entrances were so tightly jammed that even some senators found it difficult to get to their seats. The atmosphere under the crystal chandeliers was highly charged, although the precise analogies employed by newspapers to describe it depended on their ideologies. For the interventionist *Richmond Times-Dispatch*, the hearing was like the opening game of the World Series or a Rose Bowl classic; for the isolationist *Chicago Daily Tribune*, it was more like a murder trial or a circus.[111]

Leaning forward into a large microphone, Willkie delivered his prepared testimony, which he had drafted with the help of Irita Van Doren. The statement referred only obliquely to his mission to Britain, but it derived huge emotional power and immediacy from it. The only realistic approach for America, he said, was to realize that "an attack against liberty in one part of the world is a threat against liberty in another part of the world. If liberty is destroyed in Britain, this constitutes a real and immediate threat to liberty in the United States." He had criticisms of the bill, and suggested amendments to it, but urged its carriage as "the best clear chance for us to keep out of the war." Willkie's belief, shared by those "in high quarters in Britain," was that if she could stand through the summer, "then at last the effects of our long-term assistance will begin to be felt. The tide will turn." If America did not support Britain, she faced the "prospect of a future surrounded by totalitarian powers; threatened by dictators whose real desire is for conquest; betrayed by nations whose word is not to be trusted; loaded with armaments and domestic debt; and faced with a declining standard of living."[112]

In the question-and-answer session that followed, Willkie parried the attacks from hostile senators with wit and flair, alternately sitting back with his leg over the arm of his chair and leaning forward across the table, smoking and gesticulating all the while. When Senator Bennett C. Clark of Missouri asked about implications in the London newspapers that he was the leader of America's opposition, Willkie answered, "Somebody always calls you by a higher title. I always call a captain a major, too." Clark mistakenly referred to him as "Mr. President," and Willkie replied to gales of laughter, "Senator, you merely speak of what should have been." His interrogators tried to embarrass him by citing his campaign criticisms of Roosevelt, but Willkie would have none of it. When arch-isolationist Senator Gerald P. Nye of North Dakota asked him about his campaign prediction that FDR would have America at war by April 1941, Willkie waved him away. "It was a bit of campaign oratory. I am very glad you read my speeches, because the President said he did not." On a more serious note, he commented, "I struggled as hard as I could to beat Franklin Roosevelt and I tried to keep from pulling any of my punches. He was elected President. He is my President now." Most of Washington's leading reporters stayed to watch all of Willkie's "bravura performance." FDR joked to those who turned up to his 4 p.m. White House press conference that they were at "the wrong end of Pennsylvania Avenue this afternoon."[113]

Late that evening, Willkie came down to the Roosevelts' end of Pennsylvania Avenue, where they were presiding over the annual White House reception for the U.S. Army, Navy, and Marine Corps. This was the last state reception of the season, and the most colorful. Army officers wore their formal blues and the navy showed off its gold braid; medals and foreign orders were on proud display. The Marine Band, decked out in scarlet and gold, played while the officers walked down the receiving line in the Blue Room. As soon as FDR had finished shaking hands, he slipped away from the reception and repaired upstairs to his second-floor study, where he received Willkie. This oval room, its walls covered in old maritime prints and its floor cluttered with ships' models, was Roosevelt's refuge. For an hour and a half, until nearly midnight, the two rivals talked alone about Willkie's impressions of Britain and Ireland. An outside chef had been brought in to prepare some terrapin that FDR had been sent. Roosevelt ordered that no one was to interrupt this "old cronies dinner." Those who wondered what was taking place—and an unusual number of White House staffers found reasons to visit that part of the residence that night—heard "great bursts of laughter" coming from behind the closed doors. The atmosphere was not entirely free of one-upmanship, however. Roosevelt told Harold Ickes beforehand that he intended to address Willkie as "Wendell."[114]

On February 13, the Lend-Lease bill was favorably reported out of the Foreign Relations Committee; three weeks later, on March 8, it passed the Senate. Does Willkie deserve any credit for this? His boosters, such as Thomas Lamont, thought their man "pushed the Bill through."[115] FDR himself was always grateful for Willkie's efforts, slapping down Hopkins on one occasion for making a disparaging remark about Willkie, whom he said was "a godsend to this country when we needed him the most."[116] In reality, Willkie's support did not change many votes, either in the committee room or on the floor of the Senate. But his travels and his testimony deflated the bill's opponents and prevented them from making Lend-Lease a completely partisan issue or imposing unacceptable amendments. Surely his advocacy also affected the thinking of some of the twenty-two million Americans who had voted for him for president.[117]

In the weeks and months after his return, Willkie continued his evangelizing on behalf of Britain. "I am doing all I can," he wrote to a British confidante, "to help preach the doctrine over here of All-Out Aid to Britain." The Australian minister, Richard Casey, saw him at the Commodore Hotel and reported that "he is hot-foot for all possible US assistance to enable Britain to defeat Germany." In speeches and magazine articles, he described what he had "seen with his own eyes." He stayed in close contact with Lord Halifax, seeking facts and figures that could be used "to stir the public," and even advising the ambassador to encourage Churchill to flatter FDR publicly so as to assuage the president's vanity.[118] In March he visited Canada, receiving the most rapturous reception seen there since the royal visit of 1939. In Toronto, he dined with Prime Minister Mackenzie King at the York Club, enjoyed a ticker-tape parade, and addressed the Ontario legislature as well as a 17,000-strong rally at Maple Leaf Gardens. "Wendell Willkie is worth more than Spitfires," was the title of one Toronto editorial. In Montreal, twenty thousand people turned up at Windsor Station to hear him speak.[119]

All these activities, of course, did violence to Willkie's relationships with Republicans. At the Waldorf Hotel in New York, he reminded the National Republican Club that their party was "founded to preserve freedom," so it could hardly ignore the fact that a few days' travel away, "bombs are dropping, destroying cities lived in by free men, free men like us." Yet Herbert Hoover told intimates that the erstwhile nominee had "become a publicity hound and a political adventurer . . . [who] permits himself to be exploited by the Administration." The *Chicago Daily Tribune* editorialized that his decision to "hurry home and get in his licks for the war bill" showed he was an agent of Roosevelt's, and called for his "thoroughly dishonorable conduct" to be investigated by "the duped and deluded" Republican Party. The

Republican majority in the state senate of Indiana, Willkie's home state, went to the trouble of voting down a resolution commending him for his work in Britain.[120] There were persistent rumors that his travel expenses had been paid by wealthy acquaintances such as Thomas Lamont, Henry Stimson, or Helen Rogers Reid. "What price Willkie?" asked one correspondent.[121] Publicly, Willkie refused to take a backward step; privately, he was "hurt and worried" by the criticism and made repeated attempts to distance himself from the administration, although not from its policy direction.[122]

The president, on the other hand, was well pleased with his Willkie initiative, as evidenced by persistent White House attempts to obtain a copy of the original letter to Churchill. FDR strove to keep Willkie close, maintaining a friendly correspondence and sending him a copy of the letter when it was eventually located.[123] Willkie's trip to Britain and his advocacy of Lend-Lease had erased any rancor remaining from the campaign, he said. The president even tried unsuccessfully to persuade his recent rival to dedicate the new memorial at Mount Rushmore, arguing it would "give new and striking emphasis to the vital need for national unity."[124] In March, the awkwardness of the relationship was satirized in a motion picture shown to guests at the White House Correspondents' Association annual dinner, including the two men themselves. Two actors wearing Roosevelt and Willkie masks lay in a double bed together, underneath a sign reading "Bundling for Britain." When the Willkie character realized the identity of his bedmate, he cried out, "Help me, help me, help me!" The Roosevelt character just kept puffing on his cigarette.[125]

WENDELL WILLKIE'S MISSION to Britain and Ireland was, said *Time*, "one of the most extraordinary journeys in U.S. history." The *Washington Post* thought it was "a modern epic." The only parallels commentators could offer were Woodrow Wilson's voyage to the Paris Peace Conference and Theodore Roosevelt's triumphal tour of Europe after he left the White House—and neither of those men visited a war zone.[126]

Churchill recalled later that "every arrangement was made by us, with the assistance of the enemy, to let him see all he desired of London at bay." The courage and stoicism Willkie witnessed moved him deeply. On one occasion, whilst driving through Trafalgar Square in the middle of a daylight bombing raid, with two dozen German planes overhead, sirens sounding, and antiaircraft guns booming, he was startled to find the traffic unaffected and old ladies continuing to feed the pigeons under Nelson's Column.[127]

The affection was mutual. Willkie caught the imagination of the British public. The *Times* observed that "he went everywhere, saw everything, and met everybody"—from "the King to the costermongers of Lambeth Walk." With everyone, "he has left an impression of sincerity and friendship, of boundless energy and radiant high spirits, which has been immensely heartening." Willkie was "the Indiana dynamo." Rebecca West told Irita Van Doren there was "a sort of Carnival feeling about the visit." Willkie utterly overwhelmed the reporting of Harry Hopkins in the British press, which would have worried Hopkins not a bit. Hopkins avoided publicity as diligently as Willkie courted it.[128]

British cities, institutions, and individuals invited Willkie to visit them. Admirers sent him books, scarves, fur-lined gloves, whiskey, and drawings of DIY air raid shelters. As a mark of establishment acceptance, gentlemen's clubs offered him temporary membership during his stay in Britain.[129] Apparently, these were not the only favors he was offered. Back in Washington for his testimony, a surprisingly righteous Willkie told a dinner party that "moral standards have gone overboard in England" on account of the war, and that "at his hotel it was made evident to him that he would not have far to go to have all the comforts of home."[130]

Many Britons testified to the Willkie effect. The archbishop of Canterbury thanked Willkie for "the encouragement which your presence and words have given in so many parts of the country." The under secretary of the U.S. Navy, James V. Forrestal, wrote while on a visit to London, "You stand tops in England—they are conscious, fully, of the great service you have rendered." The AP correspondent Eddy Gilmore reported in February that he had just heard "a song in a nightclub about you. It was full of praise and back slaps. You really knocked them dead."

Lord Beaverbrook, a seasoned flatterer of Americans, instructed an aide to draft Willkie a congratulatory letter for his signature: "Give him a story about our war effort and it must appear to be an inside story, you know—a story that will grip him a bit . . . Then give him a little attention at the end about himself . . . The legend lives on of his visit to our country." The aide obliged. Churchill told Winant, with a good deal more sincerity, that Willkie's sympathetic mien, as well as the credential he bore, gave "the besieged people of these islands a sense of unity in American support" and "a tremendous lift to British morale."[131]

If FDR's symbolic diplomacy was directed partly at Britain, it also caused waves at home. Willkie was Roosevelt's best friend in edging Republican supporters away from isolationism. "Throughout his trip here," reported Thomas Brand to Churchill and other officials, "he always bore in mind the outlook of the Americans who are against aid to Britain rather than the people who are in favour of it." Willkie was striking a fine balance, observed his aide-de-camp, "since if he makes it too bad the American public will fear the immediate defeat of Britain, and if he makes it too favourable they will not realize the urgency for help." Brand worried that Willkie had made a spectacle of himself, but the canny American realized that human interest photographs and newsreels "were much better advance publicity for a serious statement than any number of leaders in important newspapers."[132]

Willkie's instincts were correct. The echoes of his mission, and FDR's endorsement of it, resonated long after his return. In April, the BBC broadcast another speech by Winston Churchill directed chiefly toward Americans, in which he reminded his listeners of "the lines of Longfellow which President Roosevelt had written out for me in his own hand." Now Churchill answered those lines with verses from Arthur Henry Clough "which are less well known but which seem apt and appropriate to our fortunes tonight, and I believe they will be so judged wherever the English language is spoken or the flag of freedom flies." Everyone listening in Britain and the United States understood exactly what Churchill meant by quoting them:

> For while the tired waves, vainly breaking,
> Seem here no painful inch to gain,
> Far back, through creeks and inlets making,
> Comes silent, flooding in, the main.
> And not by eastern windows only,
> When daylight comes, comes in the light,
> In front, the sun climbs slow, how slowly,
> But westward, look, the land is bright.[133]

"To Keep the British Isles Afloat"

AVERELL HARRIMAN IN LONDON, AFRICA,

AND THE MIDDLE EAST, MARCH—JULY 1941

T wo days after Harry Hopkins got back from Europe, Franklin Roosevelt summoned the liberal businessman William Averell Harriman to the White House and gave him an assignment. "I want you to go over to London," said the president, "and recommend everything that we can do, short of war, to keep the British Isles afloat."[1]

FDR had thought up Lend-Lease. He had sent Hopkins to London to explain it. Wendell Willkie had helped to sell it, especially to wary Americans. Now a third special envoy would help to deliver it.

AVERELL HARRIMAN was born on November 15, 1891, in New York City, in his family's four-story brownstone on East 51st Street and Madison Avenue, only steps away from St. Patrick's Cathedral. His father, E. H. Harriman, the "little giant" of Wall Street, was one of America's great railroad barons. A pixie of a man with a "Keystone Kops moustache" and extraordinary ambition, ruthlessness, and nerve, E.H. started his career as a five-dollar-a-week office boy. On his death, his Union Pacific and Southern Pacific railroads controlled seventy-five thousand miles of track and employed more men than the U.S. Army. E.H. collected enemies like he collected Pullman cars; one of them, Theodore Roosevelt, regarded him as an "undesirable citizen" and an "enemy of the Republic."[2]

Averell was the fourth of five surviving children born to E.H. and his wife, Mary Williamson Averell, herself the daughter of a banker and railroad man. Privileges rained down on the Harriman children like manna. Averell was educated in the finest preparatory schools, and, like Sumner Welles, he drilled with the Knickerbocker Greys. A summer vacation might be a trip across the United States in E.H.'s special train, *Utopia*, or a tour of Europe in one of the first automobiles. When E.H. wanted to shoot a Kodiak bear in Alaska, he chartered a steamship with a crew of sixty-five and took along an equal number of guests, including relatives, friends, scientists, artists, photographers, stenographers, physicians, taxidermists, and a chaplain. When Averell, traveling in Japan with his family, needed to get back to Groton School for the start of classes, E.H. diverted one of his steamships and sent the boy back with the secretary of war and future president, William Howard Taft. When Averell and his brother took an interest in rowing, E.H. set up a rowing camp for them on a private lake and brought in one of the country's best crew coaches. Averell acknowledged later that his father's character and personality had "a tremendous influence" on him. He would always remain mindful of E.H.'s injunction that he should "be something and somebody."[3]

E.H. died just as Averell entered Yale, and in his senior year he took up a seat on the Union Pacific's board of directors, as well as membership in Yale's most prestigious secret society, Skull and Bones. After graduating, he commenced a twenty-year career in business, initially in the railroad but also in a series of other industries, achieving successes along the way without ever making an E.H.-size mark anywhere. In 1917, he resigned his vice presidency at the Union Pacific to establish a shipyard on the Delaware River to build steel cargo ships for the American merchant marine, and a new town (Harriman, Pennsylvania) for the shipyard workers. Harriman won big contracts from Washington, but he "never felt entirely comfortable" about his decision to help clear the shipping bottleneck (and make a good margin) rather than serve in uniform.[4]

After the war, Harriman set up a shipping business and a private bank, which eventually merged with Brown Brothers to become Brown Brothers Harriman. He invested in various European ventures and on his inspection tours he made a practice of calling on important people. In 1924, Harriman won a concession from the government of the Soviet Union to exploit rich manganese deposits in the Caucasus. The investment was dogged by labor and political troubles, however, which were not cured by a four-hour meeting with Leon Trotsky in Moscow in 1926. Harriman found Trotsky "cold" and regretted that "there was no human interchange of any kind"; Trotsky, whose position was under severe threat from Joseph Stalin, had other things on his mind than the feelings of an American capitalist. On his way home, Harriman met with a young Benito Mussolini in Milan, in an office that was just as enormous as the one in which the dictator received Sumner Welles in Rome in 1940. In Cannes, Harriman sought out a vacationing Winston Churchill, then the chancellor of the exchequer. "I wanted an excuse to meet him," Harriman admitted, "so I talked to him about Russia." Churchill reminisced about his unsuccessful attempt in 1919–1920 to intervene in Russia and stamp out the Bolshevik Revolution.[5]

Few young businessmen would have had the confidence to stalk great men in this fashion. But Harriman was already becoming, as he would later be dubbed, "a power snob." "VIPs are Harriman's speciality," concluded a later magazine profile. "Harriman cares about rare people the way a philatelist cares about rare stamps." Like many philatelists, he acquired his hobby early.[6]

Harriman was a man of many hobbies, all of them more glamorous than stamp collecting. In games, he excelled at bridge, bezique, backgammon, canasta, and mahjong. He was an aggressive badminton player, a creditable sulky driver, a keen breeder of Labrador retrievers, an expert skier, and a genuine champion on the polo field and later the croquet court. In few of these pursuits was he a natural. He was, however, utterly relentless. He was determined to beat his opponents, come what may. As a college junior and coach of the freshman rowing crew, he took himself off to the United Kingdom for six weeks to learn "the Oxford stroke," suffering the haughtiness of the English, as well as their weather, in order to uncover their secrets. His aggression and tenacity (as well as "the best damn polo ponies in the world," as a friend observed) turned him into an eight-goal polo player who was selected for the U.S. team. Such was his intensity at croquet that he could spend an hour studying his ball, letting his opponents get a drink or even lunch while he contemplated his shot. This attitude was even more pronounced in his work, in which he pushed himself extremely hard. Dark circles were often visible under his eyes; the diplomat George F. Kennan, who later worked for Harriman, observed that he "behaves as though his body were just something that trails around with him."[7]

Harriman also had the defects of his qualities, however. He was an exceedingly serious man, especially about himself. He could be grim company—aloof, uninterested in small talk, slow to find the elegant phrase even if he were minded to look for it. Banter was not his business. He was known for falling asleep at the dinner table if he was bored. His longstanding and sympathetic aide Bob Meiklejohn conceded Harriman "was no good at human relations"; their many thousands of hours together, he recalled, yielded not a single amusing anecdote. As an employer, Harriman was not easily satisfied. He was thorough and meticulous, but a poor communicator. "He used to absolutely murder speeches," recalled one aide. He was "the world's worst speaker," concluded another. Harriman was also cheap. He rarely picked up a check or a taxi fare. As he preferred not to carry cash, his staffers were forced to dip into their own pockets to buy his newspapers and razor blades when they traveled with him, and to tip the hotel porters.[8]

If many thought Harriman unlovable, though, others found him attractive. He was a handsome devil—tall and dark, with sleek hair brushed off his forehead, and soft brown eyes. He was once included on a list of America's best-looking men. Harriman married his first wife, the willowy Kitty Lanier Lawrance, in the aftermath of a bad fall she had taken from her horse while the couple was riding on the Upper West Side near Central Park. Kitty's health never recovered, however, and the marriage was not a success. Harriman spent a good deal of time instead with cabaret singer Teddy Gerard, squiring her around Europe and maintaining her in a Greenwich Village apartment. In 1929, Averell and Kitty were divorced in Paris, where wealthy Americans could settle their affairs simply and discreetly, and the following year he married Marie Norton Whitney, ex-wife of socially prominent Cornelius Vanderbilt "Sonny" Whitney.

Marie was a great match for Averell because she was his opposite—unpretentious, irreverent, and fun. Marie was game. "She laughed, swore, chewed gum, and danced the Charleston," noted Harriman's biographer Rudy Abramson. She ran an art gallery on East 57th Street, the opening of which was attended by Henri Matisse. She also exposed Averell to people other than financiers, railroaders, polo players, and Republicans. At Arden, E.H.'s seigneurial Hudson Valley estate, Marie started a tradition of raucous Thanksgiving weekends that were attended by journalists, theater people, artists, croquet friends of Averell's, and New Dealers. Either through Averell's meanness or Marie's indifference, the food at these weekends was notoriously bad. It was "the kind you get in a second-rate, small hotel in New England," recalled one guest. People brought hampers of food and hid them in their rooms.[9]

For most of the 1930s, Harriman was chairman of the board at the Union Pacific. His most famous innovation was to open a grand ski resort in Idaho, Sun Valley, in order to generate traffic for the railroad and restore the glamour of train travel. The UP trains bringing Hollywood stars (and "unattached studio starlets") from Los Angeles certainly did that. By this stage, however, Harriman's mind was turning in another direction. He had become a Democrat after supporting the 1928 presidential campaign of Al Smith, Franklin Roosevelt's predecessor as governor of New York. With the election of FDR to the White House four years later, Harriman was drawn to Washington, D.C., like an iron filing to a magnet.[10]

Harriman had several links to the new Roosevelt administration. The two families knew each other a little, although the old Hudson River families such as the Roosevelts regarded the Harrimans' ilk as "nouveau" and Arden as "very ostentatious." Harriman was at Groton with Eleanor's younger brother, Hall, and visited the Roosevelts at their Manhattan town house and their summer home on Campobello Island. A stronger connection ran through Averell's elder sister Mary Harriman Rumsey, a remarkable woman who studied sociology at Barnard College despite E.H.'s reservations, and went on to found the Junior League in her debutante year. (She later married Charles Cary Rumsey of Buffalo, who was a cousin of Bill Donovan's wife, Ruth.) Mary Rumsey "had so damn much nervous energy," observed family friend and Cold War defense secretary Robert A. Lovett, "that if they had ever had a blackout in New York all they would have had to do was to put a couple of wires to her, and she would light the damn city up." After Roosevelt's election, Rumsey channeled that energy to Washington, taking up a post with the National Recovery Administration (NRA) and establishing a political salon in the Georgetown house she shared with her old friend Labor Secretary Frances Perkins. Harriman followed her to the capital, and for Roosevelt's first two terms he hovered on the fringes of the New Deal, flitting between his business interests and several part-time positions in government, with the NRA, the National Industrial Recovery Board, and the Commerce Department's Business Advisory Council.[11]

Harriman's most important friend at court, however, was Harry Hopkins. Harriman claimed the two met in a club car on the train from New York to Washington; others said they were brought together by Herbert Swope at his Long Island home, Keewaydin, where Hopkins also met Brendan Bracken. In the winter of 1938–1939, Harriman did Hopkins a service as chairman of the Business Advisory Council, rounding up other members of the council to support Hopkins's appointment as secretary of commerce and testifying on his behalf before the Senate Commerce Committee. "It was fine and I shall ever be grateful to you for it," wrote Hopkins.

The two men came from opposite ends of the social spectrum, but both were tough, pragmatic, and hardworking—self-consciously "doers" rather than "talkers." And Hopkins's fierce commitment to the poor was always matched by his attraction to the rich and fashionable. Harriman took Hopkins—his "guru," according to Franklin Roosevelt Jr.—to nightclubs and other "glitter spots" in New York. Harriman was not a sentimental man, but he showed uncommon affection for and gratitude to Hopkins throughout his career—as well he might, because Hopkins made him. When Roosevelt started mobilizing American industry in 1940, Harriman was disappointed not to be given a prominent job. Tenacious as always, he took a lower-level, part-time position at the Office of Production Management (OPM), made every effort to expand his brief—and stuck close to Hopkins.[12]

HARRIMAN WAS IN SUN VALLEY for a Christmas vacation when the news broke about Hopkins's mission to London. Within minutes he was on the phone to Washington seeking a spot on the plane. "Let me carry your bag, Harry," pleaded Harriman, citing his familiarity with London and his acquaintance with Churchill. He followed it up with a cable a few days later, asking, "Are you taking your secretary-valet-courier with you?" Hopkins declined, but hinted he might have something for Harriman on his return. "I'll want to talk to you when I get back," he said. "I think that some work will come out of my trip to London that you ought to get involved with." Harriman returned to his mundane job at the OPM and waited anxiously for news, occasionally bugging FDR's secretary Missy LeHand for updates.[13] Meanwhile, various power brokers in the administration weighed in on the issue. The Donovan mission the previous year had shown that Roosevelt was not always the only person involved in the appointment of his personal envoys. In this case, FDR first settled on the idea of sending someone to

Britain to expedite Lend-Lease aid, and only later was the identity and designation of that person decided.

In mid-January, word spread that John G. Winant, director of the International Labour Office, was to be the new ambassador in London, and tobacco company executive S. Clay Williams was to be minister with responsibility for production issues. A few days later, however, FDR indicated to Lord Halifax that he intended to appoint Harriman as minister, with special responsibility for industrial production.[14] However, Harriman was not interested in taking on a formal State Department post, preferring instead to work directly for the White House. The Hopkins fraternity soon interceded with the president on his behalf. On January 23, Felix Frankfurter telephoned the Treasury Department and pressed a reluctant Henry Morgenthau into service:

FRANKFURTER: I have every reason for believing . . . that Averell Harriman doesn't want to go as a Minister. He wants to go, but not as a Minister. He would feel restricted . . . He'd like to just go. See? . . . Now I wonder why that isn't an ideal arrangement, to have John Winant go as Ambassador and have Averell Harriman go as consultant at large . . .

MORGENTHAU: I see . . .

FRANKFURTER: Well, Henry, you can count on that being absolutely true, that Averell Harriman does not want to go as a Minister and that he'll go if he's just sent at large.

MORGENTHAU: Well don't lean too heavily on me because I doubt if I'll get a chance to talk to the President tonight.

FRANKFURTER: Well, I didn't mean tonight—maybe tomorrow.

MORGENTHAU: All right.[15]

The other member of the tag team, Harry Hopkins, soon hopped into the ring, sending the president two cables from London. In the first, he expressed the hope that whoever was appointed to deal with mobilization questions would "not be burdened with the diplomatic responsibilities which are required of a person second in command at this Embassy." A few days later, he chimed in again, this time to praise the current minister, Herschel Johnson, who "has a very wide acquaintance in London and . . . is doing an excellent job." "I hesitate to be making recommendations that do not fall within my responsibility," he said a little unconvincingly. But he concluded, "I do hope it can be worked out so that Johnson can remain the person second in command to the Ambassador."[16]

The matter was settled when Hopkins arrived back in the United States on February 16.[17] Hopkins had told the Australian high commissioner in London, Stanley Bruce, that the president should "send over someone in whom he had complete confidence to keep in close touch with all that was being done here." He promised to "press upon . . . the President . . . the desirability of sending some first class person over here."[18] The man Hopkins had in mind for that job was Averell Harriman.

On February 18, FDR saw Harriman at the White House and charged him with helping to "keep the British Isles afloat." The president was "a bit foggy as to whom I was to work with on this side as he had not set up the lend-lease organization," recalled Harriman, but he was made to understand that he would not report to OPM and would be "entirely independent of the State Department." Furthermore, the president "said I was to communicate with him on any matters that I thought were important enough."[19] Harriman would take him at his word.

In his announcement of the Harriman mission at a press conference that same afternoon, FDR demonstrated his customary playfulness, revealing little about the relationship between his representative and the new U.S. ambassador—but much about the sui generis nature of Rooseveltian envoys:

> FDR: You saw Averell Harriman when he went out . . . Oh, I suppose you
>   will all ask about his title, so I thought I would invent one. I talked
>   over with him what his title would be, and we decided it was a pretty
>   good idea to call him an "Expediter." There's a new one for you. I

believe it is not in the diplomatic list or any other list. So he will go over as "Defense Expediter."

That doesn't conform with anything you ever heard of before—but that doesn't mean it isn't an excellent idea. We won't send his name to the Senate—it won't be that kind of job . . . He will be Defense Expediter, and he is going in about two weeks . . .

REPORTER: Mr. President, what is Mr. Harriman's relation to our Embassy over there? Does he represent you directly?

FDR: I don't know, and I don't give a—you know! *(Laughter)*

REPORTER: Mr. President, how does he report?

FDR: I don't know, and I don't care.

REPORTER: Is it part of the Office of Production Management?

FDR: I suppose he will report to the proper authorities.

REPORTER: That means you.[20]

After years of positioning, Harriman was now in the main game. He was a Washington player, not just a bit player. He set about calling on senior administration officials and military leaders, including General George Marshall, Admiral Harold "Betty" Stark, the chief of naval operations, and Major General Henry H. "Hap" Arnold, the chief of the Army Air Corps. Henry Stimson told him over lunch at his residence, Woodley, that he favored outright repeal of the Neutrality Act, universal military training, and the sending of munitions to Britain on a large scale, in U.S. naval convoys if necessary. Cordell Hull arrived at his meeting with Harriman forty-five minutes late from a cabinet meeting, looking "weary and worried." Yet Harriman recorded that the secretary of state was "personally extremely kind in his attitude" and seemed to take the announcement of yet another special mission in his stride.[21]

What was this mission precisely? Plainly, FDR intended Harriman to provide on-the-ground assistance to Hopkins, who was to become the de facto Lend-Lease administrator, but the details of the role were opaque. Roosevelt's way, Harriman observed later, was to give his lieutenants "the direction of his mind" rather than "precise orders." This preserved an envoy's flexibility, but "also enabled him to disown you if anything went wrong."[22] In the absence of clear instructions, Harriman began to define the role himself. After his first White House meeting, he thought the job was primarily to speed up the flow of information in both directions.[23] His sessions with the military confirmed this view. Rather than "requests that come late in the evening over a bottle of port," the services required "information on which to base their judgment as to whether a particular munition was of greater value in American or in British hands." Harriman concluded that he must help Churchill to communicate his approach to Washington. "Without understanding and acceptance of his war strategy our military men will 'drag their feet.' "[24] Harriman would later redefine his job in more expansive terms.

Harriman had a farewell lunch with the president at his desk in the White House on March 7. Roosevelt was suffering from a cold and appeared to Harriman to be "tired and mentally stale." He asked his visitor to inquire into the food situation in Britain, explaining the need for the British to consume vitamins, cheese, and pork; but Harriman was more intrigued by the food situation in front of him. Cuisine at the Roosevelt White House was famously awful. Eleanor's handpicked housekeeper, Mrs. Henrietta Nesbitt, late of the League of Women Voters, believed in simple food and ignored FDR's many complaints about her cooking. (Occasionally the president rebelled and obtained the services of an outside chef, as in the case of the terrapin served to Wendell Willkie.) A witness observed that Mrs. Nesbitt "stood over the cooks" in the White House kitchen, "making sure that each dish was overcooked or undercooked or ruined in one way or another." Ernest Hemingway thought that White House food was "the worst I've ever eaten."[25]

On this particular day, Mrs. Nesbitt served spinach soup that looked to Harriman "like hot water poured over chopped up spinach," cheese soufflé for a main course (with a side dish of spinach), and pancakes with butter and maple syrup for dessert. "It struck me as the most unhealthy diet" for the ailing Roosevelt, recalled Harriman, "particularly as we discussed the British food situation and their increasing needs for vitamins, proteins and calcium!" Harriman concluded, with a rare light touch, that "in the British interest . . . fortification of the President's diet should be first priority."[26]

In between mouthfuls of spinach, Roosevelt told Harriman "he was ready to go as far as the American public opinion would permit," but he was clearly uncomfortable with the idea of the U.S. Navy escorting convoys of merchant vessels sailing for Britain, for fear it would lead to a shooting war with the Germans. FDR needed time in order to prod opinion further in the right direction, wear down isolationist opposition in Congress, and put the economy on a war footing. Instead of convoying, he described various creative "compromise" ideas for assisting the British to protect their supply lines. One was to send American merchantmen sailing in convoy as far as Iceland, where the British could transfer the supplies into their own ships for the final run home. Another was for American aircraft carriers or passenger ships to transport fighters to the African coast, where they could take off and join British forces in the Middle East. Harriman was not impressed. "All in all, I left feeling that the President had not faced what I considered to be the realities of the situation—namely that there was a good chance Germany, without our help, could so cripple British shipping as to affect her ability to hold out." Harriman's main hope was Hopkins—"the one man in [an] official position who appears to be ready to force a decision for decisive action on every front."[27]

Reflecting on his appointment a decade later, Harriman suggested he was tapped because "Roosevelt knew and trusted me."[28] This is not convincing. FDR had known him for decades, yet he declined to appoint him to meaningful positions during his first two terms. Furthermore, the trust Roosevelt reposed in Harriman had taken a bit of a dent recently. In a meeting with Willkie, Roosevelt had confided genially that Harriman had donated $5,000 to his campaign (in some tellings of the story, the sum was

$25,000). Willkie responded with a grin that Harriman had donated an equal amount to his. Harriman's explanation was that he had contributed only to Willkie's nomination fight, not his general election campaign. Still, Roosevelt made sure to let his chastened envoy know that he knew.[29]

The better explanation for the appointment is that Hopkins persuaded FDR that Harriman had the executive skills to get the job done—that he was, in one observer's words, a "go-getter who could produce results in double-time."[30] Harriman had one other qualification for the task: he was a vocal advocate of American assistance to the European democracies. From the outbreak of the war in Europe, Harriman had spoken out in favor of aiding Britain, and in the period in which Roosevelt was considering his appointment he delivered bellicose speeches in New York and Washington.[31] One British official said "he knew of no one in the United States more rabidly keen on our cause."[32] That was fine by FDR. He wanted someone who believed in his work.

AT THE SAME TIME that Roosevelt was having lunch with his latest personal envoy, his new London ambassador, Gil Winant, was just settling into his post. Winant was an unusual American politician. At the time of his appointment as ambassador, his public profile was so modest that one wag declared that Americans could not have told you whether his name "represented an Australian tennis star or a new variety of apple." *Time* observed that he "has long been half-on, half-off the U.S. public scene, with his friends constantly predicting a great role for him just as he would quietly step out of the limelight."[33] Winant was born into money and married into more of it. He served as a flyer in the First World War; taught history at his old prep school, St. Paul's in Concord; and was elected three times as governor of New Hampshire as a liberal Republican.[34] In 1935, Roosevelt made Winant, a supporter of the New Deal, the chairman of the Social Security Board, and later urged him to take up the position of director of the International

Labour Office (ILO) in order that he might have "eyes and ears in a very well-placed listening post during a critical period."[35] Roosevelt never stopped fishing for intelligence.

Winant was intense, awkward, and painfully shy. He was Lincolnesque in appearance—tall and dark, with sunken eyes and sharp cheekbones—but not in eloquence. An observer described him as "a man of slow gestures, always digging his hands in his pockets or twisting and turning awkwardly, as if he had caught his arms in the lining of his coat sleeves, while he expresses flawless liberal sentiments in a slow, pained voice." Winant was a stranger to high society despite his money; his friends marveled at his skill in finding "so many pale blue shirts with frayed cuffs and collars." The U.S. ambassador to Italy, William Phillips, observed that Winant had "the best will in the world" but found it hard "to translate good intentions into actions." His meetings always ran overtime; confusion ruled in his office. And yet for all his frailties, he had the gifts of sympathy and compassion. "When Winant enters the room, everyone somehow feels better," said an acquaintance from his ILO days. He was a softhearted man, recognizing suffering in others and helping them where he could.[36]

Indeed, there was an otherworldly aspect to John Winant. A British diplomat ventured that he had "a sense of social service which amounts almost to a religious conviction." In trying to capture the man, observers often groped for the spiritual, comparing him to a monk, a mystic, a martyr, a pilgrim, a puritan, a prophet, and a knight errant.[37]

Why would Franklin Roosevelt put an ascetic social justice campaigner in the London embassy? His principal motive, as historian David Reynolds has argued, was to establish closer links with the British left and the Labour Party, which he believed would be the dominant political force after the war.[38] Winant's appointment had been urged on FDR by many leaders of the British left who knew him from the ILO, including Ernest Bevin and Harold Laski. Many in the State Department perceived the selection as insurance against a future Labour government, and saw the dreaded influence of Felix Frankfurter in the decision.[39] FDR himself told Wendell Willkie that he had selected Winant for the London job because he anticipated "a social revolution" in Britain—or as Winant described it, "a leveling process." Roosevelt had his various ties and connections to Churchill: but what about those who came after Churchill? He told Joe Kennedy that in light of labor's growing influence, "it might be well to send somebody over there who spoke their language."[40]

At first glance, the appointment of Harriman and Winant in short order hardly gives the impression of coherent policymaking on the part of the president. But this classic piece of Rooseveltian administrative chaos had order at its heart. Harriman was sent to London to help Britain win the war; Winant was dispatched in preparation for the peace. The Democrat was to work with the Tories; the Republican was to commune with the socialists. As Assistant Secretary of State Breckinridge Long recorded in his diary, "FDR is starting two horses in the race."[41]

FRANKLIN ROOSEVELT SIGNED H.R. 1776 into law at 3:50 p.m. on Tuesday, March 11, ten minutes after the bill had been delivered to the White House. Historians have likened this to "a declaration of economic warfare on the Axis." FDR immediately approved a list of war materials to be sent from U.S. Army and Navy stocks to Europe. Shortly he would ask Congress for an appropriation of $7 billion to commence production of ships, tanks, warplanes, guns, munitions, and other materials for Britain and her allies.

For the president, this was a personal triumph. Lend-Lease would provide lifesaving aid to the British; it would also accelerate the conversion of American industry to defense production. The passage of such an ambitious and innovative measure, after bitter debates and amendment fights, revealed his immaculate sense of timing and his mastery of legislative tactics. It also showed his determination to shift the terms of the public conversation on the war.

"Let not dictators of Europe or Asia doubt our unanimity now," Roosevelt declared in a speech at the Willard Hotel in Washington on March 15.

"We have just now engaged in a great debate. It was not limited to the halls of Congress. It was argued in every newspaper, on every wave length, over every cracker barrel in all the land; and it was finally settled and decided by the American people themselves. Yes, the decisions of our democracy may be slowly arrived at. But when that decision is made, it is proclaimed not with the voice of any one man, but with the voice of one hundred and thirty millions. It is binding on us all. And the world is no longer left in doubt."[42]

Winston Churchill was certainly in no doubt as to the significance of America's decision. Lend-Lease was, he said, the third climacteric of the war—and "the most unsordid act in the whole of recorded history."[43]

ONE DAY BEFORE THE SIGNING of the Lend-Lease bill, the man responsible for helping to implement it had boarded the *Atlantic Clipper* at LaGuardia for the first leg of his journey to England. Averell Harriman carried a letter of appointment from the president, which provided him with a new and grander title—"Special Representative"—and the diplomatic rank (although not the administrative responsibilities) of minister.[44]

Harriman was well traveled, but this was the first time he had flown over the ocean, and he felt "very much the adventurer." The Clipper carried the usual colorful mix of passengers. Wealthy diplomat Anthony J. Drexel Biddle Jr., recently accredited as U.S. ambassador to the European governments in exile in London, was on board with his wife and two secretaries. (The Biddles traveled with thirty-four pieces of luggage; additional pieces had been shipped ahead.) There were also Bolivian tin kings, foreign correspondents on their way to join the British Army of the Nile, a highly cultured Spanish lady taking her English husband to Barcelona for an eye operation, an arms manufacturer of Austrian birth and dubious motives, and a honeymooning couple. Harriman wrote his wife that a mystery novel "could be woven around the characters."[45]

The *Atlantic Clipper* took the usual route to Lisbon, via Bermuda and the

Azores. The passengers sighted Portugal on the afternoon of March 12, a thick cloud bank covering the coast "like icing on a cake." As he flew up the Tagus River to Lisbon, with the blue water giving way to green, Harriman was reminded of California. Colorful houses and an occasional church were scattered through the hills and gullies and down the slopes to little beaches. He spent the next three days cooling his heels at the spies' hotel of choice, the Palácio, waiting for a seat on a KLM flight to Bristol—and "fuming at the foolishness of officialdom" when Biddle's higher diplomatic rank got him on an earlier flight. As a consolation prize, Harriman had dinner with another of FDR's agents, Bill Donovan, who was also passing through Lisbon.

When Harriman was finally summoned to the airfield, he had the "eerie experience" of walking right past a German plane parked on the tarmac, painted entirely black except for a large white swastika. The reality of war was becoming apparent to him. The windows of his Dutch aircraft, a Douglas DC-3 painted in camouflage colors, were blocked with security shades when it started its descent toward the English coast. The final run was made very low, to ensure the plane was not misidentified by British defenses. At 3:30 p.m. on March 15, Harriman stepped down onto English soil.[46]

"Believe me, the American people mean business," Harriman promised the correspondents who were waiting for him. Then he boarded Winston Churchill's Flamingo aircraft, which the prime minister had sent to meet him, for the flight to Chequers. Two Hurricane fighters accompanied them.[47] At Chequers, the usual charm and hospitality shown to prominent American visitors was on display. Harriman was an immediate hit with Clementine, who was delighted he had brought a handful of tangerines from Lisbon: rationing meant that citrus fruits were rarely seen in Britain, even at the prime minister's table. The envoy was shown upstairs to see Churchill, who had taken to his bed with a cold, and he explained his mission as well as the competing demands on U.S. supplies. "My . . . usefulness in pleading Britain's case," Harriman told the PM, would "depend entirely upon the extent of my knowledge and understanding of her position and needs."

Churchill knew an ally when he saw one, and his response was both re-assuring and flattering: "You shall be informed. We accept you as a friend. Nothing shall be kept from you."[48]

No wonder that Harriman felt "like a country boy plopped right into the center of the war." Unlike Sumner Welles or Harry Hopkins, he had always been strictly a second-string operator in Washington. Now, through the vagaries of Roosevelt's envoy diplomacy, he was literally sitting at the feet of the great man of the hour.[49]

After dinner, Churchill gave Harriman one of his famous scene-setters. The scene in March 1941 was gloomy. Harriman had arrived in Europe at the start of the fighting season. Since its stunning victories in 1940, the Wehrmacht wore a dark aura of sinister effectiveness. Everyone in Europe wondered where the mailed fist would land next; the answer would soon prove to be Greece and Yugoslavia. If the chances of an invasion of Britain had subsided, nonetheless she was under vicious attack from the air and the sea. In early March, the Luftwaffe commenced its "tour of the ports"—an attempt to close Britain's harbors through the application of high explosive. At the same time, Germany intensified its assault on British shipping in the North Atlantic, carried out by surface raiders, aircraft, and increasing numbers of U-boats, often hunting in wolf packs. Hitler's forces, Churchill told Harriman, were sinking Britain's merchant vessels three times faster than its shipyards could replace them. Britain was losing ships at the rate of half a million tons a month, a dangerous statistic for a country that imported more than half its food and almost all its raw materials. In the "Battle of the Atlantic"—so named by Churchill himself, with one eye on the Americans—Hitler sought to starve Britain into submission. Now the prime minister invited his newest American friend to attend meetings of the war cabinet's Battle of the Atlantic Committee.[50]

Unlike the missions of Roosevelt's other envoys, the Harriman mission was a long-term appointment rather than a flying visit. Harriman quickly set about establishing his life in London. He took a suite at the Dorchester and borrowed a Bentley and a driver from a well-wisher. He started to assemble a small staff, drawn mainly from various Washington agencies. Harriman always prided himself on running a lean operation, and his mission comprised initially just a handful of people, rising to thirty by the middle of 1941. They included military personnel; a statistician; an engineer; experts in shipping, food, and economics; as well as some gifted amateurs. To begin with, the mission was housed in the U.S. embassy at 1 Grosvenor Square, but it soon moved into an adjoining apartment building, with a door punched through the common wall to enable traffic between the two. Harriman's own office, formerly the living room of an elegant flat, was outfitted with mahogany and leather furniture from Britain's Department of Works. The Harriman mission ran its own payroll, receiving funding from the President's Emergency Fund, and later the Office of Lend-Lease Administration, rather than the State Department.[51]

Harriman brought his personal secretary from the Union Pacific with him to London. Bob Meiklejohn was a Republican, a Freemason, and a bean counter, efficient and pedantic. Harriman's daughter described him sharply as "a man who was devoid of humor and of any interest other than keeping his accounts, and figuring how much more his twin brother was making." It is true that Meiklejohn was mad for his records. On one of his first nights in London, he recorded in his diary that he "had a grand time figuring my accounts. Bought an account book and before I knew it had a regular bookkeeping system worked out, Meiklejohn-style, with a journal and accounts. Looks like a good system and indicates I am not living beyond my resources." He did not limit his records to revenues and expenditures, either. He carefully noted down his haircuts, drew floor plans of his apartment, and prepared lists of "strange English vocabulary." Usefully, he also recorded his impressions of individuals, events, and travels connected with the Harriman mission.[52]

Averell Harriman's job was to expedite aid to Britain. He operated independently of embassy authority, reporting directly to Harry Hopkins in the

White House. Harriman determined Britain's most urgent needs, identified obstructions that were impeding the flow of supplies down the pipeline, and conveyed his recommendations to Washington—along with an appropriate sense of urgency. He made two early contributions to the British effort in the Battle of the Atlantic. In late March, Hitler extended Germany's zone of naval combat as far west as Iceland. Harriman recommended the transfer of a number of American destroyers or cutters to the Royal Navy to bridge the gap. Having only just done the Destroyers-Bases Deal, Roosevelt could not spare any more destroyers, but he squeezed ten cutters out of the U.S. Coast Guard. They hardly turned the tide of battle, but they helped. Churchill, always quick to show gratitude to the Americans, told the president the "cutters will be a Godsend."[53] Harriman was also involved in organizing the repair of damaged British ships in American dockyards, which relieved the immense strain on British yards. Once the president had agreed to the British request, Harriman worked with Washington to schedule the repairs and reduce the ships' time out of action. Soon British aircraft carriers, battleships, and armed merchant cruisers were being repaired and reconditioned in dry docks in New York, Philadelphia, and Norfolk.[54]

But Harriman also assumed more glamorous responsibilities. As George Kennan observed later, Roosevelt's envoy was "endowed with a keen appreciation for great personal power." Bearing a presidential mandate and with FDR's invitation to correspond ringing in his ears, he acted increasingly as the president's surrogate in London, quite beyond questions of supply. If his day job had him down among the weeds, the nature of his position in the United Kingdom allowed him to climb the treetops. His diary was rich with appointments with cabinet ministers and aristocrats. "I never knew I had so many friends and acquaintances in England," he marveled in a letter to his wife, Marie. There were invitations to lunches, dinners, cocktails, and "weekends to last till doomsday."[55]

Harriman gravitated naturally toward the summit. He spent seven weekends with the Churchill family in his first eight weeks in the country, and dined with the prime minister in London at least once a week. Harriman was an instant fan of Churchill's, telling Marie he was "tremendously impressed by the clarity of his conceptions of the problems of this war and the bold courageous decisions he is making every hour."[56] The feeling was mutual. Churchill's daughter Mary recalled that "whatever Averell had been like everybody here would have felt that it was their God-given duty to bloody well get on with him and make the best of it." But in fact, "it was no hardship. He was urbane and agreeable." Harriman was much more fun in London than he had ever been at home. In fact, he was the perfect American houseguest. He was wealthy, handsome, and good at games—bezique with Winston and backgammon and croquet with Clemmie. The PM's wife was a formidable croquet player, regarded within the family as unbeatable. Consequently, there was "total joy," recorded an insider, when "Averell took her on . . . and absolutely thrashed her."[57] Most important of all, though, Harriman was sympathetic.

IT IS HARD NOT TO SYMPATHIZE with your hosts when they are being bombed, and you along with them. In late March, Churchill had Harriman and Biddle to dinner at the Number 10 Annexe. The party was interrupted by a heavy air raid that killed 504 Londoners and injured three times that number. The standard operating procedure in this circumstance was for the prime minister to hunker down. Instead, Churchill gave his guests helmets and led them to the roof of the nearby Air Ministry to watch the show. It was a "fantastic climb," recalled Churchill's secretary Eric Seal, up ladders and stairwells and through a tiny manhole at the top of a tower. German planes were droning overhead, antiaircraft guns firing continually, and fire engines racing past. While explosions lit up the London skyline, Churchill quoted Tennyson's prescient lines on aerial war, written well before the invention of the aircraft:

Heard the heavens fill with shouting, and there rain'd a ghastly dew
From the nations' airy navies grappling in the central blue.

There was "great excitement amongst the Americans," wrote Seal, "who felt they were at last in the war!"[58]

In April, the gloom thickened. Moscow and Tokyo signed a neutrality pact, which made Washington anxious that Japanese forces would soon be on the move southward. German panzer columns wheeled across Greece and Yugoslavia in a matter of weeks. In Libya, General Erwin Rommel chased most of the British forces, their ranks thinned by Churchill's decision to defend Greece, back to the Egyptian border and seemed to threaten Suez. These Axis advances around the edges of the Mediterranean, as well as debilitating losses to British shipping in the Atlantic, caused Roosevelt to toughen his position. Most importantly, he began to ease America into the Battle of the Atlantic.

Here the president faced an acute dilemma. As historian Ian Kershaw has noted, "It made little sense to provide goods for Britain if they were merely to find their way to the bottom of the Atlantic. But helping to protect the transit of the vital material against the raids of U-boats ran the obvious and increasing risk of dragging the United States into the war"—an outcome that was opposed by more than eight out of ten Americans. Roosevelt needed to find a path, then, between benevolent neutrality and belligerency. He still did not believe that public opinion would support the use of U.S. warships to escort British convoys across the Atlantic. Instead, he extended America's security zone eastward to the 26th meridian, halfway between Africa and Brazil. This was an historic assumption of responsibility: previously Washington had counted on the Royal Navy to safeguard the Atlantic. Now America's self-declared defensive waters incorporated most of the North Atlantic, including the Azores and Greenland, which was brought under U.S. protection. Within this vast expanse, FDR ordered the U.S. Navy to conduct wide-ranging patrols and broadcast the positions of Axis vessels it encountered. In a White House press conference, he compared the battleships, cruisers, and carriers of the Atlantic Fleet to scouts sent out ahead of a wagon train to check the location of hostile Indians.

Roosevelt expanded America's reach in other ways, too. In the wake of British successes in East Africa, he removed the Red Sea and the Gulf of Aden from the official combat zone. This meant that American-flag vessels, previously banned from the area by the Neutrality Act, could begin supplying British forces in the Middle East directly, which freed up British merchantmen for more Atlantic crossings.[59]

The president's more aggressive posture was welcomed by Harriman, who had urged the Middle East decision on Washington, and who continued his forthright advocacy of the British cause. "England's strength is bleeding," he warned Roosevelt in his first lengthy report home. "In our own interest I trust our navy can be directly employed before our partner is too weak." When Churchill aide John Colville asked him whether Roosevelt's April announcements might mean war between Germany and the United States, he replied, "That's what I hope."[60]

In the meantime, Harriman did what he could to quicken the pace of interactions between the two capitals. He was, he told FDR, "a general hand holder for all with problems about which they think America might help." He advised British officials on how, and to whom, they should present their problems in Washington.[61] He worked with Hopkins to make sure that important American visitors to Britain saw the right people and received the right impressions. Hopkins was always Harriman's greatest ally. No wonder Harriman urged his Washington mentor to take care of himself: "You must not wear yourself out, you are too important to the situation. Everyone here constantly speaks of you and all look upon you as their truest friend."[62]

Harriman urged Professor Lindemann that Roosevelt be supplied with the same shipping statistics and charts on the Battle of the Atlantic as were available to Churchill so that "he could see the fight progressing."[63] He counseled Churchill on American public opinion, and even pressed on him a summary of American news coverage which concluded that "the urgency of the need for convoys is still not fully appreciated."[64] Given that U.S. policy on convoying was in a state of flux, such a suggestion from a presidential envoy to a foreign head of government may be regarded as sailing close to the wind. Naturally, the British were deeply grateful for this assistance. Churchill minuted the cabinet secretary, "I am all for trusting Mr Harriman fully and working with him on the most intimate terms." On the other hand, Churchill and his aides were determined to retain the power of private correspondence with their own purchasing officials in Washington and were dead against showing all their cables to the Harriman mission.[65] If American officials were determined to protect their supplies, British officials were determined to protect their secrets.

Harriman also became a more visible symbol of American assistance to Britain, accompanying the prime minister on inspection tours of cities that had been devastated by bombing. As he had with Hopkins, Churchill made a practice of introducing Harriman as the president's personal envoy. Over the Easter weekend, he took Harriman and Winant to visit cities in southwest England and Wales that had been stops on the Luftwaffe's tour of the ports. Unlike Roosevelt, who traveled in a cocoon of Secret Service men, Churchill's security depended on surprise: he would arrive unannounced in a town, protected only by a couple of detectives. In the Welsh coal port of Swansea, flattened in three nights in February, Harriman watched as the news of Churchill's visit spread and people poured out of broken buildings to see him. "Down the street he came in an old Ford car . . . smiling, a long cigar stuck deep in his teeth, waving on both sides at once, looking each one in the eye." At the Swansea Guildhall he reviewed the Home Guard, stopping to inquire after a decoration, "From the last war, eh?" In the hospital he passed through "a throng of cheering nurses" to visit the wards, greeting a ship's captain who had been machine-gunned by a Focke-Wulf fighter, and a ten-year-old girl with a broken leg in traction. At the docks, he was surrounded by a crowd of longshoremen whose rowdy reputation had troubled his detectives. Churchill had not yet adopted his "V for victory" sign. Instead, he put his hat on the end of his cane and twirled it around in the air to attract a crowd. "Stand back, my men, let the others see," he commanded. The dockworkers whooped, and parted.[66]

After the party dropped in on a secret rocket research station in Aberporth on the Cardiganshire coast, their train lay overnight in a siding outside their next destination, Bristol—Wendell Willkie's port of departure two months earlier. From there, Churchill and his Americans had a perfect view as the Luftwaffe did its work, raining high explosives and incendiaries down on the city and its docks. The raiders faced a fierce barrage from ground defenses and British night fighters, but with the aid of a full moon they persisted for hours. When they ran out of bombs, they used their machine guns. This would later be known as the Good Friday Raid. At times, as many as eight bombers could be counted above Bristol at once; they flew so low that one fire watcher thought he could have hit them with stones.[67]

When the visitors entered Bristol the next morning, many parts of the city were still in flames. Periodically, delayed-action bombs exploded with a crump. Some streets were blocked by rubble; others were flooded by burst water mains. The tram network had been knocked out. Commander "Tommy" Thompson recalled that "women were busy cooking breakfast in half-demolished houses or over stoves in front gardens. Almost every bombed house had a Union Jack stuck somewhere in the ruins." Everywhere, the party saw dead and wounded being dug out of Bristol's remains. A number of churches were blazing, but the airy Gothic St. Mary Redcliffe—thought by Queen Elizabeth I to be "the fairest, the goodliest, and the most famous parish church in England"—stood untouched among the devastation.

The sight of Churchill driving around seated atop an open car, waving his hat, sent a wave of excitement through the city. Because the prime minister's visit was unheralded, many presumed he had come upon hearing of the raid. Crowds of people gathered around him, waving and cheering. "Pug" Ismay recalled that "they wanted to touch the hem of his garment." Thompson had never seen Churchill more deeply moved: "He kept murmuring to himself, 'Wonderful people . . . wonderful people.'" Winant noticed that Churchill switched from his usual "Cheerio" to a more somber "God bless you." Yet there was also laughter among the ruins. When he thought Churchill was out of earshot, Harriman remarked to Ismay that the PM seemed popular with middle-aged women. The subject of this slight wheeled on Harriman in indignation. "What did you say? Not only with the middle-aged women; with the young ones too."[68]

The original purpose of Churchill's visit was to preside, as the chancellor of the University of Bristol, over a ceremony to confer honorary doctorates on Ambassador Winant and the Australian prime minister, Robert Menzies, who was also in the traveling party, as well as Harvard president James Conant in absentia. Bomb damage to the Great Hall forced a move to a smaller room in the university's fine Gothic tower. Through its broken windows, guests at the ceremony could smell the smoke and see the flames as firemen hosed down smoldering buildings. High walls nearby appeared to totter. As befitting the occasion, attendees wore their academic gowns: scarlet for members of the university senate and the two honorary graduands, dark robes for the rest, with hoods trimmed with ermine or rabbit fur. From Churchill's sloping shoulders hung the black-and-gold robes that had once belonged to his father, Randolph, when he served as chancellor of the exchequer. But this was an unusual ceremony, for most of the learned guests had been up all night fighting fires and were pale with fatigue. Underneath their robes they still wore their Home Guard battle dress, Air Raid Precautions warden uniforms, and firemen's outfits, and they were wet and grimy from their labors.[69]

In defiance of their circumstances, however—and the enemy—no part of the ancient rite was overlooked. The procession included the sword bearer, the lord mayor, and the sheriff of Bristol, various professors and administrators, two bedells, the ceremonial mace, and behind the chancellor, his train-bearer. When Winant and Menzies came before Churchill, one by one, he placed his hands over their closed hands and intoned, "By the authority of the University of Bristol, in virtue of the power vested in me, I admit you to the degree of Doctor of Laws *honoris causa*."

"I see the spirit of an unconquerable people," said Churchill in his address to the ceremony. "I see a spirit bred in freedom, nursed in tradition, which has come down to us through the centuries and will enable us most surely at this moment, this turning point in the history of the world, to bear our part in such a way that none of our race who come after us will have any reason to cast reproaches upon their sires." In reply, Winant recalled Burke's letter to the sheriffs of Bristol about the treatment of American revolutionaries—one of the great statements in defense of representative government. Churchill ended the proceedings by saying, "I declare this congregation closed. God save the King!"[70]

Harriman was moved by the day's events to draft a cable to FDR describing the ceremony. (It was a mark of the weird dualism of his life in Britain that he wrote these notes on the back of a memorandum entitled "Subject: Butter and Dried Butter Fat.") He noted that at no time of the day did Churchill falter. But as the train pulled out of Bristol station, the prime minister dropped back into his seat and held a newspaper over his face in order to hide his tears. "They have such faith," he said. "It is a grave responsibility." All Winant could think of was "the sunlight and soft green of the English spring" out the train window, which was such a startling contrast to the bleak scene they had left behind them.[71]

BACK IN LONDON LATER THAT WEEK, Harriman experienced one of the biggest night blitzes of the war. On the evening of April 16, the Luftwaffe sent 450 planes to drop their bombs, incendiaries, and parachute-mines on the capital. When Bob Meiklejohn heard the first glass breaking at 9 p.m., he locked up his secret cables, donned his helmet, and climbed to the embassy roof, where he got "a fine view in all directions." He saw huge explosions that "looked as if whole houses were sailing up in the air," and "dozens of high explosive bombs being poured into the fires and lifting regular geysers of flame into the air." A column of fire from the Battersea Power Station "seemed to go up miles." He admitted that when aircraft started diving in his direction he "did a couple of tumbling acts . . . to dodge bombs that fell blocks away." Streets were ripped up and cratered: the *Sydney Morning*

Herald's London correspondent reported that automobiles "rocked as if on an Australian bush road."[72]

From a room high up in the Dorchester, where he was attending a dinner party, Harriman watched as clusters of German flares drifted down, lighting "parts of the city like Broadway & 42nd Street." Robert Menzies, also in the Dorchester that evening, recalled that a dozen bombs landed within a hundred yards of the hotel and on several occasions "the whole building seemed to bounce with the force of the concussion." Finally, when "a bomb hit so close that it almost blew us back into the room," Harriman and his friends adjourned to the relative safety of his suite in the bowels of the hotel. When he made it to bed, he reported to Marie, "my sleep was intermittent."[73]

It was probably not only high explosives that kept Harriman up, however. It seems likely that on this night he began an affair that would turn out to be the most significant of his life. The next morning, John Colville went out to inspect the results of the raid. "London looks bleary-eyed and disfigured," he recorded. There was "a great gash in the Admiralty"; Jermyn Street, the historic home of fine shirtmakers and bootmakers, was wrecked; Mayfair had "suffered badly." Menzies, also out that morning, found "craters and fallen masonry in the streets," "a great plume of red smoke" rising from Selfridge's, and gas mains blazing in Piccadilly. Everywhere, pedestrians "crunched over acres of broken glass." Walking in the sun on Horse Guards Parade, off Whitehall, Colville also noticed something else: Averell Harriman and the comely Pamela Churchill, walking hand in hand. "Well I wonder," he thought to himself.[74]

Colville was right to wonder. The president's special envoy was sleeping with the prime minister's daughter-in-law.

PAMELA DIGBY CHURCHILL was a flirtatious twenty-one-year-old with "Raeburnesque red curls and freckles" and very bright eyes. "Every man in London was attracted by her," recalled a former war correspondent. "She was honey drawing flies." Less than a month after she had met Randolph

Churchill, a lieutenant in the 4th Hussars and notorious gambler, boozer, and womanizer, they were engaged to be married. When she gave birth to young Winston in October 1940—the first baby delivered at Chequers in two centuries—Randolph was rumored to be in the arms of another woman. (A few months later, at his first meeting with Hopkins, the prime minister pointed proudly to a picture of Pamela and his grandson.) When Randolph was posted to Egypt, the couple's finances decimated by his gambling losses, she took a job at the Ministry of Supply and moved into the Dorchester. The baby was parked with a nanny at Cherkley Court, the home of her godfather, Lord Beaverbrook. Many years later, Pamela remembered "walking down the Dorchester's corridors thinking, here I am . . . totally free . . . wondering who will walk into my life." Then one evening she entered a room and found "the most beautiful man I'd ever seen in my life, called Averell Harriman . . . sometimes things sort of click, click, click."

No doubt there was an instant physical attraction, despite the thirty-year age difference. But it was also a good match. He was, her friends told her, "the most important American in London"; she knew everyone who mattered, starting with her in-laws. Through her, Pamela recalled later, Averell "kind of came into the family through the back door." Perhaps each saw a little of themselves in the other. After all, both were chancers, trading up in spectacular fashion. His plodding government career and her dull country-life upbringing were now behind them: they were right in the thrilling, throbbing heart of things.[75]

When the bombing was intense, Pamela and her flatmate would sometimes retreat to Wendell Willkie's old bombproof suite on the first floor, now occupied by her friend Robert Menzies. On the night of the April 16 raid, however, she ended up staying in Harriman's suite, and probably in his bed. Such things were not uncommon in London in 1941. The war, which disrupted many of the rhythms of British life, also suspended the normal rules of morality for many people. As Harriman put it, "there was nothing like a blitz to get something going."

For a while at least, Harriman and Pamela were able to keep their relationship secret. The social routines of the Churchill family thrust them together, although Pamela was careful not to sign the visitors' book at Chequers when they were both there for the weekend.[76]

Harriman soon had the perfect cover in the person of his daughter Kathleen, who arrived in London in May after gaining a visa with Harry Hopkins's help. She got a job with the Hearst news organization and also acted as her father's hostess and social secretary. Churchill took her presence in Britain as an expression of confidence, one that was doubly welcome because the traffic of children of important people usually went in the opposite direction.[77] Kathleen and Pamela, both in their early twenties, hit it off, and when Harriman took a larger suite at the Dorchester, they both moved in with him. This convenient arrangement soon extended to a sixteenth-century country cottage, Petersfield Farm, located a few miles from Beaverbrook's place in Surrey, where the threesome spent bucolic weekends. The farm was "a good alibi," Pamela recalled later. Later still they decamped from the Dorchester and moved into an apartment in Grosvenor Square, near the embassy. Kathleen quickly figured out what was happening, but she said nothing. Illicit liaisons were not uncommon in her world and neither her father nor her stepmother, Marie, were innocent of them.[78]

Clementine and Winston Churchill, who got on famously with Pam, may have been more naïve. It is not clear whether they were aware of the state of things at the time. John Colville thought they would have been "horrified" and "indignant" if they had known of the "little pattering of feet along the corridors at night." Winston only ever alluded to the issue once, saying to Pamela, "You know, they're saying a lot of things about Averell in relation to you." Pamela told historian Arthur Schlesinger later that her "blood froze," but she responded breezily that "a lot of people have nothing else to do in wartime but indulge in gossip." "I quite agree," said her father-in-law, and that was the end of the conversation. There was talk that some in Washington were concerned about the affair, but there was little risk of the press breaking such a story. Franklin Roosevelt usually took an amused interest in the personal foibles of his acquaintances. In this case, according to Hopkins, FDR "knew all about it, and laughed about it."[79]

There was precious little laughter in May 1941, another troubled month for the Allies. In the Mediterranean, Malta was bombed and Crete invaded; in the Western Desert, Rommel won further victories, although he could not lever the besieged port of Tobruk from the hands of its Australian, British, and Indian defenders.

Against the backdrop of this dismal news, Roosevelt's caution was creating angst among the hawks in his administration. He sought to discourage Japanese expansionism through engagement and diplomatic signaling: exploratory talks between Cordell Hull and Tokyo's ambassador to the United States, Kichisaburo Nomura; flag-flying in Australasia; and increased aid to China. But he did not want to provoke Japan into a confrontation that would soak up U.S. resources. The Atlantic remained his preoccupation. If, as historian Robert Dallek argues, the president had concluded by now that America would eventually have to join that fight, "he remained painfully uncertain about how to proceed." In a speech on May 27, FDR warned that the Allies must retain "control of the seas" and proclaimed an "unlimited national emergency," but he was silent on what this actually meant. It was certainly not a declaration of war; Roosevelt was not even ready to adopt a policy of escorting Allied convoys.[80]

Harriman professed to be delighted by FDR's remarks. He cabled Hopkins, "Congratulations speech. Will result in reduction certain stocks by your friends this evening with view to salutary effect your health." In fact, though, no one was more frustrated by the pace of U.S. policy than the president's resident envoy in London. The inconstancy of American public opinion made him think that "America must be a nation of ostriches," he told his wife, Marie. "Hasn't the country any pride? Are we to continue to hide behind the skirts of these poor British women, who are holding up the civil defense here?"[81] "Either we have an interest in the outcome of this war, or we have not," he said in a letter to William Bullitt. "If not, why are we supplying

England with the tools? If we have, why do we not realize that the situation could not be tougher and every day we delay direct participation . . . we are taking an extreme risk that either the war will be lost or the difficulty of winning it multiplied . . . for each week we delay."[82] The president, Harriman believed, was playing Fabius.

THE SPRING OF 1941 was a dreadful season for Franklin Roosevelt. He was run-down and unwell, with a persistent cold, stomach troubles, and a serious iron deficiency, possibly caused by bleeding hemorrhoids, which required him to have multiple blood transfusions. He took to his bed and rarely came down to the Oval Office. The health of his personal assistant and confidante of two decades, Missy LeHand, was also suffering, and she would shortly suffer incapacitating strokes that would remove her from his service. Domestic politics were heating up, too. Black leaders, angry that well-qualified African Americans were being passed over for jobs by defense contractors, were planning to march on Washington, with unpredictable consequences for race relations. Meanwhile, the troublesome labor leader John L. Lewis, who had supported Wendell Willkie in the fall, was threatening to halt production of the coal required so urgently by the defense industries.

On the war, Roosevelt was wedged uncomfortably between isolationists on one side, who regarded him as an adventurer or a traitor, and interventionists on the other, who regarded him as a laggard. Many of his closest advisers, including Stimson, Knox, Morgenthau, Ickes, and Hopkins, were urging him to step up America's involvement in the conflict. But FDR was troubled by the continuing attacks from isolationists, who were staging huge rallies across the country starring Charles Lindbergh. He was also conscious that many Americans remained disconnected from events in Europe. The record-breaking fifty-six-game hitting streak enjoyed by the New York Yankees' Joe DiMaggio in the spring and summer was a more absorbing development for many people than anything happening in Europe. DiMaggio was the "Yankee Clipper" Americans cared most about. In these circumstances, Roosevelt did not want to lead the country into war: as he told Morgenthau, he was "waiting to be pushed into" it.[83]

At the same time, FDR was fighting a rearguard battle to protect Sumner Welles from his enemies. In late April, William Bullitt laid before Roosevelt a dossier describing Welles's homosexual advances to Pullman porters on the presidential train the previous year. Bullitt warned darkly that Welles was "subject to blackmail by foreign powers," if not criminal prosecution and "a terrible public scandal" that would undermine confidence in FDR. Furthermore, "morale in the Department of State . . . was being ruined by the knowledge that a man of the character of Welles was in control of all appointments and transfers." The president admitted he knew about the incident on the train, having been briefed on it by FBI director J. Edgar Hoover. But he refused to take action against Welles, insisting that his under secretary of state was too valuable to be sacked. Bullitt demanded how Roosevelt could consider asking "Americans to die in a crusade for all that was decent in human life" if one of the crusade's leaders was "a criminal like Welles." FDR dismissed his visitor abruptly, canceled the rest of his day's appointments, and retired to the residence. A furious Bullitt left the White House determined that, one way or another, Welles would be punished for his misbehavior.[84]

Meanwhile, the European war was still occupying the attentions of Wendell Willkie. The Republican had gone back to the law when he returned from England, signing on as a partner in the corporate firm of Willkie, Owen, Otis & Bailey. From his dark-paneled downtown office in the Equitable Trust Building, next to J.P. Morgan's headquarters, he could look over New York Harbor to the army barracks and Castle Williams on Governors Island. Yet the "well-ordered quiet" that visitors observed in his office belied his restlessness. Willkie was not finished with public life. Even his law practice had a political feel to it. Among his clients were European refugees who had fled the Nazis and were petitioning the U.S. government to relax its restrictions on their personal funds, and the secretary of the Californian Communist Party, whose citizenship had been revoked because of his political beliefs. In May, Willkie gave a speech to the Freedom Rally at Madison

Square Garden in support of aid to Britain, and argued the case for internationalism in a widely read article in *Collier's* magazine. "The capital of the world of tomorrow will be either Berlin or Washington," he wrote. "I prefer Washington." Willkie concluded, "Americans, stop being afraid!"[85]

Averell Harriman was too busy enjoying himself to be afraid. He was having the time of his life in London. Kathleen reported to Marie that he was working "very hard" but was "in the best of spirits—it's hard not to be when you're in his position. He knows everyone and they all think the world of him." There was a "peculiar charm" to being an American in Britain, Kathleen observed. "Yesterday I met some soldier in a pub off Fleet Street and his one comment was, 'Just wait 'til I get back and tell them I've met an American!'"[86]

Harriman continued his practice of relaxing in the country with the Churchill court. The weekend of May 9–12, spent at Ditchley, involved the usual strange mixture of the political and personal. On Sunday evening, Churchill, Harriman, and others were watching a Marx Brothers film in the darkened sitting room. They were glad for a diversion from the grim news about the battering London had suffered the previous night—the worst of the war, in which the debating chamber of the House of Commons was gutted. That must have been like a thorn in Churchill's flesh. The screening was interrupted, however, by a telephone call conveying the sensational information that the deputy Führer, Rudolf Hess, whom Welles had met in Berlin a year earlier, had landed by parachute in Scotland. In an ill-starred attempt at peacemaking, Hess had piloted a Messerschmitt Bf 110 to Britain and bailed out near the home of the Duke of Hamilton, his chosen interlocutor. Churchill wondered whether Hess had selected Hamilton because he held the title of Lord Steward of His Majesty's Household and therefore assumed he was intimate with the head of state: "I suppose he thinks that the Duke carves the chicken and consults the King as to whether he likes breast or leg!" This obscure Scottish peer, summoned immediately to Ditchley, was unable to throw much light on the matter. It was, as Churchill later told the Commons, "one of these cases where imagination is sometimes baffled by the facts as they present themselves."[87]

All this excitement made it difficult for the prime minister to deal with a pressing family issue. His youngest daughter, eighteen-year-old Mary, was threatening to accept a marriage proposal from an aristocratic young soldier, Lord Duncannon, the Earl of Bessborough's heir. While the man was socially suitable, Winston and Clementine were dead against the match on the grounds of her youth and inexperience. Wartime marriages were notoriously unstable, as several other Churchill children could attest. With the PM otherwise occupied, Clementine asked Harriman to try to talk Mary out of the marriage. The two of them bundled up against the cold and discussed the matter while they circumnavigated the formal Italian garden, with its stone-edged beds and terra-cotta vases filled with flowers from Ditchley's green-houses. "Poor Averell," Mary recalled later. "It's one thing to be sent by your president to England but to be told to meddle in the love affairs of an hysterical girl of 18!"

Harriman, whose own parenting skills were minimal, and who had just commenced an affair with the Churchills' daughter-in-law, was not fazed by the prospect of counseling their daughter on matters of the heart. His charm was improving: when Mary told him how pro-American she felt and how much she enjoyed the company of American men, he said he'd see "if Washington wouldn't send her an American husband as part of the Lend-Lease Bill and then after the war she could turn him back to the U.S." In any case, Mary thought his advice not to rush things was "very wise." The "accumulation of Averell's worldly wisdom and his kind interest in my love life worked the trick," she recalled later, and she called the engagement off. Many years later, Harriman's friend Arthur Schlesinger observed that "he likes to be close to power, on friendly terms." With the Churchills, the terms were almost familial.[88]

———

THE WAR FOLLOWED CHURCHILL wherever he went. A fortnight later, at the height of the battle for Crete, Harriman was with the prime minister at Chequers for the start of one of the most famous naval encounters of the war.[89] It was a nervous weekend, as the new German battleship *Bismarck*, the most heavily armed ship afloat, together with the heavy cruiser *Prinz Eugen*, had entered the North Atlantic on a hunting trip. Eleven British convoys, including a troop convoy, were vulnerable to their attentions. A large number of the Royal Navy's capital ships, including the battleships *King George V* (which had welcomed Harry Hopkins aboard in January) and *Prince of Wales*, the battlecruisers *Hood*, *Repulse*, and *Renown*, and the carriers *Ark Royal* and *Victorious* were detailed to find and destroy the German warships. On the evening of Friday, May 23, Churchill and his guests waited anxiously on developments, checking regularly with the duty captain at the Admiralty. They retired late without news, and early the next morning Harriman was woken by Churchill at his door, wearing a yellow sweater over his short nightshirt, which failed to cover his pink legs. "Hell of a battle going on," he reported. "The *Hood* is sunk. Hell of a battle." All but three men of the *Hood*'s company of fifteen hundred were lost, and the *Bismarck* was steaming south toward the British convoys. On Saturday night, her British pursuers lost her in the darkness, and at Chequers, as Colville recorded, "a day of fearful gloom ensued."

Under orders from the Admiralty and the weight of Churchill's urgings, a remarkable chase ensued as the *Bismarck* headed for France alone and ships converged from everywhere on her estimated position. Finally, she was spotted by a PBY Catalina, and a Swordfish torpedo bomber from the *Ark Royal* damaged the German battleship's steering gear, leaving her unmaneuverable. On the morning of May 27, as she lay wallowing, she was ruined by heavy shells fired by a ring of British ships. The *Bismarck* was finally sent to the bottom of the sea by either a British torpedo or an order to scuttle. "I have just received news that the *Bismarck* is sunk," Churchill was able to tell the House of Commons minutes later. The reaction from members of parliament, meeting in Church House, the headquarters of the Church of England, instead of their own wrecked chamber, was exuberant. As Churchill recalled modestly in his memoirs, "They seemed content."

In the three months he had been back in Washington, Harry Hopkins had been busier than ever. He had reprised his old role of chief foreign policy counselor: he was, as a British official put it, "Roosevelt's own personal Foreign Office." FDR prized his aide's work so highly that, in a neat inversion of the typical president-staff relationship, he protected Hopkins by dealing with importunate callers himself. "I don't want you to bother Harry with that," he would say indignantly. "Harry has too much to worry about as it is."

Indeed he had, for Hopkins had also acquired two new jobs. He was the chief intermediary between Roosevelt and Churchill, advising each about the other's thinking and predicament while retaining the perfect confidence of both. He was also back on the public payroll—for the first time since he resigned as commerce secretary—as Roosevelt's informal administrator of Lend-Lease. He was, diarized Richard Casey, "the fairy godmother of Lend-Lease," receiving the wishes of His Majesty's Government (sometimes via Averell Harriman) and doing his best to grant them. Hopkins was, of course, well accustomed to the job of spending billions of dollars of public funds—it was his specialty. But now his expenditure had an international rather than a domestic focus.[90]

Robert Sherwood observed that Hopkins's "method of attack" was essentially the same as in the New Deal days, except that now, "instead of breadlines, droughts, floods or hurricanes, he was confronting the greatest disaster that had ever befallen the human race." Hopkins had a small staff—initially fewer than twenty people, growing within a few months to one hundred—but he was able to call on thousands in the various government agencies. He used every bit of his authority to speed the production, allocation, and transportation of vital war materials to the democracies. Hopkins was, said one rueful interlocutor, "Generalissimo of the Needling Brigade," quick to summon a cautious military officer or recalcitrant industrialist to the telephone in order to clear a bottleneck or deliver a dressing-down. "If we do not watch our step," said the same official, all too aware of Britain's needs and Hopkins's desire to meet them, "we shall find the White House *en route* to England with the Washington Monument as a steering-oar."[91]

Hopkins's writ ran wide, for Lend-Lease touched most departments of the federal government, indeed many aspects of American life. The dimensions of the program were gigantic. The flow of American aid would not dry up, FDR vowed, but rather "accelerate from day to day, until the stream becomes a river, and the river a torrent, engulfing this totalitarian tyranny which seeks to dominate the world." It comprised everything from motor vehicles and petroleum products to tanks, ships, and even naval bases. In 1941, the U.S. Navy Department sent a thousand American engineers and mechanics to Northern Ireland and Scotland to build four destroyer and seaplane bases for the British, at a cost of $50 million. Congress would eventually appropriate one thousand times that amount, some $50 billion, to pay for the torrent of Lend-Lease aid it provided to its allies.[92]

If Lend-Lease helped to save Europe, it also changed America. New shipyards, factories, plants, and depots sprung up across the country, financed by Lend-Lease funds, to meet the new demand. "Lend-Lease money helped to build the great Ford bomber plant at Willow Run, the Chrysler Tank Arsenal in Detroit, and Kaiser's Permanente shipyards at Richmond, California," noted Edward Stettinius, Hopkins's successor as Lend-Lease supremo. It enlarged navy yards, expanded aircraft factories, and built new shipways. It helped to switch the focus of American industry, converting the output of existing factories "from automobile wheels to gun-mounts, from fireworks to ammunition, and from cotton-mill machinery to howitzers for mountain fighting." Of course, it took time for American industry to tool up. The largest early Lend-Lease allocations were for warplanes, ordnance, and merchant ships to transport the aid, but many of these orders were not shipped until 1942. When FDR signed the Lend-Lease bill, he opened up a pipeline, but it took months to fill the pipeline with arms.

Lend-Lease was able to help the British see off one threat they faced in the spring of 1941, however: starvation. Prior to the war, the United Kingdom had imported the majority of its food, including eggs and butter from New Zealand and Denmark; fish from Norway; cheese and vegetables from the Netherlands and France; and beef, flour, and wheat from Canada, Australia, and Argentina. The war progressively eroded these imports: first, food shipments were reduced to create shipping space for war materials; then Germany's Blitzkrieg eliminated whole countries as sources of food imports; then her U-boats decimated the merchant fleet that carried the shipments to Britain. Food rationing was instituted, and by one estimate the average British adult lost ten pounds between the fall of France and the passage of Lend-Lease. Meanwhile, the national food reserves were dwindling fast.

On April 16, 1941, Roosevelt extended the Lend-Lease program to cover food. He directed his agriculture secretary to transfer to Britain immediately one hundred thousand cases of evaporated milk, eleven thousand tons of eggs, and the same quantity of cheese. Over the course of 1941, one million tons of Lend-Lease foodstuffs were shipped, including canned pork and fish, dried and canned vegetables, and various forms of dairy products. Millions of vitamin tablets were flown over the Atlantic in heavy bombers being delivered to the Royal Air Force. Food shipments comprised half the value of all Lend-Lease exports to Britain in 1941.

Averell Harriman was at the Tilbury docks at the end of May to watch the first Lend-Lease food shipment being unloaded. When it arrived, Britain had only a few weeks' reserve supply of food left. Within a couple of days, canned meat, dried eggs, evaporated milk, and cheese from America was being served in British homes. The strange meats and rehydrated dairy products did not, perhaps, meet with universal enthusiasm. Nevertheless, Lend-Lease was feeding Britain.[93]

Food supply offers a good example of how the Hopkins-Harriman axis operated to salve irritations in the bilateral relationship. The minister of food, Lord Woolton, oversaw Britain's rationing system and promoted austerity dishes, including the meatless "Woolton Pie." When the first Lend-Lease food shipment arrived, Woolton had the temerity to call publicly for Americans to reduce their consumption of dairy products, canned fish, and meat so that these goods could be sent to Britain. Hopkins cabled Harriman that Americans would take more kindly to rationing advice from the U.S. Department of Agriculture. "The burden of this message," he said, "is to tell his Lordship in a nice way to pipe down." A chastened Lord Woolton soon agreed to Harriman's request that future broadcasts to the United States be cleared with the American authorities first.[94]

Notwithstanding his collaboration with Hopkins, Harriman was frustrated by the lack of information he received from home. He wrote one friend that it felt like "a Chinese wall" separated Washington and London.[95] Harriman complained to Roosevelt that the mail was "intolerably slow" and that he received no regular updates from home, concluding, "My usefulness will be in direct proportion to the extent to which I am kept informed of the developments in fact and thought in Washington." When FDR waved him away, Harriman arranged to have his staff visit the British ministries with which they dealt each day to review the cable traffic between the two capitals.[96] But this was far from perfect, and Harriman complained to Winant that if it were not for cables he received from a friend in the OPM, he "would be completely in the dark as to what was going on in Washington." "Our information now comes from the British," said Harriman. "I would prefer to see Washington through American rather than British eyes."[97] Even FDR's own envoys suffered the effects of his unorthodox administrative methods.

IT TOOK QUITE SOME CHUTZPAH on Harriman's part to complain to Winant about his access to the councils of power, given that his presence in London had wholly undermined the ambassador's position in Churchill's circle.

In many respects, Winant's embassy was a success. When he arrived in

Britain, he was met at the Windsor train station by the king, a "special courtesy" urged on Buckingham Palace by the Foreign Office in an attempt to match FDR's dramatic precedent of sailing out to greet Lord Halifax.[98] He renewed his old friendships with figures on the British left and established a warm relationship with the British public, based on his obvious decency and sympathy for the British cause. A Briton told Harold Ickes that "Winant was the most popular ambassador . . . the United States had ever sent to England."[99]

Winant went to great lengths to identify himself with the British. He lived simply, eschewing the grand ambassadorial residence at 14 Prince's Gate, overlooking Hyde Park, in favor of a small flat in Grosvenor Square, next to the embassy. He made a point of living on British wartime rations. He was often seen walking the streets of London after an air raid, offering assistance to those left homeless. The *Times* observed that in his speeches he "associated himself fully and freely with the British effort" by using the word " 'we' where a more cautious diplomatist might have been content with 'you.' " The contrast with Joseph Kennedy could hardly have been more dramatic. Winant represented, recalled an aide to Lord Beaverbrook, "a pinnacle after an abyss."[100]

Over time, however, FDR's use of Harriman—and Harriman's way of doing business—diminished Winant's role as the official U.S. representative in London. In his memoir, Winant gave a gracious version of events, writing of Roosevelt's appointment of Harriman that it "would have been hard to have made a happier choice . . . The assignment was carried out with skill, sagacity and tireless energy . . . Civil necessities and military needs were met with dispatch, and the order of priorities showed a rare comprehension of the demands of total war."[101]

In truth, the relationship between the two men was difficult. In the opinion of the U.S. military attaché Brigadier General Lee, "Never did any Ambassador undertake a new appointment with such a handicap as another man, bearing a wide open letter from the President, which describes him as his personal representative and authorizes him to interfere in anything and everything." Lee continued, "Winant has been entirely too patient. How Kennedy would have blown up!"[102] Herschel Johnson was "enraged" that Harriman was "trespassing upon the dignity, the prerogatives and the mission of Winant." He believed that Harriman's appointment was "one of the most extraordinary pieces of lunacy that has ever come to my attention."[103] The shift in Harriman's duties, from one of expediting supply to what Lee called "a kind of whispering job between Churchill and Roosevelt," left Winant firmly on the sidelines—especially given that the envoy sent his most important cables to the White House via the navy so that the State Department would not see them.[104]

For Churchill, Lend-Lease was an existential issue, so he lavished attention on the expediter at the expense of the ambassador. Winant's relationship with the prime minister dimmed, as did his ability to contribute to important debates in London. He felt his exclusion deeply, often turning up at a friend's house late at night to pace up and down the length of the sitting room and inveigh against the latest slight he had received from Harriman.[105]

Harriman made a few attempts to ameliorate the situation. In an April letter to Roosevelt, plainly aware that Winant felt undercut, Harriman wrote of "the complete confidence and respect that your Ambassador has won from all classes of people in England . . . His sympathies are warm, his devotion complete, and his judgment sound. I appreciate the opportunity of working with him."[106] A month later, Harriman told FDR, "I have never before worked in a more congenial atmosphere than at Grosvenor Square, largely due to Gil's generous personality."[107] But although Harriman admired Winant's selflessness, he did not allow any concern for the ambassador's feelings to cramp his style. FDR also tried to reassure Winant, insisting when he returned to Washington for consultations at the end of May that he stay at the White House so they could talk at length.[108] These gestures could not conceal, however, Winant's relative insignificance in the bilateral relationship. Roosevelt was always hungry for firsthand intelligence, but he was rarely faithful to a single source, and when Winant returned to London the situation continued as before.

Plainly, Roosevelt's use of Averell Harriman as a personal envoy disrupted the work of the official U.S. representative in London. This was harsh treatment on FDR's part; after all, Winant was no State Department Anglophobe or "striped-pants boy," but the president's personal appointee, a vocal supporter of aid to Britain and the president's foreign policy. Roosevelt must have felt badly about it, for he soon sought to set things right—through the offices of another special envoy.

THE FIRST PHASE of the Harriman mission concluded in the summer of 1941 when Winston Churchill asked him to make an inspection tour of the Middle East. "I wish you could go out there and see if there is anything you can do," said the prime minister. Harriman accepted immediately—even before President Roosevelt had agreed to share his envoy. The immediate purpose of the trip was to expedite the supply of U.S. combat aircraft, tanks, and other equipment that was now being sent to British forces fighting the Germans and Italians in North Africa, and to ensure that it was being assembled properly and put to the best possible use. The British had recently faced severe reverses in Greece and Crete. With their position in Egypt and the Middle East threatened from both east and west—by Axis infiltration of Syria, a pro-Axis coup in Baghdad, and Rommel's daring actions in the Western Desert—British forces were in urgent need of matériel.[109]

Churchill had a second, broader motive, however: to turn the sympathetic Harriman into an ally on the question of continued British engagement in the theater—one with recent experience on the ground. Sharp divisions existed both within and between the British and the U.S. governments regarding the importance of the Middle East, with some of the British chiefs of staff (especially General Sir John Dill, the chief of the Imperial General Staff) and the U.S. Army concerned that Churchill's preoccupation with the eastern Mediterranean could imperil the British position in the Far East—and perhaps the British Isles themselves.[110]

Churchill looked to Harriman for support in relation to strategy, then, as well as supply. He wrote a generous letter introducing Harriman to General Sir Archibald Wavell, the British commander in chief in the Middle East. "Mr Harriman enjoys my complete confidence and is in the most intimate relations with the President and Mr Harry Hopkins," said the prime minister. "No one can do more for you . . . I commend Mr Harriman to your most attentive consideration. He will report both to his own government and to me as Minister of Defence."[111] Given that the United States was not a belligerent in the war that Churchill and Wavell were prosecuting, this was a breathtaking credential.

For Harriman, Churchill's request was irresistible. It got him away from the more mundane aspects of his London job (which were parked with Brigadier General Lee for the duration, much to the attaché's chagrin) and into the action. It was "an opportunity to make a real and perhaps vital contribution," he wrote to Marie. And it could only bring him closer to Churchill.[112]

On June 9, Harriman took off from Poole for Lisbon en route to West Africa, accompanied by two experts from the Harriman mission and the "ever faithful" Bob Meiklejohn. (In preparation for the trip, Meiklejohn had outfitted himself with a Burberry raincoat, a lightweight suit, sturdy shoes, an attaché case with a patented Braham lock for storing secret documents, and a pith helmet. He ignored the advice from a Briton just back from the region to pack his tuxedo in his new Pullman suitcase, even though "they wear them in Cairo more now than in London.")[113]

The party covered sixteen thousand miles in thirty-seven days. They flew over the Atlantic, the Gulf of Guinea, the Red Sea, and the Mediterranean, not to mention the continent of Africa. They encountered hostile aircraft from the German, Vichy French, and Italian air forces that displayed varying degrees of competence. They were even fired on by a British Tommy. They traveled on a mixed flock of aircraft, including an old PBY Catalina seaplane in which an old can doubled as a dining table and bathroom fixture; a Bristol Bombay troop carrier with an interior that was almost completely bare; and a Lockheed Lodestar that felt, at times, "like a Turkish bath."[114] This was not pleasure travel.

Their first stop was Bathurst, the capital of British Gambia, a "shabby town on a point" by Harriman's reckoning, where one of the local sports was hippopotamus hunting. There was time for lunch at the governor's blessedly cool residence with two other Western visitors, FDR's son James and Captain Lord Louis "Dickie" Mountbatten, cousin of King George, whose destroyer had been sunk under him in the battle for Crete.[115] Then they flew along the West African coast to Freetown in Sierra Leone, an important assembly point for Atlantic convoys. Almost a hundred ships lay in Freetown's harbor—cruisers, destroyers, tramp steamers, merchantmen, troop transports, and others. At sunrise, the noise of the city was "drum-shattering—a thousand farmyards at one time—a million cocks competing with each other to call attention to the obvious, that the light has come." With the light came the humidity and mosquitoes. "Heat is the big industry here," reported Harriman to his wife. When he inspected the port, he saw a Vichy French bomber come in low on a lazy reconnaissance run. A few rounds were fired at the aircraft, without effect.[116]

The twelve-hundred-mile flight under the bulge of Africa to Lagos, Nigeria, took them over Vichy French territory, as well as a number of old slave-trading forts scattered in the bushland. Harriman stayed with the American consul in Lagos and learned about the polo-playing lifestyle of the British colonial officials. "Not a bad life," was his summary, "lots of black servants, work not too hard." He also encountered some unlikely visitors who were also passing through: the prime minister of New Zealand and the king of Greece, who was on his way to exile in Britain after the German conquest of his country.[117] Then Harriman doubled back to the important deepwater port of Takoradi, on the Gold Coast, where he inspected a secret British plant for the assembly of aircraft—American Tomahawks and Mohawks, British Hurricanes and Blenheims—for service in the Middle East. From Takoradi, the party joined the ferry route these newly assembled aircraft customarily took, right across Africa.[118]

They stopped in the old walled town of Kano, in northern Nigeria, and touched down in El Fasher in the Sudan in "furnace heat" and a sandstorm.

As the bush below gave way to sand and rocks, and then to mountains, Harriman wrote to Marie that the Lockheed was "bouncing around like a rubber ball over a broken country . . . the most desolate I have ever seen . . . I can't imagine why anyone wants to bother about ruling over this area—let alone live in it." Finally, they made it to Khartoum, the meeting place of the Blue Nile and the White Nile and a rare green spot in the desert. From Khartoum they could see the plain near Omdurman where Major-General Sir Herbert Kitchener put down the Mahdist forces in 1898 and ensured Britain's control of the Sudan. Riding with the 21st Lancers at that battle was a young Lieutenant Winston Churchill. In the governor-general's residence at Khartoum, "his nibs," as Meiklejohn sometimes called Harriman, enjoyed his first bath in a long time. On June 19, the party flew straight down the Nile to the heart of the British Empire in North Africa and the headquarters of its Middle East campaign—Cairo.[119]

The city of Cairo mounted a daily assault on the senses of visiting Westerners. A Briton who arrived in the city at the same time as Harriman recorded this description:

> Here a narrow street with overhanging houses, the brouhaha of the market and the clink of very small change, there a boulevard looking as if it had been transported from Lille or the outskirts of Brussels; Rolls-Royces and Cadillacs honking their way past disdainful camels; riches and poverty jostling along together; several octaves of smells, at one moment the nursery smell of cheap carpets and blankets and cottons put out for sale in the sun, at another a stench of open drains of Venetian intensity, at yet another the aroma of coffee roasting, or again just the acrid smell of human sweat and dirty clothes.[120]

Meiklejohn's impressions of Cairo were not so nuanced. "We have slums in New York," he wrote home, "but in Egypt the slums come right out and park on your doorstep." He was even underwhelmed by the Pyramids and the Sphinx.[121]

Franklin Roosevelt talking to journalists during a tour
of his estate at Hyde Park, New York, July 4, 1937.

Franklin Roosevelt in his wheelchair
with his Scottish terrier, Fala, and a
local girl at Top Cottage, Hyde Park,
February 1941.

Franklin and Eleanor Roosevelt in Washington, D.C., on the day of his third inauguration, January 20, 1941.

Sumner Welles in his office at the State Department, c. 1940.

Cordell Hull and Sumner Welles on their way to the White House for a luncheon with Franklin Roosevelt, Washington, D.C., May 9, 1940.

Mathilde and Sumner Welles and their West Highland terrier, Toby, c. 1940.

Hermann Göring showing Sumner Welles his paintings at his hunting lodge, Carinhall, March 3, 1940.

Sumner Welles with Joseph Kennedy in London, March 11, 1940.

Lieutenant Colonel Bill Donovan, 165th U.S. Infantry Regiment (formerly "the Fighting 69th"), Hazavant, France, September 6, 1918.

Bill Donovan at 10
Downing Street, London,
December 18, 1940.

Bill Donovan after
arriving in New York on
a British flying boat, the
Clare, August 4, 1940.

Harry Hopkins,
c. 1939–1940.

Harry Hopkins boarding
the *Yankee Clipper* at
LaGuardia Field, New York,
January 6, 1941.

Winston Churchill and Harry Hopkins (wearing his old fedora) on board the Australian destroyer HMAS *Napier*, en route from Thurso to Scapa Flow, January 15, 1941.

Harry Hopkins and Winston Churchill on their inspection tour of Scotland, January 1941.

Harry Hopkins and Franklin Roosevelt in the oval study
on the second floor of the White House, June 1942.

Wendell Willkie, c. 1940.

THE WHITE HOUSE
WASHINGTON

1941

Dear Churchill

Wendell Willkie will give you this — He is truly helping to keep politics out over here.

I think this verse applies to your people as it does to us:

"Sail on, Oh Ship of State!
Sail on Oh Union strong and great.
Humanity with all its fears,
With all the hopes of future years,
Is hanging breathless on thy fate"

As ever yours
Franklin D Roosevelt

The "Ship of State" letter from Franklin Roosevelt to
Winston Churchill, dated January 20, 1941.

What a Change a Few Months Make

Cartoon depicting
Wendell Willkie delivering
the "Ship of State" letter
to 10 Downing Street,
Pittsburgh *Post-Gazette*,
January 28, 1941.

Hungerford in the Pittsburgh *Post-Gazette*

Wendell Willkie inspecting the bomb damage to the Temple area of London, January 30, 1941.

Wendell Willkie paying his fare to the conductor on a London bus, February 1, 1941.

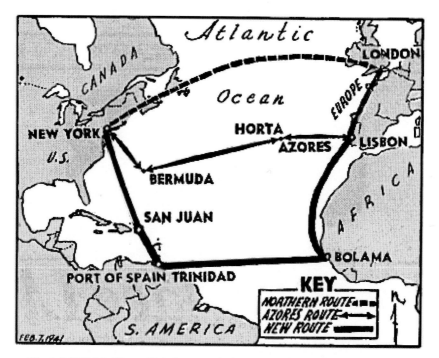

Wendell Willkie's Clipper flight home took the new southern route via Portuguese
Guinea, Trinidad, and Puerto Rico. The Azores route was used for regular
wartime runs and was taken by several presidential envoys; the
northern route was used before the war began.

Averell Harriman playing croquet, 1940.

Kathleen and Averell Harriman and Brendan Bracken, London, 1941.

Averell Harriman and John G. Winant in London, October 4, 1943. Standing between them is Lieutenant General Jacob Devers, commander in chief of U.S. forces in the European theater.

Kathleen and Averell Harriman, with Pamela Churchill at the far left, visiting a Royal Air Force base, United Kingdom, 1941.

Harry Hopkins posing with Joseph Stalin for photographer Margaret Bourke-White at the Kremlin, July 31, 1941.

Harry Hopkins and Laurence Steinhardt at Moscow Central Airport, August 1, 1941.
On the left is Soviet Deputy People's Commissar for Foreign Affairs S. A. Lozovsky.

Winston Churchill, Harry Hopkins, and British officers on the deck of
HMS *Prince of Wales* during the voyage to Placentia Bay, August 1941.

The divine service on board HMS *Prince of Wales*, August 10, 1941.
This service was the high point of the Atlantic Conference.

Harry Hopkins, "a catalytic between two prima donnas."

Franklin Roosevelt and Winston Churchill posing for photographers after the divine service. Behind the great men, Harry Hopkins is showing Averell Harriman his new homburg.

Franklin Roosevelt signing the U.S. declaration of war against Japan in the Oval Office, December 8, 1941.

Harriman was less concerned by Cairo's ambience than its disposition, finding the British officers serving there to be complacent and disorganized. A recent counteroffensive against Rommel had failed, and a few days after Harriman's arrival Churchill relieved Wavell of command and appointed General Sir Claude Auchinleck as commander in chief in his stead. Stirred into action by an inquisitive cable from Churchill, Harriman sent some bracing observations back to London and Washington from his temporary headquarters in the U.S. legation, covering various deficiencies of production, supply, and training that he had observed on his travels, in particular the weaknesses of the air ferry service. He also addressed an issue that animated many Americans: the need for a unified British military command structure in the Middle East, to improve coordination between the services.[122]

He undertook a number of side trips from Cairo. In the Western Desert he met with the commander of British forces, spoke with fighter aces, and watched tank commanders repair their vehicles. With Auchinleck, he inspected the first American-built tanks that were unloaded in Egypt. "She'll do," said the general as he pulled himself out of a tank turret after a test drive. "It's a fine weapon, maneuverable and sturdy. How many can you send us?" Harriman visited Baghdad and Basra in Iraq, now back under British control after the failure of the pro-Axis coup, and slept overnight on the roof of the British embassy in Baghdad, the coolest place available. On the flight back from Basra, he felt a "boyish thrill" upon sighting the junction of the Tigris and Euphrates Rivers—supposedly the site of the Garden of Eden. He saw Amman, capital of Transjordan—"a few hundred houses in the rock desert"—and the Suez Canal. In Jerusalem, the party met with British commanders and visited the holy sites. Harriman also flew down the Red Sea, inspecting the ports that Roosevelt had recently opened to American merchant shipping, and meeting the British commanders who had defeated the Italians. He especially liked the colonial city of Asmara, Eritrea's capital, writing Marie that its climate, "dry and cool at night," was "like Sun Valley in summer!"[123] That was surely the only similarity.

Harriman flew up to Alexandria on the Mediterranean to see some of the warships anchored in its harbor—British vessels damaged in Crete and other engagements, Greek ships, and four demobilized French capital ships. As Admiral Sir Andrew Cunningham, commander of the Mediterranean Fleet, showed them around the port in his barge, they got too close to an ammunition store and were fired on by a sentry. Luckily, the bullet went just astern of the barge.[124]

Harriman's companion for much of his time in the Middle East was none other than the man he had cuckolded, Randolph Churchill. The unknowing prime minister had commended Harriman to his son in early June, saying, "I have made great friends with him, and have the greatest regard for him. He does all he can to help us." Subsequently the plump young cavalry officer was assigned to Harriman as a personal aide while he was in Egypt. He was "not at all high hat," thought Meiklejohn, and proved popular with the visitors. Randolph knew all about Cairo's luxuries and enjoyed the attentions of a number of women around town. No one was in a better position to show the group a good time.

In fact, the two adulterers formed an unlikely mutual admiration society. Randolph told his father that Harriman "has definitely become my favourite American . . . He clearly regards himself more as your servant than Roosevelt's. I think he is the most objective and shrewd of all those who are around you." To his wife, the unsuspecting Randolph wrote cheerfully that Harriman was "absolutely charming . . . He spoke delightfully about you and I fear that I have a serious rival!" For his part, Harriman sent a sly cable to Pamela saying Randolph was the "most delightful and stimulating traveling companion. Beginning to understand your weakness for him." In one regard, however, Randolph proved unhelpful. Harriman intended to buy up all the stockings in Cairo before he left in order "to get in good with the females in London," as Meiklejohn put it. When the time came, however, Harriman had run out of piastres. Perhaps Randolph's gambling debts prevented him from making a loan, or perhaps Harriman felt he could not ask for one.[125]

Harriman and his party left Cairo for London on July 10 on board a Royal Australian Air Force (RAAF) Sunderland, a civilian flying boat that had been reengineered for submarine patrol duty. Flying the entire length of the Mediterranean in a slow and lightly armed aircraft, through a thicket of enemy air patrols, was a dangerous business. Sure enough, in the middle of the night, while the passengers slept curled up all over the floor "like a mess of cats," the Sunderland was attacked by a Messerschmitt night fighter. The Australian pilot related decades later that he returned fire and "dove into low cloud to within a couple of hundred feet of the Mediterranean, and escaped." Harriman was "extremely calm about the whole episode," the pilot recalled, merely asking "what all the racket was." Meiklejohn was equally impressed with the RAAF: "Our crew is Australian and they aren't afraid of anything."[126]

The party had one more stop before London: Gibraltar. Bad weather held them on the Rock for four days as guests of the governor, Lord Gort. Gort, known within the Grenadier Guards as "Fat Boy," proved to be quite a character. He insisted on dunking himself in a bathtub-size swimming pool each evening before dinner, adored the birds who roosted in his garden, and knew all of Gibraltar's famous Barbary apes by name. Gort showed them the Rock's impressive outer defenses, including guns, concealed pillboxes, and tank traps, and the tunnels within, with their freshwater reservoirs, sleeping quarters, kitchens, and hospitals. Harriman tried to estimate from the amount of scotch in the governor's underground headquarters how long he was prepared to hold out, and concluded it was "a long time."

The party saw the Rock's secret radar device, and went aboard two of the warships that were in at the death of the *Bismarck*: the *Renown* and the *Ark Royal*. Social life at the governor's residence was very formal. The table centerpiece consisted of three enormous gate keys dating from the Great Siege of Gibraltar in the eighteenth century. Harriman surprised his staff by appearing for dinner in a tuxedo, as they were unaware he had brought one. Meiklejohn noted that "comic relief" was provided in the form of an attempted Italian air raid, in which the Italians accidentally dropped their payload on La Línea, the Spanish town on the isthmus connecting Gibraltar with the mainland. Finally, on July 15, the Sunderland was able to get off the

Rock, and the party flew the final leg to Plymouth in daylight. Harriman was whisked off immediately to see Churchill.[127]

Harriman provided detailed observations to London and Washington on everything from the condition of various ports, highways, and railroads to the need for more hand tools, armaments, and spare parts. He recommended that the British adopt a unified command structure and that the Americans make a more definite commitment to supply the Middle East. In his memoir, Harriman enumerated the trip's "great many practical results," including the takeover of the African plane ferry route by Pan American Airways, the establishment of an American repair and supply depot in Eritrea, and various modifications made to U.S. military equipment. Despite Churchill's hopes, however, he did not have much impact on U.S. strategic discussions on the Middle East. General Marshall and Admiral Stark remained skeptical of Churchill's argument. The issue would soon be taken up again by Harry Hopkins on his next mission to London.[128]

AVERELL HARRIMAN'S MISSION, in his biographer's neat formulation, was "to tend the lifeline."[129] Franklin Roosevelt wanted him to be the London end of Hopkins's Lend-Lease operation, balancing demand and supply, and needling reluctant officials in Washington into action. In all this, he succeeded.

Some believed he went too far, and ended up serving British rather than American interests.[130] He was certainly bullish on aid to Britain. Even before he took up his post in London, he was privately critical of Roosevelt's cautious foreign policy. His sympathies were reinforced by the strenuous efforts made by the British governing class to woo him once he was in the United Kingdom. The hospitality he soaked up, his adoption by the prime minister's family, the sharing of secrets, the application of the formidable Churchillian charm—all this encouraged intense feelings of sympathy in Harriman toward his British hosts. The late-night requests over a bottle of port about which Washington had complained to Harriman were now being made to him. "I am accepted practically as a member of the Cabinet," Harriman boasted to a friend. "Whatever happens," Clementine Churchill told him, "we do not feel alone any more."[131] Harriman would have been a strong man indeed had his head not been turned by this intoxicating mix of history, flattery, danger, and sex.

The British knew that Averell Harriman chafed at the bit of neutrality and wished for deeper American involvement in the war. Shortly after Harriman's arrival, Churchill told the war cabinet he was "greatly encouraged" by the attitudes of Harriman and John Winant, both of whom "were apparently longing for Germany to commit some overt act" that would bring the United States into the war. Colville recorded the Americans' distress at the idea of "London being bombed every night [while] all the lights were on in New York."[132]

On the other hand, while Harriman admired Churchill enormously, he also prided himself on standing up to the prime minister in discussion, a practice that was hardly universal. For his part, Churchill was punctilious in his dealings with Harriman, never badgering him about U.S. entry into the war or pressing him on matters that were properly decisions for the president. He spent time with Harriman not only because he understood his influence with Hopkins, but because he liked him.[133]

In any case, Harriman's affinity for the British hardly interfered with the performance of his mission of expediting American supplies to them, indeed quite the reverse. As for Roosevelt, he was aware of Harriman's views before appointing him. The president was always comfortable with his advisers getting out in front of him on certain issues, as it drew fire away from his own person and allowed him to appeal to different constituencies simultaneously. Harriman's bellicosity did not hamper his mission, nor deflect FDR from pursuing his own foreign policy goals, in his own time.

Both men can rightly be criticized on another front, however. FDR's riding instructions to Harriman were very general. It was "an excellent mandate," Harriman said later, "in no way tying my hands."[134] He quickly took advantage of his loose presidential instructions to expand the focus of his mission. With access to Roosevelt's thinking through Hopkins, Harriman came to be seen by the British government as FDR's representative in London—to the great cost of Gil Winant and his embassy.[135]

Harriman was a complicated human being. Like the curate's egg, he was good in parts. He was loyal to his friends. He was effective. He worked phenomenally hard: a typical diary entry of Bob Meiklejohn's read, "Nothing unusual. Worked like a dog."[136] But he was also ponderous, self-regarding, and ruthlessly ambitious, as Winant discovered. His mission to London enabled him to remake himself from dull Averell to dashing Averell. It was his ladder to a life of distinction and fame. Once Harriman had his hands on the flows of power, he would never allow them to be removed.

6.

"Mister Hurry Upkins"

As Harriman flew across Africa and around the Mediterranean, Britain's fortunes were improving in the Atlantic. The summer nights afforded less hunting time to the U-boat wolf packs, and Britain's success at decrypting German naval signals helped its convoys to avoid them. The tonnage lost through the sinking of merchant ships plunged. Roosevelt's policy in mid-1941 was sharply bifurcated. With one hand, he gradually dialed up the heat on U.S. engagement in the Atlantic; with the other, he determinedly kept the situation in the Pacific off the boil. The continuation of Cordell Hull's long-running diplomatic talks with Ambassador Kichisaburo Nomura enabled the Americans to feel out Tokyo's position, delay any Japanese push toward Southeast Asia and Indochina, sow disunity among the Axis powers—and above all, to stretch things out. FDR was happy for his secretary of state to run these conversations; he was determined to devote his fullest attention, and the greatest number of his ships and supplies, to the Atlantic. "It is terribly important for the control of the Atlantic for us to help to keep peace in the Pacific," he told Harold

Ickes. "I simply have not got enough Navy to go round—and every little episode in the Pacific means fewer ships in the Atlantic."[1]

On the subject of the Atlantic, various palace factions in Washington competed for the president's ear. A group dubbed by historian Theodore Wilson the "immediatists," including Stimson, Knox, Ickes, and Stark, supported aid to Britain but also argued for a muscular U.S. military and a more aggressive national posture, if not an outright declaration of war. They were opposed by "gradualists" such as Marshall and the State Department's Adolf A. Berle, who were uncomfortable with the transfer of large amounts of matériel until the United States' own military buildup was further advanced.[2] Naturally, FDR tried to split the difference. As David Reynolds has observed, Roosevelt gradually abandoned the historic principles of "cash-and-carry" by providing Lend-Lease aid and progressively widening U.S. activities in the Atlantic, including the establishment of extensive naval patrols and, in July 1941, the occupation of Iceland by the U.S. Marines. Lend-Lease had plugged Britain's cash shortfall; now the U.S. Navy was being deployed to help ensure that American goods were carried safely to Britain.[3]

The president's rhetoric developed in line with his policies. America's forward-leaning position had once been justified as the way to avoid war; now it was the way to prevent "a Hitler-dominated world."[4] But even if FDR now accepted that America would have to join the fighting eventually—a point on which historians disagree—he was not yet ready to jump.[5]

Then Hitler let the dice fly. In the early hours of June 22, 1941, Germany's armies invaded the Soviet Union, and the war was changed completely. Operation Barbarossa was the mother of all land invasions. In the short term, it gave Britain a reprieve from the threat of invasion, which had not yet materialized but remained a source of concern, and relief from the depredations of the Luftwaffe. In turn, this relieved some of the pressure on Washington. In Asia, by contrast, it made things worse. With the Soviet Union forced into the Anglo-American column, Japan readied itself to drive south into Indochina while also preparing for a possible war with the Soviets.[6]

In the longer term, Barbarossa was to have a larger, transformative impact. For all the crimes it entailed against the Soviet peoples, it also offended grievously against German self-interest. It was Hitler's most catastrophic folly. Churchill regarded it as the fourth climacteric of the period. For the moment, however, all this was obscured by the fog of war. In the first few days, the signs were all positive for Berlin. The Germans destroyed a good portion of the Soviet air force on the ground and advanced nearly two hundred miles into Soviet territory. Most British and American officials shared Stimson's view that the Soviet Union could only resist the invader for between one and three months.[7] Roosevelt himself was ambivalent about her chances, unsure whether the attack was merely a "diversion" or presaged "the liberation of Europe from Nazi domination."[8]

Now came the dilemma: how should the West respond to Barbarossa? Churchill, the lifelong anti-Bolshevik, saw immediately where Britain's interests lay. "If Hitler invaded Hell," he remarked to John Colville the evening before the invasion, during a postprandial stroll on Chequers' croquet lawn, "I would make at least a favourable reference to the Devil in the House of Commons." When Hitler invaded the Soviet Union, Churchill did considerably more than that. He declared that Britain "shall give whatever help we can to Russia and the Russian people"; dispatched a military mission to Moscow; and concluded an agreement with the Soviets in which the two countries pledged to aid each other and, importantly, not to sue for a separate peace.[9]

The Americans were slower off the mark. Within the administration, the invasion produced a rare moment of unanimity between immediatists and gradualists. Both groups opposed the granting of substantial aid to Russia on the ground that the matériel would be better used by, respectively, British or U.S. forces.[10] In the wider community, Barbarossa scrambled the debate on the European war. On the one hand, it brought the far left in behind FDR: literally overnight, American communists went from noninterventionists to extreme interventionists. On the day of the invasion, Robert Sherwood attended a Fight for Freedom rally in Harlem. When he entered the Golden Gate Ballroom, before the news from Russia had come through, he passed through a communist-led picket line featuring placards denouncing the speakers as tools of British imperialism. When he left the building ninety minutes later, the pickets had melted away and the party had reversed its position. "The next day," he noted, "the *Daily Worker* was pro-British, pro-Lend Lease, pro-interventionist and, for the first time in two years, pro-Roosevelt."[11]

Communists did not have much pull in the United States, however. In middle America, Barbarossa undermined Roosevelt's presentation of the war as a battle between democracies and dictatorships. On the political right, it hardened further the isolationists' position. The Soviets' entry into the war "should settle once and for all the intervention issue here at home," stated General Robert Wood. "The war party can hardly ask the people of America to take up arms behind the red flag of Stalin." Isolationists were equally hostile to the idea of providing aid to Russia, preferring to leave "these two scoundrels Hitler and Stalin to fight it out." Some pointed to the advantages of Germany routing the Soviets and destroying the menace of Russian communism.[12]

Notwithstanding this tendency, the White House took two modest steps in late June, freeing up Soviet funds in the United States and announcing that the provisions of the Neutrality Act would not be applied to the Soviet Union, thereby allowing trade and aid to continue to flow. Then, in early July, amid signs of stiffer Soviet resistance, FDR took a big risk and decided to extend as much aid (albeit not yet Lend-Lease aid) to the Soviet Union as possible in the hope of prolonging her resistance until the winter.[13] In part, this decision was based on the president's positive view of the Soviets' short-term prospects, a view no doubt informed as much by FDR's congenital optimism as it was by any expert analysis. Aid to the USSR also conformed with Roosevelt's strategic logic: it would weaken Germany without costing American lives, and discourage Stalin from making another pact with Hitler.[14]

On July 10, therefore, the president told the Soviet ambassador, Constantine Oumansky, that the United States would supply his government's most urgent needs. That he still had doubts about the Soviet Union's long-term survival, though, was evidenced by his remark to Oumansky that "if the Russians could hold the Germans until October 1 that would be of great value in defeating Hitler," by tying up German troops and equipment.[15] Heavy-laden though they were, the Soviets hoped to do better than simply slow down their invaders over the summer.

Harry Hopkins was spending the summer shuttling between his various roles as foreign policy adviser, middleman between Roosevelt and Churchill, and Lend-Lease boss. His portfolio was a wide and varied one. "A good name for Harry," Roosevelt said with a laugh, "would be 'Minister of Omnium Gatherum.'" (Someone else in the room piped up, "And scatterem.") The intense activity seemed to be good for Hopkins's health. Apart from a minor relapse of his stomach trouble, he was in fine form. A beaming FDR claimed credit for the improvement, telling a friend, "Dr. Roosevelt knows what's good for Harry."[16]

Now Dr. Roosevelt asked Harry to reprise his role as special envoy and return to London. After dinner on Friday, July 11, the two men had a long talk in FDR's study on the second floor of the White House, where he had received Sumner Welles and Wendell Willkie when each returned from Europe. Speechwriter Robert Sherwood thought this room, the president's innermost sanctuary, was "the focal point of the nation and, in a sense, of the whole world." But it also had, as Labor Secretary Frances Perkins observed, "that lived-in and overcrowded look which indicated the complexity and variety of his interests and intentions." There was the handsome *Resolute* desk, a gift from Queen Victoria to President Rutherford B. Hayes, made from the timbers of HMS *Resolute*. There were also mismatched chairs, model ships, books and papers, a mechanical pipe organ that no one could operate, a Blue Eagle wastebasket from NRA days, and a lion skin from Emperor Haile Selassie's brother. Amid all this Rooseveltian detritus, the president sketched out the various elements of Hopkins's next mission.[17]

The first was to bolster the Anglo-American connection, which was sagging a little. By July, Roosevelt's incrementalist policy was causing frustration in London. Lend-Lease aid had proved valuable but not decisive, and British expectations that the United States would enter the war in the spring had been dashed. A definite note of skepticism was entering the mind of the British public about America's commitment to the cause.[18] Hopkins was a symbol of Roosevelt's good intentions. GIs were not on their way over, but Harry was.

There were specific bilateral issues to be raised. Whitehall was concerned about postwar compensation it might owe Washington for Lend-Lease, and anxious about the talks taking place between Hull and Nomura. There was also the vital question of Russia's entry into the war and how it would affect Britain and the United States.[19] Guided by his occasional Wilsonian impulses, FDR believed that the British and Soviets should not agree to postwar territorial and political adjustments, especially in relation to the Baltic states, whether in secret or in public.[20]

There was also the crucial matter of U.S. naval activities in the Atlantic. To date, Roosevelt had been prepared to order the navy to patrol the Atlantic, but not to escort convoys of merchant ships across it—a more valuable but infinitely more dangerous exercise. But now, sensing growing public support, Roosevelt had decided to proceed with a plan for protecting combined convoys; that is, convoys containing an American- or Icelandic-flag ship. He wanted to share his thinking with Churchill, via Hopkins. On a map torn from *National Geographic* magazine, the president drew a line along the 26th meridian marking the existing zone of American responsibility. Then he expanded the zone further by adding a wide bend to the right to incorporate U.S.-occupied Iceland and the waters around it. FDR's plan was limited and loose, in order to preserve his freedom of movement; he would later backtrack and postpone its implementation until he had had a chance to discuss it with Churchill. Nevertheless, within a couple of months the U.S. Navy would take over convoy protection throughout this zone, which came within a few hundred miles of the northern coast of Scotland.[21]

Hopkins was also entrusted with the job of fixing the uncomfortable situation that had arisen between Harriman and Winant. "Harriman not policy," stated Hopkins's handwritten notes from the White House.[22] The idea was to impress upon Churchill that Harriman's role was confined to Lend-Lease matters and that Winant remained the president's leading representative in London. The irony of Roosevelt instructing one personal envoy to lay down the law to another personal envoy in relation to the precedence of the properly accredited ambassador seems not to have registered with anyone.

Hopkins's final function was to settle the arrangements for the upcoming meeting between Roosevelt and Churchill. Discussions about possible dates and locations for the rendezvous had been afoot since Hopkins's January mission. Remarkably, the principals had met only once before, at a banquet at Gray's Inn in London in 1918, and it had not been a success. Churchill, who was already a senior statesman at that point, "acted like a stinker" to Roosevelt, who recalled later that he was "one of the few men in public life who was rude to me." To make matters worse, Churchill promptly forgot the meeting had ever happened. FDR was not accustomed to being forgotten.[23]

Notwithstanding that pinprick, he was anxious to see Churchill again, for their first meeting as heads of government. "I am in constant touch with Churchill," he told Canadian prime minister Mackenzie King in April. "What I feel strongly is that we should have a chance to talk together." When that chance came, though, he did not want to have to field awkward questions about U.S. entry into the war—which for Churchill was fast becoming the alpha and omega of British foreign policy. Roosevelt preferred to keep the subject veiled, and Hopkins was designated to manage the PM's expectations. "No talk about war," was the note he scribbled on White House stationery that evening.[24]

THIS WAS NOT THE ONLY BIG JOB Roosevelt gave to one of his envoys on July 11. On the same day, he signed an executive order appointing Bill Donovan his "Coordinator of Information." Donovan was charged with standing up a new spy service that was independent from the military and reported directly to the president.

For several months, Donovan had been making the case for a U.S. agency that would collect intelligence, analyze it, and devise propaganda for use against the country's adversaries. The administration was being lobbied along the same lines by British officials, including the Secret Intelligence Service's American representative, William Stephenson, as well as Rear Admiral John Godfrey from Naval Intelligence and his assistant Ian Fleming, both of whom stayed at Donovan's Georgetown home while they were in town. Bureaucratic rivals including J. Edgar Hoover and George Marshall tried to squelch Donovan's plan, but Roosevelt, who was dissatisfied with the patchy intelligence he received from the army, navy, State Department, and FBI, decided to approve it. The British expressed private delight that "our man" was in the post. Donovan set about designing his new organization and staffing it with talented and influential individuals such as FDR's speechwriter, Robert Sherwood, and his son, marine captain James Roosevelt.[25] Wild Bill was now in the big leagues.

"HOPKINS GOES TO ENGLAND very soon for a short visit," FDR cabled Winant on July 12. "Please tell Former Naval Person." Winant soon informed Washington that Churchill "was delighted to hear that Harry is coming," adding, "So am I."[26] Meanwhile, Hopkins spent his last day in the United States cramming for his trip and discussing production, shipping, and diplomatic issues with administration officials. Having recently seen Soviet ambassador Oumansky, he now dined with his British counterpart, Lord Halifax. On the morning of July 13, less than thirty-six hours after receiving his assignment from the president, Hopkins left for London. Roosevelt monitored developments closely, writing gaily on an update, "Harry H on board!" Not all of Washington was so pleased with the news of Hopkins's departure. "I am at a loss to understand why Harry should have been sent to England again, unless it was for further enhancement of his prestige," complained his old rival Harold Ickes to his diary. "No one in this administration has had a chance to build himself up to the extent that Harry has and he has done it on a very narrow margin indeed."[27]

Hopkins flew direct to Montreal and then on to Gander, Newfoundland, at the northeastern tip of the North American continent. The massive airfield at Gander—said to be the largest in the world—was a key stopover on the ferry route along which American-built aircraft were flown to Britain. Heavy weather forced an overnight stay, which enabled Hopkins to get in some restorative trout fishing with FDR's son Elliott, who was stationed there with the Army Air Corps. Then he caught a ride in a Lend-Lease B-24 Liberator heavy bomber, flying in formation with twenty others, to Scotland. The B-24 was noisy, unpressurized, and freezing cold. The vibrations from its four massive Pratt & Whitney engines and its propellers were constant. Hopkins's accommodations were located in the aircraft's cluttered bomb bay. But as a means of transportation, the B-24 also had its advantages. Pesky reporters had no idea of his movements. And it sent a certain message to his hosts to return to Britain not in a Clipper but a Liberator.[28]

Britain felt very different this time around, and not only because it was warmer. For two months, since the night the House of Commons had been smashed, London had enjoyed a vacation from air raids. The ruins were still visible, but they were no longer smoking. The streets had been tidied; restaurants were full; women wore summery cotton dresses. Signs of war were everywhere, in the form of uniforms, boarded-up windows, ration queues, and barrage balloons. But as the American journalist Raymond Gram Swing observed in a radio broadcast from London, "Having faced the worst is a great human experience. It is a liberation. The fear of the worst no longer dominates what people decide to do."[29]

The British public's preoccupation with the United States was evident in the Fourth of July celebrations held shortly before Hopkins's arrival. Surely Independence Day had never been observed like this in the British capital.

The Stars and Stripes flew alongside the Union Jack outside railway terminals, hotels, and bomb-damaged buildings. American patriotic music was piped through loudspeakers at Waterloo and Victoria Stations. One newspaper carried a U.S. flag in the corner of its front page. When the words to "My Country, 'Tis of Thee" appeared on motion picture screens, audiences rose to their feet and sang the strange lyrics to the familiar melody. Fancy restaurants served American-themed menus featuring dishes such as Philadelphia pepper pot, Baltimore fried chicken, Boston baked beans, corn on the cob, and shortcake.[30]

The great dome of St. Paul's loomed "vaster than ever against its new setting of ruined business blocks," said Raymond Swing in a July Fourth broadcast. On the same day, in a small chapel in the cathedral's crypt, Ambassador Winant attended the unveiling of a tablet in memory of the first American airman killed while wearing the uniform of the Royal Air Force. Pilot Officer William Meade Lindsay Fiske III, "Billy" to his friends, was a banker and champion bobsledder who carried the U.S. flag at the 1932 Winter Olympic Games in Lake Placid, New York, in the presence of Governor Franklin D. Roosevelt. When war came, he crossed the Atlantic and talked his way into the RAF with forged Canadian papers. He was killed in August 1940, at the height of the Battle of Britain, when his Hurricane was hit during a dogfight with Stuka dive bombers. Billy Fiske's memorial tablet was located across from a newly erected bust of George Washington, and inscribed, "An American citizen who died that England might live." Those who were gathered for the dedication, including flyers from Fiske's squadron, sang "The Battle Hymn of the Republic." No one knew, Winant observed later, that the next time they heard that hymn at St. Paul's would be at a memorial service for the commander in chief of the U.S. armed forces.[31]

All these expressions of Anglo-American solidarity barely hid the growing anxiety on the part of the British about Washington's intentions, however. A number of newspaper editorials expressed disappointment that Roosevelt's Fourth of July broadcast contained no hint of deepening U.S. involvement in the war. Hopkins was troubled by the great expectations of the British. The affectionate nickname given him by Cockneys, "Mister Hurry Upkins," was an acknowledgment of his exertions so far. It was also a plea for more.[32]

Hopkins's bomber landed at Prestwick, on the southwest coast of Scotland, on the afternoon of Thursday, July 17. Waiting at the airfield was Averell Harriman, just back from the Middle East, who had flown up when he heard of Hopkins's pending return. After his long and uncomfortable flight, Hopkins was a mess, but he headed straight down to London to see Churchill. John Colville recorded him arriving at Downing Street suddenly, "laden with ham, cheese, cigars, etc for the PM," and American cigarettes, which, to Colville's dismay, he handed to Tommy Thompson.[33] Talks between Churchill and Hopkins began immediately—on Barbarossa and its implications for Lend-Lease; the diminishing prospects of an invasion of Britain; the wisdom of defending the Middle East; and, as Churchill put it later, "the question of arranging a meeting between me and Roosevelt somehow, somewhere, soon." Hopkins produced FDR's map, and the two men discussed developments in the Atlantic.[34]

That same afternoon, "looking more dead than alive" in Alec Cadogan's assessment, Hopkins attended a meeting of the war cabinet, which heard from the military chiefs that the fighting in Russia was proving much harder than Germany had anticipated. Hopkins gave an upbeat report on the pace of the U.S. munitions program, especially merchant shipbuilding and aircraft and tank production. He also put a positive spin on the domestic political scene, concluding that while Americans were not keen on war, "if the President decided that the time had come to make war on Germany, the vast majority of the population, of all parties, would endorse his action and accord him their full support." The official minutes were silent on the question of when the United States might enter the war, but the Australian high commissioner in London, Stanley Bruce, was briefed that Hopkins told the war cabinet the "present position could not last long and suggested Japan may apply [a] match to [the] fire."[35]

Hopkins consented to the release of a public statement about his participation in the meeting, leading to comment at home. The *New York Times*
reported that the "invitation was seen as a personal compliment to Mr. Hopkins . . . and as a gesture to the United States." The *Chicago Daily Tribune*, by
contrast, thought his appearance was "more than a token": it was "an ac-
knowledgement that the British Cabinet has been running the American
war program from the beginning." Hopkins had a droll response. Asked
how he came to sit in on the deliberations of the war cabinet, he replied, "I
didn't know I was doing that. I just dropped in and saw a lot of people I'd met
when I was here before."[36]

The following morning, Hopkins held a press conference for British and
American reporters. Brigadier General Lee, who found Hopkins "thinner,
paler and more strained" than he was on his last visit, noted the contrast
between his January press briefing, in which Hopkins had been "extremely
reserved and non-committal," and this one, in which "he was much more
forthcoming and pugnacious." "Make no mistake," declared Hopkins. "Our
object is to beat this fellow, Hitler. All the oppressed people in all parts of the
world who are worrying about how the war will end can be certain that the
war cannot be lost. We are certain that the production of the United States,
coupled with that of Great Britain, will far outstrip anything that the dictator countries can achieve. And production in the United States has already
gone ahead much faster than anyone realizes." Indeed, America's defense
output, mobilized by a coalition of business tycoons and New Dealers and
fed by Lend-Lease money, was exploding.

When Hopkins reported that merchant shipping output would rise from
one million tons in 1941 to six million in 1942, there were "audible gaspings"
from the reporters. "We are going to build enough ships to bring our goods
to the United Kingdom and into every theatre of war in the world where the
democracies are fighting Hitler," promised Hopkins. There was also a "vast
program of aeroplane production" with "great new factories" to produce the
heavy bombers that can knock out targets "in the most distant parts of eastern Germany." Hopkins was sure that Britain and America could together

"build far more of those planes per month than Germany can, and better ones. The same is true of tanks." In order to "send you dairy products in great quantities," he said, the United States was undertaking "a major change in our agricultural economy." Asked about convoys, he was careful to go no further than Roosevelt's recent public statements about patrols in the U.S. security zone. But he added, "All I can say is we're going to protect our ships."[37]

Hopkins's statement had a powerful effect on British journalists, who thought it was "the most optimistic news they had had from America in a long time." They reported it on the front pages of their newspapers, under thrilling headlines in huge typefaces. The *Daily Telegraph* observed that "neutrality could hardly be more benevolent." Raymond Gram Swing told his listeners that "Hopkins didn't tell anything that wasn't known to newspapermen in Washington and to the American public—but when he put what America was doing in a single statement and stood face to face with London newspapermen, it made a big impression." Only a presidential envoy could make such an impression. Swing thought that Hopkins's message was "like vitamins for the British spirits." For isolationists back home, it was more like hemlock. Montana senator Burton Wheeler raged that Hopkins was "completely out of touch with sentiment in the United States. Both the United States and Great Britain are in a pretty bad way if we have to rely on Harry Hopkins to tell us what to do." Hopkins and the president's other advisers, he said, were "a motley crew to determine foreign policy for 130 million people in the United States."[38]

That afternoon, Hopkins spoke with Harriman and Lee at Claridge's about the British defense of the Middle East. This remained a sensitive issue in the Anglo-American relationship, but the disagreement did not play out along simple national lines. Elements of the British military dissented from Churchill's view that Egypt must be held at all costs; Roosevelt, on the other hand, was largely sympathetic to the prime minister's argument that the Middle East was as good a place as any to fight and kill German soldiers.[39] Lee and his colleagues at the U.S. embassy were worried that Hopkins would be soft-soaped by Churchill, but in fact no soaping was required. It was apparent from his comments that, like FDR, he was already inclined to support Churchill's position. Most of Washington had given up on the Middle East long ago, he told Lee and Harriman, under the influence of defeatist reports from American representatives. Many believed that sending further reinforcements out there was like "throwing snowballs into hell." But now, "with the Russians coming in and the clearing of Syria, the people in Washington are plucking up heart, and . . . the US might still be interested at this juncture."[40]

Hopkins spent the weekend at Chequers. He was pleased to discover that with the warmer weather, he no longer needed to wear his overcoat inside the old building. He was also pleased to get a new hat.[41] During his January visit, his old one, a notoriously battered, misshapen fedora "on the shady side of its fifth year," had become an object of fascination for the British public. Observers noted that it "turned up in front and flopped down over his ears." Some Britons got the impression that the "banged-up, slouched-down" headgear was "a typical American hat." Every time Hopkins's hat appeared in the London newspapers, he was "besieged by shocked English haberdashers" who wished to present him with a new one. Hopkins refused. "If I buy a new one, it will look just like this one in two weeks," he rationalized. "So what's the use? Anyway, this one is very comfortable and fulfils the purpose of any hat." He liked that he could pull it down over his ears to keep out the wind.

Well-wishers kept trying, however. In May, Sidney J. Weinberg, the legendary head of Goldman Sachs and a rare Wall Street supporter of the administration, sent Hopkins a new hat. Weinberg knew a bit about hats, having started out at Goldman as a porter, entrusted with the job of brushing the partners' hats. He wrote to an associate of Hopkins's that he had "great admiration and respect" for the envoy but "for a man of his position I don't think he made the proper impression on the English with the old hat he wore over there." Accordingly, "as a public service" he had ordered a hat made up by John Cavanagh, "maker of the finest hats in America." As a special touch, the felt was composed partly of a milk derivative produced by a corporation of which Weinberg was a director. No trace remains of Hopkins's reaction to this gift, but when he returned to London in July, his old hat went with him.

Somewhere during "the mad whirl" of his second London visit, however, the hat vanished. Some whispered that Churchill, who had "ragged Hopkins mercilessly" about the disreputable fedora, had a hand in its disappearance. In any case, when Hopkins arrived bareheaded at Chequers, Churchill told him "you can't go around like that" and presented him with a handsome, well-blocked gray homburg from his own collection, bearing the initials "W.S.C." on its inside band. At size 7⅛, the Scott & Co. hat was too large, but that had never been a problem before. "Mr Hopkins received it with thanks," according to reports, and "slapped it on his head."

ALSO AT CHEQUERS THAT WEEKEND were the usual Churchill camp followers—Bracken, Ismay, Colville, Lindemann (recently raised to the peerage as Lord Cherwell), and Averell and Kathleen Harriman—as well as army and navy chiefs, the Attlees, and Colonel Bob Laycock, who had recently led Britain's commando force on Crete (and who may have been the model for the character of Tommy Blackhouse in Evelyn Waugh's *Sword of Honour* trilogy). On Saturday, Soviet ambassador Ivan Maisky—small, with twinkling eyes and a black goatee—dropped in with a telegram from Stalin asking Churchill for increased military assistance. Maisky and Hopkins were introduced to each other and for a while they sat together in the White Parlour, named for its white-painted paneling, before a fire that Clementine had lit for Hopkins. It was probably also this weekend that Churchill offered Hopkins the privilege of an interview with the captured Nazi, Rudolf Hess. Hopkins declined for fear that the incident would leak and "give rise to embarrassing rumors of an arrangement with the Nazis."[42]

Among the guests for lunch on Sunday was Raymond Gram Swing, "a tall, stooped, tweedy, horn-rimmed man with unruly brown hair." Swing had been a daring correspondent during the First World War, who made his name when he was crossing the Sea of Marmara on a Turkish freighter during the Dardanelles campaign. A British submarine overhauled the freighter and its commander demanded the name of the Turkish vessel, asking colloquially, "Who are you?" Swing's excited reply, later immortalized in a Rudyard Kipling book, was, "I am Raymond Gram Swing of *The Chicago Daily News*." By 1941, Swing was a broadcaster on world affairs with a strong anti-Nazi position and huge audiences in the United States and Britain: Felix Frankfurter and Tallulah Bankhead were both fans. Churchill and Hopkins got on famously with Swing at lunch, and that evening they heard him praise them on the radio. Swing's broadcast captured the distance America had traveled in the past year. There were three kinds of warfare, he argued—ideological, industrial, and shooting—and the United States was in two of them.[43]

After dinner, a film was played on a new projector in Chequers' magnificent, book-lined Long Gallery: the Orson Welles classic *Citizen Kane*, based partly on the life of media magnate William Randolph Hearst. By coincidence, Hopkins had recently suggested procuring a copy of the film for FDR, thinking the president would like to see it because it "takes Hearst over the hoops." The screening at Chequers was "a violent flop," however. Churchill was so bored that he walked out before it was over. Colville, who found the film "deplorable," got into a tiff with Kathleen Harriman over it. She "thought it wonderful and said that all Americans did," he diarized. "The fact that we did not revealed to her much about English people. I replied that the fact Americans did revealed to me nothing about Americans."[44]

The party stayed up talking until three in the morning. As Kathleen Harriman observed in a letter home, Hopkins was "in the best of spirits" that weekend, and "full of fun. He's the only man I've seen so far with the PM who can say anything he wants and get away with it. Quite a different Harry, I gather, from the one in the White House! Everyone loves him over here. He's quite in his element."[45]

On Monday morning, the prime minister's party returned to London in "a great cortège of cars," stopping at the RAF's Northolt airfield on the way to watch an air show. Five heavy bombers—a Stirling, a Halifax, a Lancaster, a B-17 Flying Fortress, and a B-24 Liberator—flew past the viewing party just a few feet off the ground. Later, Hopkins and Winant met with Anthony Eden to take up the issue of secret commitments, telling the foreign secretary that Roosevelt felt strongly that no frontier commitments should be made before the war was won and the peace treaty negotiated. The United States would not want to come into the war, Hopkins warned, only to learn after the fact of the existence of secret commitments. Eden assured his visitors he was as "eager to keep my hands free as anybody," but in his diary he wrote that "the spectacle of an American President talking at large on European frontiers chilled me with Wilsonian memories."[46]

That same afternoon, Hopkins sat in on another session of the war cabinet, one that revealed the limits of British openness to Roosevelt's envoys. After hearing reports from Russia and discussing a number of uncontroversial items, Churchill indicated that Hopkins might wish to leave, as the remaining items were purely domestic in nature. A "bogus agenda" seemed to confirm this. Cadogan took up the story in his diary: "Cabinet at 5 . . . Hopkins there again. This is rather absurd, and we had to get rid of him before the end on the excuse that we were going to discuss home affairs, and then discussed—America and the Far East!"[47]

The British treatment of another issue—the speed with which Lend-Lease aircraft were being put into service—further underlined the British determination to appear responsive to the Americans. Hopkins believed "there was a feeling abroad in the United States that considerable numbers of the aircraft which they were supplying to [Britain] were not being rapidly utilised." The impression was that planes were "lying idle" because of a lack of British flight crews. Churchill set about correcting this impression. He carefully orchestrated a meeting of the relevant war cabinet committee on July 22, in which leading officials presented oral reports to Hopkins and Harriman on the extreme speed with which aircraft were being employed. He also minuted the chief of the air staff that "on the widest grounds it would be a very good thing if these [Lend-Lease] bombers were used against

Germany in bombing raids," in order to increase their visibility. No prime minister ever worked at the Anglo-American relationship more cannily or persistently than Winston Churchill.[48]

On the same day, Churchill took Hopkins for a long talk with the king. That evening, Hopkins dined with the chief of the Imperial General Staff, General Sir John Dill, along with his director of military operations, Major-General Sir John Kennedy, at Dill's flat in Westminster Gardens. Kennedy recalled that Hopkins "talked well and easily with great intelligence and spirit, though he looked a physical wreck." Smoking constantly, Hopkins painted a telling self-portrait of his role as intermediary. "The President is very like Winston in some ways—very temperamental," he said. "I regard my job as being to keep those two in close and friendly relations." One Churchill telegram, for instance, had made Roosevelt "hit the roof"; Hopkins "smoothed him down" by reminding him that the prime minister was fighting for his life. Hopkins cited another example when Churchill had given him a lecture about defeatism. "I listened to him for a bit," reported Hopkins, "and then I said, 'Now, Mr. Prime Minister, I don't want a speech—I want something I can take back to convince the President that you are right.'"[49]

The next day he reported to the president on his progress in London. "I am rapidly completing my work here," he cabled. "Have had satisfactory talks with Former Naval Person and heads of military services as well as the various supply ministries." At midday he dropped into Harriman's office on Grosvenor Square to meet with all of the expediter's staff. According to Bob Meiklejohn, Hopkins displayed a "wonderful contempt for money" in his comments, describing it as "mere bookkeeping." This comment was entirely in character for the high-rolling Hopkins, but for an enthusiastic bookkeeper like Meiklejohn, it was heresy. "If he'd ever earned an honest dollar of his own he might have more respect for it," Meiklejohn diarized in a strangled tone.[50]

ON THE AFTERNOON OF THURSDAY, JULY 24, Hopkins and Churchill settled the final details of the Atlantic Conference, the extraordinary meeting at sea between the leaders of the world's most powerful neutral and one of Europe's belligerents. In his memoir, Churchill cast things in a romantic, almost accidental light: "One afternoon in late July Harry Hopkins came into the garden of Downing Street and we sat together in the sunshine. Presently he said that the President would like very much to have a meeting with me in some lonely bay or other. I replied at once that I was sure the Cabinet would give me leave. Thus all was arranged."[51]

In reality, the rendezvous was much longed for and fussed over. Now it was decided that it would take place a fortnight hence, in Placentia Bay, off Argentia in Newfoundland. This was, in effect, Roosevelt's backyard; Churchill's commute would be much longer and more hazardous. As the historian of the conference, Theodore Wilson, observes, "For political, physical, and symbolic reasons it was necessary for Churchill to undertake the larger part of the journey—for the Old World to come, as it were, cap in hand to the New." A transatlantic phone call between the two leaders and their intermediary sealed the deal. Churchill was so excited that he forgot he was on an open line and let slip some indiscretions about the details of the parley.[52]

Late that evening, the defense of the Middle East was discussed at a revealing meeting at Downing Street. Present were the prime minister, Hopkins, Harriman, the British chiefs of staff, and three U.S. military representatives: Brigadier General Lee and two London-based "special observers" for the U.S. Army and Navy, Major General James E. Chaney and Rear Admiral Robert L. Ghormley. Lee diarized that Churchill, Harriman, and Hopkins came straight from dinner, "all looking quite comfortable, in black ties." Churchill "lit a huge cigar," Lee continued, "so big that it gave the impression he was attached to it instead of its being attached to him." Churchill opened the meeting by acknowledging that many Americans doubted the wisdom of the Middle East campaign, so he had summoned "the very best authorities he could find" to brief the Americans on British plans and have "a full and frank discussion of the position."[53]

Hopkins confirmed that many American policymakers believed Britain was making great sacrifices to maintain an indefensible position in the Middle

East. The "attitude of the President differed somewhat," reported Hopkins, in that "he realized that the enemy must be fought wherever he was found. He was therefore more inclined to support the struggle in the Middle East." Hopkins reminded the British that Americans knew little about the region: they had "never heard of Benghazi and Sollum and Mersa Matrûh"; indeed, most "are really not quite sure whether the Nile flows north or south." But "insufficient information" was a problem at the highest levels, too: the president "had never been given a comprehensive statement of the broad strategy of the Middle East campaign." A "true understanding should be reached" so that Americans could have "full confidence in a great joint enterprise."[54]

The U.S. military representatives voiced their concern that the British effort to hold the entire Middle East, which required the diversion of vast resources, could put in jeopardy the defense of transatlantic sea lanes, Singapore, and even the United Kingdom itself. Churchill replied that the present situations in the Atlantic and the Far East did not merit drawing down in the Middle East, where he felt "more comfortable about the prospects of holding our position" than he had for a long while. At this point, the British chiefs of staff chimed in, giving a uniformly upbeat account of Britain's defenses and her prospects in the Middle East. Even the army chief, Sir John Dill, supported Churchill's line, despite his private doubts. Withdrawing from the Middle East, said Dill, would shatter Allied morale and Muslim goodwill, free up German forces, and surrender control of the oilfields of the Persian Gulf and the resources of Africa. It was far better to fight the Germans in a theater where the British Empire forces had the advantages. This was Cabinet Room as echo chamber. Churchill's feeling afterward was that "our American friends were convinced by our statements and convinced by the solidarity among us."[55]

This meeting can hardly have been held, as Lee believed, for Hopkins's benefit. After all, Hopkins was not lacking in opportunities to hear Churchill's view of the Middle East. Rather, the intended audience was Lee and the other U.S. military representatives in the room, and those to whom they reported in Washington.[56] Hopkins actively sought to win them over, even setting up

Churchill to deliver one of the "comprehensive statements of broad strategy" of which he was the acknowledged master. FDR was not aware of this meeting in advance. But Hopkins was nevertheless doing his master's will, by smoothing relations between the two governments and encouraging the sometimes unruly U.S. military to get with the program.[57] That said, the British didn't get everything their own way that evening: Hopkins ignored Churchill's references to the need for a more assertive U.S. presence in the Pacific.[58]

On Friday, July 25, Hopkins was "frightfully tired" and decided to skip an excursion with Churchill, Harriman, and others to observe tank maneuvers in the countryside. Instead, he had a late breakfast in his room at Claridge's with Lee, quizzing him on how to improve the Lend-Lease machinery in Washington and London. Lee was a Harriman skeptic, and pointed out the overlapping mandates of the U.S. military attaché, the Harriman mission, and the office of the military observer, General Chaney. Hopkins revealed that the president had charged him with defusing the tension between Harriman and Winant. "I have given Harriman the most strict and explicit instructions not to touch anything which is in any way political. That is the Ambassador's business, and his alone. I also told Churchill," he said, "that we had at the moment in England the best, the finest, and most highly qualified man for ambassador that we have had for twenty-five years, and a man who is the sincere friend of Great Britain, and therefore that he must deal with Winant direct and fully in all matters which had any political aspect whatever."[59] As Sherwood noted drily, "It is doubtful that this explanation had any appreciable effect on the situation." Churchill told Harriman, like a wayward husband to his mistress, "We'll have to be more careful." But the love triangle continued as before.[60]

As his mission came to a close, Hopkins swapped some cables with Washington. In late July, as part of its post-Barbarossa push south, Japan occupied a string of Vichy bases in southern Indochina. In response, the administration froze Japanese assets in the United States, began to reinforce the Philippines, and imposed limits on oil and gas sales to Japan. Now, via Hopkins, Roosevelt briefed Churchill on another deterrence measure, his proposal to "neutralize" Indochina. The idea was that the great powers would turn the region into a neutral zone and share its resources between them. Japan would get the rice and fertilizers it needed, but only if it withdrew its military from the area. FDR presumed that Tokyo's answer would "be unfavorable but we have at least made one more effort to avoid Japanese expansion to [the] South Pacific."[61]

Tokyo's answer was indeed unfavorable. There was a larger problem, however. "What the Americans conceived of as deterrence," writes David Reynolds, "Japan saw as encirclement." Over the next two months, FDR's restrictions on oil and gas exports coalesced into a de facto oil embargo. With its oil reserves dwindling, U.S. naval power growing, and U.S. policy stiffening, Japanese military planners began to plot how to replenish their country's resources by force of arms—with an attack southward that risked war with America.[62]

HOPKINS SPENT HIS FINAL WEEKEND in the United Kingdom at Chequers. As one regular guest recalled, there were always "secretaries running around" Chequers and "important people coming and going." But the activity at the ancient house was especially frenetic that weekend. At the last minute, Hopkins had agreed to broadcast a speech on the BBC on Sunday night, and to help with the drafting he engineered an invitation for an old crony, Quentin Reynolds, the burly, untidy-looking London correspondent for *Collier's*. Churchill was also preparing an important speech that weekend, so the traveling secretaries from Number 10 were stretched. The American columnist Dorothy Thompson was present, as were Averell and Kathleen Harriman, Gil Winant, Lord Cherwell, and Air Marshal Sir Richard Peirse, head of Bomber Command. Various Churchills were in residence, along with their familiars—Winston's ill-tempered black cat Nelson, loved by the prime minister for once having chased a large dog out of the Admiralty; and Sukie, Mary's "Free French poodle." Also in attendance were Churchill family friends Sir Maurice and Lady Violet Bonham Carter, and Miss Horatia

Seymour, who had been one of Clementine's bridesmaids. Miss Seymour and Lady Violet, the daughter of Prime Minister H. H. Asquith, both staunch Liberals, accused Hopkins of "associating solely with Tories in England." Why hadn't he met any Liberals, they asked him. "I have," Hopkins replied mischievously. "As a matter of fact, I've now met both of them!"[63]

At lunch on Saturday, mutton was served, leading to a delightful exchange between Winston and Clementine that was recorded by Quentin Reynolds:

"Where did you get this mutton?"

"At the village butcher's where we always trade," she said.

"We bring our friend Hopkins down here and what do we serve him? Stringy mutton," he growled.

"Tastes all right to me," Harry said.

"English mutton is something we've always been proud of." Churchill went into a speech on the excellence of English mutton and how the present sample was terrible. "You should be able to get better mutton than this, Clemmie," he said reproachfully.

Lovely Clemmie raised her head and with a solemn face she said, "Remember, Winston, there's a war on."

Churchill just growled under his breath.[64]

Clementine took Reynolds up to Hopkins's bedroom after lunch to work on the speech. "I'm so glad you're helping Harry," she said. "We worry so about his health." She was "like a mother chicken with a chick," thought Reynolds. Hopkins was "dog-tired" and visibly ill, but he brushed off his hostess's concern by saying casually, "Got a little cold during that trip over." His drafting instructions to Reynolds indicated the balance the envoy aimed to strike in his broadcast. He "wanted to give the British public hope that big things were on the way; that substantial help was coming under Lend-Lease. But he couldn't be too specific" lest he betray ship movements to the German navy or further inflame isolationists at home who "were screaming bloody murder." Hopkins was aware of the dangers attached to the broadcast, promising FDR he would not "upset the diplomatic apple-cart, so have the State Department keep their shirts on." He knew that "anything I say will be construed as a direct message from FDR. People know I'm only the president's messenger boy." Some politicians "credit me with a Svengali-like influence over the President," he said with a smile. "If they only knew I just deliver messages."[65]

For several hours, Reynolds tapped out a draft on a typewriter, while Hopkins lay on his bed and slept. At one point Mrs. Churchill came in and reproached Reynolds for not covering Hopkins with a blanket. When Hopkins awoke and read Reynolds's draft, he laughed. "Hell, Quent, you've got me declaring war on Germany!" "We should have done it long ago," replied Reynolds. "You forget that this is the President speaking," said Hopkins, and started editing it with a pencil. The finished product was shown to Churchill, who popped into the room in the one-piece zippered garment that everyone called his "siren suit" or his "rompers." Churchill chuckled as he read it. "I'd like to make it twice as strong," said Reynolds. "So, I am sure, would our friend Hopkins," Churchill said, laughing. "But it's fine, it's fine."[66]

At dinner that evening, the air was thick with bonhomie. Churchill, dressed in a new set of rompers, spent most of the evening kidding Hopkins, who was decked out in a dinner jacket obtained from who knows where. To Reynolds's eye, Churchill regarded Hopkins as "a much-loved brother" and Mary Churchill saw him as "a favourite uncle." Clemmie continued to treat him as a patient, saying every now and again, "Why not get to bed, Harry. You have a long day tomorrow and the weather is going to be lovely. You could take a nice walk in the morning with Winston." Hopkins pretended to be hurt: "Trying to get rid of me, hey? A fine thing."[67]

Reynolds compared Churchill's dinner conversation to "a chameleon on a rock"—darting back into antiquity, forward to Lord Byron, to India, to Kipling, to Shakespeare and long passages from Hamlet, to Thomas More, and then to the First World War poet Rupert Brooke and his poem "The Fish." "That was a poet," Churchill said softly. "And he, you'll remember, was killed by the Hun." "Do you know why I hate Nazis?" Churchill asked his guests. "I hate them because they frown when they fight. They are grim and dull-faced. They don't go into battle with a song in their hearts. Now take our magnificent RAF lads. They grin when they fight. I like a man who grins when he fights." Luckily for the prime minister, the evening film was *Target for Tonight*, a documentary feature from the Crown Film Unit about Bomber Command, recently released to public acclaim. Enveloped in cigar smoke, Reynolds noticed that Churchill "was as tense as any movie fan when things looked bad for the bomber that was over Germany. He chuckled when its bombs hit their target."[68] At eleven o'clock, Clementine announced, "I've fixed your bed, Harry, and put a nice hot water bottle in it." Her efforts went unrewarded. The evening continued for another three hours, with Churchill finally declaring, "This is a half holiday: we must work tomorrow."[69]

Hopkins's principal responsibility the next day was to deliver his broadcast, which he did at 9:15 p.m. from Churchill's own microphone, in the paneled Hawtrey Room, with portraits of Elizabethan figures looking down on him:[70]

I arrived here from America one week ago on business. My business is the same as that of every other American, from the President of the United States to the man who drives a rivet or runs a lathe in an airplane factory in Los Angeles or Buffalo. That business is the safeguarding of our heritage of freedom of thought and action. Right now, Hitler is seriously threatening this heritage of ours, a heritage which is yours.

I did not come from America alone—I came in a bomber plane, and with me were twenty other bombers made in America. These airplanes tonight may be dropping bombs on Brest, on Hamburg, on Berlin, helping to safeguard our common heritage.

I came here as a representative of the President of the United States. His hatred for the things that Hitler stands for is the hatred of our people against tyranny. The people of my country feel that this world would not be worth living in if the forces of Nazi power were to prevail, and if the democracies of the world were to crumble under their fierce but futile assault.

The President, speaking for the people of the United States, is rendering Britain more than lip service. Even now as I speak sleek gray destroyers flying the American flag are plunging their bows into the waters of the North Atlantic. Once upon a time this mighty ocean separated us. Now it joins us. Tonight British and American warships are patrolling on parallel lanes with only one object in view: to guard the world's life-line.

I have been with the President when messages came to him telling of the bombing of workers' flats in the East End of London. I was with him when the news first came of the tragic bombing of Coventry and later of Plymouth. I heard the words which came not from his lips but from his heart. I watched the stern development of his determination to defeat Hitler. The President is one with your Prime Minister in his determination to break the ruthless power of that sinful psychopath of Berlin.

The President asked me to come over here. My instructions from him were these: "Find out if the material we are sending to Britain is arriving. Find out if it is what Britain wants. Let me know if there is anything more that Britain needs." This is my mission.

I have found out the things he asked me to find out. I have learned that most of the war material America has shipped to this island has arrived here—although I know only too well of some of the precious cargoes that have gone to the bottom of the sea. I have learned from your Cabinet Ministers what England needs now, and I am returning to America to report this to the President. I have found that there are certain things which you need in order to fight this war for the democracies. I am confident America can supply them . . .

Nor do we forget to look towards the East, where China is battling valiantly against the forces which menace democracy. Neither are we forgetful of the magnificent fight which the people of Russia are putting up in defence of their home land. We in America are determined to give all possible aid to China and Russia—and immediately.

The broadcast closed by continuing the public dialogue initially struck up by the Longfellow verse that FDR had sent to London with Wendell Willkie, to which Churchill had replied in his famous February speech. Now Hopkins extended the conversation:

> Your Prime Minister asked us for the tools. I promise you that they are coming; that an endless assembly belt stretches from our western coast to this island, and to the Middle East; that nothing will be allowed to interfere with the full efficiency of this supply line. The enormous amount of war material which is *en route* now will reach here safely. President Roosevelt promised that he would take steps to ensure the delivery of goods consigned to Britain. Our President does not give his word lightly.
>
> People of England—people of Britain—people of the British Commonwealth of Nations—you are not fighting alone.[71]

Hopkins had not declared war. But this was a strikingly belligerent speech, and an arresting statement of Anglo-American solidarity. U.S. policy was no longer about keeping the British Isles afloat; it was about fighting shoulder to shoulder with the British, at least in ideological and industrial terms. Surely the third kind of warfare—shooting—could not be far off.

Hopkins's address was translated into many languages and broadcast all around the empire and beyond. It was featured prominently in Egyptian newspapers. It was referred to by Churchill in the House of Commons and reported in the *New York Times*. It was printed on millions of leaflets dropped over the Continent by Bomber Command. "It took a good deal of ingenuity on the part of the British propaganda experts to explain just who Hopkins was," reports Sherwood admiringly, "but they managed to convey the implication that he represented the vanguard of an enormous American Expeditionary Force."[72] It was emblematic of the symbolic role played by Hopkins on his second mission to the United Kingdom, which was much greater than the first.

Hopkins's second mission attracted the usual criticisms from his enemies, including that he had been captured by his hosts. Harold Ickes complained that he was a "fluent promiser," and that during his time in London he had "been promising in a high, wide and handsome manner."[73] Hopkins was certainly vehement in his support for Britain—more so than he had been last time, and more so even than FDR was at this point. However, his actions in the United Kingdom were consistent with Roosevelt's instructions. Furthermore, the direction of the influence was not all one-way; the British were eager to demonstrate their openness and responsiveness.

After Hopkins had completed his broadcast, he took his leave of the prime minister and the country. In typical style, he forgot to pay his bill at Claridge's; later, he wrote to Winant asking that he do so on his behalf and also tip his valet and waiter generously, "a couple of pounds apiece."[74]

Apart from housekeeping, Hopkins's London objectives had all been substantially achieved. As the president's surrogate, he had renewed Anglo-American ties, finalized the arrangements for the upcoming summit, and delivered FDR's messages in relation to naval activity in the Atlantic, territorial deals, and Winant's position at court. After the war, Churchill wrote that Hopkins had been "the most faithful and perfect channel of communication" between the White House and Downing Street.[75] He had also become a symbol of American aid to besieged Britain.

In some ways, though, this Hopkins mission was less significant in what it achieved than what it presaged: the entangling of American and British elites, and the growing collaboration of the two governments in all spheres of the war. This process would accelerate after America entered the conflict. There would still be plenty of friction, as there is any time two sovereign countries rub up against each other. Still, this relationship was undeniably special.[76] Hopkins's July 1941 mission to Britain helped set the template.

7.

"Uncle Joe's Favorite"

HARRY HOPKINS IN MOSCOW AND AT

PLACENTIA BAY, JULY—AUGUST 1941

On the day the news came through that Germany had invaded the Soviet Union, Hopkins was at the racetrack. His first thought upon hearing the report was, "The President's policy of support for Britain has really paid off! Hitler has turned to the left." He told the Polish ambassador in Washington that Hitler's move would complicate Germany's position and ease the pressure on Britain. But there were also risks. Hopkins was concerned that Barbarossa would provide succor to isolationists in the United States, who could now appeal to anticommunist feeling in America, especially among Catholics. He also worried that the improved strategic circumstances of the British would drain the urgency from America's efforts to rearm and aid them.[1]

Like the rest of Washington, he seems to have presumed in the early days that Germany would quickly prevail. A senior U.S. military source told the *Washington Post* that only an "act of God" could save Russia from an early defeat. In the weeks after the invasion, however, Hopkins's view changed. His thinking on aiding the Soviets developed along similar lines to the president's, firming up in tandem with evidence that they were putting up a fight.[2]

The Germans' eastward advance slowed further in July, while Hopkins was in Britain. The reaction to this development back home was mixed. Newspapers were pleased by the news, but not so pleased that they supported the notion of aiding the Soviet defenders (or, as the *Chicago Daily Tribune* described them, "an Asiatic butcher and his godless crew"). The ambivalence of the nation's editors was shared by their readers: while 72 percent of Americans preferred to see the Soviets win, only 35 percent believed the United States should provide them with assistance in the same way it did Britain.[3]

Despite his reputation for caution in the face of hostile public opinion, however, Roosevelt remained determined to extend immediate, substantial aid to Stalin. Indeed, his resolution was strengthened by news from the front and personal testimony from his former ambassador to Moscow, Joseph Davies, who predicted that the Red Army would "amaze the world." But getting such a policy implemented by Washington bureaucrats, many of whom disagreed with it, was another thing altogether. Frustrated by a lack of action, and spurred on by complaints from Ambassador Oumansky and Henry Morgenthau that the Soviets were being given "the proverbial Washington 'run around,'" FDR began to lean more heavily on the departments to increase the flow of exports.[4]

AT THIS MOMENT, Hopkins staged a decisive long-distance intervention in the Washington debate. On Friday, July 25, as he was winding up his mission in the United Kingdom, he cabled Roosevelt with a startling suggestion:

> I am wondering whether you would think it important and useful for me to go to Moscow. Air transportation good and can reach there in twenty four hours. I have a feeling that everything possible

should be done to make certain the Russians maintain a permanent front even though they be defeated in this immediate battle. If Stalin could in any way be influenced at a critical time I think it would be worth doing by a direct communication from you through a personal envoy. I think the stakes are so great that it should be done. Stalin would then know in an unmistakable way that we mean business on a long term supply job.[5]

At this point, neither Roosevelt nor Hopkins contemplated a Soviet victory. Rather, as Hopkins cabled FDR from London, the "Russian business" offered a "temporary breather" to Britain and the United States—and it was worth trying to prolong the respite. Whatever Barbarossa's final outcome, assisting Moscow made sense to Hopkins. As he commented to Gil Winant, "Every German killed by a Russian will kill no Americans or British."[6]

The precise origins of Hopkins's Moscow mission are disputed. It seems unlikely that he discussed the idea with Roosevelt before he left Washington. Everyone around Hopkins thought the notion struck him suddenly in London and the decision to go was made at the last minute—so much so that he had to cancel several meetings in London, including with a member of the royal family.[7] Success has many fathers, however, and both the Soviet and U.S. ambassadors to the Court of St. James's later claimed they first suggested the mission to Hopkins. Ivan Maisky recalled that the "idea flashed through my mind" at a lunch with Hopkins that a visit to Moscow was the only way for him to get all the information he required. For his part, Winant remembered volunteering to travel to Moscow with a "message of encouragement" for Stalin, only for Hopkins to reply, after a pause, "What would you think of my going from here?"[8] (It is ironic that Winant, an ambassador who was being undermined at his post by a personal envoy, was nonetheless prepared to assume the garb of personal envoy to Stalin, despite the presence of a properly accredited ambassador in Moscow.) Perhaps these suggestions contributed to Hopkins's decision, but given his past experiences as an envoy and his preference for direct action, he needed little prompting.

The mission obviously appealed to Roosevelt, who responded immediately to Hopkins's cable: "Welles and I highly approve Moscow trip . . . I will send you tonight a message for Stalin." He also checked that Hopkins would be back in time for the Atlantic Conference. Both FDR and Churchill were anxious that their marriage broker be present at their long-awaited rendezvous. When Hopkins received Roosevelt's go-ahead late in the evening of Saturday, July 26, he was at Chequers preparing his radio broadcast for the BBC. "I had been tired up to the moment of the arrival of the message," he recalled later in an article for the *American Magazine*. But once he received his orders, he wrote, "I wasn't tired any more. I had never been in Russia. If I had any immediate concern it was to get to Moscow as fast as possible and let the gods who had been so good to me thus far take care of the rest."[9]

Early the next morning, Hopkins received a second cable from the White House containing the president's message for Stalin:

> I am sending Mr. Hopkins to Moscow in order that he may discuss with you personally . . . the vitally important question of how the assistance which the United States is able to furnish the Soviet Union in its magnificent resistance against the treacherous aggression of Hitlerite Germany may be made available most expeditiously and most effectively . . .
>
> Mr. Hopkins will communicate to me directly the views which you express to him and the particular problems involving assistance from the United States which seem to you most pressing. I ask that you treat him with the same confidence as you would if you were talking with me personally.[10]

FDR had two purposes in authorizing the Hopkins mission to Moscow.[11] The first was to investigate Russia's progress and her needs, about which Washington knew very little. Western diplomats and military attachés in Moscow had little contact with ordinary people or even officials, leaving them to base their estimates, in the words of one firsthand observer, "almost entirely on personal observation supplemented by rumor and newspaper articles." Foreigners were "completely in the dark as to what was going on."[12] To make matters worse, both the U.S. ambassador, Laurence A. Steinhardt (who did not have the benefit of a close personal relationship with Roosevelt), and the U.S. military attaché, Major Ivan Yeaton, were regarded by the Kremlin as defeatists, if not cowards. As with Joe Kennedy in London a year earlier, this increased their isolation and limited their influence.[13] The lack of reliable information obscured the administration's understanding of the USSR's needs. Roosevelt wanted Hopkins to get him the "facts" on the war, including the strength of the Soviet forces, their determination to fight, and the war materials they would require in order to hold out until the winter.[14]

Behind the issue of Russia's immediate needs stood a larger, more fundamental question: what were her prospects of holding out? Roosevelt could hardly include this question in his cable to Stalin, but he expected Hopkins to answer it. FDR was predisposed toward positivity, but he wanted his intuition backed up by evidence. Hopkins captured Roosevelt's mood of uncertain optimism in an article he drafted for *Collier's*: "He wanted to be sure—hoped to be sure—that Stalin could hold Hitler off while America and Britain were reaching the peak of defensive and offensive arming." In order to be sure, Hopkins had to see Stalin. "Stalin is Russia," wrote the envoy. "His would be the only word of authority."[15]

Hopkins's other job was to resurrect his role as intermediary, this time between Roosevelt and Stalin. The Soviet premier was a mystery to the U.S. president. "For Roosevelt," Hopkins told Maisky, "Stalin is at present just a name. He's never seen the head of your government, never talked to him, and in general has no idea of what sort of a man he is." Hopkins was to take Stalin's measure, and "to carry a personal message from the President that we would go 'all out' and give every aid possible to the Soviets."[16]

On Sunday morning, Hopkins went to Churchill's bedroom at Chequers and "told him that the next move was his . . . he'd have to figure how I was going to get to Moscow." With the Anglo-American summit looming, time was short. The prime minister telephoned the chief of the air staff, Sir

Charles Portal, and ordered him to make the arrangements. He was still in bed when the reply came through: Hopkins would depart by train that very night for Invergordon in northern Scotland, where he would board a flight for Archangel on the White Sea and then on to Moscow. Winant was dispatched to obtain a Soviet visa; meanwhile, Hopkins relayed developments to FDR, assuring him that he would be "back in time to be in Canada for your visit." The envoy passed the rest of the day like any in the country, talking to the other guests at Chequers about "books, plays, personalities" and "the war in generalities" and preparing for his BBC broadcast. If anyone other than Churchill knew about his impending mission, they gave no hint of it. "Here was British reserve at its peak," Hopkins wrote later. "Tommy" Thompson thought Hopkins "seemed surprisingly relaxed . . . the feeling of being at the centre of great events always acted as a tonic to him." This was an act. In fact, strong emotions and a great sense of responsibility were "churning" within Hopkins.[17]

Late that evening, after Hopkins had broadcast his lines from the Hawtrey Room, he repaired with Churchill to the lawn behind Chequers. As they walked back and forth in the gathering dusk, the prime minister briefed Hopkins "in the minutest detail" on the aid Britain was sending to Russia. The American asked how he should reply if Stalin asked him what cooperation Russia could expect from Britain; perhaps he was thinking about Churchill's history as a fierce anticommunist. The PM looked hard at Hopkins, his eyes grave. "Tell him, tell him . . . tell him that Britain has but one ambition today, but one desire—to crush Hitler. You can depend upon us . . . Goodbye, God bless you Harry." He laid his hand on Hopkins's arm for a moment and then disappeared into the house.[18]

Late that night Churchill, the old Tory, drafted a cable to Stalin, the old Bolshevik:

> Mr Harry Hopkins has been with me these days. Last week he asked
> the President to let him go to Moscow. I must tell you that there is a

flame in this man for democracy and to beat Hitler. He is the nearest personal representative of the President. A little while ago when I asked him for a quarter of a million rifles they came at once. The President has now sent him full instructions and he leaves my house tonight to go to you . . . You can trust him absolutely. He is your friend and our friend. He will help you to plan for the future victory and for the long term supply of Russia.[19]

Averell and Kathleen Harriman drove Hopkins from Chequers to London's neoclassical Euston railway station, with its monumental Doric arch. Little of the station was visible in the eerie London blackout, however. In the dim light Hopkins could just make out a few embassy staffers who had come to see him off and bring him his luggage from Claridge's. At the very last minute, even as the train was moving off, Winant appeared. The unfortunate ambassador had spent the afternoon trying to sort out Hopkins's visa. His Soviet counterpart, Maisky, had acquired the English habit of weekending in the country, but as a good left-winger he did so at the Bovingdon house of an exiled Spanish socialist leader, Juan Negrín. At the U.S. embassy's request, Maisky returned to London early and received Winant in his study at 10 p.m. Winant's request put the Soviet official in a bind: such permissions were usually cleared through Moscow, and in any case the visa seals were locked in a safe at a different location. Taking a chance, he wrote in Hopkins's passport by hand, "Harry Hopkins is to be permitted to cross any frontier station of the USSR without examination of luggage, as a diplomatic person. I. Maisky, Ambassador of the USSR in Great Britain." Winant tore off for Euston Station, ran up the platform, and handed the passport through the carriage window of the moving train. Hopkins was off. As his train pulled out of the darkened station, the Americans on the platform felt like "they had said good-bye to someone who was about to step into a rocket bound for interstellar space, for Russia then seemed immeasurably far away."[20]

———

HOPKINS'S RIDE FOR THE TRIP NORTH was a special five-car train with a sleeping car, dining car, and lounge car. Also on board were his two traveling companions: Brigadier General Joseph T. McNarney, a U.S. Army officer detailed by General Marshall to accompany Hopkins; and Lieutenant John R. Alison, a young Army Air Corps pilot and assistant military attaché responsible for training British pilots on the American-built P-40 Tomahawk. At noon that day, Alison had received a "cryptic call" at his squadron outside London ordering him to report to Euston Station at 11 p.m. Whitehall had decided to send some of its P-40s, still packed in their crates, to the Soviet air force, and Alison was to train the Soviets up.[21]

The young aviator was concerned by the "little tinge of yellow" in Hopkins's face but charmed by his "delightful sense of humor." "I was a very junior officer and he treated me elegantly," he recalled. "Very often they make the junior officer the bag smasher, but he treated me courteously as one of his party." Hopkins arranged to meet the other two in the lounge car for a nightcap ten minutes after leaving Euston. "What will it be?" he asked Alison when the steward approached. "Sir, I don't drink," replied Alison, who ordered a lemon squash instead. The exchange was repeated for the second round of drinks. When the steward approached for the third time, Hopkins turned to Alison with a "quizzical half-smile" on his lips and "a twinkle in his eye." "Alison," he said. "I don't care whether you drink or not but will you quit looking so damn superior!"[22]

Hopkins and his colleagues awoke the next morning, Monday, July 28, in Scotland. While they waited for the weather to clear, they drove across the rugged, beautiful moors and had tea at a shop owned by a Mrs. Simpson. After London's wartime austerities, the bread and butter, heather honey, and other delights provided by Mrs. Simpson were a treat. Then orders came through from London that the flight was to depart immediately despite the poor weather. When Hopkins came down to the waterfront and saw the big PBY Catalina wallowing at its mooring out on the Cromarty Firth, he felt both familiarity and pride. Familiarity, because he had flown in the sturdy flying boats before, including one leg of his return journey from the United Kingdom in February, when his Clipper was delayed; pride, because he had fought hard bureaucratic battles to force the U.S. Navy to relinquish some of them to the British.[23]

The PBY-5, designated by the RAF as the Catalina Mark I, was a twin-motored, high-winged, wide-bottomed flying boat manufactured in San Diego by Consolidated Aircraft, with a fuselage sixty feet long and a wing-span of a hundred feet. The PBY would become one of the Second World War's workhorses, used for long-range maritime patrol, antisubmarine warfare, search and rescue, and other roles. It was the only available aircraft with a chance of getting Hopkins to Russia and back in time for the Atlantic Conference.[24]

This particular aircraft, serial number W8416, was captained by Flight Lieutenant David "Mac" McKinley, DFC, an RAF officer from central casting except for his slight Irish accent. McKinley was one of Coastal Command's most experienced pilots, with thirty-five hundred flying hours in the PBY. The day before, he and his crew were enjoying a picnic at beautiful Loch Lomond after weeks of patrolling the North West Approaches when another aircraft from their squadron flew overhead signaling with its Aldis lamp that they should return to base. At Invergordon on the afternoon of the twenty-eighth, the station commander opened an envelope from the Foreign Office in McKinley's presence and read him his orders. McKinley was to fly Hopkins and his party to Archangel in Russia's far north, flying in a broad northerly sweep all the way up and around German-occupied Norway, past the tip of Finland (and several Luftwaffe bases), and then down over the White Sea to Archangel. For reasons of operational security, no notes were to be made or records kept, no special preparations were made for the flight that might have attracted attention, and only those charts covering McKinley's precise route were provided to him.[25]

The flight to Archangel had an inauspicious start when the Catalina's forward hatch blew open during takeoff and the anchor chain wrapped itself around the aircraft's windscreen.[26] On the second attempt, however, she got airborne. So began a flight that took nearly twenty-four hours, under the most primitive conditions. All PBYs were noisy and cramped. This one was particularly cluttered because it had been fitted with overload fuel tanks to enable it to fly the vast distance to Archangel. To accommodate the tanks and lighten the load, the aircrew had been reduced to five, which meant that none could be spared from flight duties to attend to the passengers. The RAF rations were basic—mainly sea biscuit and coffee, along with a little soup. Extreme turbulence usually put paid to any rations that had been consumed anyway. It was freezing cold, especially when the aircraft reached the Arctic region, yet the passengers had not been furnished with properly fitting flying clothes. At least Hopkins had Churchill's hat to keep his head warm.

As well as being uncomfortable, the journey was dangerous. The PBY was a slow-flying, vulnerable aircraft, especially when loaded down. This one was only lightly armed, and visibility was worryingly good in the ceaseless daylight of an Arctic summer. McKinley decided to keep well clear of the Norwegian coast and fly very low—often only a few hundred feet above the surface of the ocean—in an effort to evade enemy radar. Radio silence was maintained for most of the journey. When Hopkins asked about the chances of encountering enemy aircraft, the skipper replied that they were 50/50. "Right, there's nothing else for it," said Hopkins. "Come on, Archangel."

Hopkins maintained his good humor throughout the miserable flight, talking to the young crew about everyday subjects like school, family, and parties. He was determined not to be a burden and even acted as a steward on occasion. He spent most of his time in the waist of the flying boat, where two large plexiglass blisters provided what Alison called "picture window views." Even there, however, the crew had stashed extra lifeboats and other gear that made it difficult to get comfortable. Hopkins sat in one of the pivoted gunners' seats watching for signs of the enemy. When McKinley apologized about the rations, Hopkins patted a little medical kit he was carrying and said, "This is where my energy comes from, and it will last me for the next couple of days." From time to time, he entered the tiny galley and injected himself with some substance from the kit, probably vitamins and liver extract. At the end of the marathon, he tried unconvincingly to tell McKinley that he had had a pleasant flight. The stoic McKinley was deeply impressed with his passenger's "determination to totally disregard personal comfort," noting, "Twenty-four-hour flights in the very stern austerity furnishings of a warplane and living on hard tack rations are not ideal conditions for a man in a critical state of health."[27]

Half an hour out from Archangel, in the late afternoon of the twenty-ninth, three Soviet fighters appeared on the skyline. After the aircraft exchanged recognition signals, the Soviets closed in and escorted the Catalina into Archangel. The weather was pleasant and Hopkins noticed a beach crowded with bathers. McKinley put her down on the log-strewn Northern Dvina River in what he remembered as "a dodgy little landing, trying to move in and out of these huge baulks of timber that were floating down the river." His job was not made easier when one of the Soviet planes accidentally brushed the flying boat with its wheels in midair and took off her antenna. Once the Catalina was safely down, a small mahogany launch came alongside and directed that she be moored next to a houseboat that would serve as the crew's quarters while their passengers went on to Moscow. Later the crew heard gunfire and were told that the Soviet pilot responsible for the collision had been shot.[28]

Hopkins and his companions could not proceed to Moscow straight-away, as aircraft were not allowed to approach the capital at night. Any hopes of sleep were scotched by the insistence of the admiral in command at Archangel that the Americans join him for a banquet on the afterdeck of his yacht, a once elegant craft that was now distinctly run-down. "Dinner on the admiral's yacht was monumental," Hopkins remembered later. "It lasted almost four hours. There was an Iowa flavour to it, what with the fresh vegetables, the butter, cream, greens . . . The dinner was enormous, course after course. There was the inescapable cold fish, caviar, and vodka. Vodka has authority. It is nothing for the amateur to trifle with. Drink it as an

American or an Englishman takes whisky neat and it will tear you apart. The thing to do is to spread a chunk of bread (and good bread it was) with caviar, and, while you're swallowing that, bolt your vodka. Don't play with the stuff. Eat while you're drinking it—something that will act as a shock absorber for it."[29]

Poor Lieutenant Alison did not have the advantage of a shock absorber, however. For a while, he managed to avoid drinking the countless toasts—to Stalin, to Roosevelt, to Churchill, even to seagulls—that left one highly decorated Soviet admiral flat on his back under the table within an hour of the party starting.[30] But then a big Soviet general with an embroidered white linen tunic and "a mouthful of gold teeth" stood up, proposed a toast "to the American flyer who has come so far from his home to help us in our struggle against a common enemy," and drained his vodka glass. Alison knew that his time had come. He stood up, thanked the general, raised his own glass, and emptied it of vodka in one gulp. This was Alison's first taste of hard liquor, and the shock of it brought tears to his eyes. He sat down and put his face in his napkin while he recovered. When he came out from under the napkin, he found Hopkins looking at him from across the table with a smile on his face. "Well, Alison," he said, "that shows a definite lack of character."[31]

When he was not teasing the previously abstemious Alison, Hopkins shared "uninterrupted" talk with his hosts—all men, except for his attractive female interpreter—about books, art, and classical music. Some of them had worked at Ford's River Rouge factory in Michigan and wanted to know about the latest in American manufacturing. He got the impression they were no less confident of victory than their British allies, but instead of the Briton's "cool indifference to incidental setbacks and difficulties, the Russian is apt to go poetical." When Hopkins mentioned the approaching winter to one young Russian pilot, for instance, he replied, "There is autumn coming in nature but there is spring in our hearts." Hopkins enjoyed the conversation, but he was distracted. McKinley noticed that throughout the meal, Hopkins "kept looking at his watch and looking at the door as much as to say, when are we going to the airport?" Finally, on about the twentieth course, he was informed that he would leave for Moscow in a few hours, at 4 a.m. The Catalina aircrew were to remain in Archangel, comforted only by the attentions of their beautiful and accommodating female interpreters.[32]

After two hours' sleep, Hopkins and his party boarded an American-built Douglas DC-3 transport aircraft for the final leg of their journey. It was about the same size as the PBY but significantly more comfortable. As the DC-3 took off, its Soviet pilots gave their distinguished passenger a "special salute," a complicated maneuver in which the plane flew only a few feet off the ground, dipping each wing in turn as if to cut the grass, then rose sharply and seemed to bounce. "It may be quite an honor, even lots of fun, in Russia," Hopkins wrote later. "My own thoughts were that I had reached the end of my journey, that in another second or two Roosevelt's emissary to Stalin would be in eternity with nothing to report."

The plane covered the six hundred miles to Moscow in about four hours, again flying very low, both to avoid enemy interference and to enable it to home in on a broadcasting station in Moscow. As they passed over several hundred miles of dense forest that would be a formidable barrier even for Hitler's panzers, Hopkins was cheered by the defensive advantages lent to the Soviet Union by its geography. (His view on the prison camps that could be seen here and there went unrecorded.) Eventually the blackness of the forest gave way to collectivized farms, then to the Volga "solid with barges," "the factory towns belching their black smoke and yellow flames at us," larger and more frequent towns—and then, at last, Moscow.[33]

The morning of Wednesday, July 30, was already warm and sunny when Harry Hopkins emerged from his DC-3 on to the tarmac of Moscow Central Airport. He was greeted by Western diplomats and military officers led by the U.S. and British ambassadors, Laurence Steinhardt and Sir Stafford Cripps, a large delegation of Soviet officials, and secret police from the

NKVD, the forerunner of the KGB. The Soviets were excited by the arrival of "the personal representative and friend of President Roosevelt," whom they called "Garry Gopkins" according to their habit of converting an "h" into a "g," the closest letter in the Cyrillic alphabet. But they could not help noticing that the visitor "looked very frail, very weak, pale."[34]

Laurence Steinhardt was a New York lawyer turned diplomat, tall, ambitious, and vaguely equine in appearance. He took Hopkins back to his residence, one mile to the west of the Kremlin, and put him to bed. Spaso House, one of Moscow's "merchant palaces," had been the home of the U.S. ambassador since the establishment of diplomatic relations between the United States and the Soviet Union in 1933; since the outbreak of war, it had served as the embassy, too. Built in the late tsarist period for a wealthy merchant, the ostentatious house boasted a massive chandelier that was the talk of Moscow when it was built. Hopkins was not inclined to savor the comforts of Spaso House for too long, however. In Sherwood's words, he wanted to explore "the vast mystery which was Russia."[35]

The principal purpose of his mission, Hopkins told Steinhardt, was to see whether the military situation was as "disastrous" as many in Washington believed—and as it appeared to be in the cables sent by the military attaché, Major Ivan Yeaton. The attaché was highly suspicious of the Soviets' motives and pessimistic about their chances of holding Moscow. But Hopkins "let everybody know that the president had made a decision that we were going to help Russia," recalled John Alison later. "Policy was going to be made in the White House and his job was to see that that policy was carried out . . . He was informal, he didn't stand on strict protocol but he certainly let everybody know that he had the President's authority." Steinhardt conceded that the Soviets would be more effective in defending their homeland than they had been in attacking Finland. He protested that it was almost impossible for outsiders to get an accurate picture of the military situation, given the hostility with which they were treated by Soviet officialdom. Hopkins replied that he was determined to breach "this wall of suspicion."[36]

In fact, Hopkins held Steinhardt partly responsible for the existence of the wall. That morning, the two men called on Sir Stafford Cripps, a former Labour politician whom Churchill had sent to Moscow, hoping that as a socialist he could talk the Kremlin's language. (The British ambassador was a little cold and stiff, hence his nickname "Stuffy.") Cripps shared Steinhardt's skepticism about the Soviets' war effort, but he also believed they must be encouraged to hold out until the winter. After getting rid of Steinhardt on the pretext that he had a private message to pass on from Churchill, Hopkins told the Englishman he had "sensed the atmosphere" as soon as he arrived at Spaso House: the American officials were not taking a "broad view of the situation." Cripps was pleased to find that the two men "saw very much eye to eye about the necessities of the situation," and to hear that "Roosevelt was all out to help all he could even if the Army and Navy authorities in America didn't like it."[37]

In the afternoon, Hopkins took a sightseeing tour around Moscow. After the gaiety of London, Moscow struck new arrivals as grim and gray. The roads were good, but few private automobiles were on them. Everywhere Muscovites queued patiently and silently for trams and buses—with the same look of resignation, thought one Briton, "as cows coming in from the fields one by one at milking time." They dressed drably, having put their best outfits aside when clothes rationing began. Strict food rationing was also in place. Many children had been evacuated to the countryside; women, on the other hand, could be seen working everywhere. Soldiers were conspicuous. Hopkins observed that the standard of living in Russia was significantly lower than it was at home, and it was obvious to him that Stalin "had control over everyone in the USSR." In general, however, he was reassured. He was surprised at the lack of damage done to the capital by German air raids. Hopkins watched large supply convoys move out of Moscow to the front in a regular and systematic fashion. He marveled at "the concentration of energy" he saw in the Soviet capital. He was impressed, he told Joseph Davies later, by "the executive direction and planning which was indicated by the orderliness of all this activity."[38]

In the early evening, Hopkins headed for the undisputed center of executive direction and planning, the Kremlin. An embassy car took him, along with Steinhardt and an American interpreter, to the great triangular citadel on the hill. Secret police cars drove in front and behind. "Time and distance had been coordinated down to the inch and second," he would recall. The Kremlin was a centuries-old walled compound of palaces, barracks, and cathedrals located between Red Square, with its outlandishly beautiful St. Basil's Cathedral, and the Moscow River. Its forbidding thirty-foot-high, russet-colored walls were punctuated by soaring towers. The citadel's shape, one author noted, "was uncompromisingly sharp. On maps the Kremlin looked like a pointed tooth biting into Moscow's flesh." The current preoccupation of the authorities was to ensure that this outline could not be seen from the sky. Enormous rolls of canvas like "stage scenery," adorned with fake windows and architectural features daubed in fireproof paint, hung from the Kremlin walls. From across the river, an observer looking in the direction of the Kremlin saw only "a row of houses with gabled roofs." Lenin's mausoleum in Red Square had been turned into a wooden cottage. Nets covered in leaves and branches were draped over the Kremlin's courtyards and the façades of its buildings. The red stars that sat atop the Kremlin's spires, and the golden domes of its churches, were shrouded in gray cloth. Everything was camouflaged.[39]

Hopkins's cavalcade zoomed through the Kremlin gates and wound past ancient onion-domed cathedrals and monuments. It stopped outside the old Senate, a triangle of a building that was called the Yellow Palace in tsarist times. He was directed along many corridors and around many turns, passing countless doors on the way. Everywhere were soldiers wearing prominent Soviet decorations, including the large red enamel badge that signified a Hero of the Soviet Union. As he proceeded past groups of soldiers, they telephoned ahead to report that he was on his way. Hopkins was ushered through a dozen doors and offices containing secretaries and bodyguards until finally, at exactly six o'clock, he was brought into the presence of Joseph Stalin.[40]

———

Stalin's office was long and bare. The walls were paneled in oak to shoulder height, and hanging from them were the finest maps Hopkins had ever seen. The only other decorations were black-and-white portraits of Marx and Engels, and a pale plaster death mask of Lenin. Hopkins thought the room was "furnished with severe simplicity, but with every modern, up-to-date facility." There was a mahogany desk with five or six telephones and a panel of buttons, and a long meeting table covered in heavy green baize. The chairs were straight-backed and hard-seated. In an anteroom stood a large relief globe, perhaps ten feet high.[41]

At sixty-two, Joseph Stalin had been general secretary of the Communist Party of the USSR for nearly twenty years. In recent months he had acquired two further titles, premier (or chairman of the Council of People's Commissars), and People's Commissar of Defense. But there was nothing ornamental about the man himself. Hopkins's impression was of "an austere, rugged, determined figure in boots that shone like mirrors, stout baggy trousers, and snug-fitting blouse." Unlike everyone else in the Kremlin, the *Vozhd* (leader) wore no decorations or badges of rank on his well-cut, military-style tunic. His left arm was slightly shorter than his right and he held it near his body. He was surprisingly short; in Hopkins's generous expression he was "built close to the ground, like a football coach's dream of a tackle." His dark, bristling hair and his mustache were shot through with gray; his skin was pockmarked. At first glance he was unimpressive; in fact, more than one foreigner likened his appearance to that of a gardener. But the strength of his personality was soon evident to anyone, not least in the "hunted look" in the eyes of the people around him. Hopkins found Stalin "exceptionally able, quiet, but a strong man . . . There was no question he was the 'top man,' running the show."[42]

In late July 1941, the show was in a pretty sorry state. The first fortnight of the German invasion had been a disaster for the Soviets. Much of the air force was destroyed on the ground in the first days. German forces struck out toward Leningrad in the north, Moscow in the center, and Kiev in the south. Panzers forced their way through Soviet lines and encircled the enemy from the rear, allowing them to be enveloped and destroyed by the German infantry divisions that followed. By mid-July, the Germans had taken Smolensk, not far from Moscow's threshold. Nighttime air raids began on the Soviet capital. Estimates of Soviet losses ranged from three-quarters of a million to two million men. In the second half of the month, though, the situation stabilized a little. The Wehrmacht's offensive slowed and its logistical problems quickened; the regime did not collapse; the Red Army regrouped. The position was still desperate; indeed, the day before Hopkins's arrival the Red Army's chief of staff, General Georgii Zhukov, had been removed from his post for proposing that Kiev be abandoned. But equilibrium had been restored within the regime, as it had been within Stalin himself. Having wobbled in the first week and withdrawn to his dacha outside Moscow, he was now firmly back in command.[43]

Also present in the room when Hopkins arrived was Vyacheslav Molotov, Stalin's foreign minister. Molotov was a ruthless functionary who had lent his name, unwillingly, to the gasoline bombs the Finns had rigged up and thrown at their Soviet invaders during the 1939–1940 war. An imperturbable diplomat with what Churchill called a "smile of Siberian winter," he usually remained silent during Stalin's meetings with foreigners. Molotov struck Hopkins as "the professorial, studious type."[44]

Stalin bowed slightly to Hopkins and welcomed him, and the two men exchanged cigarettes. Stalin chain-smoked throughout the meeting, which his visitor thought helped to explain "the harshness of his carefully controlled voice." After one greeting, it was down to business. Stalin offered no small talk; when he laughed it was short and sardonic. He spoke rapidly in Russian, ignoring the interpreter, looking straight into Hopkins's eyes "as though I understood every word." Hopkins opened by explaining that he came as the personal representative of the president; his mission "was not a diplomatic one" in the sense that he "did not propose any formal understanding of any kind or character." Rather, he was here to put across a message: "The President considered Hitler the enemy of mankind and . . . he therefore wished to aid the Soviet Union in its fight against Germany." FDR believed that "the most important thing to be done in the world today was to defeat Hitler and Hitlerism," and consequently the U.S. government was determined "to extend all possible aid to the Soviet Union at the earliest possible time."[45]

The mention of Hitler had a dramatic effect on Stalin. His body tensed; his hands clenched; his person "seemed to grow larger"; his voice slowed so as to convey to Hopkins "every syllable in its implication and direct meaning." Hitler had torn up his 1939 nonaggression pact with Russia and invaded his former ally "without a word to Stalin, not a hint." The master of the Gulag said he believed that the Nazis' international behavior failed to meet the "minimum moral standard between all nations" and consequently they were "an anti-social force in the modern world." Hopkins sensed that Stalin's "cold, implacable" anger at Hitler was "a personal hatred that I have seldom heard expressed by anyone in authority . . . I think that Joseph Stalin would have liked nothing better at that moment than to have had Hitler sitting where I sat. Germany would have needed a new chancellor." The two men sat in silence until Stalin had recovered his composure.[46]

Once these questions of morality were settled, Hopkins asked about Russia's material needs: "What would Russia require that the United States could deliver immediately and . . . what would be Russia's requirements on the basis of a long war?" Stalin provided his wish list: in the first category, anti-aircraft guns and ammunition, large machine guns, and one million or more rifles; in the second, high-octane aviation gasoline, aluminum for the construction of aircraft, and certain other items. "At this point in the conversation," Hopkins reported to Roosevelt later, "Mr. Stalin suddenly made the remark, 'Give us anti-aircraft guns and the aluminum and we can fight for three or four years.'" Sherwood records that Hopkins saw great significance in "the very nature of Stalin's requests, which proved that he was viewing the war on a long-term basis. A man who feared immediate defeat would not have put aluminum so high on the list of priorities."[47]

Of course, Stalin made these requests precisely to create this impression. Years later, his interpreter, Valentin Berezhkov, observed that Stalin "was unquestionably a great actor." Stalin needed allies who believed the Soviet cause was not hopeless. When Hopkins and later foreign visitors called on him, therefore, he created an atmosphere of confidence and authority:

The chimes of the Spasskaya Tower clock barely penetrated the office where silence always reigned. The boss was radiating benevolence as he unhurriedly conversed. Nothing dramatic seemed to be occurring outside the walls of that room, nothing seemed to worry him. And that was reassuring . . . What were [his visitors] to make of Stalin's calm demeanor and the assurances he gave to Hopkins that if the Americans supplied aluminum, the Soviet Union could go on fighting even for four more years? It was obvious that Stalin had a better understanding of the situation! . . . Stalin was bluffing; but fortunately he was able to bluff it out.[48]

Hopkins was pleased with his progress, but he was anxious to get Stalin alone; perhaps he felt that the presence of Steinhardt and Molotov was preventing a meeting of minds. He later told Davies, "I saw I couldn't get anywhere in a general meeting, so I suggested that I had some messages from the President to deliver to him personally." Stalin replied, "You are our guest; you have but to command," and promised to hold himself available every evening from six o'clock. It was also agreed that Hopkins would confer with Red Army representatives later that evening and Molotov the next day. With that, the meeting adjourned. Apart from his Hitler outbursts, Hopkins thought Stalin had been "a steady, gracious, schooled diplomat."[49]

Back at Spaso House, Hopkins invited American and British reporters into the drawing room for a chat over whiskey-and-sodas. His exhaustion was obvious. "He looked pale and tired," recalled an attendee, "with one thin leg dangling over the other as he slumped in his chair. He talked faintly, his voice dwindling away at times to an inaudible murmur." The reporters complained about their inability to find out what was happening inside the Soviet Union. "Harry," said one, "for God's sake be human. Tell us something." Hopkins was not in a position to give them inside information. But if his voice was hard to make out, his message was resoundingly clear. He revealed that on the president's behalf, he had told Stalin that "whoever was fighting Hitler was on the right side of this conflict and we intended to help them." Stalin had promised that "the Soviet people will play their role in crushing Hitler."[50]

The final appointment of the day was a meeting between Hopkins, McNarney, Yeaton, and General Nikolai Yakovlev of the Soviet Field Artillery. This was supposed to be the expert discussion at which the Americans could gather the data they needed to design their aid program; in fact, the greatest insight to emerge concerned the nature of the Soviet system. The unfortunate General Yakovlev was plainly terrified of saying the wrong thing and behaved like an unwilling witness under cross-examination. He was unable to enlighten his interlocutors on almost anything, including the organization and training of antiaircraft units, the USSR's monthly output of 37-millimeter guns, or the composition of a Soviet military delegation that was then in the United States. Quizzed on the speed of the latest Soviet fighter plane, he answered, "I am an artillery man." When the Americans enquired into the weight of the heaviest Soviet tank, he replied, "It is a good tank." Yakovlev could not think of any additional items the Red Army required. Asked whether the Soviets needed items such as tanks and antitank guns, which were not on Stalin's list of requirements, he replied that he was "not empowered to say." The hapless general made sure, however, to state that Russia needed aluminum.[51]

After that uninspiring conference, Hopkins made for his bed. His body desperately needed sleep, but the Luftwaffe had other ideas. For more than a week, the capital had endured nightly air raids. The authorities' response was comprehensive. Moscow, once a city with a raucous nightlife, was thrown into deepest darkness each evening. The blackout, reported McNarney, was "magnificent. No light of any kind can be seen. It is a crime to carry a lighted cigarette on the street." Hopkins ruminated that in Britain, an air warden who saw a light in a window tapped on the owners' door to remind them to pull their curtains more tightly; in Russia, he tapped on the owners' door to arrest them. "In Moscow," he remarked, "you take to an air-raid shelter when the enemy bombers come over—or else. And you stay there until the police tell you that you may come out." This was one of the many "differences between life in a democracy and under a dictatorship." Fire-watching, too, was organized differently. A British visitor to the capital noted that "fire-watching is highly efficient for the simple reason that if a building catches fire the man in charge is held responsible and he is shot."[52]

Shortly after midnight on July 30–31, the air raid warning sounded. McNarney later told his superiors that the antiaircraft fire created an "interesting and noisy display" lasting one and a half hours, ending with "a tremendous burst from all calibers." But McNarney's terse description hardly captured the ferocity, volume, or color of the famed Moscow barrage. In a determined effort to repel the attackers, especially in the first few weeks of air raids, the Soviets launched a remarkably concentrated barrage from concentric circles of guns ringing the city. Visitors watched in awe as antiaircraft shells exploded at every height and shrapnel clattered down onto roofs like hail.[53]

The most lyrical account came from the pioneering American photographer Margaret Bourke-White, who watched one of the early raids from the roof of Spaso House:

> I have seen bombings before in other cities, but I have never before seen the entire heavens filled with shooting stars, with hanging parachute flares, with dot-dashes of tracer-gun fire, with red, white and blue Roman candles, and streamers like the tails of red comets shooting out into space. Around the complete circumference of the horizon the beams of

searchlights swung restlessly, as though a horde of insects turned over on their backs were waving their luminous legs in the air. Once while we watched, these shafts of light came together in a knot and caught in their focus a plane which glowed like a silver moth against the sky. For minutes the knot of light kept the moth imprisoned as it dipped and turned, trying to escape, until suddenly it twisted violently and fell; we had seen our first German plane shot down . . .

I had not realized that there is so much music with an air raid. The most beautiful sound is the echo of the guns, which returns on a deeper note, like the bass of a Beethoven chord. The total effect is as though two types of music were being played together—formal chords with overtones of jazz thrown in. The peculiar whistle, which one soon learns to recognize, of bombs falling in the neighborhood is like a dash of Gershwin against a classic symphonic background.[54]

On the night described by Bourke-White, the windows of Spaso House were blown out by a thousand-pound bomb that landed fifty yards away, demolishing a theater. One week later, Hopkins watched the Moscow barrage from the same spot on the roof of the embassy. "The Germans took a hand in welcoming me to Moscow," he observed archly. At dawn he would have heard, like a communist call to prayer, the loudspeakers on Moscow's roofs announcing, "The enemy has been beaten back, comrades. Go home to your rest."[55]

IN WASHINGTON THE NEXT DAY, President Roosevelt met with the Soviet military delegation about which General Yakovlev had been so ill-informed. The White House press corps was struck by the novelty of seeing the visitors' visored caps, emblazoned with the Soviet hammer-and-sickle device, hanging outside the president's office. "We discussed prospects in Russia," FDR later told reporters. "The Russian Army appears to be putting up an awfully good fight." He claimed that the Soviets had the money to pay for their military purchases so he saw no prospect of Moscow receiving Lend-Lease assistance. In a radio address a few hours later, conservative Illinois congressman Stephen A. Day called on American Catholics to repudiate the president's policies and announced he would introduce a resolution to halt U.S. aid to Moscow. FDR's decision to send Harry Hopkins to Russia, he said, was unwarranted, illegal, and unconstitutional. "We all know that none of the four freedoms exist in the Soviet Union," concluded the congressman, "and can never exist there unless the blood-soaked dictatorship of Stalin be overthrown."[56]

On the same day, Muscovites awoke to front-page newspaper reports of the Stalin-Hopkins meeting and stories emphasizing Roosevelt's pledge of immediate assistance to the USSR. Hopkins lunched with Cripps at the British embassy, a magnificent villa on the river embankment opposite the Kremlin that had once been the residence of a wealthy sugar merchant. Hopkins told Cripps about his first meeting with Stalin and they strategized about the forthcoming summit off the coast of Newfoundland. Margaret Bourke-White photographed the two men lounging on a sofa with Cripps's large Airedale terrier, Joe, playing at their feet.[57]

At 3 p.m., Hopkins and Steinhardt called on Foreign Commissar Molotov at the Kremlin. The topic for discussion was the Far East, where Japan's recent advance into Indochina had led to American sanctions and stoked fears that she might strike at Soviet Siberia. (In fact, the Japanese push into Indochina indicated they had decided not to attack the USSR.) Molotov commented that notwithstanding the Soviet-Japanese neutrality pact, Tokyo's attitude seemed "uncertain" and Moscow was "watching the situation with the utmost care." He stated that the best way of preventing Japanese aggression would be for President Roosevelt to issue a "warning," which Hopkins interpreted as being "a statement that the U.S. would come to the assistance of the Soviet Union in the event of its being attacked by Japan." Knowing FDR's aversion to such a proposal, Hopkins sidestepped it with diplomatic finesse, commenting only that Washington was "disturbed at the encroachments which Japan was making in the Far East" and "would not look with any favor" on further threatening actions.[58]

When he got back to Spaso House, Hopkins found Bourke-White in the foyer, waiting nervously to hear whether the Kremlin would allow her to photograph his second meeting with Stalin, which was taking place that evening. "Let's forget about it and go shopping," he suggested. Accompanied by the ambassador and a posse of secret police, they mounted a frontal assault on Moscow's gift stores. (The security detail proved useful when the embassy car broke down and the party needed a lift.) Hopkins inspected carvings from the Urals and little green boxes made of malachite. For his daughter Diana, he purchased an embroidered Russian peasant girl's outfit, consisting of skirt, vest, and apron, and a small clay figurine of a woman in similar dress. Steinhardt bought Hopkins his own keepsake, a small silver teapot bearing an engraving of the Kremlin. Bourke-White noticed Hopkins's "great and intelligent interest in everything he saw," especially the Russians they encountered: the way he watched their faces, their expressions, their clothes. Back at the embassy, she learned that at Hopkins's request the Kremlin had granted permission for her to photograph the meeting that night. For the first time in his life, the *Vozhd* would pose for an American photographer.[59]

At 6:30 p.m., Hopkins returned to the Kremlin in his gray business suit for his second and final meeting with Joseph Stalin. This time the two men were alone, apart from a Russian interpreter.[60] Hopkins "had made up his mind . . . to get down to brass tacks." He told Stalin that "the President was anxious to have his appreciation and analysis of the war between Germany and Russia." The Soviet leader obliged with a long and extremely detailed review of the situation. Stalin compared the numbers, equipment, and tactics of the two sides, admitting that the Soviet forces had been taken by surprise but maintaining that their morale was "extremely high," because "they are fighting for their homes and in familiar territory." Germany, he observed, had found that "moving mechanized forces through Russia was very different from moving them over the boulevards of Belgium and France." When the Germans pierced the Soviet lines, the defenders did not surrender but counterattacked at another point. Soviet "insurgents" fought behind the German front line, attacking their airfields and lines of communication. Stalin repeatedly expressed "great confidence" that when winter came, the front line would not have reached Moscow, Kiev, or Leningrad— and at that point, the "tired" Germans would have to go on the defensive.[61]

When Stalin's lengthy account was complete, the practical Hopkins moved to the subject of Western aid. The U.S. and British governments "were willing to do everything that they possibly could during the succeeding weeks to send matériel to Russia," he said, but the long-term supply issues "could only be resolved if our Government had complete knowledge, not only of the military situation in Russia, but of [the] type, number and quality of their military weapons, as well as full knowledge of raw materials and factory capacity." Consequently, Hopkins proposed that a conference be "held between our three Governments, at which the relative strategic interests of each front, as well as the interests of our several countries, [could be] fully and jointly explored." Believing it would be "unwise to hold a conference while this battle was in the balance," Hopkins suggested that it should occur in Moscow after October 1. Stalin replied that he would welcome such a conference. Hopkins had not discussed this striking idea with FDR, and he was careful to tell Stalin that he was not authorized to propose it officially. Hopkins later commended it to Roosevelt on the basis of his experience with General Yakovlev: "There is literally no one in the whole Government who is willing to give any information other than Mr. Stalin himself. Therefore, it is essential that such a conference be held with Mr. Stalin personally."[62]

They also discussed the ports of entry through which American aid could get to the Soviet Union. All of them had their problems. Archangel was difficult due to its location, although Stalin said his icebreakers could keep it open all winter. Supplies would be shipped across the Pacific to Vladivostok in the Russian Far East, where they could join the Trans-Siberian Railway; the danger there was of Japanese interception. Some matériel would have to be transported around Africa and north via the Middle East and Central Asia, although Stalin worried about the quality of the roads and railways in Iran and the loading facilities on the Caspian Sea, and urged that the U.S. military speed up construction of wharf facilities in the Persian Gulf. For the moment, all three routes would be used.[63]

Hopkins took lengthy handwritten notes of everything that Stalin said. He noticed during their meetings that Stalin was wont to take a pad and pencil—probably one of the blue pencils he favored, with "Third Five-Year Plan" printed on the side—and doodle or make notes. Hopkins decided to follow suit. He found that in the periods when Stalin was talking to the interpreter in Russian he could catch up on his notes. The "interpreting business was not such a bad thing," he admitted to Davies later. "It had its advantages."[64] Later he worked up these notes into formal minutes for distribution to the president and the secretaries of state, war, and the navy. Toward the end of the second meeting, however, Stalin said he had a "personal message" for FDR. The message concerned U.S. entry into the war and was extremely sensitive. When Hopkins wrote up this part of the conversation, therefore, he made one copy, marked it "For the President only," and recommended that it not be sent to the State Department.[65]

Stalin began this final session by stating that "the world influence of the President and the Government of the United States was enormous," and that they could give "encouragement and moral strength" to "the vast numbers of oppressed people who hated Hitler" and "countless other millions in nations still unconquered." (Stalin was silent about the vast numbers of oppressed people who hated him.) The German army and people, he said, would be "demoralized by an announcement that the United States is going to join in the war against Hitler." Such an announcement was "the one thing that could defeat Hitler, and perhaps without ever firing a shot." He even requested Hopkins to "tell the President that he would welcome American troops on any part of the Russian front," under American command. Hopkins demurred, saying that "my mission related entirely to matters of supply and that the matter of our joining in the war would be decided largely by

Hitler himself." Even in the event of American participation, he doubted the U.S. government "would want an American army in Russia." Nevertheless, Hopkins promised to pass Stalin's blunt message to Roosevelt. In subsequent public comments, Hopkins made no mention of this final exchange; indeed, he claimed that "Stalin doesn't want our Army."[66]

Toward the end of the meeting, the two men were joined by Margaret Bourke-White. The intrepid American had been picked up at her hotel in a Soviet-built limousine and taken to the Kremlin, flanked by cars full of secret police. She was driven through the grounds past saluting soldiers and then rode in a red-carpeted elevator to the second floor of the old Senate building. Like Hopkins, she was "led along the longest, most branching, most winding hall it has ever been my experience to walk through." She noticed that the doors were numbered in descending order, and when her party got to No. 2, the soldiers held it open and took her inside. The room reminded Bourke-White of "the board room of a small Midwestern factory"; in fact, it was Joseph Stalin's waiting room. After chatting for a long time with the soldiers about Georgian beauties and horse riding in the Caucasus, she was finally summoned. She adjusted the red bow she had worn in her hair to catch Stalin's eye, and was ushered into Room No. 1.[67]

At first, Bourke-White was disorientated by the gap between her expectations of Stalin and the reality before her. Her eyes "instinctively went to the ceiling, for I remembered those giant statues I had seen"; only then did she look down and see Stalin "standing very stiff and straight in the center of the rug." He was significantly shorter than Hopkins, shorter even than Bourke-White. She thought he looked gray and fatigued and was astonished to see pockmarks on his cheeks: no such imperfections ever appeared in the portraits made by Soviet photographers. Nevertheless, his "rough pitted face was so strong that it looked as if it had been carved out of stone." Bourke-White crawled around on the floor with her cumbersome camera equipment trying to find an angle "to make that stone face look human." She conscripted the interpreter into holding her reflectors and flash bulbs. When she dropped a lens, it was Hopkins who reassured her, saying, "Take your time." Stalin chuckled at the sight of Bourke-White on her hands and knees, with her head under a camera cloth. But when the session ended, so did the smile, "as though a veil had been drawn over his features. Again he looked as if he had been turned into granite, and I went away thinking that this was the strongest, most determined face I had ever seen." Later that evening Bourke-White set up a makeshift laboratory in a servant's bathroom at Spaso House and spent all night developing the pictures that would shortly appear in newspapers around the world.[68]

Hopkins's conference with Stalin ended three hours after it began. It did not finish on Stalin's word; skillfully he allowed Hopkins to terminate the visit. The premier said good-bye once, with finality and warmth but without any theatrics. Hopkins recalled that he "shook hands from Stalin's office to the doors where my car was."[69]

The Soviet leader made a strong impression on Hopkins. The American was delighted by Stalin's confidence that Russia "would ultimately destroy Hitler as Russia had destroyed Napoleon." He wrote that Stalin "seems to have no doubts. He assures you that Russia will stand against the onslaughts of the German Army. He takes it for granted that you have no doubts, either." He told Cripps later he was "surprised and encouraged" by Stalin's account; he told the press that the meeting had added to his "confidence that Hitler will lose." Hopkins also liked Stalin's nondiplomatic manner: his "clear, concise, direct" questions; his "capacity for clear and simple statements." Like his office décor and his uniform, Stalin's manner was unadorned: "he never wastes a syllable." "He talked," Hopkins remarked, "as he knew his troops were shooting—straight and hard." In his article in the *American Magazine*, Hopkins explained that in Washington and London, "such missions as mine might be stretched out into what the State Department and Foreign Office call conversations. I had no conversations in Moscow—just six hours of conversation. After that there was no more to be said. It was all cleaned up at two sittings."[70]

Hopkins was also struck by Stalin's frankness and his "extraordinary grasp of detail." He told Cripps that Stalin gave him "every figure and statistic that he asked for," in most cases from memory. To Davies, Hopkins mused that the accuracy of Stalin's recall may be "due, in part, to the fact that every phase of the industrial Five Year Plan and war preparedness had been given Stalin's personal and direct attention over a long period." Stalin was, Hopkins thought, "right on the ball"; his "finger was on the throttle."[71]

The aura of command must have been seductive to someone accustomed to the easy informality of the Roosevelt and Churchill circles. On the rare occasions that an answer eluded the *Vozhd*, Hopkins recalled later, he merely "touched a button. Instantly, as if he'd been standing alertly at the door, a secretary appeared, stood at attention. Stalin repeated my question. The answer came like a shot. The secretary disappeared just like that."[72]

Stalin's openness with Hopkins was indeed something of a revelation. This was the first proper military briefing the Soviet leader had provided to a foreigner since Barbarossa began. It contained exactly the kind of intelligence that Roosevelt craved and that his Moscow embassy had been unable to provide. Ambassador Steinhardt admitted to the president that Stalin had discussed matters "with a frankness unparalleled in my knowledge in recent Soviet history." The interpreter Berezhkov concurred that Stalin was "very candid," even going so far as to admit mistakes, which was not his habit.[73] Yet just as Stalin's demeanor was contrived to inspire confidence, so were his statements. He played down Soviet air losses and casualties and played up Soviet morale. He predicted confidently that the German offensive would halt in front of Leningrad, Moscow, and Kiev by the start of October; in fact, it enveloped Kiev in September and threatened Leningrad and Moscow until early December.[74]

On the other hand, some gilding of the lily was to be expected. Like Churchill before him, Stalin had to walk a careful line in convincing an American envoy that his country's cause was serious enough to justify aid but not so dire that aid would be pointless.[75] Hopkins no doubt applied a discount factor to Moscow's confidence, just as he did to London's. In the main, Stalin's précis was accurate, as was his larger point: that Russia was determined to resist the German attack, irrespective of the cost.

Berezhkov records that Stalin had "high expectations" of the Hopkins visit, and based on the available fragments of evidence, they were met.[76] Averell Harriman, who came to know Stalin well, said the dictator had "great respect for Harry's courage." The idea of "this frail sick man" with a "great heart" taking such a dangerous trip made "a very deep impression on Stalin."[77] Berezhkov testified that Stalin had "a special regard for Hopkins" because "he was the first who came after this terrible blow we got from the Germans." Furthermore, Hopkins's predilection for straight talk and hard work endeared him to the Soviets. Stalin was widely quoted in Moscow as saying that Hopkins was "the only man he ever met who could work harder and longer than himself." Other officials were also impressed: in late 1941 foreign correspondent Quentin Reynolds, who by then had moved from London to Moscow, heard Molotov and a colleague "talk about Hopkins with awe. They'd never seen such a bundle of dynamite in Moscow as Harry."[78]

Hopkins does seem to have made a connection with Stalin. American diplomat Charles Bohlen heard Stalin say that Hopkins was the first American to whom he had spoken "*po dushe*," or from the soul. For the rest of the war, Harriman noted, Hopkins was the only foreigner apart from Roosevelt and Churchill to whom Stalin showed "any personal warmth," invariably crossing the room to greet him. As Bohlen cautioned, however, the personal feelings of Stalin and his comrades never affected "their single-minded pursuit of their objectives."[79]

Hopkins and Steinhardt dined that evening at Stalin's favorite Caucasian restaurant, eating "a vast quantity of Georgian food," including lamb, caviar, and vodka.[80] When the air raid siren sounded during dinner, the secret police bundled the Americans off to a special bomb shelter. Stalin had already apologized to Hopkins for not looking after him better during the previous raid; he was not going to make the same mistake two nights in a row. Ordinary Russians sheltered inside Metro stations, many of which were quite beautiful, with marble pillars and elaborate ceilings. Film director Sergei Eisenstein once declared that Moscow's "Metro is exactly what Metro-Goldwyn-Mayer would think an air raid shelter should look like." Hopkins and Steinhardt were taken somewhere even more cinematic: "the deepest shelter in Moscow," a tiled room located beneath the Metro that was usually reserved for top party officials. There were comfortable sofas, sleeping cots, and a great "spread" of provisions, including champagne, chocolate, cigarettes, and more caviar. Hopkins laughed when Steinhardt told him that no such shelter had ever been placed at his disposal.[81]

THE FOLLOWING DAY, Hopkins sent FDR his first cable from Moscow: "I have had two long and satisfactory talks with Stalin and will communicate personally to you the messages he is sending. I would like to tell you now, however, that I feel ever so confident about this front. The morale of the population is exceptionally good. There is unbounded determination to win."[82] The news of Hopkins's optimism soon raced around Washington.

The cable arrived on a busy day for the president. In a conference with reporters, he labeled the Soviet resistance "magnificent, and frankly, better than any military expert in Germany thought it would be." Asked by a reporter whether he was referring to the Führer, FDR replied to general laughter, "Now don't go and spoil it." He also met with another of his executive agents, Averell Harriman, briefly back home to report on his progress in London.[83]

Unusually for the genial Roosevelt, he also gave a stern forty-five-minute lecture to his cabinet that afternoon for failing to expedite aid to the USSR. Harold Ickes recalled gleefully that the president gave the departments of State and War "one of the most complete dressings down that I have witnessed. He said that these departments had been giving Russia a 'runaround.'" Inadequate progress had been made in filling the Soviets' requests for P-40 pursuit planes, bombers, antiaircraft guns, and other supplies, for which they were willing to pay. Morgenthau noted that FDR "directed most of his fire at Stimson, who looked thoroughly miserable. Never have I heard the President more emphatic and insistent." He said he was "sick and tired" of promises, and ordered, "Get the planes right off with a bang next week."

The beleaguered Stimson, caught between an impatient president and an army that was loath to split its armaments with both Britain and Russia, complained to his diary that FDR "was really in a hoity-toity humor and wouldn't listen to argument."[84]

Hopkins's cable arrived in Washington some hours after the cabinet meeting wrapped up, so it did not influence the president's comments directly.[85] However, Hopkins's meetings in the Kremlin weighed on the president's mind and sharpened his desire for action: Ickes got the impression in the Cabinet Room that Roosevelt was "particularly anxious" about Soviet aid because of Hopkins's mission.[86] The receipt of Hopkins's cable that evening would have confirmed FDR's thinking. The following day, Welles sent a formal note to Ambassador Oumansky confirming the administration's decision to "give all economic assistance practicable for the purpose of strengthening the Soviet Union in its struggle against armed aggression." That same day, FDR assigned a favored administrator, Hopkins protégé Wayne Coy, the task of expediting delivery of the aid, instructing him to "please, with my full authority, use a heavy hand—act as a burr under the saddle and get things moving!" The task was reminiscent of Averell Harriman's job in London. In case there was any doubt as to FDR's meaning, he closed his letter with "Step on it!"[87]

Hopkins spent his last day in Moscow reviewing the results of his mission with Stafford Cripps as well as officials at Spaso House. In his cable to FDR, he mentioned a "satisfactory" meeting with Laurence Steinhardt. In truth, he was deeply underwhelmed by the U.S. ambassador. From the moment he arrived at the airport, he had been trying to shake him so he could discuss events with other observers. Cripps "pumped it in to" Hopkins that the U.S. embassy was a defeatists' haunt, which was "bad for the atmosphere" in Moscow. "It seemed to me after my conference in Russia with Stalin," Hopkins wrote privately in October, "that the President should personally deal with Stalin. It was perfectly clear that Stalin had no confidence in our Ambassador or in any of our officials in Moscow. I gathered he would have felt the same way about the State Department if he had been asked."[88]

For his part, Steinhardt was spooked by Hopkins's visit and quickly fell into line behind Roosevelt's policy. On August 1, he sent a glowing review of the mission to Washington: "The reception accorded Harry Hopkins by the Soviet Government and the unusual attention which has been devoted to him by the Soviet press clearly indicate that extreme importance has been attached to his visit by this Government . . . I am certain that the visit has been extremely gratifying to the Soviet Government and that it will prove to have exercised a most beneficial effect upon Soviet-American relations . . . [and] greatly encouraged the Soviet war effort."[89] On the same day, he confided in Cripps that he now realized how bad his military attaché, Major Yeaton, was, and foreshadowed a change in attitude at the embassy. Both his instructions to his staff and his cables home became more positive about the Soviets' prospects of holding off the Nazis until the winter. A week later, Cripps saw Steinhardt at the Swedish legation and was delighted by his colleague's Damascene conversion. "I never heard anyone more anti-Axis and pro-Russian than the American Ambassador was," Cripps diarized. "A complete change has been wrought since Harry Hopkins was here and I think [Steinhardt] must have suspected that he might be in danger of being removed unless he changed his tune!"[90]

BOTH AMBASSADORS WERE AT THE AIRPORT at 2 p.m. on Friday, August 1, to see Hopkins off, only two days after he had arrived. No one presumed to check his papers; indeed, the whole time he was in the Soviet Union no official ever asked to see the handwritten visa that had caused so much fuss for Gil Winant and Ivan Maisky. On board the Soviet aircraft with Hopkins was General McNarney, who at Hopkins's request had remained by the telephone during the envoy's conferences and otherwise made his own inquiries into the state of Russia's defenses. However, Lieutenant Alison was not with them: he was remaining in Moscow to train Soviet pilots on the P-40, an assignment approved by Stalin himself. This time when the aircraft took off, there were no "salutes for distinguished visitors."

"Now that I was done," Hopkins noted wryly, "I don't think I'd have cared." In his luggage were ninety pages of meeting notes and plentiful quantities of vodka and caviar. Something had been left behind in the rush, however: the satchel of medications on which he relied for his daily sustenance.[91]

Hopkins's aircraft arrived at Archangel shortly before 7 p.m., and he was soon at the door of the houseboat that had served as the Catalina crew's billet, asking, "Are we ready to go?" Flight Lieutenant McKinley thought he looked "absolutely worn out," with "great blue circles under his eyes." He seemed to have lost additional weight while he was in Moscow. Anxious to get back to Britain in time to hitch a ride to the Churchill-Roosevelt meeting, Hopkins insisted on commencing departure procedures immediately despite reports of bad weather that made a landing at Scapa Flow seem improbable. He asked whether the flying boat had a first-aid kit he could use in lieu of his own medicines, but McKinley explained that it was only a primitive kit for use on cuts and wounds and would hardly be of assistance to the sickly Hopkins. "If I have your assurances you'll get me there," replied the American, "that will help me more than anything else." At 10:15 p.m. the PBY was back in the air carrying Hopkins, McNarney, and another valuable cargo, a large quantity of platinum, which was used in the manufacture of aircraft and munitions. Whitehall had compared Bill Donovan to platinum; now Hopkins was bringing the real thing back to Britain with him.[92]

The flight from Archangel to Scapa followed the same perilous route as the outward journey and was even less pleasant. The flying boat took off in a gathering storm and flew up the White Sea in quickly deteriorating conditions. Driving into a nasty headwind, she bucked and slid violently for hours on end. Again, McKinley kept her low, generally two or three hundred feet above the ocean's surface. Off the Murmansk coast, she was fired on by an unidentified destroyer that did not stop throwing up flak even when McKinley flashed the Soviet recognition signal. Shrapnel hit the mainplane but caused little damage, and the flying boat dived to sea level to evade the attack. Meanwhile, its most important passenger leapt to the gun in the waist blister, crying, "If they fire at us, I'll fire back!"

Once the PBY had passed out of range of the destroyer's guns, however, Hopkins grew drowsy and slept for seven hours straight. "It was now very evident," McKinley noted later in his report, "that he was critically ill and only fit to lie down and take what rest was possible." Throughout the flight, he never complained or intruded on the crew's flight duties. "Don't waste food on me," he said when they offered him a meal. "You need it to get me to Scapa Flow." As McKinley had been unable to raise any new flight rations at Archangel, and the food was even less appetizing than on the outbound journey, this was no great sacrifice.[93]

After nearly twenty-four hours in the air, McKinley put the PBY down on the rough and turbulent waters of Scapa Flow. The weather was cold and wet and a thick fog lay over the archipelago, nearly hiding the Home Fleet from view. Little boats buzzed about and barrage balloons hung in the sky. A naval launch approached in order to pick up Hopkins and take him to the nearby HMS *King George V*, but the choppy seas prevented it from maneuvering in close enough. Hopkins suggested that if he could not be transferred by small boat, they rig up a line between the flying boat and the battleship and haul him across in a breeches buoy. "You'll be in the water more than you're in the air," said McKinley. "I don't care where I am, so long as I get on that god-damned vessel," was Hopkins's retort.

In the end, though, he decided to jump for it. The first attempt nearly resulted in disaster, when he began to leap just as the flying boat and the launch moved apart in the heavy swell. Luckily a quick-thinking crew member grabbed him around the waist and pulled him back into the body of the PBY. For the second time that year, the Royal Navy had saved Harry Hopkins from a dunking at Scapa Flow. Undeterred, he climbed on top of the hull, and when the distance closed to ten feet, he jumped. "He was taken in the arms of a couple of able seamen who stopped him crunching into the deck," recalled McKinley, "but he very nearly measured his length on the deck of the thing." He was followed soon after by his luggage, containing his precious handwritten notes from the Kremlin, which was hurled without ceremony across the open water. A few minutes later the crew of the Catalina saw Hopkins wave from the top of the gangway of the *King George V* and then disappear. "There's only one man in the world like that," thought McKinley. "There he goes."[94]

THE *KING GEORGE V* was the flagship of Admiral John Tovey, commander in chief of the Home Fleet and the man who had led the hunt for the *Bismarck*. After Hopkins had enjoyed a lively dinner with a party including Gil Winant, who had come up from London, Tovey took his guest in hand and ordered him to bed. By some reports, Hopkins looked so unwell that there were fears for his life. He did not wake up until late the following afternoon, and then spent another night at Scapa under the care of naval doctors, gradually regaining his strength.[95]

At midday on Monday, August 4, the prime minister's party arrived aboard a pair of destroyers steaming in line. It included the chief of the Imperial General Staff, General Sir John Dill; the first sea lord, Admiral Sir Dudley Pound; Air Vice Marshal Wilfred Freeman; Sir Alec Cadogan representing the Foreign Office; and "the Prof," Lord Cherwell. Churchill's mood was buoyant; he was, observed a witness, "like a boy who's been let out of school suddenly." He came onto the quarterdeck of the *Prince of Wales*, the *King George V*'s sister ship, which had also been involved in the *Bismarck* chase and was to carry him and his entourage to the Atlantic Conference. There he found Hopkins, who had already transferred aboard. The American was standing beneath a gun turret, looking pale and fragile, his loose overcoat blowing about his thin body and Churchill's homburg on his head. "Ah, my dear friend, how are you?" asked the PM, shaking hands with Hopkins. "And how did you find Stalin?" "I must tell you all about it," replied Hopkins wearily as they went below with their arms linked.[96]

Shortly after the *Prince of Wales* put to sea, Churchill signaled Roosevelt as follows:

Harry returned dead beat from Russia, but is lively again now. We shall get him in fine trim on the voyage. We are just off. It is 27 years ago today that Huns began their last war. We must make good job of it this time. Twice ought to be enough. Look forward so much to our meeting.[97]

The voyage across the Atlantic from Scapa Flow to Placentia Bay took nearly five days. Initially, the darkened *Prince of Wales* was flanked by destroyers, but they could not keep up with the battleship in the heavy seas, and on the first night the prime minister's ship lost her escort. She was naked until she was joined on Wednesday by Canadian warships that had steamed from Icelandic waters. The *Prince of Wales* had protection from another source, however: the British codebreakers at Bletchley Park, whose skill at decrypting German naval signals helped her to avoid lurking U-boat wolf packs.

The storm had other implications for the passengers. The 35,000-ton ship pitched and rolled; she vibrated at the behest of her turbines; terrific bangs and other mysterious sounds were heard. Huge seas broke over her bows and forecastle, leaving the decks awash. A reporter accompanying Churchill compared the vessel's "monstrous plunges" to a "vast steel-works . . . flying unsteadily through the air." The ship's company was accustomed to all this, but their guests were not. "Most of us were not feeling too happy," recalled one of Churchill's assistants.[98]

Apart from seasickness, which soon improved along with the weather, the prime minister's party was in good spirits. Churchill excitedly planned the details of his meeting with Roosevelt, including the turtle soup and grouse he intended to serve the president. "You'd have thought Winston was being carried up into the heavens to meet God!" Hopkins told friends later. The warrant officers' mess was commandeered for use as Churchill's private sitting and dining room; the rest of the delegation were installed as temporary members of the officers' wardroom, a clubby room that spanned the whole width of the quarterdeck. At teatime, Churchill would join his military chiefs in the wardroom, leaving them to work at the dining table while he and Hopkins settled into comfortable chairs to listen to the wireless. "I think this must be the first Chiefs of Staff meeting held to the accompaniment of Bruce Belfrage's dulcet tones," diarized a military man, referring to a famous BBC broadcaster. When the weather allowed, "the Prof" strolled the deck in his yachting cap, taking the air. Churchill alternated between working on his dispatch boxes and relaxing with a nautically themed novel or a game of backgammon with Hopkins.[99]

Dinner was served by Royal Marines in white mess jackets. Hopkins's caviar from Moscow was a special treat. Each night after dinner, films were presented in the wardroom. On one night it was *Pimpernel Smith*, starring Leslie Howard as a modern Scarlet Pimpernel figure in Nazi Germany; on another, *High Sierra*, starring Humphrey Bogart; on yet another, it was a sentimental New York comedy, *The Devil and Miss Jones*. Churchill enjoyed them all. One of his favorites, *Lady Hamilton*, a love story set during the Napoleonic Wars and starring Vivien Leigh and Laurence Olivier, was also shown. The dénouement of the film was Admiral Nelson's death at the Battle of Trafalgar. The prime minister had seen *Lady Hamilton* many times before but was utterly absorbed by it all over again. When the dying Nelson was told that the battle had been won, an observer noted that Churchill "took a handkerchief from his pocket and wiped his eyes without shame." At the film's conclusion he stood up and addressed the ship's officers, who were seated during the shows in their dining chairs, or "sixpennies," as they were christened. "I thought this would be of particular interest to you, many of whom have recently been under the fire of the enemy's guns on an occasion of equal historical importance. Good night."[100]

The most memorable film night, though, was on Tuesday. Churchill came into the wardroom, bowed to the assembled officers, and sat down in an armchair that had been placed at the front. The room went dark. But instead of a Hollywood film, there appeared on the screen a shot of a large transport aircraft landing at a foreign airfield, met by a delegation of officials. When the plane's hatch opened, who should step out but Harry

Hopkins. "Oh, there you are, Harry!" shouted a surprised and delighted prime minister, clapping his hands. "Bravo! Bravo!" Hopkins had brought a short film back with him from Moscow showing glimpses of his mission, including his arrival, pictures of him entering and exiting various buildings, and stray shots of the Russian capital. It made a contrast to the other film shown that evening, *Comrade X*, a Clark Gable comedy also set in Moscow. *Comrade X* was pulled from British cinemas because of its unflattering portrayal of Stalin's regime, but alliance sensitivities could not prevent its screening on the high seas.[101]

The night ended on a high. The *Prince of Wales* lacked a skilled projectionist, so when the reels were changed, the projector whirred, images from the film reappeared on the screen in reverse or upside down, and the lights went up. At this point, Churchill called for gramophone music and joined in the singing in his navy blue Royal Yacht Squadron uniform. He knew every verse of Noël Coward's "Mad Dogs and Englishmen" and was almost word-perfect on "Franklin D. Roosevelt Jones." A participant recalled that at the end of the night, "Mr. Churchill, smoking a cigar of a size recognised by the gunnery officer as 'a fifteen-incher,' bowed gracefully and retired on a tidal wave of benevolence."[102]

As Churchill predicted, Hopkins rallied on the voyage to Newfoundland. He spent much of each day in his sea cabin on the bridge of the *Prince of Wales*, to which he moved after finding the engine vibration too great in the grander quarters he had initially been assigned. The sea cabin was a lovely berth with a fine view. Here Hopkins could sleep in until midday and take a nap after lunch. Sometimes he took a walk on the quarterdeck; one morning he was interrupted by Churchill clad only in a nightshirt and carrying a cigar. He was assigned a personal steward and a secretary, a corporal in the RAF whom Hopkins called his "aviator." Like everyone else on board, Corporal Green thought Hopkins a "grand fellow." He was "very amiable" but "very tired," and "chatters like a monkey, only slower."[103]

Green helped Hopkins to get off various pieces of correspondence to friends in England, as well as a charming letter to his daughter Diana:

I presume by this time you are as brown as a berry, and that is as it should be when one is 8 years old . . . I have been far away, to what is said to be one of the coldest countries in the world, Russia. Strange to say I found little boys and girls swimming in the White Sea.

In another far-off country I have been to there is war, and bombs and guns going off in the night. Some day that will all be over and Mr. Hitler will be defeated. Then I shall bring you to England, and we will roam over the green hills and eat in what you will think to be very queer little restaurants. The strange part of it is, little English boys and girls think that our houses and hotels and beaches are just as queer.

I shall see you very soon now, and want you to know that I love you very much.[104]

It was in his sea cabin, too, that Hopkins worked on his most important task: converting his meeting notes from Moscow into a report for the president. Green diarized that he had "been doing work of highest importance and secrecy for Harry Hopkins," "heaps of reports" containing "much 'gen'" about Uncle Joe and his effort." Hopkins's ambition was to relate "Stalin's own words" to FDR. He had left Stalin, he recalled later, "packed with facts and figures as cold, as informative, as colorless, as mathematical as the reports I once made as head of the WPA and as barren of romance as the reports that went across my desk as Secretary of Commerce. Facts were what the President asked for." Facts were what Hopkins intended to give him.[105]

The facts he included in his reports to Churchill and Roosevelt gave him confidence that the Soviets' resistance would continue at least until the winter, during which they could resupply their armies and reorganize their defenses. Hopkins felt that the Red Army had been "very much underrated," in part because the "the Soviets 'high-hatted' military attachés" in Moscow. In the long term, all-out aid to Russia was, he believed, a wager worth making. As Averell Harriman recalled later, nothing was lost in supporting Russia and much could be gained. "In any event," Harriman noted, "there was no alternative."[106]

What was the basis for Hopkins's confidence about Russia's chances? He had not visited the front in person, nor was he able to verify Stalin's claims by reference to other sources—a point he admitted in his report to the president. Rather, he was impressed by Stalin's assurance, the nature of his requests, and his determination to fight. In this context, Stalin's palpable anger at Hitler's treachery must have helped convince Hopkins that the Soviet leader was not open to another deal with the Nazis. "I hope never to be hated as Stalin hates Hitler," he concluded.[107]

Hopkins had not gone to Moscow with an open mind anyway. He was predisposed to support aid to Russia. When he was asked once how he had come to his view based on only a few meetings, he reportedly replied that he reached his conclusion in the same way Supreme Court justice Oliver Wendell Holmes reached his verdicts: "I had a hunch where I wanted to come out and then looked around to find some reasons to justify the hunch."[108]

Back in London and Washington, word was already getting around that the mission had been a success. On August 3, Winant passed Hopkins's account to several "rather jubilant" colleagues at the U.S. embassy, and the following day Sumner Welles told the journalist Raymond Clapper that "Harry Hopkins is most enthusiastic about Russian chances now." By August 8, the Anglophile New York banker Thomas Lamont was hearing from contacts in London that Stalin had been "very calm" and had spoken "of the struggle in terms of 'next year,' which is all to the good."[109]

ON THE MORNING OF SATURDAY, AUGUST 9, the *Prince of Wales* passed through the entrance of Placentia Bay, in the southeastern corner of Newfoundland. Harry Hopkins was on the bridge in his bathrobe, peering into a thick mist. He had slept badly the night before, worrying that his Moscow notes were incomplete. "I had the Russian story for the president," he recalled later, and he wanted to get the story straight. Suddenly, "wraithlike in the fog," the crew spotted the outlines of American destroyers. Patrol planes buzzed overhead. Slowly the morning sun burned off the mist, and then, "as if revealed by the lifting of many filmy curtains," Hopkins saw the heavy cruiser USS *Augusta*, flagship of the U.S. Atlantic Fleet. He dashed back to his cabin, dressed and threw his possessions into his bag, presented his steward with the overcoat he had purchased in England as a tip, and returned to the bridge. Training his binoculars on the deck of the *Augusta*, lying at anchor a few hundred yards off, he saw the person of Franklin Delano Roosevelt.[110]

The president had devised and employed an elaborate ruse in order to get to Newfoundland in conditions of complete secrecy. The previous weekend he had boarded his yacht USS *Potomac* at New London, Connecticut, for what was billed as a ten-day "vacation cruise" off the New England coast. On Monday, the presidential yacht made harbor at Nonquitt, Massachusetts, so that Roosevelt could take a group of exiled Norwegian royals fishing, in plain view of hundreds of people. That evening, thousands of vacationers watched as the *Potomac* sailed down the Cape Cod Canal, with the presidential flag flying and a small party in civilian clothes sitting on the afterdeck, while the Secret Service and Massachusetts state troopers guarded her from the shore. Over the next week, naval dispatches claimed that the president was "enjoying the sea air from the fantail" of the *Potomac*. "All members of the party are showing effects of sunning," reported the U.S. Navy, and "responding to the New England air after the Washington summer." There was "no definite schedule" and "weather and angling prospects would determine each day's movements." In fact, this was all a cover story. On Monday, Roosevelt had transferred to USS *Augusta* for passage to Placentia Bay, accompanied by USS *Tuscaloosa* and five destroyers. FDR was delighted that he had duped everyone, including the Secret Service and the White House press corps. "Even at my ripe old age," he exulted to his cousin Daisy Suckley in a letter from the *Augusta*, "I feel a thrill in making a get-away—especially from the American press."[111]

Roosevelt's flotilla, reinforced by additional vessels, arrived at its destination early on Thursday, August 7. Formed by long peninsulas to the east and west and surrounded by low, forested hills, Placentia Bay struck the visitors as "very bleak and beautiful." Soon the bay was full of American warships, and aircraft patrolled the skies above it. The waters were especially crowded off Argentia on the eastern shore, where the Americans were building a naval base pursuant to the Destroyers-Bases Deal. As he cruised up and down the shore, FDR was well pleased with the fruit of that particular vine.[112]

The president was accompanied by his chief military advisers, General George Marshall, Admiral Harold "Betty" Stark, and Major General "Hap" Arnold, as well as the commander in chief of the Atlantic Fleet, Admiral Ernest J. King. To keep the conference intimate, however, FDR had left Secretaries Stimson, Knox, and Hull at home. Two of his sons, Ensign Franklin D. Roosevelt Jr. and Captain Elliott Roosevelt, were ordered in from their posts, presented with aiguillettes (or as FDR dubbed them, "the gold spinach"), and detailed to serve as presidential aides. Fala, Roosevelt's Scottish terrier, was also on board. On Friday afternoon, Sumner Welles, whom Roosevelt wanted to speak for the State Department, arrived by flying boat. With him on the PBY was another of FDR's envoys, Averell Harriman.[113]

By his own admission, Harriman had invited himself along. When he called at the White House in early August, he was horrified to discover that Roosevelt had no intention of including him in the American delegation. Even when Harriman protested that Churchill wanted him to be present, FDR told him, implausibly, that there were no free berths on the *Augusta*. Finally, under pressure, the president admitted that Welles would be flying up from Boston and agreed that Harriman could hitch a ride with him. Once again, Averell's brass neck was on prominent display.[114]

The first passenger from the *Prince of Wales* to come aboard the *Augusta* was Harry Hopkins, and his first words to the president were, "The Russians are confident." Shortly after eleven o'clock, Winston Churchill stepped onto the U.S. flagship's gleaming top deck and stood at attention as a Marine band played "God Save the King." Then he walked over to Franklin Roosevelt, who stood supported by his son Elliott, executed a little salute, which was duly returned by the president, and handed him a letter from King

George VI by way of a credential. Soon the formalities gave way to hand-shakes and smiles; the American lit a cigarette and the Englishman produced a cigar.[115]

Finally, after so much anticipation and so many delays, the two men had met for the first time as heads of government. This was, in a sense, the consummation of a long-distance relationship that had been sustained not only by their correspondence but through the labors of Roosevelt's special envoys, three of whom—Welles, Harriman and, most importantly, Hopkins—were present at the climax.

FOR THE NEXT THREE DAYS, the leaders and their delegations deliberated on the progress of the war in Europe. Churchill need not have fussed as much as he did about the impression he would make. Roosevelt liked him, finding him "a tremendously vital person," and in a letter to his cousin compared him to "an English Mayor LaGuardia! Don't say I said so!" (He was also "amazed" at the quantity of alcohol he consumed.) The president did less talking than was his custom, satisfied by Churchill's willingness to defer to his seniority. The two settled quickly into an easy, joking relationship. Hopkins wrote to Pamela Churchill that FDR was "ever so much impressed with your great father-in-law"; Harriman reported that the prime minister had been "in his best form" and Roosevelt was "much intrigued." It was due to Hopkins's work, Pamela ruminated later, that when these two strangers came together "they were able to meet as old friends."[116]

Nor was Hopkins's contribution to Anglo-American comity limited to the leaders. At his suggestion, Roosevelt sent a cardboard carton of treats, including fruit, cheese, and cigarettes, to every man in the ship's company of the *Prince of Wales*. Inside each of the fifteen hundred boxes was a card reading, "The President of the United States sends his compliments and best wishes."[117]

Hopkins's most substantive job at Argentia was to communicate his Moscow findings. Harriman recalled later that his friend's conviction that

Russia would hold out and not make a new peace with Germany "pervaded" the Atlantic Conference. Franklin Roosevelt Jr.'s recollections of a briefing that Hopkins gave his father on board the *Augusta* help to explain why this was so. "Harry had a very clear mind," he said later, "a very excellent simple way of expressing himself so he didn't leave any questions or any doubts. If there were any my father would ask him a question. Harry would answer very explicitly . . . He had a marvellous way of sort of setting forth his conclusions, his thinking . . . Harry had this marvellous ability to grow into any new situation and really step up to totally understand, totally dominate the details of any new problem." Apparently the president, always eager for insights into the personalities of other leaders, was pleased to hear that Stalin had some sense of humor.[118]

The power of Hopkins's testimony was supplemented by the imperatives of realpolitik, in any case. Demands from the Kremlin for a second front, which were impossible to meet, made an ambitious supply program even more of a necessity.[119] In a joint message to Stalin, therefore, that was explicitly a response to the Hopkins report, Roosevelt and Churchill formally proposed the idea of a supply conference in Moscow in order that "all of us may be in a position to arrive at speedy decisions as to the apportionment of our joint resources." The Soviet Union was, in Churchill's phrase, "a welcome guest at [a] hungry table." Lord Beaverbrook, who winged his way to Newfoundland at the last minute, was selected to represent the British point of view at the conference. FDR wanted Hopkins to head up the American delegation, but in light of his physical condition Hopkins recommended Harriman instead.[120]

Churchill had hoped that the president would use the meeting at sea to announce a dramatic escalation of U.S. involvement in the war. But FDR remained as cautious as ever, determined to retain his flexibility and avoid any charges of making undertakings without congressional approval. According to the prime minister's account to the war cabinet, Roosevelt said he would "wage war, but not declare it." He would "become more and more provocative" and "look for an 'incident' which would justify him in opening hostilities." The need for such caution was demonstrated during the conference by the shocking announcement that an extension of the Selective Training and Service Act had passed the House of Representatives by the dangerously narrow margin of a single vote.

The act that Roosevelt had signed into law in September 1940 had limited inductees' term of service to one year. By the spring of 1941, military chiefs were anxious about the impending loss of hundreds of thousands of trained personnel and their replacement by raw recruits. FDR asked Congress for an eighteen-month extension, stating that the "danger today" was "infinitely greater" than it had been a year before and the army must not be permitted "to melt away." General Marshall testified that to allow the draftees to go home in the fall would be "perilous to the national safety" and amount to the "disintegration of the Army." But many congressmen saw draft-term extension as a breach of contract between the government and the draftees (or worried that voters would see it as such). Isolationists perceived another conspiracy to involve the United States in a foreign war, and the president's decision to aid Stalin's government had increased their pique. "Good God!" exclaimed Senator Hiram Johnson. "Did we ever sink so low before as to choose one cutthroat out of two?"

The extension passed the Senate easily, but it only just squeaked through the House by 203 votes to 202; even then, it might have failed had Speaker Sam Rayburn not ignored wavering congressmen and gaveled the measure through. The closeness of the vote had, Hopkins noted, a "decidedly chilling effect" on the delegations at Argentia, especially the British. It was a sobering rejoinder to those who demanded that Roosevelt be speedier and less mindful of his opponents. At the very moment that he and Churchill were planning a new world order over which they hoped to preside, Congress had nearly denuded the United States of its defenses. No wonder, as Sherwood observed pungently, the news "dropped like enemy bombs on the decks of the *Augusta* and the *Prince of Wales*."[121]

———

There were several consolation prizes for the British. The political and military chiefs of the two countries got to know each other. While FDR balked at Churchill's idea of joint Anglo-American-Dutch warnings to forestall further Japanese expansion to the south, fearing they might precipitate a crisis, he promised to deliver a tough message to Ambassador Nomura when he got back to Washington. (As it was, the Japanese were much disturbed by the conference. One Japanese staff officer commented that it was tantamount to America's declaration of war.) Regarding the other important theater, the president confirmed that the U.S. Navy would soon escort combined convoys in the western Atlantic, as far as Iceland.[122] Most important of all, however, was the release of the Atlantic Charter.

The Atlantic Charter took the form of a "Joint Declaration by the President and the Prime Minister" setting out "certain common principles . . . on which they base their hopes for a better future for the world." Those eight principles were: the renunciation of aggrandizement by the United States and Britain; opposition to territorial changes in the absence of popular consent; support for democratic self-government, including for those peoples who had been forcibly deprived of it; access to trade and raw materials on equal terms (but "with due respect" for "existing obligations," a sop to the system of preferential trading arrangements within the British Empire); international economic collaboration; a postwar peace "after the final destruction of the Nazi tyranny," and guarantees that "all the men in all the lands may live out their lives in freedom from fear and want"; freedom of the seas; and, finally, the disarmament of nations, pending the establishment of "a wider and permanent system of general security." The charter was not a treaty or formal diplomatic instrument; indeed, some officials present thought it "not much more than a publicity hand-out." But if its immediate influence was limited, its broader effect was, as Sherwood writes, "cosmic and historic."[123] The dangerous ideas it contained would later excite oppressed peoples, inform the world's thinking on the United Nations organization, and even raise uncomfortable questions for Churchill's beloved empire.

These disturbances were mainly in the future, however. For the moment, all was serenity, especially at the divine service that took place on the quarterdeck of HMS *Prince of Wales* on Sunday, August 10, under the big guns. It was "a really lovely morning," noted one of the British participants, with "a soft breeze, the sun behind thin clouds, a beautiful shimmering grey look on the waters, and the green rocky hills all round." The president, wearing a blue double-breasted suit, and the uniformed chiefs of the U.S. fighting services came on board the British battleship, which was camouflaged and battle-damaged in contrast to the peacetime paint and immaculate trim of the American ships. A Royal Marine band played "The Star-Spangled Banner" and a guard of honor presented arms, and the Americans were greeted by the prime minister in his Royal Yacht Squadron outfit. Then Roosevelt slowly walked the length of the deck, bareheaded and erect, supporting himself on a stick and his son Elliott's arm. It took him a long time to cover the distance, and the immense effort it required was visible on his features. The word went around the ship that this was the longest walk he had attempted since his paralysis. He lowered himself into a chair under the after turret, next to the prime minister. Behind them were their advisers, including three of FDR's envoys: Hopkins, Harriman, and Welles. On either side and amidships stood mixed ranks of British and American sailors. A finer setting for what seemed to Churchill aide John Martin "a sort of marriage service between the two navies" was unimaginable.[124]

Churchill had decreed that the service should be "fully choral and fully photographic." He was not particularly churchy himself, but someone, probably Hopkins, had advised him that Roosevelt loved his hymns. Churchill's selections, "O God, Our Help in Ages Past," "Onward, Christian Soldiers," and "Eternal Father, Strong to Save," all touched on the themes of solidarity and succor. Churchill vetted the prayers in advance, having an assistant read them aloud while he dried after his bath. Two chaplains, one American and one British, offered prayers to the president and the king. The Lesson, which was read by the skipper of the *Prince of Wales*, Captain John Leach, was from the first chapter of Joshua: "There shall not any man be able to stand before thee all the days of thy life; as I was with Moses, so I will be with thee; I will not fail thee, nor forsake thee. Be strong and of good courage." Two American flying boats flew over the ship and dipped their wings in salute. "My God, this is history!" whispered one attendee. Roosevelt later told the press he was "deeply moved" by the service, during which witnesses noted that Churchill's "handkerchief stole from its pocket."[125]

Later, the prime minister asked a shipmate if he did not think the ceremony had been "a wonderful and moving sight." Then he answered his own question: "The same language, the same hymns and, more or less, the same ideals ... I have an idea that something really big may be happening—something really big.'" Although he was not generally religious, he told Harriman he felt "a divine power was bringing the two nations together."[126]

When the service ended, a number of sailors, and presently officers, approached the great men and asked to take their picture. As one onlooker said, this was a scene that a "press photographer would dream of after a good dose of hashish." Both leaders were pleased to oblige, and sat chatting to each other and smoking for half an hour while sailors crawled up to within a yard of them and let off their portable cameras. As FDR described to his cousin, "We were all photographed—front, sides and rear!" Caught on film in the background was Harry Hopkins showing his new gray homburg to Averell Harriman. Eventually the press caught on to the story of the hat's provenance, and newspaper leader writers back home had some fun with it. "Whence Came Yon Hat?" asked the *Christian Science Monitor*. For the *Chicago Daily Tribune*, this was a "Tale of Two Hats." The *Philadelphia Inquirer* identified a "'New Deal' in Hats." But the *New York Herald Tribune* made the most of it: "Churchill Lend-Leases Hat to Hopkins."[127]

That same afternoon, the prime minister donned his rompers for a brief excursion to shore, accompanied by Harriman and members of his official family. The coast was rugged and empty. "We went about like the first discoverers," recalled John Martin, "with not a soul to meet, the PM collecting a fistful of flowers." Churchill was "like a schoolboy," noted Alec Cadogan, delighting in "rolling boulders down a cliff." Much to his companions' horror, he slid over the edge himself, but no bones were broken. The party sat for an hour in a shingly little cove, Churchill musing to Harriman about "how delightful life must be at Newfoundland," before deciding that "it would be a superb existence for others than himself." A sudden drenching rainstorm hastened their return to the warships.[128]

The Atlantic Conference was the high point of Sumner Welles's professional life. It was he, not Secretary of State Cordell Hull, who sat at the president's side as he conferred with Churchill about the shape of the postwar order. Welles drafted part of the Atlantic Charter, and he and Alec Cadogan negotiated other matters on behalf of their respective masters. The acerbic Cadogan, no fan of Welles the previous year, was warming to him now. "He improves on acquaintance," Cadogan diarized, although "it is a pity that he swallowed a ramrod in his youth. But I suppose that can happen in any family with sporting tastes."[129]

As the conference wound down, Harry Hopkins sent a series of delightful notes from his sea cabin on the *Augusta* to his friends on the *Prince of Wales*, along with small gifts of oranges, lemons, candies, canned ham, and other rare foodstuffs. To Churchill, he warned, "These are really for your wife, so don't use all these on the ship's mess." To the first sea lord, Sir Dudley Pound, "This is a token payment to the Commander of the British Navy for such a smooth and delightful voyage home." To Sir John Dill, "These are not quite as good as tanks, but some of them are almost as hard to get. The tanks, I trust, will follow." To the nonsmoking, teetotaling, vegetarian Lord Cherwell, he said, "My dear Prof: These tokens cannot be put on charge. I have omitted the ham so that you may ever regret being a vegetarian." He asked Alec Cadogan to pass one of the lemons he enclosed to Anthony Eden, "along with what is left of the Far Eastern problem."[130]

He also sent over a parcel of food for delivery to Pamela Churchill in London, writing playfully in the accompanying note, "Averell tells me that I am to send these to Baby Winston, but to hell with that, I am sending these to you. I didn't see nearly enough of you over there, so why don't you get yourself made ambassadoress to the United States? You can give one of these to Kathleen if she is behaving herself." Averell was left to play the straight man in his own letter to Pamela and Kathleen: "Harry has sent quantities of food to everybody. I was going to send oranges to Baby Winston but he has stripped the ship so my package could only be a token of affection."[131]

There was great activity during the afternoon of Tuesday, August 12, as departure preparations were made. Visitors were piped over the side for the last time and boats were hoisted on board; hatches were battened down and skylights closed. Launches moved constantly between ships; secretaries ran up and down gangways. On board the *Augusta* a charming little ceremony took place. At Chequers the previous month, Hopkins had found some illuminated reproductions of the verse from Longfellow's "The Building of the Ship," which Roosevelt had sent to Churchill care of Wendell Willkie. Now these were produced, and two dozen copies were signed by the president and the prime minister.[132] Roosevelt was attended by three envoys at the Argentia conference, but a fourth was present in spirit at its close.

The *Prince of Wales* departed Placentia Bay shortly afterward, passing through lines of gray ships lined with American sailors. The prime minister watched from its quarterdeck in his siren suit, chewing on a cigar, while flying boats overhead dipped in salute and U.S. Marine bands played a jaunty "Anchors Aweigh." She was escorted as far as Iceland by American destroyers including USS *Mayrant*, whose executive officer was Ensign Franklin D. Roosevelt Jr., and made it to Scapa Flow without incident. Churchill's special train, still waiting at Thurso, took him home to London with fighter planes providing an aerial escort. When he stepped out at King's Cross Station, one of his party diarized that there was a "stampede down the platform, with the Press photographers easy winners. The heads of Cabinet Ministers could be seen popping up and through the forest of cameras and flashlights, and some kind of formal greeting was attempted without much success." Gil Winant, who, unlike Averell Harriman, had not maneuvered his way to Argentia, was also at the station but could not get through the crowd. Fortunately, Clementine Churchill, wearing a purple suit and gray furs, pointed him out to her husband. "Puffing his big cigar like a destroyer under forced draft," recorded the correspondent from the *Washington Post*, Churchill "elbowed through to greet the Ambassador."[133]

The Americans who attended the Atlantic Conference had a shorter journey home. Harriman got a ride in Lord Beaverbrook's private train to Gander. It was a record run: even Harriman, who had been taking fast train rides his whole life, feared "the train was going off the track at every curve." From Gander the pair took an RAF Liberator to New Brunswick, Beaverbrook's birthplace, and then on to Washington. Meanwhile, the *Augusta* and the rest of President Roosevelt's little fleet set a course for the Maine coast, where Sumner Welles and several of the military chiefs climbed on board a PBY for a flight to Rhode Island en route to Washington. Roosevelt and his closest advisers, including Harry Hopkins, transferred back to the presidential yacht *Potomac*, which resumed its leisurely cruise southward.[134]

Friday, August 15, found the *Potomac* anchored in Pulpit Harbor on the island of North Haven, Maine. This lovely, sheltered little inlet took its name from Pulpit Rock, an outcrop reminiscent of a church pulpit that stood authoritatively in front of the harbor's mouth. Woods and meadows sloped down to the harbor's pebbly beaches, and summer homes were perched on its shoreline. One of them, Sky Farm, belonged to the banker Thomas Lamont, who was, in addition to being a booster of Wendell Willkie's, an old friend of Franklin Roosevelt's. After first inquiring whether the president was "receiving," Lamont joined FDR and Hopkins on the yacht's fantail for a talk.[135]

The banker began by congratulating Roosevelt on the Atlantic Conference, the "most wonderful story of the century—a stroke of genius." Relaxing in his wheelchair, with a suntan and his cigarette holder to hand, the president looked satisfied. "We were a great assembly," he agreed. He confided that Churchill "surprised me very much," and said he was more encouraged "than I have been for many months." Lamont commented, "I understand Harry

Hopkins is Winston Churchill's white haired boy." "Yes yes," replied Roosevelt, "but even more so Joe Stalin's—we joke him, Churchill and I, about being 'Uncle Joe's favorite.'" Hopkins chimed in with his favorable impressions of Stalin, the Red Army, and the Russians—a "whole people determined to resist to the end." He admitted he was "completely in the dark" about the quality of the Red Army's marshals, but noted that the Soviets "declare that when snow flies, the Germans will not have taken Leningrad or Moscow or Kiev." Seeing Lamont off the yacht after the pleasant little catch-up, Hopkins warned, "We are going to have some pretty hard bumps yet."[136]

The following afternoon, vacationers in Rockland, Maine, were thrilled to see the "top-heavy, bulging, comfortable" *Potomac* come in to shore, escorted by a sleek, dangerous-looking Coast Guard cutter. The reception committee for what *Time* billed as "the greatest fishing trip that any president of the United States has ever undertaken" was a pack of impatient White House correspondents annoyed at being kept in the dark over the previous fortnight. At a press conference in the yacht's white-walled wardroom, a visibly refreshed FDR in loose gray tweeds, looking "as pleased with himself as a canary-full cat," told them soothingly about the meeting at sea. A "sallow" Hopkins, "just back from Moscow," as FDR put it, sat nearby against a bulkhead. Roosevelt told the reporters that sailors from both navies had intermingled on the quarterdeck of the *Prince of Wales*, and that Cockney accents and Texan drawls had combined to sing the hymns. It was "one of the great historic services." At 4 p.m., FDR was piped off the *Potomac* by the boatswain and driven to the train station, smiling broadly and waving his fedora gaily at the crowds, with Hopkins seated beside him. The presidential train took both men directly back to Washington.[137]

Roosevelt was not the only observer to accentuate the spiritual side of the Atlantic Conference. That Sunday, a Canadian clergyman and scholar, the Reverend Dr. Samuel Henry Prince of the University of King's College, Halifax, preached at St. Stephen's Protestant Episcopal Church on Manhattan's Upper West Side. The theme of his sermon was the prophet Elijah's injunction to his servant, "Go up now and look toward the sea." "In the last few days," said Dr. Prince, "the eyes of millions of mankind have been looking toward the sea in faith and hope, and like Elijah's servant have not been disappointed."[138]

HARRY HOPKINS'S MISSION to Moscow and Placentia Bay was one of the most remarkable ventures of the war. As the first senior Western official to visit the capital after the German invasion, he was able to gather valuable information concerning Russia's chances, her needs, and most of all her leader. Hopkins's reports had an important effect on the president's thinking. As one historian remarks, the mission was not the "turning-point" on aid to Russia, but it was the "point of no return," providing "a firm basis for an already strong inclination."[139] Hopkins provided a kind of character reference for the Soviet Union, just as Bill Donovan had earlier provided one for the United Kingdom. In both cases, the envoys testified that their host country would not be defeated before winter closed in. Hopkins's influence can be seen in the decisions reached in Washington in the first week of August and at Placentia Bay in the second week, and in the administration's increasing tendency to see Russia as a long-term prospect.

Hopkins also relayed a personal message of support to Stalin and his government. Hopkins's status as a trusted presidential emissary was plainly important in this respect, too.[140] But so was his personality. Franklin Roosevelt Jr., who saw Hopkins in action at Argentia, mused on this later:

> To my way of thinking I just don't know who else could have done the job that Harry did. Sumner Welles, no. Because Sumner Welles didn't have the marvelous charm that Harry had. Harry could disarm you. He could make you his friend in the first five minutes of a conversation and that must have been pretty rough with Stalin who was a tough old bird. But Stalin absolutely trusted Harry . . . Harry had the ability to win him over.[141]

FDR was delighted at the rapport struck up by Hopkins and Stalin, boasting to dinner guests at Hyde Park in late August that the encounter at the Kremlin had been "highly successful." Roosevelt reported that Hopkins had asked the Soviet leader why it had been so difficult for the West to get the facts it required. In the president's telling, Stalin replied, "Because I have never before trusted any emissary sent to me by a foreign power," and then proceeded to give Hopkins all the information for which he had asked.[142]

The arrival of such a powerful, persuasive envoy plainly shook up America's official representative, Laurence Steinhardt, but in so doing it cleared the communications channel between Washington and Moscow. The embassy's attitude quickly changed, although not quickly enough for Hopkins's taste. He warned Secretary Stimson against accepting Major Yeaton's opinions, and engineered the posting of a more sympathetic U.S. Army officer to Moscow to coordinate the supply of U.S. aid. Within a few months, both Steinhardt and Yeaton were recalled from the USSR.[143]

The Moscow mission also had a symbolic effect, and mainly in the direction FDR would have liked. Glowing stories and photographs ran on the front pages of Soviet newspapers, which was, as Steinhardt assured Washington, a fact "of much greater significance here than in any other country."[144] In the United States, needless to say, press coverage was less uniform. There was a certain amount of favorable editorial comment; on the other hand, an editorial survey taken on August 8 indicated that despite growing optimism about the war, some newspapers remained concerned about Stalin's bona fides. There were, it found, "signs of editorial distaste for giving more than formal support to the USSR. Some commentators regarded Mr. Hopkins's visit to Moscow . . . as laying it on a bit thick." That is an understatement. Under the headline "Our Comrades Now?," the *Wall Street Journal*, for instance, worried that Hopkins "in a casual way seems to have made this nation an ally of Soviet Russia . . . We cannot get rid of the disease of totalitarianism by strengthening one totalitarian at the expense of another. To try that is to fly in the face of common sense. Worse than that, it is to fly in the face of morals."[145]

Over time, however, the combination of Hopkins's visit to Moscow and the Atlantic Conference focused the minds of editorial writers on the strategic imperative of aiding the Soviets. A similar editorial survey conducted at the end of August indicated a marked shift in position: "Editorial writers expressed delight that the initiative had at last been wrested from the Axis. Even the shipment of supplies to Russia is accepted much more readily, now that it has been removed from the domain of discussion and made a settled policy."[146] None of that addressed the points the *Wall Street Journal* was making, of course. Regardless of its rationale in realpolitik, supporting the Soviet regime was disagreeable.

Hopkins's enthusiasm for the Soviet cause should not be confused with any personal affection for Stalin. He took a more hardheaded approach, as he explained to "Pug" Ismay in a letter from the *Prince of Wales* on the way to Argentia: "I would hardly call Uncle Joe a pleasant man, though he was interesting enough, and I think I got what I wanted, but you can never be sure about that." If anything, Hopkins was depressed by his glimpse of Soviet totalitarianism. "Before my three days in Moscow ended," he wrote in the *American Magazine*, "the difference between democracy and dictatorship was clearer to me than any words of philosopher, historian, or journalist could make it." He measured that difference in the fear in General Yakovlev's eyes and the behavior of the authorities toward the citizenry. But he was pragmatic about the limits of America's ability to bridge that difference, and he was sure that Hitler posed the greater threat. Much of the West made the same calculation. Winston Churchill was once asked by a dinner companion at Ditchley, "How *can* we be allies of the Russians?" Churchill replied, "I believe in holding the carnal until the spiritual is free."[147]

As historian Warren Kimball notes, Roosevelt is often accused of slavishly following congressional and public opinion. In August 1941, however, "he took the tougher road, going against the thrust of opinion within and without his administration by promising both aid and legitimacy to the Soviet Union."[148] He gambled on Russia—and the Hopkins mission gave him confidence that it was a wise bet. At another inflection point in the development of U.S. policy toward the war, a presidential envoy played the vital role.

Considering both the second and third Hopkins missions together, it is clear that Hopkins helped to establish the pattern of the triangular relationship between the United States, the United Kingdom, and the Soviet Union.[149] London and Moscow would provide the manpower; Washington would provide the matériel. Hopkins was at the center of this triangle. "Incredibly," observed one canny D.C. operator, "Stalin, Churchill and Roosevelt each trusted him more than they trusted each other."[150]

"We stand, all of us," said Winston Churchill in 1941, "upon the watch towers of history."[151] That summer, this was certainly the case for Harry Hopkins.

Epilogue

A fter the dramatics at Placentia Bay, the rest of August 1941 was surprisingly quiet. In September, however, the relentless march to war began again. Franklin Roosevelt took advantage of a clash off the Icelandic coast between the American destroyer USS *Greer* and a German U-boat to up the ante. Offering a somewhat colored version of the incident to a national radio audience, he characterized the attack as an act of piracy—part of a Nazi conspiracy to "seize control of the oceans" and create "a permanent world system based on force, on terror, and on murder." He announced a policy of U.S. naval escorting, and warned that German or Italian warships entering American defensive waters "do so at their own peril." U.S. warships would escort all Allied convoys—whether or not they contained an American-flag ship—in an area comprising three-quarters of the North Atlantic. Axis vessels would be attacked on sight. "When you see a rattlesnake poised to strike," he reminded his listeners, "you do not wait until he has struck before you crush him." In October and November, the president persuaded Congress, after another bitter and close-fought battle, to "unshackle" his hands and eviscerate the Neutrality Act. American merchantmen could now be armed and sent through war zones to carry supplies directly to belligerent ports.[1]

After a year of steadily enlarging its operations, the United States was now waging an undeclared naval war against Germany in the Atlantic. Lend-Lease had been followed through to its logical conclusion. Confronted by persistent opposition from isolationists and noninterventionists, Roosevelt had, argues Wayne Cole, "equivocated and masked his moves in his efforts to muffle objections." But the sum of all his incremental initiatives—increasingly wide-ranging patrols within an expanded naval zone, the defense of Greenland and Iceland, and finally convoying and shoot-on-sight—had brought America to the brink of belligerency.[2]

FDR also delivered on his commitment to help supply the Soviet war effort, which was coming under fearful pressure from the Wehrmacht. At the end of September, Averell Harriman and Lord Beaverbrook led the American and British delegations to the Moscow Conference on supply issues. "I have doubled the number of my trouble-shooters," said Roosevelt in announcing Harriman's appointment. "Harry Hopkins remains a trouble-shooter, and I add Harriman to him." Harriman took with him a personal message for Stalin from Roosevelt. "Harry Hopkins has told me in great detail of his encouraging and satisfactory visits with you," said the president. "I can't tell you how thrilled all of us are because of the gallant defense of the Soviet armies." The Moscow Conference agreed on a $1 billion program of aid to the Soviet Union and a protocol governing the division of American matériel between military chiefs in Moscow, London, and Washington.[3] The president continued to push the bureaucracy to accelerate aid to Moscow, and on November 7 he brought the Soviet Union under the provisions of the Lend-Lease Act. Later that month, frustrated at his officials' tardiness in getting aircraft to the Soviets, he instructed Hopkins to "say to them from me: Hurry, hurry, hurry!"[4]

In the end, war came to America from Asia, not Europe. Roosevelt's belief that he could restrain Tokyo without provoking it proved wrong. He misjudged Japanese intentions just as Stalin had misjudged German intentions. Tokyo chafed at Washington's de facto oil embargo and worried about preserving its naval superiority as the American war machine revved up. In the fall of 1941, Japanese leaders decided to go to war unless negotiations with Washington bore fruit. By late November, Cordell Hull's talks had achieved nothing, and a new, more bellicose administration, led by former war minister General Hideki Tojo, was in power in Tokyo. The Americans regarded Japan as an expansionist bully that had to be checked. From Japan's point of view, its only alternatives were submission to a U.S.-led coalition or resistance against it. "An American-imposed peace," recounts historian Akira Iriye, "was considered less desirable and honourable than a Japanese-initiated war." Roosevelt kept playing for time, but increasingly he and his cabinet anticipated an overt act of aggression from Japan, most likely in Southeast Asia.[5]

They were caught unawares, therefore, on Sunday, December 7, when hundreds of carrier-based Japanese aircraft struck at American warships moored in Pearl Harbor, Hawaii, more than five thousand miles to the east. Within a few hours, a sizable portion of the U.S. Pacific Fleet lay at the bottom of the harbor, including four battleships and a number of smaller vessels. Fortunately, no U.S. carriers were in port at the time of the attack. But 188 aircraft were destroyed, most of them on the ground, and 2,403 Americans were killed. Japanese attacks on other U.S. and British possessions in Asia followed with dispatch; the greatest shock for Churchill was the sinking of the battlecruiser *Repulse* and the battleship *Prince of Wales*, under whose guns he had sung hymns with Roosevelt at Argentia.[6]

ALL FIVE OF ROOSEVELT'S ENVOYS were involved in the events of December 7, 1941—and much more directly than they had been in September 1939. Once peripheral, their missions had drawn them in to the center of power.

Harry Hopkins was having lunch with the president in his oval study on the second floor of the White House when the news came through. He had just returned to the residence after a four-week stay in the hospital. FDR, wearing an old sweater he had borrowed from one of his sons, ate from a tray on his desk and fed morsels to Fala; Hopkins lounged across from him in a V-necked sweater and slacks. Roosevelt had consecrated the unseasonably warm day to rest, and hoped to spend some time on his stamp collection. Meanwhile the two men chatted about "things far removed from war." At 1:47 p.m., Frank Knox called to tell him the Navy Department was picking up news from Honolulu about an air raid. "No!" was FDR's response. Twenty-five minutes later the president telephoned Cordell Hull, who was due to meet with Japanese envoys at the State Department, and instructed him to receive them "formally and coolly and bow them out." At 3 p.m., FDR and Hopkins were joined by Knox, Henry Stimson, George Marshall, and others for a council of war. The participants were shocked, but the atmosphere was "not too tense," Hopkins recorded later that night. "All of us believed that in the last analysis the enemy was Hitler and that he could never be defeated without force of arms; that sooner or later we were bound to be in the war and that Japan had given us an opportunity."[7]

Sumner Welles was just leaving the State Department for lunch at the Mayflower Hotel when Roosevelt called him with the news. A few minutes later he sat in Hull's office while the secretary called the president to report on his meeting with the Japanese. Soon Hull left to join the conference at the White House, leaving Welles to alert U.S. embassies and foreign capitals to the situation and begin rallying the Latin American countries.[8]

Bill Donovan was in New York City watching football. The former college football star had a ticket to the final game of the NFL's regular season—a crosstown derby between the New York Giants and the Brooklyn Dodgers, played at the horseshoe-shaped Polo Grounds in Harlem. A crowd of 55,051 had turned out to watch the interborough contest and celebrate the career of the Giants' veteran running back, Alphonse "Tuffy" Leemans. The Giants had won the Eastern Division title, but on December 7 the Brooks played like champions and won 21–7, making the New Yorkers look like "dismal cellar tenants."[9]

The Polo Grounds' authorities elected not to tell the crowd what had happened in Hawaii. At the end of the first quarter, however, an announcement was made over the public address system asking Donovan to call Washington immediately, which caused "an ominous buzzing" around the ground. Donovan slipped down to the stadium's office and spoke on the telephone to his staffer James Roosevelt, who was at the White House and reported that his father wanted him in the capital right away. The coordinator of information made his excuses and left for the airport to join Vice President Henry Wallace and other senior officials on a flight to Washington.[10]

Remarkably, another of Roosevelt's envoys was also at the Polo Grounds that afternoon—Wendell Willkie. That weekend, Willkie was catching up with various political cronies, all veterans of his 1940 campaign, whom he hoped would help him again in 1944.[11] On Sunday, he went to the football game with Albert Lasker, an advertising whiz and political supporter. Others in their group included Bill Donovan, William Randolph Hearst Jr., and Byron Foy, a Chrysler executive who had married a Chrysler heiress. Willkie probably heard of the sneak attack on Hawaii from Donovan, and he must have felt keenly his exclusion from official circles when his fellow Republican left the game early for Washington. At the conclusion of the game, an announcement over the PA ordered navy and army personnel to report to their stations. Having no station to report to, Willkie went with his companions to the Foys' grand Upper East Side home to talk through the implications of the day's events. Later he returned to his own nearby apartment, where he was contacted by the *New York Times* for a comment. "I have not the slightest doubt as to what a united America should and will do," he told the newspaper's readers.[12]

Wendell Willkie must have been thinking about the presidency on December 7. As it happened, Pearl Harbor also got the president thinking about Willkie. Two days earlier, Roosevelt had drafted a letter to his former opponent inviting him to reprise his role as a "Special Representative of the President," this time to Australasia, as it would be "of real value to cement our relations with New Zealand and Australia" in light of Japan's posture in the Pacific. Canberra was enthusiastic about the idea, which had originated with Australian newspaper publisher Sir Keith Murdoch. Now FDR wrote in longhand on the bottom of his unsent letter, "This was dictated Friday morning—long before this vile attack started."[13] With Irita Van Doren's assistance, Willkie drafted a response declining the offer in light of the Japanese attack, although he had previously commented to an Australian diplomat that such a trip would provoke allegations that "he was nothing more than a 'stooge' for the President and the Administration."[14]

Several days later, Willkie visited the White House to have lunch with the president and talk about the war effort. At the last minute, despite serious consideration and rampant press speculation, Roosevelt decided not to offer him a job in his administration coordinating economic mobilization. Questioned by the press, Willkie hid his disappointment behind a smile and reminded them, "I am not running the government, although I sought to, and tried very hard." Perhaps FDR had listened to the unsentimental Harry Hopkins, who warned him that Willkie would use the war production issue as "a political football."[15]

On December 7, Averell Harriman was at Chequers, where the time was five hours ahead of Washington, dining with Winston Churchill, his daughter-in-law Pamela, his aides Commander Thompson and John Martin, Kathleen Harriman, and Gil Winant. The mood in the dignified old house was sober. The prime minister appeared tired and preoccupied, holding his head in his hands in silence for long periods. He feared that the Japanese were poised to attack a British possession in Asia, leaving the British with the "unthinkable" prospect of fighting both Germany and Japan without the armed assistance of the United States.[16]

Just before 9 p.m., Churchill's butler, Sawyers, brought in a small black fifteen-dollar radio set, a gift from Harry Hopkins, so the party could listen to the BBC news. Churchill raised the flip-top lid to activate the set and some information came through about a Japanese attack. "The Japanese have raided Pearl Harbor!" exclaimed Harriman, causing Churchill to sit up. Thompson thought the announcer had referred to the Pearl River in southern China, but the trusty Sawyers dashed in to confirm that the staff had also been listening and the target was Hawaii. Within ten minutes, the prime minister was on the telephone to Washington, asking, "Mr President, what's this about Japan?" "It's quite true," replied FDR. "They have attacked us at Pearl Harbor. We are all in the same boat now." "This certainly simplifies things," said a relieved Churchill. "God be with you." Later that night, the PM and Harriman penned a joint message to Hopkins: "Thinking of you much at this historic moment.—Winston, Averell."[17]

In his memoirs, Churchill wrote that Harriman and Winant "took the shock with admirable fortitude . . . They did not wail or lament that their country was at war. They wasted no words in reproach or sorrow. In fact, one might almost have thought they had been delivered from a long pain." As David Reynolds has revealed, Churchill's first draft of that passage was less discreet. The two Americans received the news with "exaltation," he recorded initially. "In fact they nearly danced for joy."[18]

For his part, Churchill understood immediately Pearl Harbor's significance: "So we had won after all! . . . We had won the war. England would live; Britain would live; the Commonwealth of Nations and the Empire would live. How long the war would last or in what fashion it would end no man could tell, nor did I at this moment care . . . We should not be wiped out. Our history would not come to an end. We might not even have to die as individuals. Hitler's fate was sealed. Mussolini's fate was sealed. As for the Japanese, they would be ground to powder. All the rest was merely the proper application of overwhelming force." That night, he recorded, he "slept the sleep of the saved and thankful."[19]

After taking the call from Churchill, Roosevelt completed his council of war, receiving damage reports from the navy, discussing the disposition of the army and air force with Marshall, and ordering the Justice Department to pick up Japanese nationals who were regarded as "dangerous to the peace and security of the United States." Guards were to be placed at arsenals, bridges, and munitions factories, but the president refused to countenance a military guard at the White House. When the meeting adjourned, he dictated to Grace Tully a first draft of his war message to Congress. Even on the day of the Pearl Harbor attack, FDR had not budged from his view that Germany was America's principal foe. Being anxious to preserve national unity, however, and believing on the basis of intercepts that Berlin would probably throw its lot in with Tokyo, he intended to ask Congress for a declaration of war against Japan alone and wait for Hitler to do the rest.[20]

After a light dinner with Hopkins and Tully, FDR convened the cabinet, which sat in a ring around his desk. Roosevelt's cabinet meetings were usually jovial affairs, but he opened this one by noting it was the gravest session since Abraham Lincoln had summoned his secretaries after Fort Sumter had been fired upon. His cabinet officers thought he seemed deadly serious, yet calm and somehow relieved that "his terrible moral problem had been resolved." Later he called in congressional leaders, including a prominent isolationist senator, to brief them on developments and find out when they would be ready to receive him in joint session. Sumner Welles then joined FDR for an hour to talk over the details of the war message and some diplomatic questions, recalling later that the president demonstrated "confidence and mastery" in every gesture.[21]

While all this activity was taking place in FDR's oval room, Ed Murrow was sitting on a bench in the hallway outside, chain-smoking and watching the dignitaries come and go. He and his wife, just back from London, had shared a supper of scrambled eggs with Eleanor that evening, and the president had sent a message asking him not to leave. "What the hell are you doing here?" asked Hopkins when he emerged from the study. "He told me to wait," replied Murrow. "If he said wait, you better wait," advised Hopkins. The two men went down the corridor to Hopkins's bedroom, and they talked while he got into an old pair of striped pajamas. The Japanese attack was "plainly and simply a Godsend," he told Murrow, for "by no other means could the country have been brought into the war without serious internal disunity." Just before Hopkins collapsed into his bed, Murrow recalled later, he "sat on the edge for a moment, looking extremely frail in his sagging pajamas. He spoke, in a very low tone, as if to himself, saying, 'Oh, God—If only I had the strength.' "[22]

Welles left the president's study around midnight and Murrow was finally admitted, joining FDR for a sandwich and a beer. The president asked Murrow how Britain was bearing up and he outlined the losses at Pearl Harbor. He was indignant that so many American aircraft had been destroyed on the ground. "On the ground," he repeated, banging his fist on the desk. Soon a bell rang, and Bill Donovan joined them in the study, the last visitor of this momentous day. He had been at his headquarters at 25th and E Streets all evening, assembling what information he could and sending out propaganda broadcasts to the Far East. "What do you know, Bill?" asked Roosevelt. Not much, the nascent spymaster admitted, and the talk switched to Pearl Harbor's effect on American public opinion and the defense of the Philippines. At 12:30 a.m., FDR cleared everyone out and announced he was going to bed.[23]

AT NOON THE NEXT DAY, President Roosevelt went to Congress to ask for a declaration of war against Japan. In less than twenty-four hours, reporters observed, "the whole tempo of the city had changed." The streets were thick with cars; telephone lines were jammed for hours. U.S. Marines stood on guard at the Capitol's doorways with fixed bayonets, and the "quick-eyed Secret Service men" in Roosevelt's motorcade cradled tommy guns on their laps. The large crowd milling in front of the Capitol let out a roar when his limousine approached; then it broke, with people heading to their cars to listen to his address over the radio. Inside, the House of Representatives chamber was full to bursting with senators, representatives, and, down at the edge of the well, members of the cabinet and the Supreme Court. At 12:29 p.m., Speaker Sam Rayburn rapped his gavel and, in a thunderous voice, presented "the President of the United States." For a moment there was silence, then crashing applause as FDR entered wearing a black frock coat and striped trousers, leaning on the arm of his son James. In striking contrast to the Axis capitals, only four military uniforms were spotted on the floor of the House, worn by James and the three service chiefs.[24]

From the first sentence, Roosevelt's short speech was perfectly weighted and delivered in measured tones. "Yesterday, December 7, 1941—a date which will live in infamy—the United States of America was suddenly and deliberately attacked by naval and air forces of the Empire of Japan." His face was solemn throughout and he did not acknowledge the applause until the very end. Looking down on the president from a packed gallery, where he was seated just behind Eleanor Roosevelt and Woodrow Wilson's widow, Edith, was his most trusted envoy, Harry Hopkins.[25]

Swiftly, and with only one dissenting vote, Congress resolved to declare war on Japan. For two years, Roosevelt had worn down and marginalized his isolationist opponents; Pearl Harbor finished them as a political force. The president signed the declaration of war at 4:10 p.m. that afternoon in the Oval Office.[26] Britain also declared war on Japan and her empire followed suit. Three days later, on December 11, Germany and Italy declared war on the United States. The European war was now a world war, and America was in it. Finally, Franklin Roosevelt was a war president.

IN THE YEARS AFTER PEARL HARBOR, all these characters played their parts in shaping America's war effort and her foreign policies. Franklin Roosevelt prosecuted the war against the dictators until he died within sight of victory, on April 12, 1945. He was sixty-three years old. The same month saw the deaths of Adolf Hitler and Benito Mussolini. Roosevelt's life, declared Winston Churchill in a speech to the Pilgrims in London, was "one of the commanding events in human destiny." Even in his final weeks, FDR sent special diplomatic agents to Europe to keep him in touch with events.[27]

Harry Hopkins remained with Roosevelt throughout the war, providing essential counsel and acting as his emissary on many occasions. George

Marshall called him "one of the most courageous, self-sacrificing figures of the war—the least appreciated and the most misunderstood." Churchill wrote that he played "a sometimes decisive part in the whole movement of the war. His was a soul that flamed out of a frail and failing body. He was a crumbling lighthouse from which there shone the beams that led great fleets to harbour." Hopkins helped to keep the Big Three together. After Churchill proposed a toast to Hopkins at the tripartite Tehran Conference in 1943, FDR leaned over to him and said, "Dear Harry, what would we do without you?"

The relationship cooled a little, however, when Hopkins married again and moved out of the White House at the end of 1943: Roosevelt liked his intimates to be close at hand. Hopkins then suffered a recurrence of his illness that kept him in hospital and away from FDR for half a year. Although still very sick, he was back at the president's side for the Yalta Conference in February 1945, but the two men argued on their way home on board USS *Quincy*, "a kind of weariness" having affected both their tempers. They never saw each other again, Hopkins always regretting that he had not said goodbye to Roosevelt when he left the ship. Hopkins was back at the Mayo Clinic when FDR died. His nurse was surprised when her "very cantankerous patient," a "gray-looking person" with "the feeling of grayness about him," received personal calls of sympathy from Joseph Stalin, Winston Churchill, and Charles de Gaulle.[28]

Hopkins carried out one last mission for the new president, Harry S. Truman, returning to Moscow a few weeks after VE Day to resolve a dispute with Stalin. His reaction when he was asked to go was "wonderful to behold." He was, thought his intimates, "like an old fire horse hearing the alarm." In September, Hopkins was awarded the Distinguished Service Medal in the Rose Garden at the White House, surrounded by his friends, but soon afterward he was back in hospital for the final time. The White House relayed a message from Hopkins's third wife, Louise, to his friends to warn them that he was "failing rapidly." In desperation, his son Robert called President Truman from the hospital and begged him to send his father abroad again, in the hope that that would revive him. It was too late: Harry Hopkins died on January 26, 1946, aged fifty-five. The immediate cause was his nutritional malady, but those who knew him well considered him a war casualty.[29]

Sumner Welles served as under secretary of state for nearly two more years after Pearl Harbor, managing much of America's wartime diplomacy and shouldering the burden of postwar planning. He was brought down, however, by the dissonance between his public and private selves. In August 1943, he resigned at the insistence of Cordell Hull, who was bitter about his deputy's prominence and outraged by William Bullitt's accounts of his sexual misconduct. FDR was sympathetic toward Welles, but in the end he reluctantly cut him loose. Bullitt's vendetta also destroyed its author, who was banished from Roosevelt's orbit. Later, the president encouraged Bullitt to run for mayor of his hometown of Philadelphia, then sent word to the local political bosses to "cut his throat."[30]

Welles never returned to government service. Initially he found success as a columnist, lecturer, and broadcaster. He published a good book and a bad one. He was an active supporter of the Zionist cause, and after Willkie's death he accepted the presidency of Wendell Willkie Memorial House in New York City. The long-run pattern, however, especially after his wife Mathilde's death in 1949, was a sad decline marked by drinking, illness, loneliness, sexual wantonness, and attempted suicide. He died on September 24, 1961, of pancreatic cancer, his body ruined by drink just as his career had been. He was sixty-eight. "Casually, almost indifferently," wrote his son, "he had tossed his enemies . . . the means to destroy him, and they had."[31]

Bill Donovan served as coordinator of information until June 1942, when Roosevelt renamed his agency the Office of Strategic Services. He was later promoted to major general. Donovan was an unorthodox and somewhat disorganized spymaster who presided over an equal number of successes and blunders. Because he recruited for his "league of gentlemen" from the upper echelons of American society, the OSS became known as "Oh So Social"— just as his cavalry troop had been known as the "Silk Stocking Boys." For a restless man of action with a taste for international travel and a love of cloak-and-dagger, this was a dream job. He was bitterly disappointed, therefore, when the OSS was dismantled by Truman at the end of the war and he was repeatedly overlooked to head up its successor organization, the Central Intelligence Agency.[32]

Donovan resumed his law practice, including service as a prosecutor in the Nuremberg trials, before being recalled to serve as ambassador to Thailand in 1953–1954. President Eisenhower refused his request that, in addition to ambassador, he be designated "Personal Representative of the President of the United States." Donovan suffered dementia in his final years and passed away on February 8, 1959, at the age of seventy-six. He is remembered as the father of U.S. intelligence, and his statue stands in the foyer of CIA headquarters in Langley, Virginia.[33]

Despite Wendell Willkie's reluctance to serve as Roosevelt's emissary in the Pacific in 1941, he wrote to the president the following year asking for assistance in planning a trip to the Middle East, the Soviet Union, and China. He was pleased to accept FDR's offer that he undertake the trip, later written up in the bestselling book *One World*, as a presidential envoy. Roosevelt provided a U.S. Army bomber called the *Gulliver* and a small traveling staff, and wrote personal letters of introduction to Joseph Stalin and Chiang Kai-shek. Willkie's large appetites had not diminished, and in Chungking he established a special relationship with the generalissimo's beautiful and willful wife, Madame Chiang. Willkie's envoy status caused difficulties, however, when he made controversial statements en route—calling for the Allies to open a second front in Europe, and for the end of colonialism—and FDR hinted that his personal representative's remarks were not worth reading.[34] Willkie was tiring of Roosevelt's continuing attempts to co-opt him. He also came to feel that Churchill—whom he had once called "the greatest public figure in the world"—had not given him his due, considering the "heavy political risk" he had taken for Britain.[35]

Willkie stayed in touch with the ukulele-playing reporter Eddy Gilmore, with whom he had traveled to London. In 1943, Willkie interceded with

Stalin to allow Gilmore to marry a Russian ballerina he had met in Moscow. "I never thought of myself as a cupid before," remarked Willkie, "but, on reflection, I don't see why I am not qualified." Willkie was notified of Stalin's agreement by a young Soviet diplomat, Andrei Gromyko. The couple had a daughter, whom they called Victoria Wendell Gilmore.[36]

Willkie sought the Republican nomination for the presidency again in 1944 and won the New Hampshire primary, but he withdrew after a devastating defeat in Wisconsin, a state with a strong isolationist cast. There were rumors that Roosevelt would appoint him navy secretary when Frank Knox died that April, or invite him to run for vice president on the Democratic ticket, but nothing came of them. Willkie's endorsement would have been valuable to Roosevelt in an election year, of course. Consequently, there were further twitches upon the thread: invitations to visit the White House, hints about big jobs and future partnerships. Disillusioned, Willkie turned his thoughts to newspaper publishing, but it was not to be. He died after a series of heart attacks one month before the presidential election, on October 8, 1944, aged only fifty-two. In the Old Chesterfield Arms in Mayfair, where he had bought a round of drinks for some Tommies and flirted with the barmaid, they hung black crêpe on their framed photographs of his visit. The pub's regulars, including Willkie's former darts partner, drank a toast to "a proper gent who made us feel that he was our friend."[37]

Averell Harriman, on the other hand, saw many more presidents elected. All told, he held office under four of them. From 1943 to 1946 he served as U.S. ambassador to Russia. Although he had consciously disrupted Gil Winant's embassy, he did not like it when special envoys came to Moscow and tried to go around him. "That was a horse of a different color," remembered his aide Bob Meiklejohn. Harriman succeeded Winant as ambassador to the United Kingdom in 1946, but he was soon recalled to Washington to serve as secretary of commerce.[38]

In late 1947, Winant was also back in the United States. He was in a troubled state of mind, frustrated with the condition of international politics, depressed by his marginalization after Roosevelt's death, unprepared for private life, and lonely after the end of an affair with Winston Churchill's daughter Sarah. On November 3, at his home in Concord, New Hampshire, Winant killed himself.[39] He was fifty-eight.

Harriman's career ground steadily on. "For a dull man," observed Robert Dallek, "he led an extraordinarily interesting life." As persistent as ever, he outlasted almost all other major figures from the Second World War; in the public mind, he came to overshadow his mentor Harry Hopkins, although he was undoubtedly the lesser man. Harriman served as governor of New York for a term, and was twice a candidate for the Democratic nomination for president. He later served as ambassador at large—a kind of institutionalized personal envoy—and in other posts under Presidents John F. Kennedy and Lyndon B. Johnson. As a politician, he was disastrously leaden. ("Honest Ave, the Hairsplitter," one observer called him.) As a diplomat, he was blessed by what Isaiah Berlin called "an uncanny sense of what, as a negotiator, could work, and what could not." He was entitled to take credit for many diplomatic accomplishments, and he did; yet when his biographer asked him in the 1980s what he wanted to be remembered for, he first nominated his 1941 mission to London.[40]

Harriman spent his final years with Pamela Churchill, whom he married in 1971 after their respective spouses had died. ("My, my, an old flame rekindled," was Clementine Churchill's reaction when she heard the news.) In the thirty years since their London affair had begun, Pamela had acquired a string of lovers and husbands as long and precious as a pearl necklace, including Ed Murrow, Jock Whitney, Gianni Agnelli, Prince Aly Khan, Baron Elie de Rothschild, and Leland Hayward. Averell and Pamela's marriage was happy, so much so that he even became accustomed to opening his checkbook. Averell Harriman died on July 26, 1986, at the great age of ninety-four, with Pamela by his side. Awful fights ensued between Pamela and the rest of the Harrimans over Averell's money, and even his remains. Having taken U.S. citizenship and become a legendary Democratic Party hostess and fund-raiser, she acted on Harry Hopkins's advice that she get herself made an "ambassadoress." In 1993, President Bill Clinton appointed her as his ambassador to France. Pamela Harriman died on February 6, 1997, after suffering a cerebral hemorrhage while swimming laps at Sumner Welles's Paris hotel, the Ritz.[41]

The seven European missions described in this book tell the story of the progressive hardening of Roosevelt's policies that eventually took America into the war. In the spring of 1940, the president was still grasping for means by which he could contribute to the fight for freedom; Sumner Welles's mission was an attempt to identify them. The fall of France revealed the perils of caution, and after hearing Bill Donovan's testimony and watching the Battle of Britain, Roosevelt decided to extend symbolic and material assistance to Britain by executive fiat. After winning a third term, he toughened his policy further and American assistance was converted into a great legislative and national effort, Lend-Lease.[42] A full-court press of three personal emissaries and a new ambassador was ordered to London to implement the new strategy. The envoys carried out different yet complementary tasks: Harry Hopkins explained Lend-Lease to Churchill and the British elite; Wendell Willkie spoke to the British and American publics; and Averell Harriman hurried the flow of aid. Finally, in the aftermath of Operation Barbarossa, FDR worked through Hopkins to establish the critical three-way relationship between the United States, Britain, and the Soviet Union.

Over these two years, Roosevelt took America on a long journey. By rearming and aiding the Allies, he put the country on a war footing before war was declared. As the situation in Europe became graver, U.S. involvement got deeper. There were periods of drift, certainly—but the direction of the movement, and the presidential purpose behind it, was unmistakable. The journey might have been quicker had FDR been bolder, but millions of Americans would have been left behind. The nation would have entered the war divided and angry. Instead, by the time of the surprise attack at Pearl Harbor, the United States had lost its illusions. Americans were united and ready for the fight. The president had carried the country with him.

Roosevelt did not undertake this effort single-handedly. He called on five men to act as his investigators, surrogates, and symbols in Europe. The investigative work of Donovan in London and Hopkins in Moscow was critical to the course of the war. In both cases, an optimistic FDR sought an eyewitness report before taking a gamble against the advice of a defeatist U.S. ambassador. It is hard to overestimate the importance of these decisions. The fall of France and the invasion of Russia were, as David Reynolds argues, two of the critical junctures of the war, at which FDR might have behaved differently and retreated into hemispheric defense.[43] In both cases he chose the alternative path and insisted, over the opposition of most of his counselors, that America aid Britain and the Soviet Union. Envoys were involved in both decisions.

The president also relied on Hopkins as a surrogate. Hopkins was the catalyst for stronger personal relationships between Roosevelt on the one hand and Churchill and Stalin on the other. His position in the White House entitled him to speak authoritatively on Roosevelt's behalf. His personality was also suited to both missions: his courage appealed to Churchill's romanticism, and his directness suited Stalin's brutal realism. Welles and Harriman also acted as surrogates for Roosevelt in Europe, bringing him firsthand perspectives and extending his influence.

Finally, it is striking how FDR put his envoys to symbolic use. The tension between the urgency of the European situation and the sluggishness of congressional and public opinion was extreme. Through a deluge of speeches, broadcasts, messages, and conversations, Roosevelt pushed isolationism to the margins of American life and tilted the national mood toward supporting aid to Hitler's opponents even at the risk of war. For Robert Dallek, Roosevelt's brilliance as a foreign policy president lay in his "appreciation that effective action abroad required a reliable consensus at home and his use of dramatic events overseas to win national backing from a divided country."[44] It was in this spirit that he used Willkie's mission to London and Hopkins's mission to Moscow to focus Americans' minds on the European war and strengthen the morale of the Allies. No mere ambassador could have produced headlines like FDR's envoys, or sent such pungent messages to the world. Roosevelt was an enthusiastic practitioner of symbolic diplomacy, and in Willkie—the titular head of the Republican Party—he had the ideal tool, albeit a reluctant one. Isaiah Berlin once observed that Roosevelt "believed in flexibility, improvisation, the fruitfulness of using persons and resources in an infinite variety of new and unexpected ways."[45] Anybody, it seemed—even a presidential rival—could be turned to his purposes.

In calling on these representatives, FDR neglected the government agency charged with assisting him in the conduct of U.S. foreign policy: the State Department. Roosevelt's emissaries, often traveling alone, carried out their missions with a flair no regular diplomat could have managed. Yet FDR's envoy addiction also robbed the resident heads of mission of some of their stature. That was no great loss in the cases of Joe Kennedy and Laurence Steinhardt; their pessimism had already made them unwelcome in London and Moscow and largely impotent in Washington. But it was decidedly shortsighted, and unfair, in the case of Gil Winant, who was pushed out of Churchill's inner circle by the more assertive Harriman.

HARRY HOPKINS was fond of telling a story from a conference between Roosevelt and Churchill that was held in Washington shortly after Pearl Harbor. The visitors were accommodated at the White House, and on one occasion Roosevelt accidentally surprised Churchill in the middle of his morning bath. FDR apologized and made to leave, but Churchill supposedly rose like a sea monster from the bathtub and stood before him, naked, plump, pink, and dripping. Unashamed, he declared, "The prime minister of Great Britain has nothing to conceal from the president of the United States."[46]

In fact, the Anglo-American relationship was a more contested and ambiguous thing than Churchill would have had Roosevelt, or us, believe.[47] Considerable suspicion existed between the two governments, and the British repeatedly sought to influence American policy through the medium of

FDR's envoys, for example by assigning an aide to watch over Willkie or stage-managing a war cabinet meeting to impress Hopkins. The British attitude to the release of confidential information changed markedly once they realized, with the Donovan mission, that a policy of openness could pay dividends. The Soviets were just as determined to create the right impression, whether by laying on a feast or giving a "special salute." Stalin artfully posed questions that appeared to demonstrate his resolve. Unlike Whitehall, the Kremlin was able to employ terror to ensure that everyone, including the wretched General Yakovlev, stuck to the correct line.

Roosevelt's envoys were rarely taken in by all this. Even if they had been captured, a politician of FDR's genius would hardly have been fooled. He knew the sympathies of his emissaries when he commissioned them; he was never threatened by advisers who got ahead of him. One might even ask, as does Warren Kimball: who manipulated whom?[48] FDR used his envoys to project his influence—to appeal for Allied patience with American caution, and to urge Allied ferocity in the battle against the Axis.

The five envoys were highly diverse in their politics, their professions, their relations with Roosevelt, even their tailoring. Yet they shared an internationalist mind-set. They did not constitute a bloc, but on occasion they worked together to strengthen ties between Washington, London, and, in the final months before Pearl Harbor, Moscow. With the president's blessing, they helped explain each side to the other, urging Britons and Soviets to fight on with the assurance of greater American assistance, even as they counseled their own countrymen to have confidence and hasten quickly. In Donovan's terms, they were a platoon of "sensible Colonel Houses."

The platoon commander, of course, was Franklin Roosevelt. The record of his envoys' work in Europe adds colorful new tesserae to our mosaic of the thirty-second president. For the most part, he moved his envoys around the globe with great skill and élan. Sometimes, especially in his moments of irresolution, they shifted his thinking. At other times, and especially as the great republic moved nearer to war, they were instruments of his will.

"There is a mysterious cycle in human events," believed Franklin

Roosevelt. "To some generations much is given. Of other generations much is expected. This generation of Americans has a rendezvous with destiny."[49] Sumner Welles, Bill Donovan, Harry Hopkins, Wendell Willkie, and Averell Harriman kept their rendezvous. In each of these men, for different reasons, FDR reposed special faith and confidence. He sent them to Europe in a campaign of subtle and effective diplomacy, and in the cause of freedom. Together, Roosevelt and his envoys took America into the war—and into the world.

Acknowledgments

———

Fighting the Second World War entailed blood, toil, tears, and sweat. Occasionally I felt the same was true for writing about it.

Victory would have been impossible without great armies of supporters. First among them is Scott Moyers, who agented, edited, and published this book. I would call this a hat trick; Scott would call it a triple play. Either way, he was superb and I am hugely grateful. My thanks, too, to the rest of the stellar team at the Penguin Press in New York, including Ann Godoff; Laura Stickney, who bought the book and was unfailingly enthusiastic about it; Mally Anderson; and Roland Ottewell. Thanks also to Penguin Australia's Ben Ball, a great ally.

Thank you to Andrew Wylie, an astute and valued counselor, and his colleagues at the Wylie Agency, including James Pullen.

I wrote this book at the Lowy Institute, Australia's leading think tank. I am grateful to Frank Lowy AC, the Institute's chairman and founder, and the rest of the board. My predecessor as executive director, Michael Wesley, was generous in his support of the project. Many of my colleagues, including Anthony Bubalo, Hugh White, Sam Roggeveen, Malcolm Cook, Philippa Brant, Milton Osborne, and Justin

Jones, helped me with it. A section of energetic interns pitched in, including Bronwyn Lo, Matt Hill, Ben Coleridge, Angela Evans, and Chris Croke. Joanne Bottcher was indefatigable and indispensable. Her contribution was very significant.

Thanks also to my colleagues at the Brookings Institution, Martin Indyk and Strobe Talbott.

The book had its origins in research I conducted at the University of Oxford as a Rhodes Scholar. I am grateful to the Rhodes Trust for funding my study; Balliol College and Nuffield College for providing me with congenial homes; and my supervisors Sir Adam Roberts, Yuen Foong Khong, and John Darwin.

Recreating the seven missions undertaken by Franklin Roosevelt's envoys depended largely upon archival sources spread across three continents, many of them new or only lightly used in the past. In particular, the envoys' firsthand accounts of their travels, recorded in journals, letters, and articles, were like time capsules. A brigade of archivists and librarians has provided first-rate assistance to me over the years. Its ranks are too numerous for individual citations, but special mention must be made of Bob Clark, Bob Parks, Wendell "Tex" Parks, Ray Teichman, and Matthew Hanson at the Franklin D. Roosevelt Presidential Library and Museum in Hyde Park. I must also thank the brilliant archivists at the Library of Congress, the National Archives and Records Administration, the Columbia Center for Oral History Collection, the Houghton Library, the Baker Library, the Lilly Library, the U.S. Army Military History Institute, the British National Archives, the Churchill Archives Centre, the National Archives of Australia, and the National Library of Australia. Working in the archives can be a monastic life, and I am grateful to all those who made it easier. A full list of the archives I used and the papers I consulted is included in the bibliography.

I am thankful to my interviewees, including the late Richard Holbrooke, George Mitchell, the late Arthur M. Schlesinger Jr., and William J. vanden Heuvel. Harry Hopkins's daughter Diana Hopkins Halsted was kind enough to correspond with me.

A number of distinguished international historians have helped me along the way. Thank you to Sir Martin Gilbert, Robert Dallek, Keith Jeffery, Simon Sebag Montefiore, and in particular Steven Casey, a source of encouragement and assistance since Oxford. Frank Costigliola pointed me to the revealing Verne Newton collection of videos at the Roosevelt Library. Thomas Parrish was good enough to copy Rudy Abramson's papers and send them to me in Sydney. Gillian Bennett and Patrick Salmon helped me navigate the darker corners of the Foreign & Commonwealth Office archives.

Any author addressing the Second World War nearly three-quarters of a century after it began will rely heavily on scholars who have gone before. For me, the writings of Robert E. Sherwood, David Reynolds, Robert Dallek, Sir Martin Gilbert, and Waldo Heinrichs form the canon. Luckily, because of the novelty of my special-envoy angle, I found that even well-scrubbed primary and secondary sources often contained new insights.

I would like to thank sincerely those who read my manuscript and saved me from various pratfalls: James Fallows, Graham Freudenberg, John Pollard, Emma-Kate Symons, Graeme Gill, John Bowan, Jonathan Wright, Justin Vaïsse, Stephen Harris, Sudhir Hazareesingh, and others mentioned elsewhere in these acknowledgments. The remaining stumbles are all mine.

Sir Jeremy Greenstock and Sir John Holmes, two directors of the Ditchley Foundation, along with their excellent staff, welcomed me to Ditchley Park—a very fine house that itself is almost a character in my book. Derek Chollet showed me around the West Wing of the White House. Ambassador Michael McFaul hosted me at Spaso House. Bob Carr used his good offices on my behalf. Thanks also to Lorand Bartels, David Lee, Camille Grand, François Heisbourg, Charlie Peters, David Robarge, Douglas Waller, Gerald Hensley, Svetlana Chervonnaya, Glyn Stone, Mark Pottle, John Fraser, and Kevin Barker.

Paul Keating and Owen Harries both encouraged me, in different ways, to address big, central issues rather than small, marginal ones. If you're going swimming, Owen often reminds me, swim in the deep water, not the shallows. Mark Ryan is a good friend and a sharp student of history. Thank you to my own personal brains trust—Sophie Gee, David Howarth, David Hunt, and Robert Dann.

Final edits were made at Wolf Cabin on Premier Lake, near Skookumchuck, British Columbia. Thank you to my Canadian relatives, especially my excellent mother-in-law, Janet Charlton.

Profound thanks and love go to my mother, Paddy Fullilove, a wise confidante; and my father, the late Eric Fullilove, who grew up in London during the Blitz and served in the war that Roosevelt and Churchill fought. Thanks, too, to my brother Christian Fullilove and his family for their love and support.

I have saved the best until last. My greatest discovery at Oxford was my brilliant, beautiful wife, Gillian. This book is dedicated to her, and to our darling sons, Patrick, Thomas, and Alexander.

Abbreviations in Notes
and Bibliography

AFHRA	Air Force Historical Research Agency, Montgomery, AL
BIA	Borthwick Institute for Archives, University of York, UK
BL	Baker Library, Harvard Business School, Cambridge, MA
BOD	Bodleian Library, Department of Special Collections & Western Manuscripts, University of Oxford, UK
CAC	Churchill Archives Centre, Churchill College, Cambridge, UK
CCOHC	Columbia Center for Oral History Collection, Columbia University, New York, NY
CPL	Claude Pepper Library, Florida State University, Tallahassee, FL
DGFP	Documents on German Foreign Policy
FDR	Franklin D. Roosevelt
FDRL	Franklin D. Roosevelt Presidential Library and Museum, Hyde Park, NY
FO	Foreign Office
FRUS	*Foreign Relations of the United States*
GUL	Georgetown University Library, Special Collections Division, Washington, DC

HIL	Hoover Institution Library, Stanford, CA
HL	Houghton Library, Harvard University, Cambridge, MA
LAC	Library and Archives Canada, Ottawa, Canada
LBJL	Lyndon Baines Johnson Presidential Library and Museum, Austin, TX
LC	Library of Congress, Manuscript Division, Washington, DC
LL	Lilly Library, Indiana University, Bloomington, IN
MML	Seeley G. Mudd Manuscript Library, Princeton University, Princeton, NJ
NA	National Archives, Kew, UK
NAA	National Archives of Australia, Canberra and Melbourne, Australia
NARA	National Archives and Records Administration, College Park, MD
NLA	National Library of Australia, Canberra, Australia
PA	Parliamentary Archives, London, UK
PPA	*Public Papers and Addresses of Franklin D. Roosevelt*
PPC	*Complete Presidential Press Conferences of Franklin D. Roosevelt*
UB	Cadbury Research Library, Special Collections, University of Birmingham, UK
UDL	University of Delaware Library, Special Collections Department, Newark, DE
UIL	University of Iowa Libraries, Special Collections Department, Iowa City, IA
USAMHI	United States Army Military History Institute, Carlisle, PA
UT	University of Toronto Archives, Toronto, Canada
VHL	Vere Harmsworth Library, University of Oxford, UK
YUL	Yale University Library, New Haven, CT

Notes

PROLOGUE: SEPTEMBER 1939

1. FDR note, September 1, 1939, PPF 3737, FDRL; Joseph Alsop and Robert Kintner, *American White Paper: The Story of American Diplomacy and the Second World War* (London: Michael Joseph, 1940), 78; Kenneth S. Davis, *FDR: Into the Storm, 1937–1940: A History* (New York: Random House, 1993), 460–61; John Gunther, *Roosevelt in Retrospect: A Profile in History* (London: Hamish Hamilton, 1950), 329–30. FDR's bedroom is described in Frances Perkins, *The Roosevelt I Knew* (London: Hammond & Hammond, 1948), 55–56; *Life*, January 20, 1941.

2. *Time*, August 11, 1941; Harold Nicolson, *Diplomacy* (Washington, DC: Institute for the Study of Diplomacy, School of Foreign Service, Georgetown University, 1988), 62; Alsop and Kintner, *American White Paper*, 78–82; Benjamin Welles, *Sumner Welles: FDR's Global Strategist; A Biography* (New York: St. Martin's, 1997), 126–27, 216.

3. Conrad Black, *Franklin Delano Roosevelt: Champion of Freedom* (New York: PublicAffairs, 2003), 528–31; Graham Stewart, *Burying Caesar: Churchill, Chamberlain and the Battle for the Tory Party* (London: Weidenfeld & Nicolson, 1999), 379–84; *Washington Post*, August 17, 1941; Welles, *Sumner Welles*, 216; *Los Angeles Times*, September 4, 1939.

4. H. Wendell Ellicott, "Personal Records of Alaska and the Yukon hunting trip 1939," 27–32, 48–49, 52–53, 58–59, 63–64, box 132C, Donovan Papers, USAMHI; *Chicago Daily Tribune*, August 9, 1939.

5. H. Wendell Ellicott, "Personal Records of Alaska and the Yukon hunting trip 1939," 64–65, box 132C, Donovan Papers, USAMHI; *Chicago Daily Tribune*, September 9, 1939; Justus D. Doenecke, "General Robert E. Wood: The Evolution of a Conservative," *Journal of the Illinois State Historical Society* 71, no. 3 (1978): 162–69.

6. Geoffrey C. Ward, ed., *Closest Companion: The Unknown Story of the Intimate Friendship between Franklin Roosevelt and Margaret Suckley* (Boston: Houghton Mifflin, 1995), 23, 233, 239, 244–45; Marquis W. Childs, "The President's Best Friend," *Saturday Evening Post*, April 19 and 26, 1941; Robert E. Sherwood, *The White House Papers of Harry L. Hopkins: An Intimate History*, 2 vols. (London: Eyre & Spottiswoode, 1948), I: 7.

7. Sherwood, *The White House Papers*, I: 116–20; Henry H. Adams, *Harry Hopkins: A Biography* (New York: Putnam, 1977), 161; Harry Hopkins to Averell Harriman, September 8, 1939, and November 25, 1939, both in Special Files: Public Service: Business Advisory Council: Harry Hopkins, box 147, Averell Harriman Papers, LC.

8. *New York Times*, September 2, 1939.

9. *New York Times*, September 1, 1939; FDR to Knox, December 29, 1939, PSF (Departmental): Navy: Knox: 1939–1941, FDRL; Steven Casey, *Cautious Crusade: Franklin D. Roosevelt, American Public Opinion, and the War against Nazi Germany* (Oxford: Oxford University Press, 2001), 20, 28; Sherwood, *The White House Papers*, I: 129.

10. *Life*, May 13, 1940; *Time*, July 15, 1940; *New York Times*, January 6, 1941; Ellsworth Barnard, *Wendell Willkie: Fighter for Freedom* (Marquette: Northern Michigan University Press, 1966), 132.

11. Marcia Davenport, *Too Strong for Fantasy* (London: Collins, 1968), 227, 229–31; Steve Neal, *Dark Horse: A Biography of Wendell Willkie* (Garden City, NY: Doubleday, 1984), 48–51.

12. *New York Herald Tribune*, August 27, 1939; Peter Schwed to Wendell Willkie, August 22, 1939; Willkie to Schwed, September 5, 1939, both in Correspondence, Willkie Papers, LL; Arthur Krock to Willkie, August 30, 1939, General Correspondence: Willkie, Wendell L., box 10, Van Doren Papers, LC; Barnard, *Wendell Willkie*, 134–35. Willkie's review continued, "The quality for which we envy [the Whigs] is not their morals, which were questionable, nor their principles, which were largely expedient, but their amazing vitality. They had a zest for life and few reservations as to when, where or how they should express it . . . The period of the great Whig families was one of lusty enjoyments, of full-flavored pleasures, of dangers taken with a relish."

13. Willkie to Schwed, September 5, 1939, Correspondence, Willkie Papers, LL; Neal, *Dark Horse*, 41–42.

14. Meiklejohn MS Diary, box 211, Averell Harriman Papers (hereafter "Meiklejohn MS Diary"), foreword, i, LC; Rudy Abramson, *Spanning the Century: The Life of W. Averell Harriman, 1891–1986* (New York: Morrow, 1992), 263–64; E. J. Kahn Jr., *The World of Swope* (New York: Simon & Schuster, 1965), 329.

15. Photograph dated June 11, 1939, box 881, Averell Harriman Papers, LC; *New York Times*, September 17, 1939.

16. Averell Harriman to Harry Hopkins, June 28, 1939; Hopkins to Harriman, June 30, 1939; Harriman to Hopkins, September 1, 1939; Hopkins to Harriman, September 8, 1939; Harriman to Hopkins, November 16, 1939; Hopkins to Harriman, November 25, 1939, all in Special Files: Public Service: Business Advisory Council: Harry Hopkins, box 147, Averell Harriman Papers, LC.

17. David Reynolds argues that the fall of France in June 1940 was the century's "fulcrum," contributing to the emergence of the "Special Relationship," the "rise of the superpowers," and the tendency toward European integration: David Reynolds, "1940: Fulcrum of the Twentieth Century?" *International Affairs* 66, no. 2 (1990): 325–50. See also Justus D. Doenecke, "U.S. Policy and the European War, 1939–1941," *Diplomatic History* 19, no. 4 (1995): 669; Marvin R. Zahniser, "Rethinking the Significance of Disaster: The United States and the Fall of France in 1940," *International History Review* 14, no. 2 (1992): 274–75.

18. Three excellent historiographical reviews of U.S. policy during this period are: Doenecke, "U.S. Policy and the European War," 669–98; David Reynolds, *From Munich to Pearl Harbor: Roosevelt's America and the Origins of the Second World War* (Chicago: Ivan R. Dee, 2001), 5–10; and J. Garry Clifford, "Both Ends of the Telescope: New Perspectives on FDR and American Entry into World War II," *Diplomatic History* 13, no. 2 (1989): 213–30.

19. J. Garry Clifford and Samuel R. Spencer Jr., *The First Peacetime Draft* (Lawrence: University Press of Kansas, 1986), 53.

20. Martin Gilbert, comp., *The Churchill War Papers*, 3 vols. (London: Heinemann, 1993–2000), III: 835.

21. David Reynolds, *From World War to Cold War: Churchill, Roosevelt, and the International History of the 1940s* (Oxford: Oxford University Press, 2006), 54; Waldo H. Heinrichs, *Threshold of War: Franklin D. Roosevelt and American Entry into World War II* (New York: Oxford University Press, 1988), 19–20, 36. "The Second World War actually consisted of two wars, one in Europe and the Atlantic, and the other in Asia and the Pacific," argues Akira Iriye. "The two theatres were, for the most part, distinct": Akira Iriye, *The Origins of the Second World War in Asia and the Pacific* (London: Longman, 1987), 1. Steven Casey notes that in the eleven months leading up to the attack at Pearl Harbor, FDR mentioned the Nazis on more than 150 occasions, but made only four references to Japan: Casey, *Cautious Crusade*, 12–13, 39.

22. Sherwood, *The White House Papers*, I: 10.

23. Gunther, *Roosevelt in Retrospect*, 19; Doris Kearns Goodwin, *No Ordinary Time: Franklin and Eleanor Roosevelt: The Home Front in World War II* (New York: Touchstone, 1994), 606.

24. Black, *Franklin Delano Roosevelt*, 1118; FDR to Grace Tully, November 26, 1943, Correspondence: Franklin D. Roosevelt, box 4, Tully Papers, FDRL. The backdrop for one of the skits at the 1939 Gridiron Dinner was an eight-foot-tall sphinx with Roosevelt's face, complete with cigarette holder. A delighted FDR

obtained it for display at his new presidential library: Frank Freidel, *Franklin D. Roosevelt: A Rendezvous with Destiny* (Boston: Little, Brown, 1990), 327.

25. John Morton Blum, *From the Morgenthau Diaries*, 3 vols. (Boston: Houghton Mifflin, 1959–65), I: 254; Rexford G. Tugwell, *The Democratic Roosevelt: A Biography of Franklin D. Roosevelt* (Garden City, NY: Doubleday, 1957), 14, 96–97. On FDR's elusiveness, see, e.g., Herbert Feis, "Some Notes on Historical Record-Keeping, the Role of Historians, and the Influence of Historical Memories during the Era of the Second World War," in *The Historian and the Diplomat: The Role of History and Historians in American Foreign Policy*, ed. Francis L. Loewenheim (New York: Harper & Row, 1967), 93–96; Warren F. Kimball, *The Juggler: Franklin Roosevelt as Wartime Statesman* (Princeton: Princeton University Press, 1991), 7; Heinrichs, *Threshold of War*, vii; Mark A. Stoler, "A Half Century of Conflict: Interpretations of U.S. World War II Diplomacy," *Diplomatic History* 18, no. 3 (1994): 395; John Lewis Gaddis, *Strategies of Containment: A Critical Appraisal of Postwar American National Security Policy* (New York: Oxford University Press, 1982), 8.

26. Oliver Lyttelton, *The Memoirs of Lord Chandos* (London: Bodley Head, 1962), 308.

27. Fireside Chat on Economic Conditions, April 14, 1938, PPA, VII: 248.

28. Isaiah Berlin, *Personal Impressions*, ed. Henry Hardy. 2nd ed. (London: Pimlico, 1998), 21, 26; Rosenman 1959 interview, 174–76, CCOHC; Cordell Hull, *The Memoirs of Cordell Hull*, 2 vols. (London: Hodder & Stoughton, 1948), I: 205–6; Interview with Arthur M. Schlesinger Jr., April 28, 2003.

29. Arthur M. Schlesinger Jr., *The Age of Roosevelt*, 3 vols. (Boston: Houghton Mifflin, 1957–60), II: 528.

30. King MS Diary, April 23–24, 1940, 14, LAC; Harold L. Ickes, *The Secret Diary of Harold L. Ickes*, 3 vols. (New York: Simon & Schuster, 1953–54), III: 516; Charles E. Bohlen and Robert Howard Phelps, *Witness to History, 1929–1969* (London: Weidenfeld & Nicolson, 1973), 135; Martin Weil, *A Pretty Good Club: The Founding Fathers of the U.S. Foreign Service* (New York: Norton, 1978), 103; Samuel I. Rosenman, *Working with Roosevelt* (New York: Harper, 1952), 9; "White House Wisps," box 116, Cuneo Papers, FDRL.

31. Robert Dallek, *Franklin D. Roosevelt and American Foreign Policy, 1932–1945* (New York: Oxford University Press, 1995), 532; Goodwin, *No Ordinary Time*, 602; FDR to Welles, July 11, 1940, box 262, Welles Papers, FDRL.

32. George M. Elsey, "Some White House Recollections, 1942–1953," *Diplomatic History* 12, no. 3 (1988): 359–60; Sherwood, *The White House Papers*, II: 752.

33. Warren F. Kimball, *Forged in War: Churchill, Roosevelt and the Second World War* (London: HarperCollins, 1998), 37; Bohlen interview (1873), Sherwood Papers, HL.

34. Hull, *The Memoirs*, I: 200.

35. James MacGregor Burns, *Roosevelt: The Lion and the Fox* (London: Secker & Warburg, 1956), 393; Jean Edward Smith, *FDR* (New York: Random House, 2007), 433–34; Reynolds, *From World War to Cold War*, 139. Humbler figures were also caught in FDR's web of connections. When the Australian minister to Washington, Richard Casey, was offered the job of British minister of state in the

Middle East, Roosevelt advised him that he "should accept this offer in the general interest." "Dick, this is grand," he enthused. "It will give me a direct and personal link with the Middle East I have never had before": Casey MS Diary, March 15, 1942, NAA.

36. Freidel, *Franklin D. Roosevelt*, 49.

37. Eleanor Roosevelt interview, July 13, 1954, Oral History Interviews, Small Collections, FDRL.

38. Goodwin, *No Ordinary Time*, 27–29, 379–84, 462–67, 492; Schlesinger, *The Age of Roosevelt*, II: 525–26; William L. Langer and S. Everett Gleason, *The World Crisis and American Foreign Policy*, 2 vols. (London: Royal Institute of International Affairs, 1952–53), I: 5.

39. See, e.g., Perkins, *The Roosevelt I Knew*, 29–30; Curtis Roosevelt, "Remembering FDR's Leadership," *Prologue* 38, no. 4 (2006): 36–37.

40. On Roosevelt's concerns about the effectiveness of the scrambling device on the transatlantic telephone, see Lamont, notes of conversation with FDR, February 5, 1942, 127-27, Lamont Papers, BL. See also Sherwood, *The White House Papers*, I: 445.

41. FDR to House, undated, series I, box 95, folder 3290, House Papers, YUL; FDR to House, April 10, 1935, in Elliott Roosevelt, ed., *FDR: His Personal Letters, 1928–1945*, 2 vols. (New York: Kraus Reprint Co., 1970), I: 472–73; Sherwood, *The White House Papers*, I: 225. I am indebted to the late Arthur M. Schlesinger Jr. and Godfrey Hodgson for bringing the FDR-House letters to my attention.

42. Michael Fullilove, "All the Presidents' Men," *Foreign Affairs* 84, no. 2 (2005): 14–15; Hull, *The Memoirs*, I: 200, II: 1585–86.

43. See Berle MS Diary, December 22, 1939, FDRL; FDR to Taylor, February 11 and 13, 1940, box 10, Taylor Papers, FDRL. FDR quietened Protestant opposition by designating the appointee, industrialist Myron C. Taylor, a personal representative rather than an ambassador: Long MS Diary, March 8, 1940, LC; FDR to George A. Buttrick, March 14, 1940, PPA, IX: 101–2. To maintain this fiction, the State Department refused Taylor allowances, offices, even official letterhead: Phillips MS Diary, February 11, 1940, 3703, March 19, 1940, 3795–96, April 10, 1940, 3836–37, HL; Phillips 1951 interview, 120–23, CCOHC; Hull to Taylor, March 18, 1940, 121.866A/39B, RG 59, NARA; Moffat MS Diary, March 19, 1940, HL.

44. See the documents in FRUS, 1940, I: 129–35; Berle MS Diary, March 16, 1940, FDRL. The idea was eventually abandoned on the State Department's advice: Roosevelt, ed., *FDR: His Personal Letters, 1928–45*, II: 1010.

CHAPTER 1: "A ONE-MAN AMERICAN MISSION OF CURIOSITY"

1. The previous two paragraphs draw on: Heinrichs, *Threshold of War*, 3; Kathleen Burk, "The Lineaments of Foreign Policy: The United States and a 'New World Order,' 1919–1939," *Journal of American Studies* 26, no. 3 (1992): 387; Manfred Jonas, *Isolationism in America, 1935–1941*, new ed. (Chicago: Imprint Publications, 1990), 24–31; Reynolds, *From Munich to Pearl Harbor*, 31–32; Warren F. Kimball,

The Most Unsordid Act: Lend-Lease, 1939–1941 (Baltimore: Johns Hopkins University Press, 1969), 2.

2. David Reynolds, *The Creation of the Anglo-American Alliance, 1937–41: A Study in Competitive Co-operation* (Chapel Hill: University of North Carolina Press, 1982), 30–33; Arnold A. Offner, "Appeasement Revisited: The United States, Great Britain, and Germany, 1933–1940," *Journal of American History* 64, no. 2 (1977): 380–81; Rosenman, *Working with Roosevelt*, 167.

3. Dallek, *Franklin D. Roosevelt*, 171–82; Reynolds, *From Munich to Pearl Harbor*, 42–50, 172–73; Barbara Rearden Farnham, *Roosevelt and the Munich Crisis: A Study of Political Decision-Making* (Princeton: Princeton University Press, 1997), 146–66; Casey, *Cautious Crusade*, 13; Heinrichs, *Threshold of War*, 8.

4. The previous two paragraphs draw on: Smith, *FDR*, 426; 500th press conference, November 15, 1938, PPA, VII: 597; Dallek, *Franklin D. Roosevelt*, 171, 187–98; Reynolds, *From Munich to Pearl Harbor*, 54–56, 63.

5. The previous two paragraphs draw on: Fireside Chat on the War in Europe, September 3, 1939, PPA, VIII: 463; Robert Dallek, "Woodrow Wilson, Politician," *Wilson Quarterly* (Autumn 1991): 70; Reynolds, *From Munich to Pearl Harbor*, 63–68, 173–74; Dallek, *Franklin D. Roosevelt*, 199–205; Ian Kershaw, *Fateful Choices: Ten Decisions That Changed the World, 1940–1941* (London: Penguin, 2007), 146–47.

6. Warren F. Kimball, ed., *Churchill and Roosevelt: The Complete Correspondence*, 3 vols. (London: Collins, 1984), I: 24; Kimball, *Forged in War*, 31.

7. Dallek, *Franklin D. Roosevelt*, 208–9; Freidel, *Franklin D. Roosevelt*, 324; *Time*, March 18, 1940; *Los Angeles Times*, September 19, 1939.

8. *Time*, February 19, 1940; Joseph Edward Davies, *Mission to Moscow* (London: Victor Gollancz, 1942), II: 312; *Washington Post*, April 1, 1951.

9. Welles, *Sumner Welles*, 7–8; *Chicago Daily Tribune*, February 18, 1940.

10. Welles, *Sumner Welles*, 8–10; *Washington Post*, August 17, 1941.

11. Welles, *Sumner Welles*, 9–18.

12. Ibid., 18–22, 25–29, 34–35.

13. Irwin F. Gellman, *Secret Affairs: Franklin Roosevelt, Cordell Hull, and Sumner Welles* (Baltimore: Johns Hopkins University Press, 1995), 59–61, 107; Welles, *Sumner Welles*, 1, 36–38, 57–59; Smith, *FDR*, 49–50.

14. Gellman, *Secret Affairs*, 31–32, 61–63; Welles, *Sumner Welles*, 63–107.

15. *Washington Times*, January 20, 1908; Gellman, *Secret Affairs*, 62–63, 106; Welles, *Sumner Welles*, 84, 112–15.

16. *Washington Post*, August 17, 1941; Gellman, *Secret Affairs*, 64; Welles, *Sumner Welles*, 126–27.

17. Welles, *Sumner Welles*, 123–24, 134–36, 138–41. In this period, Welles also wrote a history of the Dominican Republic, described in *Time* as "a ponderous, lifeless, two-volume work": *Time*, August 11, 1941.

18. Welles, *Sumner Welles*, 155, 196–97; Gellman, *Secret Affairs*, 21, 120–35; Mark Falcoff, "Too Impressive to Be Real," *National Interest* 52 (1998): 102–3.

19. Gellman, *Secret Affairs*, 33; Erik Larson, *In the Garden of Beasts: Love, Terror, and an American Family in Hitler's Berlin* (New York: Crown, 2011), 15; *Washington Post*, April 1, 1951.

20. Welles, *Sumner Welles*, 127–28, 197–200; Gellman, *Secret Affairs*, 136–40; *Time*, August 11, 1941; *Nation*, August 1, 1942; *New York Times*, August 3, 1941; Robert A. Divine, *Second Chance: The Triumph of Internationalism in America during World War II* (New York: Atheneum, 1967), 42.

21. Hull, *The Memoirs*, I: 202; Phillips 1951 interview, 129–30, CCOHC; Moffat MS Diary, October 6–10, 1940, HL; Long MS Diary, March 15, 1940, LC.

22. Gellman, *Secret Affairs*, 30–31, 160–61, 167–68; *Time*, March 11, 1940, and August 11, 1941.

23. *New York Times*, August 3, 1941; *Washington Post*, February 29, 1940; *Time*, August 11, 1941.

24. Ickes, *The Secret Diary*, III: 273, II: 351; Welles, *Sumner Welles*, 245.

25. 622nd press conference, February 9, 1940, PPC, XV: 139–40; *Christian Science Monitor*, February 9, 1940; *New York Times*, February 10, 1940.

26. 622nd press conference, February 9, 1940, PPC, XV: 141–43.

27. See, e.g., *News Chronicle*, February 14, 1940, noted in FO 371/24405 C2741/89/18, NA; Long MS Diary, March 12, 1940, 26, LC.

28. Hull to Welles, February 15, 1940, Special Mission to Europe, box 155, Welles Papers, FDRL; Wallace MS Diary, February 9, 1940, 2, UIL; Ickes, *The Secret Diary*, III: 138; Moffat MS Diary, February 3–12, 1940, HL.

29. The most useful sources are FDR's discussions with British ambassador Lord Lothian on February 1 and 6 and Breckinridge Long on March 12: Lothian to Neville Chamberlain, February 2 and 6, 1940, both in FO 371/24417 C1839/285/18, NA; Long MS Diary, March 12, 1940, 24–27, LC. Reynolds is dubious of FDR's claims in his conversation with Long: Reynolds, *The Creation of the Anglo-American Alliance*, 71–72. To this author, however, they read like an authentic glimpse of Roosevelt's thinking rather than a statement for posterity.

30. Both the main protagonists, Roosevelt and Welles, along with State Department officials George S. Messersmith and Adolf A. Berle, stated that the mission was Roosevelt's idea: Long MS Diary, March 12, 1940, 25, LC; Sumner Welles, *The Time for Decision* (London: Hamish Hamilton, 1944), 61–62; Clapper MS Diary, February 12, 1940, LC; Berle MS Diary, February 13, 1940, FDRL. Others believed the proposal emanated from Welles: Hull, *The Memoirs*, I: 737; Ickes, *The Secret Diary*, III: 138.

31. Long MS Diary, March 12, 1940, 25–26, LC; Fred L. Israel, *Nevada's Key Pittman* (Lincoln: University of Nebraska Press, 1963), 170–72. On Long, see Fred L. Israel, ed., *The War Diary of Breckinridge Long: Selections from the War Years, 1939–1944* (Lincoln: University of Nebraska Press, 1966), xi–xxv; Gellman, *Secret Affairs*, 231–32.

32. Dallek, *Franklin D. Roosevelt*, 220–23; Berle MS Diary, August 16 and 24, 1939, FDRL; Langer and Gleason, *The World Crisis*, I: 77–78, 87–88; Welles, *The Time for Decision*, 63–64; Sumner Welles, foreword to *Ciano's Diary, 1939–1943*, ed. Malcolm Muggeridge (London: William Heinemann, 1947), viii.

33. *Time*, August 11, 1941. See also Jean-Baptiste Duroselle, *L'Abîme: 1939–1945* (Paris: Imprimerie Nationale, 1982), 94; Phillips 1951 interview, 124, CCOHC. "It might be a good thing," FDR explained to the reporters in the Oval Office, "to

get somebody to see all the conditions in all the countries so that one mind would be able to cover the situation instead of having four separate minds reporting on separate things": 622nd press conference, February 9, 1940, PPC, XV: 140.

34. Schlesinger, *The Age of Roosevelt*, I: 408.

35. Long MS Diary, March 12, 1940, 26, LC. In a later meeting with Canadian prime minister Mackenzie King, FDR dwelled at length on Welles's accounts of his meetings with European leaders: King MS Diary, April 23–24, 1940, 5–6, LAC.

36. For example, his April 1939 call for Hitler and Mussolini to guarantee the territorial integrity of thirty-one countries for ten years, and his last-minute appeals for peace in August 1939: see Reynolds, *From Munich to Pearl Harbor*, 54; Dallek, *Franklin D. Roosevelt*, 197.

37. Lothian to Chamberlain, February 2, 1940, FO 371/24417 C1839/285/18, NA.

38. Castle MS Diary, February 13, 14, and 18, 1940, HL; Robert D. Murphy, *Diplomat among Warriors* (Garden City, NY: Doubleday, 1964), 37. The U.S. ambassador to France, William Bullitt, claimed that Welles "sold" Roosevelt on the trip "by saying it would make a hit with the ladies' peace societies": Wallace MS Diary, March 1940, 1, UIL.

39. Clifford and Spencer, *The First Peacetime Draft*, 8; Wayne S. Cole, *Roosevelt and the Isolationists, 1932–45* (Lincoln: University of Nebraska Press, 1983), 338.

40. Wayne S. Cole, "American Appeasement," in *Appeasement in Europe: A Reassessment of U.S. Policies*, ed. David F. Schmitz and Richard D. Challener (New York: Greenwood Press, 1990), 13. See also the comments of an American journalist to a British diplomat: Warner to John Balfour, March 3, 1940, FO 371/24251 A1723/605/45, NA.

41. The case for peacemaking as a motive for the Welles mission is made in: Langer and Gleason, *The World Crisis*, I: 361–62; Offner, "Appeasement Revisited," 384–93; Arnold A. Offner, "The United States and National Socialist Germany," in *The Fascist Challenge and the Policy of Appeasement*, ed. Wolfgang J. Mommsen and Lothar Kettenacker (London: Allen & Unwin, 1983), 420–24; Reynolds, *The Creation of the Anglo-American Alliance*, 71–72, 80–83; Reynolds, *From Munich to Pearl Harbor*, 74–75; J. Simon Rofe, *Franklin Roosevelt's Foreign Policy and the Welles Mission* (Basingstoke, UK: Palgrave Macmillan, 2007), 77–78, 83–84; and, to some extent, Dallek, *Franklin D. Roosevelt*, 216–18. A spirited rebuttal is provided in Stanley E. Hilton, "The Welles Mission to Europe, February–March 1940: Illusion or Realism?" *Journal of American History* 58, no. 1 (1971): 93–120. See also: Cole, *Roosevelt and the Isolationists*, 338–42; Cole, *American Appeasement*, 13.

42. Reynolds, *The Creation of the Anglo-American Alliance*, 31–32, 71–72; King MS Diary, April 23–24, 1940, 9, LAC.

43. See Rofe, *Franklin Roosevelt's Foreign Policy*, 77–78, 92–94; and FDR's comments in Morgenthau Presidential MS Diary, March 3, 1940, FDRL. On the same day that the president announced the Welles mission, his administration also invited neutrals to Washington to discuss the possibilities for postwar cooperation: Langer and Gleason, *The World Crisis*, I: 350–54.

44. Welles's writings after the fact also state that part of his remit was to ascertain the governments' views as to the possibilities of concluding a just and permanent peace: Welles, *The Time for Decision*, 61.

45. Blum, *From the Morgenthau Diaries*, II: 102; Hull to Kennedy, September 11, 1939, FRUS, 1939, I: 424. See also Casey, *Cautious Crusade*, 9, 13; Cole, *Roosevelt and the Isolationists*, 332–33. In private, FDR stressed that there could be "no inconclusive or precarious peace," which seemed to rule out a deal with Berlin in the absence of regime change: FDR memorandum, undated, Special Mission to Europe: Roosevelt, box 155, Welles Papers, FDRL; FDR to Chamberlain, February 14, 1940; FDR to Daladier, February 14, 1940, both in PSF (Departmental): State: Welles: January–May 1940, FDRL; Clapper MS Diary, April 22, 1940, LC.

46. Ribbentrop to Thomsen, February 14, 1940, DGFP, series D, VIII, 774–75; Thomsen to German Foreign Ministry, March 7, 1940, DGFP, series D, VIII, 867–68; Hilton, "The Welles Mission," 103. See also FDR's criticisms of Germany the day after the announcement: *New York Times*, February 11, 1940.

47. Hilton, "The Welles Mission," 103. Compare the bland departmental drafts attached to Welles to FDR, February 12, 1940, with the baroque final versions: FDR to Mussolini, February 14, 1940; FDR to Daladier, February 14, 1940; FDR to Chamberlain, February 14, 1940, all in PSF (Departmental): State: Welles: January–May 1940, FDRL.

48. Hilton, "The Welles Mission," 103; Kirk to Hull, February 14, 1940, FRUS, 1940 I: 8–9; Moffat MS Diary, February 25, 1940, HL; Welles, *The Time for Decision*, 73.

49. Welles was the driving force behind the January 1938 proposal and the conference of neutrals: Reynolds, *The Creation of the Anglo-American Alliance*, 69–71; Offner, "Appeasement Revisited," 384–85.

50. Stimson MS Diary, December 18, 1940, VHL.

51. Welles, *The Time for Decision*, 61; Rofe, *Franklin Roosevelt's Foreign Policy*, 90, 122; Ickes, *The Secret Diary*, III: 9; Clapper MS Diary, April 22, 1940, LC. Two persuasive characterizations of FDR's thinking are: Cole, *Roosevelt and the Isolationists*, 332–33; and George F. Kennan, *Memoirs, 1925–1950* (London: Hutchinson, 1968), 115.

52. *New York Times*, February 10, 1940; *Chicago Daily Tribune*, February 10 and 11, 1940; *Times*, February 10, 1940; Lothian to FO, February 13, 1940, FO 371/24405 C2400/89/18, NA.

53. Sure enough, rumors of his opposition found their way into the press and forced him to release a statement criticizing such "trouble-making" and complimenting Welles: R. Walton Moore to Francis B. Sayre, February 28, 1940, Personal File: 1938–1941, Moore Papers, FDRL; Hull, *The Memoirs*, I: 737–39; Hull statement, February 14, 1940, FRUS, 1940, I: 8; *Chicago Daily Tribune*, February 14 and 15, 1940; *New York Times*, February 15, 1940.

54. Moore to Sayre, February 28, 1940, Personal File: 1938–1941, Moore Papers, FDRL. See also Castle MS Diary, February 13, 1940, HL; Herbert Feis quoted in Stimson MS Diary, March 12, 1940, 29: 44–45, VHL.

55. Davies to FDR, February 10, 1940, PSF (Departmental): State: Hull: 1939–1940, FDRL. Another supporter was George S. Messersmith: Messersmith to Long, March 27, 1940, Messersmith Papers, UDL.

56. Phillips MS Diary, February 23, 1940, 3729, HL; Phillips 1951 interview, 130, CCOHC; Gellman, *Secret Affairs*, 34–35; Welles, *Sumner Welles*, 36.

57. Dallek, *Franklin D. Roosevelt*, 167–68; Kirk to Hull, February 14, 20, and 24, 1940, FRUS, 1940, I: 8–11; Hilton, "The Welles Mission," 107.

58. Gellman, *Secret Affairs*, 45–49, 123–24, 175; Murphy, *Diplomat among Warriors*, 35; Duroselle, *L'Abîme*, 94; Moffat MS Diary, February 3–12, 1940, HL; Wallace MS Diary, March 1940, 1, UIL; Ickes, *The Secret Diary*, III: 138; *New York Times*, March 24, 1940; *Chicago Daily Tribune*, March 31, 1940.

59. "Washington Merry-Go-Round" syndicated column, February 25, 1940; *Chicago Daily Tribune*, February 14, 1940; Ickes, *The Secret Diary*, III: 138.

60. *New York Times*, February 10, 1940; Langer and Gleason, *The World Crisis*, I: 363.

61. Vansittart note, February 9, 1940; Cadogan note, February 7, 1940, both in FO 371/24238 A1309/131/45, NA. See also Cadogan MS Diary, February 2, 1940, ACAD 1/9, CAC.

62. Chamberlain to Lothian, February 4, 1940; Lothian to Chamberlain, February 6, 1940; Chamberlain to Lothian, February 7, 1940, all in FO 371/24417 C1839/285/18, NA; Rofe, *Franklin Roosevelt's Foreign Policy*, 83–90; see also Belle Willard Roosevelt MS Diary, March 8, 1940, LC.

63. Murphy to Hull, February 10, 1940, FRUS, 1940, I: 6; Hilton, "The Welles Mission," 96–97; Johnson to Hull, February 12, 1940, box 262, Welles Papers, FDRL; *Times*, February 12, 1940. Ambassador Saint-Quentin showed that the French gave no ground to the British in their ability to patronize American statesmen. FDR's initiative was "showy diplomacy," he said, that suited the president's temperament and his desire for prestige: Duroselle, *L'Abîme*, 94.

64. Hilton, "The Welles Mission," 98–99; Paul Schmidt and R. H. C. Steed, *Hitler's Interpreter* (Melbourne: Heinemann, 1951), 168; *Chicago Daily Tribune*, February 25, 1940; Ulrich von Hassell, *The von Hassell Diaries, 1938–1944: The Story of the Forces against Hitler inside Germany* (London: Hamish Hamilton, 1948), 113; Thomsen to German FO, February 10, 1940, DGFP, series D, VIII, 757–58; Hitler to Mussolini, March 8, 1940, DGFP, series D, VIII, 879; Ribbentrop to Thomsen, February 14, 1940, DGFP, series D, VIII, 774–75; Elizabeth Wiskemann, *The Rome-Berlin Axis: A Study of the Relations between Hitler and Mussolini*, new and revised ed. (London: Collins, 1966), 236; German aide-mémoire, February 15, 1940, Special Mission to Europe, box 155, Welles Papers, FDRL.

65. *Time*, August 28, 1933; William H. Miller Jr., *The Great Luxury Liners, 1927–1954: A Photographic Record* (New York: Dover, 1981), 44.

66. Moffat MS Diary, "Diary of trip to Europe with Sumner Welles," introduction, HL; FDR to Welles, Special Mission to Europe, box 155, Welles Papers, FDRL; Welles, *Sumner Welles*, 198, 246; *Time*, March 11, 1940; Nancy Harvison Hooker, ed., *The Moffat Papers: Selections from the Diplomatic Journals of Jay Pierrepont Moffat, 1919–1943* (Cambridge, MA: Harvard University Press, 1956), 1–4; *New*

York Times, February 13 and 17, 1940; *Chicago Daily Tribune*, February 18, 1940; Betty Hynes, "Wisdom guides choice of Welles's first aid," Special Mission to Europe: Clippings, Welles Papers, FDRL. Foreign service officer Lucius Hartwell Johnson went along as Welles's private secretary. FDR's recently appointed personal representative to the Vatican, Myron C. Taylor, was also on board the *Rex*. The effect, William Phillips observed, to "add color to the idea that the President and the Pope have got something up their sleeves" in the way of a joint peace proposal: Phillips MS Diary, February 10, 1940, 3702, HL.

67. *New York Times*, February 16, 1936, March 23 and April 2, 1937, May 12, 1940; New York City Federal Writers' Project, *New York City Guide* (New York: Random House, 1939), 36; G. Carlyle Allison, CBC-CKY broadcast, February 28, 1940, box 262, Welles Papers, FDRL.

68. Moffat MS Diary, "Diary of trip to Europe with Sumner Welles," introduction, HL.

69. Moffat MS Diary, February 23, 1940, HL; *Life*, February 5, 1940; *New York Times*, February 18 and 24, 1940; *Chicago Daily Tribune*, February 24, 1940, *Time*, March 4, 1940.

70. Phillips MS Diary, February 25, 1940, 3735-3736, HL; *Chicago Daily Tribune*, February 26, 1940; Moffat MS Diary, February 25, 1940, HL; *Los Angeles Times*, February 26, 1940; *New York Times*, February 26, 1940; Welles, *Sumner Welles*, 246.

71. *Time*, March 11, 1940; Welles, *The Time for Decision*, 73; *Chicago Daily Tribune*, February 26, 1940; Moffat MS Diary, February 25, 1940, HL.

72. *New York Times*, February 27, 1940; Phillips MS Diary, February 26, 1940, 3737, HL; Welles, foreword to *Ciano's Diary, 1939–1943*, viii–ix, xii; William Phillips, *Ventures in Diplomacy* (London: J. Murray, 1955), 92; Report by Sumner Welles, FRUS, 1940, I: 21–117 (hereafter "Welles Report"), 21–27; *Time*, March 11, 1940; MacGregor Knox, *Mussolini Unleashed, 1939–1941: Politics and Strategy in Fascist Italy's Last War* (Cambridge: Cambridge University Press, 1982), 47–48; Ray Moseley, *Mussolini's Shadow: The Double Life of Count Galeazzo Ciano* (New Haven, CT: Yale University Press, 1999), 4, 92–93.

73. *Time*, April 5, 1937; Welles Report, 28; Phillips MS Diary, February 26, 1940, 3741, HL; Phillips, *Ventures in Diplomacy*, 150–51; Phillips to Hull, February 28, 1940, FRUS, 1940, I: 12–13.

74. *New York Times*, February 27, 1940; Welles Report, 28; Phillips MS Diary, February 26, 1940, 3741-43, HL; Phillips, *Ventures in Diplomacy*, 150–51; Clapper MS Diary, April 22, 1940, LC; Malcolm Muggeridge, ed., *Ciano's Diary, 1939–1943* (Melbourne: William Heinemann, 1947), 230.

75. Welles Report, 29–33; Malcolm Muggeridge, ed., *Ciano's Diplomatic Papers* (London: Odhams Press, 1948), 337–39; Phillips MS Diary, February 26, 1940, 3741-43, HL.

76. Pearson, handwritten notes, March 12 and April 22, 1940, Sumner Welles, box F33, Pearson Papers, LBJL; Muggeridge, ed., *Ciano's Diary*, 212–13; Sir Percy Loraine to FO, February 27, 1940, FO 371/24405 C3117/18/89, NA.

77. Knox, *Mussolini Unleashed*, 47–50; Kershaw, *Fateful Choices*, 129–38, 146–48.

78. Phillips to Hull, February 28, 1940, FRUS, 1940, I: 12–13; Phillips MS Diary, February 26, 1940, 3742–43, March 16, 1940, 3787–88, March 18, 1940, 3792, HL; Phillips, *Ventures in Diplomacy*, 151; *Time*, March 4 and 11, 1940. As Welles left, the Italian press blossomed with accounts of his cordial talks with Mussolini and Ciano: Moffat MS Diary, February 28, 1940, HL; *New York Times*, February 22, 1940.

79. *New York Times*, February 27 and 28, 1940; *Chicago Daily Tribune*, February 28, 1940; CTPS report, February 28, 1940, in Special Mission to Europe: Clippings, Welles Papers, FDRL.

80. Moffat MS Diary, February 28, 1940, HL; *New York Times*, February 28, 1940; *Time*, March 11, 1940; Welles, *Sumner Welles*, 248; Welles, *The Time for Decision*, 74.

81. Moffat MS Diary, February 29, 1940, HL; Welles, *The Time for Decision*, 74–75; *Times*, March 2, 1940.

82. *Times*, March 2, 1940; *New York Times*, March 3, 1940; Welles, *The Time for Decision*, 74–75; *Time*, March 11, 1940; *Christian Science Monitor*, March 1, 1940.

83. *Chicago Daily Tribune*, March 2, 1940; *Times*, March 2, 1940; Welles, *The Time for Decision*, 75; *Time*, March 11, 1940.

84. *Time*, March 11, 1940; William L. Shirer, *Berlin Diary: The Journal of a Foreign Correspondent, 1934–1941* (New York: Alfred A. Knopf, 1942), 235; Howard K. Smith, *Last Train from Berlin* (Sydney: Angus & Robertson, 1943), 33, 41–42. A series of illuminating articles about Berlin life were published in the *Christian Science Monitor*, January 10, 12, 15, 27, and 30, 1940.

85. Welles, *The Time for Decision*, 97; *Christian Science Monitor*, January 30, 1940.

86. Schmidt and Steed, *Hitler's Interpreter*, 169.

87. Hitler memorandum, February 29, 1940, DGFP, series D, VIII, 817–19.

88. Welles's itinerary in Berlin, Paris, and London is detailed in Special Mission to Europe: Appointment Schedules, box 153, Welles Papers, FDRL.

89. *Life*, April 1, 1940; *New York Times*, March 3, 1940; Welles Report, 33–34; Welles, *The Time for Decision*, 75; Clapper MS Diary, April 22, 1940, LC.

90. Welles Report, 34–41; memorandum of conversation, March 1, 1940, DGFP, series D, VIII, 821–29; Clapper MS Diary, April 22, 1940, LC. Welles was particularly offended by Ribbentrop's comparison of Germany's desire for hegemony in central Europe with America's Monroe Doctrine, the nineteenth-century proposition that the United States would not tolerate European interference in Western Hemisphere affairs. Welles carefully explained the Good Neighbor policy he had helped Roosevelt to devise.

91. Welles Report, 41; Pearson, handwritten notes, April 22, 1940, Sumner Welles, box F33, Pearson Papers, LBJL.

92. *Chicago Daily Tribune*, March 3, 1940; Welles Report, 43; Albert Speer, *Inside the Third Reich: Memoirs* (New York: Macmillan, 1970), 103, 113.

93. *New York Times*, March 3 and 4, 1940; Speer, *Inside the Third Reich*, 103; Welles Report, 43–44.

94. Speer, *Inside the Third Reich*, 103; Welles Report, 44; Welles, *The Time for Decision*, 83.

95. Welles Report, 44; Clapper MS Diary, April 22, 1940, LC.

96. Welles Report, 44–50; memorandum of conversation, March 2, 1940, DGFP, series D, VIII, 838–45; Offner, "Appeasement Revisited," 387; Welles, *The Time for Decision*, 89.

97. Moffat MS Diary, March 3, 1940, HL; *New York Times*, March 4, 1940; Welles Report, 50; Welles, *The Time for Decision*, 90.

98. Welles Report, 50–51; Welles, *The Time for Decision*, 90–91.

99. Welles Report, 51–52; *New York Times*, March 4, 1940; Welles, *The Time for Decision*, 91.

100. Welles Report, 52; Welles, *The Time for Decision*, 94.

101. Welles Report, 52–56; memorandum of conversation, March 3, 1940, DGFP, series D, VIII, 850–62; Welles, *The Time for Decision*, 91, 96–97. That afternoon Welles also met with Dr. Hjalmar Schacht, a minister who had fallen out of the Führer's favor: Welles Report, 56–58; Moffat MS Diary, March 2, 1940, HL; *Time*, March 11, 1940.

102. Moffat MS Diary, March 3, 1940, HL; Welles Report, 45–46, 50; Schmidt and Steed, *Hitler's Interpreter*, 169.

103. Moffat MS Diary, March 3, 1940, HL; Hans-Heinrich Dieckhoff memorandum, March 4, 1940, DGFP, series D, VIII, 864–65; Hilton, "The Welles Mission," 110–11, 116–17; Martin Gilbert, *Second World War*, new [2nd] ed. (London: Phoenix Press, 2000), 46–47; Hitler to Mussolini, March 8, 1940, DGFP, series D, VIII, 871–80; memorandum of conversation, DGFP, series D, VIII, 900–901; Wiskemann, *The Rome-Berlin Axis*, 236–40; Knox, *Mussolini Unleashed*, 81–84.

104. *New York Times*, March 3 and 4, 1940; Shirer, *Berlin Diary*, 235–36; *Time*, March 11, 1940; *Chicago Daily Tribune*, March 3, 1940.

105. *Chicago Daily Tribune*, March 4 and 5, 1940; Moffat MS Diary, March 4, 1940, HL.

106. *Chicago Daily Tribune*, March 5, 1940.

107. Ibid.; Moffat MS Diary, March 4, 1940, HL.

108. *Chicago Daily Tribune*, March 4 and 6, 1940; *New York Times*, March 5, 6, and 7, 1940; *Sydney Morning Herald*, March 6, 1940; Moffat MS Diary, March 6, 1940, HL. By coincidence, Joe Kennedy was also on the Orient-Express, which led to further press speculation: Joseph P. Kennedy unpublished memoirs, box 51, Landis Papers, LC (hereafter "Kennedy Memoirs"), 540–42; *Chicago Daily Tribune*, March 7, 1940.

109. The previous four paragraphs draw on: *Washington Post*, March 30, 1940; Sherwood, *The White House Papers*, I: 170–73; Goodwin, *No Ordinary Time*, 106–8; Address at the Laying of the Cornerstone of the Franklin D. Roosevelt Library, November 19, 1939, PPA, VIII: 580; Perkins, *The Roosevelt I Knew*, 102; Smith, *FDR*, 441–44.

110. *L'Ouest-Éclair*, March 8, 1940; *Time*, March 18, 1940.

111. Welles, *The Time for Decision*, 98; *Time*, March 11, 1940; Moffat MS Diary, March 7, 1940, HL; *Washington Post*, March 10, 1940; Alexander Werth, *The*

Last Days of Paris: A Journalist's Diary (London: Hamish Hamilton, 1940), 14–15; Massey MS Diary, April 29, 1940, UT.

112. *Time*, March 11, 1940; Werth, *The Last Days of Paris*, 15; Moffat MS Diary, March 7, 1940, HL. See also *New Yorker*, March 16, 1940; A. J. Liebling, *The Road Back to Paris* (London: Michael Joseph Ltd., 1944), 34–41.

113. Werth, *The Last Days of Paris*, 15–17; Moffat MS Diary, March 8, 1940, HL.

114. *Chicago Daily Tribune*, July 23, 1944; Walter Trohan, *Political Animals: Memoirs of a Sentimental Cynic* (Garden City, NY: Doubleday, 1975), 165.

115. Welles Report, 58–59; Welles, *The Time for Decision*, 98–99.

116. Welles, *The Time for Decision*, 99; Ernest R. May, *Strange Victory: Hitler's Conquest of France* (London: I.B. Tauris, 2000), 164.

117. Welles, *The Time for Decision*, 99–101; Welles Report, 59–66; Rofe, *Franklin Roosevelt's Foreign Policy*, 123.

118. Welles Report, 67; Welles, *The Time for Decision*, 101; Moffat MS Diary, March 7, 1940, HL; May, *Strange Victory*, 113–14, 125–26. The following day, Welles met with the finance minister and future prime minister, Paul Reynaud: Welles Report, 70–72; Welles, *The Time for Decision*, 103–4.

119. Welles, *The Time for Decision*, 104; *Chicago Daily Tribune*, March 9, 1940.

120. Bullitt to FDR, April 18, 1940, 121.840 SW/176 1/2, RG 59, NARA; see also Ickes, *The Secret Diary*, III: 216.

121. Hilton, "The Welles Mission," 114–15; Campbell to FO, March 8, 1940, FO 371/24406 C3654/89/18, NA.

122. Murphy to Hull, March 8, 1940, Special Mission to Europe: Memoranda, box 155, Welles Papers, FDRL; *New York Times*, March 8 and 9, 1940; *Time*, March 18, 1940; *Chicago Daily Tribune*, March 8, 1940.

123. Moffat MS Diary, March 10, 1940, HL; Welles, *The Time for Decision*, 104–5; *Chicago Daily Tribune*, March 11, 1940; *Times*, March 11, 1940.

124. Kennedy Memoirs, 551; Alfred Thorpe Stirling, *Lord Bruce: The London Years* (Melbourne: Hawthorn Press, 1974), 143; Liddell MS Diary, KV/4/186 (hereafter "Liddell MS Diary"), March 7 and 8, 1940, NA; Matthew Sweet, *The West End Front: The Wartime Secrets of London's Grand Hotels* (London: Faber & Faber, 2011), 27–29.

125. Kennedy Memoirs, 551; Moffat MS Diary, March 10, 1940, HL; see also Kennedy's comments in the *Times*, March 8, 1940, and the *Argus*, March 9, 1940. In 1950, Welles conceded that Kennedy's ghostwritten memoir was essentially correct insofar as it related to his mission: see Landis to Welles, September 20, 1950; Welles to Landis, November 28, 1950, both in box 51, Landis Papers, LC.

126. Vincent Massey, *What's Past Is Prologue: The Memoirs of the Right Honourable Vincent Massey* (Toronto: Macmillan, 1963), 280–81; *Chicago Daily Tribune*, October 8, 1939.

127. *Chicago Daily Tribune*, March 11, 1940; *Christian Science Monitor*, February 17, 1940; Welles, *The Time for Decision*, 108. British newspapers mainly confined themselves to assuring their readers that Welles had not come to Europe to make peace, and declaring the country's resolve to fight: see, e.g., *Times*, March 8, 11, and 12, 1940.

128. Kennedy to Hull, March 9, 1940, FRUS, 1940, I: 14–15; Cadogan, FO minute, March 7, 1940, FO 371/25254, NA; Belle Willard Roosevelt MS Diary, March 8, 1940, LC.

129. Stevenson to Hardinge, March 11, 1940, enclosing notes for the king, FO 800/324, H/XXXVII/64, NA; Andrew Roberts, *The Holy Fox: A Biography of Lord Halifax* (London: Weidenfeld and Nicolson, 1991), 191; generally see Offner, "Appeasement Revisited," 390. On Daladier's resignation, see May, *Strange Victory*, 335–36.

130. *Sydney Morning Herald*, March 12, 1940; Welles Report, 78–83, 85–87; *Times*, March 13, 1940.

131. *Chicago Daily Tribune*, March 12, 1940; *New York Times*, March 12, 17, and 29, 1940. Welles's English-born manservant Reeks also caught the imagination of the British press: *Chicago Daily Tribune*, March 13, 1940; *Life*, April 1, 1940.

132. Cadogan to Ismay, February 29, 1940, FO 371/24406 C3538/18/89; extract of War Cabinet conclusions, March 2, 1940, FO 371/24406 C3348/18/89, both in NA.

133. Martin Gilbert, *Winston S. Churchill*, revised ed., 8 vols. (London: Heinemann, 1966–88), VI: 4; Welles Report, 83–84; Minutes, War Cabinet Meeting 67 (40), March 13, 1940, 11:30 a.m., CAB 65/6, NA; *Life*, May 3, 1948.

134. Note, London, March 12, 1940, PSF (Safe): Welles Report, FDRL; Welles Report, 83–84; B. E. F. Gage, FO note, dated February 28 but probably March 28, 1940, FO 371/24407 C4618/89/18, NA.

135. Welles Report, 74–75; Cecil Beaton, *The Years Between: Diaries, 1939–44* (London: Weidenfeld & Nicolson, 1965), 56; also Welles Report, 72–74. Welles was impressed, however, by Halifax's "innate sincerity" and "character."

136. Minutes, War Cabinet Meeting 67 (40), March 13, 1940, 11:30 a.m., CAB 65/6, NA; Halifax to Lothian, March 11, 1940, FO 371/24406 C3815/89/18, NA; Halifax to Lothian, March 11, 1940, FO 371/24406 C3814/89/19, NA; Welles Report, 72–78.

137. Minutes, War Cabinet Meeting 67 (40), March 13, 1940, 11:30 a.m., CAB 65/6, NA; Halifax to Lothian, March 11, 1940, FO 371/24406 C3815/89/18, NA; Halifax to Lothian, March 11, 1940, FO 371/24406 C3814/89/19, NA; Welles Report, 72–78. Australian high commissioner Stanley M. Bruce also felt Welles was feeling for a peace proposal: Bruce to Menzies, March 14, 1940, Monthly War Files; Bruce file note, March 13, 1940, Supplementary War Files, both in Bruce Papers, NAA. On the same day, Welles expanded on his disarmament ideas to Secretary of State for Dominion Affairs Anthony Eden: note, March 13, 1940, PREM 4/25/2, NA; Anthony Eden, *The Eden Memoirs: The Reckoning* (London: Cassell & Co., 1965), 91–93.

138. Vansittart to Halifax, March 13, 1940, FO 371/24406 C3815/89/18, NA.

139. Halifax to Lothian, March 13, 1940, FO 371/24406 C3999/G, NA; Welles Report, 90; Kennedy Memoirs, 575.

140. Mr Sumner Welles' visit: Suggested list of guests, PREM 4/25/2, NA; Welles Report, 90–91; see also Moffat MS Diary, March 13, 1940, HL. On March 8, 1940, Chamberlain had asked Kermit and Belle Roosevelt for "minute particulars

about Sumner's background and upbringing": Belle Willard Roosevelt MS Diary, March 8, 1940, LC.

141. Johnson to Hull, March 23, 1940, enclosing excerpts from a parliamentary debate, 121.840 SW/172, RG 59, NARA; also Reynolds, *The Creation of the Anglo-American Alliance*, 82; Halifax MS Diary, March 11, 1940, A7.8.3, BIA.

142. Vansittart, FO minutes, March 12, 1940, FO 371/24406 C3814/89/18; March 13, 1940, FO 371/24406 C3815/89/19; March 14, 1940, FO 371/24406 C3815/89/19; March 18, 1940, FO 371/24406 C3949/89/19, all in NA. Despite his initial suspicion of the mission, Kennedy ended up a supporter, writing to Hull that Welles "did an exceptionally fine job here in getting facts from all types of people": Kennedy to Hull, March 14, 1940, Special Mission to Europe, box 154, Welles Papers, FDRL.

143. FO to Lothian, March 27, 1940, FO 371/24407 C4564/89/18, NA; FO minute, March 25, 1940, FO 371/24407 C4392/89/18, NA; also Scott, FO minute, March 30, 1940, FO 371/24407 C4695/89/18, NA. This view of Welles's behavior is borne out by a comparison of the British accounts of the March 11 and 13 meetings with Welles's own dispatches, in which he played up the British willingness to negotiate and played down his own role in pushing them to do so.

144. Moffat MS Diary, March 14 and 15, 1940, HL. Welles met briefly with Reynaud and Daladier at the Ritz before he caught his train, but the meetings were unremarkable: Welles Report, 91–92; *L'Ouest-Éclair*, March 15, 1940.

145. *Chicago Daily Tribune*, March 17, 1940; *New York Times*, March 15 and 17, 1940.

146. Welles Report, 96–104; Welles, *The Time for Decision*, 108–13; Muggeridge, ed., *Ciano's Diary*, 222; Muggeridge, ed., *Ciano's Diplomatic Papers*, 359–60. Welles later disputed Ciano's account of his comments: *Washington Post*, July 11, 1945.

147. Welles Report, 102; Muggeridge, ed., *Ciano's Diplomatic Papers*, 360; Moffat MS Diary, March 16, 1940; Knox, *Mussolini Unleashed*, 85.

148. Welles Report, 104; Welles, *The Time for Decision*, 113; *Washington Post*, July 11, 1945.

149. Muggeridge, ed., *Ciano's Diary*, 223. The British Security Service had a different, and somewhat garbled, account of the call from an unknown source: Liddell MS Diary, March 19, 1940, NA.

150. Radio Address in Connection with Christian Foreign Service Convocation, March 16, 1940, PPA, IX: 103; *New York Times*, March 17, 1941; Hull, memorandum of conversation with Lothian, March 22, 1940, FRUS, 1940, I: 19–20; Hull, *The Memoirs*, I: 739–40.

151. Knox, *Mussolini Unleashed*, 87; Kershaw, *Fateful Choices*, 148–49. In a final meeting with Welles on March 19, Ciano misrepresented Brenner as presaging "absolutely no change to Italy's non-belligerent attitude": see Moffat MS Diary, March 16 and 19, HL; Welles Report, 110–13; Muggeridge, ed., *Ciano's Diary*, 224; *Times*, March 20, 1940; Phillips, *Ventures in Diplomacy*, 151–52; Rofe, *Franklin Roosevelt's Foreign Policy*, 165–66.

152. Moffat MS Diary, March 18, 1940, HL; Welles Report, 106–8; Phillips MS Diary, March 18, 1940, 3793, HL. The next day, Welles was forced to deny an untrue report in the *New York Times* that he and the pope had discussed a Nazi

peace proposal: Moffat MS Diary, March 19, 1940, HL; *New York Times*, March 19 and 20, 1940; Berle MS Diary, March 13, 1940, FDRL; Hull, *The Memoirs*, I: 739–40; Hull to Welles and reply, March 19, 1940, FRUS, 1940, I, 18–19; *Chicago Daily Tribune*, March 19 and 20, 1940.

153. Moffat MS Diary, March 18, 1940, HL; Phillips MS Diary, March 18, 1940, 3793, HL; *Chicago Daily Tribune*, March 19, 1940.

154. The previous two paragraphs draw on: *Time*, April 1 and 8, 1940; *New York Times*, March 28 and 29, 1940; Pearson, handwritten notes, April 22, 1940, "Sumner Welles," box F33, 2 of 3, Pearson Papers, LBJL.

155. Welles Report, 21 n. 28, 113–16; *New York Times*, March 23, 1940; Hull, *The Memoirs*, I: 740; Berle MS Diary, April 3, FDRL. An indication of Welles's preoccupation with Italy was his determination to correct press reports about a map that appeared in photographs of his meeting with Reynaud, which seemed to point to a redistribution of territory that was unfavorable to Italy: see Welles to Phillips, April 3, 1940, 121.840 SW/155A, RG 59, NARA.

156. Welles Report, 116–17.

157. *New York Times*, March 29, 1940.

158. Statement on the Return of Under Secretary of State Welles from His Mission to Europe, March 29, 1940, PPA, IX: 111–12.

159. Pittman to Hull, April 3, 1940; Hull to Pittman, April 5, 1940, both in 121.840 SW/155, RG 59, NARA.

160. Interview with Arthur M. Schlesinger Jr., April 28, 2003.

161. Gellman, *Secret Affairs*, 194–95, 201–2.

162. Ibid., 201.

163. Casey, *Cautious Crusade*, 18, 27; although see Nicholas John Cull, *Selling War: The British Propaganda Campaign against American "Neutrality" in World War II* (New York: Oxford University Press, 1995), 64.

164. Sherwood, *The White House Papers*, I: 139.

165. 622nd press conference, February 9, 1940, PPC, XV: 140; King MS Diary, April 23–24, 1940, 2, 5–6, LAC; Clapper MS Diary, April 22, 1940, LC.

CHAPTER 2: "A SENSIBLE COLONEL HOUSE"

1. Roosevelt borrowed the term from Edward Weeks, the editor of the *Atlantic Monthly*: Weeks to FDR, May 17, 1940; FDR to Weeks, May 21, 1940, both in PPF 5553, FDRL.

2. "Blood, Toil, Tears and Sweat," May 13, 1940, House of Commons, in David Cannadine, ed., *Blood, Toil, Tears and Sweat: Winston Churchill's Famous Speeches* (London: Cassell & Co., 1989), 149.

3. Heinrichs, *Threshold of War*, 9–10; Kershaw, *Fateful Choices*, 91, 110–15; see also Stephen E. Ambrose, *Rise to Globalism: American Foreign Policy Since 1938*, 5th rev. ed. (Harmondsworth, UK: Penguin, 1988), 6.

4. Address at University of Virginia, June 10, 1940, PPA, IX: 263–64; Robert A. Divine, *Roosevelt and World War II* (Baltimore: Johns Hopkins University Press, 1969), 29–32.

5. Clifford and Spencer, *The First Peacetime Draft*, 10–11; Dallek, *Franklin D. Roosevelt*, 223–25; Message to the Congress Asking Additional Appropriations for National Defense, May 16, 1940, PPA, IX: 202; *New York Times*, May 20 and August 18, 1940; *Washington Post*, May 20, 1940.

6. Clifford and Spencer, *The First Peacetime Draft*, 3, 48, 55.

7. Reynolds, *The Creation of the Anglo-American Alliance*, 109–10, 112–13; Sherwood, *The White House Papers*, I: 150–52; Dallek, *Franklin D. Roosevelt*, 221–23, 228.

8. Kimball, *The Most Unsordid Act*, 57–60; Dallek, *Franklin D. Roosevelt*, 231–32; Jimmy Dunn, quoted in Moffat MS Diary, October 6–10, 1940, HL.

9. Arthur M. Schlesinger Jr., *A Life in the Twentieth Century: Innocent Beginnings, 1917–1950* (Boston: Houghton Mifflin, 2000), 305.

10. Stephen L. Harris, *Duffy's War: Fr. Francis Duffy, Wild Bill Donovan, and the Irish Fighting 69th in World War I* (Washington, DC: Potomac Books, 2006), 38–40; Douglas Waller, *Wild Bill Donovan: The Spymaster Who Created the OSS and Modern American Espionage* (New York: Free Press, 2011), 9–10; Anthony Cave Brown, *The Last Hero: Wild Bill Donovan* (New York: Times Books, 1982), 15–17; Corey Ford, *Donovan of OSS* (Boston: Little, Brown, 1970), 15.

11. Waller, *Wild Bill Donovan*, 10–12; William Jenkins, "In the Shadow of a Grain Elevator: A Portrait of an Irish Neighborhood in Buffalo, New York, in the Nineteenth and Twentieth Centuries," *Éire-Ireland: A Journal of Irish Studies* (Spring–Summer 2002): 24.

12. Waller, *Wild Bill Donovan*, 11–16; Brown, *The Last Hero*, 18–22, 24–26.

13. Waller, *Wild Bill Donovan*, 16–18; Harris, *Duffy's War*, 40–41.

14. Waller, *Wild Bill Donovan*, 18–20; Harris, *Duffy's War*, 51–53.

15. Harris, *Duffy's War*, 96–100, 147; Ford, *Donovan*, 11–12; Brown, *The Last Hero*, 37, 131–32.

16. Waller, *Wild Bill Donovan*, 22; Henry F. Pringle, "Exit 'Wild Bill': A Portrait of William J. Donovan," *Outlook and Independent*, January 9, 1929; Harris, *Duffy's War*, 351; Richard Dunlop, *Donovan: America's Master Spy* (Chicago: Rand McNally, 1982), 68, 101.

17. Harris, *Duffy's War*, 163–76, 209–10.

18. Waller, *Wild Bill Donovan*, 22–23; Harris, *Duffy's War*, 267–303, 307.

19. Harris, *Duffy's War*, 339, 349–60; Waller, *Wild Bill Donovan*, 24–29, 35.

20. Allen W. Dulles, "William J. Donovan and the National Security," Central Intelligence Agency, https://www.cia.gov/library/center-for-the-study-of-intelligence/kent-csi/vol3no3/html/v03i3a07p_0001.htm; Waller, *Wild Bill Donovan*, 23, 30; Pringle, "Exit 'Wild Bill' "; Ford, *Donovan*, 47, 56–58; *New York Times*, April 23, 28, and 29, 1919.

21. Waller, *Wild Bill Donovan*, 34–41; Ford, *Donovan*, 67–71; Dunlop, *Donovan*, 142–59.

22. Dunlop, *Donovan*, 160–69; Ford, *Donovan*, 71; Pringle, "Exit 'Wild Bill.' "

23. Waller, *Wild Bill Donovan*, 41–45, 47–48; A. W. Martin and Patsy Hardy, eds., *Dark and Hurrying Days: Menzies' 1941 Diary* (Canberra: National Library of Australia, 1993), 131; Brown, *The Last Hero*, 117–26; Smith, *FDR*, 287.

24. Waller, *Wild Bill Donovan*, 32–33, 51–54; Ford, *Donovan*, 80–83.

25. Knox to FDR, December 15, 1939, box 75B, Donovan Papers, USAMHI; FDR to Knox, December 29, 1939, PSF (Departmental): Navy: Knox: 1939–1941, FDRL; Thomas F. Troy, *Wild Bill and Intrepid: Donovan, Stephenson, and the Origin of CIA* (New Haven, CT: Yale University Press, 1996), 22–26; Waller, *Wild Bill Donovan*, 44, 54–56.

26. Martin and Hardy, eds., *Dark and Hurrying Days*, 85; Pringle, "Exit 'Wild Bill'"; Edgar A. Mowrer–Allen W. Dulles interview transcript, c. 1962, 10, 25, 27, Dulles Papers, MML; Waller, *Wild Bill Donovan*, 2; *New York Times*, May 4, 1941, and February 15, 1959.

27. Waller, *Wild Bill Donovan*, 56–57; FDR to Donovan, April 9, 1940; Donovan to FDR, April 10, 1940, both in PPF 6558, FDRL; *New York Times*, April 11, 1940.

28. Frank Knox to Annie Knox, July 6, 1940, Knox Papers, LC; *New York Times*, June 22, 1940; Troy, *Wild Bill and Intrepid*, 28–29; Deborah Davis, *Katharine the Great: Katharine Graham and Her Washington Post Empire*, 3rd ed. (New York: Sheridan Square Press, 1991), 108. The Donovans' house was later owned by Katharine Graham, publisher of the *Washington Post*.

29. Clifford and Spencer, *The First Peacetime Draft*, 3, 27, 72–78, 87, 103, 105; William Donovan, "Should the United States Adopt Compulsory Military Training as a Permanent Policy? Pro," *Congressional Digest* 20, no. 8/9 (1941): 208–9; *New York Times*, July 4, 1940.

30. Despite his later inflated claims, there is little evidence that William Stephenson, head of British Security Coordination in the United States, played any role in initiating the Donovan mission: see Troy, *Wild Bill and Intrepid*, 40–44; Gill Bennett, *Churchill's Man of Mystery: Desmond Morton and the World of Intelligence* (London: Routledge, 2006), 256, 370 n. 52. Donovan denied that he even knew Stephenson at the time of the mission: see his handwritten notation on Conyers Read, "British relations with the OSS," box 4, folder 4, Troy Papers, RG 263, NARA. Stephenson did, however, hear of the mission and inform his superiors in London of it.

31. Waller, *Wild Bill Donovan*, 59.

32. The meeting is described in William J. Donovan, "Address by Colonel William J. Donovan at the Union League of Philadelphia, April 29, 1941," *Union League of Philadelphia Annual Report* (1941): 80; Troy, *Wild Bill and Intrepid*, 45–47; Donald McLachlan, *Room 39: Naval Intelligence in Action, 1939–45* (London: Weidenfeld & Nicolson, 1968), 225–26; United States War Department, *War Report of the OSS* (New York: Walker, 1976), 5. Troy suggests the meeting took place at 5:15 p.m. on July 9, citing an ambiguous reference in Stimson MS Diary, July 9, 1940, VHL.

33. Ford, *Donovan*, 93; Hull to Joseph P. Kennedy, July 11, 1940, 470.0011 EW 1939/4570A; Hull to Herbert C. Pell, July 11, 1940, 740.0011 EW 1939/4570B, both in RG 59, NARA; Troy, *Wild Bill and Intrepid*, 30.

34. Troy, *Wild Bill and Intrepid*, 60.

35. Casey MS Diary, July 13, 1940, NAA; United States War Department, War Report, 5; *New York Times*, December 7, 1940. On Roosevelt's fifth-column concerns, see Dallek, *Franklin D. Roosevelt*, 224–27.

36. Edgar Ansel Mowrer, *Triumph and Turmoil: A Personal History of Our Time* (London: Allen & Unwin, 1970), 314–15; Mowrer-Dulles interview transcript, 5, Dulles Papers, MML; Naval Memoirs of Admiral J. H. Godfrey, Volume V, 1939–1942, Part I, GDFY 1/6 (hereafter "Godfrey Memoirs"), 19, 130, CAC; Ronald Tree, *When the Moon Was High: Memoirs of Peace and War, 1897–1942* (London: Macmillan, 1975), 126; Interview with William J. vanden Heuvel, February 6, 2012.

37. Moffat MS Diary, March 3, 1940, HL; Mowrer, *Triumph and Turmoil*, 314–15; Larson, *In the Garden of Beasts*, 74–76; Mowrer-Dulles interview transcript, 4–6, 27, Dulles Papers, MML.

38. Dallek, *Franklin D. Roosevelt*, 232; Thomas F. Troy, "Donovan's Original Marching Orders," *Studies in Intelligence* 17, no. 2 (1973): 40.

39. Mowrer-Dulles interview transcript, 3, Dulles Papers, MML; *New York Times*, December 7, 1940; Mowrer, *Triumph and Turmoil*, 314–15.

40. Kennedy Memoirs, 539, LC.

41. Hull to Kennedy, July 10, 1940, 841.00N/9; Hull to Kennedy, July 11, 1940, 740.0011 EW 1939/4570A, both in RG 59, NARA.

42. Kennedy to Hull, July 12, 1940, #2113, 740.0011 EW 1939/4571 1/3; Kennedy to Hull, July 12, 1940, #2133, 740.0011 EW 1939/4571 2/3; Kennedy to Hull, July 13, 1940, #2147, 841.00N/9 1/2, all in RG 59, NARA.

43. Welles to FDR, July 12, 1940, 740.0011 EW 1939/4571 1/3, RG 59, NARA; FDR to Knox, July 13, 1940, PSF (Departmental): Navy: Knox: 1939–1941, FDRL.

44. Hull to Kennedy, July 13, 1940, 740.0011 EW 1939/4571 1/3, RG 59, NARA.

45. Lothian to Halifax, July 10, 11 and 12, 1940; Lothian to Duff Cooper, July 13, 1940, all in FO 371/24237 A3542/90/45, NA.

46. Balfour, FO minute, July 16, 1940; see also the minute by J. V. Perowne, July 12, 1940, both in FO 371/24237 A3542/90/45, NA.

47. Lothian to Halifax, July 16 and 18, 1940, both in FO 371/24237 A3542/90/45, NA.

48. Liddell MS Diary, July 16, 1940, NA. See also Swinton to Halifax, July 15, 1940; Halifax to Lothian, July 16, 1940; Halifax to Swinton, July 22 and 23, 1940, all in FO 371/24237 A3542/90/45, NA.

49. F. Darvall to Whitehead, July 18, 1940, FO 371/24237 A3542/90/45, NA.

50. Frank Knox to Annie Knox, July 14, 1940, Knox Papers, LC; *Chicago Daily Tribune*, March 26, 1942; Casey MS Diary, July 13, 1940, NAA.

51. *New York Times*, July 15, 1940; Troy, *Wild Bill and Intrepid*, 47.

52. *New York Times*, July 16 and 18, 1940; *Chicago Daily Tribune*, August 18, 1940.

53. Clipper information enclosed with Juan Trippe to Averell Harriman, December 17, 1973, box 865, Averell Harriman Papers, LC; Meiklejohn MS Diary, March 10–11, 1941, LC; James Trautman, *Pan American Clippers: The Golden Age of Flying Boats* (Erin, ON: Boston Mills, 2007), 52–54; *Life*, November 3, 1941.

54. *New York Times*, July 15 and 21, 1940, and June 4, 1961; *Christian Science Monitor*, July 5 and August 1, 1940; John G. Winant to Bunse and "List of letters of introduction," both undated, box 81B, volume 34, Donovan Papers, USAMHI.

55. Sherwood, *The White House Papers*, I: 169–74, 177–79; Smith, *FDR*, 459–60; Black, *Franklin Delano Roosevelt*, 568–73.

56. FO minute, July 27, 1940, FO 371/24237 A3542/90/45, NA; A. G. Kirk to Rear Admiral W. S. Anderson, July 27, 1940, Kirk Papers, RG 38, NARA; Sherwood, *The White House Papers*, I: 235; *New York Times*, July 15, 1940; Liddell MS Diary, March 29, 1940, NA; Sweet, *The West End Front*, 27–29; *Chicago Daily Tribune*, October 8, 1939; Gemma Levine, *Claridge's: Within the Image* (London: Harper-Collins, 2004), 196.

57. *Chicago Daily Tribune*, July 21, 1940; *Manchester Guardian*, July 18, 1940; *Illustrated London News*, July 20, 1940; *New York Times*, July 9, 1940; Gilbert, *Second World War*, 110. One prominent diarist, Lady Violet Bonham Carter, found herself incapable even of finishing her sentence describing the French surrender: Mark Pottle, ed., *Champion Redoubtable: The Diaries and Letters of Violet Bonham Carter, 1914–1945* (London: Weidenfeld & Nicolson, 1998), 226–27.

58. *Washington Post*, July 16, 1940; *New York Times*, July 21, 1940; Gilbert, *Second World War*, 114–16; Malcolm Smith, "Battle of Britain," in *The Oxford Companion to World War II*, ed. I. C. B. Dear and M. R. D. Foot (Oxford: Oxford University Press, 2001).

59. Balfour, FO minute, undated, FO 371/24237 A3542/90/45, NA.

60. Two useful sources for the mission, which are relied on throughout the following account, are the itineraries contained in box 81B, volume 34, Donovan Papers, USAMHI.

61. Kirk to Anderson, July 27, 1940, Kirk Papers, RG 38, NARA; James R. Leutze, *Bargaining for Supremacy: Anglo-American Naval Collaboration, 1937–1941* (Chapel Hill: University of North Carolina Press, 1977), 100–101; Tree, *When the Moon Was High*, 126–27.

62. Keith Jeffery, *MI6: The History of the Secret Intelligence Service, 1909–1949* (London: Bloomsbury, 2010), 225, 442–43, 726–27; Bennett, *Churchill's Man of Mystery*, 257; Troy, *Wild Bill and Intrepid*, 43–44, 53–54. Around the same time, Donovan also caught up with Edgar Mowrer at Claridge's and suggested they "scatter out" to see what they could find: Mowrer-Dulles interview transcript, 5–6, Dulles Papers, MML.

63. *Washington Post*, March 4, 1940.

64. Balfour, FO minute, July 25, 1940; Lothian to Halifax, July 19, 1940, both in FO 371/24257 A3572/3216/45, NA.

65. James R. Leutze, ed., *The London Journal of General Raymond E. Lee, 1940–1941* (Boston: Little, Brown, 1971), 19, 21.

66. Engagement card, July 25, 1940, WCHL 6/44, CAC.

67. Vansittart to Churchill, July 23, 1940, PREM 3/463/1, NA.

68. Memorandum, undated, Trip Files: Trip to England: January 26–31, 1941, Willkie Papers, LL.

69. Itinerary and telephone message, July 25, 1940, both in box 81B, volume 34, Donovan Papers, USAMHI; Ben Macintyre, *For Your Eyes Only: Ian Fleming and James Bond* (London: Bloomsbury, 2008), 60–62; Patrick Beesly, *Very Special Admiral: The Life of Admiral J. H. Godfrey, CB* (London: Hamilton, 1980), xix–xx.

70. Kirk 1961 interview, 122, 210–11, CCOHC; Godfrey Memoirs, 129–30, CAC; Godfrey, "Interview with Colonel Donovan," August 2, 1940, ADM 199/156, NA; Godfrey to V. Cavendish-Bentinck, August 2, 1940, FO 371/252, NA.

71. Kirk to Anderson, July 27, 1940, Kirk Papers, RG 38, NARA; Armoured Division Dorking to Donovan, July 28, 1940, box 81B, volume 34, Donovan Papers, USAMHI; *Daily Herald*, August 7, 1940; "Washington Merry-Go-Round" syndicated column, December 12, 1940.

72. Will Swift, *The Kennedys Amidst the Gathering Storm: A Thousand Days in London, 1938–1940* (Washington, DC: Smithsonian Books, 2008), 226; David E. Koskoff, *Joseph P. Kennedy: A Life and Times* (Englewood Cliffs, NJ: Prentice Hall, 1974), 256–57; Itinerary and Kirk to Donovan, July 25, 1940, both in box 81B, volume 34, Donovan Papers, USAMHI; Troy, *Wild Bill and Intrepid*, 53; Leutze, ed., *The London Journal*, 28; see also Mowrer-Dulles interview transcript, 25, Dulles Papers, MML.

73. Telephone message, July 25, 1940; Cooper to Donovan, July 29, 1940, both in box 81B, volume 34, Donovan Papers, USAMHI.

74. Kirk to Donovan, July 25, 1940, box 81B, volume 34, Donovan Papers, USAMHI; Kirk to Anderson, July 27, 1940, Kirk Papers, RG 38, NARA.

75. Itineraries; E. H. Irvine to Donovan, July 27, 1940; telephone message, July 29, 1940, all in box 81B, volume 34, Donovan Papers, USAMHI; Troy, *Wild Bill and Intrepid*, 52; *Daily Herald*, August 7, 1940; Gerald Pawle and C. R. Thompson, *The War and Colonel Warden* (London: George G. Harrap, 1963), 88.

76. Telephone messages; Sevan to Donovan, July 29, 1940; Donovan to Bracken, August 27, 1940, all in box 81B, volume 34, Donovan Papers, USAMHI; Alex Danchev and Daniel Todman, eds., *War Diaries, 1939–1945: Field Marshal Lord Alanbrooke* (Berkeley: University of California Press, 2001), 96; *Daily Herald*, August 7, 1940.

77. Donovan to Bevin, August 5, 1940, box 81B, volume 34, Donovan Papers, USAMHI; *Daily Herald*, August 7, 1940. The description of Bevin draws on "The Labour Ministers," Overseas Papers, 1941, Menzies Papers, NLA; and Raymond Gram Swing's radio broadcast from London, July 25, 1941, box 16, Swing Papers, LC.

78. *Daily Herald*, August 7, 1940.

79. Waller, *Wild Bill Donovan*, 60; Dalton MS Diary, July 22 and August 2, 1940, LSE.

80. Leutze, ed., *The London Journal*, 27–28.

81. Godfrey, "Interview with Colonel Donovan," August 2, 1940, ADM 199/156, NA; Godfrey Memoirs, 129–32, CAC. See also Donovan to Slessor, August 5, 1940; Donovan to Newall, August 27, 1940, both in box 81B, volume 34, Donovan Papers, USAMHI; Langer and Gleason, *The World Crisis*, I: 715–16.

82. Godfrey, "Interview with Colonel Donovan," August 2, 1940, ADM 199/156, NA; Godfrey Memoirs, 129, 131, CAC; Donovan to Slessor, August 5, 1940, box 81B, volume 34, Donovan Papers, USAMHI; Troy, *Wild Bill and Intrepid*, 54–55.

83. Godfrey to V. Cavendish-Bentinck, August 2, 1940, FO 371/252, NA.

84. Godfrey, "Interview with Colonel Donovan," August 2, 1940, ADM 199/156, NA; Godfrey Memoirs, 130, CAC.

85. Clifford and Spencer, *The First Peacetime Draft*, 160–64, 170–72; Dallek, *Franklin D. Roosevelt*, 248–49; *New York Times*, August 3, 1940; *Washington Post*, August 3, 1940; 666th press conference, August 2, 1940, PPC, XVI: 86–89; Roosevelt, ed., *FDR: His Personal Letters, 1928–1945*, II: 1058.

86. Donovan to Slessor, August 5, 1940; Kirk to Donovan, August 14, 1940; Donovan to Newall, August 27, 1940; Donovan to Lee, August 28, 1940; Donovan to Bracken, August 27, 1940, all in box 81B, volume 34, Donovan Papers, USAMHI; *New York Times*, August 5 and 9, 1940; *Christian Science Monitor*, August 5, 1940; *Flight*, August 15, 1940; *Times*, August 5, 1940. The *Clare* was a four-motored, strengthened C-class "Empire" boat, previously named *Australia*.

87. Donovan to Lee, August 28, 1940, box 81B, volume 34, Donovan Papers, USAMHI; *New York Times*, August 5, 1940; *Los Angeles Times*, August 5, 1940; *Washington Post*, August 5, 1940; *Chicago Daily Tribune*, August 5, 1940. The flag was the civil air ensign, a light blue standard with a dark blue cross and a Union Jack in the upper left canton.

88. *New York Times*, August 5 and 6, 1940; *Washington Post*, August 5, 1940; *Chicago Daily Tribune*, August 5, 1940; Joseph P. Lash, *Eleanor Roosevelt: A Friend's Memoir* (Garden City, NY: Doubleday, 1964), 157–58.

89. *New York Times*, August 6, 1940; Frank Knox to Annie Knox, August 8, 1940, Knox Papers, LC; Donovan to Kirk, August 27, 1940, box 81B, volume 34, Donovan Papers, USAMHI; B. Mitchell Simpson, *Admiral Harold R. Stark: Architect of Victory, 1939–1945* (Columbia: University of South Carolina Press, 1989), 52.

90. *New York Times*, August 6, 1940; Stimson MS Diary, August 6, 1940, 30: 67–68, VHL. The following day, Stimson and Knox met to talk over Donovan's report: Stimson MS Diary, August 7, 1940, 30: 70–71, VHL.

91. Lothian to Halifax, August 7, 1940, FO 371/24237 A3542/90/45, NA; Menzies to Hopkinson, August 9, 1940, FO 1093/166, NA; Donovan, "Address," 81, 95; Interview with William J. vanden Heuvel, February 6, 2012.

92. The previous two paragraphs draw on: *New York Times*, August 9, 11, and 12, 1940; *Chicago Daily Tribune*, August 9 and 11, 1940; *Christian Science Monitor*, August 9 and 12, 1940; *Los Angeles Times*, August 12 and 13, 1940.

93. 668th press conference, August 9, 1940, PPC, XVI: 104; Perkins, *The Roosevelt I Knew*, 54; Goodwin, *No Ordinary Time*, 112; *Washington Post*, August 10, 1940.

94. *Los Angeles Times*, August 10, 1940; Lash, *Eleanor Roosevelt*, 159–60.

95. *Los Angeles Times*, August 10, 1940; *Life*, January 20, 1941.

96. Donovan to Tree, August 28, 1940; Donovan to Kirk, August 27, 1940; Donovan to Godfrey, August 27, 1940; Donovan to Newall, August 27, 1940; Donovan to John Bickell, August 24 and 29, 1940, all in box 81B, volume 34, Donovan Papers, USAMHI; Balfour to Nevile Butler, December 21, 1940, FO 371/24263 A5194/G, NA; *Los Angeles Times*, August 10, 1940; Dunlop, *Donovan*, 220.

97. *Christian Science Monitor*, August 10, 1940; *Washington Post*, August 11, 1940; *Chicago Daily Tribune*, August 11, 1940; *New York Times*, August 11, 1940; General Motors press release, January 17, 2009.

98. 668th press conference, August 9, 1940, PPC, XVI: 104; 669th press conference, August 10, 1940, PPC, XVI: 110–14; *Washington Post*, August 11, 1940; *New York Times*, August 11 and 12, 1940.

99. 669th press conference, August 10, 1940, PPC, XVI: 111–12; *Washington Post*, August 11, 1940; *New York Times*, August 11, 1940.

100. *New York Times*, August 13, 1940; *Los Angeles Times*, August 12, 1940; 670th press conference, August 12, 1940, PPC, XVI: 116–17.

101. Dunlop, *Donovan*, 221–22; Doenecke, "General Robert E. Wood," 169–70; ABP to Morgenthau, Morgenthau MS Diary, August 13, 1940, 293: 168, FDRL.

102. Pepper MS Diary, August 12, 1940, CPL; Stimson MS Diary, August 12, 1940, 30: 80–81, VHL; Dallek, *Franklin D. Roosevelt*, 248–49; Clifford and Spencer, *The First Peacetime Draft*, 175.

103. *Christian Science Monitor*, August 19–22, 1940; *Time*, September 2, 1940; Mowrer, *Triumph and Turmoil*, 318; *Chicago Daily Tribune*, August 18, 1940; Donovan to Bracken, August 27, 1940, box 81B, volume 34, Donovan Papers, USAMHI. Lord Lothian was unimpressed with the articles and told the Foreign Office they had not "caused any stir." However, a Whitehall official noted, "The importance to us of Colonel Donovan's visit to London is not to be measured by the 'weight' of these articles, or even of the attention they may attract in the US": Lothian to Halifax, August 26, 1940; J. V. Perowne, FO minute, September 18, 1940, both in FO 371/24237 A4153/90/45, NA.

104. Minute, December 3, 1940, AIR 8/368, NA; Ford, *Donovan*, 95. Lord Lothian wrote of Donovan's "splendid work for us"; the British foreign secretary, Lord Halifax, thought he was "one of our best and most influential friends in America": Lothian to Halifax, December 28, 1940; Halifax to Duff Cooper, undated, both in FO 371/24263 A4925/4925/45, NA.

105. Gilbert, *Winston S. Churchill*, VI: 672; Waller, *Wild Bill Donovan*, 60.

106. Sherman Miles to Donovan, August 31, 1940, box 81B, volume 34, Donovan Papers, USAMHI.

107. Miles to Donovan, September 4, 1940; Tree to Donovan, August 21, 1940; W. Y. Elliott to Donovan, September 4, 1940; Donovan to Elliott, September 18, 1940; Elliott to Donovan, October 4, 1940, all in box 81B, volume 34, Donovan Papers, USAMHI; Tree, *When the Moon Was High*, 126.

108. Donovan to Miles, October 1, 1940, and reply, both in box 81B, volume 34, Donovan Papers, USAMHI.

109. Unsigned letter to Donovan, August 29, 1940; Admiral Land to Donovan, November 5, 1940, both in box 81B, volume 34, Donovan Papers, USAMHI.

110. Donovan to Bracken, August 27, 1940; Bracken to Donovan, August 29, 1940; Edward R. Stettinius to Donovan, August 30, 1940; Donovan's secretary to Stettinius, September 4, 1940; Donovan to Bracken, September 23, 1940; Donovan to Stettinius, October 1, 1940; Donovan to FDR, October 1, 1940; Stettinius to Donovan, October 2 and 17, 1940, all in box 81B, volume 34, Donovan Papers, USAMHI. See also Bracken to Lothian, August 29, 1940, FO 371/24237 A3542/90/45, NA.

111. Sir Arthur Salter to Churchill, passing on Purvis's message, August 17, 1940, FO 371/24237 A3542/90/45, NA. Sir Archibald Sinclair agreed, writing, "We showed him a great deal and took him very largely into our confidence—I think we have had no reason to regret doing so": Sinclair to Halifax, December 7, 1940; also Halifax to Anthony Eden, December 5, 1940, both in FO 371/24263 A4925/4925/45, NA.

112. Clifford and Spencer, *The First Peacetime Draft*, 175, 214, 221; Remarks by William J. Donovan, WGN, Chicago, August 17, 1940, Compulsory Military Service Pamphlet Collection, HIL; *New York Times*, August 14 and September 15, 1940.

113. Clifford and Spencer, *The First Peacetime Draft*, 223; Donovan to Vansittart, September 26, 1940, box 81B, volume 34, Donovan Papers, USAMHI.

114. Clifford and Spencer, *The First Peacetime Draft*, 231; Dallek, *Franklin D. Roosevelt*, 223–24.

115. Cole, *Roosevelt and the Isolationists*, 363–65; Hadley Cantril, ed., *Public Opinion, 1935–1946* (Princeton: Princeton University Press, 1951), 973–74.

116. Donovan to Kirk; Donovan to Newall, both dated August 27, 1940, box 81B, volume 34, Donovan Papers, USAMHI; Balfour to Butler, December 21, 1940, FO 371/24263, NA.

117. Donovan to Tree, August 28, 1940; also Donovan to Bracken, August 27, 1940, both in box 81B, volume 34, Donovan Papers, USAMHI.

118. Mowrer, *Triumph and Turmoil*, 318; *New York Herald Tribune*, February 11, 1941; Gilbert, *Second World War*, 116–25.

119. The following section draws on Leutze, *Bargaining for Supremacy*, 95–97, 104–27; Reynolds, *The Creation of the Anglo-American Alliance*, 113–32; and Dallek, *Franklin D. Roosevelt*, 243–47.

120. Reynolds, *The Creation of the Anglo-American Alliance*, 124–27; Reynolds, *From Munich to Pearl Harbor*, 85; Cohen to LeHand, attaching the Acheson advice, August 12, 1940, PSF (Departmental): Navy: Destroyers—Naval Bases, FDRL. See also Leutze, *Bargaining for Supremacy*, 112–13.

121. Balfour to Butler, December 21, 1940, FO 371/24263, NA; Donovan to Bracken, August 27, 1940, box 81B, volume 34, Donovan Papers, USAMHI; *New York Times*, December 6 and 8, 1940. There is little evidence for Brown's claim that Donovan's law firm undertook the legal research that enabled the deal: Brown, *The Last Hero*, 151–52; Troy, *Wild Bill and Intrepid*, 58–59. He did, however, retain a copy of the Acheson advice in his files: box 141, folder 7, Donovan Papers, USAMHI.

122. J. R. M. Butler, *Lord Lothian, Philip Kerr, 1882–1940* (London: Macmillan, 1960), 297. On August 13 as the turning point, see Morgenthau Presidential MS Diary, August 14, 1940, FDRL; Dallek, *Franklin D. Roosevelt*, 245; Reynolds, *The Creation of the Anglo-American Alliance*, 124–25.

123. Jeffery, *MI6*, 443; see also Menzies to Hopkinson, April 2, 1941, FO 1093/193, NA.

124. Reynolds, *From Munich to Pearl Harbor*, 86–87; Edward R. Stettinius, *Lend-Lease: Weapon for Victory* (New York: Macmillan, 1944), 41–42.

125. "The Few," August 20, 1940, House of Commons, in Cannadine, ed., *Blood, Toil, Tears and Sweat*, 192.

126. Memorandum, undated, Trip Files: Trip to England: January 26–31, 1941, Willkie Papers, LL.
127. *Daily Herald*, August 7, 1940; Amanda Smith, ed., *Hostage to Fortune: The Letters of Joseph P. Kennedy* (New York: Viking, 2001), 458–59, 463, 480–82, 497.
128. Draft telegram and FO minutes, FO 371/24251 A4955/605/45, NA.
129. Mowrer-Dulles interview transcript, 27, Dulles Papers, MML.

CHAPTER 3: "HISTORY'S FOREMOST MARRIAGE BROKER"

1. Dallek, *Franklin D. Roosevelt*, 241; Iriye, *The Origins of the Second World War*, 114–18.
2. Clifford and Spencer, *The First Peacetime Draft*, 1–3; *Washington Post*, October 30, 1940; *New York Times*, October 31, 1940.
3. Harold Nicolson, *Diaries and Letters, 1939–1945*, ed. Nigel Nicolson (London: Collins, 1967), 125.
4. Winston Churchill, *The Second World War*, 6 vols. (London: Cassell & Co., 1948–54), II: 494–501. The letter is also reproduced in Kimball, ed., *Churchill and Roosevelt*, I: 102–9. See David Reynolds, *Lord Lothian and Anglo-American Relations, 1939–1940* (Philadelphia: American Philosophical Society, 1983), 43–48; Sherwood, *The White House Papers*, I: 222–23; Kimball, *The Most Unsordid Act*, 111–12.
5. 702nd press conference, December 17, 1940, PPC, XVI: 350, 354; Adams, *Harry Hopkins*, 197.
6. Fireside Chat on National Security, December 29, 1940, PPA, IX: 635.
7. 702nd press conference, December 17, 1940, in PPC, XVI: 354–55; see also Blum, *From the Morgenthau Diaries*, II: 208–9.
8. Fireside Chat on National Security, December 29, 1940, PPA, IX: 643. On FDR's post-election statements on the war, see: Kimball, *The Most Unsordid Act*, 121–24, 128–29; Dallek, *Franklin D. Roosevelt*, 255–58; Sherwood, *The White House Papers*, I: 223–27.
9. Kimball, *The Most Unsordid Act*, 151–52.
10. Sherwood, *The White House Papers*, I: 269–70.
11. Robert Hopkins interview, Newton Collection, FDRL; June Hopkins, *Harry Hopkins: Sudden Hero, Brash Reformer* (New York: St. Martin's, 1999), 11–14; Geoffrey T. Hellman, "House Guest," *New Yorker*, August 7 and 14, 1943.
12. George McJimsey, *Harry Hopkins: Ally of the Poor and Defender of Democracy* (Cambridge, MA: Harvard University Press, 1987), 3, 12–15; Childs, "The President's Best Friend"; Hopkins, *Harry Hopkins*, 18–21, 30; Adams, *Harry Hopkins*, 32; Robert Hopkins interview, Newton Collection, FDRL.
13. Hellman, "House Guest"; Adams, *Harry Hopkins*, 35–37.
14. McJimsey, *Harry Hopkins*, 42–43, 46, 52.
15. Sherwood, *The White House Papers*, I: 44; Childs, "The President's Best Friend."
16. Ward, ed., *Closest Companion*, 239; see also Sir Owen Dixon, *Jesting Pilate, and Other Papers and Addresses* (Sydney: Law Book Co., 1965), 143.

17. Franklin D. Roosevelt Jr. interview, January 11, 1979, Oral History Interviews, Small Collections, FDRL; Turner Catledge, "It's 'Send for Harry,'" *New York Times*, March 16, 1941. On Hopkins's loyalty to FDR, see, e.g., Sherwood, *The White House Papers*, I: 6; John G. Winant, *A Letter from Grosvenor Square: An Account of a Stewardship* (London: Hodder & Stoughton, 1947), 66; Earl of Halifax, *Fulness of Days* (London: Collins, 1957), 261; Ward, ed., *Closest Companion*, 185.

18. Hellman, "House Guest"; George Elsey and Robert Hopkins interviews, Newton Collection, FDRL; *Washington Post*, August 17, 1941; McJimsey, *Harry Hopkins*, 108; Letter from Diana Hopkins Halsted, September 26, 2011; Raymond Swing, *Good Evening* (London: Bodley Head, 1965), 232.

19. Childs, "The President's Best Friend"; James MacGregor Burns, *Roosevelt: The Soldier of Freedom* (New York: Harcourt Brace Jovanovich, 1970), 60; Hellman, "House Guest."

20. Martin and Hardy, eds., *Dark and Hurrying Days*, 125; *Washington Post*, August 17, 1941; *New York Times*, August 11, 1941; "Harry Hopkins," *Fortune*, July 1935; Hellman, "House Guest."

21. *Boston Sunday Globe*, May 25, 1941; Childs 1959 interview, 56–57, CCOHC; Thomas Corcoran quoted in "Hopkins—methods of operation," box 112, Cuneo Papers, FDRL; McJimsey, *Harry Hopkins*, 104.

22. James A. Halsted, "Severe Malnutrition in a Public Servant of the World War II Era: The Medical History of Harry Hopkins," *Transactions of the American Clinical and Climatological Association* 86 (1975): 24; McJimsey, *Harry Hopkins*, 117–26; Childs, "The President's Best Friend."

23. Halsted, "Severe Malnutrition," 9; *Chicago Daily Tribune*, August 29, 1943; McJimsey, *Harry Hopkins*, 127–28; Hellman, "House Guest"; Adams, *Harry Hopkins*, 161–63; Ickes MS Diary, July 24, 1939, 3603, LC; *Washington Post*, August 17, 1941.

24. Sherwood, *White House Papers*, I: 12; Franklin D. Roosevelt Jr. interview, January 11, 1979, Oral History Interviews, Small Collections, FDRL.

25. Stimson interview (1906b), Sherwood Papers, HL; Casey MS Diary, June 26, 1940, NAA; also Hull, *The Memoirs*, I: 922–23.

26. *New York Times*, January 10, 1941; Eleanor Roosevelt, *This I Remember* (London: Hutchinson, 1950), 190.

27. Sherwood, *The White House Papers*, I: 203–5; Hellman, "House Guest"; Adams, *Harry Hopkins*, 160; Danchev and Todman, eds., *War Diaries*, 269; Catledge, "It's 'Send for Harry'"; Childs, "The President's Best Friend."

28. This account draws principally on Welles, *Sumner Welles*, 1–3, 272–73. See also: Gellman, *Secret Affairs*, 235–38; John Morton Blum, ed., *The Price of Vision: The Diary of Henry A. Wallace, 1942–1946* (Boston: Houghton Mifflin, 1973), 68; *Washington Post*, September 18, 1940; *New York Times*, September 18, 1940.

29. Butler to FO, January 4, 1941, FO 371/26179 A101/101/45, NA; Sherwood, *White House Papers*, I: 231–32; Frankfurter interview (1886), Sherwood Papers, HL; Childs, "The President's Best Friend."

30. 706th press conference, January 3, 1941, PPC, XVII: 2; Childs, "The President's Best Friend."

31. 706th press conference, January 3, 1941, PPC, XVII: 2–6.

32. Morgenthau MS Diary, February 17, 1941, 373: 77B, FDRL; Butler to FO, January 4, 1941, FO 371/26179 A101/101/45, NA; FDR to Ickes, January 4, 1941, in Roosevelt, ed., *FDR: His Personal Letters, 1928–1945*, II: 1100; Sherwood, *The White House Papers*, I: 6.

33. Grace G. Tully, *F.D.R., My Boss* (New York: C. Scribner's Sons, 1949), 147.

34. See, e.g., Sullivan to Halifax, December 7, 1940, FO 371/24263 A5059/4925/45, NA; FO minute, December 5, 1940, FO 371/24263 A5017/5017/45, NA.

35. Bruce file note, January 29, 1941, Monthly War Files, Bruce Papers, NAA; Morgenthau MS Diary, February 17, 1941, 373: 77B, FDRL.

36. Ogden transcripts, October 7–8, 1991, box 1, Pamela Harriman Papers, LC; King MS Diary, April 23–24, 1940, 5, 11, LAC; Ickes MS Diary, May 12, 1940, 4380, LC; Reynolds, *The Creation of the Anglo-American Alliance*, 179.

37. The previous two paragraphs draw on: Butler to FO, January 3, 1941, FO 371/26177 A91/91/45, NA; Butler to FO, January 3, 1941, FO 371/26179 A101/101/45, NA; Butler to FO, January 4, 1941, FO 371/26179 A101/101/45, NA; T. North Whitehead, FO minute, January 6, 1941, FO 371/26179 A101/101/45, NA.

38. Martin and Hardy, eds., *Dark and Hurrying Days*, 130; Childs 1959 interview, 72, CCOHC.

39. Jimmy Dunn, quoted in Moffat MS Diary, January 31, 1941, HL. Frankfurter's Anglophilia was stoked during his time as the George Eastman Visiting Professor at Balliol College, Oxford, in 1933–1934.

40. Frankfurter interview (1886) and Monnet interview (1901), both in Sherwood Papers, HL; Jean Monnet, *Memoirs* (Garden City, NY: Doubleday, 1978), 166; Sherwood, *The White House Papers*, I: 232–33.

41. Casey MS Diary, January 6, 1941, NAA; Casey to Bruce, January 6, 1941, Casey Papers, NAA; Bruce to Casey, January 8, 1941, Monthly War Files, Bruce Papers, NAA; Frankfurter interview (1886), Sherwood Papers, HL.

42. Casey to Frankfurter, January 9, 1941, General Correspondence: Casey, Richard G., Frankfurter Papers, LC; Casey MS Diary, March 3 and September 24, 1941, NAA. See also Casey to Frankfurter, October 25, 1960; Frankfurter to Casey, November 1, 1960, both in General Correspondence: Casey, Richard G., Frankfurter Papers, LC.

43. Charles Lysaght, *Brendan Bracken* (London: Allen Lane, 1979), 178; Kahn, *The World of Swope*: 316–17, 329; Alfred Allan Lewis, *Man of the World: Herbert Bayard Swope: A Charmed Life of Pulitzer Prizes, Poker and Politics* (Indianapolis: Bobbs-Merrill, 1978), 228–30; Bracken to Swope, January 16, 1939, Hopkins microfilm, reel 19, Hopkins Papers, FDRL; Sir Ian Jacob interview, Newton Collection, FDRL.

44. Hopkins to Bracken, February 3, 1939; Bracken to Hopkins, March 13, 1939; Hopkins to Bracken, April 10, 1939; Bracken to Hopkins, August 25, 1940; Hopkins to Bracken, September 14, 1940, all in Hopkins microfilm, reel 19, Hopkins Papers, FDRL; John Colville, *The Fringes of Power: Downing Street Diaries, 1939–1955* (London: Hodder & Stoughton, 1985), 331; Sherwood, *The White House Papers*, I: 235; Johnson interview (1892), Sherwood Papers, HL; Gilbert, comp., *The Churchill War Papers*, III: 48.

45. *New York Times*, January 10, 1941; *Wall Street Journal*, January 9, 1941; Castle MS Diary, January 4, 1941, HL; Ickes MS Diary, January 19, 1941, 5123, LC; "Matters for Discussion in England" (1850), Sherwood Papers, HL; *Chicago Daily Tribune*, January 12, 1941. A rare supporter was Herbert Swope, who told Hopkins, "You will be a good man for the London job because your single minded devotion to the Boss and to the objectives of the war will free you from the pool of cross currents": Swope to Hopkins, January 3, 1941, box 60, folder 11, Accession I, Hopkins Papers, GUL.

46. Kimball, *The Most Unsordid Act*, 129, 132–41; Smith, ed., *Hostage to Fortune*, 528.

47. Eleanor Roosevelt to Hopkins, January 5, 1941; Frankfurter to Hopkins, January 6, 1941, both in Hopkins microfilm, reel 19, Hopkins Papers, FDRL.

48. *New York Times*, January 7, 1941; Sherwood, *The White House Papers*, I: 57.

49. *New York Times*, January 7, 1941. The novels were *The Blood of the Conquerors* by Harvey Fergusson and *The Honorable Picnic* by Thomas Roucat.

50. FDR to Hopkins, January 4, 1941, PPF 4096, FDRL.

51. The previous six paragraphs draw on: Annual Message to the Congress, January 6, 1941, PPA, IX: 663–72; *New York Times*, January 7 and 8, 1941; *Washington Post*, January 7, 1941; Rosenman, *Working with Roosevelt*, 262–64.

52. *New York Times*, January 8, 9, and 11, 1941; Hopkins to FDR and Hull, January 8, 1941, 121.841 HH/2, RG 59, NARA; Colville, *The Fringes of Power*, 331.

53. "Hopkins—methods of operation," box 112, Cuneo Papers, FDRL; Hastings Lionel Ismay, *The Memoirs of General the Lord Ismay* (London: Heinemann, 1960), 214; Sherwood, *The White House Papers*, I: 235; Colville, *The Fringes of Power*, 331; Pawle and Thompson, *The War and Colonel Warden*, 91.

54. *Daily Sketch*, January 10, 1941; *New York Times*, January 10, 1941; *Chicago Daily Tribune*, January 10, 1941; Sherwood, *The White House Papers*, I: 236–37.

55. Gilbert, comp., *The Churchill War Papers*, III: 51; Sherwood, *The White House Papers*, I: 237.

56. *Daily Herald*, January 11, 1941; Leutze, ed., *The London Journal*, 218; Sherwood, *The White House Papers*, I: 254–55.

57. Winant, *A Letter*, 66; Hopkins to FDR, January 10, 1941, box 56, folder 12, Accession I, Hopkins Papers, GUL; Reynolds, *The Creation of the Anglo-American Alliance*, 176. By contrast, Eden diarized of Hopkins that "I like him": Avon MS Diary, January 10, 1941, UB. Halifax recorded privately that his meeting with Hopkins was "very useful": Halifax MS Diary, January 10, 1941, A7.8.7, BIA.

58. The previous two paragraphs draw on: Engagement card, January 10, 1941, WCHL 6/44, CAC; Terence Feely, *Number 10: The Private Lives of Six Prime Ministers* (London: Sidgwick & Jackson, 1982), 11, 210; Anthony Seldon and Mark Fiennes, *10 Downing Street: The Illustrated History* (London: HarperCollins, 1999), 82–83; Christopher Jones, *No. 10 Downing Street: The Story of a House* (London: British Broadcasting Corporation, 1985), 137; Elizabeth Nel, *Mr. Churchill's Secretary* (London: Hodder & Stoughton, 1958), 25–27; Hopkins to FDR, January 10, 1941, box 56, folder 12, Accession I, Hopkins Papers, GUL.

59. Hopkins to FDR, January 10, 1941, box 56, folder 12, Accession I, Hopkins Papers, GUL.

60. Adam Gopnik, "Finest Hours: The Making of Winston Churchill," *New Yorker*, August 30, 2010; Churchill, *The Second World War*, III: 21; Ismay, *The Memoirs*, 215. Churchill's "searching gaze" sufficed as a job interview for his secretary John Martin: John Martin, *Downing Street: The War Years* (London: Bloomsbury, 1991), 4.

61. Engagement card, January 10, 1941, WCHL 6/44, CAC; Hopkins to FDR, January 10, 1941, box 56, folder 12, Accession I, Hopkins Papers, GUL. On Churchill's unanswered telegram, see Churchill to FDR, November 6, 1940, FO 371/24242 A4437/131/45, NA; Churchill to Lothian, November 29, 1940, FO 371/24249, NA.

62. Hopkins to FDR, January 10, 1941, box 56, folder 12, Accession I, Hopkins Papers, GUL; Colville, *The Fringes of Power*, 331.

63. Leutze, ed., *The London Journal*, 220; Sherwood, *The White House Papers*, I: 243.

64. *Daily Herald*, January 11, 1941; Cudlipp to Beaverbrook, July 22, 1946, BBK/C/175, Beaverbrook Papers, PA; *New York Times*, January 11, 1941; *Washington Post*, January 11, 1941; *Daily Mail*, January 11, 1941; Leutze, ed., *The London Journal*, 218–20.

65. Murrow interview (1902), Sherwood Papers, HL; Sherwood, *The White House Papers*, I: 237; Alexander Kendrick, *Prime Time: The Life of Edward R. Murrow* (Boston: Little, Brown, 1969), 226.

66. Tree, *When the Moon Was High*, 130, 132; Nicolson, *Diaries and Letters, 1939–1945*, 128; Louisa Kennedy, "House with a Lustrous Past," *New York Times*, March 31, 1985.

67. Tree, *When the Moon Was High*, 37; Pawle and Thompson, *The War and Colonel Warden*, 91; Colville, *The Fringes of Power*, 331–32.

68. Colville, *The Fringes of Power*, 332–33; Tree, *When the Moon Was High*, 138, 139; Mary Soames interview, Newton Collection, FDRL; Lysaght, *Brendan Bracken*, 184.

69. Lyttelton, *The Memoirs*, 165.

70. Colville, *The Fringes of Power*, 333–34; Lyttelton, *The Memoirs*, 165–66. See also W. Averell Harriman and Elie Abel, *Special Envoy to Churchill and Stalin, 1941–1946* (London: Hutchinson, 1976), 11. Sherwood disagrees: Sherwood, *The White House Papers*, I: 243.

71. Tree, *When the Moon Was High*, 37, 43–46, 134–36, 144; Nicolson, *Diaries and Letters, 1939–1945*, 128–29.

72. Tree, *When the Moon Was High*, 41–42, 133–34; Colville, *The Fringes of Power*, 334–35; Martin and Hardy, eds., *Dark and Hurrying Days*, 70; "Sketches of People," Overseas Papers, 1941, Menzies Papers, NLA; Cadogan file note, January 29, 1941, FO 371/26179 A101/101/45, NA.

73. Churchill to FDR, January 13, 1941, 121.841 HH/3, RG 59, NARA.

74. Hopkins to FDR, January 14, 1941, in Sherwood, *The White House Papers*, I: 244–45; Leutze, ed., *The London Journal*, 227.

75. Hopkins to FDR, January 14, 1941, in Sherwood, *The White House Papers*, I: 244–45.

76. Ismay, *The Memoirs*, 215; Leutze, ed., *The London Journal*, 224; Martin, *Downing Street*, 41; Lord Moran, *Winston Churchill: The Struggle for Survival*,

1940–1965 (London: Constable, 1966), 5–6. For security reasons, passengers were told not to ask for the prime minister's train but for the "eleven-thirty special."

77. Martin, *Downing Street*, 41; Leutze, ed., *The London Journal*, 226–27; John Bastock, *Australia's Ships of War* (Sydney: Angus & Robertson, 1975), 148; Geoffrey Cousins, *The Story of Scapa Flow* (London: Frederick Muller Limited, 1965), 163; Ismay, *The Memoirs*, 215–16; Ismay interview (1891), Sherwood Papers, HL; Sherwood, *The White House Papers*, I: 245.

78. Hopkins to Captain Miles, January 21, 1941, Book 3, Sherwood Collection, Hopkins Papers, FDRL; Hopkins file note, January 30, 1941, Hopkins microfilm, reel 19, Hopkins Papers, FDRL; Pawle and Thompson, *The War and Colonel Warden*, 92; Martin, *Downing Street*, 40; Ismay, *The Memoirs*, 216; Halifax, *Fulness of Days*, 237–38; Martin, *Downing Street*, 42.

79. *Times*, January 18, 1941; *New York Times*, January 19, 1941; Ismay, *The Memoirs*, 217; Ismay interview (1891), Sherwood Papers, HL. On the speeches given by Churchill and Hopkins that evening at the Glasgow City Chambers, see: Martin, *Downing Street*, 42; *Times*, January 18, 1941; *New York Times*, January 18, 19, and 21, 1941; *Glasgow Herald*, January 18, 1941; Hopkins to Hull, January 20, 1941, 121.841 HH/6, RG 59, NARA.

80. Martin, *Downing Street*, 42; Thomas Johnston, *Memories* (London: Collins, 1952), 145; *Herald Scotland*, October 19, 2010. The king later complained to Hopkins about the lord provost's unshaven features: Hopkins file note, January 30, 1941, Hopkins microfilm, reel 19, Hopkins Papers, FDRL.

81. This account of Hopkins's speech is derived from: Johnston, *Memories*, 146; Moran, *Winston Churchill*, 6; and Ismay, *The Memoirs*, 217. The biblical quotation is from Ruth 1:16.

82. John Martin and Mary Soames interviews, Newton Collection, FDRL; Moran, *Winston Churchill*, 6; Winant, *A Letter*, 20–21; Ismay, *The Memoirs*, 217.

83. Plantagenet Somerset Fry, *Chequers: The Country Home of Britain's Prime Ministers* (London: H.M.S.O., 1977), ix–x, 21, 24; D. H. Elletson, *Chequers and the Prime Ministers* (London: Robert Hale, 1970), 106–7.

84. Elletson, *Chequers*, 113; J. G. Jenkins, *Chequers: A History of the Prime Minister's Buckinghamshire Home* (Oxford: Pergamon Press, 1967), 146; Pamela Harriman and Mary Soames interviews, Newton Collection, FDRL; Ismay, *The Memoirs*, 217; Martin, *Downing Street*, 39.

85. Gilbert, comp., *The Churchill War Papers*, III: 97; *Daily Mail*, February 6, 1941; W. Ridsdale, FO minute, January 25, 1941, FO 371/26179 A101/101/45, NA.

86. Churchill, *The Second World War*, III: 22.

87. FDR to Hopkins, January 15, 1941, Book 3, Sherwood Collection, Hopkins Papers, FDRL.

88. Ickes MS Diary, January 19, 1941, 5126, LC. Ickes had been worried for some time about Kennedy speculating while in London: see Ickes MS Diary, July 24, 1939, 3609, LC. On Kennedy's financial practices, see, e.g., Peter Collier and David Horowitz, *The Kennedys: An American Drama* (London: Secker & Warburg, 1984), 42–43; Smith, ed., *Hostage to Fortune*, 57, 108–9.

89. Ickes records that he received the information from Alfred Bergman on January 14 and passed it to Grace Tully immediately. By lunchtime the following day, FDR had dictated and signed the letter for transport to London via Clipper: Ickes MS Diary, January 19, 1941, 5126, LC. On Kennedy and the Willkie campaign, see Neal, *Dark Horse*, 168–69.

90. Smith, ed., *Hostage to Fortune*, 524–29; Ickes MS Diary, January 19, 1941, 5147, LC; Langer and Gleason, *The World Crisis*, II: 268; Michael R. Beschloss, *Kennedy and Roosevelt: The Uneasy Alliance* (New York: Norton, 1980), 235–41; Kimball, *The Most Unsordid Act*, 191.

91. Lee MS Diary, July 25, 1941, USAMHI; *Star*, January 10, 1941. This summary of meetings draws on "Mr Harry Hopkins' appointments," Sherwood Collection, Hopkins Papers, FDRL.

92. Massey, *What's Past Is Prologue*, 280–81; Martin and Hardy, eds., *Dark and Hurrying Days*, 62; Amy Helen Bell, *London Was Ours: Diaries and Memoirs of the London Blitz* (London: I.B. Tauris, 2008), 30.

93. Bell, *London Was Ours*, 5; Massey, *What's Past Is Prologue*, 280–81; *Chicago Daily Tribune*, October 8, 1939; *New York Times*, February 2, 1941.

94. Cudlipp to Beaverbrook, July 22, 1946, BBK/C/175, Beaverbrook Papers, PA.

95. W. Ridsdale, FO minute, January 25, 1941, FO 371/26179 A101/101/45, NA.

96. J. Edgar Hoover to Edwin M. Watson, February 12, 1941: Book 3, Sherwood Collection, Hopkins Papers, FDRL; *Sunday Times*, February 2, 1941.

97. Cudlipp to Beaverbrook, July 22, 1946, BBK/C/175, Beaverbrook Papers, PA. Most of this letter is extracted in Sherwood, *The White House Papers*, I: 248–49.

98. Colville, *The Fringes of Power*, 340–41; Somerset Fry, *Chequers*, 31.

99. Hopkins file note, January 25, 1941, Hopkins microfilm, reel 19, Hopkins Papers, FDRL.

100. Colville, *The Fringes of Power*, 344.

101. Somerset Fry, *Chequers*, 30; Colville, *The Fringes of Power*, 345–47.

102. Colville, *The Fringes of Power*, 347; Gilbert, *Winston S. Churchill*, VI: 996.

103. FDR to Hopkins, January 26, 1941, 121.841 HH/10A, RG 59, NARA; Hopkins to Churchill, January 27, 1941, PREM 4/25/3, NA; Minutes, War Cabinet Meeting 10 (41), 5 p.m., January 27, 1941, CAB 65/17, NA. In these cables, Hopkins also received FDR's permission to extend the length of his stay in Britain.

104. Hopkins to FDR and Hull, January 27, 1941, 121.841 HH/9, RG 59, NARA; see also *New York Times*, January 25, 1941; Roberts, *The Holy Fox*, 281.

105. Massey MS Diary, January 29, 1941, UT.

106. *Daily Mail*, February 6, 1941.

107. Hopkins to FDR and Hull, January 28, 1941, 740.0011 EW 1939/8061 11/12, RG 59, NARA; Gilbert, *Second World War*, 130–31.

108. Sherwood, *The White House Papers*, I: 257–58; Hopkins to FDR and Hull, February 3, 1941, 121.841 HH/10 3/7, RG 59, NARA.

109. Childs, "The President's Best Friend"; Roosevelt, *This I Remember*, 155–56, 210; Theo Aronson, *The Royal Family at War* (London: John Murray, 1993), 4–10, 77–78, 113–14; Roy Nash, *Buckingham Palace: The Place and the People*

(London: Macdonald Futura, 1980), 102–3, 107–8. A fortnight earlier, Hopkins had made a brief introductory call on the king. He forgot to present his credentials, which were later delivered by messenger: FDR to King George VI, January 4, 1941, PPF 4096, FDRL; Johnson to Lascelles, January 14, 1941; Lascelles to Johnson, January 15, 1941, both in Sherwood Collection, Hopkins Papers, FDRL; *New York Times*, January 14, 1941.

110. Hopkins file note, January 30, 1941, Hopkins microfilm, reel 19, Hopkins Papers, FDRL; Nash, *Buckingham Palace*, 110; Roosevelt, *This I Remember*, 210; *New York Times*, May 29 and June 12, 1939.

111. Hopkins file note, January 30, 1941, Hopkins microfilm, reel 19, Hopkins Papers, FDRL; *New York Times*, June 23, September 8, and November 17, 1940. Another Hopkins file note dated the same day describes his meeting with the exiled King Haakon VII of Norway.

112. The previous three paragraphs draw on: *New York Times*, January 31, 1941; *Washington Post*, January 31, 1941; Sherwood, *The White House Papers*, I: 207–8, II: 933–34; Rosenman, *Working with Roosevelt*, 145, 148; Hopkins to FDR, January 30, 1941, 121.841 HH/11, RG 59, NARA; Radio Address on the Occasion of the President's Eighth Birthday Ball for the Benefit of Crippled Children, January 30, 1941, PPA, X: 8–9.

113. *Times*, February 1, 1941; *Daily Telegraph*, February 1, 1941. On HMS *Jervis Bay*, see Gerald Duskin and Ralph Segman, *If the Gods Are Good: The Epic Sacrifice of HMS* Jervis Bay (Annapolis, MD: Naval Institute Press, 2004).

114. Gilbert, comp., *The Churchill War Papers*, III: 165. Hopkins spent the rest of the weekend at Beaverbrook's country place in Surrey, Cherkley Court. See: Engagement Diary, February 2, 1941, BBK/K/2/81; Cherkley Court Visitors' Book, February 2/3, 1941, BBK/K/2/110, both in Beaverbrook Papers, PA; Hopkins to FDR and Hull, February 1, 1941, 121.841 HH/10 2/7, RG 59, NARA; Sherwood, *The White House Papers*, I: 253; Clive Aslet, "Cherkley Court," *Country Life*, April 19, 2007; Sally Bedell Smith, *Reflected Glory: The Life of Pamela Churchill Harriman* (New York: Simon & Schuster, 1996), 93; Joseph P. Lash, *Roosevelt and Churchill, 1939–1941: The Partnership That Saved the West* (London: Deutsch, 1977), 286; Lash, *Eleanor Roosevelt*, 208; Ben Pimlott, ed., *The Second World War Diary of Hugh Dalton, 1940–45* (London: Jonathan Cape, 1986), 159, 172.

115. Hopkins to Marshall, February 3, 1941, 121.841 HH/12, RG 59, NARA; *Chicago Daily Tribune*, May 5, 1941; Eden to Halifax, February 5, 1941, FO 371/26177 A657/91/45, NA; Hopkins to FDR and Hull, February 8, 1941, 740.0011 EW 1939/8145 4/5, RG 59, NARA; Dallek, *Franklin D. Roosevelt*, 271. See also Hopkins memorandum, January 24, 1942, Hopkins microfilm, reel 19, Hopkins Papers, FDRL.

116. Sherwood, *The White House Papers*, I: 260–62; Childs, "The President's Best Friend"; Pawle and Thompson, *The War and Colonel Warden*, 94.

117. Hopkins to Churchill, January 8, 1941, PREM 4/25/3, NA.

118. "Mr. Harry Hopkins' appointments," Book 4, Sherwood Collection, Hopkins Papers, FDRL; Sherwood, *The White House Papers*, I: 261–62; Thompson interview (1906d), Sherwood Papers, HL; Johnson to Thompson, February 8, 1941,

PREM 4/25/3, NA; Johnson to Hull, February 10, 1941, 121.841 HH/19, RG 59, NARA; *New York Times*, February 11, 12, 13, 14, 15, 16, and 17, 1941.

119. Thompson to Jarrett, January 26, 1941; Thompson to Churchill, January 30, 1941; Thompson to Churchill, February 6, 1941, all in PREM 4/25/3, NA.

120. MK to Mallet, March 5, 1941; Thompson to Martin, July 2, 1941; Martin to Mallet, July 3, 1941; Mallet to Martin, July 7, 1941, all in PREM 4/25/3, NA; *New York Times*, February 17, 1941. Officials were careful to ensure that the U.S. government did not receive the bill for the officer's expenses.

121. Hopkins to Hull, February 6, 1941, 121.841 HH/10 4/7, RG 59, NARA; *New York Herald Tribune*, February 11, 1941. Hopkins's documents included an aide-mémoire on the import situation prepared for FDR by Professor Lindemann: see Churchill note, January 29, 1941, FO 371/28937, NA.

122. *New York Herald Tribune*, February 17, 1941; *New York Times*, February 17, 1941; *Washington Post*, February 17, 1941.

123. *New York Times*, February 17, 1941; Winant, *A Letter*, 18; *Washington Post*, February 17, 1941; *Time*, February 24, 1941; Morgenthau MS Diary, February 18, 1941, 373: 73, FDRL; *New York Herald Tribune*, February 18, 1941; Harriman and Abel, *Special Envoy*, 12.

124. *New York Herald Tribune*, February 18, 1941; *Time*, February 24, 1941; Blum, *From the Morgenthau Diaries*, II: 230–31; Henry R. Luce, "The American Century," *Life*, February 17, 1941; see also FDR's comments in 719th press conference, February 18, 1941, PPC, XVII: 129–30. Morgenthau thought Hopkins looked "wonderful," with "Yorkshire pink cheeks": Morgenthau MS Diary, February 17, 1941, 373: 49–50, FDRL.

125. Halifax MS Diary, February 19, 1941, A7.8.8, BIA. Halifax also learned about the latest European developments from the envoy, writing to Churchill, "I was very glad to learn a good deal of your latest mind from Hopkins": Halifax to Churchill, February 21, 1941, PREM 4/27/9, NA.

126. Stimson MS Diary, February 26 and March 5, 1941, VHL.

127. Mary Soames interview, Newton Collection, FDRL.

128. Most historians of the alliance agree: see, e.g., Kimball, *Forged in War*, 78; David Reynolds, "Roosevelt, Churchill, and the Wartime Anglo-American Alliance, 1939–1945: Towards a New Synthesis," in *The "Special Relationship": Anglo-American Relations since 1945*, ed. William Roger Louis and Hedley Bull (Oxford: Clarendon, 1986), 22; Heinrichs, *Threshold of War*, 19.

129. Heinrichs, *Threshold of War*, 19.

130. Churchill to FDR, January 28, 1941, 740.0011 EW 1939/7979 1/2, RG 59, NARA.

131. Ickes, *The Secret Diary*, III: 429. See also Morgenthau MS Diary, February 18, 1941, 373: 73, FDRL.

132. Ickes, *The Secret Diary*, III: 429.

133. Sherwood, *The White House Papers*, I: 237; Johnson interview (1892), Sherwood Papers, HL. Harold Laski reported to FDR that he had heard "nothing but praise for [Hopkins's] forthrightness, his tact, and the quickness of his insight": Laski to FDR, February 18, 1941, General Correspondence: Roosevelt, Franklin D., Frankfurter Papers, LC. See also Averell Harriman to Marie Harriman,

March 30, 1941, box 3, Averell Harriman Papers, LC; Pimlott, ed., *The Second World War Diary*, 150.

134. Harriman memorandum, March 11, 1941, Chronological File, box 158, Averell Harriman Papers, LC; W. Ridsdale, FO minute, January 25, 1941, FO 371/26179 A101/101/45, NA.

135. On the Scapa Flow trip, see: Churchill, *The Second World War*, III: 24; Leutze, ed., *The London Journal*, 226. The prime minister made sure that Hopkins was provided with photographs from the trip: JMM to Hopkins, January 28, 1941, PREM 4/25/3, NA.

136. For example, the suggestions of transporting him home in a warship, or inviting him to Belfast on the ground that "the invitation might be flattering." Churchill thought better than to raise this issue with Hopkins: see R. Grandsen to Sir Alexander Maxwell, January 29, 1941; note to Churchill, February 3, 1941; note to C. Markbreiter (Home Office), February 5, 1941, all in PREM 4/25/3, NA.

137. See, e.g., Hopkins to FDR and Hull, January 27, 1941, 121.841 HH/10 1/7, RG 59, NARA.

138. See, e.g., Harriman memorandum, March 11, 1941, Chronological File, box 158, Averell Harriman Papers, LC.

139. See Pamela Churchill Harriman and Kathleen Harriman Mortimer interviews, Newton Collection, FDRL. FDR believed this was the key to the Hopkins-Churchill relationship: see King MS Diary, April 20, 1941, LAC.

140. Characteristically, though, Roosevelt denied to journalists that he and Hopkins were in contact: 711st press conference, January 17, 1941, PPC, XVII: 79.

CHAPTER 4: "SAIL ON, OH SHIP OF STATE!"

1. Cole, *Roosevelt and the Isolationists*, 379–82, 385, 414; Neal, *Dark Horse*, 187; Clifford, "Both Ends of the Telescope," 228.

2. Kimball, *The Most Unsordid Act*, 154–55; Neal, *Dark Horse*, 187; 710th press conference, January 14, 1941, PPC, XVII: 76.

3. Davenport, *Too Strong for Fantasy*, 230; Gardner Cowles, *Mike Looks Back: The Memoirs of Gardner Cowles, Founder of Look Magazine* (New York: Gardner Cowles, 1985), 65.

4. The previous two paragraphs draw on: Neal, *Dark Horse*, 1–4; Barnard, *Wendell Willkie*, 9–12, 15–16, 22, 30–31; Joseph Barnes, *Willkie: The Events He Was Part of, the Ideas He Fought For* (New York: Simon & Schuster, 1952), 21–22, 26.

5. The previous two paragraphs draw on: Barnard, *Wendell Willkie*, 23–26, 28–30, 33–37, 39–42, 44–46; Hubert Kay, "Wendell Willkie: A Big Businessman with Liberal Ideas Gets a Republican Presidential Boom," *Life*, May 13, 1940.

6. The previous two paragraphs draw on: Neal, *Dark Horse*, 14, 25, 28–37; Barnard, *Wendell Willkie*, 51–55, 75, 78–124; Barnes, *Willkie*, 21–22, 26.

7. The previous two paragraphs draw on: *New York Times*, February 23, 1939; Neal, *Dark Horse*, 54, 56–62; Davenport, *Too Strong for Fantasy*, 233; *Washington Post*, August 18, 1940; Kay, "Wendell Willkie."

8. Lamont to Gordon Wasson, September 9, 1940, 137-24, Lamont Papers, BL; Neal, *Dark Horse*, viii; Kay, "Wendell Willkie"; Davenport, *Too Strong for Fantasy*, 230–31.

9. Neal, *Dark Horse*, 68–71; Barnard, *Wendell Willkie*, 164–65.

10. Richard Norton Smith, *Thomas E. Dewey and His Times* (New York: Simon & Schuster, 1982), 302–5; Barnard, *Wendell Willkie*, 169–75, 180–81; Neal, *Dark Horse*, 74–79, 87–116; Charles Peters, *Five Days in Philadelphia: The Amazing "We Want Willkie!" Convention of 1940 and How It Freed FDR to Save the Western World* (New York: PublicAffairs, 2005), 76, 95–97, 102–8; Davenport, *Too Strong for Fantasy*, 237–41; *New York World-Telegram*, February 6, 1941.

11. Neal, *Dark Horse*, ix, 142–43, 146, 149–53, 157–58, 176–77, 181; Barnard, *Wendell Willkie*, 225–26, 250–51; Davenport, *Too Strong for Fantasy*, 241–44; Marquis W. Childs, "The Education of Wendell Willkie," in *The Roosevelt Era*, ed. Milton Crane (New York: Boni & Gaer, 1947), 472; Clifford and Spencer, *The First Peacetime Draft*, 194–96, 201–4.

12. Neal, *Dark Horse*, 178, 184; Barnard, *Wendell Willkie*, 273–76; Barnes, *Willkie*, 242; *New York Times*, January 6 and 13, 1941.

13. *New York Times*, January 13, 1941; Address to Women's National Republican Club, January 18, 1941, Speeches: January 1941–March 1942, Willkie Papers, LL.

14. *New York Times*, January 13 and 20, February 12, 1941; *Washington Post*, January 20, 1941.

15. Neal, *Dark Horse*, 37–44; "The FDR Tapes: Secret Recordings Made in the Oval Office of the President in the Autumn of 1940," *American Heritage* 33, no. 2 (1982): 9–24. See also Ickes MS Diary, February 8, 1941, 5199–200, LC.

16. Willkie to Frankfurter, March 3, 1938; Frankfurter to Willkie, March 4, 1938; Frankfurter MS Diary, January 16, 1941, all in General Correspondence: Willkie, Wendell, L., microfilm reel 68, Frankfurter Papers, LC. See also T. H. Brand to Sir David Scott, February 6, 1941, PREM 4/26/6, NA.

17. Balfour, FO minute, February 7, 1941, in FO 371/26200 A743/G, NA.

18. Neal, *Dark Horse*, 189; Barnes, *Willkie*, 243.

19. Frankfurter MS Diary, January 16, 1941, General Correspondence: Willkie, Wendell, L., microfilm reel 68, Frankfurter Papers, LC.

20. Stimson MS Diary, January 8, 11 and 13, 1941, 32: 91–92, 98–99, 101–2, VHL. See also Stimson to Willkie, November 10, 1940, Correspondence: Stimson, Henry L., Willkie Papers, LL.

21. Quoted in Stimson to George, November 12, 1940, Correspondence: Stimson, Henry L., Willkie Papers, LL. Hull renewed his offer of information at the Gridiron Dinner in Washington in December 1940: *New York Herald Tribune*, January 20, 1941.

22. Hull to Willkie, January 10, 1941; Hull to Herbert C. Pell, January 10, 1941, both in Trip Files: Trip to England: November 19, 1940–January 19, 1941, Willkie Papers, LL; Hull to Johnson, January 21, 1941, 032 WW/8, RG 59, NARA.

23. Hull to FDR, January 10, 1941, PPF 7023, FDRL; *New York Times*, January 19 and 20, 1941. Stimson claimed in his diary that he urged FDR in cabinet to meet with Willkie and the president "gladly consented": Stimson MS Diary, January 17,

1941, 32: 111, VHL. However, the Ickes diary reveals that FDR had already reached that decision by January 15: Ickes MS Diary, January 19, 1941, 5147–48, LC.

24. Stimson MS Diary, January 17, 1941, 32: 111, VHL.

25. *New York Times*, January 20, 1941; *Washington Post*, January 20, 1941; *Time*, January 27, 1941.

26. On FDR's opinion of Willkie, see Roosevelt, *This I Remember*, 176–77; Tully, *F.D.R.*, 58, 239, 279; Gunther, *Roosevelt in Retrospect*, 337–38; Ross T. McIntire and George Creel, *White House Physician* (New York: G. P. Putnam's Sons, 1946), 126–27. On Willkie's cable to Edith and his opinion of FDR, see the interviews with Edith, Philip, and Edward Willkie, and George Henley, Notes: Relations with Roosevelt, Barnard Papers, LL; also Casey MS Diary, February 16, 1941, NAA.

27. Sherwood, *The White House Papers*, I: 234–35; Schlesinger, *The Age of Roosevelt*, II: 513; *Washington Post*, January 20, 1941; *New York Times*, January 20, 1941.

28. *New York Times*, January 20, 1941; *Chicago Daily Tribune*, January 20, 1941; Sherwood, *The White House Papers*, I: 4. We have to rely on Willkie's account of this conversation for the veracity of Roosevelt's cruel "half-man" remark.

29. *Washington Post*, January 20, 1941; *New York Times*, January 20, 1941; Sherwood, *The White House Papers*, I: 234–35.

30. FDR to Churchill, dated January 20 but actually January 19, 1941, WCHL 13/1, CAC; Kimball, ed., *Churchill & Roosevelt*, I: 131; Churchill, *The Second World War*, III: 24–25. A slightly different version, dictated by FDR from memory, is in PPF 7023, FDRL.

31. *Washington Post*, January 20, 1941; *Chicago Daily Tribune*, January 20, 1941; *Los Angeles Times*, January 20, 1941; *New York Times*, January 20, 1941.

32. Sherwood, *The White House Papers*, I: 235.

33. Regarding FDR's ambition to expand Americans' view of international affairs, see Reynolds, *From Munich to Pearl Harbor*, 178–83.

34. Perkins, *The Roosevelt I Knew*, 95–96.

35. Ickes, *The Secret Diary*, III: 415; see also Ickes MS Diary, January 19, 1941, 5147–48, LC.

36. Ickes, *The Secret Diary*, III: 427–28.

37. *New York Times*, January 23, 1941. See also *New York Herald Tribune*, January 26, 1941; *Boston Post*, January 28, 1941.

38. Balfour, FO minute, January 13, 1941 (original underlining), FO 371/26200 A252/252/45, NA.

39. Whitehead, FO minute, January 16, 1941; Balfour to Butler, January 13, 1941; Butler to FO, January 13, 15, and 20, 1941; FO to Butler, January 17, 1941, all in FO 371/26200 A252/252/45, NA.

40. J. V. Perowne, FO minute, January 20, 1941, FO 371/26200 A252/252/45, NA. The Nazi newspaper *Der Angriff* said Willkie was in the pocket of "the mammoth banker Morgan" and supported by "the strong fist of Henry Morgenthau": *New York Times*, January 24, 1941.

41. Sir Eric Seal, note, January 19, 1941, PREM 4/26/6, NA; Johnson to Hull, January 20, 1941, 032 WW/3, RG 59, NARA. For Willkie's reply, see Hull to Johnson,

January 20, 1941, 032 WW/7, RG 59, NARA; Colville to Churchill, January 20, 1941, PREM 4/26/6, NA. Examples of Churchill being consulted include: JMM to Churchill, January 21, 1941; Thompson to Churchill, January 27, 1941; Seal to Churchill, January 27, 1941, all in PREM 4/26/6, NA.

42. Thompson to Churchill, January 27, 1941, PREM 4/26/6, NA.

43. Thompson to Churchill, January 23, 1941; Bridges to Thompson, January 23, 1941, both in PREM 4/26/6, NA; Balfour, FO minute, January 20, 1941, FO 371/26200 A252/252/45, NA.

44. Balfour, FO minute, January 22, 1941; Balfour to Johnson, January 23, 1941, both in FO 371/26200 A252/252/45, NA.

45. *Christian Science Monitor*, January 27, 1941. See Lamont to Churchill, January 16, 1941, 137-24, Lamont Papers, BL; Helen Rogers Reid to Churchill, January 21, 1941, PREM 4/26/6, NA; and William L. Chenery to Churchill, January 21, 1941, Trip Files: Trip to England: January 20–25, 1941, Willkie Papers, LL.

46. See, e.g., Douglas Fairbanks Jr. to Anthony Eden, January 17, 1941, FO 954/29, NA; George Cameron to Sir Robert Vansittart, January 13, 1941; Denis Conan Doyle to Duff Cooper, January 16, 1941; Albert Ainsworth to Lord Reith, January 17, 1941; Stimson to Sir Walter Layton, January 14, 1941; Stimson to Sir Arthur Salter, all in Trip Files: November 19, 1940–January 19, 1940, Willkie Papers, LL; McTeach to Herbert Morrison, January 20, 1941; Samuel A. Welldon to Sir Oliver Lyttelton, January 20, 1941, both in Trip Files: Trip to England: January 20–25, 1941, Willkie Papers, LL; Thomas Lamont to Sir Montagu Norman, January 20, 1941; Lamont to Sir Archibald Sinclair, January 20, 1941, both in 137-24, Lamont Papers, BL. Arthur Krock's letter to Brendan Bracken suggested that when Willkie "departs from the captains and the kings you can tell him more, if you will, than they can": Krock to Bracken, January 20, 1941, Unfiled correspondence, 1929–1944: 1941: Willkie Papers, LL.

47. See John Gordon to Willkie, January 13, 1941, Trip Files: Trip to England: November 19, 1940–January 19, 1941; Bartley C. Crum to Willkie, January 14, 1941, Correspondence: Crum, Bartley C.: 1941; Leon Fraser to Keynes, Trip Files: Trip to England: January 20–25, 1941; Mrs. John English Hale to Willkie, January 26, 1941, Trip Files: Trip to England: January 26–31, 1941, all in Willkie Papers, LL; Lamont to Lord Bicester of Morgan Grenfell, January 17, 1941, 137-24, Lamont Papers, BL; Leon Fraser to Lord Kindersley of Lazard Brothers, January 20, 1941, Trip Files: Trip to England: January 20–25, 1941, Willkie Papers, LL. Helen Rogers Reid of the *Herald Tribune* sent cables to the owners of the *Observer*, the *Times*, and the *Daily Telegraph*, and to personal friends including Vincent Massey, Lady Ward, and Lady Colefax: Reid, undated memorandum, Trip Files: Trip to England: January 20–25, 1941, Willkie Papers, LL. Finally, see Lamont to Lord Catto and Lord Bicester, both on January 17, 1941; Lamont to Viscount Astor, Lady Colefax, and the Dowager Marchioness of Reading, all on January 20, 1941, 132-24, all in Lamont Papers, BL.

48. See Reid, undated memo; Nast to Lord Camrose, January 15, 1941; Nast to Rex Benson, January 20, 1941, all in Trip Files: Trip to England: January 20–25, 1941, Willkie Papers, LL.

49. Trans-Atlantic Clipper Sailing Instructions, January 22, 1941, Trip Files: Trip to England: January 20–25, 1941, Willkie Papers, LL; *New York Times*, January 23, 1941.

50. A point made in Neal, *Dark Horse*, 193.

51. T. H. Brand to Sir David Scott, February 11, 1941, FO 371/26200 A716/G, NA; Willkie to Pan-American Airways, January 18, 1941, Trip Files: Trip to England: November 19, 1940–January 19, 1941; Peggy Gilmore to Willkie, undated, Correspondence: Gilmore, Eddy, both in Willkie Papers, LL; *Washington Post*, January 20, 1941.

52. *Washington Post*, January 23, 1941.

53. *New York Times*, January 23 and 24, 1941.

54. *Washington Post*, January 24, 1941.

55. *New York Times*, January 25, 1941; Tree, *When the Moon Was High*, 159; Robert Rhodes James, ed., *Chips: The Diaries of Sir Henry Channon* (London: Weidenfeld & Nicolson, 1967), 292.

56. Tree, *When the Moon Was High*, 159-160.

57. Tree, *When the Moon Was High*, 160; *New York Herald Tribune*, January 26, 1941; *Washington Post*, January 26, 1941.

58. *Chicago Daily Tribune*, January 27, 1941; *New York Times*, January 27, 1941; *Times*, January 27, 1941; Pawle and Thompson, *The War and Colonel Warden*, 94.

59. *Chicago Daily Tribune*, January 27, 1941; *Times*, January 27, 1941; *New York Times*, January 27, 1941; *Christian Science Monitor*, January 27, 1941; Pawle and Thompson, *The War and Colonel Warden*, 94; *Life*, February 7, 1949.

60. Beaton, *The Years Between*, 49, 52; James, ed., *Chips*, 272; Massey, *What's Past Is Prologue*, 289–90.

61. *Chicago Daily Tribune*, January 27, 1941; *New York Times*, January 26 and February 2, 1941; Martin and Hardy, eds., *Dark and Hurrying Days*, 61; see also Halifax MS Diary, May 17, 1941, A7.8.8, BIA.

62. *Time*, February 3, 1941; *New York Times*, January 28, 1941; *Chicago Daily Tribune*, January 28, 1941; *Boston Post*, January 28, 1941; *Christian Science Monitor*, January 27, 1941; *Times*, January 28 and February 6, 1941; *Daily Herald*, January 28, 1941.

63. Avon MS Diary, January 28, 1941, UB; Halifax Secret MS Diary, February 17, 1941, A7.8.19, BIA; *Christian Science Monitor*, January 27, 1941.

64. Eden, *The Reckoning*, 253–54.

65. *Christian Science Monitor*, January 27, 1941; Beaton, *The Years Between*, 58–59; *Times*, January 28, 1941; *Daily Herald*, January 28, 1941.

66. Engagement card, January 27, 1941, WCHL 6/44, CAC; *New York Times*, February 12, 1941; Address to National Republican Club, February 12, 1941, Speeches: January 1941–March 1942, Willkie Papers, LL.

67. *Boston Post*, January 28, 1941; *Chicago Daily Tribune*, January 28, 1941; *Daily Herald*, January 28, 1941; Gilbert, *Winston S. Churchill*, VI: 997–98; *New York Times*, January 28, 1941. Dominion high commissioners in London were told the Churchill-Willkie meeting was "most helpful": Bruce file note, January 29, 1941, Monthly War Files, Bruce Papers, NAA.

68. John Colville, *Footprints in Time* (London: Collins, 1976), 145.

69. Churchill to FDR, January 28, 1941, 740.0011 EW 1939/7979 1/2, RG 59, NARA. Willkie rounded off his marathon first day in London with an uneventful meeting with his fellow envoy Harry Hopkins at the Dorchester: see Hopkins to FDR and Hull, January 27, 1941, 121.841 HH/10 1/7, RG 59, NARA; *New York Times*, January 28, 1941; *Boston Post*, January 28, 1941; Johnson interview (1892), Sherwood Papers, HL.

70. Reynolds, *The Creation of the Anglo-American Alliance*, 182–85; Sherwood, *The White House Papers*, I: 272–73.

71. *New York Times*, January 29, 1941; *Chicago Daily Tribune*, January 29, 1941; *Times*, January 29, 1941. With one eye firmly on electoral politics, Willkie also called on Cardinal Hinsley, the primate of the Catholic Church in Britain, at Westminster Cathedral. Afterward he admitted that the visit was occasioned by "the importance of Catholic opinion in the US," in particular the fact that most Catholic Americans were of Irish, German, or Italian origin: Balfour, FO minute, February 7, 1941, FO 371/26200 A743/G, NA; *Washington Post*, January 29, 1941. He also discussed war finances with Sir Montagu Norman of the Bank of England, and had lunch with a group of Labour Party ministers, one of whom told him he had relatives in Elwood. "I know every one of them!" claimed Willkie: *New York Times*, January 29, 1941.

72. *New York Times*, January 29, 1941; *Times*, January 29, 1941; *Chicago Daily Tribune*, January 29, 1941. Other British officials also did what they could to make Willkie feel welcome. The lord mayor suggested to Downing Street that he be offered the freedom of the City of London; the chief whip sought Churchill's opinion on whether he should accorded the rare honor of addressing Parliament: Seal to Churchill, January 27, 1941; JMM to Churchill, January 28, 1941, both in PREM 4/26/6, NA.

73. "Lord Beaverbrook's dinner," January 28, 1941, Trip Files: Trip to England: January 26–31, 1941, Willkie Papers, LL; *Sunday Times*, February 2, 1941.

74. "Appointments," January 29, 1941, Trip Files: Trip to England: January 26–31, 1941, Willkie Papers, LL; Laski to FDR, February 18, 1941, General Correspondence: Roosevelt, Franklin D., Frankfurter Papers, LC.

75. *Daily Herald*, January 30, 1941; *News Chronicle*, January 30, 1941; Casey MS Diary, February 16 and 19, 1941, NAA; Brand to Scott, February 6, 1941, PREM 4/26/6, NA. As a gift, the TUC gave Willkie a signed book on the Tolpuddle Martyrs, a group of Dorset laborers transported to Australia in 1834 for the crime of establishing a union.

76. *Chicago Daily Tribune*, January 30, 1941; *New York Times*, January 30, 1941; *Life*, February 17, 1941.

77. *New York Times*, January 30 and 31, 1941; *Christian Science Monitor*, January 30, 1941; *New York Herald Tribune*, January 30, 1941; *Chicago Daily Tribune*, January 30, 1941; *News Chronicle*, January 30, 1941.

78. *Times*, January 31, 1941; *Daily Herald*, January 31, 1941; *New York Times*, January 31, 1941; *Sydney Morning Herald*, January 31, 1941.

79. *New York Times*, January 31, 1941; *Times*, January 31, 1941.

80. Massey MS Diary, January 29 and 30, 1941, UT.
81. *Times,* February 1, 1941; *New York Times,* February 1 and 2, 1941; *Sydney Morning Herald,* February 3, 1941.
82. Hull to Johnson, January 30, 1941, 032 WW/16, RG 59, NARA; Johnson to Hull, January 31, 1941, 032 WW/17, RG 59, NARA; *New York Times,* February 12, 1941.
83. The following three paragraphs draw principally on Kimball, *The Most Unsordid Act,* 165–78, 185–87, 191–92, 203. See also Cole, *Roosevelt and the Isolationists,* 417, 419.
84. *New York Times,* February 1, 1941; *Times,* February 6, 1941; *Sydney Morning Herald,* February 3, 1941; Philip D. Caine, *Spitfires, Thunderbolts, and Warm Beer: An American Fighter Pilot over Europe* (Dulles, VA: Potomac Books, 2005), 59–60.
85. *New York Times,* February 2, 1941; *Sydney Morning Herald,* February 3, 1941; Neal, *Dark Horse,* 197; Brand to Scott, February 11, 1941, FO 371/26200 A716/G, NA.
86. Gilbert, *Winston S. Churchill,* VI: 1000; Elletson, *Chequers,* 108, 115–16; Beaverbrook to Churchill, June 6, 1941, PREM 4/26/6, NA; Martin and Hardy, eds., *Dark and Hurrying Days,* 63; *New York Times,* February 10, 1941.
87. Edward Weeks interview, Notes: English Visit, Barnard Papers, LL. See also: Clementine Churchill to Willkie, undated but probably February 1, 1941, Unfiled correspondence, 1929–1944: 1941, Willkie Papers, LL. Eden liked Willkie better when he saw him at Chequers: Avon MS Diary, February 1, 1941, UB.
88. *News Chronicle,* January 30, 1941.
89. Norman Longmate, *Air Raid: The Bombing of Coventry, 1940* (London: Hutchinson, 1976), 13–15, 180–81, 190, 210, 212.
90. *New York Times,* February 3, 1941; *Daily Herald,* February 3, 1941; Longmate, *Air Raid,* 93–95; Henry Andrews to Gerald Pinsent, February 5, 1941, FO 371/26200 A743/G, NA.
91. *Daily Herald,* February 3, 1941; *Times,* February 3, 1941, *New York Times,* February 3, 1941.
92. *New York Times,* February 4, 1941; *Times,* February 4, 1941; *Washington Post,* February 25, 1941.
93. The previous two paragraphs draw on: U.S. Consul George Tait to Hull, February 4, 1941, 032 WW/30, RG 59, NARA; *Daily Herald,* February 4, 1941; *New York Times,* February 4, 1941; *Manchester Guardian,* February 4, 1941; Brand to Scott, February 11, 1941, FO 371/26200 A716/G, NA. See also Willkie to Lord Mayor of Manchester, Trip Files: Trip to England, February 1–5, 1941, Willkie Papers, LL.
94. John Cowles to Barnard, November 25, 1953, Correspondence: 1953, Barnard Papers, LL; Brand to Scott, February 6, 1941, PREM 4/26/6, NA.
95. Cowles to Barnard, November 25, 1953, Correspondence: 1953, Barnard Papers, LL; Davenport to Willkie, February 2, 1941, FO 371/26200 A717/252/45, NA; see also Kaye to Willkie, January 23, 1941, Trip Files: Trip to England: January 20–25, 1941, Willkie Papers, LL.
96. Cowles to Barnard, November 25, 1953, Correspondence: 1953, Barnard Papers, LL; Beaverbrook to Churchill, June 6, 1941, PREM 4/26/6, NA; Robert G. Menzies, *Afternoon Light: Some Memories of Men and Events* (Melbourne: Cassell

Australia, 1967), 37; U.S. Minister David Gray to Hull, February 7, 1941, 032 WW/29, RG 59, NARA; *New York Times*, February 5, 1941; *Times*, February 5, 1941.

97. *Irish Times*, February 5, 1941; Gray to Hull, February 7, 1941, 032 WW/29, RG 59, NARA; *Christian Science Monitor*, February 5, 1941; Martin and Hardy, eds., *Dark and Hurrying Days*, 107; Nicolson, *Diaries and Letters, 1939–1945*, 219.

98. Hopkins file note, January 30, 1941, Hopkins microfilm, reel 19, Hopkins Papers, FDRL; Nicolson, *Diaries and Letters, 1939–1945*, 219–20.

99. "Ireland: Report of a Visit by the Prime Minister of the Commonwealth of Australia," April 9, 1941, Overseas Papers, 1941, Menzies Papers, NLA.

100. Nicolson, *Diaries and Letters, 1939–1945*, 219.

101. This account of the Willkie–de Valera conversation draws on Willkie's various descriptions of it, found in Andrews to Pinsent, February 5, 1941, FO 371/26200 A743/G, NA; Brand to Scott, February 6, 1941, PREM 4/26/6, NA; Brand to Scott, February 11, 1941, FO 371/26200 A716/G, NA; Castle MS Diary, February 19, 1941, HL; J. V. Perowne, FO minute, February 5, 1941, FO 371/26200 A743/G, NA; Ickes, *The Secret Diary*, III: 439; Nicolson, *Diaries and Letters, 1939–1945*, 142–43. Also Cowles to Barnard, November 25, 1953, Correspondence: 1953, Barnard Papers, LL.

102. *Christian Science Monitor*, February 5, 1941; Gray to Hull, February 4, 1941, 032 WW/21, RG 59, NARA; *New York Times*, February 5, 1941; *Chicago Daily Tribune*, February 5, 1941; *Irish Times*, February 5, 1941.

103. Edward Willkie interview, Notes: English Visit, Barnard Papers, LL; *New York Times*, February 2 and 10, 1941; *Times*, February 2, 1941; Barnard, *Wendell Willkie*, 281.

104. The following is derived from these firsthand accounts: Balfour, FO minute, February 5, 1941; Andrews to Pinsent, February 5, 1941, both in FO 371/26200 A743/G, NA; West to Van Doren, February 9, 1941, General Correspondence: West, Rebecca, box 9, Van Doren Papers, LC; Nicolson, *Diaries and Letters, 1939–1945*, 142–43. (In his writings, Nicolson was very cutting about politicians and other amateurs who sought to engage in diplomacy: Nicolson, *Diplomacy*, 39–40, 52–53.) Willkie wrote a playful telegram to Van Doren after the dinner party claiming that West's "deliberate judgment of my age is 42": Willkie to Van Doren, February 5, 1941, General Correspondence: Willkie, Wendell L., box 10, Van Doren Papers, LC.

105. Sir Robert Vansittart, FO minute, February 7, 1941, FO 371/26200 A743/252/45, NA.

106. Andrews to Pinsent, February 5, 1941, FO 371/26200 A743/G, NA; *Washington Post*, February 5, 1941; *New York Times*, February 5, 1941; *Times*, February 6, 1941; *Los Angeles Times*, February 6, 1941; Neal, *Dark Horse*, 162–63; "Comment by Wendell Willkie on Berlin story from the German Minister of Propaganda," March 13, 1941, Speeches: January 1941–March 1942, Willkie Papers, LL.

107. Seal to Churchill, February 3, 1941, PREM 4/26/6, NA; *New York Times*, February 5, 6, and 10, 1941; *Time*, February 24, 1941; Hull to Johnson, January 31, 1941, 032 WW/19, RG 59, NARA.

108. *Los Angeles Times*, February 7, 1941; *New York Times*, February 7 and 10, 1941; *Chicago Daily Tribune*, February 8, 1941; Mary Earhart Dillon, *Wendell Willkie, 1892–1944* (Philadelphia: Lippincott, 1952), 239–40.

109. *Time*, February 17, 1941; *New York Times*, February 10, 1941; Kimball, *Most Unsordid Act*, 206.

110. "Give Us the Tools," February 9, 1941, BBC, London, in Cannadine, ed., *Blood, Toil, Tears and Sweat*, 212–13.

111. Neal, *Dark Horse*, 202–4; Barnard, *Wendell Willkie*, 285; *Chicago Daily Tribune*, February 12, 1941; Childs, "The Education," 478; *Richmond Times-Dispatch*, February 12, 1941.

112. Willkie to Van Doren, February 1, 1941, General Correspondence: Willkie, Wendell L., box 10, Van Doren Papers, LC; "Statement of Wendell Willkie before Senate Foreign Relations Committee," February 11, 1941, Speeches: January 1941–March 1942, Willkie Papers, LL.

113. *Richmond Times-Dispatch*, February 12, 1941; *New York Times*, February 16, 1941; *Time*, February 24, 1941; 717th press conference, February 11, 1941, PPC, XVII: 118.

114. *New York Times*, February 12, 1941; *Los Angeles Times*, February 12, 1941; *Time*, February 24, 1941; Sherwood, *The White House Papers*, I: 204; Tully, *F.D.R.*, 58; Roosevelt, *This I Remember*, 178; James Roosevelt and Sidney Shalett, *Affectionately, F.D.R.: A Son's Story of a Courageous Man* (Westport, CT: Greenwood Press, 1975), 291; Ickes, *The Secret Diary*, III: 428. Landon Thorne made a separate report to Stimson and the War Department: Stimson MS Diary, February 9–10, 1941, 33: 18–19, VHL.

115. Kimball, *The Most Unsordid Act*, 208–11, 216–17; Lamont to Lord Halifax, November 2, 1942, 137-25, Lamont Papers, BL.

116. Sherwood, *The White House Papers*, II: 633. See also: Rosenman, *Working with Roosevelt*, 274; Perkins, *The Roosevelt I Knew*, 96.

117. *Washington Post*, February 23, 1941; Barnard, *Wendell Willkie*, 290.

118. Lamont to Halifax, November 2, 1942, 137-25, Lamont Papers, BL; Willkie to Ellen Parkinson, MP, April 2, 1941, Trip Files: Trip to England: February 6, 1941–June 4, 1942, Willkie Papers, LL; Casey MS Diary, February 27, 1941, NAA; Willkie, "America, Stop Being Afraid!," *Collier's*, May 10, 1941; Halifax to FO, July 8, 1941, FO 954/29, NA; Halifax Secret MS Diary, February 17, 1941, A7.8.19, BIA.

119. U.S. Consul General Herbert C. Hengstler to Hull, March 26, 1941, 032 WW/31, RG 59, NARA; *Globe and Mail*, March 24 and 25, 1941; *Evening Telegram*, March 25, 1941; *Life*, April 7, 1941; Neal, *Dark Horse*, 209–10.

120. Barnard, *Wendell Willkie*, 288–89; Barnes, *Willkie*, 253; Castle MS Diary, February 12, 1941, HL; *Chicago Daily Tribune*, February 13, 1941; Neal, *Dark Horse*, 207.

121. Robert S. Byfield to Robert C. Hardy, May 7, 1941; Willkie to Byfield, May 20, 1941; Willkie to William R. Davis, May 20, 1941; Davis to Willkie, May 25, 1941; Willkie to Davis, May 27, 1941, all in Correspondence: Davis, William R., Willkie Papers, LL; W.P. Knight to Willkie, January 19, 1941, Trip Files: Trip to England: November 19, 1940–January 19, 1941, Willkie Papers, LL.

122. Frankfurter MS Diary, January 16, 1941, General Correspondence: Willkie, Wendell, L., microfilm reel 68, Frankfurter Papers, LC.

123. Grace Tully to Willkie, August 29, 1941; Grace Graham to Tully, December 3, 1941; FDR to Willkie, January 28, 1942, all in PPF 7023, FDRL.

124. *New York Times*, February 12, 1941; FDR to Willkie, August 25, 1941; Willkie to FDR, August 29, 1941, both in Correspondence: Roosevelt, Franklin D., Willkie Papers, LL.

125. *New York Times*, March 16, 1941; *Los Angeles Times*, March 16, 1941.

126. *Time*, February 17, 1941; *Washington Post*, February 8, 1941.

127. Churchill, *The Second World War*, III: 23; Nicolson, *Diaries and Letters, 1939–1945*, 141–42. See also Bruce to Acting PM, February 1, 1941, Monthly War Files, Bruce Papers, NAA; Eden, *The Reckoning*, 254.

128. *Times*, February 5 and 6, 1941; Commander Ronald Kinnear RN to Charles Kinnear, February 2, 1941, Trip Files: February 6, 1941–June 4, 1942, Willkie Papers, LL; Henry Clay quoted in Crum to Willkie, March 14, 1941, Correspondence: Crum, Bartley, Willkie Papers, LL; *Life*, February 17, 1941; West to Van Doren, February 9, 1941, General Correspondence: West, Rebecca, box 9, Van Doren Papers, LC; *Los Angeles Times*, February 6, 1941.

129. See the various lists contained in Trip Files: Trip to England: January 26–31, 1941; Trip Files: Trip to England: February 1–5, 1941; Trip Files: Trip to England, February 6, 1941–June 4, 1942, all in Willkie Papers, LL.

130. Ickes, *The Secret Diary*, III: 439.

131. The previous two paragraphs draw on: Cosmo Gordon Lang to Willkie, February 5, 1941, Trip Files: Trip to England: February 1–5, 1941, Willkie Papers, LL; Forrestal to Willkie, undated but probably May or June 1941, Correspondence: Forrestal, James, Willkie Papers, LL; Eddy Gilmore to Willkie, February 21, 1941 and September 3, 1944, both in Correspondence: Gilmore, Eddy, Willkie Papers, LL; Beaverbrook to Thompson, undated, and Beaverbrook to Willkie, May 19, 1941, BBK/D/463, Beaverbrook Papers, PA; Beaverbrook to Willkie, May 19, 1941, Trip Files: February 6, 1941–June 4, 1942, Willkie Papers, LL; Winant, *A Letter*, 20.

132. Brand to Scott, February 6, 1941, PREM 4/26/6, NA; also Brand to Scott, February 11, 1941, FO 371/26200 A716/G, 3, NA. Both reports were initialed by Churchill.

133. "Westward, Look, the Land Is Bright," April 27, 1941, BBC, London, in Cannadine, ed., *Blood, Toil, Tears and Sweat*, 224.

CHAPTER 5: "TO KEEP THE BRITISH ISLES AFLOAT"

1. Harriman and Abel, *Special Envoy*, 3; Reminiscences, October 12, 1953, box 872, Averell Harriman Papers, LC.

2. Abramson, *Spanning the Century*, 22, 31, 63–64, 84–86; Robert A. Lovett interview, July 16, 1983, Abramson Papers.

3. Harriman and Abel, *Special Envoy*, 37, 40–42; Abramson, *Spanning the Century*, 53, 66–70, 74–77; E. J. Kahn Jr., "Plenipotentiary—II," *New Yorker*, May 10, 1952; Averell Harriman interview, December 10, 1984, Abramson Papers.

4. Abramson, *Spanning the Century*, 90, 103–19; Harriman and Abel, *Special Envoy*, 6; Robert A. Lovett interview, July 16, 1983, Abramson Papers; Kahn, "Plenipotentiary—II."

5. Abramson, *Spanning the Century*, 141–57; Harriman and Abel, *Special Envoy*, 48–51; Reminiscences, October 12, 1953, box 872, Averell Harriman Papers, LC.

6. Kahn, "Plenipotentiary—II."

7. Ibid.; Abramson, *Spanning the Century*, 99–100, 164–70, 173–85, 264; Harriman and Abel, *Special Envoy*, 34–36; John Colville interview, undated; Peter Duchin interview, May 11, 1983; Robert A. Lovett interview, July 16, 1983, all in Abramson Papers; Reminiscences, July 12, 1982, box 1105, Averell Harriman Papers, LC; George F. Kennan, quoted in *Washington Post*, December 7, 1975.

8. Robert Meiklejohn interview, undated; Waldeman Nielsen interview, May 2, 1983, both in Abramson Papers; Kathleen Harriman to Marie Harriman, October 14, 1941, Chronological File, box 160, Averell Harriman Papers, LC; Chris Ogden, *Life of the Party: The Biography of Pamela Digby Churchill Hayward Harriman* (Boston: Little, Brown, 1994), 344; E. J. Kahn Jr., "Plenipotentiary—I," *New Yorker*, May 3, 1952.

9. The previous two paragraphs draw on: *Boston Evening Transcript*, April 12, 1941; Kathleen Harriman Mortimer interview, undated; Donald Klopfer interview, undated; Dorothy Schiff interview, February 7, 1985, all in Abramson Papers; Abramson, *Spanning the Century*, 109–11, 170–77, 183–85, 262–65; *New York Times*, April 18, 1915, and February 22, 1930; Nancy H. Yeide, "The Marie Harriman Gallery (1930–1942)," *Archives of American Art Journal* 39, no. 1/2 (1999): 3–11; *Time*, October 13, 1930.

10. Abramson, *Spanning the Century*, 221–32; Harriman and Abel, *Special Envoy*, 54.

11. Franklin D. Roosevelt Jr. interview, undated; Robert A. Lovett interview, July 16, 1983, both in Abramson Papers; Reminiscences, October 12, 1953, box 872, Averell Harriman Papers, LC; Kahn, "Plenipotentiary—I"; Harriman and Abel, *Special Envoy*, 53–55; Abramson, *Spanning the Century*, 246–60.

12. The previous two paragraphs draw on: Harriman and Abel, *Special Envoy*, 12–14; Reminiscences, October 12, 1953, box 872, Averell Harriman Papers, LC; Hopkins to Harriman, January 31, 1939; Harriman to Hopkins, June 28, 1939, both in Special Files: Public Service: Business Advisory Council: Harry Hopkins, box 147, Averell Harriman Papers, LC; James Roosevelt, Herbert B. Swope Jr., James L. Rowe, and Franklin D. Roosevelt Jr. interviews, all undated, in Abramson Papers; Abramson, *Spanning the Century*, 267–68, 270–73.

13. Harriman and Abel, *Special Envoy*, 10; Harriman to Hopkins, January 5 and 11, 1941, Hopkins microfilm, reel 19, Hopkins Papers, FDRL; Reminiscences, October 12, 1953, box 872, Averell Harriman Papers, LC.

14. Butler to FO, January 21, 1941, FO 371/26224 A409/409/45, NA; Halifax to FO, January 25, 1941, FO 371/26224 A409/409/45, NA; see also a reporter's question in 712th press conference, January 21, 1941, PPC, XVII: 86; *New York Times*, January 21, 1941; Smith, ed., *Hostage to Fortune*, 526.

15. Morgenthau MS Diary, January 23, 1941, 350: 186–90, FDRL.

16. Hopkins to FDR and Hull, January 27, 1941, 121.841 HH/9, RG 59, NARA; Hopkins to FDR and Hull, February 1, 1941, 124.41/105 1/2, RG 59, NARA.

17. Regarding the position, see FDR's comments in 719th press conference, February 18, 1941, PPC, XVII: 128; *New York Times*, February 19, 1941. Regarding the person, both Harriman and Ickes were convinced that Hopkins was the prime mover behind the choice of Harriman: Harriman and Abel, *Special Envoy*, 14; Ickes MS Diary, March 1, 1941, 5269, LC.

18. Bruce file note, January 29, 1941, Monthly War Files, Bruce Papers, NAA.

19. Harriman and Abel, *Special Envoy*, 3; Reminiscences, October 12, 1953, box 872; "Memorandum of conversation with the President," March 11, 1941, Chronological File, box 158, both in Averell Harriman Papers, LC.

20. 719th press conference, February 18, 1941, PPC, XVII: 128–31.

21. Harriman and Abel, *Special Envoy*, 14–17; Harriman memorandum, March 1, 1941; "Memorandum of conversation with Secretary of State Cordell Hull," March 11, 1941, both in Chronological File, box 158, Averell Harriman Papers, LC; Stimson MS Diary, March 1, 1941, 33: 48, VHL.

22. Reminiscences, October 12, 1953, box 872, Averell Harriman Papers, LC; Schlesinger, *A Life*, 307.

23. Harriman memorandum, February 21, 1941, Chronological File, box 158, Harriman Papers, LC.

24. "Memorandum on conversations before leaving Washington for London," March 11, 1941, Chronological File, box 158, Averell Harriman Papers, LC.

25. "Memorandum of conversation with the President," March 11, 1941, Chronological File, box 158, Averell Harriman Papers, LC; Harriman and Abel, *Special Envoy*, 17–18; Smith, *FDR*, 336–38.

26. "Memorandum of conversation with the President," March 11, 1941, Chronological File, box 158, Averell Harriman Papers, LC.

27. Ibid. On FDR's thinking at this point, see Heinrichs, *Threshold of War*, 16.

28. Reminiscences, October 12, 1953, box 872, Averell Harriman Papers, LC.

29. Irita Van Doren interview, December 30, 1954, Notes: Relations with Roosevelt, Barnard Papers, LL; Walter Isaacson and Evan Thomas, *The Wise Men: Six Friends and the World They Made: Acheson, Bohlen, Harriman, Kennan, Lovett, McCloy* (London: Faber & Faber, 1986), 188; Franklin D. Roosevelt Jr. interview, undated, Abramson Papers.

30. Elliott Roosevelt and James Brough, *A Rendezvous with Destiny: The Roosevelts of the White House* (London: W. H. Allen, 1977), 293.

31. See, e.g., Harriman speech to the National Industrial Conference Board, Washington, D.C., September 28, 1939, Speeches, box 746, Averell Harriman Papers, LC; Harriman to Hopkins, June 6, 1940, Hopkins microfilm, reel 19, Hopkins Papers, FDRL; Harriman speeches to the Yale Club, New York City, February 4, 1941, and the Traffic Club, Washington, D.C., February 14, 1941, both in Chronological File, box 158, Averell Harriman Papers, LC. Harriman told a Briton he "wanted to go on record" before departing for the United Kingdom "so that he would not be accused on returning home of having 'fallen for the British'": Balfour, FO minute, March 22, 1941, FO 371/26177 A1901/91/45, NA.

32. Hamilton to Balfour, March 1, 1941, FO 371/26177 A1901/91/45, NA. See also Purvis to London Supply Committee, March 13, 1941, FO 371/28794 W1805/37/49, NA. However, the British were concerned that the appointment might damage Britain's ordered arrangements for communicating war information to the Americans: FO to Halifax, April 4, 1941, FO 371/28937 W5351/1163/49, NA.

33. *Christian Science Monitor*, February 6, 1941; *Time*, February 17, 1941.

34. This summary of Winant's life draws on Bernard Bellush, *He Walked Alone: A Biography of John Gilbert Winant* (The Hague: Mouton, 1968); *New York Times*, February 16, 1941; *Times*, February 8, 1941.

35. Reported in R. A. Butler, FO minute, January 24, 1941, FO 371/26224 A409/409/45, NA.

36. This description draws on Martin and Hardy, eds., *Dark and Hurrying Days*, 89; Massey, *What's Past Is Prologue*, 338; *Time*, February 17, 1941; Phillips 1951 interview, 135, CCOHC; *New York Times*, February 16, 1941; also Pimlott, ed., *The Second World War Diary*, 173, 258.

37. T. North Whitehead, FO minute, January 22, 1941, FO 371/26224 A409/409/45, NA. The religious analogies are contained in: Moran, *Winston Churchill*, 125; Arthur Krock quoted in Butler to FO, January 21, 1941, FO 371/26224 A409/409/45, NA; Kathleen Harriman to Marie Harriman, October 14, 1941, Chronological File, box 160, Averell Harriman Papers, LC; *Time*, March 31, 1941; Martin and Hardy, eds., *Dark and Hurrying Days*, 89; Harold Butler writing in the *Times*, February 8, 1941.

38. See generally David Reynolds, "Roosevelt, the British Left, and the Appointment of John G. Winant as United States Ambassador to Britain in 1941," *International History Review* 4, no. 3 (1982): 393–413.

39. Young to Miller, November 6, 1940, FO 371/24263 A4898/4898/45, NA; D. J. Scott, FO minute, January 23, 1941, FO 371/26224 A409/409/45, NA; Moffat MS Diary, January 31, 1941, 2–3, Ottawa I, 1940–1941, HL; Laski to FDR, February 18, 1941, General Correspondence: Roosevelt, Franklin D., Frankfurter Papers, LC; Casey MS Diary, February 21, 1941, NAA. Frankfurter regarded Winant as "a very dear and old friend": Morgenthau MS Diary, January 23, 1941, 350: 187, FDRL.

40. Brand to Scott, February 11, 1941, FO 371/26200 A716/G, NA; Casey MS Diary, February 16 and 21, 1941, NAA; Halifax Secret MS Diary, February 17, 1941, A7.8.19, BIA; *Washington Post*, February 8, 1941; Smith, ed., *Hostage to Fortune*, 526.

41. Long MS Diary, February 15, 1941, LC.

42. The previous three paragraphs draw on: Kimball, *The Most Unsordid Act*, 216–20, 232–33, 235; *New York Times*, March 12, 1941; Langer and Gleason, *The World Crisis*, II: 253; Address at Annual Dinner of White House Correspondents' Association, March 15, 1941, PPA, X: 61, 63.

43. Gilbert, comp., *The Churchill War Papers*, III: 835, 1427.

44. FDR to Harriman, March 6, 1941, OF 4341, FDRL. Harriman also bore a diplomatic passport—something that was, in Breckinridge Long's phrase, "pretty hard to chisel out of this Department": Long to Hopkins, April 29, 1941, General Correspondence: Hopkins, Harry, 1941, box 147, Long Papers, LC.

45. Reminiscences, October 12, 1953, box 872; Averell Harriman to Marie Harriman, undated, box 3, both in Averell Harriman Papers, LC; Meiklejohn MS Diary, March 12, 1941, LC. See also *New York Times*, March 11, 1941; Abramson, *Spanning the Century*, 278–79.

46. The previous two paragraphs draw on: Meiklejohn MS Diary, March 12 and 15, 1941, LC; Averell Harriman to Marie Harriman, undated, box 3; Reminiscences, October 12, 1953, box 872; Appointment Diary, March 14, 1941, box 157, all in Averell Harriman Papers, LC; Harriman and Abel, *Special Envoy*, 21; Dunlop, *Donovan*, 271–72. Bill Donovan was on his way home from the Balkans and the Middle East, where he had been on a new assignment for Secretary Knox: see Troy, *Wild Bill and Intrepid*, 77–92; Jay Jakub, *Spies and Saboteurs: Anglo-American Collaboration and Rivalry in Human Intelligence Collection and Special Operations, 1940–45* (Basingstoke, UK: Macmillan, 1999), 10–19; Waller, *Wild Bill Donovan*, 63–67.

47. *New York Times*, March 16, 1941; R. P. Meiklejohn, "Report on the Harriman Mission," 1946, Special Files: Public Service: World War II: Subject File, box 165, Averell Harriman Papers, LC (hereafter "Meiklejohn Report"), 7; Meiklejohn MS Diary, March 15, 1941, LC.

48. Harriman 1959 interview, 22, CCOHC; Reminiscences, October 12 and 22, 1953, box 872; Averell Harriman to Marie Harriman, April 30, 1941, box 3, all in Averell Harriman Papers, LC; Harriman and Abel, *Special Envoy*, 21–22.

49. Reminiscences, October 12, 1953, box 872, Averell Harriman Papers, LC.

50. Heinrichs, *Threshold of War*, 15, 27–30; Churchill, *The Second World War*, III: 38–39; Harriman and Abel, *Special Envoy*, 22.

51. Meiklejohn MS Diary, March 19 and May 5–9, 1941, LC; Meiklejohn to Nathaniel P. Davis, July 29, 1941, Chronological File, box 160, Averell Harriman Papers, LC; Meiklejohn Report, 2–3, 5; Rowe to FDR, March 5, 1941, OF 4341, FDRL; Harriman and Abel, *Special Envoy*, 26.

52. Kathleen Harriman Mortimer interview, December 19, 1987; Robert Meiklejohn interview, undated, both in Abramson Papers; Meiklejohn MS Diary, April 1, 4, 15, and 30, May 5–9, June 5, July 11, 1941, LC.

53. Heinrichs, *Threshold of War*, 42–43, 48; Churchill to FDR, March 30, 1941, in Kimball, ed., *Churchill and Roosevelt*, I: 156.

54. Harriman and Abel, *Special Envoy*, 57; Heinrichs, *Threshold of War*, 48; Reminiscences, October 12, 1953, box 872, Averell Harriman Papers, LC; Stettinius, *Lend-Lease*, 118–20.

55. Kennan, *Memoirs*, 233; Meiklejohn Report, 8; Averell Harriman to Marie Harriman, April 30, 1941, box 3, Averell Harriman Papers, LC.

56. Harriman and Abel, *Special Envoy*, 23; Averell Harriman to Marie Harriman, April 30, 1941, box 3, Averell Harriman Papers, LC.

57. Mary Soames interview, undated; Kathleen Harriman Mortimer interview, June 24, 1987; John Colville interview, undated, all in Abramson Papers.

58. Appointment Diary, March 19, 1941, box 157, Averell Harriman Papers, LC; Gilbert, *Winston S. Churchill*, VI: 1038–39; Colville, *The Fringes of Power*, 366.

59. The previous three paragraphs draw on: Heinrichs, *Threshold of War*, 46–49, 51–52, 57; Waldo Heinrichs, "President Franklin D. Roosevelt's Intervention in the Battle of the Atlantic, 1941," *Diplomatic History* 10, no. 4 (1986): 320–21; Dallek, *Franklin D. Roosevelt*, 261; Kershaw, *Fateful Choices*, 187, 235, 301; Smith, *FDR*, 491–92; 738th press conference, April 25, 1941, PPC, XVII: 288–89.

60. Harriman to Hopkins, March 24, 1941, Chronological File, box 158, Averell Harriman Papers, LC; Harriman to FDR, April 10, 1941, PPF 6207, FDRL; Harriman to Hopkins, April 14, 1941, Harriman (Incoming Cables, 1941–1942), Sherwood Collection, Hopkins Papers, FDRL; John Colville interview, undated, Abramson Papers; Colville, *The Fringes of Power*, 374.

61. Harriman to FDR, May 7, 1941, PSF (Diplomatic): Great Britain: Harriman, W. A.: 1941–1942, FDRL. See also Harriman to R. G. Menzies, April 30, 1941, Chronological File, box 159, Averell Harriman Papers, LC.

62. Harriman to Hopkins, April 24, 1941, Chronological File, box 159, Averell Harriman Papers, LC.

63. Lindemann to Churchill, March 25, 1941, CHAR 20/258A, CAC.

64. Harriman to Churchill, April 15, 1941, Chronological File, box 159, Averell Harriman Papers, LC.

65. Gilbert, *Winston S. Churchill*, VI: 1034; departmental minutes, March 20 and April 2, 1941, CAB 115/12, NA.

66. Harriman notes, April 11, 1941, box 159; Reminiscences, October 12, 1953, box 872, both in Averell Harriman Papers, LC; Pawle and Thompson, *The War and Colonel Warden*, 149.

67. Pawle and Thompson, *The War and Colonel Warden*, 102; Colville, *The Fringes of Power*, 373; Ismay interview (1891), Sherwood Papers, HL; *Washington Post*, April 13, 1941.

68. The previous two paragraphs draw on: Pawle and Thompson, *The War and Colonel Warden*, 102; Winant interview (1907), Sherwood Papers, HL; Martin and Hardy, eds., *Dark and Hurrying Days*, 111; Colville, *The Fringes of Power*, 373; Ismay interview (1891), Sherwood Papers, HL; *Washington Post*, April 13, 1941; Reminiscences, October 12, 1953, box 872, Averell Harriman Papers, LC; Winant, *A Letter*, 45–46.

69. Martin and Hardy, eds., *Dark and Hurrying Days*, 111; *Time*, April 21, 1941; Winant, *A Letter*, 47–48; Harriman, draft cable to FDR, dated April 11 but actually April 12, 1941, box 159, Averell Harriman Papers, LC; Colville, *Footprints in Time*, 154; Winant interview (1907), Sherwood Papers, HL; Pawle and Thompson, *The War and Colonel Warden*, 102–3.

70. The previous two paragraphs draw on: University of Bristol, Degree Congregation, April 12, 1941, Procedure and Processions, Overseas Papers, 1941, Menzies Papers, NLA; *Chicago Daily Tribune*, April 13, 1941; Winant, *A Letter*, 47–48.

71. Harriman, draft cable to FDR, dated April 11 but actually April 12, 1941, box 159; Reminiscences, October 12, 1953, box 872, both in Averell Harriman Papers, LC; Harriman and Abel, *Special Envoy*, 29–30; Winant, *A Letter*, 48. Harriman made an anonymous donation to the rebuilding of Bristol: Clementine

Churchill to Harriman, April 15, 1941, Chronological File, box 159, Averell Harriman Papers, LC.

72. *Life*, April 28, 1941; Meiklejohn MS Diary, April 15, 1941, LC; *Sydney Morning Herald*, April 18, 1941.

73. Averell Harriman to Marie Harriman, April 17, 1941, box 3, Averell Harriman Papers, LC; Martin and Hardy, eds., *Dark and Hurrying Days*, 113.

74. Colville, *The Fringes of Power*, 375; Martin and Hardy, eds., *Dark and Hurrying Days*, 114; John Colville interview, undated, Abramson Papers. See also Frank Costigliola, *Roosevelt's Lost Alliances: How Personal Politics Helped Start the Cold War* (Princeton: Princeton University Press, 2012), 113–15.

75. The previous two paragraphs draw on: Beaton, *The Years Between*, 53; Larry LeSueur interview, April 27, 1987, Abramson Papers; Abramson, *Spanning the Century*, 309, 311–12; Ogden, *Life of the Party*, 100; Ogden transcripts, October 1 and March 8, 1991, Pamela Harriman Papers, LC; Lynne Olson, *Citizens of London: The Americans Who Stood with Britain in Its Darkest, Finest Hour* (New York: Random House, 2010), 98.

76. The previous two paragraphs draw on: Ogden transcripts, July 7 and October 1, 1991, Pamela Harriman Papers, LC; Kathleen Harriman Mortimer interview, undated, Abramson Papers.

77. Hopkins to Berle, April 29, 1941, Special Assistant to the President, 1941–1945: Harriman, Hopkins Papers, FDRL; Harriman 1959 interview, 3, CCOHC; Averell Harriman to Marie Harriman, April 30, 1941, box 3, Averell Harriman Papers, LC.

78. Averell Harriman to Marie Harriman, June 9, 1941, box 3, Averell Harriman Papers, LC; Ogden transcript, October 1, 1991, Pamela Harriman Papers, LC; Smith, *Reflected Glory*, 89, 99–100; Olson, *Citizens of London*, 102–3.

79. John Colville interview, undated, Abramson Papers; Ogden transcript, October 26, 1991, Pamela Harriman Papers, LC; Arthur M. Schlesinger Jr., *Journals, 1952–2000*, ed. Andrew Schlesinger and Stephen Schlesinger (New York: Penguin, 2007), 343. See also the sly reference in Hopkins to Beaverbrook, September 26, 1942, BBK/C/175, Beaverbrook Papers, PA.

80. The previous two paragraphs draw on: Gilbert, *Second World War*, 179–88; Dallek, *Franklin D. Roosevelt*, 264–73; Heinrichs, *Threshold of War*, 83–85; Heinrichs, "President Franklin D. Roosevelt's Intervention," 320–23; Radio Address Announcing Unlimited National Emergency, May 27, 1941, PPA, X: 190, 193.

81. Harriman to Hopkins, May 29, 1941, Harriman (Incoming Cables, 1941–1942), Sherwood Collection, Hopkins Papers, FDRL; Averell Harriman to Marie Harriman, May 6, 1941, box 3, Averell Harriman Papers, LC.

82. Bullitt to Harriman, April 29, 1941; Harriman to Bullitt, May 21, 1941, both in Chronological File, box 159, Averell Harriman Papers, LC. See also Harriman to W. M. Jeffers, May 30, 1941; Harriman to James Roosevelt, June 11, 1941, both in Chronological File, box 159, Averell Harriman Papers, LC.

83. The previous two paragraphs draw on: Costigliola, *Roosevelt's Lost Alliances*, 120; Smith, *FDR*, 493–95; Freidel, *Franklin D. Roosevelt*, 370–71; Sherwood, *The White*

House Papers, I: 292–93, 298–99; Cole, *Roosevelt and the Isolationists*, 428; *New York Times*, April 1 and May 14, 1941; *Los Angeles Times*, November 12, 1941; Morgenthau Presidential MS Diary, May 17, 1941, FDRL; see also Orville H. Bullitt, ed., *For the President, Personal and Secret: Correspondence between Franklin D. Roosevelt and William C. Bullitt* (Boston: Houghton Mifflin, 1972), 512. I am grateful to Scott Moyers for alerting me to Joe DiMaggio's batting streak.

84. Bullitt, ed., *For the President*, 512–14; Gellman, *Secret Affairs*, 235–41.

85. *Washington Post*, April 17, 1941; *New York Times*, December 2, 4, and 14, 1941; Willkie remarks to Freedom Rally, May 8, 1941, Speeches: January 1941–March 1942, Willkie Papers, LL; Wendell L. Willkie, "Americans, Stop Being Afraid!," *Collier's*, May 10, 1941.

86. Kathleen Harriman to Marie Harriman, May 17, 1941, Chronological File, box 159, Averell Harriman Papers, LC.

87. Churchill, *The Second World War*, III: 43–44; Pawle and Thompson, *The War and Colonel Warden*, 107–8; Tree, *When the Moon Was High*, 149; Gilbert, *Winston S. Churchill*, VI: 1087.

88. The previous two paragraphs draw on: Mary Soames and Arthur M. Schlesinger Jr. interviews, both undated, Abramson Papers; Tree, *When the Moon Was High*, 45–46; "A Weekend with the Churchills," *Boise Capital News*, July 9, 1941. There are good accounts of this incident in Thomas Parrish, *To Keep the British Isles Afloat: FDR's Men in Churchill's London, 1941* (New York: Smithsonian Books, 2009), 235–37, and Abramson, *Spanning the Century*, 300–301.

89. This account draws on: Churchill, *The Second World War*, VI: 270–86; Lawrence Hogben, "Sinking the 'Bismarck,'" *London Review of Books* 23, no. 8 (2001): 36–37; Harriman and Abel, *Special Envoy*, 33–34; Reminiscences, October 12, 1953, box 872, Averell Harriman Papers, LC; Colville, *The Fringes of Power*, 390–92; Ismay, *The Memoirs*, 220–21; Winant, *A Letter*, 184–86.

90. The previous two paragraphs draw on: Sherwood, *The White House Papers*, I: 202, 267–69; Coy interview (1878), Sherwood Papers, HL; Casey MS Diary, April 11, 1941, NAA.

91. Sherwood, *The White House Papers*, I: 268, 278, 282, 284; Stettinius, *Lend-Lease*, 89.

92. Stettinius, *Lend-Lease*, 86, 126–27; Kershaw, *Fateful Choices*, 233.

93. The previous four paragraphs draw on: Stettinius, *Lend-Lease*, 90–93; Harriman to Hopkins et al., March 24, 1941, Chronological File , box 158, Averell Harriman Papers, LC; Meiklejohn Report, 11–11A; Harriman and Abel, *Special Envoy*, 56–57; *Observer*, June 1, 1941.

94. *Times*, April 26, 1941; Parrish, *To Keep the British Isles Afloat*, 222–23; *New York Times*, May 31, 1941; Harriman to Hopkins, June 5, 1941, Chronological File, box 159, Averell Harriman Papers, LC. Lord Woolton's strictures were felt in the most elevated households in the land. John Colville, whose mother was a lady-in-waiting to Queen Mary, the mother of George VI, attended a dinner at the queen's beautiful house in Badminton. "In obedience to Lord Woolton," he recorded, "we only had two courses but four pages and footmen to serve them": Colville, *The Fringes of Power*, 421.

95. Harriman to William Batt, April 12, 1941, Chronological File, box 159, Averell Harriman Papers, LC.

96. Harriman to FDR, April 10, 1941; Hull to FDR, April 21, 1941; FDR to Harriman, April 22, 1941, all in PPF 6207, FDRL; Meiklejohn Report, 7.

97. Harriman to Winant, May 27, 1941, Chronological File, box 159, Averell Harriman Papers, LC.

98. The revealing exchanges between the Foreign Office and the palace are in FO 371/26224 A1017/409/45, A1018/409/45, and A1735/409/45, NA; see also Winant, *A Letter*, 18–19.

99. Ickes MS Diary, June 15, 1941, 5617, LC; see also George VI to FDR, June 3, 1941, PSF (Diplomatic): Great Britain: King and Queen, FDRL.

100. Abramson, *Spanning the Century*, 302; *Times*, May 15, 1941; David Farrer, *G—for God Almighty: A Personal Memoir of Lord Beaverbrook* (London: Weidenfeld & Nicolson, 1969), 71.

101. Winant, *A Letter*, 54–55.

102. Leutze, ed., *The London Journal*, 359; the final two sentences are from Lee MS Diary, July 30, 1941, 2, USAMHI.

103. Quoted in Lee MS Diary, July 20, 1941, 4, USAMHI.

104. Leutze, ed., *The London Journal*, 340; Robert Meiklejohn interview, undated, Abramson Papers.

105. Tree, *When the Moon Was High*, 157.

106. Harriman to FDR, April 10, 1941, PPF 6207, FDRL.

107. Harriman to FDR, May 7, 1941, PSF (Diplomatic): Great Britain: Harriman: 1941–1942, FDRL.

108. Averell Harriman to Marie Harriman, March 30, 1941, box 3, Averell Harriman Papers, LC; Winant, *A Letter*, 138–39.

109. Harriman and Abel, *Special Envoy*, 62–63; Churchill to FDR, June 3, 1941, CHAR 20/39, CAC; Harriman to Churchill, June 4, 1941, Chronological File, box 159; Reminiscences, October 12, 1953, box 872; Harriman to James Roosevelt, June 11, 1941, Chronological File, box 159, all in Averell Harriman Papers, LC. See also R. P. Meiklejohn, "Report on Trip to Middle East," June 15, 1946, box 212, Averell Harriman Papers, LC (hereafter "Meiklejohn Middle East Report"), 1, 3; *Christian Science Monitor*, June 12, 1941; *Washington Post*, June 6, 1941.

110. Meiklejohn Report, 16; Reynolds, *The Creation of the Anglo-American Alliance*, 208–10.

111. Harriman and Abel, *Special Envoy*, 63.

112. Leutze, ed., *The London Journal*, 301; Averell Harriman to Marie Harriman, June 6, 1941, box 3, Averell Harriman Papers, LC.

113. Meiklejohn Middle East Report, 3–5; Averell Harriman to Marie Harriman, June 9, 1941, box 3, Averell Harriman Papers, LC; Meiklejohn MS Diary, June 6, 1941, LC.

114. "Middle East Trip Itinerary," undated, Chronological File, box 159; Averell Harriman to Marie Harriman, June 12 and 18, 1941, box 3, both in Averell Harriman Papers, LC; Meiklejohn Middle East Report, 10; Meiklejohn MS Diary, June 19 and 30, 1941, LC.

115. Averell Harriman to Marie Harriman, June 12, 1941, box 3; Meiklejohn to Pemberton, July 17, 1941, box 3, both in Averell Harriman Papers, LC; Meiklejohn MS Diary, June 12, 1941, LC.

116. Averell Harriman to Marie Harriman (letter and cable), June 13, 1941, box 3, Averell Harriman Papers, LC; Meiklejohn MS Diary, June 12 and 13, 1941, LC; Meiklejohn Middle East Report, 5.

117. Meiklejohn MS Diary, June 14 and 15, 1941, LC; Averell Harriman to Marie Harriman, June 18, 1941; Meiklejohn to Pemberton, July 17, 1941, both in box 3, Averell Harriman Papers, LC; Meiklejohn Middle East Report, 6.

118. Meiklejohn MS Diary, June 15, 1941, LC; Meiklejohn Middle East Report, 6.

119. Averell Harriman to Marie Harriman, June 18, 1941; Meiklejohn to Pemberton, July 17, 1941, both in box 3, Averell Harriman Papers, LC; Meiklejohn MS Diary, June 16, 18 and 19, 1941, LC; Harriman and Abel, *Special Envoy*, 64.

120. Lyttelton, *The Memoirs*, 232–33.

121. Meiklejohn to Pemberton, July 17, 1941, box 3, Averell Harriman Papers, LC.

122. Churchill to Harriman, June 30, 1941; Harriman to Churchill, July 1, 1941; Harriman to FDR, July 5, 1941; Harriman to FDR, July 9, 1941, all in Chronological File, boxes 159–60, Averell Harriman Papers, LC; Harriman and Abel, *Special Envoy*, 65, 68–69.

123. Meiklejohn MS Diary, June 20, 24 and 26, July 6–7 and 10, 1941, LC; Harriman BBC broadcast, November 23, 1941, box 1101; Meiklejohn to Pemberton, July 17, 1941, box 3; Averell Harriman to Marie Harriman, July 12, 1941, box 3; Appointment Diary, box 157, all in Averell Harriman Papers, LC; Harriman and Abel, *Special Envoy*, 69.

124. Meiklejohn MS Diary, July 1–2, 1941, LC; Meiklejohn to Pemberton, July 17, 1941, box 3; Harriman to Churchill, July 1, 1941, Chronological File, box 160, both in Averell Harriman Papers, LC.

125. The previous two paragraphs draw on: Winston Churchill to Randolph Churchill, June 8, 1941, CHAR 1/362, CAC; Meiklejohn to Pemberton, July 17, 1941, box 3, Averell Harriman Papers, LC; Meiklejohn MS Diary, June 23, July 1 and 10, 1941, LC; Ogden, *Life of the Party*, 130–32; Olson, *Citizens of London*, 118–19; Harriman to Pamela Churchill, undated, box 5, Pamela Harriman Papers, LC.

126. Meiklejohn MS Diary, July 10–11, 1941, LC; Robert Meiklejohn interview, undated, Abramson Papers; Hugh M. Birch to Pamela Harriman, August 6, 1986, box 5, Pamela Harriman Papers, LC.

127. The previous two paragraphs draw on: Lyttelton, *The Memoirs*, 229; Meiklejohn MS Diary, July 11–12, 14–15, 1941, LC; Meiklejohn to Pemberton, July 17, 1941, box 3, Averell Harriman Papers, LC; Meiklejohn Middle East Report, 10.

128. Harriman to Churchill, July 1, 1941; Harriman to FDR, July 5 and 9, 1941; "Observations on Middle East," July 16, 1941; "Middle East Situation," undated; "Memorandum: Trip to Alexandria and Western Desert," July 25, 1941, all in Chronological File, boxes 159-160, Averell Harriman Papers, LC; Harriman to Churchill, July 16, 1941, PREM 3/217/2, NA; Harriman and Abel, *Special Envoy*, 71–72; Abramson, *Spanning the Century*, 287; Harriman, memoranda of conversations with Marshall, Stark, and Stimson, August 6, 1941, Abramson Papers.

129. Abramson, *Spanning the Century*, 303.
130. See, e.g., Fraser Harbutt, "Churchill, Hopkins, and the 'Other' Americans: An Alternative Perspective on Anglo-American Relations, 1941–1945," *International History Review* 8 (1986): 237–39.
131. Harriman to W. M. Jeffers, May 30, 1941; Clementine Churchill to Harriman, April 15, 1941; also Kathleen Harriman to Marie Harriman, May 17, 1941, all in Chronological File, box 159, Averell Harriman Papers, LC.
132. Gilbert, *Winston S. Churchill*, VI: 1036; John Colville interview, undated, Abramson Papers.
133. Harriman 1959 interview, 14–15, 19–20, CCOHC; Reminiscences, October 14, 1953, box 872, Averell Harriman Papers, LC; John Colville interview, undated, Abramson Papers.
134. Harriman and Abel, *Special Envoy*, 19, 229. Harriman made similar comments to Arthur Schlesinger: Interview with Arthur M. Schlesinger Jr., April 28, 2003.
135. In August, Roosevelt admitted that Harriman's position had "normally and naturally enlarged itself," and referred to him as a "general troubleshooter": 765th press conference, August 29, 1941, PPC, XVIII: 125–26.
136. Meiklejohn MS Diary, July 3, 1941, LC.

CHAPTER 6: "MISTER HURRY UPKINS"

1. Heinrichs, *Threshold of War*, 53, 75, 116; Ickes, *The Secret Diary*, III: 567.
2. Theodore A. Wilson, *The First Summit: Roosevelt and Churchill at Placentia Bay, 1941*, rev. ed. (Lawrence: University Press of Kansas, 1991), 40–42.
3. Reynolds, *From Munich to Pearl Harbor*, 102; Gilbert, *Second World War*, 190, 208.
4. Reynolds, *From Munich to Pearl Harbor*, 182–83; Radio Address Announcing Unlimited National Emergency, May 27, 1941, PPA, X: 192.
5. Dallek argues that FDR had come to this conclusion by May 1941; Harper argues the turning point was the German invasion of Russia in June 1941; Heinrichs believes that the president made the mental shift to active belligerency, which he must have known would result in war, at the Atlantic Conference in August 1941; Wilson argues that by August FDR was resigned to war but hoped not to involve U.S. ground troops; Casey thinks that by the fall of 1941 he felt it desirable that the United States formally enter the war; Reynolds suggests that he hoped to avoid participation right up until the attack on Hawaii: Dallek, *Franklin D. Roosevelt*, 265, 285, 530; John Lamberton Harper, *American Visions of Europe: Franklin D. Roosevelt, George F. Kennan, and Dean G. Acheson* (Cambridge: Cambridge University Press, 1994), 73–76; Heinrichs, *Threshold of War*, 159; Wilson, *The First Summit*, 23; Casey, *Cautious Crusade*, 14–15; Reynolds, *The Creation of the Anglo-American Alliance*, 217–20.
6. Reynolds, *The Creation of the Anglo-American Alliance*, 204; Heinrichs, *Threshold of War*, 116; Dallek, *Franklin D. Roosevelt*, 273–74; Iriye, *The Origins of the Second World War*, 140–44.

7. Gilbert, comp., *The Churchill War Papers*, III: 835; Gilbert, *Second World War*, 199–201; Sherwood, *The White House Papers*, I: 303–4; Kimball, *The Juggler*, 15; Mary E. Glantz, *FDR and the Soviet Union: The President's Battles over Foreign Policy* (Lawrence: University Press of Kansas, 2005), 63–75.

8. Roosevelt, ed., *FDR: His Personal Letters, 1928–1945*, II: 1177. Richard Casey encountered this kind of ambivalence throughout Washington: Casey to Canberra, June 23, 1941, Casey Papers, NAA.

9. Churchill, *The Second World War*, III: 331; Colville, *The Fringes of Power*, 404; Langer and Gleason, *The World Crisis*, II: 531–37.

10. See, e.g., Langer and Gleason, *The World Crisis*, II: 537–39; and Berle MS Diary, July 30–31, 1941, FDRL.

11. Cole, *Roosevelt and the Isolationists*, 435; Sherwood, *The White House Papers*, I: 303.

12. Cole, *Roosevelt and the Isolationists*, 434–35; Letter, June 22, 1941, in FO 371/ 29485 N3283/78/38, NA; Jan Ciechanowski, *Defeat in Victory* (Garden City, NY: Doubleday, 1947), 24–27.

13. Raymond H. Dawson, *The Decision to Aid Russia, 1941: Foreign Policy and Domestic Politics* (Chapel Hill: University of North Carolina Press, 1959), 121–22, 139–50; Langer and Gleason, *The World Crisis*, II: 541, 545–46.

14. Wilson, *The First Summit*, 248 n. 13; Kimball, *The Juggler*, 34; Dawson, *The Decision to Aid Russia*, 139.

15. Memorandum of meeting, July 10, 1941, FRUS, 1941, I: 788–89.

16. Lash, *Eleanor Roosevelt*, 269; *Washington Post*, August 18, 1941; Adams, *Harry Hopkins*, 227.

17. Sherwood, *The White House Papers*, I: 204, 309; Perkins, *The Roosevelt I Knew*, 56; *Life*, September 2, 1940.

18. Wilson, *The First Summit*, 23–24.

19. Dwight William Tuttle, *Harry L. Hopkins and Anglo-American-Soviet Relations, 1941–1945* (New York: Garland Publishing, 1983), 86–87; Kimball, *Forged in War*, 90.

20. Sherwood, *The White House Papers*, I: illustration facing 320; Wilson, *The First Summit*, 22; Langer and Gleason, *The World Crisis*, II: 553–54; Berle MS Diary, July 17, 1941, FDRL. A few days later, he reiterated the point in a cable to Churchill: FDR to Churchill, July 14, 1941, FRUS, 1941, I: 342.

21. Sherwood, *The White House Papers*, I: illustration facing 273, 309–11; Heinrichs, *Threshold of War*, 85, 114–17, 156, 167; Heinrichs, "President Franklin D. Roosevelt's Intervention," 325–29, 332; Reynolds, *The Creation of the Anglo-American Alliance*, 206–7, 214–15; Lash, *Roosevelt and Churchill*, 372–73; Halifax Secret MS Diary, July 12, 1941, A7.8.19, BIA.

22. Sherwood, *The White House Papers*, I: illustration facing 320.

23. Smith, ed., *Hostage to Fortune*, 411, 496; Black, *Franklin Delano Roosevelt*, 91; Sherwood, *The White House Papers*, I: 351; Theodore A. Wilson, "The First Summit: FDR and the Riddle of Personal Diplomacy," in *The Atlantic Charter*, ed. Douglas Brinkley and David R. Facey-Crowther (Basingstoke, UK: Macmillan, 1994), 2–3.

24. King MS Diary, April 20, 1941, LAC; Sherwood, *The White House Papers*, I: 312, illustration facing 320; Wilson, *The First Summit*, 22–23.

25. The previous two paragraphs draw on: Waller, *Wild Bill Donovan*, 69–73; Menzies to Hopkinson, June 19, 1941, FO 1093/238, NA.

26. FDR to Winant, July 12, 1941, John G. Winant, Special Assistant to the President, Hopkins Papers, FDRL; Winant to FDR and Hull, July 16, 1941, FRUS, 1941, I: 343.

27. Hopkins Pandick Diary, July 11–12, 1941, box 52, Part I, Hopkins Papers, GUL; Sherwood, *The White House Papers*, I: 310; FDR note on telephone message, July 14, 1941, Book 4, Sherwood Collection, Hopkins Papers, FDRL; Ickes MS Diary, July 20, 1941, 5768–69, LC.

28. Sherwood, *The White House Papers*, I: 310; Elliott Roosevelt, *As He Saw It* (New York: Duell, Sloan & Pearce, 1946), 27; Meiklejohn MS Diary, July 31 and August 1, 1941, LC; *New York Times*, July 16, 1941.

29. Raymond Gram Swing broadcasts, July 4 and 14, 1941; undated but probably late July 1941, all in box 16, Swing Papers, LC.

30. *Christian Science Monitor*, July 5, 1941; *New York Times*, July 5, 1941.

31. Raymond Gram Swing broadcast, July 4, 1941, box 16, Swing Papers, LC; Winant, *A Letter*, 126–27; *New York Times*, July 5, 1941; *Observer*, February 3, 2002.

32. *Christian Science Monitor*, July 5, 1941; Harriman and Abel, *Special Envoy*, 12; *Time*, August 11, 1941.

33. Appointment Diary, July 17, 1941, box 157, Averell Harriman Papers, LC; Meiklejohn MS Diary, July 16, 1941, LC; Sherwood, *White House Papers*, I: 310; Colville, *The Fringes of Power*, 415. Bob Meiklejohn wrote to a friend, "Harry Hopkins arrived here today on a surprise visit so things will start popping more than ever": Meiklejohn to Pemberton, July 17, 1941, box 3, Averell Harriman Papers, LC.

34. Churchill, *The Second World War*, III: 377; Sherwood, *The White House Papers*, I: 311, 313.

35. Cadogan MS Diary, July 17, 1941, ACAD 1/10, CAC; Minutes, War Cabinet Meeting 71 (41), 5:30 p.m., July 17, 1941, CAB 65/19, NA; Bruce to Menzies, July 18, 1941, Monthly War Files, Bruce Papers, NAA.

36. *New York Times*, July 18, 1941; *Chicago Daily Tribune*, July 19, 1941.

37. The previous two paragraphs draw on: Leutze, ed., *The London Journal*, 342–43; Raymond Gram Swing broadcast, July 18, 1941, box 16, Swing Papers, LC; *New York Times*, July 19, 1941; *Chicago Daily Tribune*, July 19, 1941; *Times*, July 19, 1941; Arthur Herman, *Freedom's Forge: How American Business Produced Victory in World War II* (New York: Random House, 2012), 154.

38. *New York Times*, July 19 and 20, 1941; Raymond Gram Swing broadcast, July 18, 1941, box 16, Swing Papers, LC.

39. Reynolds, *The Creation of the Anglo-American Alliance*, 208–10.

40. Leutze, ed., *The London Journal*, 343; Bernard Fergusson, ed., *The Business of War: The War Narrative of Major-General Sir John Kennedy* (London: Hutchinson, 1957), 153.

41. The following account draws on: *Philadelphia Inquirer*, August 18, 1941; *Washington Post*, August 17, 1941; *New York Herald Tribune*, August 18, 1941;

Christian Science Monitor, August 19, 1941; *New York Times*, August 17, 1941; *Times*, August 14, 2006; Weinberg to Batt, May 5, 1941, Book 4, Sherwood Collection, Hopkins Papers, FDRL; Catledge, "It's 'Send for Harry'"; Hellman, "House Guest"; Sherwood, *The White House Papers*, I: 325.

42. Sherwood, *The White House Papers*, I: 310; Colville, *The Fringes of Power*, 415–16; Quentin Reynolds, *Only the Stars Are Neutral* (Sydney: Angus & Robertson, 1942), 61; Ivan M. Maisky, *Memoirs of a Soviet Ambassador: The War, 1939–1943* (London: Hutchinson, 1967), 177–79; Elleston, *Chequers*, 121; Leutze, ed., *The London Journal*, 344.

43. *Time*, January 8, 1940; David H. Culbert, "Radio's Raymond Gram Swing: 'He Isn't the Kind of Man You Would Call Ray,'" *Historian* 35, no. 4 (1973): 589–90; Rudyard Kipling, *Sea Warfare* (London: Macmillan, 1916), 120–22; Swing, *Good Evening*, 212–14; Kathleen Harriman to Marie Harriman, dated July 30 but probably July 21, 1941, Chronological File, box 160, Averell Harriman Papers, LC.

44. D. J. Wenden and K. R. M. Short, "Winston S. Churchill: Film Fan," *Historical Journal of Film, Radio and Television* 11, no. 3 (1991): 198; Somerset Fry, *Chequers*, 31, 64; Sherwood, *The White House Papers*, I: 286; Kathleen Harriman to Marie Harriman, dated July 30 but probably July 21, 1941, Chronological File, box 160, Averell Harriman Papers, LC; Colville, *The Fringes of Power*, 416; Jenkins, *Chequers*, 119; photograph caption, WCHL 6/61, CAC.

45. Kathleen Harriman to Marie Harriman, dated July 30 but probably July 21, 1941, Chronological File, box 160, Averell Harriman Papers, LC.

46. Colville, *The Fringes of Power*, 417; Kathleen Harriman to Marie Harriman, dated July 30 but probably July 21, 1941, Chronological File, box 160, Averell Harriman Papers, LC; Avon MS Diary, July 21, 1941, UB. In his diary, Eden wrote "Winstonian" rather than "Wilsonian," but he corrected himself in his memoirs: Eden, *The Reckoning*, 273. The Americans returned to the topic of frontier commitments at the Atlantic Conference: Wilson, *The First Summit*, 160–62.

47. Minutes, War Cabinet Meeting 72 (41), 5pm, July 21, 1941, CAB 65/19, NA; Kimball, *The Juggler*, 32; Pimlott, ed., *The Second World War Diary*, 255; Cadogan MS Diary, July 21, 1941, ACAD 1/10, CAC.

48. Minutes, War Cabinet Defence Committee (Supply) Meeting, 5 p.m., July 22, 1941, Book 4, Sherwood Collection, Hopkins Papers, FDRL; Gilbert, comp., *The Churchill War Papers*, III: 968.

49. Hopkins to FDR, July 23, 1941, 121.841 HH/26, RG 59, NARA; *New York Times*, July 23, 1941; Fergusson, ed., *The Business of War*, 117, 155–56.

50. Hopkins to FDR, July 23, 1941, 121.841 HH/26, RG 59, NARA; Meiklejohn MS Diary, July 23, 1941, LC.

51. Churchill, *The Second World War*, III: 380. I follow Gilbert in dating the garden meeting to July 24: Gilbert, comp., *The Churchill War Papers*, III: 978.

52. Wilson, *The First Summit*, 14–15; Colville, *The Fringes of Power*, 419.

53. Leutze, ed., *The London Journal*, 349–50; Minutes, Middle East meeting, 10 p.m., July 24, 1941, Book 1, Sherwood Collection, Hopkins Papers, FDRL (hereafter "Middle East minutes").

54. Middle East minutes; Leutze, ed., *The London Journal*, 349; Sherwood, *The White House Papers*, I: 314.

55. Middle East minutes; Churchill, *The Second World War*, III: 379.

56. Leutze, ed., *The London Journal*, 349; McJimsey, *Harry Hopkins*, 173.

57. See Hopkins's cable the following day explaining the event: Hopkins to FDR, July 25, 1941, PSF (Safe): Hopkins, Harry, FDRL.

58. Tuttle, *Harry L. Hopkins*, 93–94.

59. Lee MS Diary, July 25, 1941, USAMHI.

60. Sherwood, *The White House Papers*, I: 312; Reminiscences, October 12, 1953, box 872, Averell Harriman Papers, LC; Harriman and Abel, *Special Envoy*, 26.

61. Dallek, *Franklin D. Roosevelt*, 274–75; Reynolds, *From Munich to Pearl Harbor*, 140–43, 150–51; FDR to Hopkins, July 26, 1941, PSF (Safe): Hopkins, Harry, FDRL.

62. Reynolds, *From Munich to Pearl Harbor*, 133, 150–51; Heinrichs, *Threshold of War*, 177–78, 180–83.

63. Kathleen Harriman to Marie Harriman, dated July 30 but probably July 21, 1941, Chronological File, box 160, Averell Harriman Papers, LC; Gilbert, comp., *The Churchill War Papers*, III: 989; Reynolds interview (2441); Thompson interview (1906d), both in Sherwood Papers, HL; Quentin Reynolds, *By Quentin Reynolds* (London: Heinemann, 1964), 198–99, 201; Reynolds, *Only the Stars Are Neutral*, 14, 16; Leutze, ed., *The London Journal*, 353; Pawle and Thompson, *The War and Colonel Warden*, 123.

64. Reynolds interview (2441), Sherwood Papers, HL.

65. Reynolds interview (2441), Sherwood Papers, HL; Hopkins to FDR, July 26, 1941, Book 4, Sherwood Collection, Hopkins Papers, FDRL.

66. Reynolds interview (2441), Sherwood Papers, HL; Reynolds, *By Quentin Reynolds*, 203; Sherwood, *The White House Papers*, I: 320; Reynolds, *Only the Stars Are Neutral*, 15.

67. Reynolds interview (2441), Sherwood Papers, HL; Reynolds, *Only the Stars Are Neutral*, 16.

68. Reynolds interview (2441), Sherwood Papers, HL; Reynolds, *Only the Stars Are Neutral*, 16–21; Gilbert, *Second World War*, 216; Reynolds, *By Quentin Reynolds*, 205–7.

69. Reynolds interview (2441), Sherwood Papers, HL; Martin, *Downing Street*, 56.

70. Elletson, *Chequers*, 123; Jenkins, *Chequers*, 94; Sherwood, *The White House Papers*, I: 320–21.

71. Hopkins broadcast, July 27, 1941, McJimsey Papers, GC.

72. Sherwood, *The White House Papers*, I: 322; Kirk to Hull, July 29, 1941, 740.0011 EW 1939/13510, RG 59, NARA; *New York Times*, July 28, 1941; Gilbert, comp., *The Churchill War Papers*, III: 1008.

73. Ickes MS Diary, July 20, 1941, 5768; August 2, 1941, 5818, both in LC; Sherwood, *The White House Papers*, I: 292.

74. Hopkins to Winant, August 9, 1941, Hopkins microfilm, reel 19, Hopkins Papers, FDRL.

75. Churchill, *The Second World War*, III: 21–22.

76. See, e.g., Robert M. Hathaway, *Ambiguous Partnership: Britain and America, 1944–1947* (New York: Columbia University Press, 1981), 8–9.

Chapter 7: "Uncle Joe's Favorite"

1. Sherwood, *The White House Papers*, I: 302–3; Letter, June 22, 1941, in FO 371/29485 N3283/78/38, NA; Ciechanowski, *Defeat in Victory*, 24–27.
2. *Washington Post*, June 22 and 27, 1941. Joseph Davies briefed Hopkins in person and in writing on the need to "furnish all possible aid to Russia in the fight against Hitler": Davies, *Mission to Moscow*, II: 312, 315–17.
3. Alan Barth, survey of editorial opinion, July 24, 1941, PSF (Departmental): Treasury: Morgenthau: Editorial Opinion, FDRL; *Chicago Daily Tribune*, August 16, 1941; Ralph B. Levering, *American Opinion and the Russian Alliance, 1939–1945* (Chapel Hill: University of North Carolina Press, 1976), 43; Cantril, ed., *Public Opinion*, 411.
4. Davies, *Mission to Moscow*, II: 314; Langer and Gleason, *The World Crisis*, II: 558–60; Dallek, *Franklin D. Roosevelt*, 279; memoranda of meetings with Oumansky, July 17 and 24, 1941, FRUS, 1941, I: 794–97.
5. Hopkins to FDR, July 25, 1941, PSF (Safe): Hopkins, Harry, FDRL; see also Sherwood, *The White House Papers*, I: 317–18.
6. Hopkins to FDR, July 25, 1941, PSF (Safe): Hopkins, Harry, FDRL; Winant interview (1907), Sherwood Papers, HL.
7. Sherwood, *The White House Papers*, I: 318; Reminiscences, October 12, 1953, box 872, Averell Harriman Papers, LC; Ismay interview (1891), Sherwood Papers, HL; *New York Times*, July 31, 1941. There is no mention of a prior conversation in Hopkins's papers. Kimball disagrees with this interpretation: Kimball, *The Juggler*, 33.
8. Maisky, *Memoirs*, 179–80; Winant, *A Letter*, 148; Winant interview (1907), Sherwood Papers, HL. Davis and Lindley suggest the idea was Churchill's; however, the prime minister was unenthusiastic about Hopkins making such a dangerous journey, particularly at the risk of missing the Atlantic Conference: Forrest Davis and Ernest K. Lindley, *How War Came: An American White Paper, from the Fall of France to Pearl Harbor* (New York: Simon & Schuster, 1942), 252–53; Sherwood, *The White House Papers*, I: 317; Wilson, *The First Summit*, 33.
9. FDR to Hopkins, July 26, 1941, PSF (Safe): Hopkins, Harry, FDRL; Hopkins draft cable to FDR, July 26, 1941, Book 4, Sherwood Collection, Hopkins Papers, FDRL; Hopkins, "The Inside Story of My Meeting with Stalin," *American Magazine*, December 1941 (hereafter "Hopkins, 'Inside Story'"), 114.
10. Welles to Hopkins, July 26, 1941, 740.0011 EW 1939/1348 4A, RG 59, NARA. A slightly different draft of this cable is in PSF (Safe): Hopkins, Harry, FDRL.
11. See FDR to Stimson, August 30, 1941, FRUS, 1941, I: 826–27.
12. Report of Brigadier General Joseph T. McNarney on trip to Moscow, July 8, 1941, AG350.05, RG 407, NARA (hereafter "McNarney Report"), tab E; Lee MS Diary, August 4, 1941, USAMHI; Hopkins second additional report of July 31 meeting, McJimsey Papers, GC; John Alison oral history transcript, April 22–28, 1979,

107–9, AFHRA. See also Simon M. Burgess, *Stafford Cripps: A Political Life* (London: Victor Gollancz, 1999), 140; Israel, ed., *The War Diary*, 209–10.

13. Glantz, *FDR and the Soviet Union*, 60, 63–67; David Mayers, "The Great Patriotic War, FDR's Embassy Moscow, and Soviet-U.S. Relations," *International History Review* 33, no. 2 (2011): 308; Harriman memorandum of conversation with Stalin, September 30, 1941, BBK/D/100, Beaverbrook Papers, PA.

14. Hopkins draft article for *Collier's*, October 7, 1941, Book 4, Sherwood Collection, Hopkins Papers, FDRL (hereafter "Hopkins draft article for *Collier's*"). This draft article was prepared with the assistance of a journalist. See also Welles to Steinhardt, July 27, 1941, 740.0011 EW 1939/13551, RG 59, NARA; *New York Times*, July 31, 1941; Welles to Hopkins, July 26, 1941, 740.0011 EW 1939/1348 4A, RG 59, NARA.

15. Hopkins draft article for *Collier's*; Hopkins, "Inside Story," 114.

16. Maisky, *Memoirs*, 180; Davies MS Diary, September 8 and 10, 1941, LC.

17. Hopkins, "Inside Story," 114; Sherwood, *The White House Papers*, I: 319; Hopkins to FDR, July 27, 1941, Book 4, Sherwood Collection, Hopkins Papers, FDRL; Pawle and Thompson, *The War and Colonel Warden*, 123.

18. Hopkins, "Inside Story," 114; Pawle and Thompson, *The War and Colonel Warden*, 123.

19. Churchill to Stalin, July 28, 1941, FO 954/24, NA.

20. Reminiscences, October 18, 1953, box 872, Averell Harriman Papers, LC; Johnson interview (1892), Sherwood Papers, HL; Winant, *A Letter*, 148–49; Maisky, *Memoirs*, 180–81; Thompson interview (1906d) and Winant interview (1907), both in Sherwood Papers, HL; Sherwood, *The White House Papers*, I: 321.

21. John Alison interview, Newton Collection, FDRL; McNarney Report; Leutze, ed., *The London Journal*, 357; Hopkins to FDR, July 27, 1941, Book 4, Sherwood Collection, FDRL; *Daily Telegraph*, June 15, 2011.

22. Alison interview, Newton Collection, FDRL; Alison oral history transcript, AFHRA.

23. Hopkins, "Inside Story," 115; *New York Times*, February 15 and 16, 1941; Ted Cowling, *The Journey: Per Ardua ad Astra, through Hardship to the Stars* (Wellington, UK: Laundry Cottage, 2005), 88; Sherwood, *The White House Papers*, I: 324.

24. Robert Cleworth, ed., *The Fabulous Catalina: A Collection of Catalina and Flying Boat Anecdotes from Veterans and Relatives of Those Who Flew These Machines* (Roseville, NSW: J. R. Cleworth, 2006), xi, 253; Personal communications with Neil Owen, Oban War and Peace Museum, June 2011; Hopkins, "Inside Story," 115; David McKinley interview, Newton Collection; FDRL. The terms "PBY" and "Catalina" are here used interchangeably.

25. John Alison and David McKinley interviews, Newton Collection; FDRL; Personal communications with Neil Owen, Oban War and Peace Museum, June 2011; Report by Flight Lieutenant David McKinley, Book 4, Sherwood Collection, Hopkins Papers, FDRL (hereafter "McKinley Report"); Cowling, *The Journey*, 82, 89; *Daily Telegraph*, May 2, 2002.

26. The following two paragraphs draw on: McKinley and Alison interviews, Newton Collection, FDRL; McKinley Report; Hopkins, "Inside Story," 115; Cowling, *The Journey*, 87, 90–91; Sherwood, *The White House Papers*, I: 325–26.

27. Hopkins, "Inside Story," 115; Alison and McKinley interviews, Newton Collection, FDRL; McKinley Report; Halsted, "Severe Malnutrition," 26; Costigliola, *Roosevelt's Lost Alliances*, 123–24.

28. Cowling, *The Journey*, 91, 93–94; McKinley and Alison interviews, Newton Collection, FDRL; Hopkins, "Inside Story," 115.

29. Hopkins, "Inside Story," 115; also Alison interview, Newton Collection, FDRL.

30. Alison and McKinley interviews, Newton Collection, FDRL.

31. Alison interview, Newton Collection, FDRL; Alison oral history transcript, 79–80, AFHRA.

32. Hopkins, "Inside Story," 115–16; McKinley interview, Newton Collection, FDRL; Cowling, *The Journey*, 92–95.

33. The previous two paragraphs draw on: Hopkins, "Inside Story," 116; McNarney Report; Alison oral history transcript interview, 80, AFHRA; Harold Balfour Moscow MS Diary 1941, Special Files: Public Service: World War II: Harriman Mission, Harriman Papers (hereafter "Balfour Moscow MS Diary"), September 28, 1941, LC.

34. Valentin Berezhkov interview, Newton Collection, FDRL; Valentin M. Berezhkov, *At Stalin's Side: His Interpreter's Memoirs from the October Revolution to the Fall of the Dictator's Empire* (Secaucus, NJ: Carol Publishing Group, 1994), 200; *New York Times*, July 31, 1941; Steinhardt to FDR, Hull and Welles, August 1, 1941, 740.0011 EW 1939/13605, RG 59, NARA. On the Russians' pronunciation of Hopkins's name, see Margaret Bourke-White, *Shooting the Russian War* (New York: Simon & Schuster, 1942), 205; Henry C. Cassidy, *Moscow Dateline, 1941–1943* (London: Cassell & Co., 1943), 93.

35. Mayers, "The Great Patriotic War," 302–3; Bohlen and Phelps, *Witness to History*, 88–89; Peter S. Bridges, "Spaso House," *Foreign Service Journal* April (1964): 28–29; Sherwood, *The White House Papers*, I: 327.

36. Sherwood, *The White House Papers*, I: 327–28; Glantz, *FDR and the Soviet Union*, 63–67; Alison interview, Newton Collection, FDRL; Alison oral history transcript, 116–17, AFHRA.

37. Cripps MS Diary, July 30, 1941, BOD; Burgess, *Stafford Cripps*, 150–51; Gabriel Gorodetsky, *Stafford Cripps' Mission to Moscow, 1940–42* (Cambridge: Cambridge University Press, 1984), 200–201.

38. Alison interview, Newton Collection, FDRL; Balfour Moscow MS Diary, September 28, 1941, LC; Ismay, *The Memoirs*, 232; Cathy Porter and Mark Jones, *Moscow in World War II* (London: Chatto & Windus, 1987), 76, 89–90; Alexander Werth, *Russia at War, 1941–1945* (London: Barrie & Rockliff, 1964), 178, 183; Davies MS Diary, September 8, 1941, LC; *New York Times*, July 31, 1941; Hopkins, "Inside Story," 116. Unlike some visitors, Hopkins was not misled by the rundown condition of many Moscow buildings. The American diplomat Charles Thayer wrote later that it could be hard to tell "where Socialist construction left

off and German bombing began": Charles W. Thayer, *Bears in the Caviar* (London: Michael Joseph, 1952), 211–12.

39. Hopkins, "Inside Story," 116; Constantine Pleshakov, *Stalin's Folly: The Secret History of the German Invasion of Russia, June 1941* (London: Weidenfeld & Nicolson, 2005), 23–24; Balfour Moscow MS Diary, September 28, 1941, LC; Bourke-White, *Shooting the Russian War*, 189; Cassidy, *Moscow Dateline*, 65; Porter and Jones, *Moscow in World War II*, 61.

40. Bourke-White, *Shooting the Russian War*, 211–13; Hopkins, "Inside Story," 116; Simon Sebag Montefiore, *Stalin: The Court of the Red Tsar* (London: Weidenfeld & Nicolson, 2003), 118; Berezhkov, *At Stalin's Side*, 204.

41. Sebag Montefiore, *Stalin*, 118; Pleshakov, *Stalin's Folly*, 26–27; Ian Grey, *Stalin, Man of History* (London: Weidenfeld & Nicolson, 1979), 328; *Time*, January 1, 1940, and September 22, 1941; Davies MS Diary, September 8, 1941, LC; Georgii Konstantinovich Zhukov, *The Memoirs of Marshal Zhukov* (London: Jonathan Cape, 1971), 280–81; *Life*, October 5, 1942; Margaret Bourke-White, *Portrait of Myself* (New York: Simon & Schuster, 1963), 183.

42. Hopkins, "Inside Story," 14; Balfour Moscow MS Diary, October 1, 1941, LC; Bourke-White, *Shooting the Russian War*, 213–15; Reynolds, *Only the Stars Are Neutral*, 83; Berezhkov, *At Stalin's Side*, 201; Ismay, *The Memoirs*, 234; Davies MS Diary, September 8, 1941, LC.

43. Geoffrey Roberts, *Stalin's Wars: From World War to Cold War, 1939–1953* (New Haven, CT: Yale University Press, 2006), 85, 89, 99; R. A. C. Parker, *The Second World War: A Short History* (Oxford: Oxford University Press, 1997), 67–68; Sebag Montefiore, *Stalin*, 371–85, 387–88; John Erickson, *Stalin's War with Germany: The Road to Stalingrad* (London: Weidenfeld & Nicolson, 1975), I: 124–26, 138–42.

44. McNarney Report, tab A; *Washington Post*, July 31, 1941; Derek Watson, "Molotov, the Making of the Grand Alliance and the Second Front 1939–42," *Europe-Asia Studies* 54, no. 1 (2002): 78–79; Berezhkov, *At Stalin's Side*, 204–5; Davies MS Diary, September 8, 1941, LC.

45. Hopkins, "Inside Story," 116; Hopkins report on July 30 meeting, Book 4, Sherwood Collection, Hopkins Papers, FDRL (hereafter "Hopkins Report, July 30 meeting"), 1.

46. Hopkins, "Inside Story," 14–15, 114, 117; Hopkins Report, July 30 meeting, 1–2.

47. Hopkins Report, 30 July meeting, 2–3, FDRL; McNarney Report, tab A; Sherwood, *The White House Papers*, I: 345.

48. Berezhkov, *At Stalin's Side*, 205–6; see also Berezhkov interview, Newton Collection, FDRL.

49. Hopkins Report, July 30 meeting, 5, FDRL; Davies MS Diary, September 8, 1941, LC; Hopkins, "Inside Story," 15, 116.

50. Bourke-White, *Shooting the Russian War*, 211; Cassidy, *Moscow Dateline*, 94; Alexander Werth, *Moscow '41* (London: Hamish Hamilton, 1942), 100–101; Hopkins, "Inside Story," 116; McNarney Report, tab A; *Washington Post*, July 31, 1941.

51. Hopkins report of Yakovlev meeting, July 30, 1941, Book 4, Sherwood Collection, Hopkins Papers, 1–3, FDRL; McNarney Report, tab B.

52. Werth, *Russia at War*, 182; Porter and Jones, *Moscow in World War II*, 76, 89–90; McNarney Report, tab D; Hopkins, "Inside Story," 116; Balfour Moscow MS Diary, September 28, 1941, LC; Werth, *Moscow '41*, 100.

53. McNarney Report, tab D; Werth, *Russia at War*, 182; Bourke-White, *Shooting the Russian War*, 115; Alison interview, Newton Collection, FDRL; Balfour Moscow MS Diary, October 2, 1941, LC.

54. Bourke-White, *Shooting the Russian War*, 86, 89.

55. Ibid., 90–92, 124; *New York Times*, August 1, 1941; *Newsweek*, August 11, 1941; Hopkins, "Inside Story," 116.

56. *New York Times*, August 1, 1941; *Christian Science Monitor*, August 1, 1941; *Washington Post*, August 1, 1941; *Chicago Daily Tribune*, August 1, 1941; Dawson, *The Decision to Aid Russia*, 190.

57. *New York Times*, August 1, 1941; Cripps MS Diary, July 31 and August 1, 1941, BOD; Sherwood, *The White House Papers*, I: 332; Gorodetsky, *Stafford Cripps' Mission*, 201–2; Bourke-White, *Shooting the Russian War*, 206–7.

58. Hopkins report on Molotov meeting, 740.0011 EW 1939/14920 1/2, RG 59, NARA; Steinhardt report on Molotov meeting, Book 4, Sherwood Collection, Hopkins Papers, FDRL; Gilbert, *Second World War*, 216.

59. Bourke-White, *Shooting the Russian War*, 207–9; *New York Times*, August 2, 1941; Letter from Diana Hopkins Halsted, September 25, 2011.

60. *Chicago Daily Tribune*, August 1, 1941. The interpreter's identity is mysterious. Sherwood and others following his lead identify him as the former foreign commissar and future ambassador to the United States, Maxim Litvinov: Sherwood, *The White House Papers*, I: 334. However, Hopkins did not mention Litvinov's presence in his notes, his reports to Roosevelt and Davies, or his later article on the meeting. Bourke-White, who was at the meeting, says the interpreter was actually a "suave young man" who was not related to Maxim Litvinov but shared his surname and was known in diplomatic circles as "Young Litvinov": Margaret Bourke-White, "A Photographer in Moscow," *Harper's Magazine*, March 1942, 418; Bourke-White, *Shooting the Russian War*, 213, 215. According to Stalin's visitors log, the interpreter's name was M. M. Potrubach: A. A. Chernobaev, ed., *Na Priëme u Stalina: Tetradi (Zhurnaly) Zapisei Lits, Priniatykh I. V. Stalinym (1924–1953 gg.)* (Moscow: Novyi Khronograf, 2008), 344–45, 688. I am indebted to Graeme Gill and Svetlana Chervonnaya for their help with this puzzle.

61. Davies MS Diary, September 8, 1941, LC; Hopkins report of July 31 meeting, Book 4, Sherwood Collection, Hopkins Papers (hereafter "Hopkins Report, July 31 meeting"), Part I, 1–12, FDRL.

62. Hopkins Report, July 31 meeting, Part II, 1–3, FDRL; Davies MS Diary, September 10, 1941, LC; see also Hopkins second additional report of July 31 meeting, McJimsey Papers, GC. Gorodetsky gives Cripps substantial credit for the supply conference idea: Gorodetsky, *Stafford Cripps' Mission*, 198–203.

63. Hopkins Report, July 31 meeting, Part I, 11, FDRL; Davies MS Diary, September 10, 1941, LC; Roger Munting, "Lend-Lease and the Soviet War Effort," *Journal of Contemporary History* 19, no. 3 (1984): 497–98.

64. Hopkins handwritten notes from July 31 meeting, Book 4, Sherwood Collection, Hopkins Papers, FDRL; Davies MS Diary, September 8, 1941, LC; Pleshakov, *Stalin's Folly*, 27; Bourke-White, *Shooting the Russian War*, 212.

65. Hopkins Report, July 31 meeting, Part III, 1–3; Hopkins to FDR, August 20, 1941, Book 4, Sherwood Collection, Hopkins Papers, FDRL; Sherwood, *The White House Papers*, I: 342–43. It appears that Part III never reached the State Department: Langer and Gleason, *The World Crisis*, II: 565 n. 80; FRUS, 1941, I: 813, n. 60.

66. Hopkins Report, July 31, meeting, Part III, 1–3; Hopkins, "Inside Story," 117. According to Berezhkov, Stalin felt "profoundly slighted" by the refusal of his offer to Hopkins, and later Harriman, to accept U.S. troops on the eastern front: Berezhkov, *At Stalin's Side*, 242.

67. Bourke-White, *Shooting the Russian War*, 208, 211–13.

68. Ibid., 213–19; *Life*, September 8, 1941.

69. Hopkins, "Inside Story," 14, 117.

70. Davies MS Diary, September 8, 1941, LC; Hopkins, "Inside Story," 14, 15, 117; Cripps MS Diary, August 1, 1941, BOD; *New York Times*, August 1, 1941.

71. Davies MS Diary, September 8 and 10, 1941, LC; Cripps MS Diary, August 1, 1941, BOD.

72. Hopkins, "Inside Story," 117.

73. Langer and Gleason, *The World Crisis*, II: 566; Steinhardt to FDR, August 1, 1941, 740.0011 EW 1939/13605, RG 59, NARA; Berezhkov interview, Newton Collection, FDRL.

74. Glantz, *FDR and the Soviet Union*, 79; Wilson, *The First Summit*, 251 n. 51.

75. A point made in Kimball, *The Juggler*, 27–28.

76. Berezhkov, *At Stalin's Side*, 5. The Soviet archives appear to be silent on the Stalin-Hopkins meetings: Geoffrey Roberts, "Litvinov's Lost Peace, 1941–1946," *Journal of Cold War Studies* 4, no. 2 (2002): 26 n. 10.

77. Harriman, foreword to Adams, *Harry Hopkins*, 17; Harriman 1969 interview, 249, CCOHC.

78. Valentin Berezhkov interview, Newton Collection, FDRL; Bohlen interview (1873), Sherwood Papers, HL; Reynolds interview (2441), Sherwood Papers, HL; Reynolds, *Only the Stars Are Neutral*, 5.

79. Bohlen and Phelps, *Witness to History*, 244; Reminiscences, October 22, 1953 and February 3, 1954, both in box 872, Averell Harriman Papers, LC.

80. Hopkins, "Inside Story," 117; *New York Times*, August 2, 1941.

81. *Life*, September 22, 1941; Davies MS Diary, September 10, 1941, LC; Bourke-White, *Shooting the Russian War*, 81, 83, 218; Sherwood, *The White House Papers*, I: 332; McNarney Report, tab D.

82. Hopkins to FDR, August 1, 1941, 740.0011 EW 1939/13601, RG 59, NARA.

83. 760th press conference, August 1, 1941, PPC, XVIII: 72; *New York Times*, August 2, 1941.

84. Ickes MS Diary, August 2, 1941, 5814–16, LC; Morgenthau Presidential MS Diary, August 4, 1941, 952–53, FDRL; Stimson MS Diary, August 1, 1941, 35: 1–2, VHL; Reynolds, *From Munich to Pearl Harbor*, 138–39.

85. It arrived at 8:50 p.m.: Hopkins to FDR, August 1, 1941, 740.0011 EW 1939/13601, RG 59, NARA.
86. Ickes MS Diary, August 2, 1941, 5815–16, LC.
87. Welles to Oumansky, August 2, 1941, FRUS, 1941, I: 815–16; FDR to Coy, August 2, 1941, PSF (Diplomatic): Russia: 1941, FDRL; Dawson, *The Decision to Aid Russia*, 159–62. Most authorities find a causal connection between Hopkins's mission and Roosevelt's decisions in early August: Reynolds, *From Munich to Pearl Harbor*, 138; Wilson, *The First Summit*, 44–45. On the other hand, see Langer and Gleason, *The World Crisis*, II: 563.
88. Cripps MS Diary, July 30, August 1 and 2, 1941, BOD; *New York Times*, August 1, 1941; *Chicago Daily Tribune*, August 2, 1941; Hopkins to FDR, August 1, 1941, 740.0011 EW 1939/13601, RG 59, NARA; Reminiscences, October 19, 1953, box 872, Averell Harriman Papers, LC; Hopkins memorandum, October 30, 1941, Book 5, Sherwood Collection, Hopkins Papers, FDRL.
89. Steinhardt to FDR, Hull and Welles, August 1, 1941, 740.0011 EW 1939/13605, RG 59, NARA.
90. Cripps MS Diary, August 2, 3, 4, and 9, 1941, BOD; Langer and Gleason, *The World Crisis*, II: 567.
91. McNarney Report; Cripps MS Diary, August 2, 1941, BOD; Hopkins, "Inside Story," 114; *New York Times*, August 3, 1941; Hopkins Report, July 30 meeting, 3–4; Wilson, *The First Summit*, 49; Hopkins draft article for *Collier's*; Sherwood, *The White House Papers*, I: 348.
92. McNarney Report; McKinley interview, Newton Collection, FDRL; McKinley Report.
93. The previous two paragraphs draw on: McKinley Report; Hopkins, "Inside Story," 117; Cowling, *The Journey*, 100, 102; McKinley interview, Newton Collection, FDRL.
94. The previous two paragraphs draw on: McKinley Report; Cowling, *The Journey*, 101–2; Winant, *A Letter*, 149; Sir Ian Jacob MS Diary, JACB 1/9 (hereafter "Jacob MS Diary"), August 4, 1941, CAC; McKinley interview, Newton Collection, FDRL. Sources differ as to whether Hopkins spent his time at Scapa aboard *King George V*, *Prince of Wales*, or *Nelson*, but McKinley's eyewitness report that it was *King George V* seems the most compelling. That this was his host's flagship lends it weight. Thompson mentions that Hopkins was later transferred to the *Prince of Wales* for Churchill's arrival: Thompson interview (1906d), Sherwood Papers, HL.
95. Winant, *A Letter*, 149–50; Thompson interview (1906d), Sherwood Papers, HL; Sherwood, *The White House Papers*, I: 350; Hopkins, "Inside Story," 17; Winant to FDR, August 3, 1941, 740.0011 EW 1939/13615, RG 59, NARA.
96. HMS *Prince of Wales* Ship's Log, August 4, 1941, ADM 53/114891, NA; Jacob MS Diary, August 4, 1941, CAC; H. V. Morton, *Atlantic Meeting: An Account of Mr. Churchill's Voyage in H.M.S. Prince of Wales, in August 1941, and the Conference with President Roosevelt Which Resulted in the Atlantic Charter* (London: Methuen, 1943), 30, 38; Hopkins draft article for *Collier's*.
97. Gilbert, comp., *The Churchill War Papers*, III: 1033.

98. The previous two paragraphs draw on: Wilson, *The First Summit*, 55, 69; Flight Sergeant Geoffrey Green MS Diary, GREE 1 (hereafter "Green MS Diary"), August 5, 6, 7, and 8, 1941, CAC; Morton, *Atlantic Meeting*, 54; Jacob MS Diary, August 5, 1941, CAC.

99. Martin, *Downing Street*, 57; Jacob MS Diary, August 4, 5 and 6, 1941, CAC; Sherwood, *The White House Papers*, I: 351; Morton, *Atlantic Meeting*, 43–44, 59; Gilbert, *Winston S. Churchill*, VI: 1156; Hopkins draft article for *Collier's*.

100. Morton, *Atlantic Meeting*, 44, 48–51, 69, 76, 79–80; Martin, *Downing Street*, 57; Jacob MS Diary, August 4, 6, 7 and 8, 1941, CAC; Pawle and Thompson, *The War and Colonel Warden*, 127.

101. Morton, *Atlantic Meeting*, 48, 61–62; Jacob MS Diary, August 5, 1941, CAC.

102. Pawle and Thompson, *The War and Colonel Warden*, 127; Morton, *Atlantic Meeting*, 48, 62.

103. Thompson interview (1906d), Sherwood Papers, HL; Sherwood, *The White House Papers*, I: 350; Green MS Diary, August 5, 6, 7, and 10, 1941, CAC.

104. Sherwood, *The White House Papers*, I: 353.

105. Green MS Diary, August 7, 1941, CAC; Cadogan MS Diary, August 4, 1941, ACAD 1/10, CAC; Hopkins draft article for *Collier's*; Churchill, *The Second World War*, III: 381.

106. Davies MS Diary, September 8, 1941, LC; Reminiscences, October 18, 1953, box 872, Averell Harriman Papers, LC.

107. Hopkins Report, July 31 meeting, Part I, 12; Hopkins, "Inside Story," 117; Stettinius, *Lend-Lease*, 113.

108. Louis W. Koenig, *The Invisible Presidency* (New York: Rinehart, 1960), 331–32.

109. Leutze, ed., *The London Journal*, 361; Clapper MS Diary, August 4, 1941, LC; Lamont note, August 8, 1941, 209-16, Lamont Papers, BL.

110. Hopkins draft article for *Collier's*; Hellman, "House Guest"; Jacob MS Diary, August 9, 1941, CAC.

111. FDR memorandum, August 23, 1941, PSF (Safe): Atlantic Charter, FDRL; Wilson, *The First Summit*, 1–6, 18–20; *New York Times*, August 6 and 7, 1941; *Chicago Daily Tribune*, August 8 and 9, 1941; Ward, ed., *Closest Companion*, 140.

112. FDR memorandum, August 23, 1941, PSF (Safe): Atlantic Charter, FDRL; Green MS Diary, August 9, 1941, CAC; Jacob MS Diary, August 9, 1941, CAC; Ward, ed., *Closest Companion*, 140.

113. FDR memorandum, August 23, 1941, PSF (Safe): Atlantic Charter, FDRL; Wilson, *The First Summit*, 92.

114. Harriman 1959 interview, 34–35, CCOHC.

115. Kimball, *Forged in War*, 92; Morton, *Atlantic Meeting*, 88–89; Wilson, *The First Summit*, 78–79.

116. Harriman and Abel, *Special Envoy*, 75; Ward, ed., *Closest Companion*, 141; King MS Diary, November 1–2, 1941, LAC; Roosevelt, *As He Saw It*, 28–29; Sherwood, *The White House Papers*, I: 364; Hopkins to Pamela Churchill, August 27, 1941, Hopkins microfilm, reel 19, Hopkins Papers, FDRL; Harriman to Kathleen Harriman and Pamela Churchill, [August 1941], Chronological File,

box 160, Averell Harriman Papers, LC; Pamela Harriman interview, Newton Collection, FDRL.

117. Hopkins to FDR, August 4, 1941, CHAR 20/41, CAC; Jacob MS Diary, August 4 and 9, 1941, CAC; Green MS Diary, August 9, 1941, CAC; Morton, *Atlantic Meeting*, 91–92.

118. Reminiscences, October 18, 1953, box 872, Averell Harriman Papers, LC; Franklin D. Roosevelt Jr. interview, January 11, 1979, Oral History Interviews, Small Collections, FDRL; Lash, *Eleanor Roosevelt*, 267.

119. Langer and Gleason, *The World Crisis*, II: 667.

120. FDR and Churchill to Stalin, August 12, 1941, Major correspondents: FDR: Atlantic Charter, 1941, Welles Papers, FDRL; Gilbert, comp., *The Churchill War Papers*, III: 1061; Sherwood, *The White House Papers*, I: 360; Harriman 1959 interview, 38, CCOHC.

121. The previous three paragraphs draw on: Dallek, *Franklin D. Roosevelt*, 285; Wilson, *The First Summit*, 183–84; Kenneth S. Davis, *FDR: The War President, 1940–1943: A History* (New York: Random House, 2000), 251–53, 273; Burns, *Roosevelt: The Soldier of Freedom*, 120; Smith, *FDR*, 502–3; *Time*, August 18, 1941; Paul Saunders, "The Speaker and the Draft," *American History* 36, no. 3 (2001): 45–46; Hopkins draft article for *Collier's*; Sherwood, *The White House Papers*, I: 368.

122. Wilson, *The First Summit*, 141–44, 206–11; Langer and Gleason, *The World Crisis*, II: 665, 670–77; Heinrichs, *Threshold of War*, 155–56; Heinrichs, "President Franklin D. Roosevelt's Intervention," 330; Reynolds, *The Creation of the Anglo-American Alliance*, 214–17; Iriye, *The Origins of the Second World War*, 155–57.

123. Wilson, *The First Summit*, 178–79; Sherwood, *The White House Papers*, I: 363–64.

124. Jacob MS Diary, August 10, 1941, CAC; Morton, *Atlantic Meeting*, 87, 98–99; Wilson, *The First Summit*, 97–98; Martin, *Downing Street*, 58.

125. Martin, *Downing Street*, 58; Tuttle, *Harry L. Hopkins*, 115; Wilson, *The First Summit*, 98–99; Morton, *Atlantic Meeting*, 99–103; Green MS Diary, August 10, 1941, CAC; *Washington Post*, August 17, 1941; Churchill, *The Second World War*, III: 384.

126. Morton, *Atlantic Meeting*, 107; Harriman memorandum, August 10, 1941, Chronological File, box 160, Averell Harriman Papers, LC.

127. Morton, *Atlantic Meeting*, 103–4; Jacob MS Diary, August 10, 1941, CAC; Ward, ed., *Closest Companion*, 141; *Christian Science Monitor*, August 19, 1941; *Chicago Daily Tribune*, August 18, 1941; *Philadelphia Inquirer*, August 18, 1941; *New York Herald Tribune*, August 18, 1941.

128. Harriman memorandum, August 10, 1941; Averell Harriman to Pamela Churchill and Kathleen Harriman, [August 1941], both in Chronological File, box 160, Averell Harriman Papers, LC; Gilbert, *Winston S. Churchill*, VI: 1159–60; Martin, *Downing Street*, 59; David Dilks, ed., *The Diaries of Sir Alexander Cadogan, O.M., 1938–1945* (London: Cassell & Co., 1971), 398.

129. Wilson, *The First Summit*, 160–75; Dilks, ed., *The Diaries*, 399.

130. Hopkins to Churchill, August 11, 1941; Hopkins to Pound, August 11, 1941; Hopkins to Dill, August 11, 1941; Hopkins to Cadogan, August 11, 1941, all in Hopkins microfilm, reel 19, Hopkins Papers, FDRL.

131. Hopkins to Pamela Churchill, August 11, 1941, Hopkins microfilm, reel 19, Hopkins Papers, FDRL; Averell Harriman to Pamela Churchill and Kathleen Harriman, [August 1941], Chronological File, box 160, Averell Harriman Papers, LC.

132. Green MS Diary, August 12, 1941, CAC; Hopkins to Early, September 12, 1941, Hopkins microfilm, reel 19, Hopkins Papers, FDRL; also FDR to Hull, April 9, 1941, PSF (Departmental): Hull, FDRL; Churchill to Minister of Information and private office, April 24, 1941, PREM 4/26/6, NA.

133. Green MS Diary, August 12, 15, and 18, 1941, CAC; Wilson, *The First Summit*, 187-88, 193-96; Jacob MS Diary, August 19, 1941, CAC; *Washington Post*, August 20, 1941.

134. Memorandum regarding meeting between the President and the Prime Minister, [August 1941], Chronological File, box 150, Averell Harriman Papers, LC; Harriman 1959 interview, 45-46, CCOHC; Wilson, *The First Summit*, 198-99.

135. Edward M. Lamont, *Ambassador from Wall Street: The Story of Thomas W. Lamont* (Lanham, MD: Madison Books, 1993), 471.

136. Lamont, notes of conversation with FDR and Hopkins, August 15, 1941, 127-26, Lamont Papers, BL.

137. *New York Times*, August 17, 1941; *Time*, August 25, 1941; *Washington Post*, August 17, 1941; 761st press conference, August 16, 1941, PPC, XVIII: 76-77, 80; Wilson, *The First Summit*, 201-4.

138. *New York Times*, August 18, 1941.

139. Herbert Feis, *Churchill, Roosevelt, Stalin: The War They Waged and the Peace They Sought* (Princeton: Princeton University Press, 1957), 13. *Life* declared that in sharing confidences with the Soviet premier, Hopkins had penetrated "a seclusion more mysterious than the Dalai Lama's": *Life*, September 22, 1941.

140. See, e.g., Valentin Berezhkov interview, Newton Collection, FDRL.

141. Franklin D. Roosevelt Jr. interview, January 11, 1979, Oral History Interviews, Small Collections, FDRL.

142. Belle Willard Roosevelt MS Diary, "Unfinished notes," undated but probably August 1941, LC. The dinner took place at Hyde Park on August 23, 1941.

143. McJimsey, *Harry Hopkins*, 189; Glantz, *FDR and the Soviet Union*, 67, 85-86; Lash, *Eleanor Roosevelt*, 264; Costigliola, *Roosevelt's Lost Alliances*, 126; Davis and Lindley, *How War Came: An American White Paper*, 255.

144. Steinhardt to FDR, Hull and Welles, August 1, 1941, 740.0011 EW 1939/13605, RG 59, NARA.

145. Sherwood, *The White House Papers*, I: 346; Alan Barth, survey of editorial opinion, August 8, 1941, PSF (Departmental): Treasury: Morgenthau: Editorial Opinion, FDRL; *Wall Street Journal*, August 1, 1941.

146. Alan Barth, survey of editorial opinion, August 22, 1941, PSF (Departmental): Treasury: Morgenthau: Editorial Opinion, FDRL.

147. Hopkins to Ismay, August 7, 1941, Hopkins microfilm, reel 19, Hopkins Papers, FDRL; Hopkins, "Inside Story," 114, 116; Tree, *When the Moon Was High*, 133.
148. Kimball, *The Juggler*, 39.
149. A point made in Tuttle, *Harry L. Hopkins*, 107.
150. "Harry L. Hopkins," box 131, Cuneo Papers, FDRL.
151. Gilbert, comp., *The Churchill War Papers*, III: 51.

EPILOGUE: DECEMBER 1941

1. Dallek, *Franklin D. Roosevelt*, 287–92; Heinrichs, *Threshold of War*, 166–68; Fireside Chat to the Nation, September 11, 1941, PPA, X: 384–91; Reynolds, *The Creation of the Anglo-American Alliance*, 216; Cole, *Roosevelt and the Isolationists*, 446–53.
2. Cole, *Roosevelt and the Isolationists*, 423–24.
3. 765th press conference, August 29, 1941, PPC, XVIII: 126; *Washington Post*, August 30, 1941; FDR to Stalin, September 29, 1941, Harriman-Beaverbrook Mission, Sherwood Collection, Hopkins Papers, FDRL; Dallek, *Franklin D. Roosevelt*, 294–99.
4. FDR to Stettinius, November 7, 1941, FRUS, 1941, I: 857; Dawson, *The Decision to Aid Russia*, 282–84; Sherwood, *The White House Papers*, I: 400.
5. Freidel, *Franklin D. Roosevelt*, 378, 395; Reynolds, *From Munich to Pearl Harbor*, 158–66; Dallek, *Franklin D. Roosevelt*, 299–311; Iriye, *The Origins of the Second World War*, 159–61, 165–66, 173–78.
6. Heinrichs, *Threshold of War*, 218–19; Black, *Franklin Delano Roosevelt*, 687–89; Gilbert, *Second World War*, 272–76; Churchill, *The Second World War*, III: 551.
7. Hopkins memoranda, December 7, 1941, and January 24, 1942, both in Hopkins microfilm, reel 19, Hopkins Papers, FDRL; Sherwood, *The White House Papers*, I: 384–85; Gunther, *Roosevelt in Retrospect*, 347; Forrest Davis and Ernest K. Lindley, "How War Came," *Ladies' Home Journal*, July 1942.
8. Welles, *Sumner Welles*, 313–14; United States Congress, *Report of the Joint Committee on the Investigation of the Pearl Harbor Attack* (Washington, DC: U.S. Government Printing Office, 1946), 440 n. 1; *New York Times*, December 10, 1941.
9. *New York Times*, December 8, 1941, and December 7, 1980; Waller, *Wild Bill Donovan*, 84.
10. *New York Times*, December 8, 1941, and December 7, 1980; *Chicago Daily Tribune*, December 8, 1941; Ford, *Donovan*, 117; Dunlop, *Donovan*, 331.
11. His diary contained appointments with Ralph H. Cake, a Republican national committeeman from Oregon, and Connecticut Republicans Samuel F. Pryor, J. Kenneth Bradley, and former governor Raymond E. Baldwin: Willkie MS Diary, December 7 and 8, 1941, Willkie Papers, LL.
12. Mervyn LeRoy, *Mervyn LeRoy: Take One* (New York: Hawthorn Books, 1974), 159–60; *Chicago Daily Tribune*, May 31, 1952; *New York Times*, December 8, 1941; *Washington Times*, December 1, 1991.

13. FDR to Willkie, December 5, 1941, Special Correspondence: Willkie, Wendell L., box 11, Van Doren Papers, LC; Welles to FDR, December 5, 1941, PPF 7023, FDRL; Campbell to FO, undated, FO 371/26200 A1084/254/45, NA; Casey MS Diary, February 17 and 27, April 1 and December 15, 1941, NAA.

14. Willkie to FDR, 10 December, Correspondence: Roosevelt, Franklin D., Willkie Papers, LL; Barnard interview with Irita Van Doren, Notes: Relations with Roosevelt, Barnard Papers, LL; Casey MS Diary, February 27, 1941, NAA; Barnard, *Wendell Willkie*, 136.

15. *Christian Science Monitor*, December 15, 1941; *New York Times*, December 16 and 18, 1941; *Washington Post*, December 16, 1941; Barnard, *Wendell Willkie*, 321–25; Sherwood, *The White House Papers*, I: 487.

16. Harriman and Abel, *Special Envoy*, 111–12; Winant, *A Letter*, 198; Jenkins, *Chequers*, 101–2; Dallek, *Franklin D. Roosevelt*, 299–300; Hopkins memorandum, January 24, 1942, Hopkins microfilm, reel 19, Hopkins Papers, FDRL.

17. Churchill, *The Second World War*, III: 537–39; Sherwood, *The White House Papers*, I: 443; Winant, *A Letter*, 198–99; Harriman and Abel, *Special Envoy*, 111–12; Martin, *Downing Street*, 66–67; John Martin and Kathleen Harriman Mortimer interviews, Newton Collection, FDRL.

18. Churchill, *The Second World War*, III: 538; David Reynolds, *In Command of History: Churchill Fighting and Writing the Second World War* (New York: Random House, 2005), 264. A few days later Harriman told a dinner companion he hoped that "American cities will be blitzed, so as to wake the people up": James, ed., *Chips*, 314.

19. Churchill, *The Second World War*, III: 539–40.

20. Hopkins memorandum, December 7, 1941, Hopkins microfilm, reel 19, Hopkins Papers, FDRL; Dallek, *Franklin D. Roosevelt*, 312; Black, *Franklin Delano Roosevelt*, 1125; *Washington Post*, December 8, 1941.

21. Hopkins memorandum, December 7, 1941, Hopkins microfilm, reel 19, Hopkins Papers, FDRL; Perkins, *The Roosevelt I Knew*, 304–5; Stanley Weintraub, *Long Day's Journey into War: December 7, 1941* (New York: Plume, 1991), 462; Roosevelt, *This I Remember*, 187; Gunther, *Roosevelt in Retrospect*, 351; Kendrick, *Prime Time*, 239; Cole, *Roosevelt and the Isolationists*, 503.

22. Murrow thought it was "the most poignant utterance he had ever heard in his life": Murrow interview (1902), Sherwood Papers, HL; *Saturday Evening Post*, December 10, 1949; Kendrick, *Prime Time*, 239–40; Gunther, *Roosevelt in Retrospect*, 352; A. M. Sperber, *Murrow: His Life and Times* (New York: Freundlich Books, 1986), 206–7; Roosevelt, *This I Remember*, 187.

23. *Saturday Evening Post*, December 10, 1949; Gunther, *Roosevelt in Retrospect*, 352; Sperber, *Murrow*, 206–7; Kendrick, *Prime Time*, 240; Waller, *Wild Bill Donovan*, 84–85; Hopkins memorandum, December 7, 1941, Hopkins microfilm, reel 19, Hopkins Papers, FDRL.

24. *New York Times*, December 9, 1941; *Washington Post*, December 9, 1941.

25. Address to the Congress Asking That a State of War Be Declared Between the United States and Japan, December 8, 1941, PPA, X: 514; *New York Times*, December 9, 1941; *Washington Post*, December 9, 1941.

26. *New York Times*, December 9, 1941.

27. Sherwood, *The White House Papers*, II: 923; Rosenman, *Working with Roosevelt*, 518–20, 539–40, 542–48.

28. The previous two paragraphs draw on: *New York Times*, January 31, 1946; Churchill, *The Second World War*, III: 20–21; Bohlen and Phelps, *Witness to History*, 244; Frank Costigliola, "Broken Circle: The Isolation of Franklin D. Roosevelt in World War II," *Diplomatic History* 32, no. 5 (2008): 706–7; Sherwood, *The White House Papers*, II: 862–63; Robert Hopkins and Mary Jo Mihm interviews, Newton Collection, FDRL.

29. Sherwood, *The White House Papers*, II: 874–906, 916; Bohlen interview (1873), Sherwood Papers, HL; Harriman and Abel, *Special Envoy*, 459, 463–75; Louise Hopkins to Beaverbrook, January 1946, BBK/C/175, Beaverbrook Papers, PA; Robert Hopkins interview, Newton Collection, FDRL; Reynolds interview (2441), Sherwood Papers, HL.

30. Welles, *Sumner Welles*, 341–54; Gellman, *Secret Affairs*, 302–31, 345; Ward, ed., *Closest Companion*, 226, 242–44; Costigliola, *Roosevelt's Lost Alliances*, 187–90.

31. Welles, *Sumner Welles*, 357–74, 380; Gellman, *Secret Affairs*, 389–96.

32. Waller, *Wild Bill Donovan*, 93–97, 115–16, 333–38, 352–53; Ford, *Donovan*, 127–28; Brown, *The Last Hero*, 298–99.

33. Waller, *Wild Bill Donovan*, 341–48, 360–73, 377–82, 386; Ford, *Donovan*, 315–18, 326–27, 332–33.

34. See Willkie to FDR, July 29, 1942; FDR to Marshall, July 31, 1942; FDR to Willkie, August 2, 1942; FDR to Stalin, August 22, 1942, all in PSF (Subject): Willkie: 1940–1942, FDRL; FDR to Chiang Kai-shek, August 21, 1941, PPF 7023, FDRL; Wendell L. Willkie, *One World* (London: Cassell & Co., 1943); Neal, *Dark Horse*, 231–33, 255–56; Cowles, *Mike Looks Back*, 87–90; Hannah Pakula, *The Last Empress: Madame Chiang Kai-shek and the Birth of Modern China* (New York: Simon & Schuster, 2009), 410–12, 416–18, 432–34; Barnard, *Wendell Willkie*, 360–64, 370–73; Sherwood, *The White House Papers*, II: 632–34; *Saturday Evening Post*, February 27, 1943; *Look*, March 9, 1943.

35. See, e.g., FDR to Willkie, March 6, 1943; Willkie to FDR, March 19, 1943, both in PPF 7023, FDRL; Address to National Republican Club, New York City, February 12, 1941, Speeches: January 1941–March 1942, Willkie Papers, LL; Lamont to Halifax, November 2, 1942, 137-25, Lamont Papers, BL.

36. Peggy Gilmore to Willkie, undated; Eddy Gilmore to Willkie, June 11, 1943; Willkie to Stalin, June 14, 1943; Andrei Gromyko to Willkie, June 19, 1943; Eddy Gilmore to Willkie, July 10, 1943; Eddy Gilmore to Willkie, September 3, 1944, all in Correspondence: Gilmore, Eddy, Willkie Papers, LL; Eddy Gilmore, *Me and My Russian Wife* (Garden City, NY: Doubleday, 1954), 141–42, 155–56; *Time*, August 12, 1946; *New York Times*, June 10, 1953, and October 7, 1967; *Chicago Daily Tribune*, September 30, 1956; Neal, *Dark Horse*, 186.

37. Neal, *Dark Horse*, 298–310, 313–24; Barnard, *Wendell Willkie*, 478–87, 493, 499; *New York Times*, October 9, 1944.

38. Abramson, *Spanning the Century*, 348–405, 409–22; Robert Meiklejohn interview, undated, Abramson Papers.

39. Olson, *Citizens of London*, 384–86; Bellush, *He Walked Alone*, 225–30.
40. Personal communication from Robert Dallek, December 18, 2011; Abramson, *Spanning the Century*, 487–503, 516–69, 581–87, 635–42; Lee H. Burke, *Ambassador at Large: Diplomat Extraordinary* (The Hague: Nijhoff, 1972), 56–81; Berlin to Pamela Harriman, undated, box 5, Pamela Harriman Papers, LC; Averell Harriman interview, undated, Abramson Papers.
41. Abramson, *Spanning the Century*, 683–85; Smith, *Reflected Glory*, 255–56, 260–77, 290–304, 308–9, 314–18, 380–437; Ogden, *Life of the Party*, 329–31, 337–45, 358, 403–7, 441–61; *New York Times*, February 6, 1997; *Washington Post*, February 6, 1997; Ben Bradlee to Pamela Harriman, October 10, 1986, and undated reply, both in box 5, Pamela Harriman Papers, LC.
42. A distinction made in Reynolds, *From Munich to Pearl Harbor*, 116.
43. Reynolds, *From Munich to Pearl Harbor*, 177–78.
44. Dallek, *Franklin D. Roosevelt*, 530.
45. Berlin, *Personal Impressions*, 21.
46. Sherwood, *The White House Papers*, I: 446; Pawle and Thompson, *The War and Colonel Warden*, 150.
47. Contrast the "perfect understanding" described in Churchill, *The Second World War*, II: 22, with more recent histories: Reynolds, *The Creation of the Anglo-American Alliance*; Hathaway, *Ambiguous Partnership*; and Christopher Thorne, *Allies of a Kind: The United States, Britain, and the War against Japan, 1941–1945* (Oxford: Oxford University Press, 1978).
48. Kimball, *The Juggler*, 204 n. 7.
49. Acceptance of the Renomination for the Presidency, June 27, 1936, PPA, V: 235.

Bibliography

Archival papers

AUSTRALIAN ARCHIVES

National Archives of Australia, Canberra and Melbourne
  Stanley Melbourne Bruce Papers
  Richard G. Casey Papers
National Library of Australia, Canberra
  Sir Robert Menzies Papers and MS Diary

CANADIAN ARCHIVES

Library and Archives Canada, Ottawa
  William Lyon Mackenzie King MS Diary
University of Toronto Archives, Toronto
  Vincent Massey Papers

UNITED KINGDOM ARCHIVES

Bodleian Library, Department of Special Collections & Western Manuscripts, University of Oxford
  Sir Stafford Cripps MS Diary

Borthwick Institute for Archives, University of York
    1st Earl of Halifax MS Diary and Secret MS Diary
Cadbury Research Library, Special Collections, University of Birmingham
    1st Earl of Avon MS Diary
Churchill Archives Centre, Churchill College, Cambridge
    Chartwell Papers (CHAR)
    Churchill Papers (CHUR)
    Churchill Additional Collection (WCHL)
    Churchill Press Cuttings Collection (CHPC)
    Sir Alexander Cadogan MS Diary (ACAD)
    Sir John Colville MS Diary (CLVL)
    Major General William J. Donovan Papers (DOVN)
    John H. Godfrey Papers (GDFY)
    Flight Sergeant G. Green MS Diary (GREE)
    Sir Ian Jacob MS Diary (JACB)
Vere Harmsworth Library, University of Oxford
    Henry L. Stimson MS Diary [Microfilm copy]
National Archives, Kew
    Admiralty Papers
      ADM 53: Ships' Logs
    Air Ministry Papers
    Foreign Office Papers
      FO 371: Political and Diplomatic Files
      FO 800: Private Office Papers
      FO 954: Private Office Papers of the Earl of Avon
      FO 1093: Permanent Under-Secretary's Department
    Prime Minister Winston S. Churchill Papers
      PREM 3: Prime Minister's Operational Correspondence and Papers
      PREM 4: Prime Minister's Confidential Correspondence and Papers
    Security Service Papers
      KV 4: Security Service Policy Files
    War Cabinet Papers
      CAB 65: War Cabinet Conclusions and Minutes
      CAB 66: War Cabinet Memoranda

CAB 115: War Cabinet Central Office for North American
    Supplies Minutes and Papers
Parliamentary Archives, London
    Beaverbrook Papers

UNITED STATES ARCHIVES

Air Force Historical Research Agency, Montgomery, AL
    Special Observer Corps Papers
    John R. Alison Interview Transcript (1979)
Baker Library, Harvard Business School, Cambridge, MA
    Thomas W. Lamont Papers
Columbia Center for Oral History Collection, Columbia University, New
    York, NY
    Marquis W. Childs Interview Transcript (1959)
    Marquis W. Childs Interview Transcript (1969)
    W. Averell Harriman Interview Transcript (1959)
    W. Averell Harriman Interview Transcript (1969)
    W. Averell Harriman Interview Transcript (1979)
    Alan G. Kirk Interview Transcript (1961)
    Arthur Krock Interview Transcript (1950)
    William Phillips Interview Transcript (1951)
    Samuel I. Rosenman Interview Transcript (1959)
    Henry A. Wallace Interview Transcript (1951)
Cowles Library, Drake University, Des Moines, IA
    John Cowles Papers
University of Delaware Library, Special Collections Department, Newark
    George S. Messersmith Papers
Georgetown University Library, Special Collections Division, Washington, DC
    Harry L. Hopkins Papers
    James D. Mooney Papers
Grinnell College Libraries, Department of Special Collections, Grinnell, IA
    George T. McJimsey Papers
Hoover Institution Library, Stanford, CA
    Compulsory Military Service Pamphlet Collection

Houghton Library, Harvard University, Cambridge, MA
 William Castle MS Diary
 J. Pierrepont Moffat Papers
 William Phillips Papers
 Robert E. Sherwood Papers
University of Iowa Libraries, Special Collections Department, Iowa City
 Henry A. Wallace MS Diary
Lyndon Baines Johnson Presidential Library, Austin, TX
 Drew Pearson Papers
Library of Congress, Manuscript Division, Washington, DC
 Joseph Alsop Papers
 Raymond P. Clapper Papers
 Russell W. Davenport Papers
 Joseph E. Davies Papers
 Felix Frankfurter Papers
 W. Averell Harriman Papers
 Pamela C. Harriman Papers
 Roy W. Howard Papers
 Everett Strait Hughes Papers
 Harold L. Ickes Papers and MS Diary
 Frank Knox Papers
 James M. Landis Papers
 Owen Lattimore Papers
 Breckinridge Long Papers
 Clare Boothe Luce Papers
 Belle Willard Roosevelt MS Diary
 Raymond Gram Swing Papers
 Irita Van Doren Papers
 William Allen White Papers
Lilly Library, Indiana University, Bloomington
 Ellsworth Barnard Papers
 Claude Bowers Papers
 Wendell L. Willkie Papers
Seeley G. Mudd Manuscript Library, Princeton University, Princeton, NJ
 Allen W. Dulles Papers

National Archives and Records Administration, College Park, MD
    RG 38: Records of the Chief of Naval Operations
    RG 59: General Records of the Department of State
    RG 263: Records of the Central Intelligence Agency
    RG 407: Records of the Adjutant General's Office
Courtesy of Thomas Parrish
    Rudy Abramson Papers
Claude Pepper Library, Florida State University, Tallahassee
    Claude Pepper MS Diary
Franklin D. Roosevelt Presidential Library and Museum, Hyde Park, NY
    Eleanor Roosevelt Oral History Project
    Franklin D. Roosevelt Papers as President
        Official File (OF)
        President's Personal File (PPF)
        President's Secretary's File, Departmental File [PSF (Departmental)]
        President's Secretary's File, Diplomatic File [PSF (Diplomatic)]
        President's Secretary's File, Safe File [PSF (Safe)]
        President's Secretary's File, Subject File [PSF (Subject)]
    Oral History Interviews, Small Collections
    Henry H. Adams Papers
    Adolf A. Berle Jr. Papers and MS Diary
    Ernest Cuneo Papers
    William R. Davis Papers
    Felix Frankfurter Papers
    Harry L. Hopkins Papers
    Joseph P. Lash Papers
    R. Walton Moore Papers
    Henry J. Morgenthau Jr. Papers, MS Diary, and Presidential MS
      Diary
    Verne Newton Collection
    Herbert C. Pell Papers
    Myron C. Taylor Papers
    Grace Tully Papers
    Sumner Welles Papers
    John G. Winant Papers

United States Army Military History Institute, Carlisle, PA
>   Charles L. Bolte Papers
>   William J. Donovan Papers
>   Office of the Chief of Military History, Personal Papers
>   Raymond E. Lee Papers
>   War College Curriculum Collection
Yale University Library, New Haven, CT
>   Edward M. House Papers

Newspapers and magazines

American Magazine
Argus
Boston Evening Transcript
Boston Globe
Boston Post
Chicago Daily News
Chicago Daily Tribune
Christian Science Monitor
Collier's
Daily Herald
Daily Mail
Daily Sketch
Daily Telegraph
Evening Telegram
Globe and Mail
Illustrated London News
Irish Times
Life
Look
Los Angeles Times
Manchester Guardian
News Chronicle

New Yorker
New York Herald Tribune
New York Times
New York World-Telegram
Observer
Philadelphia Inquirer
Richmond Times-Dispatch
Saturday Evening Post
Sunday Times
Sydney Morning Herald
Times
Wall Street Journal
Washington Post
Washington Times
Time

Interviews and correspondence

Letter from Diana Hopkins Halsted, September 25, 2011
Interview with Richard Holbrooke, April 19, 2010
Interview with George Mitchell, June 3, 2011
Interview with Arthur M. Schlesinger Jr., April 28, 2003
Interview with William J. vanden Heuvel, February 6, 2012

Selected books and articles

Abramson, Rudy. *Spanning the Century: The Life of W. Averell Harriman, 1891–1986.* New York: Morrow, 1992.
Adams, Henry H. *Harry Hopkins: A Biography.* New York: Putnam, 1977.
Alsop, Joseph, and Robert Kintner. *American White Paper: The Story of American Diplomacy and the Second World War.* London: Michael Joseph, 1940.
Ambrose, Stephen E. *Rise to Globalism: American Foreign Policy Since 1938.* 5th rev. ed. Harmondsworth, UK: Penguin, 1988.

Aronson, Theo. *The Royal Family at War*. London: John Murray, 1993.

Aslet, Clive. "Cherkley Court." *Country Life*, April 19, 2007.

Barnard, Ellsworth. *Wendell Willkie: Fighter for Freedom*. Marquette: Northern Michigan University Press, 1966.

Barnes, Joseph. *Willkie: The Events He Was Part of, the Ideas He Fought For*. New York: Simon & Schuster, 1952.

Bastock, John. *Australia's Ships of War*. Sydney: Angus & Robertson, 1975.

Beaton, Cecil. *The Years Between: Diaries, 1939–44*. London: Weidenfeld & Nicolson, 1965.

Beesly, Patrick. *Very Special Admiral: The Life of Admiral J. H. Godfrey, CB*. London: Hamilton, 1980.

Bell, Amy Helen. *London Was Ours: Diaries and Memoirs of the London Blitz*. London: I.B. Tauris, 2008.

Bellush, Bernard. *He Walked Alone: A Biography of John Gilbert Winant*. The Hague: Mouton, 1968.

Bennett, Gill. *Churchill's Man of Mystery: Desmond Morton and the World of Intelligence*. London: Routledge, 2006.

Berezhkov, Valentin M. *At Stalin's Side: His Interpreter's Memoirs from the October Revolution to the Fall of the Dictator's Empire*. Secaucus, NJ: Carol Publishing Group, 1994.

Berlin, Isaiah. *Personal Impressions*. Edited by Henry Hardy. 2nd ed. London: Pimlico, 1998.

Beschloss, Michael R. *Kennedy and Roosevelt: The Uneasy Alliance*. New York: Norton, 1980.

Black, Conrad. *Franklin Delano Roosevelt: Champion of Freedom*. New York: PublicAffairs, 2003.

Blum, John Morton. *From the Morgenthau Diaries*. 3 vols. Boston: Houghton Mifflin, 1959–65.

———, ed. *The Price of Vision: The Diary of Henry A. Wallace, 1942–1946*. Boston: Houghton Mifflin, 1973.

Bohlen, Charles E., and Robert Howard Phelps. *Witness to History, 1929–1969*. London: Weidenfeld & Nicolson, 1973.

Bourke-White, Margaret. "A Photographer in Moscow." *Harper's Magazine*, March 1942.

———. *Portrait of Myself*. New York: Simon & Schuster, 1963.

———. *Shooting the Russian War*. New York: Simon & Schuster, 1942.

Bridges, Peter S. "Spaso House." *Foreign Service Journal*, April 1964.

Brown, Anthony Cave. *The Last Hero: Wild Bill Donovan*. New York: Times Books, 1982.

Bullitt, Orville H., ed. *For the President, Personal and Secret: Correspondence between Franklin D. Roosevelt and William C. Bullitt*. Boston: Houghton Mifflin, 1972.

Burgess, Simon M. *Stafford Cripps: A Political Life*. London: Victor Gollancz, 1999.

Burk, Kathleen. "The Lineaments of Foreign Policy: The United States and a 'New World Order,' 1919–1939." *Journal of American Studies* 26, no. 3 (1992): 377–91.

Burke, Lee H. *Ambassador at Large: Diplomat Extraordinary.* The Hague: Nijhoff, 1972.

Burns, James MacGregor. *Roosevelt: The Lion and the Fox.* London: Secker & Warburg, 1956.

———. *Roosevelt: The Soldier of Freedom.* New York: Harcourt Brace Jovanovich, 1970.

Butler, J. R. M. *Lord Lothian, Philip Kerr, 1882–1940.* London: Macmillan, 1960.

Caine, Philip D. *Spitfires, Thunderbolts, and Warm Beer: An American Fighter Pilot over Europe.* Dulles, VA: Potomac Books, 2005.

Cannadine, David, ed. *Blood, Toil, Tears and Sweat: Winston Churchill's Famous Speeches.* London: Cassell & Co., 1989.

Cantril, Hadley, ed. *Public Opinion, 1935–1946.* Princeton: Princeton University Press, 1951.

Casey, Steven. *Cautious Crusade: Franklin D. Roosevelt, American Public Opinion, and the War against Nazi Germany.* Oxford: Oxford University Press, 2001.

Cassidy, Henry C. *Moscow Dateline, 1941–1943.* London: Cassell & Co., 1943.

Catledge, Turner. "It's 'Send for Harry.'" *New York Times,* March 16, 1941.

Chernobaev, A. A., ed. *Na Priëme u Stalina: Tetradi (Zhurnaly) Zapisei Lits, Priniatykh I.V. Stalinym (1924–1953 gg.).* Moscow: Novyi Khronograf, 2008.

Childs, Marquis W. "The Education of Wendell Willkie." In *The Roosevelt Era,* edited by Milton Crane. New York: Boni & Gaer, 1947.

———. "The President's Best Friend." *Saturday Evening Post,* April 19 and 26, 1941.

Churchill, Winston. *The Second World War.* 6 vols. London: Cassell & Co., 1948–54.

Ciechanowski, Jan. *Defeat in Victory.* Garden City, NY: Doubleday, 1947.

Cleworth, Robert, ed. *The Fabulous Catalina: A Collection of Catalina and Flying Boat Anecdotes from Veterans and Relatives of Those Who Flew These Machines.* Roseville, NSW, Australia: J. R. Cleworth, 2006.

Clifford, J. Garry. "Both Ends of the Telescope: New Perspectives on FDR and American Entry into World War II." *Diplomatic History* 13, no. 2 (1989): 213–30.

Clifford, J. Garry, and Samuel R. Spencer Jr. *The First Peacetime Draft.* Lawrence: University Press of Kansas, 1986.

Cole, Wayne S. "American Appeasement." In *Appeasement in Europe: A Reassessment of U.S. Policies,* edited by David F. Schmitz and Richard D. Challener. New York: Greenwood Press, 1990.

———. *Roosevelt and the Isolationists, 1932–45.* Lincoln: University of Nebraska Press, 1983.

Collier, Peter, and David Horowitz. *The Kennedys: An American Drama.* London: Secker & Warburg, 1984.

Colville, John. *Footprints in Time.* London: Collins, 1976.

———. *The Fringes of Power: Downing Street Diaries, 1939–1955.* London: Hodder & Stoughton, 1985.

Costigliola, Frank. "Broken Circle: The Isolation of Franklin D. Roosevelt in World War II." *Diplomatic History* 32, no. 5 (2008): 677–718.

———. *Roosevelt's Lost Alliances: How Personal Politics Helped Start the Cold War.* Princeton: Princeton University Press, 2012.

Cousins, Geoffrey. *The Story of Scapa Flow*. London: Frederick Muller Limited, 1965.

Cowles, Gardner. *Mike Looks Back: The Memoirs of Gardner Cowles, Founder of Look Magazine*. New York: Gardner Cowles, 1985.

Cowling, Ted. *The Journey: Per Ardua ad Astra, through Hardship to the Stars*. Wellington, UK: Laundry Cottage, 2005.

Culbert, David H. "Radio's Raymond Gram Swing: 'He Isn't the Kind of Man You Would Call Ray.'" *Historian* 35, no. 4 (1973): 587–606.

Cull, Nicholas John. *Selling War: The British Propaganda Campaign against American "Neutrality" in World War II*. New York: Oxford University Press, 1995.

Dallek, Robert. *Franklin D. Roosevelt and American Foreign Policy, 1932–1945*. New York: Oxford University Press, 1995.

———. "Woodrow Wilson, Politician." *Wilson Quarterly* (Autumn 1991): 106–14.

Danchev, Alex, and Daniel Todman, eds. *War Diaries, 1939–1945: Field Marshal Lord Alanbrooke*. Berkeley: University of California Press, 2001.

Davenport, Marcia. *Too Strong for Fantasy*. London: Collins, 1968.

Davies, Joseph Edward. *Mission to Moscow*. London: Victor Gollancz, 1942.

Davis, Deborah. *Katharine the Great: Katharine Graham and Her Washington Post Empire*. 3rd ed. New York: Sheridan Square Press, 1991.

Davis, Forrest, and Ernest K. Lindley. "How War Came." *Ladies' Home Journal*, July 1942.

———. *How War Came: An American White Paper, from the Fall of France to Pearl Harbor*. New York: Simon & Schuster, 1942.

Davis, Kenneth S. *FDR: Into the Storm, 1937–1940: A History*. New York: Random House, 1993.

———. *FDR: The War President, 1940–1943: A History*. New York: Random House, 2000.

Dawson, Raymond H. *The Decision to Aid Russia, 1941: Foreign Policy and Domestic Politics*. Chapel Hill: University of North Carolina Press, 1959.

Dilks, David, ed. *The Diaries of Sir Alexander Cadogan, O.M., 1938–1945*. London: Cassell & Co., 1971.

Dillon, Mary Earhart. *Wendell Willkie, 1892–1944*. Philadelphia: Lippincott, 1952.

Divine, Robert A. *Roosevelt and World War II*. Baltimore: Johns Hopkins University Press, 1969.

———. *Second Chance: The Triumph of Internationalism in America during World War II*. New York: Atheneum, 1967.

Dixon, Sir Owen. *Jesting Pilate, and Other Papers and Addresses*. Sydney: Law Book Co., 1965.

Doenecke, Justus D. "General Robert E. Wood: The Evolution of a Conservative." *Journal of the Illinois State Historical Society* 71, no. 3 (1978): 162–75.

———. "U.S. Policy and the European War, 1939–1941." *Diplomatic History* 19, no. 4 (1995): 669–98.

Donovan, William J. "Address by Colonel William J. Donovan at The Union League of Philadelphia, April 29, 1941." *Union League of Philadelphia Annual Report* (1941): 79–95.

———. "Should the United States Adopt Compulsory Military Training as a Permanent Policy? Pro." *Congressional Digest* 20, no. 8/9 (1941): 208–9.

Dulles, Allen W. "William J. Donovan and the National Security." Central Intelligence Agency, https://www.cia.gov/library/center-for-the-study-of-intelligence/kent-csi/vol3no3/html/v03i3a07p_0001.htm.

Dunlop, Richard. *Donovan: America's Master Spy.* Chicago: Rand McNally, 1982.

Duroselle, Jean-Baptiste. *L'Abîme: 1939–1945.* Paris: Imprimerie Nationale, 1982.

Duskin, Gerald, and Ralph Segman. *If the Gods Are Good: The Epic Sacrifice of HMS Jervis Bay.* Annapolis, MD: Naval Institute Press, 2004.

Eden, Anthony. *The Eden Memoirs: The Reckoning.* London: Cassell & Co., 1965.

Elletson, D. H. *Chequers and the Prime Ministers.* London: Robert Hale, 1970.

Elsey, George M. "Some White House Recollections, 1942–1953." *Diplomatic History* 12, no. 3 (1988): 357–64.

Erickson, John. *Stalin's War with Germany: The Road to Stalingrad.* London: Weidenfeld & Nicolson, 1975.

Falcoff, Mark. "Too Impressive to Be Real." *National Interest* 52 (1998): 100–105.

Farnham, Barbara Rearden. *Roosevelt and the Munich Crisis: A Study of Political Decision-Making.* Princeton: Princeton University Press, 1997.

Farrer, David. *G—for God Almighty: A Personal Memoir of Lord Beaverbrook.* London: Weidenfeld & Nicolson, 1969.

"The FDR Tapes: Secret Recordings Made in the Oval Office of the President in the Autumn of 1940." *American Heritage* 33, no. 2 (1982): 9–24.

Federal Writers' Project, New York City. *New York City Guide.* New York: Random House, 1939.

Feely, Terence. *Number 10: The Private Lives of Six Prime Ministers.* London: Sidgwick & Jackson, 1982.

Feis, Herbert. *Churchill, Roosevelt, Stalin: The War They Waged and the Peace They Sought.* Princeton: Princeton University Press, 1957.

———. "Some Notes on Historical Record-Keeping, the Role of Historians, and the Influence of Historical Memories during the Era of the Second World War." In *The Historian and the Diplomat: The Role of History and Historians in American Foreign Policy,* edited by Francis L. Loewenheim. New York: Harper & Row, 1967.

Fergusson, Bernard, ed. *The Business of War: The War Narrative of Major-General Sir John Kennedy.* London: Hutchinson, 1957.

Ford, Corey. *Donovan of OSS.* Boston: Little, Brown, 1970.

Freidel, Frank. *Franklin D. Roosevelt: A Rendezvous with Destiny.* Boston: Little, Brown, 1990.

Fullilove, Michael. "All the Presidents' Men." *Foreign Affairs* 84, no. 2 (2005): 13–18.

Gaddis, John Lewis. *Strategies of Containment: A Critical Appraisal of Postwar American National Security Policy.* New York: Oxford University Press, 1982.

Gellman, Irwin F. *Secret Affairs: Franklin Roosevelt, Cordell Hull, and Sumner Welles.* Baltimore: Johns Hopkins University Press, 1995.

Gilbert, Martin, comp. *The Churchill War Papers.* 3 vols. London: Heinemann, 1993–2000.

———. *Second World War.* New [2nd] ed. London: Phoenix Press, 2000.

———. *Winston S. Churchill.* Revised ed. 8 vols. London: Heinemann, 1966–88.

Gilmore, Eddy. *Me and My Russian Wife.* Garden City, NY: Doubleday, 1954.

Glantz, Mary E. *FDR and the Soviet Union: The President's Battles over Foreign Policy.* Lawrence: University Press of Kansas, 2005.

Goodwin, Doris Kearns. *No Ordinary Time: Franklin and Eleanor Roosevelt: The Home Front in World War II.* New York: Touchstone, 1994.

Gopnik, Adam. "Finest Hours: The Making of Winston Churchill." *New Yorker,* August 30, 2010.

Gorodetsky, Gabriel. *Stafford Cripps' Mission to Moscow, 1940–42.* Cambridge: Cambridge University Press, 1984.

Great Britain. Foreign Office. *Documents on German Foreign Policy.* Series D. Vol. VIII. London: H.M.S.O., 1954.

Grey, Ian. *Stalin, Man of History.* London: Weidenfeld & Nicolson, 1979.

Gunther, John. *Roosevelt in Retrospect: A Profile in History.* London: Hamish Hamilton, 1950.

Halifax, Earl of. *Fulness of Days.* London: Collins, 1957.

Halsted, James A. "Severe Malnutrition in a Public Servant of the World War II Era: The Medical History of Harry Hopkins." *Transactions of the American Clinical and Climatological Association* 86 (1975): 23–32.

Harbutt, Fraser. "Churchill, Hopkins, and the 'Other' Americans: An Alternative Perspective on Anglo-American Relations, 1941–1945." *International History Review* 8, no. 2 (1986): 236–82.

Harper, John Lamberton. *American Visions of Europe: Franklin D. Roosevelt, George F. Kennan, and Dean G. Acheson.* Cambridge: Cambridge University Press, 1994.

Harriman, W. Averell, and Elie Abel. *Special Envoy to Churchill and Stalin, 1941–1946.* London: Hutchinson, 1976.

Harris, Stephen L. *Duffy's War: Fr. Francis Duffy, Wild Bill Donovan, and the Irish Fighting 69th in World War I.* Washington, DC: Potomac Books, 2006.

"Harry Hopkins." *Fortune,* July 1935.

Hassell, Ulrich von. *The von Hassell Diaries, 1938–1944: The Story of the Forces against Hitler inside Germany.* London: Hamish Hamilton, 1948.

Hathaway, Robert M. *Ambiguous Partnership: Britain and America, 1944–1947.* New York: Columbia University Press, 1981.

Heinrichs, Waldo. "President Franklin D. Roosevelt's Intervention in the Battle of the Atlantic, 1941." *Diplomatic History* 10, no. 4 (1986): 311–32.

———. *Threshold of War: Franklin D. Roosevelt and American Entry into World War II.* New York: Oxford University Press, 1988.

Hellman, Geoffrey T. "House Guest." *New Yorker,* August 7 and 14, 1943.

Herman, Arthur. *Freedom's Forge: How American Business Produced Victory in World War II.* New York: Random House, 2012.

Hilton, Stanley E. "The Welles Mission to Europe, February–March 1940: Illusion or Realism?" *Journal of American History* 58, no. 1 (1971): 93–120.

Hogben, Lawrence. "Sinking the 'Bismarck.'" *London Review of Books* 23, no. 8 (2001): 36–37.

Hooker, Nancy Harvison, ed. *The Moffat Papers: Selections from the Diplomatic Journals of Jay Pierrepont Moffat, 1919–1943*. Cambridge, MA: Harvard University Press, 1956.

Hopkins, Harry. "The Inside Story of My Meeting with Stalin." *American Magazine*, December 1941.

Hopkins, June. *Harry Hopkins: Sudden Hero, Brash Reformer*. New York: St. Martin's, 1999.

Hull, Cordell. *The Memoirs of Cordell Hull*. 2 vols. London: Hodder & Stoughton, 1948.

Ickes, Harold L. *The Secret Diary of Harold L. Ickes*. 3 vols. New York: Simon & Schuster, 1953–54.

Iriye, Akira. *The Origins of the Second World War in Asia and the Pacific*. London: Longman, 1987.

Isaacson, Walter, and Evan Thomas. *The Wise Men: Six Friends and the World They Made: Acheson, Bohlen, Harriman, Kennan, Lovett, McCloy*. London: Faber & Faber, 1986.

Ismay, Hastings Lionel. *The Memoirs of General the Lord Ismay*. London: Heinemann, 1960.

Israel, Fred L. *Nevada's Key Pittman*. Lincoln: University of Nebraska Press, 1963.

———, ed. *The War Diary of Breckinridge Long: Selections from the War Years, 1939–1944*. Lincoln: University of Nebraska Press, 1966.

Jakub, Jay. *Spies and Saboteurs: Anglo-American Collaboration and Rivalry in Human Intelligence Collection and Special Operations, 1940–45*. Basingstoke, UK: Macmillan, 1999.

James, Robert Rhodes, ed. *Chips: The Diaries of Sir Henry Channon*. London: Weidenfeld & Nicolson, 1967.

Jeffery, Keith. *MI6: The History of the Secret Intelligence Service, 1909–1949*. London: Bloomsbury, 2010.

Jenkins, J. G. *Chequers: A History of the Prime Minister's Buckinghamshire Home*. Oxford: Pergamon, 1967.

Jenkins, William. "In the Shadow of a Grain Elevator: A Portrait of an Irish Neighborhood in Buffalo, New York, in the Nineteenth and Twentieth Centuries." *Éire-Ireland: A Journal of Irish Studies* (Spring–Summer 2002): 14–37.

Johnston, Thomas. *Memories*. London: Collins, 1952.

Jonas, Manfred. *Isolationism in America, 1935–1941*. New ed. Chicago: Imprint Publications, 1990.

Jones, Christopher. *No. 10 Downing Street: The Story of a House*. London: British Broadcasting Corporation, 1985.

Kahn, E. J., Jr. "Plenipotentiary—I." *New Yorker*, May 3, 1952.

———. "Plenipotentiary—II." *New Yorker*, May 10, 1952.

———. *The World of Swope*. New York: Simon & Schuster, 1965.

Kay, Hubert. "Wendell Willkie: A Big Businessman with Liberal Ideas Gets a Republican Presidential Boom." *Life*, May 13, 1940.

Kendrick, Alexander. *Prime Time: The Life of Edward R. Murrow*. Boston: Little, Brown, 1969.

Kennan, George F. *Memoirs, 1925–1950*. London: Hutchinson, 1968.

Kennedy, Louisa. "House with a Lustrous Past." *New York Times*, March 31, 1985.

Kershaw, Ian. *Fateful Choices: Ten Decisions That Changed the World, 1940–1941*. London: Penguin, 2007.

Kimball, Warren F., ed. *Churchill and Roosevelt: The Complete Correspondence*. 3 vols. London: Collins, 1984.

———. *Forged in War: Churchill, Roosevelt and the Second World War*. London: HarperCollins, 1998.

———. *The Juggler: Franklin Roosevelt as Wartime Statesman*. Princeton: Princeton University Press, 1991.

———. *The Most Unsordid Act: Lend-Lease, 1939–1941*. Baltimore: Johns Hopkins University Press, 1969.

Kipling, Rudyard. *Sea Warfare*. London: Macmillan, 1916.

Knox, MacGregor. *Mussolini Unleashed, 1939–1941: Politics and Strategy in Fascist Italy's Last War*. Cambridge: Cambridge University Press, 1982.

Koenig, Louis W. *The Invisible Presidency*. New York: Rinehart, 1960.

Koskoff, David E. *Joseph P. Kennedy: A Life and Times*. Englewood Cliffs, NJ: Prentice Hall, 1974.

Lamont, Edward M. *Ambassador from Wall Street: The Story of Thomas W. Lamont*. Lanham, MD: Madison Books, 1993.

Langer, William L., and S. Everett Gleason. *The World Crisis and American Foreign Policy*. 2 vols. London: Royal Institute of International Affairs, 1952–53.

Larson, Erik. *In the Garden of Beasts: Love, Terror, and an American Family in Hitler's Berlin*. New York: Crown, 2011.

Lash, Joseph P. *Eleanor Roosevelt: A Friend's Memoir*. Garden City, NY: Doubleday, 1964.

———. *Roosevelt and Churchill, 1939–1941: The Partnership That Saved the West*. London: Deutsch, 1977.

LeRoy, Mervyn. *Mervyn LeRoy: Take One*. New York: Hawthorn Books, 1974.

Leutze, James R. *Bargaining for Supremacy: Anglo-American Naval Collaboration, 1937–1941*. Chapel Hill: University of North Carolina Press, 1977.

———, ed. *The London Journal of General Raymond E. Lee, 1940–1941*. Boston: Little, Brown, 1971.

Levering, Ralph B. *American Opinion and the Russian Alliance, 1939–1945*. Chapel Hill: University of North Carolina Press, 1976.

Levine, Gemma. *Claridge's: Within the Image*. London: HarperCollins, 2004.

Lewis, Alfred Allan. *Man of the World: Herbert Bayard Swope: A Charmed Life of Pulitzer Prizes, Poker and Politics*. Indianapolis: Bobbs-Merrill, 1978.

Liebling, A. J. *The Road Back to Paris*. London: Michael Joseph Ltd., 1944.

Longmate, Norman. *Air Raid: The Bombing of Coventry, 1940*. London: Hutchinson, 1976.

Luce, Henry R. "The American Century." *Life*, February 17, 1941.

Lysaght, Charles. *Brendan Bracken*. London: Allen Lane, 1979.

Lyttelton, Oliver. *The Memoirs of Lord Chandos*. London: Bodley Head, 1962.

McIntire, Ross T., and George Creel. *White House Physician.* New York: G. P. Putnam's Sons, 1946.

Macintyre, Ben. *For Your Eyes Only: Ian Fleming and James Bond.* London: Bloomsbury, 2008.

McJimsey, George. *Harry Hopkins: Ally of the Poor and Defender of Democracy.* Cambridge, MA: Harvard University Press, 1987.

McLachlan, Donald. *Room 39: Naval Intelligence in Action, 1939–45.* London: Weidenfeld & Nicolson, 1968.

Maisky, Ivan M. *Memoirs of a Soviet Ambassador: The War, 1939–1943.* London: Hutchinson, 1967.

Martin, A. W., and Patsy Hardy, eds. *Dark and Hurrying Days: Menzies' 1941 Diary.* Canberra: National Library of Australia, 1993.

Martin, John. *Downing Street: The War Years.* London: Bloomsbury, 1991.

Massey, Vincent. *What's Past Is Prologue: The Memoirs of the Right Honourable Vincent Massey.* Toronto: Macmillan, 1963.

May, Ernest R. *Strange Victory: Hitler's Conquest of France.* London: I.B. Tauris, 2000.

Mayers, David. "The Great Patriotic War, FDR's Embassy Moscow, and Soviet-U.S. Relations." *International History Review* 33, no. 2 (2011): 299–333.

Menzies, Robert G. *Afternoon Light: Some Memories of Men and Events.* Melbourne: Cassell Australia, 1967.

Miller, William H., Jr. *The Great Luxury Liners, 1927–1954: A Photographic Record.* New York: Dover, 1981.

Monnet, Jean. *Memoirs.* Garden City, NY: Doubleday, 1978.

Moran, Lord. *Winston Churchill: The Struggle for Survival, 1940–1965.* London: Constable, 1966.

Morton, H. V. *Atlantic Meeting: An Account of Mr. Churchill's Voyage in H.M.S. Prince of Wales, in August, 1941, and the Conference with President Roosevelt Which Resulted in the Atlantic Charter.* London: Methuen, 1943.

Moseley, Ray. *Mussolini's Shadow: The Double Life of Count Galeazzo Ciano.* New Haven, CT: Yale University Press, 1999.

Mowrer, Edgar Ansel. *Triumph and Turmoil: A Personal History of Our Time.* London: Allen & Unwin, 1970.

Muggeridge, Malcolm, ed. *Ciano's Diary, 1939–1943.* Melbourne: William Heinemann, 1947.

———, ed. *Ciano's Diplomatic Papers.* London: Odhams Press, 1948.

Munting, Roger. "Lend-Lease and the Soviet War Effort." *Journal of Contemporary History* 19, no. 3 (1984): 495–510.

Murphy, Robert D. *Diplomat among Warriors.* Garden City, NY: Doubleday, 1964.

Nasaw, David. *The Patriarch: The Remarkable Life and Turbulent Times of Joseph P. Kennedy.* New York: The Penguin Press, 2012.

Nash, Roy. *Buckingham Palace: The Place and the People.* London: Macdonald Futura, 1980.

Neal, Steve. *Dark Horse: A Biography of Wendell Willkie.* Garden City, NY: Doubleday, 1984.

Nel, Elizabeth. *Mr. Churchill's Secretary.* London: Hodder & Stoughton, 1958.

Nicolson, Harold. *Diaries and Letters, 1939–1945.* Edited by Nigel Nicolson. London: Collins, 1967.

———. *Diplomacy.* Washington, DC: Institute for the Study of Diplomacy, School of Foreign Service, Georgetown University, 1988.

Offner, Arnold A. "Appeasement Revisited: The United States, Great Britain, and Germany, 1933–1940." *Journal of American History* 64, no. 2 (1977): 373–93.

———. "The United States and National Socialist Germany." In *The Fascist Challenge and the Policy of Appeasement,* edited by Wolfgang J. Mommsen and Lothar Kettenacker. London: Allen & Unwin, 1983.

Ogden, Chris. *Life of the Party: The Biography of Pamela Digby Churchill Hayward Harriman.* Boston: Little, Brown, 1994.

Olson, Lynne. *Citizens of London: The Americans Who Stood with Britain in Its Darkest, Finest Hour.* New York: Random House, 2010.

Pakula, Hannah. *The Last Empress: Madame Chiang Kai-shek and the Birth of Modern China.* New York: Simon & Schuster, 2009.

Parker, R. A. C. *The Second World War: A Short History.* Oxford: Oxford University Press, 1997.

Parrish, Thomas. *To Keep the British Isles Afloat: FDR's Men in Churchill's London, 1941.* New York: Smithsonian Books, 2009.

Pawle, Gerald, and C. R. Thompson. *The War and Colonel Warden.* London: George G. Harrap, 1963.

Perkins, Frances. *The Roosevelt I Knew.* London: Hammond & Hammond, 1948.

Peters, Charles. *Five Days in Philadelphia: The Amazing "We Want Willkie!" Convention of 1940 and How It Freed FDR to Save the Western World.* New York: PublicAffairs, 2005.

Phillips, William. *Ventures in Diplomacy.* London: J. Murray, 1955.

Pimlott, Ben, ed. *The Second World War Diary of Hugh Dalton, 1940–45.* London: Jonathan Cape, 1986.

Pleshakov, Constantine. *Stalin's Folly: The Secret History of the German Invasion of Russia, June 1941.* London: Weidenfeld & Nicolson, 2005.

Porter, Cathy, and Mark Jones. *Moscow in World War II.* London: Chatto & Windus, 1987.

Pottle, Mark, ed. *Champion Redoubtable: The Diaries and Letters of Violet Bonham Carter, 1914–1945.* London: Weidenfeld & Nicolson, 1998.

Pringle, Henry F. "Exit 'Wild Bill': A Portrait of William J. Donovan." *Outlook and Independent,* January 9, 1929, 47.

Reynolds, David. "1940: Fulcrum of the Twentieth Century?" *International Affairs* 66, no. 2 (1990): 325–50.

———. *The Creation of the Anglo-American Alliance, 1937–41: A Study in Competitive Co-operation.* Chapel Hill: University of North Carolina Press, 1982.

———. *From Munich to Pearl Harbor: Roosevelt's America and the Origins of the Second World War.* Chicago: Ivan R. Dee, 2001.

———. *From World War to Cold War: Churchill, Roosevelt, and the International History of the 1940s.* Oxford: Oxford University Press, 2006.

———. *In Command of History: Churchill Fighting and Writing the Second World War.* New York: Random House, 2005.

———. *Lord Lothian and Anglo-American Relations, 1939–1940.* Philadelphia: American Philosophical Society, 1983.

———. "Roosevelt, Churchill, and the Wartime Anglo-American Alliance, 1939–1945: Towards a New Synthesis." In *The "Special Relationship": Anglo-American Relations since 1945,* edited by William Roger Louis and Hedley Bull. Oxford: Clarendon, 1986.

———. "Roosevelt, the British Left, and the Appointment of John G. Winant as United States Ambassador to Britain in 1941." *International History Review* 4, no. 3 (1982): 393–413.

Reynolds, Quentin. *By Quentin Reynolds.* London: Heinemann, 1964.

———. *Only the Stars Are Neutral.* Sydney: Angus & Robertson, 1942.

Roberts, Andrew. *The Holy Fox: A Biography of Lord Halifax.* London: Weidenfeld & Nicolson, 1991.

Roberts, Geoffrey. "Litvinov's Lost Peace, 1941–1946." *Journal of Cold War Studies* 4, no. 2 (2002): 23–54.

———. *Stalin's Wars: From World War to Cold War, 1939–1953.* New Haven, CT: Yale University Press, 2006.

Rofe, J. Simon. *Franklin Roosevelt's Foreign Policy and the Welles Mission.* Basingstoke, UK: Palgrave Macmillan, 2007.

Roll, David L. *The Hopkins Touch: Harry Hopkins and the Forging of the Alliance to Defeat Hitler.* New York: Oxford University Press, 2013.

Roosevelt, Curtis. "Remembering FDR's Leadership." *Prologue* 38, no. 4 (2006): 30–39.

Roosevelt, Eleanor. *This I Remember.* London: Hutchinson, 1950.

Roosevelt, Elliott. *As He Saw It.* New York: Duell, Sloan & Pearce, 1946.

———, ed. *FDR: His Personal Letters, 1928–1945.* 2 vols. New York: Kraus Reprint Co., 1970.

Roosevelt, Elliott, and James Brough. *A Rendezvous with Destiny: The Roosevelts of the White House.* London: W. H. Allen, 1977.

Roosevelt, Franklin D. *Complete Presidential Press Conferences of Franklin D. Roosevelt.* 25 vols. in 12. New York: Da Capo, 1972.

———. *Public Papers and Addresses of Franklin D. Roosevelt.* Compiled by Samuel I. Rosenman. 13 vols. London: Macmillan, 1938–50.

Roosevelt, James, and Sidney Shalett. *Affectionately, F.D.R.: A Son's Story of a Courageous Man.* Westport, CT: Greenwood Press, 1975.

Rosenman, Samuel I. *Working with Roosevelt.* New York: Harper, 1952.

Saunders, Paul. "The Speaker and the Draft." *American History* 36, no. 3 (2001): 42–46.

Schlesinger, Arthur M., Jr. *The Age of Roosevelt.* 3 vols. Boston: Houghton Mifflin, 1957–60.

———. *Journals, 1952–2000.* Edited by Andrew Schlesinger and Stephen Schlesinger. New York: Penguin, 2007.

———. *A Life in the Twentieth Century: Innocent Beginnings, 1917–1950.* Boston: Houghton Mifflin, 2000.

Schmidt, Paul, and R. H. C. Steed. *Hitler's Interpreter*. Melbourne: Heinemann, 1951.

Sebag Montefiore, Simon. *Stalin: The Court of the Red Tsar*. London: Weidenfeld & Nicolson, 2003.

Seldon, Anthony, and Mark Fiennes. *10 Downing Street: The Illustrated History*. London: HarperCollins, 1999.

Sherwood, Robert E. *The White House Papers of Harry L. Hopkins: An Intimate History*. 2 vols. London: Eyre & Spottiswoode, 1948.

Shirer, William L. *Berlin Diary: The Journal of a Foreign Correspondent, 1934–1941*. New York: Alfred A. Knopf, 1942.

Simpson, B. Mitchell. *Admiral Harold R. Stark: Architect of Victory, 1939–1945*. Columbia: University of South Carolina Press, 1989.

Smith, Amanda, ed. *Hostage to Fortune: The Letters of Joseph P. Kennedy*. New York: Viking, 2001.

Smith, Howard K. *Last Train from Berlin*. Sydney: Angus & Robertson, 1943.

Smith, Jean Edward. *FDR*. New York: Random House, 2007.

Smith, Malcolm. "Battle of Britain." In *The Oxford Companion to World War II*, edited by I. C. B. Dear and M. R. D. Foot. Oxford: Oxford University Press, 2001.

Smith, Richard Norton. *Thomas E. Dewey and His Times*. New York: Simon & Schuster, 1982.

Smith, Sally Bedell. *Reflected Glory: The Life of Pamela Churchill Harriman*. New York: Simon & Schuster, 1996.

Somerset Fry, Plantagenet. *Chequers: The Country Home of Britain's Prime Ministers*. London: H.M.S.O., 1977.

Speer, Albert. *Inside the Third Reich: Memoirs*. New York: Macmillan, 1970.

Sperber, A. M. *Murrow: His Life and Times*. New York: Freundlich Books, 1986.

Stettinius, Edward R. *Lend-Lease: Weapon for Victory*. New York: Macmillan, 1944.

Stewart, Graham. *Burying Caesar: Churchill, Chamberlain and the Battle for the Tory Party*. London: Weidenfeld & Nicolson, 1999.

Stirling, Alfred Thorpe. *Lord Bruce: The London Years*. Melbourne: Hawthorn Press, 1974.

Stoler, Mark A. "A Half Century of Conflict: Interpretations of U.S. World War II Diplomacy." *Diplomatic History* 18, no. 3 (1994): 375–403.

Sweet, Matthew. *The West End Front: The Wartime Secrets of London's Grand Hotels*. London: Faber & Faber, 2011.

Swift, Will. *The Kennedys amidst the Gathering Storm: A Thousand Days in London, 1938–1940*. Washington, DC: Smithsonian Books, 2008.

Swing, Raymond. *Good Evening*. London: Bodley Head, 1965.

Thayer, Charles W. *Bears in the Caviar*. London: Michael Joseph, 1952.

Thorne, Christopher. *Allies of a Kind: The United States, Britain, and the War against Japan, 1941–1945*. Oxford: Oxford University Press, 1978.

Trautman, James. *Pan American Clippers: The Golden Age of Flying Boats*. Erin, ON: Boston Mills, 2007.

Tree, Ronald. *When the Moon Was High: Memoirs of Peace and War, 1897–1942*. London: Macmillan, 1975.

Trohan, Walter. *Political Animals: Memoirs of a Sentimental Cynic*. Garden City, NY: Doubleday, 1975.

Troy, Thomas F. "Donovan's Original Marching Orders." *Studies in Intelligence* 17, no. 2 (1973): 36–69.

———. *Wild Bill and Intrepid: Donovan, Stephenson, and the Origin of CIA*. New Haven, CT: Yale University Press, 1996.

Tugwell, Rexford G. *The Democratic Roosevelt: A Biography of Franklin D. Roosevelt*. Garden City, NY: Doubleday, 1957.

Tully, Grace G. *F.D.R., My Boss*. New York: C. Scribner's Sons, 1949.

Tuttle, Dwight William. *Harry L. Hopkins and Anglo-American-Soviet Relations, 1941-1945*. New York: Garland Publishing, 1983.

United States. Congress. *Report of the Joint Committee on the Investigation of the Pearl Harbor Attack*. Washington, DC: U.S. Government Printing Office, 1946.

United States. Department of State. *Foreign Relations of the United States*. Washington, DC: U.S. Government Printing Office.

United States. War Department. Strategic Services Unit. History Project. *War Report of the OSS*. New York: Walker, 1976.

Waller, Douglas. *Wild Bill Donovan: The Spymaster Who Created the OSS and Modern American Espionage*. New York: Free Press, 2011.

Ward, Geoffrey C., ed. *Closest Companion: The Unknown Story of the Intimate Friendship between Franklin Roosevelt and Margaret Suckley*. Boston: Houghton Mifflin, 1995.

Watson, Derek. "Molotov, the Making of the Grand Alliance and the Second Front, 1939-42." *Europe-Asia Studies* 54, no. 1 (2002): 51–85.

Weil, Martin. *A Pretty Good Club: The Founding Fathers of the U.S. Foreign Service*. New York: Norton, 1978.

Weintraub, Stanley. *Long Day's Journey into War: December 7, 1941*. New York: Plume, 1991.

Welles, Benjamin. *Sumner Welles: FDR's Global Strategist: A Biography*. New York: St. Martin's, 1997.

Welles, Sumner. "Foreword." In *Ciano's Diary, 1939–1943*, edited by Malcolm Muggeridge. London: William Heinemann, 1947.

———. *The Time for Decision*. London: Hamish Hamilton, 1944.

Wenden, D. J., and K. R. M. Short. "Winston S. Churchill: Film Fan." *Historical Journal of Film, Radio and Television* 11, no. 3 (1991): 197–214.

Werth, Alexander. *The Last Days of Paris: A Journalist's Diary*. London: Hamish Hamilton, 1940.

———. *Moscow '41*. London: Hamish Hamilton, 1942.

———. *Russia at War, 1941-1945*. London: Barrie & Rockliff, 1964.

Willkie, Wendell L. "Americans, Stop Being Afraid!" *Collier's*, May 10, 1941.

———. *One World*. London: Cassell & Co., 1943.

Wilson, Theodore A. "The First Summit: FDR and the Riddle of Personal Diplomacy." In *The Atlantic Charter*, edited by Douglas Brinkley and David R. Facey-Crowther. Basingstoke, UK: Palgrave Macmillan, 1994.

———. *The First Summit: Roosevelt and Churchill at Placentia Bay, 1941*. Rev. ed. Lawrence: University Press of Kansas, 1991.

Winant, John G. *A Letter from Grosvenor Square: An Account of a Stewardship*. London: Hodder & Stoughton, 1947.

Wiskemann, Elizabeth. *The Rome-Berlin Axis: A Study of the Relations between Hitler and Mussolini*. New and revised ed. London: Collins, 1966.

Yeide, Nancy H. "The Marie Harriman Gallery (1930–1942)." *Archives of American Art Journal* 39, no. 1/2 (1999): 3–11.

Zahniser, Marvin R. "Rethinking the Significance of Disaster: The United States and the Fall of France in 1940." *International History Review* 14, no. 2 (1992): 252–76.

Zhukov, Georgii Konstantinovich. *The Memoirs of Marshal Zhukov*. London: Jonathan Cape, 1971.

Index

Index

Credits

TEXT

Epigraph: Reproduced with permission of Curtis Brown, London, on behalf of the Estate of Sir Winston Churchill. Copyright © Winston S. Churchill.

Page 277: Speech by Harry Hopkins to British upon arrival in London, July 27, 1941, George T. McJimsey Papers, Grinnell College. Printed by permission of George T. McJimsey.

IMAGE INSERT

Page 1: ABOVE: © Bettmann/CORBIS. BELOW: Franklin D. Roosevelt Presidential Library and Museum.

Page 2: ABOVE: Franklin D. Roosevelt Presidential Library and Museum. BELOW, LEFT: Harris & Ewing Collection, Prints & Photographs Division, Library of Congress, LC-DIG-hec-28141. BELOW, RIGHT: Harris & Ewing Collection, Prints & Photographs Division, Library of Congress, LC-DIG-hec-28631.

Page 3: ABOVE: Harris & Ewing Collection, Prints & Photographs Division, Library of Congress, LC-DIG-hec-28404. BELOW: © Bettman/CORBIS.

Page 4: ABOVE: Topical Press Agency/Getty Images. BELOW: National Archives, Photo No. 111-SC-25158.

Page 5: ABOVE: AP Photo/Associated Press. BELOW: AP Photo/Associated Press.

Page 6: ABOVE: Harris & Ewing Collection, Prints & Photographs Division, Library of Congress, LC-DIG-hec-28064. BELOW: NYWT&S Collection, Prints & Photographs Division, Library of Congress, LC-USZ62-135306.

Page 7: ABOVE: AP Photo/Associated Press. BELOW: Franklin D. Roosevelt Presidential Library and Museum.

Page 8: ABOVE: Franklin D. Roosevelt Presidential Library and Museum. BELOW: Harris & Ewing Collection, Prints & Photographs Division, Library of Congress, LC-DIG-hec-28898.

Page 9: ABOVE: Courtesy of Churchill Archives Centre of Churchill College, Cambridge. Churchill Additional Papers, WCHL 13/1. BELOW: Courtesy of the Pittsburgh *Post-Gazette*.

Page 10: AP Photo/Eddie Worth.

Page 11: ABOVE: AP Photo/Eddie Worth. BELOW: *Chicago Daily Tribune,* Feb. 7, 1941.

Page 12: ABOVE, LEFT: Richard C. Wood/Getty Images. ABOVE, RIGHT: AP Photo/Graphic Photo Union. BELOW: National Archives, Photo No. 208-PU-89FF-27.

Page 13: ABOVE: Bettmann/CORBIS. BELOW: Margaret Bourke-White/Getty Images.

Page 14: ABOVE: Franklin D. Roosevelt Presidential Library and Museum. BELOW: Franklin D. Roosevelt Presidential Library and Museum.

Page 15: ABOVE: Courtesy of the Imperial War Museum. BELOW: National Archives, Photo No. 80-G-26865.

Page 16: ABOVE: Franklin D. Roosevelt Presidential Library and Museum. BELOW: Franklin D. Roosevelt Presidential Library and Museum.